The Appraisal of Real Estate

The Appraisal of Real Estate

Ninth Edition

American Institute of Real Estate Appraisers
430 North Michigan Avenue
Chicago, Illinois 60611-4088

Acknowledgments
Director of Publications: Karla L. Heuer
Development Writer: Michael R. Milgrim, Ph.D

For Educational Purposes Only
The opinions and statements set forth herein do not necessarily reflect the viewpoint
of the American Institute of Real Estate Appraisers or its individual members, and
neither the Institute nor its editors and staff assume responsibility for such expres-
sions of opinion or statements.

Printed in the United States of America
92 91 90 89   7   6   5   4   3

Library of Congress Cataloging in Publication Data

The Appraisal of real estate.
  Bibliography: p.
  Includes index.
  1. Real property—Valuation. I. American Institute of Real Estate Appraisers.
HD1387.A663   1987   333.33'2   87-17423
ISBN 0-911780-87-4

TABLE OF CONTENTS

Foreword

As the twenty-first century approaches, increasingly sophisticated methods and procedures have become a familiar hallmark of the appraisal profession. The accelerating tempo of change in economic, fiscal, and technological environments has created greater complexity in real estate appraisal. I am especially proud, therefore, to introduce the ninth edition of *The Appraisal of Real Estate* in anticipation of the practice of appraisal in the upcoming century. It is my firm belief that the ninth edition meets the needs of both students entering the field and those of seasoned appraisers. It presents a comprehensive overview of current appraisal techniques and, at the same time, keeps sight of the fundamental principles that have long guided the development of our profession.

The revision was inaugurated with a survey of 1,100 professors and instructors who teach from *The Appraisal of Real Estate*. Their suggestions for an improved textbook were executed by MAI and RM practitioners whose expertise in the marketplace is manifested throughout the book. The integration of concept and practice, textbook case and realistic application, make *The Appraisal of Real Estate* a unique book. The changes between the eighth and ninth editions are many and diverse. Because of the importance of the consideration of real property rights in an appraisal, the ninth edition includes a new chapter on fee simple and partial interests, and introduces a real property rights adjustment in the application of the sales comparison and cost approaches. This edition also provides an in-depth discussion of the driving concept of market value. The ninth edition features a new chapter on land or site valuation and one on advanced applications of yield capitalization. In addition, there are guidelines for market analysis projections and updated information that reflects current economic conditions, tax policies, and the Appraisal Institute's revised Code of Professional Ethics and Standards of Professional Practice.

Richard Marchitelli, MAI, Chairman of Publications, guided the monumental decision-making process, which over three years was essential to assure that the content of this new edition is useful and contemporary. Readers will benefit from his astute insights and those of the following contributors and reviewers: E. Nelson Bowes, MAI; Douglas C. Brown, MAI; James H. Bulthuis, MAI; Robert C. Cantwell, IV, MAI; Sheila Crowell; Max J. Derbes, Jr., MAI; John D. Dorchester, Jr., MAI; Stephen F. Fanning, MAI; Clifford E. Fisher, Jr., MAI; Kenneth G. Foltz, MAI; W. West Foster, MAI; James E. Gibbons, MAI; Terry V. Grissom, MAI; J. R. Kimball, MAI; Peter F. Korpacz, MAI; David J. Lau, MAI; A. Scruggs Love, Jr., MAI; C. David Matthews, MAI; Terrell R. Oetzel, MAI; Anthony Reynolds, MAI; Judith Reynolds, MAI; Mark I. Roth; J. Carl Schultz, Jr., MAI; Gary P. Taylor, MAI; Eugene W. Stunard, MAI; and Janice F. Young, MAI.

Mary Jo Thomas, RM; Richard Marchitelli, MAI; and Peter D. Bowes, MAI, were final reviewers of the entire manuscript. The Appraisal Institute is particularly grateful for their contributions of knowledge, experience, time, and energy.

Richard C. Wolcott, MAI
1987 President
American Institute of Real Estate Appraisers

1 Real Property and Its Appraisal

Under all is the land. This statement implies more than a physical reality. Land is the surface of the earth and the major source of all mineral, vegetable, and animal matter; it is the foundation for the social and economic activities of people as well as a commodity and the root of wealth.

Because land is essential to life and human society, it is the subject of various disciplines, including geography, law, sociology, and economics. Each of these disciplines employs somewhat different concepts of real estate. Geography focuses on describing the physical elements of land and the distribution and activities of the people who use it. Law considers land as the subject of ownership. Sociology focuses on the dual nature of land: as a resource to be shared by all people and a commodity to be owned, traded, and used by individuals. In economics, land is regarded as one of the four agents of production, along with labor, capital, and coordination. Land represents all the natural elements of a nation's wealth.

The concept of land value is an economic concept. A common understanding of the attributes of land is shared by geographers, lawyers, sociologists, and economists.

1. Each parcel of land is unique in its location and composition.
2. Land is physically immobile.
3. Land is durable.
4. The supply of land is finite.
5. Land is useful to people.

Real estate appraisers also recognize these attributes of land. They are concerned with the concepts of land used in other disciplines because these concepts provide the basic perceptions on which real estate value rests. In real estate appraisal the emphasis is on real estate markets, which result from the actions of people who respond to, and often are directed or limited by, all the important attributes of land delineated in other disciplines.

CONCEPTS OF LAND

Geographic

An understanding of land begins with recognizing its diverse physical characteristics and how these characteristics combine in a particular area. Developing a sense of land also includes an awareness of how physical characteristics influence the use of land.

Land is affected by a number of processes. Ongoing physical and chemical processes modify the land's surface, biological processes affect the distribution of all life forms, and socioeconomic processes direct human habitation and activity on the land. Together, these processes influence land capability and, therefore, land use.

Land may be used for many purposes, including agriculture, commerce, industry, habitation, and recreation. Land-use decisions are influenced by climate, topography, and the distribution of natural resources, population centers, and industry. Land use is also affected by economic conditions, population pressures, technological practices, and cultural influences. The influence of each of these factors varies, depending on the geographic area.

Geographic considerations are particularly significant to appraisers. The importance of land's physical characteristics—e.g., climate, geology, soils, water, and vegetation—is obvious, but the distribution of people, facilities, and services and the movement of goods and people are equally important. The geographic concept of land, which emphasizes matters such as resources and resource bases, industrial location, and actual and potential markets, provides much of the background knowledge required in real estate appraisal.

Legal

A society's cultural, political, governmental, and economic attitudes are reflected in its laws. The legal profession does not focus on the physical characteristics of land, but on the rights and obligations associated with various interests in land. Law maintains the right of individuals to own and use land for material gain, while it also protects the right of all people to use the land. In other words, the law recognizes the conflict between private ownership and public use.

"Whose is the land, his it is, to the sky and the depths." This ancient maxim is the basis for the following legal definition.

> Land includes not only the ground, or soil, but everything that is attached to the earth, whether by course of nature, as are trees and herbage, or by the hand of man, as are houses and other buildings. It includes not only the surface of the earth, but everything under it and over it. Thus, in legal theory, a tract of land consists not only of the portion on the surface of the

earth, but is an inverted pyramid having its tip, or apex, at the center of the earth, extending outward through the surface of the earth at the boundary lines of the tract, and continuing on upward to the heavens.[1]

This definition may seem to suggest that land ownership implies complete possession from the center of the earth to the ends of the universe. In practice, however, ownership is limited. For example, the U.S. Congress has declared that the federal government has complete and exclusive sovereignty over the nation's airspace and that every citizen has "a public right to freedom of transit in air commerce through the navigable air space of the United States."[2] Because ownership can be limited, ownership rights are the subject of law, and the value of these rights is the subject of appraisal.

The laws that govern the use and development of land in America give the landowner the greatest possible freedom in deciding how to use the land. The owner's rights are restricted only if they unreasonably harm the rights of others. The definition of reasonable use has been argued in many court cases.

Legal matters of particular concern to appraisers include easements, access regulations, use restrictions, and the recording and conveyance of titles. Appraisers must be familiar with local and state laws because the jurisdiction over lands is vested primarily at the local and state levels.

Social

As the physical characteristics and legal limitations of land increasingly affect its use, society has become more concerned with how land is used and how rights are distributed. Because the supply of land is fixed, the increased demand for land exerts pressure for land to be used more intensively. Conflicts often arise between groups with different views on proper land use. Some people believe that land is a resource to be shared by all. They want to preserve the land's scenic beauty and important ecological functions. Others view land primarily as a marketable commodity; they believe that society is best served by private, unrestricted ownership. Because land is both a resource and a commodity, there are no clear-cut solutions to this conflict.[3]

Both points of view have legal support. As a resource, land is protected for the good of society. As a marketable commodity, the ownership, use, and disposal of land are regulated so that individual rights are not violated.

In 1876 the U.S. Supreme Court established government's right to regulate "the manner in which [a citizen] shall own his own property when such regulation

1. Robert Kratovil and Raymond J. Werner, *Real Estate Law*, 8th ed. (Englewood Cliffs, N.J.: Prentice-Hall, Inc., 1983), p. 6.

2. The Air Commerce Act of 1926 (formerly 49 USC 171 *et seq.*); the Civil Aeronautics Act of 1938 (formerly 49 USC 401 *et seq.*); and the Federal Aviation Act of 1958 (see 49 USC 401).

3. Richard N. L. Andrews, *Land in America* (Lexington, Mass.: D.C. Heath and Company, 1979) p. ix.

becomes necessary for the public good." The court quoted the words of England's Lord Chief Justice Hale: "When private property is 'affected with a public interest,' it ceases to be *juris privati* only."[4]

Throughout American history, land ownership has been recognized as fundamental. John Adams wrote, "If the multitude is possessed of real estate, the multitude will take care of the liberty, virtue, and interest of the multitude in all acts of government."[5]

In the public interest, society may impose building restrictions, zoning and building ordinances, development and subdivision regulations, and environmental controls. Environmental controls include provisions to protect the air and water from wastes, dirt, chemicals, and excessive noise. To preserve land in its natural state, there are regulations that protect wetlands, beaches, and navigable waters.

Economic

Land is a physical substance with inherent ownership rights that can be legally limited for the good of society. Land is also a major *source* of wealth, which, in economic terms, is measured in money or exchange value. Land and its products have economic value only when they are converted into goods or services that are useful, desirable, and paid for by consumers. The economic concept of land as a source of wealth and an object of value is central to appraisal theory.

The economic concept of land reflects a long history of thought on the sources and bases of value, which is referred to as value theory.[6] Value theory contributes to the definitions of value used in appraisal reports and appraisal literature, and it is an important part of the philosophy that underlies professional appraisal practice. The development of value theory and its relationship to other systems of thought, which form the ideological basis of real estate appraisal, are discussed in Chapter 2.

THE DISCIPLINE OF APPRAISAL

Geographic, legal, social, and economic concepts of land all relate to the real estate appraiser's concept of land. Land, legally defined to include everything attached to the land, constitutes real estate. Appraisers study the value of physical real estate and its accompanying ownership rights, recognizing that real estate exists within the

---

4. 94 U.S. 113 (1896). Quoted in Richard F. Babcock and Duane A. Feurer, "Land as a Commodity 'Affected with a Public Interest' " in Andrews, p. 110.

5. Andrews, p. 31.

6. Paul F. Wendt, *Real Estate Appraisal: Review and Outlook* (Athens: University of Georgia Press, 1974), p. 17.

context of our society as a whole. Because the potential uses of land are influenced by geographic, legal, social, and economic factors, these considerations form the background against which appraisal activities are conducted.

REAL ESTATE, REAL PROPERTY, AND PERSONAL PROPERTY

To begin the study of real estate appraisal, an important distinction must be made between the terms *real estate* and *real property*. Although these concepts are different, some state laws treat them as synonymous.

Real estate is the physical land and appurtenances affixed to the land, e.g., structures. Real estate is immobile and tangible. The legal definition of real estate includes land and all things that are a natural part of land (e.g., trees and minerals), as well as all things that are attached to it by people (e.g., buildings and yard improvements). All permanent building attachments (e.g., plumbing, electrical wiring, heating installations) as well as built-in items (e.g., cabinets and elevators) are usually considered part of the real estate.

Real property includes all interests, benefits, and rights inherent in the ownership of physical real estate. A right or interest in real property is also referred to as an *estate*. Specifically, *an estate in land is the degree, nature, or extent of interest that a person has in it.*

Interests vary, so real property is said to include a "bundle of rights" that are inherent in the ownership of real estate. Ownership rights include the right to use real estate, to sell it, to lease it, to enter it, to give it away, or to choose to exercise all or none of these rights. The bundle of rights is often likened to a bundle of sticks, with each stick representing a distinct and separate right or interest. Private enjoyment of these rights is guaranteed by the U.S. Constitution subject to certain limitations and restrictions.

It is possible to own all of the rights in a parcel of real estate or only some of them. The extent of ownership determines the kind of interest, or estate, that is held. A person who owns all the property rights is said to have *fee simple title. A fee simple estate implies absolute ownership unencumbered by any other interest or estate.*

Partial interests in real estate are created by selling, leasing, or otherwise limiting the bundle of rights in a fee simple estate. Partial estates include leased fee and leasehold estates.

A leased fee estate is an ownership interest held by a landlord with the right of use and occupancy conveyed by lease to others; the rights of lessor (the leased fee owner) and leased fee are specified by contract terms contained within the lease. An appraisal assignment may call for the appraisal of a fee simple estate or a partial interest such as a *leasehold estate held by a lessee (the tenant and renter) and conveying the right of use and occupancy for a stated term and under certain conditions.* Leased fee interests are frequently valued by considering their income components and comparing them with other leases. (A detailed discussion of the valuation of partial interests is presented in Chapter 6.)

All estates in real property are subject to four powers of government: taxation, eminent domain, police power, and escheat.

Taxation is the right of government to raise revenue through assessments on valuable goods, products, and rights. Because the U.S. Constitution effectively precludes the federal government from taxing real property directly, the right of taxation is reserved for state and local governments.

Eminent domain is the right of government to take private property for public use upon the payment of just compensation. This right can be exercised by an entity acting under governmental authority such as a housing authority or public utility. *Condemnation is the act or process of enforcing the right of eminent domain.*

Police power is the right of government under which property is regulated to protect public safety, health, morals, and general welfare. Zoning ordinances, building codes, air and land traffic regulations, and health regulations are based on police power.

Escheat is the government right that gives the state titular ownership of a property when its owner dies without a will or any ascertainable heirs.

The government also controls *overflight, the air space over a property through which aircraft may pass so long as the property's occupants suffer no inconvenience beyond established standards.*

In addition to government restrictions on property, private legal agreements may also impose limitations. One type of agreement is a restriction inserted in a deed. Private restrictions can limit the use or manner of development and even the manner in which ownership can be conveyed. The purchaser of a property may be obligated to use the property subject to a private restriction such as an easement, right-of-way, or party-wall agreement.

The individual rights in the bundle of rights can be sold, leased, transferred, or otherwise disposed of separately, subject to government limitations and private restrictions. Certain parcels of land give their owners a number of options. For example, one property owner could sell or lease the mineral rights to his property and retain the rights to use the surface area. Another owner could lease the property's surface rights to one party and the subsurface rights to another. A third owner could sell or lease the air rights to a property for construction or avigation (i.e., air traffic control). Thus, the ownership of certain rights can be severed from the ownership of the rest of a property and be sold, leased, or given to other parties.

Appraisers must not only understand the distinction between real estate and real property, but they must also differentiate between real estate and personal property.

Personal property is a movable item of property that is not permanently affixed to, or part of, real estate. Personal property is not endowed with the rights of real property ownership. Items of personal property include furniture and furnishings, e.g., refrigerators, freestanding shelves, that are not built into the structure. Under specific lease terms, items such as bookshelves and venetian blinds may be installed in apartments or rented houses by the tenant and remain personal property to be removed at the termination of the lease.

PERSONAL PROPERTY

(H. Armstrong Roberts, Inc.)

Although personal property generally consists of tangible items, called *chattels personal* in the legal profession, an intangible personal property right, called *chattels real*, may be created by a lease.[7]

It is sometimes difficult to determine whether an item should be considered personal property or real estate. Often, the courts must resolve the conflict. *A fixture is an article that was once personal property, but has since been installed or attached to the land or building in a rather permanent manner; it is regarded in law as part of the real estate.* Therefore, a fixture is endowed with the rights of real property ownership and is part of the real estate.

Although fixtures are real estate, trade fixtures are not. *A trade fixture, also called a chattel fixture, is an article that is owned and attached to a rented space or building by a tenant and used in conducting a business.* Thus, trade fixtures are not real estate endowed with the rights of real property ownership; they are, however, personal property regardless of how they are affixed.

Examples of trade fixtures include restaurant booths and bars, gasoline station pumps and storage tanks, and the lanes and pinsetters in bowling alleys. In industrial real estate, the term can be used to refer to fixed building equipment

---

7. Historically, personal property also included ownership rights to real estate for a fixed number of years, such as a tenant's interest. These were called *chattels real*, to distinguish them from movable personal objects, which were called *chattels personal*. Today, it is more common to refer to a lessee's interest as an interest in, or right to, real estate.

installed for human comfort (e.g., plumbing, lighting, heat, and air-conditioning) and to industrial equipment (e.g., air hoses, water pipelines, craneways, and bus ducts). A trade fixture is to be removed by the tenant when the lease expires unless this right has been surrendered in the lease.

To decide whether an item is a trade fixture, and therefore personal property, or part of the real estate, courts use the following criteria:

1. The manner in which the item is affixed. Generally, an item is considered personal property if it can be removed without serious injury to the real estate or itself. There are exceptions to this rule.
2. The character of the item and its adaptation to the real estate. Items that are specifically constructed for use in a particular building or installed to carry out the purpose for which the building was erected are generally considered permanent parts of the building.
3. The intention of the party who attached the item. Frequently, the terms of the lease reveal whether the item is to be permanent or to be removed at some future time.[8]

Appraisers must know whether an item is personal property or a fixture to decide if it will be included in the property value indication. If an item is classified as a fixture, and therefore part of the real estate, its contribution to value is included in the value estimate; if it is personal property, it contributes nothing to the real estate value. Because this distinction is not always obvious, appraisers should know how courts in their jurisdictions define fixtures.

APPRAISAL PRACTICE

In our complex society, professional real estate appraisers perform a variety of functions and services. They estimate several types of defined value and may advise clients and participate in decisions about real estate.

An appraisal is an unbiased estimate of the nature, quality, value, or utility of an interest in, or aspect of, identified real estate and related personalty. Appraisal involves selective research into appropriate market areas; the assemblage of pertinent data; the application of appropriate analytical techniques; and the use of knowledge, experience, and professional judgment to develop an appropriate solution to the appraisal problem.

The nature of the real estate problem in question indicates whether the appraisal is a valuation or an evaluation. *Valuation is the process of estimating the market value, insurable value, investment value, or other properly defined value of an identified interest or interests in a specific parcel or parcels of real estate as of a given date.* Valuation assignments include market value estimates of fee simple estates, leasehold estates, preservation easements, and many others. *Evaluation is a*

---

8. Kratovil and Werner, pp. 18-23.

study of the nature, quality, or utility of a parcel of real estate or interests in, or aspects of, real property, in which a value estimate is not necessarily required. Evaluation assignments include land utilization studies, supply and demand studies, economic feasibility studies, highest and best use analyses, and marketability or investment considerations that relate to proposed or existing developments.

In a valuation assignment, the appraiser communicates to the client an estimate of real property value which reflects all pertinent market evidence. In an evaluation assignment, current market activity and evidence are used to form a conclusion that is not a specific value indication. In both types of assignments, conclusions are derived from appropriate data analysis that conforms with standards of professional practice.

The application of appraisal procedures and the communication report of the appraiser's conclusions are guided by the nature of the assignment. To avoid misunderstandings between the client and the appraiser, it is important to determine whether the assignment is a valuation or an evaluation.

PURPOSE AND USE OF AN APPRAISAL

The purpose of an appraisal is the stated scope of an appraisal assignment, i.e., to estimate a defined value of any real property interest, or to conduct an evaluation study pertaining to real property decisions.[9] The purpose of an appraisal is established by the client's question. It points to the information that the client needs to answer specific questions pertaining to real property. If the client's questions are understood, the purpose of the appraisal can be clearly and fully stated in terms of the information requested.

When an estimate of value is required in an appraisal, the type of value sought must be defined at the outset. The defined value may be market value, insurable value, going-concern value, assessed value, use value, or investment value. The distinctions among these terms are discussed in Chapter 2.

The purpose of a valuation appraisal establishes the foundation for the final value conclusion, which does not change to accommodate the use of the appraisal. The structure of an appraisal report may be adapted to the intended use of the valuation estimate, but the valuation estimate itself will not change. For example, the valuation of a single-family property might be reported in a short form for use in a purchase or sale, a long form for mortgage financing, a brief narrative report for rehabilitation decisions, or a full narrative report for use in litigation. Whatever the circumstances, the numbers associated with the defined value type will be the same.

The use of an appraisal is the manner in which a client employs the information contained in an appraisal report. The use of an appraisal is determined

---

9. Specific legal definitions of the terms *appraisal* and *appraisal assignment* are cited in the Code of Professional Ethics and Standards of Professional Practice of the American Institute of Real Estate Appraisers. Members of the Appraisal Institute and candidates for Institute designations should be familiar with these definitions.

by the client's needs. For example, a client may want to know the market value of a residence to avoid paying too much for it or accepting too little for its sale. Corporate clients may need to ascertain the rent levels or demographic trends in an area to help determine the advisability of relocating there. Insurance companies and private citizens may wish to know the insurable value of buildings, and a developer may need to know the supply and demand factors in a community before constructing an apartment complex there.

An appraisal provides the basis for a decision concerning real property, so the use of an appraisal depends on the decision the client wishes to make. In defining the appraisal problem, the appraiser should develop an understanding of the client's requirements that is acceptable to both parties and consistent with accepted standards of professional practice.

An appraisal may be requested in a number of situations. The following list does not include all uses for appraisals, but it does indicate the broad scope of professional appraisal activities.

Transfer of ownership

- To help prospective buyers set offering prices
- To help prospective sellers determine acceptable selling prices
- To establish a basis for real property exchanges
- To establish a basis for reorganizing or merging the ownership of multiple properties
- To determine the terms of a sale price for a proposed transaction

Financing and credit

- To estimate the value of the security offered for a proposed mortgage loan
- To provide an investor with a sound basis for deciding whether to purchase real estate mortgages, bonds, or other types of securities
- To establish a basis for a decision to insure or underwrite a loan on real property

Just compensation in condemnation proceedings

- To estimate the market value of a property as a whole—i.e., before the taking
- To estimate the market value of the remainder after the taking
- To estimate the damages to the property

Tax matters

- To estimate assessed value
- To separate assets into depreciable (or capital recapture) items such as buildings, and nondepreciable items such as land, and to estimate applicable depreciation (or capital recapture) rates
- To determine gift or inheritance taxes

Investment counseling and decision making

- To set rental schedules and lease provisions
- To determine the feasibility of a construction or renovation program
- To help corporations or third parties purchase homes for transferred employees
- To serve the needs of insurers, adjusters, and policyholders
- To facilitate corporate mergers, the issuing of stock, or the revision of book value
- To estimate liquidation value for forced sale or auction proceedings
- To counsel clients on investment matters, by considering their goals, alternatives, resources, constraints, and timing
- To advise zoning boards, courts, and planners, among others, on the probable effects of proposed actions
- To arbitrate between adversaries
- To determine supply and demand trends in a market
- To ascertain the status of real estate markets

SUMMARY

Land is the subject of a variety of disciplines. The uniqueness, fixity, durability, finiteness, and usefulness of land are acknowledged in the fields of geography, law, sociology, and economics. Geography is concerned with the physical characteristics, demographic patterns, and economic uses of land, while the legal profession is concerned with land ownership. In sociology the competition between private and public interests over the use and distribution of land is considered, and in economics land is regarded as an agent of production and a source of wealth.

The distinction between *real estate* and *real property* is fundamental to appraisal. Real estate includes the physical land and all appurtenances affixed to the land. Real property includes all the interests, benefits, and rights inherent in the ownership of physical real estate.

Ownership rights can be held, leased, sold, transferred, or otherwise disposed of as a whole or fractionally. The ownership of real property rights unencumbered by any other interest is known as a *fee simple estate*. An ownership interest held by a landlord with the right of use and occupancy conveyed to a tenant by a lease is a *leased fee estate*. The right of use and occupancy held by a tenant is known as a *leasehold estate*.

All real property is subject to four powers of government: taxation, eminent domain, police power, and escheat.

The distinction between *personal property* and *real estate* is very important to appraisers. Personal property is a movable item of property that is not permanently affixed to, or part of, the real estate. Fixtures are considered real estate, but trade fixtures are personal property.

An *appraisal* is an unbiased estimate of the nature, quality, value, or utility of an interest in, or aspect of, identified real estate and related personalty. Valuation and evaluation are two different kinds of appraisal assignments; the distinction between them is derived from the nature of the real estate problem. *Valuation* is the process of estimating the market value, insurable value, investment value, or other properly defined value of an identified interest or interests in a specific parcel or parcels of real estate as of a given date. *Evaluation* is a study of the nature, quality, or utility of a parcel of real estate or interests in, or aspects of, real property, in which a value estimate is not necessarily required.

The *purpose of an appraisal* is based on the client's needs for information about the defined value of a real property interest. The *use of an appraisal* is the manner in which the client employs this information. The appraisal conclusion is communicated in accordance with the purpose of the appraisal, but it is not adjusted to accommodate the use of the appraisal. Appraisals are needed in situations involving the transfer of ownership, financing, estimates of just compensation in condemnation proceedings, tax settlements, the determination of rent and leasing provisions, insurance matters, feasibility and marketability considerations, investment decision making, and zoning or planning initiatives.

2 The Nature of Value

The concept of value pervades every segment of the real estate industry. Value considerations are of central importance in a broad and diverse range of real estate activities. Value is an economic term that is often used imprecisely in common speech, but it has a specific meaning which distinguishes it from the related concepts of price, market, and cost.

DISTINCTIONS AMONG PRICE, MARKET, COST, AND VALUE

Appraisers make important distinctions among the terms price, market, cost, and value. The term *price*, usually used to refer to a sale or transaction price, applies to exchange; a price is an accomplished fact. *A price represents the amount a particular purchaser agrees to pay and a particular seller agrees to accept under the circumstances surrounding their transaction.*

Generally, the circumstances of a transaction reflect conditions within one or several markets. *A market is a set of arrangements in which buyers and sellers are brought together through the price mechanism.* A market may be defined in terms of geography, products or product features, number of available buyers and sellers, or other arrangements of circumstance.

A real estate market is the interaction of individuals who exchange real property rights for other assets, such as money. Specific real estate markets are defined on the basis of property type, location, income-producing potential, a typical investor profile, a typical tenant profile, or other attributes considered by those participating in the exchange of real property. The market for new, single-family residences selling for $100,000 and the market for older apartment buildings located six miles from the central business district and available for complete renovation are examples of specific real estate markets.

The term *cost*, as used by appraisers, applies to production, not exchange; it may be either an accomplished fact or a current estimate. Appraisers distinguish among several types of costs: direct costs, indirect costs, construction costs, and development costs.

Direct costs are expenditures for the labor and materials necessary to construct a new improvement. Direct costs are also called *hard costs*. A contractor's overhead and profit are generally considered direct costs.

Indirect costs are incurred in construction and refer to expenditures for items other than labor and materials. Indirect costs include administrative costs; expenses incurred by the owner for professional fees, financing, taxes, and interest and insurance during construction; and lease-up costs, which are the net expenses of operating the project until it reaches a stable occupancy level. Indirect costs are sometimes referred to as *soft costs*.

Construction cost, or contractor's bid price, normally includes the direct costs of labor and materials plus the contractor's indirect costs.

Development cost is the cost to create a property, including the land, and bring it to an efficient operating state, as distinguished from the cost to construct the improvements.

These real estate-related expenditures are directly linked to the price of goods and services in competitive markets. For example, the costs of roofing materials, masonry, architectural plans, and rented scaffolding are determined by the interaction of supply and demand in specific areas and are subject to the influence of social, economic, governmental, and environmental forces.

Price, market, and cost relationships also incorporate concepts of value. Value can have many meanings in real estate appraisal; the applicable definition depends on the context and usage.[1] Because value exists at a given moment, an appraisal reflects value at a particular point in time. In its simplest form, *value as of a given time represents the monetary worth of property, goods, or services to buyers and sellers*. To avoid confusion, professional appraisers do not use the word *value* alone; instead they refer to "market value," "use value," "investment value," "assessed value," or other specific kinds of value. Market value is the focus of most real property appraisal assignments and its estimation is the purpose of most appraisals.

MARKET VALUE, USE VALUE, AND OTHER VALUES

Market Value

The concept of market value is of paramount importance to the business and real estate communities. Vast sums of debt and equity capital are committed annually in

---

1. See Halbert C. Smith, "Value Concepts as a Source of Disparity Among Appraisals," *The Appraisal Journal*, April 1977.

real estate investments and mortgage loans on the basis of market value estimations. Real estate taxation, litigation, and legislation also reflect an ongoing, active concern with market value issues. In virtually every aspect of the real estate industry and its regulation at local, state, and federal levels, considerations of market value are of vital importance to economic stability.

Precisely for these reasons, the definition of market value used by appraisers and by the clients they serve must be clearly understood and communicated. However, in real estate appraisal, definitions of market value can and do represent different beliefs and assumptions about the marketplace and the nature of value. Market value is inherently a simple concept—it is an objective value created by the collective patterns of the market—but the ultimate definition of market value is a controversial issue. Thought on the subject continues to evolve, sometimes in terms of rather fine distinctions.

Differences in market value definitions fall into several categories:

1. All-cash and terms equivalent to cash versus non-cash-equivalent financing terms
2. Specified property rights versus the real estate
3. The price versus the highest price
4. The most probable price versus the highest price
5. Equilibrium value versus market value

Current definitions of market value reflect different schools of thought about the points listed above. One school subscribes to the belief that market value is best measured only in terms of all cash. This opinion had its origin in the first half of the twentieth century when economic conditions were remarkably stable. During that period mortgage rates remained nearly level, real estate prices rose slowly, and fee simple interest was usually the subject of an appraisal. Because of these and other prevalent conditions, consideration of financial terms in estimating market value was limited, and market value in appraisals most frequently implied all-cash transactions.

A second school of thought emerged in the latter part of the twentieth century with changes in real estate financing and increasingly complex real property interests. Long-term, fixed-rate loans have become increasingly supplemented or replaced by more complicated financing instruments. Clients now frequently request estimates of the market value of property subject to leases, easements, or mortgages. Therefore, real estate analysts have focused their attention on the importance of interrelationships of debt and equity interests and fee-simple, leased-fee, and lease-hold interests.

Financing terms, which may or may not be equivalent to cash, affect value. Value affected by financing or leases can be market value, because it is value created by the activity of the collective market.

A market value appraisal is always valuation of specified rights in the subject property rather than valuation of the physical entity of the real estate. The specified property rights can be the fee simple estate, the as-leased or as-mortgaged estate, or some other interest in the real estate.

Webster defines market value as "a price at which both buyers and sellers are willing to do business."[2] *Random House Dictionary of the English Language* defines the term as "what a property can be sold for on the open market."[3] Market value is defined similarly in other general dictionaries. Professional appraisers must recognize that in general commerce and in the law, the amount of this defined "price" depends on custom, encumbrances, and conditions, or the impositions of regulation, statute, or appellate court. These differences are not necessarily inadvertent.

Although there is considerable logic and simplicity in the concept of market value as "most probable selling price," this is a notion that includes duress. If duress is present, it is reflected in a transaction price, and price may not be market value.

The concept of market value as the "highest price" under a set of specific conditions, as opposed to the concept of market value as a modal or central tendency under the same conditions, is also controversial. For a market to exist, there must be enough buyers, sellers, and product to provide competition; out of this will develop a central tendency and a highest tendency. The notion of the "highest price" was originally rooted in the idea that market value should be the highest possible price represented by the central tendency and was not thought to be the highest possible price within the range of data; however, a definition that includes the word *highest* is perhaps subject to misinterpretation.

Equilibrium value is the price that would be available in the market if supply and demand were in balance. When the forces of supply and demand are out of equilibrium, market value can and does differ significantly from market value in a more balanced situation. During the Great Depression, for example, when values fell dramatically, many people believed or wanted to believe that there was intrinsic value in properties although it was not then obtainable in the market. When the market is extremely active, prices rise above the level some people believe is normal or intrinsic. In all cases, however, market value is the price that is available in the market. Intrinsic value is regarded by some practitioners and theorists to be meaningless in relation to market value.

Despite the differing schools of thought, it is generally agreed that market value results from collective value judgments rather than isolated judgments. A market value estimate must be based on objective observation of the collective actions of the marketplace. The standard of measurement of these actions is necessarily cash; the increments or diminutions in market value caused by financing and other terms are measured against the all-cash value.

A definition that incorporates concepts that are most widely agreed upon, such as willing, able, and knowledgeable buyers and sellers who act prudently, gives an appraiser a choice among three bases: 1) all cash, or 2) terms equivalent to cash, or 3) other precisely revealed terms, and still requires increments or diminutions from the all-cash market value to be quantified in terms of cash. Such a definition is the following:

---

2. *Webster's Ninth New Collegiate Dictionary* (Springfield, Mass.: Mirriam-Webster Inc., 1983), p. 728.

3. *Random House Dictionary of the English Language*, unabr. ed. (New York: Random House, 1967), p. 878.

> The most probable price, as of a specified date, in cash, or in terms equivalent to cash, or in other precisely revealed terms, for which the specified property rights should sell after reasonable exposure in a competitive market under all conditions requisite to fair sale, with the buyer and seller each acting prudently, knowledgeably, and for self-interest, and assuming that neither is under undue duress.

Some appraisers cite this definition verbatim in their appraisal reports and clarify separately if the value is stated in cash, or in terms equivalent to cash, or in other terms. Other appraisers use only one phrase about the value in the definition— that is, if appropriate, instead of "in cash," they substitute "in terms arithmetically equivalent to cash" or "in terms precisely revealed below."

The *Standards of Professional Practice* of the Appraisal Institute require that the following items directly related to a market value definition must be included in every appraisal report.

1. Identification of the specific property rights to be appraised.
2. Statement of the effective date of the value opinion.
3. Specification of whether cash, or terms equivalent to cash, or other precisely described financing terms are being assumed as the basis of the appraisal.
4. If the appraisal is conditioned upon financing or other terms, specification of whether the financing or terms are at, below, or above market interest rates and/or contain unusual conditions or incentives. The terms of above- or below-market interest rates and/or other special incentives must be clearly set forth; their contribution to, or negative influence on, value must be described and estimated; and the market data supporting the valuation estimate must be described and explained.

Although the definition above includes non-cash-equivalent financing terms within the scope of market value of appraised property rights, these rights are valued in relation to cash. Increments or diminutions in market value attributable to financing terms are measured against the all-cash standard, and the dollar amount of variance from the cash standard must be reported.

Market value definitions are found in a wide variety of sources, including appraisal texts, real estate dictionaries, and court decisions. One of the best known definitions came out of a court decision from the Supreme Court of California, the Heilbron case. This definition has been widely employed in appraisal literature.

> The highest price estimated in terms of money which the land would bring if exposed for sale in the open market, with reasonable time allowed in which to find a purchaser, buying with knowledge of all of the uses and purposes to which it is adapted and for which it was capable of being used.
>
> [*Sacramento Southern R.R. Co. v. Heilbron* 156 Cal. 408, 104 p. 979 (1909).]

In litigation matters appraisers must use the exact definition of market value that applies in the jurisdiction in which the services are being performed. In addition, since government and regulatory agencies from time to time define or interpret market value, persons performing appraisal services for such agencies or institutions subject to their control are cautioned to use the applicable definition.

Two recent definitions that are refined attempts to capture the essence of the market value concept are worth examining. The first is

> The price in cash and/or other identified terms for which the specified real property interest is expected to sell in the real estate marketplace under all conditions requisite to a fair sale.[4]

This definition does not include any reference to a specified date. The second definition is

> The value or distribution of values inferrred by a competent observer from sufficient patterns of clearly understood, correctly reported, representative, and uncompelled transactions found in an adequate market which is either identical or sufficiently congruent to the market in which the property will be traded.[5]

This definition does not refer to the date of value or property rights, but assumes that this is understood.

Use Value

The realities of current real estate and mortgage practices not only place new emphasis on market value, but also require more frequent consideration of other kinds of value. One of these, use value, is a concept based on the productivity of an economic good. *Use value is the value a specific property has for a specific use.* Use value focuses on the contributory value of the real estate to the enterprise of which it is a part, without regard to its highest and best use or the monetary amount that might be realized upon its sale. Use value may vary, depending on the management of the property and external conditions such as changes in the business. For example, a manufacturing plant designed around a particular assembly process may have one use value before a major change in assembly technology and another use value afterward.

Real property may have a use value *and* a market value. An older factory that is still used by the original firm may have considerable use value to that firm, but only a nominal market value for another use.

Use-value appraisal assignments may be performed to value assets, including real property, for mergers, acquisitions, or security issues. This type of assignment is particularly common in appraising industrial real estate when the existing business enterprises include real property.

Court decisions and specific statutes may also create the need for use-value appraisals. For instance, many states require agricultural-use appraisals of farmland for property tax purposes rather than value estimates based on highest and best use.

---

4. See Peter F. Korpacz and Richard Marchitelli, "Market Value: A Contemporary Perspective," *The Appraisal Journal*, October 1984, and "Market Value: Contemporary Applications," *The Appraisal Journal*, July 1985.

5. Jared Shlaes, "The Market in Market Value," *The Appraisal Journal*, October 1984.

When appraising a type of property that is not commonly exchanged or rented, it may be difficult to determine whether an estimate of market value or use value is appropriate. Such properties, called *limited market properties*, can cause special problems for appraisers. *A limited market property is a property that has relatively few buyers at a particular time.* Large manufacturing plants, for example, are limited-market properties that typically appeal to relatively few potential purchasers.

Many limited-market properties include structures with unique physical designs, special construction materials, or layouts that restrict their utility to the use for which they were originally built. These properties usually have limited conversion potential and, consequently, are often called *special purpose* or *special design properties*. Examples of such properties include houses of worship, museums, schools, public buildings, and clubhouses.

Limited market properties may be appraised for market value based on their current use or the most likely alternative use. Due to the relatively small market and the lengthy market exposure needed to sell such properties, there may be little evidence to support a market value estimate based on their current use. Nonetheless, if a market exists, the appraiser must search diligently for whatever evidence of market value is available.

If a property's current use is so specialized that there is no demonstrable market for it, but the use is viable and likely to continue, the appraiser may render an estimate of use value. Such an estimate should not be confused with a market value estimate. If no market can be demonstrated, or if data are not available, the appraiser cannot estimate a market value, and should state this in his or her report. However, it is sometimes necessary to estimate market value in these situations for legal purposes. In these cases, appraisers must comply with the legal requirement, relying on their judgment rather than direct market evidence.

Investment Value

While use value focuses on the specific use of a property, investment value represents the value of a specific investment to a particular investor. As used in appraisal assignments, *investment value is the value of an investment to a particular investor based on his or her investment requirements.* In contrast to market value, investment value is value to an individual, not value in the marketplace.

Investment value reflects the subjective relationship between a particular investor and a given investment. It differs in concept from market value, although investment value and market value indications may be similar. When measured in dollars, investment value is the price an investor would pay for an investment in light of its perceived capacity to satisfy his or her desires, needs, or investment goals. To estimate investment value, specific investment criteria must be known.

An investment value appraisal may be sought by the potential purchaser of an existing investment or income-producing property, or by the developer of a new property.

Going-Concern Value

Going-concern value is the value created by a proven property operation; it is considered a separate entity to be valued with an established business. This value is distinct from the value of the real estate only. Going-concern value includes an intangible enhancement of the value of an operating business enterprise which is associated with the process of assembling the land, building, labor, equipment, and marketing operation. This process leads to an economically viable business that is expected to continue.

Going-concern appraisals are commonly conducted for hotels and motels, restaurants, bowling alleys, industrial enterprises, retail stores, and similar properties. In appraising these properties, the physical real estate assets are integral parts of an ongoing business, so market values for the land and the building are difficult, if not impossible, to segregate from the total value of the business.

Insurable Value

Insurable value is based on the replacement and/or reproduction cost of physical items that are subject to loss from hazards. *Insurable value is that portion of the value of an asset or asset group that is acknowledged or recognized under the provisions of an applicable loss insurance policy.* This value is often controlled by state law and varies from state to state.

Assessed Value

Assessed value applies in ad valorem taxation and refers to the value of a property according to the tax rolls. The assessed value schedule may not conform to market value, but it usually is calculated in relation to a market value base.

FACTORS OF VALUE

Value is extrinsic to the commodity, good, or service to which it is ascribed; it is created in the minds of individuals who constitute a market. The relationships that create value are complex, and values change with changes in the factors that are most influential. Typically, four interdependent economic factors create value: utility, scarcity, desire, and effective purchasing power. All four factors must be present for a property to have value.

Utility

Utility is the ability of a product to satisfy a human want, need, or desire. All properties must have utility to tenants, owner-investors, or owner-occupants. Residential properties satisfy the need for shelter; the useful benefits of these properties are called amenities. Usually, the value of amenities is related to their desirability and utility to the owner-occupant, but their value can also be converted into income in the form of rent. The benefits from income-producing properties can usually be measured in cash flow. The influence of utility on value depends on the characteristics of the property. Size utility, design utility, location utility, and other specific forms of utility can significantly influence property value.

The benefits of real property ownership derive from the bundle of rights that an owner possesses. Restrictions on ownership rights may inhibit the flow of benefits and, therefore, lower the property's value. Similarly, a property can only achieve its highest value if it can legally perform its most useful function. Environmental control regulations, zoning regulations, deed restrictions, or any other limitation on the rights of ownership can enhance or detract from a property's utility and value.

Scarcity

Scarcity is the present or anticipated supply of an item relative to the demand for it. In general, if demand is constant, the scarcity of a commodity makes it more valuable. Land, for example, is still generally abundant, but useful, desirable land is relatively scarce and, therefore, has greater value. No object, including real property, can have value unless scarcity is coupled with utility. Air, which has a high level of utility, has no definable economic value because it is abundant.

Desire

Desire is a purchaser's wish for an item to satisfy human needs (e.g., shelter, clothing, food, companionship) or individual wants beyond essential life support needs. Desire, along with utility and scarcity, is considered in relation to purchasing power.

Effective Purchasing Power

Effective purchasing power is the ability of an individual or group to participate in a market—that is, to acquire goods and services with cash or its equivalent. A valid estimate of the value of a property includes an accurate judgment of the market's ability to pay for the property.

SUPPLY AND DEMAND

The complex interaction of the four factors that create value is reflected in the basic economic principle of supply and demand. The utility of a commodity, its scarcity or abundance, the intensity of the human desire to acquire it, and the effective power to purchase it all affect the correlation between the supply of and demand for the commodity in any given situation.

Demand for a commodity is created by its utility and affected by its scarcity. Demand is also influenced by desire and the forces that create and stimulate desire. Although human longing for things may be unlimited, desire is restrained by effective purchasing power. Thus, the inability to buy expensive things affects demand.

Similarly, the supply of a commodity is influenced by its utility and limited by its scarcity. The availability of a commodity is affected by its desirability. Land is a limited commodity, and the land in an area that is suitable for a specific use will be in especially short supply if the perceived need for it is great. Sluggish purchasing power keeps the pressure on supply in check. If purchasing power expands, the supply of a relatively fixed commodity will dwindle and create a market-driven demand to increase the supply.

THE HISTORY OF VALUE THEORY

The development of modern value theory began in the eighteenth and nineteenth centuries when economic thinkers of the classical school first identified the four agents of production—labor, capital, coordination, and land—and examined the relationships between the basic factors that create value and supply and demand. Classical theory was largely based on the contributions of the Physiocrats, whose ideas were put forth in reaction to the mercantilist doctrines that dominated earlier economic thought.

Mercantilism focused on wealth as a means of enhancing a nation's power. National wealth was equated with an influx of bullion into the national treasury. Mercantilists sought to maintain a favorable balance of trade by selling goods to accumulate gold, the chief medium of exchange. Between the fifteenth and eighteenth centuries, economic activity in western Europe was associated with overseas exploration, colonization, and commerce. Mercantilist doctrine promoted strong, central economic controls to maintain monopolies in foreign trade and ensure the economic dependency of colonies.

Physiocratic thinkers of the mid-eighteenth century objected to the commercial and national emphasis of mercantilism. They stressed other considerations in formulating a theory of value. Agricultural productivity, not gold, was identified as the source of wealth, and land was cited as the fundamental productive agent. The Physiocrats also identified the importance of factors such as utility and scarcity in determining value.[6]

---

6. Francois Quesnay (1694-1774) and Anne Robert Turgot (1727-1781) put forth an individualistic, agrarian-based concept of economic behavior without centralized state control. They popularized the phrase *laissez-faire* (let people do as they choose), which underscores their individualistic approach. Quesnay's concept of economic rent introduced the role of competition in determining price and influencing profits. Turgot suggested that "subjective elements," not competition, more directly determined value. Turgot referred to these elements as "the ability to satisfy a want, the ease with which a commodity could be obtained, its scarcity, and other considerations." See Eric Roll, *A History of Economic Thought*, 3rd ed. (Englewood Cliffs, N.J.: Prentice-Hall, Inc., 1964), p. 134.

18TH CENTURY PRODUCTION

(Historical Pictures Service, Chicago)

The Classical School

The classical school expanded and refined the tenets of Physiocratic thought, formulating a value theory that attributed value to the cost of production. The Scottish economic thinker, Adam Smith (1721-1790), suggested that capital, in addition to land and labor, or productivity, constituted a primary agent of production. Smith acknowledged the role of coordination in production, but did not study its function as a primary agent. Smith believed that value was created when the agents of production were brought together to produce a useful item. In *The Wealth of Nations* (1776), the first systematic treatment of economics, Adam Smith considered value as objective phenomenon. By virtue of its existence, an item was assumed to possess utility. Scarcity also imparted exchange value to goods. The "natural price" of an object generally reflected how much the item cost to produce. In contemporary appraisal practice, the classical cost of production theory of value has influenced the cost approach.

Later economic thinkers who are regarded as members of the classical school offered theoretical refinements on the cost of production theory of value, but none contested its basic premises. David Ricardo (1772-1823) developed a theory of rent based on the concept of marginal land and the law of diminishing returns. Land residual returns were referred to as *rent*. Ricardo's theory has contributed significantly to the concept of highest and best use and the land residual technique used in the income capitalization approach to value.

ADAM SMITH

(Historical Pictures Service, Chicago)

Thomas Malthus (1776-1834) elaborated on Ricardo's theory of rent and, in the process, identified value in use, value in exchange (price), and intrinsic value. Although his contribution represents a departure from the cost of production theory of value, it did not alter prevailing economic thought.

Jean Baptiste Say (1767-1832) rejected the relationship between labor and value, concentrating on utility as the determinant of value. Say focused on the role of the entrepreneur in providing management and coordination as an agent of production.

John Stuart Mill reworked Adam Smith's ideas in *The Principles of Political Economy* (1848), which became the leading economic text of its time. Mill defined the relationship between interest and value in use, which he referred to as "capital value"; the role of risk in determining interest; and the inequities of "unearned increments" accruing to land.[7]

Confident of the analysis of the cost of production theory, John Stuart Mill (1806-1873) asserted, "Happily, nothing in the laws of value remains for the present or any future writer to clear up; the theory of the subject is complete."

Challenges to the Classical Theory

In the second half of the nineteenth century, two serious challenges to classical value theory were put forward. One was the labor theory of value, an extreme position

---

7. For further discussion of value theory, see James H. Burton, *Evolution of the Income Approach* (Chicago: American Institute of Real Estate Appraisers, 1982).

JOHN STUART MILL

(Historical Pictures Service, Chicago)

zealously espoused by Karl Marx (1818-1883). Marx claimed that all value is the direct result of labor and that increased wages to labor would lower capitalistic profits. Marx envisioned an inevitable struggle between the social classes which would eventually result in a violent political upheaval.

The other challenge was presented by the marginal utility, or Austrian, school, which was critical of both the classical and Marxian theories. The central concept of marginal utility links value to the utility of, and demand for, the marginal, or additional, unit of an item. Thus, if one more unit than is needed or demanded appears in a given market, the market becomes diluted and the cost of production becomes irrelevant. Value is regarded as a function of demand prices, with utility as its fundamental precept.

William Stanley Jevons (1835-1882), a founder of modern statistics and a principal representative of this school, wrote "Labor once spent has no influence on the future value of any article: it is gone and lost forever." Eugen von Boehm-Bawerk (1835-1882), a member of the Austrian school, defined value as "that significance a good acquires in the contribution of utility toward the well-being of an individual."[8] Marginal utility is the theoretical basis for the concept of contribution.

The Neoclassical Synthesis

These formidable challenges to the classical theory of value inspired economists to reconsider the problem. In the late nineteenth and early twentieth centuries, the

---

8. W. Stanley Jevons, *The Theory of Political Economy*, 5th ed. (New York: Augustus M. Kelley, 1965), p. 164; Burton, p. 17.

neoclassical school successfully merged the supply-cost considerations of the classicists with the demand-price theory of marginal utility. Alfred Marshall (1842-1924) is credited with this synthesis, which underlies contemporary value theory.[9]

Marshall compared supply and demand to the blades of a pair of scissors, neither of which could ever be separated from the determination of value. However, he stressed the critical importance of time in working out an adjustment between the two principles. Marshall maintained that market forces tend toward an equilibrium where prices and production costs meet. Utility-demand considerations operate in the limited span of a given market. In the short term, supply is relatively fixed and value is a function of demand. Cost-supply considerations, however, extend over a broader period, during which production flows and patterns are subject to change. Marshall believed that a perfect economic market would eventually result and that price, cost, and value would all be equal.[10]

Marshall was the first major economist to consider the techniques of valuation, specifically the valuation of real estate. In this regard, his writings, and the writings of those who built upon his work, are important sources for understanding the distinction between value theory and valuation theory, or "the method of estimating, measuring, or predicting a defined value." (The development of valuation theory and the three approaches used in the valuation process are discussed in Chapter 4.)

SUMMARY

Because the concept of value is central to appraisal, clear distinctions must be drawn among related terms such as price, market, cost, and value. A *price* represents the amount a particular purchaser agrees to pay and a particular seller agrees to accept under the circumstances surrounding a transaction. A *market* is a set of arrangements in which buyers and sellers are brought together through the price mechanism. Real estate markets involve the exchange of property rights for other assets, such as money. *Cost* applies to production rather than exchange, and can be divided into direct, or hard, costs and indirect, or soft, costs, as well as construction and development costs. *Value* represents the monetary worth of property, goods, or services to buyers and sellers.

Although *market value* is a simple concept, different beliefs and assumptions about the marketplace and the nature of value render any ultimate definition controversial. Market value definitions fall into five categories. The following definition incorporates the concepts that are most widely accepted:

---

9. In 1890, Marshall published *Principles of Economics*, which succeeded Mill's *Principles of Political Economy* as the foremost text on economic thought. In this book, Marshall advocated a dynamic theory of value to explain real world events. See Marshall, *Principles of Economics*, 8th ed. (London: MacMillan and Company, 1920) Reprint. (Philadelphia: Porcupine Press, 1982), pp. 288-290, 664-669.

10. See Robert L. Heilbroner, *The Worldly Philosophers*, rev. ed. (New York: Simon and Schuster, 1964), pp. 178-179, and Paul F. Wendt, *Real Estate Appraisal: Review and Outlook* (Athens: University of Georgia Press, 1974), pp. 18-19.

the most probable price, as of a specified date, in cash, or in terms equivalent to cash, or in other precisely revealed terms, for which the specified property rights should sell after reasonable exposure in a competitive market under all conditions requisite to fair sale, with the buyer and seller each acting prudently, knowledgeably, and for self-interest, and assuming that neither is under undue duress.

The Appraisal Institute's *Standards of Professional Practice* require that an estimate of market value 1) include a statement that specifies whether the financing terms are at, below, or above market interest rates and whether unusual conditions or incentives are present, and 2) quantify contribution to, or negative influence on, value.

Other types of value are also considered in real estate: use value, investment value, going-concern value, insurable value, and assessed value. *Use value* focuses on the real estate's contributory value to the enterprise of which it is a part, without regard to the property's highest and best use. *Investment value* is the value of an investment to a particular investor, based on his or her investment requirements. *Going-concern value* is the value created by a proven property operation in which the physical real estate assets are an integral part of an ongoing business. *Insurable value* is the portion of value that is covered by casualty insurance. *Assessed value* refers to the property's value according to the tax rolls.

Four interdependent factors create value: utility, scarcity, desire, and effective purchasing power. The interaction of these four factors affects the balance of supply and demand. Various schools of economic thought have contributed to the development of modern value theory. The classical school represented by Adam Smith departed from mercantilist theory by attributing value to the cost of production. The labor theory of value, set forth by Karl Marx, and the opposing concept of marginal utility, which linked value to demand, both challenged the classical theory of value. The neoclassical economics of Alfred Marshall combined classical supply-cost considerations with the demand-price theory of the marginal utility school.

3 Foundations of Appraisal

$\mathbf{T}$he characteristics of land and real property that underlie appraisal activity reflect our society's attitudes and beliefs. Because real estate has value, the possession and successful management of real estate create opportunities for citizens to achieve economic goals that are perceived as desirable by society as a whole. Greater financial stability, freedom from excessive restrictions, and higher returns on investments are a few of the goals that can be achieved by participating in real estate markets.[1]

In determining their level of participation in the market, individuals consider their wants and needs as well as the choices available to them at different times. These choices, which represent the variety of market characteristics, help support a free market economy in which both individual and collective decisions contribute to the nation's economic success.

Similarly, the production of goods, services, and income that comprise the consumable portion of our economy depends on the combined effects of several essential economic ingredients. These ingredients are the agents of production: labor, capital, coordination, and land. The combination of human effort, tangible wealth, production systems, and natural resources permits society to pursue its economic goals.

The collective human action that shapes the operation of the market reflects the pursuit of economic goals. To analyze the many dynamic and interactive factors that influence people's attitudes and beliefs about value, the fundamental concepts of anticipation and change must be addressed.

---

1. Constance Perin, *Everything in Its Place; Social Order and Land Use in America* (Princeton, N.J.: Princeton University Press, 1977).

ANTICIPATION

Anticipation is the perception that value is created by the expectation of benefits to be derived in the future. In the real estate market, the current value of a property is not based on its historical prices or the cost of its creation; rather, value is based on market participants' perceptions of the future benefits of acquisition.

The value of owner-occupied property is primarily based on the expected future advantages, amenities, and pleasures of ownership and occupancy. The value of income-producing real estate is based on the anticipated income it will produce in the future. Therefore, real property appraisers must be aware of local, regional, and national real estate trends that affect the perceptions of buyer and seller and their anticipations of the future. Historical data on a property or a market are relevant only insofar as they help interpret current market anticipations.

CHANGE

Change is the result of the relationship between cause and effect that affects real property value. Although change is inevitable and constant, the process may be gradual and not easily discernible. In active markets, change may occur rapidly; new properties may be put up for sale and others may be sold on a daily basis. Abrupt changes may be precipitated by plant closings, tax law revisions, or the start of new construction. The pervasiveness of change is evident in the dynamic real estate market, where the social, economic, governmental, and environmental forces that affect real estate are in constant transition. As these forces change, so do individual property values. Appraisers attempt to identify any current or anticipated changes in the market that could affect current property values, but because change is inevitable, appraisal value estimates are valid only for the time specified in the appraisal report.

The inevitability of change is also evident in the physical, functional, and economic impairments observed in buildings as they age. These impairments create *depreciation, a loss in property value from any cause.* Depreciation may be seen as the difference between the cost to reproduce or replace a property and its value. In general, losses in property value derive from deterioration or obsolescence. Because deterioration and obsolescence begin the moment a building or improvement is completed, the varieties of each have unique implications in appraisal. (A detailed discussion of deterioration and obsolescence is presented in Chapter 17.)

The appraisal principles of supply and demand, substitution, balance, and externalities help to explain shifts in value and to identify value trends. These principles are founded in general economics, and can be applied in an individual context to the unique physical and legal characteristics of a particular parcel of real property. When these principles are in proper accord, they indicate highest and best use, a concept of great significance in real property appraisal.

SUPPLY AND DEMAND

In economic theory, the principle of supply and demand states that the price of a commodity, good, or service varies directly, but not necessarily proportionately, with demand, and inversely, but not necessarily proportionately, with supply. In real estate, the appraisal principle of supply and demand states that the price of real property varies directly, but not necessarily proportionately, with demand, and inversely, but not necessarily proportionately, with supply. Thus, increasing the supply of an item or decreasing the demand for an item tends to reduce the price obtainable in the market; the opposite is also true. The relationship between supply and demand may not be directly proportional, but the interaction of these forces is fundamental to economic theory. The interaction of suppliers and demanders, or sellers and buyers, constitutes a market.

Figure 3.1   Supply and Demand Curve

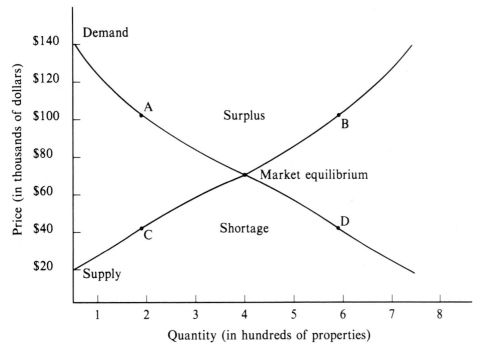

Quantity (in hundreds of properties)

The relationship between supply and demand can be shown by plotting the supply of and demand for a particular category of real estate in a given market. Prices increase as demand increases and decline as demand declines. As prices increase, sellers expand supply; as prices decline, sellers cut back on supply.

Point B indicates that 600 properties are being offered for sale at $100,000, but Point A shows that there are only enough buyers to purchase 200 properties at this price. Point C indicates that 200 properties are being offered for sale at $40,000, and Point D shows that there are enough buyers to purchase 600 properties at $40,000.

Market equilibrium has been achieved only for the 400 properties priced at $70,000.

Usually, property values vary inversely with changes in supply. If properties for a particular use become more abundant than they were in the past, their value declines; by contrast, if properties become more scarce, their value increases. The supply of and demand for commodities always tend toward equilibrium. At this theoretical point, market value, price, and cost are equal.

In real estate, supply is the amount of a type of real estate available for sale or lease at various prices. Typically, more of an item will be supplied at a higher price and less at a lower price. Therefore, the supply of an item at a particular price, at a particular time, and in a particular place refers to that item's relative scarcity, which is a basic factor of value. The supply of real estate is a function of the capital needed to bring a parcel of land to a given use relative to the current price for existing properties providing that use. For example, as the price of houses increases, builders may find it profitable to build on land that was previously considered too expensive to develop.

Because real property is both a physical commodity and a service, the supply of real estate refers to the amount of service, or use, space as well as the quantity of physical space. Consequently, those involved in real estate are primarily concerned with the supply of land suitable for a specific use, not the total number of acres available. The supply of real estate incorporates both the *quality* and *quantity* of service space provided. The quality of space may affect property value even more than its quantity. Quality is a function of the tangible attributes of a property, such as size, shape, and condition, and its intangible attributes, or amenities. Proper comparisons can be made only between properties that are similar both qualitatively and quantitatively.

Generally, the quantity of space supplied for a given use is slow to adjust to changes in price levels. The length of time needed to build new structures, the large amount of capital required, and government regulations often hamper a supplier's ability to meet changes in the market. However, the quality of service space can change rapidly because suppliers can convert nonproductive space to alternative uses, defer maintenance, and partition existing space into smaller units.

Demand is the desire and ability to purchase or lease goods and services. In real estate, demand is the amount of a type of real estate desired for purchase or rent at various prices. Typically, less of an item will be demanded at a higher price, and more will be demanded at a lower price. Property values tend to vary directly with shifts in demand; prices tend to increase if demand increases and other factors remain constant. Usually, the relationship between demand and price is not fixed. This changing relationship is described as the elasticity of demand.

Because the supply of real property for a specific use is difficult to adjust, especially in a short time, values are most affected by current demand. Demand, like supply, can be motivated by the desire for real estate characterized in terms of both quantity and quality. Demand that is supported by purchasing power results in effective demand, which is the relevant market consideration. Typically, there is a direct, but not proportional, relationship between demand and price. If demand increases and supply remains constant, prices tend to increase; if demand falls, prices tend to fall. Appraisers must interpret market behavior to ascertain the existing relationship between the supply of, and the demand for, the type of property being appraised.

COMPETITION

The concept of competition is related to the principle of supply and demand. *Competition between buyers or tenants is the interactive efforts of two or more potential purchasers or tenants to secure a purchase or lease. Between sellers or landlords, competition is the interactive efforts of two or more potential sellers or landlords to effectuate a sale or lease.* It is fundamental to the dynamics of supply and demand in a free enterprise, profit-maximizing, economic system.

Competition causes continual shifts in the levels of commodities that are available and, therefore, affects the levels of demand for these commodities. Buyers and sellers of real property operate in a competitive market setting, so, in essence, each property competes with all other properties that are suitable for the same use. For example, a profitable motel faces competition from newer motels nearby; existing residential subdivisions compete with new subdivisions; and downtown retail properties compete with suburban shopping centers.

Over time, competitive market forces tend to reduce unusually high, or excess, profits. Profit encourages competition, but excess profits tend to breed detracting competition. For example, the first store to open in a new and expanding area generates more profit than considered typical for that type of enterprise. Owners of similar retail enterprises may then gravitate to the area to compete for the surplus profits, and, eventually, there may not be enough business to support all the stores. A few stores may earn normal profits, but others will fail. The effects of competition and market trends on profit levels are especially important to appraisers making income projections for the income capitalization approach to value.

SUBSTITUTION

The principle of substitution states that when several similar or commensurate commodities, goods, or services are available, the one with the lowest price attracts the greatest demand and widest distribution. This principle assumes rational, prudent market behavior with no undue cost because of delay. According to the principle of substitution, a buyer will not pay more for one property than for another that is equally desirable.

Property values tend to be set by the cost of acquiring an equally desirable substitute property. The principle of substitution recognizes that buyers and sellers of real property have other options, i.e., other properties are available for similar uses. The substitution of one property for another may be considered in terms of use, structural design, or earnings. The cost of acquisition may be the cost to purchase a similar site and construct a building of equivalent utility, assuming no undue cost due to delay; this is the basis of the cost approach. On the other hand, the cost of acquisition may be the price of acquiring an existing property of equal utility, again assuming no undue cost due to delay; this is the basis of the sales comparison approach.

The principle of substitution is equally applicable to properties purchased for their amenity-producing capabilities—e.g., residential properties—and those purchased for their income-producing capabilities. In regard to income-producing property, substitution refers to alternate investment property that produces equivalent investment returns with equivalent risk. The limits of property prices, rents, and rates tend to be set by the prevailing prices, rents, and rates for equally desirable substitutes. The principle of substitution is fundamental to all three traditional approaches to value—sales comparison, cost, and income capitalization.

OPPORTUNITY COST

The concept of *opportunity cost, the cost of options foregone or opportunities not chosen*, is related to the principle of substitution. Opportunity cost is particularly significant in estimating the rates of return necessary to attract capital. By analyzing and comparing the prospective rates of return offered by alternative investment opportunities, an appraiser can estimate an appropriate rate of return for the property being appraised.

BALANCE

The principle of balance holds that real property value is created and sustained when contrasting, opposing, or interacting elements are in a state of equilibrium. This principle applies to relationships among various property components as well as the relationship between the costs of production and the property's productivity. Labor, capital, coordination, and land are the agents of production, but for most real properties, the critical combination is the land and the building. The point of economic balance is achieved when the combination of land and building is optimal, i.e., when no marginal benefit or utility is achieved by adding another unit of capital. *The law of increasing returns* holds that larger amounts of the agents of production produce greater net income up to a certain point. At this point, *the point of decreasing returns*, the maximum value is developed. Any additional expenditures will not produce a return commensurate with the additional investment, according to *the law of decreasing returns*.

The fertilization of farmland provides a simple example. Applying fertilizer to the land increases crop yield only up to a point. The optimum amount of fertilization is achieved when the value of the crops does not increase with additional expenditures for fertilizer. This is the point of balance.

The principle of balance also involves the relationship between the property as a whole and its environment. Balance affirms that a proper economic mix of types and locations of land uses in an area creates and sustains value.

The principle of balance and the related concepts of contribution, surplus productivity, and conformity are interdependent and crucial in estimating highest and best use and market value. These concepts form the theoretical foundation for estimating all forms of depreciation in the cost approach, making adjustments in the sales comparison approach, and calculating expected earnings in the income capitalization approach.

CONTRIBUTION

When appraisers apply the principle of balance to component property parts, they study the concept of contribution. *The concept of contribution states that the value of a particular component is measured in terms of its contribution to the value of the whole property, or as the amount that its absence would detract from the value of the whole.* The cost of an item does not necessarily equal its value. A swimming pool that costs $10,000 to install does not necessarily cause the value of a residential property to increase by $10,000. Rather, the pool's dollar contribution to value is measured in terms of how valuable its benefit or utility is in the market. Its contribution to value may be lower or higher than its cost. Thus, in some cases, a property's market value may not increase even though the physical real estate has undergone alteration, modification, or rehabilitation.

The existing improvements may not reflect a proper balance for the total property. Especially in areas of rapid transition, a property's present use may represent underutilization of the land. Nevertheless, an existing, less optimal use, called an *interim use*, will continue until it is economically feasible for a developer to absorb the costs of converting the property by razing or rehabilitating the existing improvements.

SURPLUS PRODUCTIVITY

Surplus productivity is the net income that remains after the costs of labor, capital, and coordination have been paid. The surplus is attributable to land rent and tends to fix land value. The concept of surplus productivity is the basis for the residual concept of land returns and for residual valuation techniques.

CONFORMITY

Conformity is the appraisal principle that holds that real property value is created and sustained when the characteristics of a property conform to the demands of its market. The styles and uses of the properties in an area may conform for several reasons, including economic pressures; the shared preferences of owners for certain types of structures, amenities, and services; and the enforcement of uniform standards by means of zoning. Through local zoning ordinances, the government encourages conformity by restricting land use. Standards of conformity are set by the market and are therefore subject to change. Zoning codes, however, tend to establish conformity in basic property characteristics, including size, style, and design. A particular market also sets standards of conformity, especially in terms of price. Usually, the value of an overimproved property will decline, or regress, toward the value level of surrounding, conforming properties; the value of an underimproved property may increase, or progress, toward the prevailing market standard.

EXTERNALITIES

The principle of externalities states that economies or diseconomies outside a property may have a positive or negative effect on its value. When external economies affect a great number of people, the product or service will probably be provided by government. Bridges, highways, police and fire protection, and other essential services can be provided more cheaply through common purchase by the government than through separate acquisition by individuals.

EXTERNAL INFLUENCES ON RESIDENTIAL PROPERTY
(H. Armstrong Roberts, Inc.)

External diseconomies result when the costs of inconveniences are imposed on other people by an individual or a firm. A person who litters, for example, imposes the cleanup costs on others.

Real estate is affected by externalities more than any other economic good, service, or commodity. Because it is physically immobile, real estate is subject to many types of external influences. These influences may be international or national in origin or they may emanate from the region, community, or neighborhood. Externalities may be as broad as international currency and gold prices or as narrow as a neighbor's standard of property maintenance. An appraiser should observe and analyze how external influences affect the parcel of real estate being appraised.

At the international and national levels, trade policy, manufacturing efficiency, interest rates, and socioeconomic priorities can greatly affect real estate values. For example, a combination of these influences caused many U.S. real estate values to fall or stagnate in the early 1980s. Foreign imports depressed some U.S. industries, and old plants and equipment tended to make U.S. manufacturing operations less efficient than their foreign counterparts. High interest rates depressed home buying and industrial expansion, and decreased emphasis on homeownership as a national priority resulted in more competition for credit. Borrowers who wanted to buy a home had to compete for capital with government and industry.

At the regional level, real estate values in the early 1980s fared better in some areas than in others. In general, the population migration to the Sunbelt tended to enhance values there at the expense of older regions in the north, where values tended to stabilize or decline. Industrial areas with manufacturing operations that were susceptible to foreign competition suffered more than areas that were less reliant on such industries. By the mid 1980s the decline in oil prices brought about a recession in the Sunbelt. In addition, the great volume of construction activity over the previous decade resulted in an oversupply of office buildings. Simultaneously, the northern Rustbelt experienced economic recovery. In this section of the country, the fall-off in construction coupled with pent-up demand has led to higher real estate prices.

At the community and neighborhood levels, property values are affected by local laws, local government policies and administration, property taxes, economic growth, and social attitudes. Different property value trends are frequently noted among communities in the same region and among neighborhoods in the same community. Appraisers should be familiar with external events at all levels and be able to assess their impact on individual property values.

FORCES THAT INFLUENCE REAL PROPERTY VALUES

The value of real property reflects and is influenced by the interaction of basic forces that motivate human activity. These forces are divided into four major categories: *social* trends, *economic* circumstances, *governmental* controls and regulations, and *environmental* conditions. The forces are dynamic; they exert pressure on human activities and in turn are affected by these activities. The interaction of all the forces influences the value of every parcel of real estate in the market.

To estimate value, an appraiser interprets how the market views a particular property; the scope of investigation is not limited to static, current conditions. Rather, the appraiser analyzes trends in the forces that influence value to determine the direction, speed, duration, strength, and limits of these trends.

Social Forces

Social forces are exerted primarily through population characteristics. The demographic composition of the population reveals the potential, basic demand for real estate services; therefore, proper analysis and interpretation of demographic trends are imperative in real estate appraisal. Real property values are affected not only by population changes and characteristics, but also by the entire spectrum of human activity. The total population, the rate of family formations and dissolutions, and age distributions strongly influence real property values.

Economic Forces

Economic forces are also significant to real property value. Appraisers analyze the fundamental relationships between current and anticipated supply and demand and the economic ability of the population to satisfy its wants, needs, and demands through its purchasing power. Many specific market characteristics are considered in the analysis of economic forces—e.g., employment, wage levels, industrial expansion, the economic base of the region and the community, price levels, and the cost and availability of mortgage credit. Most of these are considered demand-side economic characteristics. Supply-side economic characteristics include the stock of available vacant and improved properties, new development under construction or being planned, occupancy rates, the rental and price patterns of existing properties, and construction costs. Other economic trends and considerations may be studied as the appraiser's analysis focuses on successively smaller geographic areas.

Governmental Forces

Governmental, political, and legal actions at all levels have a great impact on property values. The legal climate at a particular time or in a particular place may overshadow the natural market forces of supply and demand. The government provides many necessary facilities and services that affect land-use patterns. Therefore, appraisers must diligently identify and examine the potential value influences of

- Public services such as fire and police protection, utilities, refuse collection, and transportation networks
- Local zoning, building codes, and health codes, especially those that obstruct or support land use
- National, state, and local fiscal policies
- Special legislation that influences general property values (e.g., rent control laws, statutory redemption laws, restrictions on forms of ownership such as condominiums and timeshare arrangements, homestead exemption laws, environmental legislation regulating new developments, and legislation affecting the types of loans, loan terms, and investment powers of mortgage lending institutions)

Environmental Forces

Both natural and man-made environmental forces influence real property values. Environmental forces that may be analyzed for real estate appraisal purposes include climatic conditions such as snowfall, rainfall, temperature, and humidity; topography and soil; natural barriers to future development, such as rivers, mountains, lakes, and oceans; primary transportation systems, including federal and state highway systems, railroads, airports, and navigable waterways; and the nature and desirability of the immediate area surrounding a property.

The environmental forces that affect a specific real property value may be best understood in relation to the property's location. *Location is the time-distance relationship, or linkage, between a property or neighborhood and all possible origins and destinations of residents coming to or going from the property or neighborhood.* Time and distance are measures of relative access. To analyze locational forces, the linkages between the property and important points or places outside the property are identified, and the distance and time required to cover those distances by the most commonly used types of transportation are measured. Depending on the area and the property type, the appraiser may investigate the property's access to public transportation, schools, stores, service establishments, parks, recreation and cultural facilities, places of worship, sources of employment, product markets, suppliers of production needs, and processors of raw materials.

An understanding of all value-influencing forces is fundamental to the appraisal of real property. Although the four forces are discussed separately here, they work together to affect property values. These forces provide the background against which appraisers view every parcel of real property. (Value influences are discussed in detail in Chapters 7 and 8.)

HIGHEST AND BEST USE

By identifying and interpreting the market forces that affect a specific property in a local and regional context, the appraiser determines the property's highest and best use. Highest and best use is a fundamental concept in real estate appraisal because it focuses market analysis on the subject property and allows the appraiser to consider the property's optimum use in light of market conditions on a specific date.

Highest and best use reflects a basic assumption about real estate market behavior—that the price a buyer will pay for a property is based on his or her conclusions about the most profitable use of the site or property. Therefore, sites and improved properties tend to be put to their highest and best uses. However, the determination of a property's highest and best use set forth in an appraisal may or may not conform with the existing use. The determination of highest and best use must be based on careful consideration of prevailing market conditions, trends affecting market participation and change, and the existing use of the subject property.

Highest and best use has been defined as

> the reasonably probable and legal use of vacant land or an improved property, which is physically possible, appropriately supported, financially feasible, and results in the highest value.

Because the use of land can be limited by the presence of improvements, highest and best use is determined separately for the land or site as though vacant and available to be put to its highest and best use, or for the property as improved.

The first determination reflects the fact that land value is derived from potential land use. Land has limited value unless there is a present or anticipated use for it; the amount of value depends on the nature of the land's anticipated use, according to the concept of surplus productivity. Among all reasonable, alternative uses, the use that yields the highest present land value, after payments are made for labor, capital, and coordination, is generally regarded as the highest and best use of the land as though vacant.

For the purpose of analysis, the appraiser assumes that the parcel of land in question is vacant. Even a site with a large building on it can be made vacant by demolishing the building. The question to be answered is: If the land were vacant, what new improvement should be constructed on the site?

The highest and best use of a property as improved refers to the optimal use that could be made of the property including all existing structures. The implication is that the existing improvement should be renovated or retained as is so long as it continues to contribute to the total market value of the property, or until the return from a new improvement would more than offset the cost of demolishing the existing building and constructing a new one. For example, a large, old house could continue to be used as a single-family residence, or it could be converted into apartments or offices. The decision depends on the rents or prices that could be charged for the existing property under the alternative uses and how these amounts compare with the costs of conversion. Although the existing improvement does not represent the highest and best use of the site as though vacant, it should not necessarily be demolished, or demolished yet.

The determination of the highest and best use of land as though vacant is useful for land or site valuation; determining the highest and best use of an improved property provides a decision regarding continued use or demolition of the property.

The relationship between the supply of, and demand for, land adaptable to a particular use is significant in determining highest and best use. If a more profitable use must be delayed due to insufficient present demand, an *interim use* will continue until or unless the value of the land as if vacant plus the cost of demolishing the existing improvements exceeds the total value of the improved property at its current use.

DEMOLITION OF A BUILDING

(H. Armstrong Roberts, Inc.)

When properties are devoted to temporary, interim uses, the concept of consistent use must be addressed. *Consistent use is the concept that land cannot be valued on the basis of one use while the improvements are valued on the basis of another.* Improvements must contribute to the land value to have any value themselves. Improvements that do not represent the land's highest and best use, but do have substantial remaining physical lives, may have an interim use of temporary value or they may have no value at all. In fact, the improvements could even have negative value if substantial costs would be incurred for their removal. (Highest and best use is discussed in detail in Chapter 12.)

REAL ESTATE MARKETS

Appraisers consider value in the context of real estate markets, so delineating real estate markets and submarkets is an essential part of appraisal. Many evaluation studies are conducted to determine and interpret the characteristics of markets for investors and developers. In valuation assignments, particularly in estimations of market value, an appraiser's understanding of the market for a specific property provides the criteria with which to research, select, and interpret the comparability of other properties. In a market value appraisal assignment, the appraiser identifies and analyzes the market or markets that influence the subject property. To provide credible evaluation conclusions and estimates of market value, real estate appraisers must thoroughly understand the real estate market or markets that are relevant to each assignment.

Buyers and sellers of real estate interact in different areas for different reasons and different types of property. Thus, real estate markets are divided into categories based on the differences among property types and their appeal to different market participants. The markets for various categories of real estate are further divided into submarkets, which correspond to the preferences of buyers and sellers. Differentiating real estate markets facilitates their study.

All real estate markets are influenced by the attitudes, motivations, and interactions of buyers and sellers of real property, which, in turn, are subject to many social, economic, governmental, and environmental influences. Real estate markets may be studied in terms of their geographic, competitive, and supply-and-demand characteristics which relate to overall real estate market conditions.

The identification and interpretation of real estate markets is an analytical process. Because real estate markets bring buyers and sellers together to allocate an increasingly scarce resource—land—it is important that appropriate analytical methods and techniques be applied in appraisal assignments. Appraisers frequently rely on analytical methods to study the complex interrelationships among the factors that create value in the minds of market participants.

Appraisers determine the utility and scarcity of property, as well as the desire and effective purchasing power of those who seek to acquire property rights, answering questions about real estate markets and submarkets. Their appraisal education and experience tell them which questions to ask and which procedures to follow in gathering information. As the body of appraisal knowledge continues to expand, new analytical methods and techniques can be applied to the data gleaned from market investigation.

Characteristics of Real Estate Markets

Real estate markets do not possess the same economic characteristics as markets for other goods and services, which are efficient markets. The efficiency of a market is based on assumptions about the behavior of buyers and sellers and the characteristics of the products traded.

The goods or services in an efficient market are essentially homogeneous items that can be readily substituted for one another. In contrast, each parcel of real estate is unique and its location is fixed. No two parcels of real estate are physically identical. Although some parcels may be economically similar and could be substituted for one another, they differ geographically. The essential features of real estate preclude its diverse markets from being highly efficient.

In an efficient market there is a large number of buyers and sellers who create a competitive, free market, and none of these participants has a large enough share of the market to have a direct and measurable influence on price. In real estate markets, only a few buyers and sellers may act at one time, within one price range, and at one location for any type of property. The high relative value of real estate requires great purchasing power, so real estate markets are very sensitive to changes in wage levels, the stability of income, and the number of individuals employed. Construction costs, housing costs, and rent levels are all affected by market participants' ability to pay.

In an efficient market, prices are relatively uniform, stable, and low. They are often the primary consideration in purchase or sale decisions because quality tends to be uniform at a set price. In real estate markets, prices are relatively high and very few purchasers have enough money to pay for property in cash. Therefore, types of financing offered, the amount of mortgage money available, interest rates, down payment requirements, and typical loan duration affect the decision to purchase real estate. If a property cannot be financed favorably, it usually will not be bought. Investors are less likely to buy income-producing property if the debt service exceeds a certain percentage of gross income.

An efficient market is self-regulating. There are very few government restrictions on open and free competition. Real estate markets, on the other hand, are not self-regulating. Federal, state, county, and local regulations govern the ownership and transfer of real estate; contract and deed restrictions further regulate the sale and purchase of property. A deed restriction, for example, may require that houses in a subdivision contain at least 2,000 square feet of area.

Supply and demand are never far out of balance in an efficient market because the market tends to move toward balance through the effects of competition. Although the supply of, and demand for, real estate also tend toward equilibrium, this point is theoretical and seldom achieved. The supply of real estate suitable for a specific use is slow to adjust to market demand, unlike the supply of less durable commodities. Furthermore, shifts in demand may occur while new real estate units are being constructed, so an oversupply, rather than market equilibrium, may result.

Units of real estate that are comparable in size and quality do tend to sell at comparable prices; if supply and demand are in relative balance, real estate prices tend to be stable. But if the demand for real estate increases suddenly, an additional supply cannot be provided quickly. Similarly, if demand declines suddenly, the excess supply cannot be quickly removed from the market.

In real estate markets, supply and demand *are* considered causal factors and price is the result of their interaction. Price changes usually are preceded by changes in market activity. Often, supply or demand may shift suddenly in a period of no activity or increased activity.

Buyers and sellers in an efficient market are knowledgeable and fully informed about market conditions, the behavior of others, past market activity, product quality, and product substitutability. Any information needed on bids, offers, and sales is readily available. Buyers and sellers of real estate may not be well informed. Most people do not buy and sell real estate frequently, so they are not very familiar with the procedure or knowledgeable about how to judge a property. Information on bids, offers, and sales of a particular property or similar properties may not be readily available to buyers and sellers.

Buyers and sellers in an efficient market are brought together by an organized market mechanism, such as the New York Stock Exchange, and it is relatively easy for sellers to enter into the market in response to market demand. In real estate markets, however, demand may be volatile due to sudden shifts in population. A sudden influx of population in an area may result in high prices because it will take months or years to construct new buildings and increase development. A sudden migration due to unfavorable economic conditions can result in an oversupply and lower prices.

Finally, in an efficient market, goods are readily consumed, quickly supplied, and easily transported. Real estate is a durable product and, as an investment, it may be relatively unmarketable and illiquid. Real estate is not usually sold quickly because its sale involves large sums of money and the appropriate financing may not always be readily secured. The supply of real estate is relatively inflexible and, because it is fixed in location, the supply cannot be adjusted quickly on a national or regional level.

Real estate markets are not efficient and, due to imperfections such as a lack of product standardization and the time required to produce a new supply, it is difficult to predict their behavior accurately. Recognizing that real estate markets do not operate like markets for other commodities, appraisers must analyze the significant aspects of market activity that are indicated by the market's inefficiency. Therefore, real estate market analysis focuses on the motivations, attitudes, and interaction of market participants as they respond to the particular characteristics of real estate and to external influences that affect its value. This focus underscores the importance of objective real estate appraisal in a free market economy and the responsibility of appraisers to the communities they serve.

Types of Real Estate Markets

Different real estate markets are created by participants' needs, desires, motivations, locations, and ages, and the types, locations, designs, and zoning restrictions of property.

Five real estate markets can be identified to correspond to five broad categories of property:

1. Residential
2. Commercial
3. Industrial
4. Agricultural
5. Special-purpose

Each market for a particular type of property can be subdivided into smaller, more specialized, markets called *submarkets.* Submarkets for urban, suburban, and rural residential property can be further divided in terms of the purchasers' preference for high-, medium-, or low-priced properties. Offices, stores, loft buildings, parking garages, motels, hotels, and shopping centers, which are all commercial properties, typically appeal to different groups of buyers and sellers. Industrial properties include factories, warehouses, and mining operations. The market for agricultural properties can be divided into markets for pasture, timberland, cropland, orchards, and ranchlands. Special-purpose properties include parks, cemeteries, houses of worship, clubs, golf courses, historic or recreational government properties, and public utilities.

The process of identifying and analyzing submarkets within a larger market is called market segmentation. A submarket can be created by changes in the demand side of the market; for example, a type of property may be in demand by a particular group. Families looking for homes and companies in need of warehouses may be considered real estate markets. The properties within these large markets are heterogeneous because residences and warehouses can be large or small, old or new, well designed or poorly designed. A market is divided into a number of smaller, more homogeneous submarkets by recognizing the different product preferences of buyers and sellers. These preferences may include building size and design, price range, and property location.

Real estate appraisers identify and research market segments by considering locational, demographic, socioeconomic, psychological, and product-related characteristics. They may use survey research techniques to discover, quantify, analyze, and form conclusions about the composition of particular submarkets. (For further information on market segmentation and the urban growth patterns on which it is based, see the discussion of city origins and growth patterns in Chapter 7.)

APPROACHES TO MARKET STUDY

Three major elements affect and help create real estate markets: location, competition, and the demand unit. Appraisers study markets from these three viewpoints to understand market participants; their actions reveal patterns that can be used to identify trends in market behavior.

Location

A real estate market can be identified by its location. To ascertain the market for a particular property, an appraiser delineates the surrounding physical or political boundaries within which related economic decisions are made.[2] The market area is delineated in terms of the distance and travel time to or from common destinations and origins.

A property may have an international, national, regional, statewide, urban, rural, district, and neighborhood market. In appraising a large industrial plant, for example, an appraiser might study the national or international market for this type of property. The space involved, the price level or price range of similar properties, and the current or intended use of the real estate help determine the geographic

---

2. The economic location concept is elaborated in *situs* theory, which describes the relationship between the total urban environment and the specific use of a parcel of land at a particular time. Economic location analysis involves more than simply identifying the physical position of one property in relation to another. Rather, locational analysis considers the economic activities in a defined neighborhood or trade area, the relationship among these activities, the accessibility of people and goods or services to the focus of these activities, and the environment or surroundings through which these people, goods, and services must pass. See Richard B. Andrews, *Urban Land Economics and Public Policy* (New York: Free Press, 1971).

extent of the market for a property. The market for office buildings in major commercial cities, for example, is probably broader geographically than the market for single-family residences in rural communities.

Competition

Real estate transactions occur in a competitive environment. This competiton is a function of two interrelated components: the number of available properties that appeal to potential purchasers and the number of potential purchasers, or renters, who constitute the market for these properties. Competition influences the behavior of market participants. It is a function of supply and demand and, therefore, can be studied in terms of the availability and prices of similar properties. Competition also results from the behavior of market participants. Buyers compete to obtain the most personally satisfying or useful property at the most advantageous price; sellers compete to sell their property at the price that is most advantageous to them.

Because prices are affected by the supply of, and demand for, property, appraisers study the number of available properties and the approximate number of buyers and sellers who are active in a market during a particular time period. If there are few properties for sale and many potential buyers, it is a seller's market and prices tend to rise. If there are many properties for sale and few buyers, it is a buyer's market and prices tend to fall. Price is considered a credible value indicator when several similar, competing parcels of real estate are offered for sale and several competing, competent buyers are available to purchase the units. Thus, alternative or competitive choices influence the competition of market participants.

Appraisers also analyze market competition by noting the prices asked by sellers, offered by buyers, accepted by sellers, and paid by buyers. They may find that parcels of real estate that are comparable in size, condition, and desirability of location tend to sell or rent for similar prices at a given time in a particular community or neighborhood. This equalization of prices is caused by competition between sellers or lessors and buyers or lessees. Properties of different sizes and conditions located in dissimilar areas tend to sell or rent for different prices because adjustments are made by market participants.

Demand Unit

A market can also be viewed in terms of the economic units that are or may be eligible to express demand for the product. All demand for real estate and real estate resources is based on people; the rate of change in the number of potential buyers in a particular market or submarket is one determinant of future demand. Appraisers look at the number of potential buyers in a specific population who are financially capable of purchasing or leasing particular types of real estate. For example, the potential market for retail space is determined by accurately assessing how many people are likely to shop in an area or at a particular store or shopping center. People with money or credit create value by demanding a service or good; people with financial resources create effective demand.

Demand is influenced by changes in the level of property prices or rents, the expectations of consumers, the prices of competing budget items, net new family or household formations, net emigration or immigration, market preferences, typical ages within the population, asset holdings or savings, and real income growth.

MARKET ANALYSIS

Market analysis is the identification and study of a pertinent market. From a market study or analysis, an appraiser can develop an overview of the demand for real estate and analyze the general market demand for a single type of real estate—e.g., shopping centers, office buildings, condominiums, or multifamily apartments. In this analysis, the appraiser identifies the present and probable supply of and demand for a particular property type.

Market analysis is important in all appraisal assignments. Appraisers use the evidence obtained from market analyses to support estimates of value and to perform marketability studies, feasibility studies, and other evaluation assignments. In a marketability study, the present and future demand for a particular property and its absorption rate (i.e., the rate at which properties can be marketed) are studied. A marketability study uses information on competition in price, quality, and property characteristics to determine whether a property can be marketed. The likelihood of a property's financial success or failure is analyzed in a feasibility study, which should include the findings of a properly analyzed market study. A property may have many marketable attributes such as a good location and fertile soil, but its financial success may depend on economic conditions that make its purchase or use unfeasible.

In an appraisal assignment, a market is delineated and identified only after the area and the influences that create a market are studied. Because people generally acquire or use real estate for specific purposes, the market usually can be delineated by the type of use—e.g., single-family residential, commercial, or light industrial. The purchase of these properties may be motivated by investment goals or speculation. To designate a particular market or submarket, an appraiser answers the following questions:

- Where are the properties located?
- What kinds of properties are competitive with, and similar to, the subject property?
- What is the geographic range of properties that can effectively compete with the subject property?
- How does the principle of substitution apply to the comparable properties?

An appraiser first determines whether the scope of the market for a property is international, national, regional, or local. Single-family residences, small commercial and industrial properties, and small farms and ranches usually appeal to local and regional markets. Large apartment projects, industrial plants, regional shopping centers, and government parcels often appeal to international, national, or regional markets. Once the scope of the market is determined, the appraiser studies the pertinent characteristics of market participants.

It is particularly difficult to delineate a market for raw land. Raw land can appeal to segments of several markets and is often purchased by subdividers or developers who may be real estate brokers, construction contractors, or speculators. If the land is subdivided, it is platted into lots; if it is developed, streets and utilities are installed. Raw land can be developed for industrial parks, mobile home parks, shopping centers, strip centers, institutional and recreational uses, and residential subdivisions. Like most real estate, undeveloped land in good locations may be in short supply and in great demand, but the high price of land and the high costs of construction can diminish development activity. In delineating a market for raw land, appraisers must not only consider the effects of costs, but also the impact of local zoning laws and state and federal use restrictions that can affect the land's availability for specific uses.

Many buyers purchase land and hold it for resale without further improvement. This type of investment, which is called *speculation*, is based on the potential for land appreciation. Speculators often purchase unimproved land such as prairie or forestland, land in agricultural use, vacant urban lots, or even parking lots; they may also purchase residential, commercial, industrial, and special-purpose properties in hopes of obtaining a profit at resale.

After studying a subject property and the location and available supply of similar, competitive properties, an appraiser can delineate a market and determine the appropriate submarket based primarily on the competitiveness and location of the properties and the supply of and demand for the property type.

In an appraisal to estimate market value, accurate market analysis is necessary because conclusions pertaining to property value are drawn from the market. In conducting a market analysis to estimate market value, an appraiser designates the market area of the subject property and then studies the impact of market conditions within the area by analyzing supply and demand.

The market conditions examined by an appraiser are dictated by the subject property and its use. For example, a manufacturing property is analyzed in terms of labor, transportation, raw materials, power, utilities, taxes, government regulations, and the sales territory for its products. To value an apartment complex, population growth and community trends, wage levels in certain age groups, the percentage of the population owning and renting homes, employment data, the existing supply of competitive rent levels, and the availability of financing at given interest rates are studied.

General market conditions are studied in relation to the market for the subject property and its location. Although the usual market for some properties is local, more out-of-state and foreign buyers may be participating in the market. Although international and national market conditions may strongly affect the value of a subject property, these conditions are probably having the same effect on comparable properties. Thus, although the market for a property may be broad, the appraiser's analysis usually centers on the local community and neighborhood.

Figure 3.2   Market Analysis

FUNCTIONS

Basis for *value conclusions* drawn from the market

Basis for *feasibility, marketability, and other evaluation studies*

COMPONENTS

Delineation of market area according to

1. Type of use (residential, commercial, industrial, agricultural, recreational, special purpose, or raw land for subdivision/development or speculative holding)
2. Location of property
3. Kinds of similar properties
4. Geographic range of competitive properties (local, regional, national, international)
5. How the principle of substitution applies to the comparable properties

Examination of effect of market conditions on delineated area

1. Current and anticipated supply and demand situation
2. Relation of market conditions to use of the property

In every appraisal assignment, a knowledge of supply and demand will help the appraiser investigate the particular community, region, or state. To analyze the supply of competing properties, the following items must be studied:

- Volume of new construction
- Availability and price of vacant land
- Construction and development costs
- Current offerings of available properties (old and new)
- Competition
- Standing stock
- Owner occupancy versus tenant occupancy
- Causes and number of vacancies
- Conversions to alternate uses
- Special economic conditions and circumstances

- Availability of mortgage money and financing
- Impact of building codes, zoning ordinances, and other regulations on construction volume and cost[3]

The investigation of demand is a study in demography, focusing on the number of market participants and their ages, sex, households, disposable income, preferences, and behavior patterns. The following factors are important in any analysis of demand.

- Demographic data relating to population, rate of increase or decrease, and age distribution
- Income and wages
- Employment types and unemployment rate
- Geographic factors (e.g., climate, topography, and natural or man-made barriers)
- Financial considerations such as savings and lending
- Land use and city growth
- Cultural institutions
- Educational facilities
- Health and medical facilities
- Fire and police protection
- Transportation facilities, highway systems, and costs of transportation
- Tax structure and administration

Any analysis undertaken for subdivision and development purposes must include an estimate of the demand for the specific category of real estate involved (e.g., residential units or retail space). A demand estimate begins with the past and projected population characteristics of the proposed subdivision, in terms of both size and income. The U.S. Census Bureau has facilitated the collection of demographic data by filing most of its information on computer tapes. Other private and public sources may provide past and projected population data. Comparisons should be made between the demographic data obtained and the actual subdivision information (e.g., building permit data) kept by the city building inspection department. Market sales and absorption data obtained from city planning or public works departments should also be compared with demographic data.

To estimate housing demand for units in a subdivision over a projected five-year period, which is the time frame in which most developers and builders work, an appraiser may follow these steps:[4]

---

3. Jerome Knowles, Jr., "City and Neighborhood Data and Analysis," *The Appraisal Journal*, April 1967, p. 261.

4. The steps for estimating housing, retail space, and office space demand that are outlined here are based on procedures demonstrated by J.R. Kimball and Barbara S. Bloomberg in "The Demographics of Subdivision Analysis," *The Appraisal Journal*, October 1986; and J.R. Kimball in "Office Space Demand Analysis," *The Appraisal Journal*, October 1987.

1. Identify the neighborhood in which the subdivision is located. Census tracts are frequently used for this purpose.
2. Select data on the types of housing units that would appeal to the income group(s) for which the subdivision is designed.
3. Project the total number of housing units and vacant structures in five years, based on projected demographic data.
4. Calculate the total number of housing units that will be in demand over the next five years and do an annual breakdown.
5. Compare the demand estimate with the building permit data from recent years.
6. Determine the income required to meet the expenses of mortgage payments, maintenance, insurance, and taxes on the projected housing units. Consider local lending practices and interest rates.
7. Project the number of households that fall into the required income category, using projected demographic data.
8. Adjust the total number of housing units in demand (calculated in Step 4) for projected vacancy.

The projected number of households in the required income category (obtained in Step 7) and the total number of housing units adjusted for vacancy (obtained in Step 8) provide a range for the demand estimate.

Figure 3.3   Projections of Total U.S. Population 1985-1995

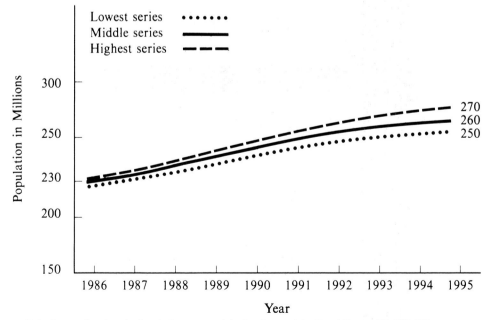

Projections are based on the data in *Projections of the Population of the United States 1983-2080*, U.S. Department of Commerce, Bureau of the Census.

To estimate the demand for retail space over a projected five-year period, an appraiser might follow these steps:

1. Determine the type of retail facility intended for the subdivision (e.g., a shopping center).
2. Define the service area around the subdivision (e.g., a circle with a two-mile radius).
3. Determine the amount of existing retail space, both currently leased and vacant, in the defined service area.
4. Identify the supportable gross leasable space in the same area using projected demographic data.
5. Compare the supportable gross leasable space (obtained in Step 4) with the existing retail space (obtained in Step 3). If there is not already a surplus of existing retail space, the difference between the two will be the additional space needed.
6. Adjust the estimate for additional space (obtained in Step 5) to accommodate retail income from outside the service area.

To estimate the demand for office space in a particular district over a projected five-year period, an appraiser analyzes the relationship between supply and demand in the overall market area and the district's share of the projected demand. Then the date when the project will reach stabilized occupancy can be forecast. The projected demand for office space in the overall market area is formulated in five steps. The appraiser

1. Projects employment for the overall market area by subtracting current estimates of the size of the work force in various economic and occupational sectors from demographic projections for the past five years.
2. Calculates the number of office space occupants in each economic and occupational sector over the past five years by establishing the ratio between the number of office workers and the number of total workers in each sector. Because only two-thirds of all office workers occupy space in freestanding office buildings, each ratio is multiplied by 0.67. With these adjusted ratios, the number of office workers in each sector can be determined and the total number of office workers from all sectors can be calculated.
3. Converts the number of office occupants into a theoretical, annual demand for office space. On the average, an office worker needs 250 square feet of office space. Therefore, the total number of office workers is multiplied by 250 and then divided by five (i.e., the number of years over which growth in the work force is projected).
4. Compares the theoretical demand for office space with the existing supply of office space, which includes all existing, vacant space as well as proposed space and space under construction. The appraiser subtracts the total available supply from the projected demand to arrive at the

unsatisfied demand for office space. Then the total available supply is divided by projected annual demand to determine the absorption period. At the end of the absorption period, additional space will be required.

5. Checks the accuracy of the demand projection against historic demand patterns.

To determine a particular district's share of the overall demand projection, development patterns in the district must be analyzed. Suburban office construction has exceeded construction in central business districts, but not all suburbs share equally in this growth. Development patterns in areas that closely resemble the district in terms of the population's educational and income levels should be compared.

The appraiser may develop a ratio by dividing the amount of existing office space in the district by the amount of office space in the overall market area. The projected demand for office space in the overall market area is multiplied by this ratio. This projected demand is compared with the existing supply, and the accuracy of demand projections are checked against historic patterns. These are the same procedures used to analyze demand and absorption in the overall market area.

To forecast the date when the project will reach stabilized occupancy, the appraiser must estimate the construction period and an absorption rate based on historic performance. Historic performance is interpreted and used to forecast expectations. Detailed data on occupancy may describe not only district and neighborhood patterns, but also absorption rates for different types of buildings (e.g., low-, mid-, and high-rise) and for different occupants (e.g., anchor tenants or non-anchor tenants).

Various other techniques can be used to estimate demand.

SUMMARY

A number of important principles underlie people's understanding of value. These principles provide the rationale for market behavior and, therefore, help explain changes in property value. The principle of *anticipation* is the perception that value is created by the expectation of future benefits. The principle of *change* holds that social, economic, government, and environmental forces affect value as do any physical deterioration and functional obsolescence of the property. The principle of *supply and demand* states that the price of real property varies directly, but not necessarily proportionately, with demand, and inversely, but not necessarily proportionately, with supply. *Competition* between buyers or tenants is the interactive efforts of two or more potential purchasers or tenants to secure a purchase or a lease; between sellers or landlords, it is the interactive efforts of two or more potential sellers or landlords to effectuate a sale or lease. Competition is fundamental to the operation of supply and demand.

The principle of *substitution* affirms that when several similar or commensurate commodities, goods, or services are available, the one with the lowest price will attract the greatest demand and the widest distribution. *Opportunity cost*, a related concept, is the cost of options foregone or opportunities not chosen. The principle of *balance* holds that real property value is created and sustained when contrasting, opposing, or interacting elements are in a state of equilibrium. These elements may include the physical components of the property (i.e., land and improvements), the costs of production or development, and the relationship between the property and its environment. The *laws of increasing and decreasing returns* govern how balance is established. The concepts of *contribution, surplus productivity,* and *conformity* are related to the principle of balance. Because real estate is physically immobile, its value is subject to the positive and negative effects of *externalities*, the economies or diseconomies that exist outside a property.

Four basic forces interact to influence the value of real property: social trends (population characteristics), economic circumstances (demand-side and supply-side economic indicators), governmental controls and regulations (e.g., public services, zoning and building codes, tax policies, and specific real estate laws), and environmental conditions (e.g., climate, topography, soil, natural barriers to development, the availability of transportation systems and the suitability of the *location* in terms of linkage, and the attractiveness of the location).

The premise of *highest and best use* is predicated on the assumption that buyers and sellers set prices for properties based on their conclusions about the most profitable use of the site or property. Highest and best use is the reasonably probable and legal use of vacant land or an improved property, which is physically possible, appropriately supported, financially feasible, and results in the highest value. Highest and best use is determined separately for the land or site as though vacant and available for the anticipated use, and for the property as improved. The related concept of *consistent use* states that the land and improvements must be valued on the basis of the same use.

Real estate markets do not possess the same economic characteristics as markets for goods and services. Real estate markets are not efficient because real estate is not a homogeneous, readily substitutable item. Few buyers and sellers are involved in a real estate market at any given time, in any given price range or location. Real estate prices are fairly high, so most transactions involve financing. Many government regulations apply to real estate; therefore, the market cannot be self-regulating. The real estate market is slow to reach supply-demand equilibrium. Market participants are not always well informed, and shifts in the demand for real estate can be volatile. Real estate is an immobile, durable product, and its supply is relatively stable.

Appraisers study the behavior of market participants, both buyers and sellers, to identify patterns and trends. There are five general real estate markets: residential, commercial, industrial, agricultural, and special-purpose. *Market segmentation* is the process by which submarkets within a larger market are identified and analyzed.

Three elements shape real estate markets and the behavior of market participants: location, competition, and the demand unit. *Location* refers to the area in which relevant economic decisions are made. The area's boundaries are set by time and distance relationships. *Competition*, which is a function of supply and demand, depends on the availablility of properties and the number of potential purchasers or renters in the market. It is reflected in the prices proposed, offered, accepted, and paid for comparable parcels of real estate. The *demand unit*, an economic unit that can or does express the demand for a product, is based on demography, which defines the potential number of present and future buyers in a market.

Market analysis provides the information needed for value estimates and for marketability and feasibility studies. Market analysis delineates and identifies a market or submarket on the basis of location and the characteristics, geographic range, and substitutability of competitive properties. Market analysis also relates specific market conditions to the formation of property value.

4 The Valuation Process

$\mathbf{T}$he concepts that are fundamental to appraisal thought also serve as a rationale for the actions appraisers perform when addressing their clients' needs. These actions represent *the valuation process, a systematic procedure employed to provide the answer to a client's question about real property value.* The valuation process is both a model and a mirror of appraisal activity and, as such, it reflects many attitudes, beliefs, techniques, and methods that relate to questions of value.

The theory of valuation, as distinct from the theory of value, began to take form in the late nineteenth century. Alfred Marshall (1842-1924), the British economist who formulated the synthetic neoclassical theory of value, also anticipated and developed many of the concepts employed in contemporary appraisal practice. These concepts include the estimation of site value by capitalized income, the impact of depreciation on returns on buildings and land, and the influence of different building types and land uses on site value. Marshall is also credited with identifying the three traditional approaches to value: market comparison, replacement cost, and capitalization of income. Irving Fisher (1867-1947), an influential American economist associated with the neoclassical school, fully developed the income theory of value, which is the basis for the income capitalization approach used by modern appraisers.[1]

MODERN APPRAISAL THEORY

The writings of Marshall, Fisher, and other economists of the late nineteenth and early twentieth centuries were read by scholars and business professionals interested in economic thought. At the same time, the field of real estate appraisal was emerging

---

1. Paul F. Wendt, *Real Estate Appraisal: Review and Outlook* (Athens: University of Georgia Press, 1974), pp. 18-19.

and a few practitioners were gaining experience estimating market value, and other kinds of value, for properties of various types. In the 1920s and 1930s, several events helped to establish appraisal as a young, but viable, real estate specialization in the United States.

ALFRED MARSHALL

(Historical Pictures Service, Chicago)

One motivating force was the introduction of land economics as an academic discipline. Land economics developed from the interrelationship of several disciplines and attracted scholars and students who contributed significantly to real estate and appraisal literature over the next 40 years. This influential group included Richard T. Ely (1854-1943), the founder of land economics as an academic subject, Frederick Morrison Babcock (b.1898), Ernest McKinley Fisher (1893-1981), and Arthur J. Mertzke (1890-1970). Each of these men participated in research and publication programs that advanced real estate education.

Ely, Babcock, and Fisher contributed to the Land Economics Series planned by the National Association of Real Estate Boards, the predecessor of the NATIONAL ASSOCIATION OF REALTORS®. The Land Economics Series was the first major publication effort designed to provide real estate professionals with current technical information. The first texts in this series were Fisher's *Principles of Real Estate* (1923), Ely and Moorehouse's *Elements of Land Economics* (1924), and Babcock's *The Appraisal of Real Estate* (1924).[2]

---

2. See A. M. Weimer, "A Note on the Early History of Land Economics," *AREUEA Journal*, Fall 1984; and Pearl Janet Davies, *Real Estate in American History* (Washington, D.C.: Public Affairs Press), pp. 126, 154, and 161.

Another significant event in appraisal history was the publication of *Real Estate Appraising* by Arthur J. Mertzke in 1927. In this book Mertzke used Alfred Marshall's ideas to produce a tangible link between value theory and valuation theory. In the words of one scholar,

> Mertzke translated the economic theory of the equivalence between long-run costs, normal value, and capitalized-income values (under specifically assumed conditions of perfect competition and economic equilibrium) into a working appraisal theory.[3]

Mertzke helped establish a clear emphasis on the three approaches to value and explained the use of capitalization rates as indexes of security.

The preeminence of the three approaches to value in the "appraisal process" was underscored in publications by K. Lee Hyder (1888-1947), Harry Grant Atkinson (1890-1979), and George L. Schmutz (1893-1958).[4] Each of these works set forth systematic procedures for applying the sales comparison, cost, and income capitalization approaches under appropriate conditions to answer clients' questions about value. Schmutz presented this process in diagram form, suggesting a model in which appraisal activity leads to a conclusion of value. Later, this model was incorporated into *The Appraisal of Real Estate*, published by the American Institute of Real Estate Appraisers in 1951.

In the years following these early works, appraisal theory has continued to evolve. Today, technical education requirements have become more demanding and appraisers now make use of many analytical methods and techniques. Applying these methods and techniques to an expanding data base presents new challenges and raises questions as to how applicable the valuation model is to actual appraisal assignments, how well it analyzes the forces that affect value, and how accurately it describes the role of the three approaches in determining value estimates.

THE VALUATION PROCESS

The valuation process begins when an appraiser fully identifies the appraisal problem and ends when he or she reports the solution to the client.

Each real property is unique and many different types of value can be estimated for a single property. The most common appraisal assignment is undertaken to estimate market value; the valuation process contains all the appropriate steps for this type of assignment. The model also provides the framework for estimating any other defined value. Furthermore, evaluation assignments often call for value estimates which are derived through application of the valuation process.

---

3. Wendt, p. 218.

4. K. Lee Hyder, "The Appraisal Process," *The Appraisal Journal*, January 1936; Harry Grant Atkinson, "The Process of Appraising Single-Family Homes," *The Appraisal Journal*, April 1936; and George L. Schmutz, *The Appraisal Process* (North Hollywood, Calif.: the author, 1941).

The valuation process is accomplished by following specific steps; the number of steps used depends on the nature of the appraisal assignment and the data available. However, the model indicates a pattern that can be used in any appraisal assignment to perform market research and data analysis, to apply appraisal techniques, and to integrate the results of these activities into an estimate of defined value.

Research begins after the appraisal problem has been defined. The analysis of data relevant to the problem commences with an examination of trends observed at all market levels—international, national, regional, community, and neighborhood. This examination should lead to an understanding of the interrelationships among the principles, forces, and factors that affect real property value in a specific area. It also provides raw data from which to extract numerical measurements and other evidence of market trends—e.g., positive or negative percentage changes in property value over a number of years, the percentage of population movement into an area, and the number of employment opportunities and their effect on the purchasing power of potential property users. These data can be employed in appraisal techniques to estimate a defined value.

Traditionally, appraisal techniques are the specific procedures through which the three approaches are used to derive separate indications of real property value. Other procedures such as the use of inferential statistics and economic models also contribute to appraisal methods. One or more approaches to value may be used, depending on their applicability to a particular appraisal assignment.

In assignments to estimate market value, the ultimate goal of the valuation process is a well-supported value conclusion that reflects the appraiser's study of all factors that influence the market value of the property being appraised. To achieve this goal, an appraiser studies a property from three different viewpoints, which correspond to the three traditional approaches to value.

1. The value indicated by recent sales of comparable properties in the market—the sales comparison approach
2. The current cost of reproducing or replacing the improvements, minus the loss in value from depreciation, plus land value—the cost approach
3. The value of a property's earning power based on the capitalization of its income—the income capitalization approach

The three approaches are *interrelated*; each involves the gathering and analysis of sales, cost, and income data that pertain to the property being appraised. Each approach is outlined briefly in this chapter and discussed in detail later in the text. From the approaches applied, the appraiser derives separate indications of value for the property being appraised. One or more of the approaches may not be applicable to a specific assignment or may be less significant due to the nature of the property, the decisions of the client, or the data available.

To complete the valuation process, the appraiser integrates the information drawn from market research and data analysis and from the application of appraisal techniques in the three approaches to form a conclusion. This conclusion may be presented as a single estimate of value or as a range in which the value may fall. An effective integration of all these elements depends on the appraiser's skill, experience, and judgment.

The valuation process is depicted in Figure 4.1.

Figure 4.1   The Valuation Process

Definition of the Problem					
Identification of real estate	Identification of property rights to be valued	Date of value estimate	Use of appraisal	Definition of value	Other limiting conditions

Preliminary Analysis and Data Selection and Collection	
General	**Specific (Subject and Comparables)**
Social	Site and improvements
Economic	Sales and listings
Government	Cost and depreciation
Environmental	Income/expense and capitalization rate

Highest and Best Use Analysis
Land as though vacant
Property as improved

Land Value Estimate

Application of the Three Approaches		
Sales comparison	Cost	Income capitalization

Reconciliation of Value Indications and Final Value Estimate

Report of Defined Value

DEFINITION OF THE APPRAISAL PROBLEM

The first step in the valuation process is to develop a concise statement of the appraisal problem. This sets the limits of the appraisal and eliminates any ambiguity about the nature of the assignment. The problem statement should include

1. Identification of the real estate
2. Identification of the property rights to be valued

3. Date of the value estimate
4. Use of the appraisal
5. Definition of value
6. Other limiting conditions

Identification of the Real Estate

A property is first identified by a common address, a location, or other descriptive data that enable it to be located or referred to by recognized landmarks. At this point in the appraisal, the property is only identified; a complete physical description is provided later. An appraiser can identify a property succinctly by using an outline.

Reference:	The Kennedy Building, commercial offices
Common address:	2600 South Zephyr Denver, Colorado
Identity of the physical entity:	Lots 7-10, inclusive, Sterns Addition, Fifth Filing, City and County of Denver, Colorado

If, instead, the property is identified with a legal description, the description is the client's responsibility and should be prepared by a qualified individual. Legal descriptions of real estate are usually derived from land surveys and preserved in public records in accordance with local or state law. Appraisers should be familiar with the specific system or systems used to describe land in particular areas. Systems of land description include the metes and bounds system, the rectangular or government survey system, and the lot and block system.

Identification of the Property Rights To Be Valued

The valuation of real property includes both the physical real estate and the rights that one or more individuals, partnerships, or corporations may have or contemplate having in the ownership or use of the land and improvements. An appraiser may estimate the value of a fee simple estate or of partial interests created by the severance or division of ownership rights. Special attention must be given to any limitations on ownership rights, such as easements, encroachments, liens, or leases. Financing must also be considered because fee simple estates, leasehold estates, and leased fee estates can all be mortgaged. The specific rights to be valued and the probable or actual financing must be ascertained at the start of the assignment because the complexity of these rights and terms will determine the procedures, skills, and time required to complete the assignment.

The fee simple estate is often valued before partial interests are considered. However, the dollar value of the fee simple estate is not necessarily equal to the sum of the values of all partial interests; the value of a partial interest may differ from the value of its contribution to the whole. For instance, a one-half interest in a property may have a value that is significantly less than 50% of the fee simple value; this lower value could be a direct result of dividing the fee simple estate. In estimating the market value of a partial interest in real property, direct market evidence that reflects market attitudes toward the particular aspects of that partial interest is usually sought.

Date of the Value Estimate

The date of a value estimate must be specified because the influences on real property value are constantly changing. Although conditions observed at the time of the appraisal may persist for a considerable time after that date, an estimate of value is considered valid only for the exact date specified. Relatedly, market value is generally seen as a reflection of market participants' perceptions of future economic conditions. These perceptions are based on market evidence as of a specific point in time. Value influences reflect economic conditions at a particular time, and sudden changes in business and real estate markets can dramatically influence value.

Most appraisals call for current value estimates but, in some cases, a valuation as of some date in the past is required. Retrospective appraisals may be required for inheritance tax (date of death), insurance claims (date of casualty), income tax (date of acquisition), law suits (date of loss), and other reasons. It is sometimes necessary to estimate a property's value as of March 1, 1913, the date when the federal income tax was established, to calculate the capital gain on a property owned since that date.

In condemnation proceedings, appraisers may estimate property value as of the date of filing the declaration or petition to condemn, the date of trial, or another date stipulated by the parties involved or by the court.

Because historical market data are often available, market value can be estimated in retrospect. However, forecast or prospective market value estimates may be made. Comparable rents, expenses, construction costs, and sales information as of a future date are, of course, unknown. An appraiser may make a prospective market value estimate provided the appraiser clearly identifies the time frame and the market conditions upon which the forecast is based.

Use of the Appraisal

The use of an appraisal is the manner in which a client employs the information contained in an appraisal report. The client may specify the use of the appraisal when requesting it; if not, the appraiser must ask for it. Because an appraisal provides the basis for a decision, the nature of the decision affects the character of the assignment and the subsequent report. A value estimate may be needed to determine the

- Price at which to buy or sell
- Amount of a loan
- Basis for taxation
- Terms of a lease
- Value of real property assets in financial statements
- Basis for just compensation in eminent domain proceedings

To avoid wasted effort, the appraiser and the client must have a mutual understanding of the use and ownership of the appraisal report and its conclusions.

Definition of Value

The purpose of the valuation process is to estimate the value of a real property interest, so the specific type of value and the interests involved must be clearly identified. The statement of purpose in the final report of defined value specifies the stated scope of the valuation assignment, i.e., an estimate of a defined value of a real property interest. Types of appraised value include market value, use value, going-concern value, investment value, assessed value, and insurable value.

A written statement of the defined value to be estimated must be included in every appraisal report. This precise statement establishes the question to be answered for the client, the appraiser, and all readers of the report. It explains the data selected for consideration and the methods employed to analyze the data, thus supporting the logic and validity of the final value estimate. The statement also specifies whether the value estimate is reported in terms of cash, terms equivalent to cash, or other precisely revealed terms.

Other Limiting Conditions

The identification of the real estate and the property rights to be appraised, the date of the value estimate, the use of the appraisal, and the definition of value are limiting conditions that govern the appraisal. There are other limiting conditions as well. Such statements are used for the appraiser's protection and the information and protection of the client and others using the report. For example, an appraisal report may state that the valuation of subsurface oil, gas, or mineral rights is not part of the appraisal. Another limiting condition might be that the appraiser is not required to provide court or hearing testimony or to attend court unless arrangements are made a reasonable time in advance. Other limiting conditions might specify that no engineering survey was made or that, except as specifically stated, property data were taken from sources considered to be reliable. (For further examples, see the discussion of assumptions and limiting conditions in Chapter 24.)

PRELIMINARY ANALYSIS AND DATA SELECTION AND COLLECTION

After defining the problem, the appraiser is ready to do a preliminary analysis of the character and scope of the assignment and the amount of work that will be required to gather the necessary data. The preliminary analysis and work plan depend on the assignment and the type of property being valued. For example, much more information will be required in the valuation of a large apartment building than in the valuation of a single-family residence.

To complete an assignment quickly and efficiently, each step in the valuation process must be planned and scheduled. The amount of time and personnel needed will vary with the amount and complexity of the work. Some assignments may be completed in only a few days; for more complex appraisal problems, weeks or months may be spent gathering, analyzing, and applying all pertinent data.

For some assignments, the appraiser may be able to perform all the work personally; for others, the assistance of other staff members or appraisal specialists may be needed. Sometimes the assistance of specialists in other fields is necessary. For example, in valuing a rural property the appraiser's findings may be augmented by the professional opinion of a soil engineer. Recognizing when work can or must be delegated improves efficiency and final accuracy.

A planned work schedule is helpful, particularly for large, complicated assignments. A clear and precise understanding of individual responsibilities will help expedite an assignment. Because the appraiser bears the ultimate responsibility, he or she must see the assignment in terms of its total context as well as its numerous details. With a comprehensive view, the appraiser can recognize the type and volume of work to be done and schedule and delegate it properly.

The appraiser's work plan usually includes an outline of the proposed appraisal report. The report's major divisions are delineated and the data and procedures involved in each division are noted. Using this outline, data can be assembled intelligently and the appropriate amount of time can be allocated to each step in the valuation process.

Two types of data are gathered for appraisals: general and specific. General data consist of information on the principles, forces, and factors that affect property value. This information describes trends in the social, economic, governmental, and environmental forces that affect property value. *A trend is a series of related changes brought about by a chain of causes and effects.* Trends such as population shifts, declining office building occupancy rates, or increased housing starts in an area are identified by analyzing general data. General data can contribute significantly to an appraiser's understanding of the marketplace.

Specific data relate to the property being appraised and to comparable properties. These data include physical, locational, cost, and income and expense information on the properties as well as the details of comparable sales. Financial arrangements that could affect selling prices are also considered.

The amount and type of data collected for an appraisal depend on the approaches used to estimate value. These approaches, in turn, relate directly to the appraisal problem. In a given valuation assignment, more than one approach to value may be appropriate and necessary to determine a value indication. However, the problem or problems to be addressed may require that one approach be given greater emphasis in making a final value estimate. The appraiser's judgment and experience in conducting a particular type of assignment and the quantity and quality of data available for analysis may determine which approach or approaches are used.

All meaningful data are collected for a purpose. Any influences, pertinent facts, or conclusions about trends should be clearly indicated in the report and related specifically to the property being appraised. Because the data selected form the basis for the appraiser's judgments, a thorough explanation of the significance of the data ensures that the reader will understand these judgments.

HIGHEST AND BEST USE ANALYSIS

Analysis of the highest and best use of the land as though vacant and of the property as improved is essential in the valuation process. Through highest and best use analysis, the appraiser interprets the market forces that influence the subject property and identifies the use on which the final value estimate is based. (Highest and best use analysis is discussed in detail in Chapter 12.)

Analyzing the highest and best use of the land as though vacant serves two functions. First, it helps the appraiser identify comparable properties. The property being appraised is always compared with similar properties that have sold recently in the market. The comparable properties' highest and best use of the land as though vacant should be similar to that of the subject property. Potentially comparable properties that do not have similar highest and best uses are usually eliminated from further analysis.

The second reason to analyze the property's highest and best use as though vacant is to identify the use that would produce maximum income to the land after property income is allocated to the improvements. In the cost approach and some income capitalization techniques, a separate value estimate of the land is required. Estimating the land's highest and best use as though vacant is a necessary part of deriving a land value estimate.

There are also two reasons to analyze the highest and best use of the property as improved. The first is to help identify comparable properties. Comparable improved properties should have the same or similar highest and best uses as the improved subject property.

The second reason to analyze the highest and best use of the property as improved is to decide whether the improvements should be demolished, renovated, or retained in their present condition. They should be retained as long as they have some value and the return from the property exceeds the return that would be realized by a new use, after deducting the costs of demolishing the old building and constructing a new one. Identification of the existing property's most profitable use is crucial to this determination.

LAND VALUE ESTIMATE

Land value is directly related to highest and best use. The relationship between highest and best use and land value may indicate whether an existing use is the highest and best use of the land.

Land value may be a major component of total property value. Appraisers often estimate land value separately, even when valuing properties with extensive building improvements. Land value may change at a different rate than building value. Improvements are almost always subject to depreciation after the effects of inflation are removed. For many appraisals, a separate estimate of land value is required.

Although a total property value estimate may be derived in the sales comparison or income capitalization approaches without separating land and improvement values, it may be necessary to estimate land value separately to isolate the contributory value of the land to the total property. In the cost approach, the value of the land must be estimated separately and specifically stated.

In the valuation process, the land value estimate is a separate step, which may be accomplished by applying sales comparison or income capitalization techniques. The most reliable way to estimate land value is by sales comparison. When few sales are available, or when the value indications produced through sales comparison need substantiation, other procedures may be used to value land. In all, six procedures can be used to obtain land value indications.

1. *Sales comparison.* Sales of similar, vacant parcels are analyzed, compared, and adjusted to provide a value indication for the land being appraised.
2. *Allocation.* Sales of improved properties are analyzed, and the prices paid are allocated between the land and the improvements. Allocation can be used in two ways—to establish a typical ratio of land value to total value, which may be applicable to the property being appraised, or to isolate either the land or the building's value contribution from the sale for use in comparison analysis.
3. *Extraction.* Land value is estimated by subtracting the estimated value of the improvements from the known sale price of the property. This procedure is frequently used when the value of the improvements is relatively low or easily estimated.
4. *Subdivision development.* The total value of undeveloped land is estimated as if the land were subdivided, developed, and sold. Development costs, incentive costs, and carrying charges are subtracted from the estimated proceeds of sale, and the net income projection is discounted over the estimated period required for market absorption of the developed sites.
5. *Land residual technique.* It is assumed that the land is improved to its highest and best use. All expenses of operation and the return attributable to the other agents of production are deducted, and the net income imputed to the land is capitalized to derive an estimate of land value. An

alternate land residual technique is applied by valuing the land and improvements and deducting the cost of the improvements and any entrepreneurial profit. The remainder is the residual land value.

6. *Ground rent capitalization.* This procedure is used when land rental and capitalization rates are readily available such as in well-developed areas. Net ground rent, the net amount paid for the right to use and occupy the land, is estimated and divided by a land capitalization rate. The capitalization process, which can be applied to either actual or estimated rents, relies on rates that can be supported in the market. This procedure may be seen as an extension of direct sales comparison, but, where applicable, it provides a specific unit of comparison.

APPLICATION OF THE THREE APPROACHES

The valuation process is used to develop a well-supported estimate of a defined value, which is based on consideration of all pertinent general and specific data. Appraisers estimate property value by applying specific appraisal procedures which reflect three distinct methods for analyzing data mathematically—sales comparison, cost, and income capitalization. One or more of these approaches are used in all estimations of value; the approaches employed depend on the type of property, the use of the appraisal, and the quality and quantity of data available for analysis.

All three approaches are applicable to many appraisal problems. However, one or more of the approaches may have greater significance in a specific assignment. For example, the cost approach may be inappropriate in valuing properties that show substantial accrued depreciation because the physical deterioration, functional obsolescence, and external obsolescence of older buildings are difficult to estimate. The sales comparison approach cannot be applied to very specialized properties such as garbage disposal plants because comparable data may not be available. The income capitalization approach is rarely used to value owner-occupied residential interests, although it may be used with market support. Income capitalization can be particularly unreliable in a commercial or industrial property market where user-occupants outbid investors.

Sales Comparison Approach

The sales comparison approach is most useful when a number of similar properties have been sold recently or are currently for sale in the subject property market. Using this approach, an appraiser produces a value indication by comparing a subject property with similar properties, called *comparable sales.* The sale prices of properties that are judged to be most comparable tend to indicate a range in which the value indication for the subject property will fall.

An appraiser estimates the degree of similarity or difference between the subject property and comparable sales by considering various elements of comparison.

1. Real property rights conveyed
2. Financing terms
3. Conditions of sale
4. Market conditions
5. Location
6. Physical characteristics
7. Income-producing characteristics
8. Other characteristics (e.g., access and zoning)

Dollar or percentage adjustments are then made to the sale price of each comparable property, with consideration for the real property interest involved. Adjustments are made to the sale prices of the comparables because the values of the comparables are known, while the value of the subject property is not known. Through this comparative procedure, the appraiser estimates one or more kinds of value as of a specific date.

Data such as income multipliers and income rates may also be extracted from sales comparison analysis. In the sales comparison approach, appraisers consider these data, but do not regard them as elements of comparison. These data are applied in the income capitalization approach.

Cost Approach

The cost approach is based on the premise that the value of a property can be derived by adding the estimated value of the land to the current cost of constructing a reproduction or replacement for the improvements and then subtracting the amount of depreciation (i.e., deterioration and obsolescence) in the structures from all causes. If entrepreneurial profit has been realized, it is added to the value indication. This approach is particularly useful in valuing new or nearly new improvements and properties that are not frequently exchanged in the market. Cost approach techniques can also be employed to derive information needed in the sales comparison and income capitalization approaches to value.

The current costs to construct the improvements can be obtained from cost estimators, cost estimating publications, builders, and contractors. Depreciation is measured through market research and the application of specific valuation procedures. Land value is estimated separately in the cost approach.

Income Capitalization Approach

In the income capitalization approach, the present value of the future benefits of property ownership is measured. A property's income streams and its resale value, or reversion, are capitalized into a present, lump-sum value. Two basic formulas are used in this approach.

$$\frac{\text{Income}}{\text{Rate}} = \text{Value}$$

$$\text{Income} \times \text{Factor} = \text{Value}$$

Like the sales comparison and cost approaches, the income capitalization approach requires extensive market research. Research and data analysis for this approach are conducted against a background of supply and demand relationships, which provide information on trends and market anticipation.

An investor in an apartment building, for example, anticipates an acceptable return *on* the investment as well as a return *of* the invested funds. The level of return needed to attract investment capital fluctuates with changes in the money market and the levels of return offered by alternative investments. Appraisers must be alert to the changes in investor requirements indicated by the current market for investment properties and by changes in the more volatile money markets which may suggest forthcoming trends.

The specific data that an appraiser investigates for this approach might include the property's gross income expectancy, the expected reduction in gross income due to vacancy and collection loss, the anticipated annual operating expenses, the pattern and duration of the property's income stream, and the anticipated resale value or the value of other real property interest reversions. After income and expenses are estimated, the income streams are converted into present value through capitalization or discounting. The rates used for capitalization or discounting are derived from acceptable rates of return for similar properties.

RECONCILIATION OF VALUE INDICATIONS

The final analytical step in the valuation process is the reconciliation of the value indications into a single dollar figure or a range in which the value will most likely fall. The nature of the reconciliation depends on the appraisal problem, the approaches that have been used, and the reliability of the value indications derived.

When all three approaches are used, the appraiser examines the spread among the three, separate indications. A wide spread may indicate that one or more of the approaches is not truly applicable to the appraisal problem. The appraiser must always consider the relative dependability and applicability of each approach in reconciling the value indications into a final estimate of defined value. In the reconciliation the appraiser can explain variations among the indications derived from the different approaches and account for any inconsistencies between the value conclusions and methods with which they were derived.

REPORT OF DEFINED VALUE

The final estimate of a defined value is the goal of the valuation process. The assignment is not complete, however, until the conclusion is stated in a report and presented to the client. Usually, a written report includes all the data considered and analyzed, the methods used, and the reasoning that led to the final value estimate. A concise valuation analysis enables the reader to understand the problem and the factual data and to follow the reasoning behind the appraiser's conclusion of value. The value estimate is the appraiser's opinion, reflecting the experience and judgment that he or she applied to the study of the assembled data.

An appraisal report is the tangible expression of an appraiser's service. In preparing a report, an appraiser should give particular attention to writing style, organization, presentation, and overall appearance.

SUMMARY

The *valuation process* is a systematic procedure employed to provide the answer to a client's question about real property value. It is a model of appraisal activity, reflecting an understanding of value and the methods used in value estimation.

The theory of valuation took form in the late nineteenth century. Alfred Marshall identified the three approaches to value used by contemporary appraisers, and Irving Fisher formulated the theory on which the income capitalization approach is based. Throughout the twentieth century, appraisal theory has continued to evolve and respond to the needs of market participants.

The first step in the valuation process is the *definition of the appraisal problem*, which includes identification of the real estate and property rights to be valued, specification of the date and use of the appraisal, definition of the value sought, and identification of other limiting conditions.

Property identification can be accomplished with a common address, a location, or a legal description. The *property rights* are identified by the ownership (i.e., individual, partnership, or corporation and limitations on these rights such as easements), the financial interests (e.g., mortgage and equity) or the legal estate (e.g., fee simple, leased fee, or leasehold).

Specification of the date of the *value estimate* communicates the point in time when the value estimate is relevant, whether it is a current value, a prospective value, or an historical value estimated for inheritance tax, income tax, insurance claims, law suits, or capital gains. The *use of the appraisal* is decided by the client and affects the character of the assignment. An appraisal may be used to estimate a price at which to buy or sell, to set the amount of a loan, to prepare tax returns, to fix rent, to estimate real property assets for financial statements, or to determine just compensation in eminent domain proceedings.

The *definition of value* in most appraisals is market value, but use value, going-concern value, investment value, assessed value, or insurable value may also be sought. A statement of *other limiting conditions* identifies specific qualifications of the appraisal that were not cited previously.

Once the appraisal problem is defined, other steps in the valuation process may be carried out. The *preliminary analysis* is an overview of the character and scope of the assignment. The *selection and collection of data* provide general data on value influences and *trends* as well as specific data on the market, financing, cost, income and expenses, and physical or locational features of the property being appraised.

Highest and best use analysis of the *land as though vacant* helps the appraiser identify comparable properties and derive an estimate of land value. Highest and best use analysis of the *property as improved* is useful in identifying comparable properties and determining whether the existing improvements should be retained, renovated, or demolished. A *land value estimate* is required when the land's contribution to total property value is sought, or when improvements are valued separately, as in the cost approach. There are six procedures for estimating land value.

1. Sales comparison
2. Allocation
3. Extraction
4. Subdivision development
5. Land residual technique
6. Ground rent capitalization

Three approaches can be applied to the analysis of data to derive a well-supported value conclusion. Although the approaches are interrelated, the property type and use will determine which approach or approaches are most appropriate. The *sales comparison approach* is useful when data on recently sold or currently offered properties similar to the subject property are available. These comparable data are adjusted to reflect the differences between the comparable properties and the subject property.

The *cost approach* is effective in valuing new improvements and properties that are not frequently exchanged in the market. In this approach a separate land value estimate is added to an estimate of the current cost to construct a reproduction or replacement of the improvements. Entrepreneurial profit is also added when applicable. From this total, the estimated depreciation and obsolescence from all causes is subtracted.

The *income capitalization approach* is used to appraise income-producing properties. The present value of the future benefits of property ownership is measured, and the property's anticipated income stream and resale value, or reversion, are capitalized into a present value. There are two basic formulas: income/rate = value and income x factor = value.

Reconciliation of the value indications derived from the approaches used may provide a single value indication or a range of most probable values. In this process, the reliability of the value indications and the applicability of the approaches are explained. Reconciliation also provides an opportunity to resolve variations and inconsistencies among the value indications and the methods with which they were derived.

The *report of defined value* provides the client with a summary of the data analyzed, the methods used, and the reasoning that led to the value estimate. The appraisal report should be carefully written, well organized, and clearly presented.

5 Money Markets and Capital Markets

In business, money is the exchange medium employed in selling and purchasing goods and services. The parties to a business transaction agree on the value of the good or service and this value is expressed in terms of money. Each nation has a monetary currency, which may be hard currency (e.g., gold, silver, or copper), paper, or a combination of the two. The relative values of currencies are established through trading and international banking agreements. Real estate is priced in terms of money and real estate investments are money, so the value of money influences real estate prices. Therefore, it is imperative that appraisers understand monetary values.

The term *money* is difficult to define and various definitions are used by economists. Some believe that money is "currency in the hands of the public plus demand deposits at commercial banks"; others say that money is "currency plus demand and time deposits at commercial banks." (Time deposits are funds that can be withdrawn only after proper notification.) Money has also been defined as "currency plus demand and time deposits plus the liabilities of non-bank financial intermediaries."[1] Most of the money in circulation is in checking accounts. Whether the money supply is defined in terms of currency, account balances, or both, its value is influenced by its availability.

MONEY SUPPLY AND DEMAND

Supply and demand relationships set the cost, or price, of money. When money is

---

1. Howard R. Vane and John L. Thompson, *Monetarism—Theory, Evidence and Policy* (New York: Halsted Press, 1979), p. 49.

plentiful, the price is modest; when it is scarce, the cost rises. The price of money is expressed as an interest rate—i.e., the cost to borrow funds. This relationship is particularly important in the real estate industry because most investments are created by combining debt and equity funds. When the demand for money is high and its supply is low, capital costs, or interest rates, tend to increase. These higher interest rates affect real property values.

There is a significant difference between money and other commodities on the supply side of the pricing formula. The demand for money is a product of natural economic forces, but its supply is mechanically regulated by the Federal Reserve (the Fed). As the manager of supply, the Fed has the power to regulate general interest rate levels, which strongly influence the discount rates and overall capitalization rates used in real estate valuation.

Trading Money Instruments

A money market is the interaction of buyers and sellers who trade short-term money instruments. Short-term money instruments include federal funds, Treasury bills, Treasury notes, and other government securities; repurchase agreements and reverse repurchase agreements; certificates of deposit; commercial paper; bankers' acceptances; municipal notes; and Eurodollars. Although it is called a "market," the money market is not formally organized like the New York Stock Exchange. Rather, it is an "over-the-counter" operation that provides accurate and readily available national and international trading information through computerization. Because the Federal Reserve System regulates the money supply, it influences trading activity in the money market on a daily basis. The money market, in turn, greatly affects the real estate industry because short-term financing is needed for construction and development. The availability and cost of money regulates the real estate industry's magnitude and pace.

A capital market is the interaction of buyers and sellers trading long- or intermediate-term money instruments. Long- and intermediate-term instruments usually mature in more than one year and include bonds or debentures, stocks, and mortgages and deeds of trust. Although stocks are capital market items, they are equity investments with no maturities. The distinction between money markets and capital markets is not sharp because both involve trading in funds for varying terms and both are sources of capital for all economic activities, including real estate.

In money markets and capital markets, the relationships between various instruments stem from differing interest rates, maturities, and investment qualities. In "normal" periods, an individual who invests in a long-term instrument is believed to assume greater risk than one who invests in a short-term instrument. Therefore, the long-term investor is compensated with higher yields. In other words, long-term instruments usually offer higher yields than short-term instruments. This situation is graphically portrayed in a normal yield curve.

Figure 5.1   Low Inflationary Period

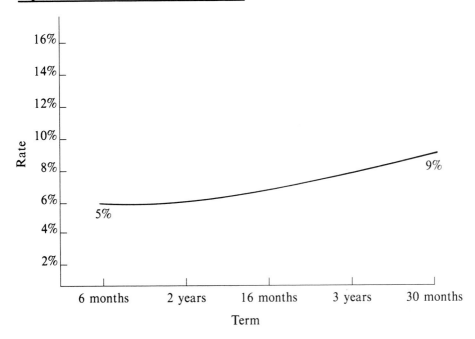

The relationship can be reversed. In periods of high inflation, investors are reluctant to take long-term positions. They fear that escalating interest rates will erode their capital, so they try to keep their money in short-term instruments. The Federal Reserve, however, wants to combat inflation, so it causes *interest* rates to rise. This action is intended to be temporary, lasting just long enough to dampen investors' inflationary expectations. As a result, short-term yields are greater than long-term yields, and the yield curve is said to be "inverse."

Fractional Reserve Banking

When a commercial bank makes a loan to a business or an individual, it credits that business or personal checking account with the amount of the transaction. In a sense, banks manufacture money through this loan process because they create money by monetizing debt. Commercial banks effectively fund a large volume of loans by entering the money market. They raise the required cash by selling their paper—e.g., certificates of deposit—to a broad group of investors. Of course, the money-creating activities of banks are restricted because the Federal Reserve requires that they maintain reserves equal to specified percentages of their deposits. If a bank has a 20% reserve requirement, each dollar of its reserves can support four dollars of deposits, which can be created by extending four dollars in loans and crediting them to the borrowers' accounts. This arrangement is called *fractional reserve banking* and it is used by central banking systems throughout the world.

**Figure 5.2   High Inflationary Period Yield Curves—
Certificates of Deposit**

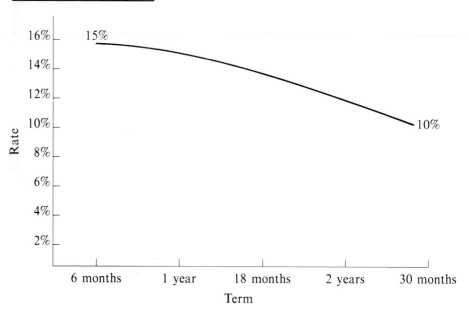

FEDERAL RESERVE SYSTEM

In 1913 the U. S. Congress passed the Federal Reserve Act, which created the Federal Reserve System, a central bank to control monetary affairs. The framers of the act studied central banking in other countries and attempted to create a banking system that avoided either political or private hegemony. The Federal Reserve System is an independent banking system that manages money and credit to promote orderly growth of the economy. The system's independence distinguishes it from central banks in most other countries, which are government entities. Although the Fed is independent, it functions within the general structure of the U.S. government. Thus, the system operates in accordance with national economic policies, but has the power to exercise its judgment independently.

The Fed is composed of 12 regional banks, which serve the 12 Federal Reserve regional districts, and a number of member banks, which include all nationally chartered commercial banks and many state-chartered banks. The Fed is directed by a seven-member board of governors, who are appointed by the President and confirmed by the U.S. Senate for 14-year terms. The geographic distribution and occupations of board members are considered in their selection. Only one member from each region can serve at a time, so no region is overrepresented on the board. To avoid conflicts of interest, bank officers, directors, and stockholders cannot serve on the Federal Reserve Board.

Figure 5.3 Federal Reserve System

Federal Open Market Committee	Board of Governors	Federal Advisory Council
7 governors, 5 federal reserve bank presidents	7 governors appointed by the President and confirmed by the Senate	12 members, 1 from each federal reserve bank

12 Federal Reserve Banks
9 directors on each board:
Member banks elect 6 (3 from banking and 3 from commerce, agriculture, or industry) and Board of Governors appoints 3

6,200 Member Banks
(represents 85% of U.S. banking activity)

Credit Regulation

Reserve requirements, discount rates, and the Federal Open Market Committee are three credit-regulation devices that the Fed uses to promote orderly economic growth. Because the Federal Reserve regulates money and credit, which are the lifeblood of the real estate industry, appraisers should be familiar with the Fed's regulations and practices.

Reserve Requirements

Within statutory limits, the Federal Reserve Board can fix the amount of reserves that member banks must maintain. One requirement of membership in the system is that member banks cannot make all their deposit liabilities available for business loans; they must agree to keep part frozen in reserve accounts at Federal Reserve banks. The Federal Reserve changes the amount of its reserve requirements from time to time and these changes expand or contract the volume of money and credit available. If the Fed wants to restrict the money supply, it increases deposit reserve obligations; if it wants to increase the supply, it lowers the obligations. In recent years, demand deposits have been subject to a reserve requirement of approximately 15%, and time funds have been subject to a reserve requirement between 3% and 8%.

Federal Discount Rate

The discount rate is another major credit-regulation tool. Members of the Federal Reserve System have an important advantage over other banks because they can borrow from the Fed and obtain funds for their customers even in periods of great demand. To get these loans, member banks agree to pay Federal Reserve interest at its established discount rate. The borrowing privilege of member banks is not unrestricted, however. The Fed denies loan requests when it believes that borrowing is not in the best interests of the national or regional economy. When credit is refused, it is said that "the discount window is closed." The borrowing privilege is a vehicle for expanding the monetary supply; its curtailment limits or contracts credit. When the discount rate is low, banks are encouraged to borrow and the amount of money available to the economy expands. When the discount rate is high, member banks are reluctant to borrow and credit is generally restricted. Thus, the federal discount rate helps determine *the prime rate, the interest rate that a commercial bank charges for short-term loans to borrowers with high credit ratings*. The federal discount rate is generally about two percentage points below the prime rate.

Federal Open Market Committee

The Fed's third credit-regulation tool is the Federal Open Market Committee (FOMC). The FOMC is probably the most extensively used and most potent of the Federal Reserve's credit-regulating devices. The committee is composed of the Federal Reserve Board of Governors, the president of the New York Federal Reserve Bank, and four district reserve bank presidents who serve for one-year terms on a rotating basis. The FOMC buys and sells U.S. government securities in the open market, thereby exerting a powerful influence on interest rates. In fact, through its daily operations, the FOMC maintains short-term money rates at selected target levels. When the committee buys securities, money is infused into the market in an amount that is approximately six times the purchase volume. The FOMC buys securities from bond dealers with Federal Reserve checks, which the dealers deposit in their accounts in the commercial banking system. These payments increase balances in member banks' reserve accounts, permitting greater loan activity at these banks, which, in turn, increases the money supply by expanding checking account balances. Thus, economic growth and expansion are encouraged. When the FOMC sells securities, it causes funds to be removed from member banks' reserve accounts, which reduces the supply of money and credit. Thus, economic growth is discouraged.

Usually, the FOMC meets once a month to set monetary policy strategies. The minutes of these meetings are kept secret for 30 days, and then published. Before the minutes become public, money dealers watch the actions of the committee to infer its current policy. Financial market participants may be guided by the opinions of experts, called *Fed watchers*, who often correctly predict Fed policy by analyzing the committee's activities. Real estate investors and appraisers, whose success may depend on correct market interpretation, may also follow and use the extensive information provided by Fed watchers.

FISCAL POLICY

While the Fed determines monetary policy, the Department of the Treasury manages the government's financial activities. The Treasury's strategies and actions make up national fiscal policy. Essentially, the U.S. Treasury raises funds and pays bills. To raise funds, the Treasury generates currency, collects taxes, and borrows money. Expenditures for national projects and activities are made pursuant to congressional appropriations.

When income matches or exceeds spending, balance is promoted throughout the economy. This condition is desirable, but rare. When the outflow of funds exceeds collections, the result is a federal deficit. Heavy spending that is not covered by taxes produces deficits, which are financed by the sale of public debt instruments such as bonds, bills, and notes by the Treasury. When deficits are monetized by selling large amounts of debt, the Fed is tacitly expected to cooperate by supplying the banking system with sufficient reserves to accommodate the debt sales program and still leave enough credit for the private sector.

In theory, expenditures should expand the economy, increasing government tax collections and eventually producing an operating surplus that will reduce government debt. In practice, however, spending has grown much faster than revenues, producing deficits that, during the late 1970s and early 1980s, led to severe inflation. Throughout this experience, the Fed supplied the money needed to fund the Federal deficit. Financial institutions became concerned that excessive borrowing by the Treasury might use up credit supplies, short-changing private sector needs and crowding out smaller borrowers. These developments were damaging to the real estate industry, which was threatened by the loss of long-term mortgage capital due to the volatility of money markets and capital markets.

While disinflation and economic recovery in the mid-1980s helped to stabilize the real estate industry, the growth of the Federal deficit shows no sign of abating. Large amounts of this debt are monetized by foreign investment which can be expected to continue, provided interest rates remain high enough to ensure profitability in light of the devaluation of the dollar. The concensus in financial circles is that the growth of the Federal deficit constitutes the threat of a resurgence of inflation.

MONEY MARKET INSTRUMENTS

The prices of financial instruments, which are established in a free and active money market, determine their investment yields. These yields consist of the instruments' face, or stated, interest rates plus any price discounts earned, or minus any price premiums paid. Money cost is properly called an interest rate because when a borrowing instrument is created, it carries that day's market interest level for the maturity involved.

If a six-month-term instrument is sold when it is three months old, and prevailing interest rates are higher than when the instrument was created, the buyer will not be satisfied with the face, or coupon, rate. To make a deal, the seller will have to discount the paper; the investment yield to the buyer will then be the face rate plus amortization of the discount. If lower interest rates prevail at the time of sale, the buyer cannot purchase at the coupon rate, because the seller will demand a premium. The yield to the buyer will then be the face rate minus amortization of the premium paid. These conditions are reflected in the real estate market where buyers price property to provide good prospects for what they believe to be competitively attractive yields on the equity invested.

Money markets are especially important to real estate development activities. Construction loans are short-term mortgages with variable interest rates that are tied to market indexes. For example, borrowing costs in the market might be two to four percentage points above the floating *prime rate*, which is the short-term loan rate that commercial banks offer to favored customers. It is not unusual for building loan rates to be adjusted monthly with a floor, or minimum, rate, but no cap, or upper limit. When the demand for short-term money is intense and supply is limited, market interest rates escalate and construction funds become extremely expensive. The high real estate project costs that result can destroy economic feasibility and cause project failures and bankruptcies. The anticipated cost and availability of short-term funds is a key consideration for developers, and their perceptions cause real estate activity to expand or contract. Appraisers must factor projected construction loan costs, or "soft costs," into their cost approach valuations, particularly when appraising projects that will require more than a year to complete.

In money markets, a wide variety of instruments and arrangements is offered and sold by the federal government, banks, corporations, and local governments. Some important items are federal funds, Treasury bills, Treasury notes, other government securities, repurchase and reverse repurchase agreements, certificates of deposit, commercial paper, bankers' acceptances, municipal notes, and Eurodollars.

Federal Funds

When member banks experience intense loan demand, their reserve account balances may fall below the Federal Reserve System's requirements. To increase their reserves, these banks can borrow at the Fed's "discount window" or from other banks that have experienced slack demand and have excess reserves to loan for a short term. The borrowed or loaned money is called *federal funds* because it is used to meet Federal Reserve requirements. To obtain federal funds, banks may deal directly with one another or they may employ brokers to arrange the transactions.

The federal funds rate is influenced by any or all of the Federal Reserve's credit-regulation devices as well as supply and demand between banks. It is a key rate and its movements generate sympathetic trends in other money market and capital market costs. The rates for various instruments in these markets differ largely because of differences in their investment qualities and maturities. The federal funds rate is of particular interest to Fed watchers because it is the only money cost that is directly manipulated by the Federal Reserve System. It is clear that money and capital markets follow and react to variations in the federal funds rate.

Treasury Bills

A Treasury bill is a short-term, direct debt obligation of the U.S. government, usually having a maturity of three months, six months, or one year. Treasury bills are issued in denominations of $10,000, $15,000, $100,000, $500,000, and $1 million. These instruments do not bear a coupon interest rate; they are sold at a discount, which provides investor earnings. The yield on a Treasury bill is calculated for a 360-day year, but maturities are based on a 52-week year.

Treasury bills are backed by the full faith and credit of the U.S. government and are sold at frequent auctions. In preparing bids, purchasers study recent levels and movements in the federal funds rate to determine the direction of monetary policy. This plainly demonstrates the close relationship between these money rates.

Treasury bills greatly influence real estate activity. In the early 1980s, banks and savings and loan associations received regulatory permission to sell government-backed, six-month savings certificates at yields equal to or 25 basis points above the six-month Treasury bill yield established at the most recent auction. The arrangement was introduced to help these institutions attract savings funds, which they would channel into home mortgage loans. If the thrift industry could not compete for savings funds, mortgage fund shortages were expected to occur. The thrift industry was later deregulated and the program was eliminated, but Treasury bill rates are still the principal guide for short-maturity loan costs, particularly in the construction and development sectors of the real estate industry.

Other Government Securities

U.S. Treasury notes, which have longer maturities than most money market instruments, are traded in money and capital markets. They are backed by the full faith and credit of the U.S. government and are issued in maturities of one to ten years. Many issues fall in the two- to four-year range. Treasury notes are issued in denominations of $1,000, $5,000, $10,000, $100,000, and $1 million. They are interest bearing and carry a face rate.

After Treasury notes are issued, they are traded freely and priced to reflect current market yields. In these transactions, the remaining maturities are frequently short and the rates indicated fit typical patterns for similar money market investments.

Because of their long maturities, the earning rates on Treasury notes influence the rate levels of real estate "bridge" mortgages. Bridge mortgages are real estate loans that owners might obtain for two- to four-year periods while they are waiting for more favorable, longer-term financing or converting rental properties to condominium or cooperative ownership.

Other important securities are created and sold by government-sponsored agencies such as the Federal National Mortgage Corporation, the Federal Farm Credit System, the Federal Home Loan Bank, the World Bank, and the Federal Land

Bank. These instruments are supported by borrowing lines from the U.S. Treasury. They are freely and actively traded over the counter and offer yields slightly higher than those offered by direct Treasury obligations.

Repurchase Agreements and Reverse Repurchase Agreements

Repurchase agreements and reverse repurchase agreements are short-term financing arrangements made by securities dealers, banks, and the Federal Reserve System in which a person who needs funds for a short period uses his or her portfolio of money market investments as collateral and sells an interest in the portfolio with the obligation to repurchase it, with interest, at a specified future time. These agreements provide borrowers with needed liquidity and lenders with securities as collateral. Individuals and businesses with excess short-term cash invest in repurchase agreements. The time of repurchase may be in one day or up to several months in the future.

The Fed has used this procedure in fine-tuning money markets to achieve selected interest rate levels. By arranging a purchase from a securities dealer who is obligated to repurchase in a few days, the Fed temporarily creates additional bank reserves because the dealer deposits the transaction proceeds in a commercial bank. A reverse repurchase agreement is created when the Fed sells securities to dealers who must sell them back with interest. In this way the Fed temporarily withdraws reserves from the banking system because the dealer will pay with a check drawn on a commercial bank account.

Repurchase agreements enable corporations to lend excess cash for short periods. This is especially important because these businesses cannot engage in Federal Reserve funds trading, which is usually reserved for banking organizations. The interest rates in repurchase agreements are determined by prevailing supply and demand conditions in short-term money markets. They are also influenced by the quality of the collateral, which is usually excellent.

Certificates of Deposit

Certificates of deposit (CDs) are financial instruments that represent time deposits with banking organizations. Certificates of deposit may be for terms of one month, three months, six months, one year, or up to seven years. Most large certificates of $100,000 or more are for one- or three-month terms. A CD is a contract between a bank or savings and loan and a depositor in which the institution agrees to pay negotiated rates of interest and the depositor agrees to maintain the deposit for a fixed period of time. A CD is backed only by the credit of the issuing bank, which is usually supported by FDIC insurance. Many CDs are negotiable and can be traded.

Although the interest rate on a CD is negotiated, the Federal Reserve imposed constraints on CD rates for many years through its Regulation Q. However, in the early 1980s deregulation legislation relaxed or removed these limitations, and Congress established the Depository Institutions Deregulation Committee to assure equality among all financial institutions.

Commercial Paper

Commercial paper is a corporation's promissory notes to borrow short-term funds for current operations. By trading commercial paper, organizations with excess cash can lend to those in need of money. This money market sector is well organized, and transaction data on prices and interest rates are widely and quickly disseminated by computer. Dealers specializing in commercial paper "make markets" and are able to consummate deals quickly and efficiently. Because commercial paper is backed only by the credit of the corporations issuing it, only the largest, soundest companies can use it effectively. Due to the vagaries of money supply and demand conditions, commercial paper rates are frequently lower than bank loan costs; hence, large corporations benefit from the ability to use commercial paper.

In the real estate industry, commercial paper is used to raise short-term construction funds. For example, a real estate investment trust (REIT) might issue commercial paper to raise the money to fund construction loans. For the REIT, the key consideration is that interest rates on the commercial paper be sufficiently below construction mortgage rates to give the trust enough earnings to handle expenses and provide a satisfactory profit. Commercial paper is exempt from federal securities regulations provided 1) it is for a short term, 2) the funds are for current operations, and 3) there is an unequivocal "takeout" commitment for the loan. When these requirements are met, the Securities and Exchange Commission will issue "no action" letters.

Bankers' Acceptances

A bankers' acceptance is a bank's obligation or promise to pay. The main difference between commercial paper and bankers' acceptances is that commercial paper is backed by the corporation's credit only, while the corporation and the bank both stand behind bankers' acceptances. Thus, the latter carries less risk, which often causes yields on bankers' acceptances to be less than yields on commercial paper.

Bankers' acceptances are short-term, noninterest-bearing notes that are sold at discount and redeemed at par, or the face amount, like Treasury bills. Most bankers' acceptances are created in the course of foreign trade, so large banks with foreign departments participate in this market. These instruments are not directly related to real estate operations, but they reflect trends in short-term interest rates for investments of varying quality.

Municipal Notes

Municipal notes are short-term obligations of villages, cities, counties, etc., used to finance current operations until satisfactory long-term funds are obtained. Because municipal notes are exempt from federal and state taxation, they are favored by money investors. This tax advantage has caused the interest rates on these notes to be relatively low. The earning rates on municipal notes may indicate real estate investor's requirements for after-tax yields. Although real estate investments are generally for longer terms, the rates on these notes do offer some useful insights into investment strategies.

Eurodollars

Eurodollars are dollars deposited outside the United States. This monetary element has grown enormously since World War II. The growth of Eurodollars has been aided by the fact that U.S. trading deficits are paid in dollars, world oil bills are settled in dollars, and increasing numbers of multinational business operations are using and requiring dollars. Banks and businesses that require short- to intermediate-term financing have profitably borrowed this type of capital.

While the REIT industry expanded, many trusts secured Eurodollar loans to fund mortgage lending operations. Eurobond and debenture issues of five to seven years have been employed, but maturities of one to six months are more common. When supply and demand conditions generate favorable interest levels, Eurodollar loans can provide bridge financing for real estate ventures.

Yield Levels

Appraisers use published daily financial reports to follow the money market for indications of changing monetary values. These reports provide information on various debt and equity instruments and their yield rates. This information indicates the general state of the economy and can be expected to affect real estate industry operations. Figure 5.4 is a sample report from the *New York Times* daily financial section. It shows the yield levels evidenced in the day's trading. Other publications also provide this type of information.

CAPITAL MARKET INSTRUMENTS

Traditional capital market operations are described in this section, but readers must keep in mind that the conditions influencing the use of long-term, fixed-rate instruments may change over time. Appraisers and other market analysts must be aware of market changes and interpret how they may affect the financing arrangements discussed below.

Figure 5.4

Key Rates
In percent

	Yesterday	Previous Day	Year Ago
PRIME RATE	**8.25**	8.25	8.50
DISCOUNT RATE	**5.50**	5.50	6.50
FEDERAL FUNDS	**6.56**	6.66	6.39
3-MO. TREAS. BILLS	**5.68**	5.55	5.73
6-MO. TREAS. BILLS	**5.79**	5.64	5.79
7-YR. TREAS. NOTES	**8.29**	8.21	7.11
30-YR. TREAS. BONDS	**8.72**	8.61	7.27
TELEPHONE BONDS	**9.67**	9.69	9.21
MUNICIPAL BONDS*	**8.05**	8.04	7.93

* Municipal Bond Index, The Bond Buyer
Salomon Brothers estimates for bellwether issues

Bonds

A bond is a capital market instrument issued with a fixed interest rate for a term of one year or more. The U.S. government, business corporations, states, and municipalities, among others, issue bonds to raise long-term capital for operations and development. Earnings from government-issued bonds are not free from federal taxation, but they are often exempt from local taxes. Generally, the short-term funding discussed earlier is used for project development, and long-term arrangements are made when the project is completed.

Bonds are usually sold with a par value of $1,000; if the issue carries an interest rate of 12%, each bond will earn $120 per year. The buyer will receive this earnings rate and at maturity, in 20 or 30 years, will be repaid the $1,000 principal.

The bond market is closely related to real estate investment activities. Real estate is normally bought with a combination of equity capital and medium- to long-term debt funds, called *mortgage money.* Most real estate deals are structured with a substantial amount of mortgage money and a smaller amount of equity, or venture, funds. Institutions with long-term capital to invest usually survey bond markets, then examine mortgage opportunities, and finally make investment decisions to secure the best earnings for the risk involved.

Correlating bond market yields and mortgage capital costs is an intriguing study. Until the 1970s and early 1980s when high inflation caused money market volatility, there was a close correlation between good-quality mortgages and AA-rated utilities bonds. The unstable financial conditions of this period reduced the availability of long-term, fixed-interest capital and created a need for new real estate investment analysis methodologies. Today, mortgage-equity combinations may involve debt funds with variable interest rates, and property feasibility studies must account for these expected rate changes. To do so, appraisers must develop interest rate forecasts that cover the projected investment term.

The municipal bond yields observed in daily trading reflect the after-tax earnings requirements of investors. A popular proxy for these bonds is the Bond Buyers Index, which is found in the financial press. Figure 5.5 is extracted from "New Bond Issues," a regular feature of the *New York Times*, which contains information on maturities, risk ratings, and daily price changes. The quoted yields are calculated from indicated prices and interest rates, assuming full payment at maturity. Some bonds are traded on organized exchanges such as the New York Stock Exchange, but many others are handled over the counter.

Figure 5.5

New Bond Issues

TUESDAY, JULY 21, 1987

Issues	Moody's Rating	Current Bid&Asked	Chng	Yield
UTILITY BONDS				
Pac Bell 9¼s26	A1	93-93½	-¾	9.90
Pac G & E 9.40s19	A1	92½-92⅞	-1⅜	10.15
CORPORATE BONDS				
Amoco 8⅝s16	Aaa	91-91½	-⅝	9.48
Sears Roe 6s00	Aa2	74½-75	-½	9.40
Union Pac 8½s17	A1	87¼-87¾	-⅜	9.77
INTERMEDIATE NOTES				
Boeing 8⅜s96	Aa3	95½-96	-½	9.05
Chevron 8¾s96	Aa3	97½-97⅞	-⅝	9.10
GMAC 8⅞s96	Aa-1	97¼-97¾	-¼	9.25
INTERNATIONAL ISSUES				
Hydro Que 8¼s26	A1	86¾-87¼	-1¼	9.49
Nov Scotia 8⅞s16	A2	91½-92	-1	9.70
World Bank 8⅞s26	Aaa	92¾-93¼	-1¼	9.53

Source: First Boston Corp.

Stocks

A stock is an ownership share in a company or corporation. A stock corporation is a common legal entity in which investors provide organizational capital by subscribing to shares that represent ownership and a right to all proprietary benefits but are subject to the prior claims of operating expenses and debt service on capital raised by selling bonds, debentures, and other money market instruments. Shareholder benefits consist of any cash or stock dividends declared, augmented by share price appreciation or diminished by depreciation.

Marketing mechanisms in the form of stock exchanges—e.g., the New York Stock Exchange and the American Stock Exchange (Amex)—were established to give business ventures ready access to capital sources and to provide flexibility and ease in trading shares. Through continuous refinement of exchange operations, orderly market conditions have been established and share values, dividends declared, and other important financial data are published on a regular basis.

Mortgages

A mortgage is a legal instrument for pledging a described property interest for the repayment of a loan under certain terms and conditions. A mortgage constitutes a lien on the interest pledged. Mortgage loans supply most of the capital employed in real estate investments. A borrower gives a lender a lien on real estate as assurance that the loan will be repaid. If the borrower fails to make payment, the lender can foreclose the lien and acquire the real estate, thereby offsetting the loss. Traditionally, mortgage loans were made for long terms of 20 to 30 years and carried fixed interest rates. A level-payment mortgage, which requires the same dollar amount of payment to be made each period for the entire loan term, is a popular contract. The payments are calculated to pay interest at the rate selected and to amortize the loan fully over its term so that less of each successive payment is required for interest and more is available for debt reduction. Other payment arrangements are also used. The parties to a mortgage are usually free to contract in any fashion they desire, subject only to limitations of usury and public policy.

A borrower may pledge real estate to more than one lender, thereby creating several liens; in such cases, the order of the liens is important. The first loan contract executed and recorded is the first mortgage, which has priority over all subsequent transactions. Second and third mortgages are sometimes referred to as *junior liens*; because they involve more lending risk than first mortgages, higher rates of interest are charged for secondary financing.

Mortgages fall into three major categories: guaranteed, insured, and conventional. Veterans Administration (VA) home mortgages are the most notable example of guaranteed mortgages, but other state and national government agencies also provide guarantees. Federal Housing Authority (FHA) mortgages are the most extensively used insured loans, but other government bodies and private insurance companies offer loan insurance as well. Conventional mortgages are neither insured nor guaranteed. Although regulations vary from state to state, in most states institutional lenders are limited to a 75% to 80% conventional loan-to-value ratio. Private mortgage insurance (PMI), however, is available for loans that exceed 75% to 80% loan-to-value ratios.

Mortgage terms are set by contractual agreement between a lender and a borrower, and are subject to usury limitations. In the early 1980s, the Fed's monetary policy generated such high interest rates that usury ceilings had to be raised or eliminated. Without these actions, mortgage money would have become unavailable. Congress sets interest rate limits for VA and FHA mortgages. Because loan procedures may change too slowly to keep pace with rapidly changing money markets, the practice of paying points has emerged. Points are a percentage of the total loan amount that the lender is paid up front to enhance the loan yield and make it competitive with current capital market rates.

The effects of competition for capital are clearly evident in mortgage markets. In the early 1980s, yields soared and changes were so frequent that investors preferred to acquire short-term, liquid investments, which offered generous rates and maximum flexibility. In a volatile climate, investors resist long-term positions and fixed-rate instruments because they provide little protection against inflation. In response to erratic conditions, contracts such as variable-rate mortgages, adjustable mortgages, and rollover mortgages were created. These mortgage instruments provide for periodic adjustment of interest rates to keep yields competitive with those available in capital markets. Although these contracts may cover long periods, the payment requirements change at frequent intervals so real estate owners cannot budget for fixed debt service. In managing a property subject to a variable-rate mortgage, an owner may feel impelled to arrange leasing programs that permit rapid rental adjustments to offset increases in mortgage payments caused by money market fluctuations.

Deeds of Trust

While a mortgage is a contract between a borrower and a lender, a deed of trust involves a third party. *Hence, a deed of trust is defined as a legal instrument similar to a mortgage that, when executed and delivered, conveys or transfers property title to a trustee.* In such an arrangement, a borrower conveys or transfers property to a trustee for the benefit of a lender. A deed of trust states the trustee's name and the lender's name. The borrower conveys title to the trustee, but retains the right to use and occupy the property. In many states where deeds of trust are used, they are recorded in the county and given to the lender or trustee for safekeeping until the loan is paid off.

Deeds of trust are also used to circumvent foreclosure proceedings against a defaulting debtor. A *trust agreement* accompanies the deed and sets forth the terms of the security and instructions to the trustee. If the buyer defaults, a public sale by the trustee in accordance with state law provides funds to compensate the trustee and repay the debt with interest. In some states, deeds of trust are used in place of mortgage contracts.

Nonmoney Credit Instruments

Land contracts, frequently called *installment sale contracts* or *contracts for deed*, are instruments that provide for the future delivery of a property deed to a buyer after certain conditions are met. A seller finances the sale of a property by permitting the buyer to pay for it over a period of time, but the title is delivered only after all payments are made. In the event of default, the buyer normally forfeits all payments made and the seller may also elect to hold the buyer to his or her contract. Because such contracts are sometimes not recorded, a buyer usually ensures that the agreement contains provisions to protect against any liens or encumbrances that may be filed against the property before title passes.

The purchase-money mortgage is a common real estate financing device that is similar to the installment sale contract. With this instrument, a buyer can finance all or much of a property's cost by arranging for the seller to accept a purchase-money mortgage as part of the purchase price. The contract specifies the required interest rate, the amortization payments, and a date for final and full repayment. To facilitate a transaction, a seller may take back a purchase-money mortgage so that the buyer does not have to obtain funds from other sources. The buyer takes title immediately and becomes the property owner. If the buyer defaults on a payment or some other requirement, the seller may foreclose. When used for land acquisition, a purchase-money mortgage should contain release clauses that specify the principal payments that must be made to release parts of the property from the lien of the mortgage. Other procedural matters such as the order in which lots may be released are normally set forth as well.

RELATIONSHIPS BETWEEN MONEY MARKET AND CAPITAL MARKET RATES

Rates

Observation of daily trading activity over a period of time may reveal relationships among the earning rates of various instruments traded in money and capital markets. For example, there may be a relatively constant spread of 50 basis points between the yields on three-month and six-month Treasury bills. However, market volatility can cause the spread between these yields to increase or decrease at times. Similarly, the spread between three-month and six-month commercial paper may widen to 70 basis points and remain steady at that level for several months. These observations are significant because they reveal how the length of an instrument's maturity influences its yield.

The federal funds rate is a foundational rate. In money and capital markets, fluctuations in this rate are closely followed and produce sympathetic reactions in prices and yields. Another key investment yield is reflected in the weekly auction of Treasury bills. Because these instruments represent top credit quality and short maturity, their yields establish a base from which market participants measure all short-term money costs, including real estate construction loan rates. Money market and capital market rate relationships are created by prime investment considerations, which include borrowers' credit, loan maturity, monetary supply and demand conditions, and existing and anticipated inflation rates. All of these factors are important in risk rating various investments. With an understanding of rate relationships, appraisers can correlate real estate investment risk with the risks associated with actively traded capital market instruments, using the abundance of pricing and yield information that is available.

Pattern of Rates

Traditionally, long-term instruments have provided the most generous yields. In the early 1980s, however, financial market trading reflected an inverse yield curve, and short-term rates exceeded longer-term investment returns. The steep debt service requirements created by high interest rates drained business earnings and reduced equity returns. Consequently, many real estate ventures at that time were not economically feasible. When money costs declined, many projects that were previously infeasible became practical and profitable.

Cycles, Trends, and Inflation

Money and capital market conditions are cyclical. As the economy expands, competition for capital intensifies, the costs of goods and services increase, and inflation escalates. Then the Fed tightens money and credit until the economy slows down. The demand for funds subsides, interest rates decline, and economic conditions become sufficiently stable for businesses to begin new expansion. When the frequency of the economic cycle accelerates and its range increases, business and money conditions change drastically and rapidly. This creates an unattractive economic environment for long-term investments.

Inflation is often described as price escalations throughout the economy; when goods and services become increasingly expensive, inflation accelerates. Inflation is also described as the proliferation of monetary units—i.e., a currency expansion. These descriptions are inextricably related. When monetary units proliferate with no apparent growth in underlying wealth, the value of each unit declines; more units are required in exchange for goods and services, and price levels rise.

A good illustration of how inflation affects real estate can be seen in the single-family residential market. In the late 1970s, the supply of money in the United States expanded sharply; simultaneously, the median prices of new and used dwelling units escalated drastically, and these prices were accepted and supported by healthy demand.

The economic importance of inflation also can be seen in the concept of "real" interest rates. Nominal interest rates, like those reported daily in the financial press, are said to be composites of the "real" cost of funds, or real interest rate, and the premiums that investors demand to protect their currency value from being eroded by inflation. Thus, the nominal rate equals the real interest rate plus an inflation premium. Economists suggest that the real interest rate has remained steady at 3% to 4%. Therefore, if the capital market shows a nominal rate of 11% for 10-year U.S. Treasury notes, the real interest rate concept would indicate an inflation premium of 7%.

$$
\begin{array}{ll}
4\% & \text{(real interest rate)} \\
+\ 7\% & \text{(inflation premium)} \\
\hline
11\% & \text{(nominal rate)}
\end{array}
$$

This example demonstrates how investors' perceptions of inflation can affect prices in market trading and change the interest rates on instruments of different maturities.

Traditional real estate investment practices involve the use of two types of capital—debt and equity—and a typical venture is structured with a substantial mortgage amount and a smaller equity contribution. Before 1970, the largest suppliers of mortgage funds were thrift institutions such as savings banks and savings and loan associations and life insurance companies. However, the high interest rates of the 1970s and early 1980s had a negative effect on these organizations' mortgage positions. Their portfolio yields became inadequate, their liquidity diminished, and their mortgages were being repaid with funds that were cheaper than those originally loaned. High interest rates also caused depositors to withdraw their money, so traditional mortgage lenders were unable to offer as many loans. The term *disintermediation* was coined to describe these inflation-generated conditions.

Business and Real Estate Cycles

Obviously, money market and capital market activities and trends affect the real estate industry. The years following World War II (1946-1966) were characterized by discernible patterns in real estate and general business cycles. As business prospered, the demand for capital intensified, inflation tended to accelerate, and an oversupply of goods and services was being produced. Then Federal Reserve monetary policy and other economic controls were used to slow the pace of the economy and a recession ensued.

When Congress wanted to develop economic revival programs, the industry invariably selected to provide economic stimulation was real estate, particularly home building. Programs to provide abundant moderately priced mortgage money were developed. These programs usually involved loan insurance or guarantees to induce capital managers to participate. Because there was a substantial demand for housing, the programs were well received and residential development expanded, increasing employment in all economic sectors. Manufacturers of hardware, supplies (e.g., heating, plumbing, and electrical), paints, furniture, equipment, and other goods experienced business improvement. The economy finally revived, then inflation started to accelerate, and the cycle was repeated. When loan insurance and guarantee programs supplied inexpensive long-term capital, real estate prospered and the general economy expanded.

SOURCES OF CAPITAL FOR REAL ESTATE

The different aspirations of equity and debt investors are revealed in their market actions. The debt investor participates in bonds or mortgages, usually pursuing conservative paths in search of certain income and repayment of principal. This type of investor expects a priority claim on investment earnings and often looks for security in the form of a lien on the assets involved. While a debt investor is relatively passive, an equity investor is active. Such an investor is more willing to assume risk, so the funds used for equity investment are known as *venture capital.*

Inflation tends to change traditional investor attitudes. Institutions that normally restrict their real estate positions to debt in the form of mortgages become dismayed when they realize that the rates of return they bargained for, and once deemed adequate, are woefully low. They also realize that the expensive money they loaned will be repaid with cheap, inflated dollars. In the early 1980s, these conditions impelled institutional investors to alter their investment policies and seek real estate equity positions, which they believed to be reasonable hedges against inflation. In those years, many financial authorities thought that long-term, fixed-rate debt capital would become a thing of the past. The economic and monetary changes of the mid-1980s, however, suggest a return to more traditional investor attitudes and policies.

Equity

Equity investors realize that their earnings are subordinate to a project's operating expenses and debt service requirements. Equity income earnings are called *dividends*, but they are only one part of the total return that the investor anticipates. Investors also expect that the value of their original investment will increase, although there is a risk that it will remain stable or decline.

Trusts

A trust is a temporary, conditional, or permanent fiduciary relationship in which the legal title to, and control of, property are placed in the hands of a trustee for the benefit of another person. Trust entities are used extensively to amass equity funds for real estate investment. One frequently employed trust is the Massachusetts business trust, in which holders of shares of beneficial interest have no personal liability for the trust's actions. Usually, this protection is achieved by using a corporate form of doing business. This type of trust also allows shareholders to avoid the double income taxation incurred in the use of corporations. A corporate entity is taxed on its earnings, and from its after-tax net income it distributes dividends to shareholders, who are then personally taxed on that income. The earnings on a Massachusetts business trust, however, are passed through to beneficial shareholders; no income tax is paid by the trust and only a single tax is paid by the shareholders. Investors have found these income and tax pass-through arrangements very attractive.

Real estate investment trusts (REITs) have been successful in pooling the funds of small investors to acquire real estate investment positions that could not be handled by these people individually. These trusts offer shareholders freedom from personal liability, the benefit of expert management, and readily transferred shares. To qualify for a tax pass-through, a REIT must pay dividends of at least 90% of its net income. With complicated income-measuring practices, trusts have attempted to pay almost all net income and, therefore, have been precluded from establishing reserves for possible losses.

Partnerships

A common vehicle for pooling real estate equity funds is a partnership. *A partnership is a business arrangement in which two or more persons jointly own a business and share in its profits and losses.* There are two kinds of partnerships—general and limited.

A general partnership is an ownership arrangement in which all partners share in investment gains and losses and each is fully responsible for all liabilities. A general partner's complete liability for the acts of the other partners and responsibility for debts incurred by them is one major disadvantage of this type of business arrangement. General partners may legally participate in full, active management of the partnership's business. The most attractive feature of a general partnership is that the real estate investment's tax shelter benefits of depreciation and interest may be passed through to partners.

A limited partnership is an ownership arrangement consisting of general and limited partners; general partners manage the business and assume full liability for partnership debt, while limited partners are passive and liable only to the extent of their own capital contributions. Limited partnerships are popular because they permit an uneven distribution of tax-shelter benefits. Although limited partners' financial liability is restricted to their capital contributions, they may receive tax benefits in excess of that amount.

Syndications

Another popular arrangement for raising real estate equity capital is a syndication. *A syndication is a private or public partnership that pools funds for the acquisition and development of real estate projects or other business ventures.* Private syndications are limited to small groups of investors and are relatively free from government regulation. Public syndications involve large groups of investors and generally operate interstate, so they are subject to Security Exchange Commission (SEC) registration regulations. Due to their large investor groups, public syndications can amass great amounts of equity funds by gathering contributions from people who do not have the resources to handle a venture alone.

Often a syndication is organized or promoted by a general partner, who has full financial liability for the partnership's activities. The other syndicate investors are limited partners. To attract a large number of investors, syndication agreements may provide for an unequal distribution of investment benefits, allocating the major share of tax shelter benefits to syndicate-share purchasers, not the general partner.

Joint Ventures

A joint venture is a combination of two or more entities that join to undertake a specific project. Although a joint venture often takes the form of a general or limited partnership, it differs from a partnership in that it is intended to be temporary and does not involve other ventures. The parties may later embark on other ventures, but each venture is the subject of a separate contractual agreement. General and limited partnership arrangements are popular in real estate joint ventures because they permit uneven distribution of tax-shelter benefits. Tenancy in common is a form of joint ownership that is usually employed in small property holdings.

A joint venture arrangement is frequently used in large real estate projects. One party, usually a financial institution, supplies most of the required capital and the other party provides building or management expertise. Life insurance companies and pension trusts have joined with entrepreneurial building organizations in joint ventures to develop large offices, shopping malls, and other major real estate projects. If the financial partner wants the restricted liability of a limited partner, it must be willing to forego active project management. Home or condominium builders may participate in joint ventures with the service corporations of savings and loan associations. Combinations such as these have produced a substantial amount of much-needed housing.

Pension Funds

Private and government-operated pension funds comprise a huge and rapidly growing source of investment capital. Usually, the pension contributions of employers and employees are placed with a trustee, who is obliged to invest and reinvest prudently, accumulate funds, and pay designated plan benefits to retirees. The trustee may be a government body, a trust company, an insurance company, or an individual. In performing these duties, an individual trustee may employ the trust departments of commercial banks, insurance companies, and other financial institutions.

U.S. pension funds totaled approximately $1.71 trillion in 1985, and they are expected to increase steadily through the next decade. A capital source of such huge proportions cannot fail to have a major impact on the general economy and the real estate industry. Pension trusts are the only group that can feasibly consider longer-term investments because their funds are collected and their pension benefits are paid out over an extended period of time.

Traditionally, pension funds have been most involved in securities investments such as stocks and bonds. The development of pass-through securities by the Government National Mortgage Association, however, has made it easier for pension funds to invest in mortgages, and they have taken sizable positions. Pension trusts have also shown some willingness to invest in real estate equities by purchasing or participating in the real estate investments created by life insurance companies and commercial banks. Banks and life insurance companies acquire high-quality real estate equities, pool the investments in separate accounts, and for a fee, supply the necessary portfolio management. Pension trusts commit funds to these accounts and share in all earnings, which consist of both income returns and sales profits.

Life Insurance Companies

Through normal insurance sales and operations, life insurance companies accumulate large amounts of funds which they place in diverse investments. Insurance companies are substantial mortgage lenders, and they make many real estate equity investments for their own accounts and as managers of separate accounts. Their investment officers regard equities as attractive earning situations that offer growth potential and reasonable protection against the capital erosion caused by inflation.

International Equity Capital

The investment activities of foreign individuals, countries, financial institutions, and pension funds also provide equity capital for the real estate industry. These "offshore" capital sources have become increasingly important to U.S. real estate. Foreign investors often take a long-term investment view, bidding up prices, accepting relatively low initial cash flow returns, and looking to future income and value growth to supply a major part of their anticipated total equity return. Many of these investors do not hesitate to make 100% equity acquisitions when the properties involved are attractive and have exciting growth potential. Many of these investors will undoubtedly mortgage at a later time, when monetary conditions improve and lower interest rates permit positive leveraging.

International capital comes from a variety of sources, including the oil-rich nations of the Middle East and financial institutions and individuals in Western Europe. Although these entities have supplied needed equity capital to realty ventures in this country, they still represent a very small fraction of total U.S. real estate investment.

Debt

Because mortgage money is so important in real estate, investors, appraisers and counselors must be familiar with the sources and costs of debt capital.

Savings and Loan Associations

Savings and loan associations, along with mutual savings banks, life insurance companies, credit unions, and others, are financial intermediaries. They receive savings deposits, lend them at interest, and distribute dividends to depositors after paying operating expenses and establishing appropriate reserves.

Savings and loan associations may be state or federally chartered. Federal savings and loan associations are supervised by the Federal Home Loan Bank Board (FHLBB), which was created in 1932 to provide credit to thrift and home financing institutions. The agency's main functions are to relieve liquidity problems and to provide the savings and loan industry with a constant flow of funds. Savings and loan associations promote thrift, pool savings, and invest funds in home mortgages.

There is a close relationship between the health of savings and loan associations and the market for residential real estate. When short-term interest rates are high, savers withdraw funds and reinvest them in higher-yielding, short-term money market instruments and funds. Because savings and loan associations are financial intermediaries, high interest rates reduce the availability of mortgage funds and increase their cost.

Commercial Banks

Commercial banks are privately owned institutions that offer a variety of financial services to businesses and individuals. They may be state or federally chartered. Commercial banks are managed by boards of directors, who are selected by stockholders but are subject to regulation by state agencies and the Federal Deposit Insurance Corporation (FDIC). The FDIC is an independent agency that insures individual deposits in all state and federally chartered banks in the Federal Reserve System.

In keeping with their role as short-term lenders, commercial banks have traditionally supplied construction and development loans. They usually require construction borrowers to obtain commitments from long-term, permanent lenders, obliging them to "take out" a loan when the project is completed. Large commercial banks make a limited number of permanent mortgage loans, usually on commercial and industrial properties. In small communities, commercial banks are also expected to supply their customers with home loans.

One important real estate credit function of commercial banks is warehousing mortgages for mortgage bankers and other financial institutions. The banks provide mortgage bankers with short-term loans secured by their mortgage inventories. This arrangement gives mortgage bankers the liquidity to continue their lending operations while they try to sell the accumulated mortgages to a permanent lender.

Life Insurance Companies

Life insurance companies are large suppliers of real estate mortgage credit; they are of two principal types—mutual or stock. Mutual life insurance companies are owned by policyholders, who share in net earnings by receiving dividends that can be used to reduce their premium expenses. The profits of stock life insurance companies belong to shareholders, who may or may not be policyholders.

Life insurance companies have always invested heavily in real estate. Their activities include both mortgage lending and property ownership. Life insurance companies usually acquire real estate positions that are long term and relate well to their regular business, in which policy premiums are collected over extended periods. The recent development and popularity of "universal" life insurance has deprived companies of much long-term investment capital. In this insurance arrangement, the policyholder, not the company, directs the investment of policy reserves.

The mortgage investments of life insurance companies cover the full range of realty types—e.g., residences, apartments, offices, shopping malls, hotels, and industrial properties. Because many companies have great financial resources, they have been important in mortgaging large income-producing properties. These large companies prefer loans on offices and shopping malls; they have less interest in rental apartments.

Life insurance companies may acquire full ownership of real estate for their own investment accounts or for the separate investment accounts that they manage for pension trusts. Although real estate ownership may amount to only 3% to 5% of a company's assets, a large dollar investment is involved because major life companies may have billions of dollars in assets.

Mutual Savings Banks

Mutual savings banks are located in many states and are regulated by the FDIC and various state banking departments. They are very similar to mutual savings and loan associations, promoting thrift and investing substantial amounts of savings in real estate mortgages. In general, they have broader investment powers than savings and loan associations. With deregulation in the early 1980s, mutual savings banks began to expand their scope of activity, which now almost equals that of commercial banks. Mutual savings banks have grown substantially and continue to experience rapid change; they control assets of more than $100 billion.

Savings banks are important mortgage lenders on local and national levels. When the FHA became dominant in home mortgage lending, savings banks participated extensively in FHA programs. Like savings and loan associations, mutual savings banks have supplied large amounts of mortgage funds for the one- to four-family residential real estate market. Savings banks have reasonably broad investment powers, but they usually concentrate on mortgages, which may account for 65% to 75% of a bank's assets. They also invest in government bonds, corporate bonds, and, to a minor degree, real estate and stock equity investments.

Thrift institutions have been in the unfortunate position of borrowing short and lending long—i.e., their deposits are of the demand type, but they are invested in long-term mortgages. When unusually large amount of funds are withdrawn, liquidity is threatened and banks must borrow at high costs to meet their obligations. The earnings squeeze results from the ongoing trend to deregulate the interest rates that may be paid on savings. When interest rate ceilings are lifted, banks and savings and loan associations must pay high competitive dividend rates to keep the funds they previously received and invested in low-yield, fixed-rate mortgages. Such a situation erodes the institutions' net worth and limits their lending. For the real estate industry, this means less mortgage money is available and any money that is found costs a great deal. When interest rates escalate, fewer aspiring home purchasers qualify as acceptable credit risks because debt service would consume too much of their disposable income. These conditions depress home building and sales.

Junior Mortgage Originators

Real estate investments are not only structured with first mortgages, but also with second, third, and fourth mortgages. Junior mortgages can be used to raise substantial amounts of mortgage funds and to achieve various investment goals, such as creating additional leverage and facilitating sales in money markets that are not conducive to refinancing first mortgages. In most jurisdictions, loans must be legally recorded to establish their priority. The first lien recorded takes priority over any that are subsequently filed. When a mortgagor defaults, junior lien holders must keep the senior positions financially current or they run the risk of being cut off by foreclosure of the prior liens. Obviously, junior mortgages involve greater risks than senior liens, and therefore, they command higher interest rates.

Legal regulations usually preclude banks, savings and loan associations, and life insurance companies from making large junior mortgage loans. However, various regulatory "leeway" or "basket" clauses permit institutions to make junior mortgage loans in amounts that do not exceed 3% or 4% of institutional assets. Other private lenders such as REITs, financing companies, and factoring organizations provide secondary financing as a regular line of business. They offer expensive secondary financing in the form of junior mortgages or subordinated land sale-leasebacks, and they are not supervised as banks and life insurance companies are.

Secondary Mortgage Market

When intense competition causes capital shortages that depress the general economy and curtail mortgage market activity, government and monetary authorities often see housing activity as the most effective way to improve the situation. Government and private organizations may stimulate home building by creating facilities that are known collectively as the *secondary mortgage market*. This market allows mortgagees to sell a package of mortgages at prices consistent with existing money market rate conditions. The sales of mortgages free up capital, create liquidity, and permit mortgagees to lend when they might otherwise lack funds.

Federal National Mortgage Association. A major influence on the secondary mortgage market is exerted by the Federal National Mortgage Association (FNMA). The FNMA's principal purpose is to help the housing industry by purchasing mortgages from primary mortgage markets, thus increasing the liquidity of primary lenders. It issues long-term debentures and short-term discount notes to raise most of its funds. Two important FNMA programs are the over-the-counter program, in which the FNMA posts the prices it will pay for the immediate delivery of mortgages, and the free market system commitment auction, in which separate but simultaneous auctions are held for FHA, VA, and conventional mortgages.

Federal Home Loan Mortgage Corporation (FHLMC). The Federal Home Loan Mortgage Corporation was created in 1970 to increase the availability of mortgage funds and to provide greater flexibility for mortgage investors. The organization is directed by the Federal Home Loan Bank Board. The FHLMC facilitates the expansion and distribution of capital for mortgage purposes by conducting both purchase and sales programs.

In its purchase programs, the FHLMC buys single-family and condominium mortgages from approved financial institutions. This allows a selling, banking, or mortgage banking organization to remain liquid in times of credit stringency and continue making mortgage funds available for housing. Although FNMA programs include insured and guaranteed mortgages, the corporation's main thrust is in conventional mortgage fields. Both whole mortgages and participations are purchased by the FHLMC.

In its sales programs, the FHLMC sells its mortgage inventories, acquiring funds from organizations that have excess capital. Through its purchases, the FHLMC supplies these funds to other organizations that have shortages. Because its operations are conducted nationally, the FHLMC generates mortgage capital availability throughout the United States.

Government National Mortgage Association (GNMA). Another agency that influences the secondary mortgage market is the Government National Mortgage Association. Its operations have made much mortgage capital available to housing markets. While the FNMA is a private corporation, the GNMA is a government organization that gets financial support from the U.S. Treasury. The GNMA provides special assistance in mortgage programs for loans that could not be handled without extraordinary support. It also manages and liquidates certain mortgages acquired by the government. Its most important role in the secondary market, however, is in the Mortgage Backed Security Program.

The GNMA is authorized to guarantee the timely payment of principal and interest on long-term securities that are backed by pools of insured or guaranteed mortgages. The most popular security is a pass-through arrangement in which mortgage payments are passed on to the holder of the security. In this program, mortgage originators pool their loans in groups of $1 million or more, issue covering securities, and obtain a GNMA guarantee. Through this program, investors who do not have the capacity to originate mortgages can become involved in home finance markets. Because of their excellent investment attributes, GNMA securities are traded extensively. Money and capital market investors regard the investment yields indicated by the GNMA as the current return on top-quality liquid paper.

The recent development of Collateralized Mortgage Obligations (CMOs) as a major investment banking operation was prompted by GNMA guarantee arrangements. These instruments are bonds issued and sold in the capital markets. They are attractive because the debt involved is usually collateralized by GNMA certificates covering pools of residential mortgages. Because of GNMA participation, these bonds receive an AAA, highest-quality risk rating and can be sold at attractively low interest rates. As CMOs have proliferated, they have involved collateral other than GNMA certificates, including FNMA, FHLMC, and even conventional institutional mortgages. This vehicle has been a huge source of liquidity for the mortgage industry and has monetized the mortgage element in real estate investment.

Private sector transactions. Although most secondary mortgage market activity has been generated by the FNMA, the GNMA, and the FHLMC, the private sector has also played a role. Banks and insurance companies with mortgage-originating capability often sell loan portfolios, or participations, to private or institutional investors. Some REITs have purchased mortgages from institutions, thereby supplying the sellers with the liquidity needed to continue their lending programs.

The development and growth of private mortgage insurance programs have facilitated private secondary mortgage activity. In the residential field, private programs have successfully insured mortgage loan increments that exceed legal ratios. This has encouraged private secondary market operations, which could not have occurred otherwise.

Debt and Equity Relationships

In money markets and capital markets, when risks are comparable, funds flow to the investment that offers the best prospective yield. Risks are related to rewards; if capital is to be attracted, competitive yields must be offered. Debt and equity investments have different characteristics and appeal to different investors. A survey of these investment attributes is presented here to clarify the distinction between a real estate venture's mortgage and equity components.

Equity yield is cash flow or dividend income that is augmented by growth or diminished by depreciation. This is true whether the investment is a real estate equity or a common stock. From 1955 to 1975, most real estate appraisers and analysts based their opinions about competitively attractive equity yields on real estate market data. Throughout this period, capital was generally available at modest and stable costs.

After 1975, an inflation-induced recession slowed real estate investment activity, reducing the availability of market data for appraisal purposes. The information that was gathered was difficult to interpret because rapid, intense monetary changes quickly impaired its market relevance. If, for example, the general interest rate changes 10 times in one year, it is difficult to attach much importance to a capitalization rate that has been extracted from a sale transaction completed just six months ago. The adjustments required are too large to be reliable.

In an unstable economic climate, appraisers are well advised to search money markets and capital markets for data to support the conclusions developed from real estate data. There are hundreds of thousands of daily transactions in financial markets and billions of dollars are involved. These transactions reflect the discounting of economic futures by well-informed investors and provide useful guidance and insight for investment analysts. The general decline in interest rates since 1983 has restored some importance to real estate market data in equity yield analysis, but analysis of financial markets may still be meaningful.

The largest equity market is the trading of common stocks. Transactions are reported daily, and share prices and current dividend rates are revealed. Most substantial newspapers carry full details of stock market operations, and other financial publications offer abundant information about corporate earnings and general business conditions in commercial and industrial organizations. These data provide the basis for risk rating the securities issued by businesses. The rating task is often performed by professionals such as Standard & Poor's and Moody's, whose opinions are widely published and respected by the financial community.[2] Other information is furnished by the securities analysts of major banking institutions, brokerage companies, and the investment banking industry. Their opinions are readily available to the investment world. Financial analysts generally follow groups of companies, examining their business affairs in detail and forecasting their prospects for earnings and growth.

Analysts' reports and financial publications do not reveal prospective stock yields, but they do provide information from which investment indexes can be drawn. Because value is the present value of future income and reversion combined, a key element of value is anticipated appreciation or depreciation. In the stock market, securities analysts are the best sources of the in-depth information on which the investment world bases its growth or depreciation forecasts. In this regard, securities analysts are like real estate appraisers who support their value estimates by discounting market-supported income and reversion forecasts.

The second, larger component in real estate investment is the debt capital segment, or mortgage funds. Again, capital markets offer abundant information on investor yield requirements for a great variety of debt instruments with assorted maturities and risk ratings. In the bond and debenture markets, there are hundreds of thousands of daily transactions involving billions of dollars. Each transaction represents one investor's discounting of perceived future economic conditions. The entire volume of transactions presents an excellent picture of well-informed anticipations for debt capital performance.

There are differences in the investment yields produced by debt and equity instruments. With a debt instrument, the original lender is entitled to an interest rate, either fixed or variable, and full payment of the loan amount at maturity. The arrangement may involve periodic payments of interest only and full repayment of the principal at maturity, as in the case of bonds, or it may involve periodic payments that combine interest and debt reduction, as in most mortgage loans. If the original lender sells the investment during its contractual term, a different yield will be realized. If money market conditions are tight and interest rates are higher than when the loan was originated, the lender must sell the position at a discount. If money is freer and rates are lower, the lender may be able to sell at a premium. The purchaser collects interest in the original contract dollar amount, but the earnings rate is related to a new investment basis. When the loan is repaid at maturity, the purchaser receives the full face amount, plus any discount involved in the acquisition, or minus any premium paid. The instrument's investment yield comprises the interest collected, plus or minus any gain or loss realized at loan maturity and repayment.

---

2. Standard and Poor's Corporation and Moody's Investor Services, Inc. publish a variety of data on the performance of stocks and bonds. For a listing of these publications, see Appendix D, Periodicals.

SUMMARY

Because the price of real estate is expressed in terms of money, appraisers must understand how the value of money influences prices. Supply and demand relationships determine the value of money. When supply is abundant, the interest rate, which is the cost of borrowing money, is low. When the supply is limited, the interest rate rises. The demand for money is the product of natural economic forces, but its supply is regulated by the *Federal Reserve System* (the Fed).

A principal source of capital for real estate is the *money market*, the interaction of buyers and sellers who trade short-term money instruments. The Fed exerts a dominant influence on money market activity. Interest rates on short-term money market instruments affect the financing available for construction and development. A second source of capital for real estate is the *capital market*, the interaction of buyers and sellers who trade long- or intermediate-term money instruments (i.e., those with maturities of more than one year). The distinction between the money market and the capital market, however, is not sharp.

Banks "create" money by monetizing debt. The amounts that banks may lend is limited by the *fractional reserve requirements* of the Fed. To restrict the money supply, the Fed raises reserve deposit obligations; to increase the supply, it lowers the obligations. The Fed also controls the supply of credit by regulating the *federal discount rate*, which is the interest rate that banks pay on the funds they borrow. In turn, the federal discount rate helps determine the *prime rate*. The buying and selling of U.S. government securities by the *Federal Open Market Committee* is a third way in which the Fed influences interest rates and the supply of credit. The purchase of these securities with Federal Reserve checks increases the reserve accounts of member banks, thereby expanding the available supply of credit. The sale of government securities removes funds from these reserve accounts and reduces the supply of credit.

Through fiscal policy, the Department of the Treasury raises revenues to cover federal expenditures. Spending has grown faster than revenues, producing inflation and a federal deficit that must be monetized by the Fed. This deficit consumes credit that would otherwise be available to the private sector.

Short-term money market instruments include *federal funds, Treasury bills, Treasury notes, repurchase agreements and reverse repurchase agreements, certificates of deposit, commercial paper, bankers' acceptances, municipal notes, and Eurodollars*. If a money market instrument is sold before it matures, the yield consists of the face, or stated, interest rate and a discount or premium determined by the rates prevailing at the time of sale. Yield levels are reliable economic indicators and exert an important influence on real estate activity.

Long- or intermediate-term capital market instruments include *bonds, stocks, mortgages,* and *deeds of trust*. The bond market is closely related to real estate activities because bonds and mortgages compete for the same investment capital. A mortgage is a legal instrument for pledging a described property interest for the repayment of a loan under certain terms and conditions. Mortgage loans supply most of the capital used in real estate investments.

The relationships among the earning rates of instruments actively traded in money and capital markets and the yield on real estate investments are functions of the risk rating of investments. The rates on federal funds and Treasury bills are key indicators of short-term yields. Although long-term instruments have generally provided the highest yields, in the early 1980s severe inflation produced an inverse yield curve and short-term rates exceeded longer-term returns.

Capital and money markets respond to the business cycle. *Inflation*, characterized by price escalation and currency expansion, accelerated in the late 1970s. Thrift institutions, the major suppliers of mortgage capital, suffered because loans were being repaid with funds that were cheaper than those originally loaned. *Disintermediation*, the transfer of money from low interest-bearing accounts to higher interest-bearing accounts, destabilized the flow of mortgage funds.

The capital invested in the real estate industry may be divided into debt and equity positions. Debt investment has prior claim to the earnings of an enterprise and is often secured by a lien on the assets involved. Debt investors receive fixed or variable interest on the money invested in bonds or mortgages and the principal is repaid at maturity. Equity investment is known as *venture capital* because it involves greater risk. Equity earnings are subordinate to operating expenses and debt service, but equity investors are compensated with dividends and possible appreciation in the value of their investments.

Vehicles for assembling real estate equity funds include *trusts*, *partnerships* (general and limited), *syndications*, *joint ventures*, *pension funds*, *life insurance companies*, and *international equity capital*. Sources of real estate debt investment are savings and loan associations, commercial banks, life insurance companies, mutual savings banks, junior mortgage originators, and the secondary mortgage market.

The different characteristics of debt and equity investments appeal to different kinds of investors. The inflation of the late 1970s changed attitudes toward real estate investment. Institutions that had traditionally funded debt positions began to seek equity positions as hedges against inflation. Economic and monetary conditions of the mid 1980s, however, show a return to more traditional investor attitudes.

The trading of common stocks, which represents the largest equity market, provides data with which to analyze the competitiveness and risk of real estate equity investments. Transactions in the bond and debenture markets reflect investors' perceptions of future economic conditions and the anticipated performance of debt capital investment in real estate.

6 Fee Simple and Partial Interests

According to the bundle of rights theory, complete real property ownership, or title in fee, consists of a group of distinct rights. Each of these rights can be separated from the bundle and conveyed by the fee owner to other parties in perpetuity or for a limited time period. When a right is separated from the bundle and transferred or mortgaged, a partial, or fractional, property interest is created.[1]

Appraisers must understand partial interests to define appraisal problems. At the start of any appraisal assignment, the property rights to be valued must be clearly identified. Valuations of partial interests are often required because many forms of real estate ownership and lease agreements involve less than the complete bundle of rights. Evaluations of partial interests are needed in a wide range of real estate decisions.

Property interests may be examined from many perspectives because the ownership, legal, economic, and financial aspects of real estate overlap.

From an ownership perspective, property interests can be divided in various ways. For example, several parties may have undivided partial ownership rights in a specific property through joint tenancies, tenancies in common, or tenancies by the entirety. A land trust is a vehicle for partial property interests in which a group of property owners continues to operate and manage a property, but the legal title is conveyed to a trustee. Other legal arrangements and title-holding entities that divide property rights among groups of owners include corporations, partnerships, cooperative corporations, condominiums, and interval ownerships or timeshares. In these arrangements, property rights or interests are divided among several parties, and an appropriate legal entity is chosen to hold the property title.

---

1. For an historical view of how real property interests relate to U.S. law, see C. Reinold Noyes, *The Institution of Property* (London: Longmans, Green and Company, 1936).

Separate economic and legal interests derived from the bundle of rights are involved in many kinds of income-producing estates, and each of these interests is distinct in its form and content. Leased fee, leasehold, and subleasehold estates are created when leases are conveyed in accordance with established legal procedures.

The leasing of real estate is one practical and familiar application of the bundle of rights theory. An owner of a complete bundle of rights (the lessor) may convey to a tenant (the lessee) rights to use and occupy a property for a fixed period of time. In return, the tenant agrees to pay periodic rent.

The U.S. Constitution establishes the right of freedom of contract, which allows for flexibility in lease arrangements. A variety of lease contract clauses and provisions have been developed, used, and in many cases, tested for meaning through litigation. The flexibility of leasing arrangements has resulted in leasing practices that are responsive to changing economic and financial conditions.

In valuing the economic and legal interests created by leases, appraisers must consider two basic factors: the relationship between contract rent and market rent and the credit rating of the tenant. Both of these factors strongly influence the selection of discount rates, and have a lesser effect on the forecast of future benefits.

The financial aspects of property interests have a major impact on real estate investment practices. The analysis of mortgage and equity components is of particular importance. Mortgage funds are secured debt positions, while equity is venture capital. Mortgage and equity components may be subdivided into fee simple, leased fee, and leasehold interests. They may also be broken down according to the proportions of land and building in the overall property. Other possible financial arrangements include senior and subordinated debt, sale-leaseback finance, and equity syndications.

The ownership, legal, economic, and financial perspectives from which lease interests and other fractional property interests can be described illustrate the complexity and usefulness of the bundle of rights. A thorough understanding of the property rights to be valued in an appraisal assignment is needed not only to define the problem, but also to produce an appropriate solution.

TYPES OF PROPERTY INTERESTS

Fee Simple Estates

Possession of a title in fee establishes the interest in property known as the *fee simple estate*—i.e., *absolute ownership unencumbered by any other interest or estate*. A fee simple estate is subject only to the limitations imposed by the governmental powers of taxation, eminent domain, police power, and escheat.

Owners in fee simple may choose to improve or not to improve their property. They may also retain ownership or transfer property title by selling the property or giving it away. When a fee owner dies, the property passes to his or her heirs or to others named in the will. This creates *an estate, a right or interest in property.* Inherited property interests are frequently the subject of valuation and evaluation assignments.

Life Estates

A life estate is defined as the total rights of use, occupancy, and control, limited to the lifetime of a designated party. The designated party is known as the *life tenant* and is obligated to maintain the property in good condition and pay all applicable taxes. Life estates can be created by wills or deeds of conveyance. For example, a fee owner may leave a will that gives land to his widow for her remaining lifetime and, at her death, the land is passed on to their children. Thus, the widow acquires a life estate and functions as a life tenant. A living fee owner may deed his property to a family member and, by the terms of the conveyance, retain a life estate for himself. This practice eliminates the expense of probating the will after the owner dies.

Lease Interests

Lease interests result when the bundle of rights is divided by a lease. The lessor and the lessee each obtain interests, which are stipulated in contract form and are subject to contract law. The divided interests resulting from a lease represent two distinct, but related, estates of property—the leased fee estate and the leasehold estate. These estates do not remain in perpetuity or exist for the life of the tenant; rather, they are personal property, and the tenant is given the right to use the real estate for specific purposes over a period of time.

The leased fee estate is the lessor's, or landlord's, estate. *A leased fee estate is an ownership interest held by a landlord with the right of use and occupancy conveyed by lease to others; the rights of lessor (the leased fee owner) and leased fee are specified by contract terms contained within the lease.* Although the specific details of leases vary, a leased fee generally provides the lessor with rent to be paid by the lessee under stipulated terms; the right of repossession at the termination of the lease; default provisions; and the rights to sell, mortgage, or bequeath the property during the lease period. When a lease is legally delivered, the lessor must surrender possession of the property to the tenant for the lease period and abide by the lease provisions.

The leasehold estate is the lessee's, or tenant's, estate. *A leasehold estate is the right to use and occupy real estate for a stated term and under certain conditions as conveyed by the lease.* When a lease is transmitted, a tenant usually acquires the rights to possess the property for the lease period, to sublease the property if desired, and to improve the property under the restrictions specified in the lease. In return, the tenant is obligated to pay rent, surrender possession of the property at the termination of the lease, and abide by the lease provisions.

LEASES

Lease Terms

A lease is both a contract and a conveyance. It is a conveyance by which the landlord gives the tenant the right to occupy the property for the term specified in the lease. It imposes a contractual obligation on the tenant to pay rent to the landlord, and it may contain other promises and agreements between the landlord and the tenant. The legal interest of the tenant, the leasehold estate, is considered personal property.[2]

Leases that cover a period of one year or more must be in writing. In some states, leases for shorter periods may be verbal. A lease should describe the rented property with certainty, specifying the geographic location, street address, and condition of the premises. The signatures of the lessor and the lessee effectively establish the legal power of a lease. The tenant's possession generally provides notice that the rights of the leasehold estate are being exercised. Long-term leases are usually recorded documents.

Most leases contain clauses pertaining to the duration of tenancy, rent, security deposits, insurance, payment of public utilities, right of entry, assignment and subleasing arrangements, maintenance and repair arrangements, fixtures, taxes, eminent domain, default, and renewal options. Other contractual clauses may address purchase options, rent escalations, alterations, and use restrictions.

Lease clauses can influence property value. Therefore, it is imperative that appraisers read and understand all leases that affect the property interests being appraised. In some instances it may be advisable or necessary for an appraiser to consult an attorney for assistance in interpreting lease provisions.

By leasing real estate, a lessor receives some advantages, including the receipt of a certain income or annuity, favorable income tax considerations, and the benefit of tenant-built improvements. These can, and frequently do, enhance property value and provide the owner with a hedge against inflation. The potential advantages for a lessee include a minimum equity investment in property, an alternative to costly financing, favorable tax considerations, and reduced management responsibility.

Tenancy

When the bundle of rights is divided into property interests, tenancy is created. In real estate *tenancy* has two meanings: *1) the holding of property by any form of title, and 2) the right to use and occupy property as conveyed in a lease.* The first definition usually refers to co-ownership of real estate; the second definition concerns the nature of the relationship between a landlord and a tenant.

---

2. Robert Kratovil and Raymond J. Werner, *Real Estate Law*, 8th ed. (Englewood Cliffs, N.J.: Prentice-Hall, Inc., 1983), p. 579.

Co-ownership may be described as joint tenancy, tenancy by the entirety, or tenancy in common. *Joint tenancy is joint ownership by two or more persons with right of survivorship.* Under this arrangement, each party has an identical interest and right of possession. *Tenancy by the entirety is an estate held by a husband and wife in which neither has a disposable interest in the property during the lifetime of the other, except through joint action.* It has the same survivorship provision as a joint tenancy, but tenancy by the entirety applies only to spouses. *Tenancy in common is an estate held by two or more persons, each of whom has an undivided interest.* In this estate, the undivided interest may or may not be equally shared by the holders and there is no right of survivorship.

The valuation of undivided partial interests poses a problem for appraisers. Because no party can exercise complete control, the interest of each party is usually not worth as much as the corresponding fraction of the property's market value. Minority interests have little market appeal, so the appraiser must decide how to judge the appropriate adjustment. Because each party can bring legal action to divide the property, which is known as *partition*, the cost of this proceeding is one measure of value diminution. However, a sale in partition is a forced event, so it does not reflect free market action. Due to the lack of pertinent market transactions, valuations of co-ownerships are often somewhat subjective.

An appraiser may value an undivided partial interest by the sales comparison approach, if market data are adequate, or by the income capitalization approach. The difference between the property's earning capacity and the cost of its operation and maintenance may be regarded as the monetary benefit of ownership. To estimate the probable duration of the income from a life estate, an appraiser must rely on life expectancy statistics from actuarial studies. Once the benefits and duration of the estate are established, an appropriate discount rate can be selected and applied.

The length of the relationship between a landlord and a tenant varies and is periodic in nature. *Tenancy from period to period* and *tenancy for years* are two legally recognized ways to describe this relationship. In tenancy from period to period, the leasehold interest owner pays rent periodically and each payment renews the interest for an additional period. The ultimate length of the leasehold interest is not stated. In a tenancy for years, the beginning and end of the estate are clearly specified. If the tenant does not default, the estate continues until it expires on the specified termination date.

Rental Payments

There are two basic kinds of leases, which are distinguished by who is financially responsible for property expenses. Gross leases and net leases delineate different responsibilities. *A gross lease is a lease in which the landlord receives stipulated rent and is obligated to pay all or most of the operating expenses and real estate taxes. A net lease is a lease in which the tenant pays all property charges in addition to the stipulated rent.* Typical property charges include real estate taxes, insurance premiums, assessments, and the costs of maintenance and structural repairs. In net lease arrangements the tenant assumes the risk that taxes may increase or the building may be destroyed. If the building is destroyed, the tenant may be obligated to rebuild the building and to continue paying rent during its construction.

The level and schedule of rental payments also vary. *A flat rental, or level payment, is a specified level of rent that continues throughout the lease term.* In contrast, the payments required by a step-up or step-down lease change at specific points in time. *A step-up or step-down lease provides for a certain rent for an initial period, followed by an increase or decrease in rent over stated periods.* Other types of leases may stipulate that adjustments be made, although not necessarily at specified intervals. *An index lease provides for periodic rent adjustments based on the change in an economic index.* The Consumer Price Index (CPI) is frequently used to set rent levels in long-term leases. *A revaluation lease provides for rent adjustments at periodic intervals based on a revaluation of the real estate.* Rent payments can be annual, semi-annual, quarterly, monthly, weekly, or even daily. They may be required at the beginning of the specified rental period (ordinary annuities) or at the end (annuities due).

An appraiser valuing a partial interest must know what is expected of the lessor and the lessee in fulfilling the obligations delineated by the lease. Lease terms shape the quantity and quality of future benefits likely to flow to the interests created by the contract. Thus, the agreement provides that the lessor will receive specified rent or services during the term of the lease and a reversion of the tenant's rights of use and occupancy when the lease expires. The contract gives the tenant exclusive rights of use and occupancy during the lease term, subject to rent or service obligations. Many other divisions of rights are common. For example, an original tenant may sublet the property and both the leased fee and leasehold positions may be mortgaged. (Analysis of income and expenses and the procedures for valuing leased fee estates are discussed in Chapters 18, 19, and 20.)

A lease sets rental terms and presumably indicates gross income to the leased fee. As mentioned previously, appraisers estimating the market value of leased fee interests must always consider two factors: the relationship between contract rent (the actual rental income specified in a lease) and market rent (the rental income a property would most likely command in the open market), and the credit rating of the tenant.

The lease for a single-tenant building may obligate the tenant to pay rent in excess of market levels. If the tenant has a low credit rating, an appraiser may not give much consideration to the lease arrangement. If the same lease provisions are assumed by a tenant that is a major business entity with a triple A credit rating, the appraiser would give significant weight to the lease terms. The outlook for future income benefits is much clearer in this case, and the value of the leased fee may exceed the market value of the property unencumbered by the lease.

Other complex interrelationships may create quite different situations. For example, a below-market contract rent to be paid by a tenant with a poor credit rating may be more certain than an above-market contract rent to be paid by a tenant with a good credit rating.

Lease terms sometimes create advantages for the leasehold position to the detriment of the leased fee position. If the lessee has a rent advantage, this is assured by the leasehold interest, which often has a value in the market. A leased fee burdened with a fixed rent that is below market rates may be worth less than the unencumbered fee estate.

Several specialized lease interests are briefly discussed in the following section.

SPECIALIZED LEASE INTERESTS

Leasehold Position

The most important obligation associated with the rights to the use and occupancy of a leasehold interest is the payment of rent. *Contract rent is the actual rental income specified in a lease.* Rent is commonly paid by the tenant or tenants to the lessor according to a specified schedule. A leasehold interest usually has value when contract rent is less than market rent. *Market rent is the rental income that a property would most probably command in the open market.* Only in an ideally negotiated lease would contract rent equal market rent.

When market rent exceeds contract rent, the leasehold interest may have value, assuming that the lease term is long enough to be marketable and the lease allows for subletting or assignment. When contract rent exceeds market level, the leasehold may have a negative value.

Subleasehold Position

Normally, a tenant is free to sublease all or part of a property, but many leases require that the lessor's consent be obtained. *A sublease is an agreement in which the lessee in a prior lease conveys the right of use and occupancy of the property to another. An assignment is a written transfer of the rights of use and occupancy of the property to be held by another legal entity or to be used for the benefit of creditors.* Leases usually provide that the lessor's consent "will not unreasonably be withheld." Over the years, court decisions have established that subleasing is relatively free. To deny permission, lessors usually must show that the security of their position would be impaired.

In a sublease, the original lessee is "sandwiched" between a lessor and a sublessee. The original lessee's interest has value when the contract rent is less than the rent collected from the sublessee.

Different discount rates are used in valuing different lease interests because the rates selected reflect the risk involved. Generally, a lessor's interest, the leased fee, entails less risk than a lessee's interest, the leasehold. The lessee, in turn, assumes less risk than the sublessee, whose position is exposed to the greatest risk.

A lease contract may contain a provision that explicitly forbids subletting. Without the right to sublet and a term that is long enough to be marketable, a leasehold position cannot be conveyed and, therefore, has no market value and may diminish the value of the leased fee. The leasehold position does, however, have a use value to the lessee.

Mortgaged Lease Interests

Leasehold mortgaging is a type of mortgage-equity financing in which a lessee, or tenant, agrees to subordinate the leasehold interest to a mortgage covering leasehold improvements placed on the property. It is important to remember that, in this situation, it is the lessee, not *the lessor*, who is subordinating the leased fee to a mortgage. The leasehold mortgagee may be protected by a "nondisturbance" clause in the lease or by a subordination of the lease to the leasehold mortgage. A "nondisturbance" clause gives the mortgagee the right to cure any default(s) by the lessee upon appropriate notice. In a lease subordination arrangement, the leasehold mortgagee can foreclose on the leasehold interest subject to the lease. Often leasehold mortgages are obtained by lessee developers with the lessors' consent as part of a ground lease, which grants the right to use and occupy the land.

A leasehold mortgagee who finances building improvements should be certain that the *ground rent, the rent paid for the right to use and occupy land*, is not too high to represent a competitively attractive yield on the land value. The mortgagee should also make certain that the lease terms include the right to cure any lessee default. If compelled to foreclose, the leasehold mortgagee can then take possession of the leasehold interest, subject to the terms of the lease, and the improvements, and is only obliged to pay the required ground rent.

In current investment practice, investors seek maximum financing for favorable leveraging and the best tax shelter. Leases, the mortgaging of lease interests, and subordinations provide the necessary tools. For major investment projects, a more complex set of arrangements may be worked out. For example, a property may be divided into a leased fee and a leasehold interest. The mortgage is arranged on the leased fee and a leasehold mortgage is arranged to construct improvements. By using different legal entities, one party can hold both the fee position and the leasehold position. In this situation, expert legal advice will be needed to ensure that the documentation supports the separation of the interests and does not effect a merger.

When appraising a leasehold estate subject to a mortgage, difficulties can arise because the rent provisions of the ground lease may be tied to the CPI, debt service on the fee mortgage may be variable, and debt service on the leasehold mortgage may contain an equity kicker.

OTHER FRACTIONAL INTERESTS

The bundle of rights includes interests other than those created by leases for the use and occupancy of physical real estate. Property ownership may also be divided by vertical interests, easements, and transferable development rights (TDRs), each of which can be considered separately in sales, leases, mortgages, and other realty transactions.

Vertical Interests

An important dimension of real property ownership concerns the distinction between subsurface and air rights.[3] *A subsurface right is the right to the use and profits of the underground portion of a designated property.* The term usually refers to the right to extract minerals from below the earth's surface and to construct tunnels for railroads, motor vehicles, and public utilities. *Air rights are the property rights associated with the use, control, and regulation of air space over a parcel of real estate.* Both of these fractional interests represent portions of a fee simple estate, but each embodies the idea of land as a three-dimensional entity.

The vertical division of real property is based on the legal conception of land as a volume of space with boundless height and depth.[4] This is significant because technological developments continue to expand our ability to utilize the earth's subsurface and atmosphere. In urban areas in particular, engineering advances have dramatically affected land use and, therefore, highest and best use considerations. The development of steel-framed building construction, the passenger elevator, deep tunnel excavation techniques, and communications technology are some examples of technological changes that have helped shape our urban landscape.

These changes also reflect the forces and factors affecting value. As the density of building in urban areas increases, fewer sites are available for new construction and land values escalate. This trend has produced a growing interest in developing air rights. As early as 1902, the air rights associated with highly valued land along the New York Central Railroad in New York City were beginning to be developed. Park Avenue is one outstanding example of real estate development built on the acquisition of air rights. Many other examples of development established on air rights can be found in urban areas around the world.

When a large building is to be constructed in a space to which air rights apply, the base of the site is visualized as a platform constructed at some level (e.g., 30 or 40 feet) above the present surface. In the case of Park Avenue development, the platform is actually located below grade, just above the railroad tunnel. The platform must be supported by columns, which normally rest on a caisson foundation built underground. In this manner, a number of discrete, interrelated "lots" are created; the air, column, and caisson lots associated with different portions of the three-

---

3. Rights to surface areas may be divided by horizontal subdivision, *the division of a tract of land into smaller parcels for sale or lease.* A horizontal subdivision, however, is not a partial interest. Usually, a large tract held in fee simple estate is divided into a number of smaller units, which are also held in fee simple estate. Rights-of-way over surface areas may be conveyed by easements, which are discussed later in this chapter.

4. B. Harrison Frankel, "Three-Dimensional Real Property Law: The Truth About 'Air Rights,'" *Real Estate Law Journal,* Spring 1984.

dimensional space comprise the land or site in question. Figure 6.1 illustrates a division of vertical space.

Figure 6.1   Three-Dimensional Division for Air or Tunnel Rights

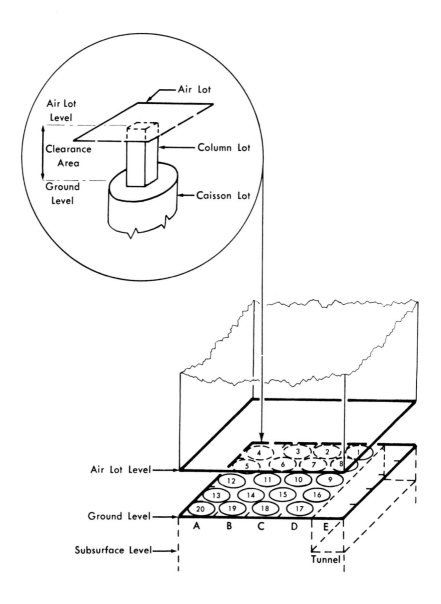

As an example, these may be identified as air rights above air lot level; column lots between air lot level and ground (1-20); caisson lots below ground level (1-20); tunnel rights between ground level and subsurface (E).

Air rights can be transferred in various ways. Often, the air rights to one property are shifted to another within the same building zone under legal planning regulations. The transfer of air rights allows developers to adjust the density of land use without putting adverse pressure on owners, neighborhoods, or districts. This practice underscores the importance of local zoning authorities, who regulate building heights, functions, setbacks, and other variables involved in the development of air rights.

Air rights can be sold in fee, with the seller retaining one or more easements for a specialized use, such as the operation of a railroad. Air rights may also be subdivided; in this case the owner of the fee sells or leases only the land and air that are to be occupied by a particular improvement.

Air rights were subdivided to construct The Merchandise Mart in Chicago which is shown in Figure 6.2. The structure was built between 1928 and 1931 in air space above The Chicago and Northwestern Railroad. The owners of the Mart, which is one of the world's largest mercantile buildings, actually possess 458 caisson lots extending 100 feet below ground, 458 column lots, a small surface parcel that houses building equipment, and the air lot 23 feet above Chicago's city datum, where the building is constructed. The Merchandise Mart typifies the traditional development of air rights over existing railroad track, but other developments may be more creatively designed.

Figure 6.2   The Merchandise Mart in Chicago

(H. Armstrong Roberts, Inc.)

Easements

Easements represent another division of property ownership. *An easement is an interest in real property that conveys use, but not ownership, of a portion of an owner's property.* Easements frequently permit a specific portion of a property to be used for access to an adjoining property or as a public right-of-way. Although surface easements are the most common, subterranean and overhead easements are used for public utilities, subways, and bridges.

Clearly, a property that acquires an easement is the beneficiary of additional rights; one that is subject to an easement is burdened. Easement rights can be conveyed in perpetuity or for a limited time period. An easement can be created by a contract between private parties or it can be arranged by states, municipalities, or public utilities through the exercise of eminent domain. In any case, a valuation is needed to estimate the price the easement beneficiary should pay to the burdened party.

An easement that affords ingress and egress to an otherwise landlocked parcel increases its value. Easement rights to a development's recreational facilities normally enhance the value of plots that have this advantage. The value of an easement is usually estimated as some part of the amount of value it adds to the property it benefits; the burdened property's loss in value can also be used to indicate the value of an easement. The value of an easement reflects the basic economic concept of contribution. No one would pay more for an easement than the amount of value gained by the property it benefits. Similarly, no one would pay the exact amount of the benefit to break even. The holder of an easement realizes a gain by paying less than the added value.

When an easement is acquired by a public utility company for overhead power lines, valuation becomes more complicated. In all cases, however, an easement is a partial interest in the burdened real property estate. It is created by a deed and has measurable value.

Preservation easements are used to protect certain historic properties by prohibiting physical changes to the property. Usually, the owner must maintain the condition of the property at the time the easement is donated or immediately after a proposed restoration. Under federal law, a preservation easement can be deeded to properly qualifying nonprofit organizations or government agencies. In such instances, the property owner donates the easement and receives an income tax reduction that can be equal to, but not more than, the market value of the real property rights donated.

The economic theory that underlies the valuation of preservation easements is generally the same as that which governs eminent domain appraising, although the acquirer of a preservation easement receives rather than takes rights. Each easement document contains specific controls and restrictions. An appraiser must carefully analyze a deed of easement to determine how it affects the encumbered property. The effect of historic district controls or individual landmark designations should be related to the subject property and to the provisions of the easement.

Transferable Development Rights

Transferable development rights (TDRs) emerged in the real estate industry during the 1970s. *A transferable development right is a development right that cannot be used by the landowner but can be sold to landowners in another location.* Some TDRs are used to preserve property uses for agricultural production, open space, or historic buildings. Through a TDR, a preservation district and a development district are identified. Landowners in the preservation district are assigned development rights which they cannot use to develop their land, but can sell to landowners in the development district. These landowners can use the rights to build at higher densities than zoning laws in the development district would normally permit.

Appraisers can value TDRs with ordinary sales comparison techniques if there is a sufficient number of transactions to constitute a market. When the market is inadequate, appraisers may use the income capitalization approach. In such cases, the economic concept of contribution provides a foundation, and the value added to a property through the acquisition of a TDR is adjusted for administrative, legal, and other costs incurred. Some, though not all, of the property's net value increase can be attributed to the TDR; no one is likely to undertake such a complicated procedure without the prospect of a reasonable profit.

SPECIALIZED FRACTIONAL OWNERSHIP

Condominiums

A condominium is a form of fee ownership of separate units or portions of multiunit buildings that provides for formal filing and recording of a divided interest in real property. A condominium unit is a separate ownership, and title is held by an individual owner. The unit may be separately leased, sold, or mortgaged. A condominium owner also has title to a partial interest in a total project, whether it is a residential or commercial property. The owner possesses a three-dimensional space within the outer walls, roof or ceiling, and floors and, along with other owners, has an undivided interest in common areas—e.g., the land, the public portions of the building, the foundation, the outer walls, and the spaces provided for parking and recreation. The owners of units in a condominium project usually form an association to manage the real estate in accordance with adopted bylaws. The expenses of management and maintenance are divided pro rata among the owners, who pay a monthly fee.

To value individual condominium units, appraisers generally use the sales comparison approach. Recent sales of units of comparable size, location, and quality are the best indicators of value. To value entire condominium projects, whether they are new constructions or conversions, appraisers usually apply the income capitalization approach using discounted cash flow analysis. The amount and timing of all capital outlays, expected monetary receipts, and returns are estimated, and these amounts are discounted at a rate consistent with competitive investment yields. The estimates of future sellout prices and the timing of sales are key elements in the procedure.

Cooperative Ownership

In certain areas, the cooperative ownership of apartments is popular. Cooperative ownership provides the selling owner/developer or converter with an attractive price and gives purchasers control of their living accommodations. *Cooperative ownership is a form of ownership in which each owner of stock in a cooperative apartment building or housing corporation receives a proprietary lease on a specific apartment and is obligated to pay a rental which represents the proportionate share of operating expenses and debt service on the underlying mortgage, which is paid by the corporation.*

A "co-op" is established when a stock corporation is organized to issue an authorized number of shares at a specified par value. The corporation takes title to an apartment building and prices the various apartments. The price per unit determines the number of shares that an apartment occupant must purchase to acquire a proprietary lease. The lease obligates the occupant to pay a monthly maintenance fee, which may be adjusted at times by the corporation's board of directors. The fee covers the expenses of management, operations, and maintenance of public areas. Because the shareholders can vote their shares in electing directors, they have some control over property conditions.

Recently, a new method for financing cooperatives has emerged in some areas. Condominium owners have always held individual mortgages on their units, but, in the past, cooperative corporations arranged mortgages on entire apartment properties. Cooperative shareholders had to fund their purchases with 100% equity or borrow the money from commercial banks on short-term, personal notes. Now, however, a cooperative corporation can arrange a mortgage on the total property, and individual apartment shareholders can mortgage their stock for up to 75% of its value. These new mortgage arrangements have made cooperative apartment properties much more marketable.

If the market for cooperative apartments is active, appraisers can value apartment units by the sales comparison approach. However, appraisers must remember that prices are influenced by the amount and terms of the mortgage financing that the corporation has placed on the building. In recent years, co-op mortgages have ranged from 25% to 50% of total value, with the balance financed by individual apartment shareholders as pure equity or with cooperative apartment mortgages. Often corporate bylaws impose limitations on the property's marketability, which can affect the validity of comparable sales data.

Timesharing

Fractional interests created by timesharing have been marketed extensively in recent years. *Timesharing is the sale of limited ownership interests in residential apartments or hotel rooms.* Like condominium ownership, timesharing conveys an interest in real property with the purchaser receiving all the rights inherent in ownership. The ownership is limited, however, because the purchaser receives a deed that conveys title to a unit for a specific part of a year.

There are two forms of timesharing; it is imperative that the appraiser distinguish between them when appraising timeshare projects or analyzing timeshare comparables. The first form of ownership is known as *timeshare, time-span,* or *tenancy in common* ownership. In this arrangement, purchasers receive a deed to an undivided interest in a particular unit as tenants in common. Each purchaser agrees to use the unit only during the time period stipulated in his or her deed. This form of timeshare is like a long-term lease on a unit for a specific period each year. The purchaser does not have an equity interest in the property but, rather, a leasehold interest for a specified time.

The second form of timesharing is *interval ownership.* An interval owner receives an estate for a specified time period, which lasts for the duration of the project. When the useful life of the project expires, interval owners become tenants in common.

A timeshare owner receives a title in fee that covers exclusive use of a specific apartment for a specified interval and the right to use public spaces and common areas. The title can be recorded and the interest can be mortgaged. Interval owners pay operating expenses, including a proportionate share of taxes, insurance, and other costs, and a fee for common area maintenance (CAM) and management. In many projects, 50 one-week intervals are created; the remaining two weeks of each year are reserved for major repairs and maintenance.

The partial interests created by timesharing are valued through sales comparison. Timesharing is relatively new, so appraisers may not find comparable sales in all areas, although comparables are abundant in resort and vacation areas. In valuing timeshares, appraisers must consider 1) the time required for sellout, 2) seasonal variations that affect sales, 3) all direct and indirect costs to create a facility that will command the prices anticipated, and most important, 4) the element of competition.

LEGAL ENTITIES AFFECTING OWNERSHIP

Stock Corporations

One common form of partial ownership is a stock corporation. A stock corporation may be organized to hold title to a single asset, such as a parcel of real property, or it may have a portfolio of investments. Corporate ownership is divided into partial interests by selling shares to an investment group. Any specific stock holding represents a percentage of total corporate ownership, which is derived from the ratio between the number of shares owned by a particular interest and the total number of shares issued by the corporation. The percentage is an ownership share in the corporation, and its book value is usually found by multiplying the corporate net worth by the ownership percentage.

The market value of a share of stock in a corporation that has a parcel of real estate as its sole asset may be higher or lower than its book value. *Book value is defined as the capital amount at which property is shown on the account books.* Book value usually equals the original cost of the asset after subtracting reserves for depreciation and adding allocations for capital recapture. Book value and market value are usually not the same, so the values of the pro rata shares of ownership associated with each differ.

Fractional corporate interests—i.e., shares of stock—typically sell for less than their pro rata value because a minority interest does not have the ability to control the investment. In a closely held corporation such as a real estate venture, additional discounts are required to reflect illiquidity because the market for shares is often limited.

Because stock market values often represent a discount from actual corporate net worth, the accounting profession and the Securities and Exchange Commission allow publicly owned real estate corporations to show both the book values and the current market values of assets on their annual financial statements. This practice, which is sometimes referred to as *current value accounting*, frequently reveals that present market values greatly exceed book values (i.e., cost less accumulated depreciation). Therefore, a corporation may have greater net worth than is indicated by book figures. Publicly owned real estate corporations employ professional appraisers to estimate the current market values used in these reports.

The International Assets Valuation Standards Committee (TIAVSC) was formed in 1980 to establish worldwide standards for the valuation of fixed assets in financial statements. Under international accounting standards, fixed assets are divided into tangible assets, intangible assets, and financial assets. Many in the accounting and financial communities believe that evaluations of the current and historical performance of businesses should be made with reference to the current value of their assets. In the United States, historical costs are commonly used to report the value of fixed assets.

Land Trusts

Trusts are sometimes used as legal vehicles for partial ownership interests in real property. *A land trust is often a legal vehicle for partial ownership interests in real property in which independently owned properties are conveyed to a trustee. Land trusts may be used to effect a profitable assemblage or in some cases to facilitate the assigning of property as collateral for a loan.* The trustee holds legal title in the property for a specified time and performs only the functions outlined in the trust agreement. The trustee may or may not actively manage the property or collect rent;

when not carried out by the trustee, these duties remain with the beneficiaries, who are the original owners. One important legal aspect of a trust arrangement is that a judgment against a beneficiary is not a lien against the real estate.

To value a beneficiary's partial interest, an appraiser must first estimate the market value of the total property. The appraiser then adjusts the estimate to account for any effect on value that may result from the trust indenture provisions, which identify the rights and obligations of beneficiaries. The beneficiary's minority position will call for significant downward adjustment.

General and Limited Partnerships

Partnerships are used extensively in real estate acquisition because they pool funds for property ownership and operation. In a general partnership, all partners share in business gains and each is fully responsible for all liabilities.

To value a partner's partial interest, an appraiser estimates the market value of the partnership's total real property assets and adjusts the estimate to reflect the partner's percentage of ownership. Other adjustments are made in light of the terms of the partnership agreement, which define the partners' rights and liabilities in sales and liquidations. The ability or inability to control business operations (i.e., to decide when to sell, to select property managers, and to approve or disapprove prospective leases) has a major effect on the value of a general partnership. Another important aspect of a partnership is that it automatically terminates when a general partner dies. Because the provisions of partnership contracts shape and limit ownership benefits, they also influence the value of the partial interests involved.

Limited partnerships have both general partners and limited partners. The general partners manage the business and assume full liability for partnership obligations. The liability of each limited partner, however, is restricted to his or her capital contributions.

The investment value of limited partnership interests, or syndicate shares, often includes income tax shelter benefits. It is not unusual for such an investment to offer small income returns, at least during the early years, when the value of the investment is perceived to be largely in the income tax benefits of building depreciation, mortgage interest, and other tax shelters. These tax deductions may offset the investor's income from other passive sources of income that are subject to certain limitations and restrictions. The resulting tax deferrals are seen as earnings of the partnership interest, even though the dollars involved do not flow from partnership property.

Frequently tax law changes alter the value of various shelter benefits. Early property disposition or foreclosure can damage shelter advantages due to tax law recapture provisions. These considerations should be weighed in rating the risk of partnership investments. The Tax Reform Act of 1986 significantly reduced the income sheltering benefits offered by real estate.

Equity Syndications

Another popular financial division of property interests is the equity syndication. *A syndication is a private or public partnership that pools funds for the acquisition and development of real estate projects.* Syndications, which may be referred to as partnerships, are established when an individual or group purchases interests in real estate for the purpose of transferring them to a limited partnership. The limited partnership interests are then sold to investors.

Such arrangements appear simple, but they may be very complex because syndications frequently purchase more than real estate, and the value of the interests in real estate and the aggregate value of the limited partnership interests differ in quality as well as quantity. Syndications create property interests, which are grouped as "securities." Their value depends not only on the underlying real estate, but also on the additional, or more limited, rights created by contracts and other nonrealty considerations. Accordingly, the valuation of syndicated property, other than market valuation of fee simple rights, involves valuing more than real estate.

The interests of real estate and the interests of the limited partnership differ in value because many non-real estate items or conditions are involved. In addition to the real estate interests conveyed, most sales of limited partnership interests by a syndicator include other items such as management services, the ability to invest in a major property that an investor might not be able to invest in alone, and the potential for improved liquidity. Potential capital appreciation and eligibility for tax benefits, which are not limited to syndications, also influence investors and may affect market value. These factors and conditions are difficult to isolate, so analyses of comparable sales may be difficult.

Decreased inflation, the prosecution of abusive tax shelters, and the failure of financial institutions have brought some mortgage and syndication practices into question. Appraisers must exercise great care in determining the exact nature of the interests to be valued in any assignment involving partnerships; they should avoid presenting the market values of syndication interests as though they represent an assembled ownership of real estate assets.[5]

SUMMARY

Property rights consist of ownership, legal estate, economic benefits, and financial components. Ownership may be held by an individual, a partnership, or a corporation, and undivided ownership rights may belong to two or more parties in tenancies. Legal estate and economic benefits refer to the disposition of the rights to property use and occupancy as well as the income generated from rent or percentage of profits.

---

5. Guide Note 1 to the Appraisal Institute's Standards of Professional Practice addresses the valuation of real estate interests intended for syndication and the valuation of real estate partnership interests.

The financial components of a property consist of the equity and mortgage funds that secure it. The equity and mortgage components of property may be further divided into *leased fee* and *leasehold interests* or into land and building portions.

A *fee simple estate* represents absolute ownership unencumbered by any other interest or estate, and subject only to the powers of government. Ownership of a fee simple estate can be retained, sold, bestowed, or bequeathed. A *life estate* is created by a will or deed of conveyance, which assigns life tenancy and provides for the property to be bequeathed when the life tenant dies.

Lease interests result when property rights are separated by legal contracts. The rights of the *lessor*, the leased fee owner or landlord, generally include the right to collect rent for the lease period; to repossess the property when the lease expires or the tenant defaults; and to dispose of the property through a sale, mortgage, or bequest during the lease period. The *lessee*, the leaseholder or tenant, has the right to use and occupy the property for the lease period and may have the right to sublease it and improve it. In return, the lessee is obligated by contract to pay rent, to surrender possession when the lease ends, and along with the lessor, to abide by the lease conditions. Other lease provisions may address required security deposits; payments for utilities, maintenance and repair; rent escalations; and renewal or purchase options.

Tenancy is the right to use and occupy property as conveyed by a lease. The length of the leasing period may be renewed periodically or it may be clearly specified. Tenancy can also refer to a variety of arrangements involving property ownership by two or more persons—e.g., *joint tenancy*, *tenancy by entirety*, and *tenancy in common*. The valuation of co-ownerships involving undivided partial interests may be especially difficult because no one party can exercise complete control.

Leases may be *gross* or *net leases*, depending on whether the landlord or the tenant pays the operating expenses and taxes for the property. Lease provisions may call for level payments (flat rental), step-up or step-down payments, or payments that are periodically adjusted to an economic index or to a revaluation of the property.

The market value of a leased fee interest depends on how *contract rent* relates to *market rent* and on the credit rating of the tenant. A leasehold interest may acquire value if the lease allows for subletting or assignment and the term is long enough to be marketable. *Subleasehold* and *sandwich leasehold positions* are created through subleasing and assignment. *Leasehold mortgaging* is often arranged for lessee developers who, with the lessor's consent, subordinate their leasehold interest to any mortgage covering the cost of improvements they build on the property.

Partial interests also include vertical interests, easements, transferable development rights (TDRs), and interests resulting from specialized fractional ownership. Vertical interests refer to *subsurface rights* (e.g., for mining or construction of transportation tunnels) and *air rights* for the use, control, and regulation of air space. *Easements* generally permit use of a portion of a property for access (e.g., for public utility lines, subways, or bridges). Preservation easements, which are deeded by donors to nonprofit organizations or government agencies in return for tax write-offs, prohibit certain physical changes to historic properties.

Fractional ownership arrangements include condominiums, cooperatives, and timesharing. *Condominium* owners hold title to individual units and have an undivided interest in common areas. They share management and maintenance expenses on a pro rata basis. In *cooperatives*, tenant proprietors, or stockholders, pay a proportionate share of operating expenses and debt service on a mortgage that is held by the cooperative. In a *timesharing* arrangement, an individual owner's interest in a residential unit, either as a tenant in common or an interval owner, is limited to a specific part of the year.

Stock corporations, land trusts, general and limited partnerships, and equity syndications are legal entities that create partial ownership interests. Corporate shareholders own stock, but the market value of this stock is generally different from its *book value*. *Land trusts*, which are formed to effect a profitable assemblage or to assign a property as loan collateral, convey legal title to a trustee, while property management and rent collection are retained by the beneficiaries. *Partnerships* are classified as general or limited depending on the partners liability for possible losses. *Equity syndications* are partnerships set up to pool funds for the acquisition and development of real estate projects. Syndications are created by contracts and provide more benefits than real estate ventures.

7 Data Collection and Analysis

The identification of property interests and all other aspects that define the appraisal problem provide direction for collecting useful data. Appraisers need patience, judgment, and researching skills to direct the preliminary steps of data collection and analysis and to gather and manage information. In appraisal, the quality and quantity of information available for analysis are as important as the methods and techniques used to process the data and complete the assignment. Therefore, the ability to distinguish between different kinds of data, to research reliable data sources, and to manage information efficiently is essential to appraisal practice.

GENERAL DATA

General data include information on social, economic, governmental, and environmental forces that affect property value. This information is part of the store of knowledge with which appraisers approach their assignments. All general data are ultimately understood in terms of how they affect the economic climate in which real property transactions occur. In analyzing general data, appraisers observe the operation of appraisal principles by studying the interaction of the four forces that affect property values in an area. Although the four forces provide convenient categories for examining general data, it is their interaction that creates trends and ultimately influences property value.

Economic Trends

The related series of changes that comprise a trend are studied and used as historical evidence to support forecasts. Forecasting is an art that employs scientific processes to identify or quantify future events or conditions. Forecasts may be developed from mathematics and statistics, observation and judgment, or a combination of these two. In making forecasts, appraisers try to discern and consider all pertinent factors affecting future conditions. Appraisers do not attempt to make predictions and, therefore, they should distinguish between forecasts that reflect personal judgment and those that are directly related to empirical market observations.

Appraisers must recognize and understand the economic trends that affect the value of real property. It is not enough to know that economic changes have occurred; the probable direction, extent, and impact of these changes must also be studied to identify and forecast trends.

The particular trends considered by appraisers vary with the appraisal problem and the type of real estate being appraised. To estimate the market value of a shopping center with the income capitalization approach to value, for example, the base rent and overage rent under a percentage lease must be forecast. [1] The shopping center's total potential gross income depends on trends in the number of households in the trade area, the income of the households, and their typical expenditures on the goods and services supplied by the center; the availability of alternative shopping facilities also must be considered.

International Economic Trends

In the world economy, the economic well-being of one nation may directly and indirectly affect many other nations. There is much foreign investment in U.S. real estate partly because land prices are relatively low and the stability of the U.S. government gives foreign investors some measure of protection. Thus, inflation and political instability in other countries influence the demand for, and value of, real estate in the United States.

The greater the intensity and duration of an economic trend, the wider its influence. Basic trends in national and international economic indicators—e.g., the balance of foreign trade, rates of foreign exchange, commodity price levels, wage levels, interest rates, industrial production levels, and the volume of retail sales—all merit consideration.

National and Regional Economic Trends

The state of the national economy is basic to any real estate appraisal. National economic conditions are indicated by the gross national product, national income, the balance of payments to other nations, price level indexes, interest rates, aggregate employment and unemployment statistics, the number of housing starts and building permits issued, the dollar volume of construction, and other general data. A time

---

1. See Chapter 6 for the definition of a percentage lease and Chapter 19 for definitions of base rent and overage rent.

series of economic indicators, which describes and measures changes or movements over a period of time, may reveal fluctuations around a longer-term trend and help put current statistics in perspective.

Federal programs and tax policies can affect the value of real estate. The need for financial institutions to compete for loanable funds with one another and with money market mutual funds has increased lending rates and resulted in an adjustment of demand in the market. The 1981 Economic Recovery Tax Act permitted accelerated cost recovery for buildings held for the production of income or for use in one's trade or business. The Tax Reform Act of 1986, however, has reinstated the straight-line depreciation system. Investment tax credits for the rehabilitation of older, nonresidential real estate and for historic preservation projects enhance the profitability of investment property and, ultimately, affect its value.

The national economy also reflects the economic condition of the nation's various geographic regions. A region's economic health depends on the status of its economic activity. This activity, in turn, is the aggregate of economic activities in individual areas and communities within the region's geographical boundaries. Minor disruptions in the economic growth of one community, however, may not appreciably affect the region if the regional and national economies are strong.

The extent to which an appraiser is concerned with the national or regional economy, in addition to the economy of the city or neighborhood, depends on the size and type of property being appraised. For example, a large regional shopping center that serves a trade area of 500,000 people and an automobile assembly plant that employs 5,000 workers are more sensitive to the general state of the economy than are medical-dental office buildings or retail service operations in suburban residential areas.

Local Economic Trends

The analysis of a local economy often focuses on trends in population, employment, and income. Population change, net household formation, the diversity of the economic base of the community, the level and stability of employment, wage rates, and household or family income all indicate the basic economic strength of a community.

The conditions and prospects of the local economy are relevant to most appraisal assignments. The value of real estate in a community is influenced by the demand for its use. The demand for various types of real estate, including vacant land, depends on the population of the market that the real estate serves, the effective purchasing power of this population, and their desire to own real estate. Demand may change for various types of real estate and between real estate and nonrealty investment sources.

Employment and economic base analysis. The population and income in a region or a community depend on the employment that constitutes the economic base of the area. *The economic base is the economic activity of a community that enables it to attract income from outside its borders.* This ability to attract income gives the community an advantage over other communities and makes it relatively more successful in providing products or services.[2] The advantage of a community may be due to its proximity to commodity markets, the presence of natural resources, the availability of a trained work force, the climate, or a government decree that establishes the community as a county seat or state capital. As a result of this advantage, most of the community's work force may be engaged in specialized activities such as the production of durable goods or assembly and distribution.

The nature of employment in a community or region can affect population growth, the level and stability of income, the willingness of the population to spend disposable income, and the risk associated with investments in the area. These characteristics affect the demand for, and value of, all types of real estate. A community that has a diversified economic base with various types of employment is more attractive to investors than a single-industry town. The stability offered by a diversified local economy can reduce the risk of a real estate investment and increase property value.

City origins and growth patterns.   Appraisers recognize that growth and change in an urban community can affect neighborhoods, districts, and other areas differently. An appraiser must be aware of the factors that contribute to urban growth patterns to analyze the neighborhood or district where the subject property is located and to determine how the area affects the quantity, quality, and duration of the property's future income stream or amenities that create value.

The structure of urban land uses in a community usually reflects, to some extent, the origin of the settlement; this is known as the *siting factor*. Some U.S. cities were established at transportation centers such as seaports, river crossings, or the intersection of trade routes. Other cities were founded near power sources useful to manufacturing, and still others were located for defensive, commercial, or political reasons. As the national standard of living improved, climate and other natural advantages became siting factors responsible for the development of retirement areas, recreational resorts, and other specialized communities. From its initial site, a community grows outward in a pattern dictated by the nature and availability of developable land, the evolution of technology, and the government's ability and willingness to provide essential public services.[3]

Communities that have a scarcity of land, such as San Francisco and New York, experience an increase in the density of land use. Development corridors channel new construction to usable land. New technology in building materials and construction methods makes it possible to construct high-rise buildings in cities without bedrock and those subject to earth tremors.

---

2. For further discussion of economic base analysis and the significance of demographic change, see Anthony Downs, "Characteristics of Various Economic Studies," and Jerome Dasso, "Economic Base Analysis for the Appraiser," in *Readings in Market Research for Real Estate* (Chicago: American Institute of Real Estate Appraisers, 1985). See also Morton J. Schussheim, "The Impact of Demographic Change on Housing and Community Development," *The Appraisal Journal*, July 1984.

3. Various conceptual models of urban growth are used to describe land use patterns. These "social ecology" models include the concentric zone theory, the sector (wedge) theory, the multiple nuclei theory, and the radial (axial) corridor theory. For a more complete discussion of urban growth patterns, see W. B. Martin, "How to Predict Urban Growth Patterns," *The Appraisal Journal*, April 1984.

Transportation improvements and the proliferation of automobiles have also shaped modern cities. Improved transportation allows urban settlements to grow in size and to serve larger markets. At the same time, the pattern of city growth is influenced by the local transportation network; growth radiates from the central business district along major transportation routes, with great dispersion created by major freeway systems.

Local Market Considerations

To understand how national and even international economic demographic trends influence property value, an appraiser studies how the region and community where the subject property is located may respond to these trends. The appraiser should examine the economic structure of the region and the community, the comparative advantages that each possesses, and the attitudes of local government and residents toward growth and change. For example, the increasing number of elderly households in the nation is less significant to property values in Minnesota than to values in Sunbelt states, which attract more of these residents. A community with a no-growth policy may have substantially different local demographics and economic potential than one that does not discourage growth.

Regional economics have an influence on local market conditions, but local markets do not necessarily parallel regional markets. Macroeconomic studies, which are concerned with broad areas such as cities and regions, are important to an understanding of real estate and real estate trends. However, these studies should not be confused with microeconomic studies, which appraisers perform to evaluate the factors influencing the market value of a particular real estate parcel. For example, regional trends may suggest an expected increase in population, but the local data available to the appraiser indicates that the particular area will not benefit from this trend. While both studies are important, local trends are more likely to influence property value directly.

Demographics

The population and its geographic distribution are basic determinants of the need for real estate. Households must have shelter, and the production and distribution of goods and services require plants, stores, hotels, hospitals, warehouses, and offices. An appraiser should be aware of the potential for change in the aggregate population and in the demographic attributes of the population that constitutes the market for the subject property. Population growth is affected by birth rates, death rates, and migration. In turn, these determinants of aggregate population reflect the rate of household formation, the age distribution of households, the state of medical technology, the standard of living, social mores, and the regulations imposed on immigration.

Aggregate population growth is distributed among regions in response to changing economic opportunities. In the past, people migrated from the South to the North and the Northeast, and from rural areas to urban areas. During the economic boom in the Sunbelt of the 1970s, the movement north was reversed. Recent economic recovery in the northern part of the country has diminished southward migration. The migration to suburban areas has slowed due to transportation costs and the expense of providing municipal services and utilities to these outlying areas. As a result, there is an increasing demand for housing in older, close-in neighborhoods in some cities.

Real estate improvements are provided in response to the demand generated by a population with effective purchasing power. *A household, persons who occupy a group of rooms or a single room that constitutes one housing unit,* imposes a basic demand for housing units. With income and a desire for ownership, households transform their needs into effective demand. In analyzing a local housing market, a knowledge of trends in the formation of households and household characteristics is crucial. The age, size, income, and other characteristics of households must be considered to determine the demand for housing.

The demand for commercial and industrial real estate is created by a population's demand for the goods and services to be produced or distributed at these sites. An appraiser must be aware of changes in the characteristics and distribution of the population that consumes the goods and services, as well as changes in the work force that produces them. A changing population coupled with technological advances can rapidly alter the demand for the services provided by property, which can affect property value.

Government Regulations and Societal Attitudes

General data include information about social attitudes and government regulations and actions that embody these attitudes. In response to social attitudes, the government establishes land use regulations and provides public services such as transportation systems and municipal utilities. Appraisers accumulate information on zoning, master plans, environmental impacts, transportation systems, and local annexation policies, as well as other data that reveal governmental and societal attitudes toward real estate.

Local zoning ordinances regulate land use and the density of development. In some areas, retroactive zoning is employed to remove uses that are nonconforming by giving owners time to alter property use. Zoning also can be used to preserve the architectural character of an area. With varying degrees of success, communities regulate zoning to halt or slow growth. To coordinate new development, they may expand capital improvement programs and construct sewage treatment facilities, fire stations, streets, and public recreational facilities. Zoning may also be used to enforce a community's master plan, which is usually based on economic growth projections and is sometimes modified for political reasons. The appraiser should be aware of the assumptions on which the master plan is based and of the potential for revision.

Environmental concerns have prompted increased regulation of land development at state and local levels. Zoning ordinances and building codes have long imposed additional costs on developers. To preserve the quality of the environment, developers are required to consider the impact of large developments on the ecology of a particular area and on the larger environmental system. They may be required to improve public roads, construct sewage treatment facilities, preserve natural terrain, or take other actions to conform to the recommendations of local, regional, or state planning agencies. These regulations can add significantly to the time required to complete a development and, therefore, increase its final cost. The value of subdivision land is obviously influenced by environmental regulations, which can affect the amount of time required to develop and sell the sites.

The creation or modification of a transportation system is a government action based on an analysis of the direct and indirect impact of the system on users and nonusers. An improvement in the transportation system can affect the accessibility of a site and, thus, its value. Improved transportation routes often cause new areas to be developed, which affects the value of other sites that must compete with the increased supply. To a great extent, the suburbanization of an urban population results from improvements in highways, commuter railroads, and bus routes.

The movement of commercial and retail enterprises between downtown areas and the suburbs has changed real estate markets and placed new emphasis on zoning systems, the administration of local government, and public expenditures. The highway system has opened certain regions to development and has increased their comparative advantage by decreasing the cost of transporting products to markets.

A municipality's willingness to annex and provide public services to outlying areas can affect the direction and amount of development. Conversely, sewer moratoriums have been used effectively to control local growth. This type of restriction can increase the value of developments that are already in place if demand is pressing on a limited supply.

To estimate value properly, the appraiser should understand the government regulations and actions that affect the subject property. The comparable properties selected should be similar to the subject property in terms of zoning, accessibility, and other characteristics.

Purchasing Power

Households obtain personal income from wages and salaries, yields on savings and other investments, profits from businesses, and private and government pensions. Many American households receive a significant proportion of their personal income in the form of government transfer payments such as social security, unemployment compensation, and farm subsidies. *Disposable income, the personal income remaining after deducting income taxes and all other payments to the government*, is either spent or saved. The amount of disposable income spent on goods and services indirectly determines the demand for properties such as shopping centers, industrial plants, office buildings, and warehouses.

Price Levels

Price-level changes influence the quantity of goods and services that can be purchased. Nominal prices that have been adjusted for changes in the price level are called "real" prices. The sale prices, rents, operating expenses, construction costs, and interest rates used to estimate market value, and the appraiser's final value estimate, are typically expressed in nominal dollars, unadjusted for price-level changes.

Investments vary in their ability to retain real or constant value during inflationary periods. Owners of income-producing real estate often attempt to keep the real value of their property constant by including escalator clauses in leases. These clauses allow rents to be adjusted according to an inflation index so that the tenant pays for increases in operating expenses.

Many lenders are unwilling to accept the risk of changing price levels and look for protection against that portion of inflation that may not be fully covered in the mortgage interest rate. Many institutions making loans on income-producing property continue to ask for equity participation in the property's income and for a mortgage interest rate that includes a premium for anticipated inflation. Other lenders may use a floating rate tied to the prime rate or some other economic indicator. These loan provisions affect the net operating income and before-tax cash flows of properties and, therefore, the value indications derived using the income capitalization approach.

Building Fluctuations

Housing starts and the construction of commercial and industrial properties fluctuate in response to business cycles, wars, and the cost and availability of financing. These fluctuations follow the long-term trend of new construction, which has been moving upward. These short-term fluctuations result in temporary misallocations of supply, which can depress rents and prices.

The standing stock of housing units at any point in time consists of all units occupied by households and those that are vacant. The stock is continually altered by the construction or conversion of units in response to developers' perceptions of the demand for new housing and by the need to replace existing units.

Six months to two years may pass between the time the developer decides to supply units and the time they enter the market. During this period, changing conditions may reduce demand, and the units coming on the market may remain unrented and unsold, thus increasing vacancy rates. Developers may continue to produce additional units for some time, even in the face of rising vacancies. Once these excess units are produced, they remain on the market and can depress rents or prices until demand increases to remove the surplus. When the market tightens, the supply of units lags behind the increase in demand, resulting in abnormally low vacancy rates and upward pressure on rents and prices. Ultimately, supply materializes as developers respond.

Fluctuations in the local supply and demand of real estate are influenced by regional and national conditions. Therefore, an appraiser looks for regional and national trends that may indicate a positive or negative change in property values at the local level. Although all regions may not experience the same slump in construction, tight monetary policy affects the cost and availability of mortgage credit and exerts a moderating influence on supply, even in a rapidly growing region.

Commercial real estate is affected by business conditions and the cost and availability of financing. Business firms pass their high financing costs on to consumers, which may restrict residential construction. If the demand for the goods and services produced or supplied by a business remains strong, the firm can raise prices and continue to expand even when credit is tight and interest rates are high.

The appraiser must recognize that a property's value as of a specific date may rise or fall during a fluctuation in building activity. Because market value is influenced by the balance of supply and demand at the time of the appraisal, the appraiser should make certain that the client understands the economic conditions that affect the subject property's value at a specific time.

Building Costs

The cost of reproducing a building tends to follow the general price levels established over a long period, but these price levels vary from time to time and from place to place. Building costs generally decline in times of deflation and increase in periods of inflation. These costs are affected by material and labor costs, construction technology, architect and legal fees, financing costs, building codes, and public regulations such as zoning ordinances, environmental requirements, and subdivision regulations.

The cost of construction can alter the quantity and character of demand and, therefore, the relative prices in real estate submarkets. The high cost of new buildings increases the demand for, and prices of, existing structures. When the cost of new structures increases, rehabilitation of existing buildings may become economically feasible. High building costs increase prices in single-family residential submarkets, which can increase the demand for rental units and their prices. The size and quality of the dwelling units demanded decrease when building costs increase more rapidly than purchasing power.

Taxes

Real estate taxes are based on the assessed value of real property, hence the term *ad valorem* (according to value) taxes. The assessed value of property is normally based on, but not necessarily equivalent to, its market value. If, for example, the tax rate is $60 per $1,000 of valuation, the assessed value is equal to market value, and the taxes are based on 50% of assessed value, then the annual real estate tax equals 3% of assessed value.

$$\frac{\$60}{\$1,000} \times 50\% = 3\%$$

If assessed value is not consistent with market value, the formula is modified to reflect the inconsistency. In jurisdictions where ad valorem real estate tax assessments have an established or probable relationship to market value, appraisal services may be required to resolve tax appeals.

In some communities, the trend in real estate taxes is an important consideration. In cities where public expenditures for schools and municipal services have increased, this heavy tax burden can affect real estate values adversely. Under these circumstances, new construction may be discouraged. There may be several tax districts in a metropolitan area, each with a different policy. The relative advantage of effective ad valorem taxation in an area is most important in analyzing how taxes affect value.

Although income taxes are not usually treated as an expense in appraisal calculations, they can influence property value. Currently, homeowners can deduct mortgage interest and property taxes when they itemize deductions in computing ordinary taxable income. This tax benefit influences the overall price level of single-family residences and condominiums. The ability to recover costs by rising accelerated depreciation in calculating the taxable income of investment property and other types of property, which was in effect between 1981 and 1986, also influenced the market's perception of the value of these property types.

Different levels of sales taxes and earnings taxes can also affect the relative desirability of properties. Although these taxes may be uniform within a state, properties in different states often compete with one another. For example, for several years Vermont imposed relatively low taxes and attracted many more new residents and industries than surrounding New England states. This increased demand probably enhanced property values in Vermont relative to values in surrounding states.

Financing

Because the cost and availability of financing help to determine the demand for, and supply of, real estate, financing affects real estate values. The cost includes the rate of interest on the mortgage instrument, deed of trust, or installment contract, as well as any points, discounts, equity participations, or other charges that the lender requires to increase the effective yield on the loan. The availability includes all nonprice determinants that affect the borrower's ability to obtain financing, including the loan-to-value ratio, the housing expense-to-income ratio required for loans on single-family homes, and the debt coverage and breakeven ratios required for loans on income-producing properties. (Loan-to-value, housing expense-to-income, debt coverage, and breakeven ratios are discussed in Chapter 20.) The cost and availability of financing typically have an inverse relationship; high interest rates and other costs usually are accompanied by a decrease in the availability of credit.

The cost and availability of credit for real estate financing influence both the quantity and quality of the real estate demanded and supplied. When interest rates are high and mortgage funds are limited, households that would have been in the home ownership market find that their incomes cannot support the required expenses. Purchases are delayed and smaller homes with fewer amenities are bought. The cost of land development financing and construction financing is reflected in the higher prices asked for single-family homes, which results in a further reduction in the quantity demanded.

The rental market is affected by the demand pressure of households that continue to rent and by the high cost of supplying new units, which results in part from financing costs. Occupancy rates and rents rise. Businesses try to pass on their higher occupancy costs to customers by increasing the prices of products or services. If they cannot fully recover the increased occupancy cost, the quantity of commercial and individual space demanded is reduced.

Sources of General Data

The general data needed to appraise real property are available from a wide variety of sources. A substantial amount of information is compiled and disseminated by federal, state, and local agencies; trade associations and private business enterprises may also provide data.

The largest body of data comes from the federal government. The *Economic Report of the President* published by the Council of Economic Advisors, includes data and analysis of housing starts and financing. *Economic Indicators* is a monthly publication prepared by the Council of Economic Advisors for the Joint Economic Committee. The *Federal Reserve Bulletin* and *Historical Chart Book*, which are published by the Federal Reserve Board, contain information on the gross national product, national income, mortgage markets, interest rates, and other financial statistics; installment credit; sources of funds; business activity; the labor force, employment, and industrial production; housing and construction; and international finance. The National Office of Vital Statistics compiles and disseminates statistics on birth and death rates.

The U.S. Department of Commerce, Bureau of the Census, publishes the *Census of Population,* the *Census of Housing*, the *Census of Manufacturers*, the *Census of Agriculture*, the *Annual Housing Survey*, and the *Statistical Abstract of the United States*, as well as various series on current population, population estimates, and population projections; consumer income; and housing completions, housing permits, and other housing statistics. These publications provide detailed information on population and housing characteristics for the nation, states, counties, metropolitan statistical areas (MSAs), municipalities, census tracts, and blocks in metropolitan areas. Interim reports on selected population, income, and housing data are also published by the Bureau of the Census. (See Chapter 8, footnote 1, for references on using census and other data in neighborhood and district analysis.)

The U.S. Department of Commerce, Bureau of Economic Analysis, publishes the *Survey of Current Business*. This is a source for data on the Consumer Price Index, the wholesale price index, mortgage debt, and the value of new construction. The U.S. Department of Housing and Urban Development issues reports on FHA building starts, financing, and housing programs administered by the department. It also disseminates FHA vacancy surveys for selected metropolitan areas. The

U.S. Department of Labor, Bureau of Labor Statistics, publishes the *Monthly Labor Review,* which contains the Consumer Price Index, wholesale prices, and monthly and annual employment and earnings figures.

At state and local levels, departments of development, local and regional planning agencies, and regional or metropolitan transportation authorities can provide appraisers with data on population, households, employment, master plans, present and future utility, and transportation systems. Often they also publish directories of manufacturers that list, by county, the names of firms, their products, and their employment figures.

A state's Bureau of Employment Service can provide county data on employment, unemployment, and wage rates. Chambers of Commerce offer a variety of information on local population, households, employment, and industry, which they often obtain from other secondary sources such as the census.

Trade associations can also be very useful sources. The NATIONAL ASSOCIATION OF REALTORS® compiles information on existing home sales for the nation as a whole and for individual regions. The national association and its affiliates put out many publications with data useful to appraisers. The National Association of Homebuilders disseminates information on new housing starts as well as prices, construction costs, and financing. *Sales and Marketing Management Magazine, Survey of Buying Power* contains information on households, income distribution, and retail sales by county and for selected cities.

Other meaningful data can be gathered from private sources such as banks, utility companies, university research centers, private advisory firms, multiple listing services, and cost services such as E. H. Boeckh and Marshall Valuation Service. These sources offer a variety of information on bank debt, department store sales, employment indicators, land prices, corporate business indicators, mortgage money costs, wage rates, construction costs, deeds, mortgage recordings, and the installation of utility meters.

In recent years, many databases have been developed for access by small computers. These databases cover a broad range of topics and offer many options for appraisers performing general or specialized research. The information available is virtually unlimited and includes topics such as current and historical news; industry analyses and reports; corporate earnings and analyses; local, regional, and national Yellow Page listings; publication indexes and articles; and much more.

General data are an integral part of an appraiser's office files. By cataloging and cross-indexing data obtained from various sources, the appraiser has quick access to important information. General data such as multiple listing information and census data can be stored and accessed by computer. Many local and regional planning and development agencies computerize information on housing inventory and vacancies, demolitions and conversions, commercial construction, household incomes, new land use by zoning classification, population and demographics, and housing forecasts by geographic area.

Recent developments in computer software and hardware have resulted in low-cost, high-performance databasing combinations for appraisers. Hundreds of individual programs are now used with desktop systems in appraisal offices. Some databases are contained in a single computer, while others are shared by several computers or terminals through local or telecommunication networks. Improvements in telecommunication programs and facilities, word processing, and electronic spreadsheets have facilitated appraisal analysis and report writing, as well as the use of database information.[4]

SPECIFIC DATA

Specific data include details about the property being appraised, comparable sales and rental properties, and relevant local market characteristics. In appraisals these data are used to determine highest and best use and to make the specific comparisons and analyses required to estimate market value. The specific data about a subject property provided in its land and building descriptions help the appraiser select comparable specific data pertaining to sales, rentals, construction costs, and local market characteristics.

In analyzing general data, national, regional, and local trends in value are emphasized; in an analysis of specific data, the characteristics of the subject property and comparable properties are studied. From relevant comparable properties, an appraiser extracts specific sale prices, rental terms, income and expense figures, rates of return on investment, construction costs, the expected economic life of improvements, and rates of depreciation. These figures are used in calculations that lead to an indication of value for the subject property.

An appraiser needs specific data to apply each of the three approaches to value. The appraiser uses the data to derive adjustments for value-influencing property characteristics, to isolate meaningful units of comparison, to analyze capitalization rates, and to measure accrued depreciation. By extracting relevant data from the large quantity of data available, an appraiser develops a sense of the market. This perception is essential to apply appraisal judgment in the valuation process and in the final reconciliation of value indications. The validity of a final estimate of market value depends to a great extent on how well it can be supported by market data.

Specific data are analyzed through comparison. In each approach to value, certain items must be extracted from market data to make comparisons. Specific data are analyzed to determine if these items are present and if they can be used to make reliable comparisons with the subject property. If, for example, the subject property is an apartment building of three-bedroom units, the appraiser may be able to use data from sales of similar apartment buildings to make adjustments for the time of sale, the location, and physical property characteristics. The appraiser may

---

4. For discussions of databasing and information processing, see Mary J. Dum, "Using an Electronic Spreadsheet in the Appraisal Office," *The Appraisal Journal*, July 1982; John D. Dorchester, Jr., "The Next Era in Appraisal: Opportunity vs. Obsolescence," *The Appraisal Journal*, January 1985; and Mark I. Roth, "Computer Connection," *The Appraisal Journal*, April 1985. Timely information can be found in *The Quarterly Byte*, a computer newsletter published by the American Institute of Real Estate Appraisers.

also need to analyze data on competitive properties that have not sold recently to obtain information on the rental rates and expenses for apartment buildings in the area.

The appraiser's analysis of highest and best use for the land as though vacant and the property as improved determines what comparable specific data are collected and analyzed. The nature and amount of research needed for a specific assignment depend on the property type and the purpose of the appraisal. The appraiser should gather all available data that may be pertinent to the assignment, organize the data, and perform a preliminary analysis before applying any analytical techniques.

Investigation of Market Transactions

A detailed description and classification of the characteristics and components of a property can be found in its land and building analyses. These analyses help the appraiser select and analyze the data used in the sales comparison, cost, and income capitalization approaches. The data used for comparison in the three approaches should be derived from properties that are similar to the appraised property. To use sales as a valid basis for further analysis, the appraiser inventories the relevant characteristics and components of the properties selected as comparable.

To select comparable sale properties, an appraiser examines public records, published sources, office files, and information from buyers, sellers, and other knowledgeable persons. Interviews with property owners may reveal relevant sales that have not been recorded. REALTORS®, salespeople, developers, and other appraisers are also good sources of sales and rental data. The selection of comparables is directed to some extent by the availability and scope of the data. Investigation of an active market usually reveals an adequate and representative number of transactions within a restricted area and time period.

The geographic area from which comparable sales can be selected depends on the property type. In valuing certain types of retail property, only properties with main street frontage may be pertinent. For many large industrial properties and most investment properties, the entire community should be studied; for larger properties, the national market may be relevant. For a residential appraisal, adequate data may occasionally be found within a block of the subject property. Even in these cases, however, the appraiser should consider the broader market to place the subject property and the comparables in a general market context.

In selecting market data for analysis, an appraiser focuses on transactions pertinent to the subject property's specific market. In general, comparable properties are those that compete with the property being appraised or have a demonstrable effect on prices or other relevant components of the market in question. With computer analysis, a large number of properties can be studied in the course of a single assignment, which may generate a more significant understanding of each property's contribution to, and influence on, a given market.

Appraisers seek data that will facilitate accurate comparisons, but because every real estate parcel is unique, absolute comparability is impossible. The comparability of properties varies, so the appraiser may find it necessary to place less confidence on a given comparable. Nevertheless, the appraiser may still want to consider this comparable for its evidence of, and effect on, the marketplace.

Appraisers have a special responsibility to consider carefully the comparability of all data used in a valuation assignment. They must fully understand the concept of comparability and should avoid comparing properties with different highest and best uses, limiting their search for comparables, or selecting inappropriate factors for comparison.

The first determinant of useful data is their degree of comparability. A second determinant is the quantity of information available, and a third, but equally important, factor is the authenticity and reliability of the data. An appraiser must not assume that all data pertinent to an assignment are completely reliable. Sales figures, costs, and other information subject to misrepresentation should be scrutinized for authenticity.

When comparable sales data in the subject property's immediate area are limited, the appraiser may need to extend the data search to adjacent neighborhoods and similar communities. When the selection of data is limited to an unacceptably narrow sample of current market activity, the appraiser may decide to use sales that are less current or to interview brokers, buyers, sellers, owners, and tenants of similar properties in the area to obtain evidence of potential market activity—i.e., listings of offers to sell and purchase. With proper adjustment, these may also be used as comparables.

An appraiser gathers broad information about a market from its pattern of sales. Important market data can be revealed by many significant characteristics:

- Number of sales
- Period of time covered by the sales
- Availability of property for sale
- Rate of absorption
- Rate of turnover (i.e., volume of sales and level of activity)
- Characteristics and motivations of buyers and sellers
- Terms and conditions of sale
- Use of property before and after its sale

While analyzing data to select comparable sales, an appraiser begins to form certain conclusions about the general market, the subject property, and the possible relationships between the data and the subject property. The appraiser ascertains market strengths and weaknesses; the probable supply of, demand for, and marketability of properties similar to the property being appraised; and the variations and characteristics that are likely to have the greatest impact on the value of properties in the market. Thus, an appraiser analyzes data against a background of information about the particular area and the specific type of property.

The information needed to apply the cost and income capitalization approaches must often be obtained from market sources other than sales. This information may also be used to refine adjustments made in the sales comparison approach. In the investigation of general and neighborhood data, an appraiser learns about trends in construction costs, lease terms, typical expenses, and vacancy rates. Examining trends in the market where the subject property is located provides additional specific data that can be used to derive value indications and successfully complete evaluation assignments.

Sources of Specific Data

Like sources of general data, sources of specific data are diverse. Although much data can be obtained from public records and published sources, personal contact with developers, builders, REALTORS®, financial and legal specialists, property managers, local planners, and other real estate professionals also provides useful information. For this reason, practicing appraisers need communication skills as well as analytical techniques to research sales, improvement costs, and income and expense data thoroughly and complete appraisal assignments.

Sources of sales data include public records; published news; REALTORS®, appraisers, managers, and bankers; multiple listing books; listings and offers; and other local sources.

Public records.   An appraiser searches public records for a copy of the property deed. The deed provides important information about the property and the sales transaction, including the full names of the parties involved and the transaction date. A legal description of the property, the property rights included in the transaction, and any outstanding liens on the title are shown.

Occasionally, the names of the parties may suggest unusual motivations for the sale. For example, a sale from John Smith to Mary S. Jones may be a transfer from a father to a daughter; a sale from John Smith, William Jones, and Harold Long to the SJL Corporation may not be an arm's-length transaction arrived at by unrelated parties under no duress.

In some states the law requires that the consideration paid upon transfer of title be shown on the deed. However, this consideration does not always reflect the actual sale price. To reduce transfer taxes, some purchasers (e.g., of motels or apartments) deduct the estimated value of personal property from the true consideration paid. Because these personal property values are sometimes inflated, the recorded consideration for the real property may be less than the true consideration. In one deed the indicated consideration may be overstated to obtain a higher loan than is warranted; in another, the consideration may be understated to justify a low property tax assessment. Although some states require that the true and actual consideration be listed on the deed, other states allow the consideration to be reported as "$10 and other valuable consideration."

The local tax assessor's records may include property cards for the subject property and comparables properties, with land and building sketches, area measurements, sale prices, and other information. In some locations, legal or private publishing services issue information about revenue stamps and other facts pertaining to current transfers.

Published news. Most city newspapers feature real estate news. Although some of the news may be incomplete or inaccurate, an appraiser can use it to confirm details because the names of the negotiating brokers and the parties to a transaction are usually published.

REALTORS®, appraisers, managers, and bankers. These professionals often provide information about real estate transactions and may suggest valuable leads. Such sources may be definitive, but if the information obtained from real estate professionals is third-party data, the appraiser should look for separate verification.

Multiple listing books. Books of multiple listings are published in many communities. They enumerate the properties listed for sale during a calendar year or fiscal quarter and cite their listing prices. The books give fairly complete information about properties, including photographs, descriptions, and brokers' names. However, details about a property's square footage, basement area, or exact age may be inaccurate or excluded. In certain areas, multiple listing books can be purchased. Multiple listing services sometimes publish the sale prices of properties that have been sold.

Listings and offers. Whenever possible, an appraiser should gather information on listings of other properties offered for sale. The appraiser can request that his or her name be added to the mailing lists of banks, brokers, and others who offer properties for sale. Classified ads of properties offered for sale provide asking prices and suggest the strength or weakness of the local market for a particular type of property or the activity in a particular area. Offers to purchase may also be obtained from brokers or managers. Listings are generally higher than actual transaction prices; offers are generally somewhat lower.

Improvement Cost Data

Useful information about construction costs may be obtained from many sources. Contractors and suppliers of construction materials can provide cost information about recently constructed buildings that are similar to the subject property. Cost estimators may also be consulted for information on the costs involved in constructing building improvements. Appraisers should be aware that published cost estimates may or may not include indirect costs such as loan interest during construction.

In an active market, cost information can be obtained by interviewing local property owners who have recently added building or land improvements similar to those found on the subject property. If work contracts and accounting records of recently improved properties are available, they can provide significant details.

Cost estimates are made by assembling, cataloging, and analyzing data on actual building costs. Detailed costs should be classified in general categories, such as residential construction or commercial building costs, and separate figures should be provided for special finishes or equipment. Costs for individual structured components should also be researched and filed.

Several cost-estimating services publish cost manuals that break down costs into square-foot and cubic-foot measures. Unit costs for building types usually start with a building of a certain size (i.e., a base area or volume) which serves as a benchmark. Then additions or deductions are made to account for the actual number of square feet or cubic feet in the subject property. Data provided by cost-estimating services can be used to confirm estimates developed from local cost data.

Cost manuals are updated periodically by including cost index tables that reflect changes in the cost of construction over a period of years. Cost indexes convert a known cost as of a past date into a current cost estimate. However, there is a practical limitation in applying this procedure because, as the time span increases, the reliability of the current cost indication tends to decrease. Sometimes cost index tables can be used to adjust costs for different geographic areas.

The use of cost index tables can pose problems because it may be difficult to ascertain which components are included in the reported original cost. Furthermore, capital expenditures for improvements added after original construction must also be considered, and added improvements may affect the estimates of cost and accrued depreciation.

Some appraisers rely almost entirely on published cost manuals; others maintain files of specific cost comparables that are similar to their files of sale comparables. These files may be based on information furnished by contract-reporting services. Contract-reporting services may give building areas or supply a general building description, the low bids, and the contract award. The appraiser can then obtain any missing information, such as the breakdown of office and warehouse space, and classify the building type for filing. When cost comparable files are carefully developed and managed, they can supply authentic square-foot costs on buildings of all types for use in appraisal assignments.

Income and Expense Data

To derive pertinent income and expense data, an appraiser investigates comparable sales and rentals as well as competitive income-producing properties in the same market. For investment properties, current and recent incomes are reviewed and vacancy and collection losses and typical operating expenses are studied. Finally, data on the mortgage terms, or debt service, should be examined and refined by the appraiser to make forecasts of future incomes and expenses.

Published information on property values for several consecutive years can suggest the rate of appreciation or depreciation for various property types. Interviews with owners and tenants in the area can provide lease and expense data. Lenders may be contacted for information on available terms of financing.

An appraiser tries to obtain all income and expense data for the income properties used as comparables. These data should be tabulated in a reconstructed operating statement and filed by property type. (See Chapter 19 for a suggested format for reconstructed operating statements.)

Like expense data, rental information is difficult to obtain. Therefore, appraisers should take every opportunity to add rents to their rental databases. Long-term leases are usually on public record. A separate county index that cites the parties to recorded leases and the volume and page numbers of recorded leases may also be available. Sometimes this information is listed with deeds and mortgages, but it is usually coded for easy identification. In certain cities, abstracts of recorded leases are printed by private publishing services. Classified ads may also provide rental information. Many appraisers periodically check advertised rentals and record rental information by property type or area. It is convenient to file rental data under the same classifications used for sales data.

Income and expense comparables should be filed chronologically and by property type so they can be retrieved easily and used to estimate the expenses for a similar type of property. Income and expense figures should be converted into units of comparison for analysis. For example, income may be reported in terms of rent per apartment unit, per room, per hospital bed, or per square foot. Income is usually stated in terms of dollars per unit(s) over a specified time period. Expenses for insurance, taxes, painting, decorating, and other maintenance charges can be expressed in the same units of comparison used for income, or they can be expressed as a percentage of the effective gross rent. The unit of comparison selected must be used consistently throughout the analysis.

Data for rental property may show vacancy rates and operating expenses as a percentage of the effective gross income. These data are essential in valuing income-producing property. The age and type of construction and any utilities provided by the owner should be specified.

Capitalization Rates

Capitalization rates are another essential type of market data. They are rates or multiples (e.g., a gross rent multiplier for a single-family property) that are extracted from market data. When net operating income and sale price information are available, an overall rate (R_O) can be calculated; if mortgage information is also available, the equity capitalization rate (R_E) can be calculated. Whenever possible, an appraiser should calculate these rates from available data and consider their meaning in the analysis. In making comparisons, the rates are analyzed in light of the similarity between the comparable sale's characteristics to the characteristics of the subject property. (The derivation of capitalization rates is discussed in detail in Chapters 20 and 21.)

The overall and equity capitalization rates derived from sales can also be used as bases for deriving other capitalization rates. If possible, overall property rates and equity yield rates should be extracted from market evidence. It is important that these rate indications be considered when adequate market information is available.

ORGANIZATION AND ARRAY OF DATA

Understanding the content and sources of general and specific appraisal data facilitates their analysis in valuation and evaluation assignments. Before undertaking any analysis, however, an appraiser must organize all the specific data accumulated in the investigation. A market data grid is a carefully constructed spreadsheet that provides

a tabular representation of market data organized into useful and measurable categories. If the information to be analyzed is very complex, the appraiser may need to
design several market data grids to isolate and study specific data.

On the initial grid, the appraiser lists each characteristic of the subject and
comparable properties that has been isolated. The market data grid should include
the total sale price of each comparable property and the date of each sale, which can
be expressed in relation to the subject property's date of valuation (e.g., one month
ago or 16 months ago). The grid also includes information about the property rights
conveyed, the financial arrangements of the sale, and any unusual motivation that
may have resulted in a negotiating advantage for the buyer or the seller, such as a
desire to liquidate a property for inheritance tax or a desire to acquire a particular
property for expansion. Because financial arrangements and unusual motivations can
significantly influence a property's sale price, they must be carefully examined.

The grid may also contain other market data that are significant to the
appraisal assignment. Such data might include reproduction costs for building and
land improvements; development costs; the amount of accrued depreciation; the
indicated economic life of improvements similar to those on the subject property;
income data (e.g., market rent estimates, gross income, net operating income, and
pre-tax cash flow or equity dividend); rates of return; the percent of land value
appreciation evident in the area; and the average value of commodities or services
provided by properties similar to the property being appraised.

The initial market data grid can include all characteristics of the subject and
comparable properties, sales transactions, and pertinent market data from sources
other than sales. However, an appraiser may choose to use one grid for comparable
sales information and other grids for information derived from other sources. The use
of serveral grids allows the appraiser to isolate various aspects of individual sales and
the total market that may be significant in the valuation problem. Isolating these
specifics provides an early indication of the information the appraiser will be able to
derive from the collected data and identifies variations among properties that may be
significant to their value.

In examining the initial market data grid, the appraiser may find that
certain data are not pertinent and will not be useful in applying the approaches to
value. Additional data may be required and the appraiser may need to create other
grids to include more information or to isolate the data required for specific
approaches. Appraisers should see data analysis as a developing process and the grid
as a tool that facilitates and helps advance this process through the approaches to
valid indications of property value.

Figures 7.1 and 7.2 show sample grids for the organization and array of
market data. Figure 7.1 is a comparable sales data grid that can serve as a basis for
analyzing data in the sales comparison approach to value. (Further discussion and
examples of the use of market data grids for comparing and adjusting market data in
the sales comparison approach are provided in Chapter 14.) Figure 7.2 shows how the
basic market data grid can be used to organize and array data on rental properties,
which may be helpful in deriving and applying market rent estimates in the income
capitalization approach to value.

Figure 7.1   Market Data Grid

Element	Subject	Sale 1	Sale 2	Sale 3	Sale 4	Sale 5
Sale price	?	——	——	——	——	——
Property rights conveyed	——	——	——	——	——	——
Financing	——	——	——	——	——	——
Conditions of sale (motivation)	——	——	——	——	——	——
Date of sale (market conditions)	——	——	——	——	——	——
Location	——	——	——	——	——	——
Gross building area (*GBA*)	——	——	——	——	——	——
Rentable area	——	——	——	——	——	——
Land area	——	——	——	——	——	——
Lease expiration dates	——	——	——	——	——	——
Rent concessions	——	——	——	——	——	——
Escalation	——	——	——	——	——	——
Market rent	——	——	——	——	——	——
Potential gross income (*PGI*)	——	——	——	——	——	——
Effective gross income (*EGI*)	——	——	——	——	——	——
Net operating income (*NOI*)	——	——	——	——	——	——
Income multiplier	——	——	——	——	——	——
Overall cap rate (R_O)	——	——	——	——	——	——
Equity cap rate (R_E)	——	——	——	——	——	——
Property yield rate (Y_O)	——	——	——	——	——	——
Equity yield rate (Y_E)	——	——	——	——	——	——

Units of Comparison

Units of comparison are used in analyzing data for all three approaches. In the sales comparison approach, the sale price may be divided by the unit of comparison. In the cost approach, the total cost of construction and total accrued depreciation are divided by the unit of comparison. In the income capitalization approach, the income and expense items and the net operating income may be divided by the chosen unit of comparison. Several different units of comparison may be used in each approach, depending on the information needed and the focus of the analysis. However, the unit of comparison selected must be consistently applied to the subject property and all comparable sales properties in each analysis.

The fundamental features of data analysis in the sales comparison, cost, and income capitalization approaches are described in the following section.

DATA ANALYSIS

Sales Comparison Approach

In the sales comparison approach to value, an appraiser analyzes data gathered primarily from comparable sales. The purpose of this analysis is to identify variations between the subject property and the comparable sale properties so that the value of

Figure 7.2   Organization and Array of Market Data for Rental Properties

Element	Subject	Sale 1	Sale 2	Sale 3	Sale 4	Sale 5
Sale price	?	$600,000	$920,000	$850,000	$990,000	$920,000
Property rights conveyed	Leased fee	Leased fee	Leased fee	Leased fee	Leased fee	Leased fee
Amount seller received	?	$600,000	see[a]	$850,000	see[b]	$920,000
Cash equivalent price	?	$600,000	$800,000	$850,000	$900,000	$920,000
Unit of comparison (number of sq. ft.)	400,000	200,000	320,000	430,000	380,000	480,000
Dollars per sq. ft. of *GBA*	?	$3.00	$2.50	$1.98	$2.37	$1.92
Conditions of sale (motivation)[c]	?	Arm's-length	Arm's-length	+10%	Arm's-length	Arm's-length
Date (market conditions)[d]	?	Current	+6%	Current	+2%	Current
Location[e]	Corner lot	Similar	+5%	Similar	+5%	Similar
Size[f]	Small lot	−5%	−2%	Similar	Similar	+2%
Other physical characteristics[g]	High ground	Similar	Similar	Similar	+5%	Similar
Zoning[h]	C-3	Similar	Similar	+10%	Similar	15%
Contract rent[i]	Same as market rent	Similar	Similar	+30%	Similar	Similar

(continued)

a. In Sale 2, the seller received $120,000 in cash and a note for $800,000 (including any interest) payable in 18 months; cash equivalent value of the note is $680,000.

b. In Sale 4, the seller received $200,000 in cash and a note for $790,000, with a 20-year amortization schedule, quarterly payments including 8.5% interest, a seven-year call provision, and a balloon arrangement.

c. In Sale 3, the seller had to dispose of the property to settle an estate.

d. Considering the rate of inflation and the popularity of the neighborhood, a 2% increase is indicated for a one-year-old sale and a 6% increase is indicated for a two-year-old sale.

e. Sales 2 and 4 are not corner lots; the subject and the other sales are.

f. Within this range of sizes, small plots are worth more per square foot than large plots due to greater demand.

g. Sale 4 includes one-half acre of floodplain land.

h. Sale 3 includes two acres of land with R-5 zoning; the subject and the other sales are all zoned C-3. Sale 5 includes a nonexclusive vehicle right-of-way for the use of the subject property.

i. Sale 3 is leased at a rent that is 8.5% below market rent and there are three years remaining on the lease term.

Figure 7.2   Organization and Array of Market Data for
Rental Properties (continued)

Element	Subject	Sale 1	Sale 2	Sale 3	Sale 4	Sale 5
Dollars per sq. ft. of *GBA* after addition of percentage adjustments	?	$2.85	$2.72	$2.57	$2.65	$2.25
Rent per sq. ft. of *GBA*	?	$.30	N/A	$.18	$.24	N/A
Gross rent multiplier (*GRM*)	?	10.0	N/A	11.0	9.9	N/A
Percentage of *NOI*	?	81%	N/A	74%	82%	N/A
Overall capitalization rate (R_O)	?	8.10%	N/A	8.14%	8.12%	N/A
Mortgage capitalization rate (R_M)	?	9.2%	9.4%	10.5%	10.1%	9.6%
Equity capitalization rate (R_E)	?	7.4%	7.3%	7.6%	7.5%	7.4%

these variations can be measured. The analysis of sales data reveals which features the market perceives to be valuable. It also suggests mathematical computations that can be applied to the known values of the comparables to arrive at the unknown whole or per-unit value of the subject property.

The first step in data analysis is the selection of one or more appropriate units of comparison. In appraising single-family residential property, adjustments are typically made to the total property sale price; therefore, the basic unit of comparison is the total property. However, the total property unit is seldom used in appraising nonresidential properties because of significant size variations.

Typically, different units of comparison are used with different property types. Comparisons can be made on the basis of the price, cost, income, or expenses per unit, depending on the approach in which the comparable property is being analyzed. The following list shows common property types and the typical units of comparison used in their appraisal.

Single-family residences

- Entire property
- Square foot
- Room
- Potential or effective gross rent multiplier

Vacant land

- Entire property
- Square foot
- Front foot
- Potential subdivided lot
- Building units per acre

Agricultural properties

- Acre
- Animal unit (AU)—for pastureland
- Hundred weight (cwt), tons, or bushel per acre—for farmland
- Thousand board feet (MBF)—for timberland

Apartments

- Square foot of livable area
- Apartment
- Room
- Potential or effective gross income multiplier

Warehouses

- Square foot
- Cubic foot
- Loading dock or door
- Potential or effective gross income multiplier

Factories

- Square foot
- Cubic foot
- Machine unit
- Potential or effective gross income multiplier

Offices

- Square foot
- Office
- Room
- Desk
- Potential or effective gross income multiplier

Hospitals

- Square foot
- Bed

Theaters

- Square foot
- Seat

After the appropriate unit of comparison is chosen, the appraiser reviews the data to determine which characteristics of the properties and which sales transactions should be used in the sales comparison approach. The dates of the sales indicate which properties will provide the best initial indication of change in value over time. Ideally, this indication would be derived from records of the sale and subsequent resale of a property that was not substantially changed between the sales.

Further data analysis suggests where the appraiser should begin to solve for the value contributed by individual property characteristics. Because properties usually have many separate components, the appraiser tries to find a single component for which a value can be derived. For example, if the market data grid shows that two properties vary only in that one is fully landscaped and the other is not, the appraiser can estimate the contributory value of the landscaping by comparing the two sales. Then another market variable can be isolated from other sales with a second calculation. (Further discussion of paired data set analysis can be found in Chapter 14.)

Thus, the analysis of sales is progressive. An appraiser isolates and solves for one variable at a time, comparing known indications against unknown characteristics. This analytical process gives the appraiser an indication of the data that will be most useful in applying the sales comparison approach and suggests the pattern of calculations that will be needed to derive a value indication. Moreover, a careful review of market data may reveal that additional data are needed to substantiate the value indication reached through the sales comparison approach, or that more weight should be attributed to the value indications derived through the cost and income capitalization approaches.

Cost Approach

To apply the cost approach, appraisers often use sales data and cost and depreciation information derived from the market. Both types of information may contribute significantly to the cost approach, and each may serve as a check on the other. An analysis of sales data can supplement cost and depreciation data obtained from other sources. Sales analysis can provide direct indications of accrued depreciation, profit margin, and the value contribution of buildings or land improvements. The cost of an improvement recently added to a sale property may indicate current construction costs.

To develop cost estimates from data obtained through observation and interviews, the appraiser must ascertain precisely what the reported expenditure represents in relation to the total actual cost of property changes. If entrepreneurial profit is evident, it should be included in the appraisal estimate. Quoted costs for improvements may not reflect the owner's related risk, labor and equipment costs, financial charges, the costs of land preparation, engineering costs, or other indirect expenses. The appraiser must also recognize that cost estimates for the reproduction or replacement of improvements as of the appraisal date, which are developed in data analysis, may not reflect any profit that the current owner realized due to a change in the property. Of course, final cost estimates should include this profit if it is evident in the market.

Income Capitalization Approach

Comparable sales data, comparable rental data, and income and expense statements provide a variety of information for use in the income capitalization approach. Much of the data needed for this approach is derived from interviews with individuals who are familiar with the subject property or comparable sale and rental properties. An appraiser may also interview owners and managers of similar properties for information on typical rents, lease terms, vacancy rates, management fees, and other operating expenses.

If an appraiser is valuing an apartment in an area where there is a relative scarcity of apartment sales or property data, the appraiser may study apartments located elsewhere to suggest income and expense trends and indications of the various relationships between income and value. If sufficient comparability exists, these data can provide support for the analysis.

When the data available provide an adequate knowledge of the income, expenses, and mortgage terms associated with each sale, the appraiser can derive an estimate of the net operating income (*NOI*) and pre-tax cash flow, or equity dividend, for each sale property. The overall capitalization rate and equity capitalization rate reflected in each sale can then be calculated.

This calculation is meaningful only if the appraiser uses the same income and expense categories to derive net operating incomes from comparable sales and to project the net operating income of the subject property. If, for example, an allowance for replacement is made in the expense statement for one comparable property and not in the others, the overall capitalization rate derived for that property will not be comparable to the rates derived for other properties.

By analyzing the market-derived overall capitalization rate and equity capitalization rate indicated in each comparable sale, the appraiser can develop an appropriate rate or rates to use in deriving a value indication of the subject property with direct capitalization techniques. When adequate comparable sale and rental data are available, it is often possible to calculate both an overall capitalization rate and an equity capitalization rate for the subject property. Although yield capitalization may produce a more detailed analysis, market-derived rates should be analyzed and explained in market value appraisals. If the results obtained with direct and yield capitalization methods differ, the appraiser must find market support for his or her conclusions and explain them in light of the market. (Yield capitalization techniques are discussed in Chapter 21.)

SUMMARY

Data collection and analysis are as important to the completion of an appraisal as the methods and procedures employed to estimate value. The information used by appraisers consists of general data on social, economic, governmental, and environmental forces and specific data on the property being appraised, comparable sales and rental properties, and relevant local market characteristics.

An appraiser studies general data to understand the interaction of value influences and to forecast economic trends. General data include economic indicators (e.g., the balance of trade or payments, the gross national product, production levels, wage levels, the volume of retail sales, the prime interest rate, the CPI, and the unemployment rate), government programs (e.g., planning activities, the provision of public utilities, municipal services, and transportation systems), tax policies, and regulations (e.g., zoning, subdivision guidelines, and environmental safeguards). General data reflect economic conditions at the international, national, regional, and local level.

The *economic base* of a community is the economic activity that enables it to attract income from outside its borders. It determines local population growth and the disposable income available for consumption or investment, which affects household formation and purchasing power. To consider the impact of macroeconomic influences on microeconomic conditions, the appraiser examines how inflationary expectations relate to local price levels and construction costs, how the current phase of the business cycle relates to area building starts, how income and real estate taxes relate to local property values, and how monetary policy and capital availability relate to local financing rates.

Sources of general data include government publications sponsored by the Council of Economic Advisors; the Federal Reserve Board; the Department of Commerce, Bureau of the Census and Bureau of Economic Analysis; and the Department of Labor, Bureau of Labor Statistics. General data can also be obtained from state and local governments, Chambers of Commerce, trade associations, research institutions, multiple listing services, and databases.

An appraiser uses specific data to apply the three approaches to value and to ensure that the final conclusion reflects the market. Specific data on comparable properties identify value-influencing property characteristics, units of comparison, sale prices and rents, operating expenses, capitalization rates, construction costs, the anticipated economic life of the improvements, and accrued depreciation. The focus of data collection and analysis is defined by the appraiser's determination of the highest and best use of the property. Specific data are evaluated on their comparability, availability, and reliability.

Specific data provide basic information about market transactions (e.g., the number of sales, periods of sales, the availability of properties for sale, absorption rates, the volume of sales or turnover rate, the motivation of buyers and sellers, the terms and conditions of sale, prior and subsequent use of the comparable property, and other significant factors affecting the market). This information can indicate the strength or weakness of the market (i.e., the relationship between supply and demand) and the marketability of the subject property.

Sources of specific sales data include public records, newspapers, real estate professionals, multiple listing services, and published property listings and offers. An appraiser may obtain specific cost data from contractors, suppliers of building materials, or cost-estimating manuals. In valuing investment properties, appraisers study data on property income, operating expenses, vacancy and collection losses, and mortgage terms or debt service. These data are available from public sources, such as recorded leases, and advertised rentals and private sources, such as owners and tenants. When relevant data are known, overall capitalization rates and equity capitalization rates can be derived.

The organization and array of specific data on a market data grid, which is a spreadsheet for tabular representation, facilitates the isolation of the variable characteristics of the subject and comparable properties and the interpretation of their effects on value. The same units of comparison should be used to describe the property characteristics of the subject and comparable properties. The analysis of specific data indicates which information will be most useful and whether additional data will be required for substantiation.

In a sales comparison analysis, the appraiser isolates the factors that are responsible for variations between the values of the subject property and comparable properties. The appraiser begins by determining the price of each comparable and the dates of sale, to account for market conditions. Then he or she reviews information on the property rights and financial arrangments involved and on the conditions of sale, to clarify the motivations of the buyer and the seller. The data should also identify any other differences in the characteristics of the subject and comparable properties.

In a cost analysis, the appraiser precisely delineates all expenditures that contribute to the total reproduction or replacement cost of the improvements. Estimates of accrued depreciation, any entrepreneurial profit, and the contribution of the improvement to the property should be supported with market evidence.

In an income capitalization analysis, capitalization rates must be derived from the market. The data on income, operating expenses, vacancy and collection losses, and mortgage terms should reflect the experiences of comparable properties. The categories of analysis should be measured consistently.

8   Neighborhoods and Districts

Social, economic, governmental, and environmental forces influence property values in the vicinity of a subject property which, in turn, directly affect the value of the subject property itself. Therefore, it is necessary to delineate the boundaries of the area of influence to conduct a thorough analysis. These boundaries are identified by determining the area within which the forces affect all surrounding properties in the same way they affect the property being appraised. Although physical boundaries may be drawn, the significant boundaries are those that fix the limits of influences on property values. By coincidence, these limits may be physically observable.

The area of influence is commonly called a neighborhood. *A neighborhood is a group of complementary land uses.* A residential neighborhood, for example, may contain single-family homes and commercial properties that provide services for local residents. A clear distinction can be drawn between a neighborhood and a district. *A district is a type of neighborhood that is characterized by homogeneous land use.* Districts are commonly composed of apartments or commercial, industrial, or agricultural properties.

To identify neighborhood or district boundaries, an appraiser examines the subject property's surroundings. The investigation begins with the subject property and proceeds outward, identifying all relevant actual and potential influences on the property's value that can be attributed to its location. The appraiser extends the geographic search far enough to encompass all influences that the market perceives as affecting the value of the subject property. At the physical point where no factors influencing the value of the subject and surrounding properties are found, the boundaries for analysis are set. The appraiser's conclusions regarding the impact of the neighborhood or district on the subject property's value are significant only when area boundaries are properly delineated.

Neighborhood or district analysis provides a framework, or context, in which property value is estimated. It identifies the area of analysis and establishes the potential limits within which the appraiser searches for data to be used in applying

161

the three approaches to value. Realistic boundaries allow the appraiser to identify comparable properties in the same neighborhood or district; the sale prices of these properties usually require little or no adjustment for location.

Neighborhood or district analysis helps the appraiser determine stability of an area and may indicate future land uses and value trends.

CHARACTERISTICS OF NEIGHBORHOODS AND DISTRICTS

A neighborhood exhibits a greater degree of uniformity than a larger area. Obviously, no group of inhabitants, buildings, or business enterprises can possess identical features or attributes, but a neighborhood is perceived to be relatively uniform.

The relative uniformity of a neighborhood is reflected in many ways. A large number of shared features may be reflected in a neighborhood, including similar building types and styles, population characteristics, economic profiles of occupants, and zoning regulations that affect land use. The variables that suggest similarity are not limited to physical characteristics. The social, economic, and governmental forces operating within a neighborhood contribute as much to its definition as the physical environment. The diverse and varied nature of neighborhoods reflects this fact. Similarity may also be indicated by the dominant land use, rent and occupancy levels, the credit strength of occupants, and the ages of buildings.

VARIETY OF LAND USES IN RESIDENTIAL NEIGHBORHOOD

(H. Armstrong Roberts, Inc.)

NEIGHBORHOOD AND DISTRICT BOUNDARIES

Neighborhood and district boundaries identify the physical area that influences the value of a subject property. These boundaries may coincide with changes in prevailing land use, occupant characteristics, or physical characteristics such as structures, street patterns, terrain, vegetation, and lot sizes. Because changes in natural or physical features often coincide with changes in land use, transportation arteries (e.g., highways, major streets, and railroads), bodies of water (e.g., rivers, lakes, and streams), and changes in elevation (e.g., hills, mountains, cliffs, and valleys) often represent significant boundaries.

The neighborhood of a house in a single-family subdivision usually ends where land uses change to commercial, apartment, or industrial use. However, another house in the same subdivision that is nearer to these different land uses may be influenced by them; therefore, the neighborhood of this house may not end at the same point.

In defining a district, variations in relevant characteristics may indicate that more limited boundaries should be established for investigation. For example, in an urban area many high-rise apartment buildings may be constructed along a natural lakeshore and separated from other land uses by major transportation arteries. In this type of district, there may be great variation in the prices of apartments of different sizes with different views, parking availability, proximity to public transportation, and building ages. These variations, which suggest limited district boundaries, must be identified to reveal market and submarket characteristics.

The properties in closest proximity to a subject property tend to exert the greatest influence on its value. Any property, even a commercial one, that is on the fringe of a residential area and near attractive, well-maintained, desirable properties tends to have a higher value than it would if it were located near less attractive, poorly maintained, undesirable properties.

Legal, political, and economic organizations collect data for standardized or statistically defined areas, so information about income and educational levels may be available for cities, counties, tax districts, census tracts, or special enumeration districts. Although these data may be relevant, they rarely conform to the area boundaries identified for property valuation. If secondary data are used to help identify neighborhood boundaries, the appraiser should verify and supplement the data with primary research.

To identify neighborhood and district boundaries, an appraiser follows several steps.

1. *Examine the area's physical characteristics.* The appraiser should drive or walk around the area to develop a sense of place, noting the degree of similarity in land uses, types of structures, architectural styles, and maintenance and upkeep. Using a map of the area, the appraiser can identify points where these characteristics change and note any physical barriers—e.g., major streets, hills, rivers, or railroads—that coincide with these points.

2. *Draw preliminary boundaries on a map.* The appraiser should draw lines on the map to connect the points where physical characteristics change. The physical barriers that coincide with or are near the shifts in physical characteristics can be identified.

3. *Test preliminary boundaries against demographic data.* If possible, the appraiser should obtain accurate data on the ages, occupations, incomes, and educational levels of neighborhood residents. Every 10 years the Bureau of the Census, U.S. Department of Commerce collects data on population and housing characteristics, employment, and earnings.[1]

Reliable data may also be available from local chambers of commerce, universities, and research organizations.

In unusual cases, an appraiser might consider sampling area residents to obtain an indication of relevant characteristics. The appraiser may also interview neighborhood occupants, business people, brokers, and community representatives for their perceptions of how far the neighborhood extends. Through experience, the appraiser learns to observe changes in how neighborhoods are perceived.

CHANGE

In neighborhood and district analysis, an appraiser recognizes the propensity for change and tries to determine how a particular neighborhood may be changing. Appraisers usually consider historic growth trends and composition when analyzing patterns of change. When values in a neighborhood are increasing, the appraiser must determine whether the subject property's value can be expected to exceed, equal, or lag behind the neighborhood trend. Similarly, if neighborhood values are stable or declining, the appraiser analyzes the value of the subject property relative to these trends.

Evidence of Change

Neighborhood change is often indicated by variations within the neighborhood. New uses may indicate potential increases or decreases in a neighborhood's property values. For example, a neighborhood in which some homes are well maintained and others are not may be undergoing either decline or revitalization. The introduction of different uses, such as rooming houses or offices, into a single-family residential neighborhood also indicates potential change.

---

1. For discussions on applying census and other data to neighborhood and district analysis, see William Schenkel, "Refining Valuation Estimates with Census Data," *Real Estate Appraiser,* September/October 1973; and Arnold L. Redman and C. F. Sirmans, "Regional/Local Economic Analysis: A Discussion of Data Sources," *The Appraisal Journal,* April 1977.

DISTINCT CHANGE IN LAND USE WITH ARTERIAL AND NATURAL BOUNDARIES
(H. Armstrong Roberts, Inc.)

Changes in one neighborhood are usually influenced by changes in other neighborhoods and in the larger area of influence. In any relatively stable city, the rapid growth of one neighborhood or district may adversely affect a competing neighborhood or district. A city may grow until its center is not accessible from its more remote districts. In such instances, new, competing business centers may be established to serve the needs of outlying areas.

Suburban business centers may have an adverse effect on a city's central business district. Newer residential areas may affect older areas. The added supply of new homes may induce residents to shift from old homes to new ones and place older homes on the market. This increase in supply may affect the market values of all homes in the area. If the location of a neighborhood makes it attractive for conversion to a more intensive use, the existing improvements may be extensively remodeled or torn down to make way for redevelopment.

City growth causes changes in the utility of both vacant and improved parcels of real estate. Utility may be increased or decreased, and changes in value may result. No neighborhood or district is static; although change usually proceeds slowly, it is always occurring.

Neighborhood and District Life Cycle

Because neighborhoods and districts are perceived, organized, constructed, and used by human beings, each has a dynamic quality of its own. Appraisers describe this quality as the *life cycle* of a neighborhood or district. The complementary land uses that comprise neighborhoods and the homogeneous land uses that comprise districts typically evolve through four stages.

1. *Growth—a period during which the neighborhood gains public favor and acceptance*

2. *Stability—a period of equilibrium without marked gains or losses*
3. *Decline—a period of diminishing demand*
4. *Revitalization—a period of renewal, modernization, and increasing demand*

Although these stages describe the evaluation of neighborhoods and districts in a general way, they should not be overemphasized as guides to market trends. Many neighborhoods and districts remain stable for a very long time; decline is not necessarily imminent in all older areas. Unless decline is caused by a specific external influence—e.g., the construction of a new highway that changes traffic patterns—it may proceed at a barely perceptible rate and can be interrupted by a change in use or a revival of demand. There is no set life expectancy for a neighborhood or district, and the life cycle stages are not always sequential. At any point in the cycle, a major change can interrupt the order of the stages. For example, a major change can cause a neighborhood that is in a stage of growth to decline precipitously rather than stabilize.

After a period of decline, a neighborhood may undergo a transition to other land uses or its life cycle may begin again due to revitalization. Neighborhood revitalization often results from organized rebuilding or restoration undertaken to preserve architectural heritage. It may also be caused by a natural rekindling of demand. The rebirth of an older, inner-city neighborhood, for example, may simply be due to changing preferences and life styles, with no planned renewal program.

Gentrification and Displacement

One relatively recent neighborhood phenomenon is *gentrification, in which middle- and upper-income people purchase neighborhood properties and renovate or rehabilitate them.* The residents displaced by this process are often lower-income individuals, who moved into these older, urban neighborhoods when middle- and upper-income groups left or began to find the neighborhoods unappealing and unattractive. Often two or more low-income households would occupy what was formerly a single-family residence. Such neighborhoods often became blighted.

Gentrification appears to be the result of a preponderance of smaller families and single persons who choose to live in a city and enjoy the proximity to its activities.

ANALYSIS OF VALUE INFLUENCES IN NEIGHBORHOODS

The forces that influence value, which are manifested in the similar characteristics of properties in a neighborhood, are important in neighborhood analysis. These similar characteristics identify influences that have affected value trends in the past and may affect values in the future. The forces that influence value are also manifest in districts and, therefore, are important in district analysis. The discussion that follows focuses on neighborhoods, but generally applies to districts as well.

NEIGHBORHOOD RENOVATION

(H. Armstrong Roberts, Inc.)

Social Considerations

A neighborhood's character may be revealed in the reasons why occupants live or work in the area. Occupants are attracted to a locale for its status, physical environment, services, affordability, and convenience.

In performing a neighborhood analysis, an appraiser identifies relevant social characteristics and influences. To identify and describe these characteristics, the appraiser must be aware that the characteristics that have the greatest influence on property values in a neighborhood tend to overlap. The overall desirability of the subject neighborhood in relation to other, competing neighborhoods is, of course, reflected in their respective price levels.

In neighborhood analysis, relevant social characteristics include

- Population density, which is particularly important in central business districts and high-rise residential neighborhoods
- Occupant skill levels, which are particularly important in industrial or high-technology districts
- Occupant age levels, which are particularly important in residential neighborhoods
- Occupant employment types, including types of unemployment (e.g., temporary, seasonal, or chronic)
- Extent or absence of crime
- Extent or absence of litter
- Quality and availability of educational, medical, social, recreational, cultural, and commercial services
- Presence or absence of community or neighborhood organizations (e.g., improvement associations, block clubs, crime watch groups)

It is difficult, if not impossible, to identify and measure the social preferences of the many individuals who comprise a given market and to relate these preferences to an effect on property value. Therefore, an appraiser should not place too much reliance on social influences in arriving at a value conclusion. From an appraiser's viewpoint, the social characteristics of a residential neighborhood are significant only when they are considered by the buying public and can be objectively and accurately analyzed. Although race, religion, and national origin are social characteristics, they have no direct relationship to real estate values. Professional appraisers know that they must perform unbiased neighborhood analyses.

Economic Considerations

Economic considerations relate to the financial capacity of neighborhood occupants to rent or own property, to maintain it in an attractive and desirable condition, and to renovate or rehabilitate it when needed. The economic characteristics of neighborhood residents and the physical characteristics of the area and of individual properties may indicate the relative financial strength of area occupants and how this strength is reflected in neighborhood development and upkeep.

Ownership and rental data can provide clues to the residents' financial capability. The income levels revealed by recent census information, newspaper surveys, and private studies may indicate the prices at which occupants can afford to rent or purchase property. Vacancy statistics compiled by newspapers, the U.S. Postal Service, and other fact-finding agencies as well as other significant information, such as the number of properties for rent or sale in classified newspaper ads, help an appraiser estimate the strength of demand and the extent of supply.

The existence of vacant lots or acreage suitable for development in an area may suggest future construction activity or indicate a lack of demand. Current construction creates trends that affect the value of existing improvements. A careful study of these trends can help an appraiser predict the probable future desirability of an area. Block-by-block information helps identify the direction of growth. A neighborhood may be developing, static, declining, or in a period of revitalization. A trend may be a local phenomenon or it may affect the entire community. A change in the economic base on which a community depends (e.g., the addition or loss of a major employer) is frequently reflected in the rate of population growth or decline. Sales demand tends to remain strong and rental occupancy levels are high when the population is growing; demand weakens and occupancy levels decrease when the population is declining.

To analyze a neighborhood's economic characteristics, an appraiser modifies general analytic procedure to include the identification and analysis of economic trends—preferably over a three- to five-year period. Then the appraiser decides which economic variables significantly determine value differences among neighborhoods and compares the current economic characteristics of competing neighborhoods.

The economic characteristics that an appraiser may consider include

- Occupant income levels
- Extent of occupant ownership
- Property rent levels
- Property value levels
- Vacancy rates for various types of property
- Amount of development and construction
- Effective ages of properties
- Changes in property use

Governmental Considerations

Governmental considerations relate to the laws, regulations, and taxes that impinge on neighborhood properties and the administration and enforcement of these constraints. Some buyers are interested in neighborhoods that are subject to effective zoning laws, building codes, and housing and sanitary codes. The property tax burden associated with the benefits provided and the relative taxes and benefits provided by other neighborhoods are also considered. The enforcement of applicable codes, regulations, and restrictions should be equitable and effective. An appraiser gathers data about the governmental characteristics of the neighborhood and compares them with the characteristics of other, competing neighborhoods.

Tax burdens in different neighborhoods can vary significantly and variations in taxes are a significant basis for comparison. Sometimes, the level of special assessments in a location can become so heavy that the marketability of property is seriously affected. The benefits resulting from these assessments may not enhance the obtainable sale prices of properties in proportion to their cost; nevertheless, the cost must be offset. As a rule, properties that are subject to special assessments can be expected to bring lower sale prices than comparable properties that are not subject to these taxes. For example, consider two identical properties located in the same block on different streets that are each worth $75,000 free of encumbrances. If one is subject to a special assessment lien of $3,000, its market value subject to the lien may be $72,000, even though an uninformed buyer might not discount for the lien.

Divergent tax rates may also affect market value. Local taxes may favor or penalize certain property types. Therefore, an appraiser should examine the local structure of assessed values and tax rates to compare the tax burdens created by various forms of taxes and ascertain their apparent effect on the values of different types of real estate.

Counties or cities may have the authority to impose optional taxes such as sales and earnings taxes on residents. When the sales and local earnings taxes applicable to competing communities vary, the relative desirability of the communities may be affected. Variations in optional taxes often have a more pronounced influence on the marketability and value of commercial and industrial property than real estate taxes do.

Most communities have detailed zoning ordinances, which are designed to implement a comprehensive plan. Zoning laws typically identify zones or districts where certain land uses are permitted and others are prohibited. The broadest zoning categories are residential (often indicated by R), commercial (indicated by C), and industrial (indicated by I). These categories are divided into subcategories, such as R1a for detached, single-family residences constructed on lots of a specified minimum size, shape, and frontage. Smaller lots may be allowed in areas zoned R1b, while R2 zoning may allow duplexes, and R3 zoning might designate low-density apartments. The zoning code for a moderate-sized city may consist of several hundred pages which identify and explain the various zones. An appraiser should examine the zoning requirements for the neighborhood in question and attempt to assess their adequacy and enforcement provisions.

Private restrictions on land use may be established by private owners through provisions in deeds or plat recordings. These restrictions may specify lot and building sizes in a subdivision, permitted architectural styles, and property uses. Condominium bylaws also restrict property use. An appraiser should make certain that private restrictions do not limit property uses inordinately. In the absence of zoning, the appraiser should determine if private restrictions are adequate to protect long-term property values.

Governmental characteristics to be considered in neighborhood analysis include

- Tax burden relative to services provided, compared with other neighborhoods in the community
- Special assessments
- Zoning, building, and housing codes
- Quality of fire and police protection, schools, and other governmental services

Environmental Considerations

Environmental considerations consist of any natural or man-made features that are contained in or affect the neighborhood and its geographic location. Important environmental considerations include building size, type, density, and maintenance; topographical features; open space; nuisances and hazards emanating from nearby facilities such as shopping centers, factories, and schools; the adequacy of public utilities such as street lights, sewers, and electricity; the existence and upkeep of vacant lots; general maintenance; street patterns, width, and maintenance; and the attractiveness and safety of routes into and out of the neighborhood.

Certain buildings may be overimprovements or underimprovements due to their excessive or deficient cost, quality, or size relative to their sites and surrounding properties. For example, a six-bedroom, four-bathroom house in an area of three-bedroom, one-bath houses might be an overimprovement, or it may signal a trend toward larger homes in the area. Overimprovements may be worth less than their cost new, particularly in middle- and lower-income neighborhoods.

Topographical features can have positive or negative effects on neighborhood property values. The presence of a lake, river, bay, swamp, or hill in or near a neighborhood may give the area a scenic advantage. A hill may mean little in a mountainous area, but in a predominantly flat area an elevated or wooded section can enhance property value. A river subject to severe flooding may cause the value of homes along its banks to decline due to the risk of such a hazard. Sometimes a river, lake, or park serves as a buffer between a residential district and commercial or industrial enterprises. Land features may give a neighborhood protection against wind, fog, or flood, or they may expose it to damage.

PHYSICAL ENVIRONMENTAL FEATURES

(H. Armstrong Roberts, Inc.)

Excessive traffic, odors, smoke, dust, or noise from commercial or manufacturing enterprises can limit a residential neighborhood's desirability.

Gas, electricity, water, telephone services, and storm and sanitary sewers are essential to meet the standard of living in municipal areas. A deficiency in any of these services tends to decrease property values in a neighborhood. The availability of utilities also affects the direction and timing of neighborhood growth or development.

A neighborhood's environmental characteristics cannot be judged on an absolute scale; rather, they must be compared with the characteristics of other, competing neighborhoods. An appraiser asks: Do the terrain, vegetation, street patterns, structural density, property maintenance, public utilities, and other attributes of one neighborhood render it more or less desirable than other neighborhoods? What is the relative desirability of the neighborhood's location?

Location

Location represents the time-distance relationships, or linkages, between a property or neighborhood and all other possible origins and destinations of people going to or coming from the property or neighborhood. Time and distance are measures of relative access. Usually, all the properties in a neighborhood have the same or very similar locational relationships with common origins and destinations. These relationships are graphically depicted in Figure 8.1.

Figure 8.1   Situs Relationships

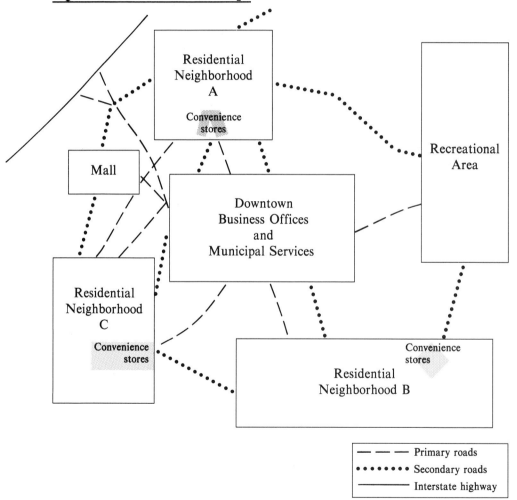

To analyze the impact of the location of a neighborhood, an appraiser must identify important linkages and measure their time-distances by the most commonly used types of transportation. The most suitable type of transportation usually depends on the preferences and needs of neighborhood occupants. It is not enough to note that transportation exists; the type of service provided and how it addresses the needs of neighborhood occupants must be considered.

Linkages should be judged in terms of how well they serve the typical users of real estate in the neighborhood. For example, in analyzing a single-family residential neighborhood, an appraiser considers where typical occupants need to go. If adequate facilities are not available for necessary linkages, the neighborhood will not be regarded as favorably as competing neighborhoods that have better linkages. For single-family residential neighborhoods, linkages with schools, grocery stores, and employment centers are usually the most important; linkages with recreational facilities, houses of worship, restaurants, and retail stores are less important. When current zoning does not restrict changes from the present land use, or when a change in the predominant land use is evident, an appraiser may need to determine linkages in terms of both the current and anticipated predominant land use in the neighborhood.

Public transportation is important because some people do not own automobiles and others prefer not to use them often. Thus, residential properties in remote areas with unreliable or infrequent public transportation may command lower rentals and prices than properties that are more conveniently located or have better service. The distance to public transportation is considered in relation to the people who will use it.

A study of neighborhood transportation facilities must consider the territory through which users must pass. People would rather avoid poorly lighted streets and rundown areas. Generally, the closer a property is to good public transportation, the wider its market.

The market's perception of the desirability of location in different neighborhoods can be studied by analyzing comparable sales. The dollar and percentage differences among the sale prices of similar properties in different locations can provide the basis for this analysis.

Some important environmental characteristics to be considered in neighborhood analysis are

- Land-use patterns
- Lot size and shape
- Terrain and vegetation
- Street patterns and width
- Density of structures and amount of open space
- Property maintenance and upkeep
- Availability and quality of utilities
- Nuisances and hazards (e.g., odors, noises, vibrations, fog, smoke, and smog)
- Access to public transportation
- Access to schools
- Access to stores and service establishments
- Access to parks and recreational facilities
- Access to houses of worship
- Access to workplaces

OBJECTIVITY IN NEIGHBORHOOD ANALYSIS

Appraisers should describe all amenities and detrimental conditions that are revealed in neighborhood or district analysis specifically and impartially. For example, a general reference to "pride of ownership" is too vague and subjective to indicate any actual effect on property value. Such references ascribe motives and attitudes to people, which should be avoided. Rather than generalities, the appraiser should record specific, impartial observations made during a personal inspection of the neighborhood. Descriptive phrases such as "many broken windows," "tall weeds present," "no litter present," and "well-kept lawns" convey direct value-influencing information.

Appraisers' conclusions regarding neighborhood conditions and their effects on property values are considered by buyers, sellers, brokers, lenders, courts, arbiters, public officials, and other decision makers and advisers. Appraisers are often asked to provide specific evidence of neighborhood conditions and trends and to explain their findings in a written report.

DISTRICTS

The unique characteristics of districts require that special factors be considered in addition to those analyzed in residential neighborhoods. The specific value influences affecting apartment districts, commercial districts, industrial districts, agricultural districts, and other types of districts differ and frequently are not the same as the influences affecting single-family residential neighborhoods. One important factor that affects land value in all districts is the availability of public utilities, including sanitary and storm sewers and municipal or well water. Prevailing levels of real estate and personal property taxes also influence the desirability of districts and may be reflected in real estate values.

The four forces that influence real estate value affect districts. The following sections address topics that relate to the analysis of various types of districts.

Apartment Districts

In large cities, an apartment district usually covers an extensive area; in smaller cities, the district may be dispersed or limited in size. Apartment design may be multistory, garden, row, or townhouse; and units may be rented or privately owned as cooperatives and condominiums.

Although apartment districts differ from single-family residential areas, they are subject to many similar influences. Therefore, an appraiser can identify the characteristics and amenities that affect an apartment district in a manner similar to that applied to a single family residential neighborhood, but with a change of emphasis. In an apartment district, desirability and value may be influenced by

- Access to workplaces

- Transportation service
- Access to shopping centers and cultural facilities
- School facilities
- Neighborhood reputation
- Residential atmosphere, neighborhood appearance, and protection against unwanted commercial and industrial intrusion
- Proximity to parks, lakes, rivers, or other natural features
- Supply of vacant apartment sites that are likely to be developed and could potentially make present accommodations more desirable or less desirable
- Parking for tenants and guests
- Economic and social status of tenants
- Vacancy and tenant turnover rate

These characteristics and other pertinent data form the basis for an appraiser's study of rental housing. In some cities, statistics concerning the supply of apartments, vacancy rates, and rent levels are available. When statistics are not available, the appraiser must gather data through research.

Commercial Districts

A commercial district is a group of offices or stores that influences the use and value of a commercial property being appraised. Commercial districts include the enterprises along a local business street or freeway service road, a development adjacent to a traffic intersection, a regional or neighborhood shopping center, and a downtown central business district (CBD).

To analyze a commercial district, an appraiser identifies its trade area—i.e., the area the businesses serve. A commercial district and its property values are affected by factors that influence the values of surrounding properties. Therefore, the type and character of nearby land uses affect a commercial district.

For example, trends in population growth, suburbanization, and the use of private automobiles have made shopping centers important sources of commercial activity. Until the mid-1970s, inexpensive energy encouraged outward urban expansion. Large regional shopping centers and smaller community centers began to replace central business districts. Commercial businesses in shopping centers often benefitted from their association with complementary establishments, but businesses in downtown areas and strip developments did not fare so well. Commercial activity in many downtown areas has declined, but in some cases this has led to revitalization of CBDs.

During the late 1970s and early 1980s, increased energy costs had dampened outward development in some cities. Most of the new shopping centers constructed in this period were in smaller cities. Since 1983 the CBDs of certain cities have been revitalized and development has been encouraged by the general decline in interest rates.

In analyzing a commercial districts's trade area, an appraiser focuses on the quantity and quality of the purchasing power of the population likely to use the shopping area. An appraiser also considers other elements, including

- Significant locational considerations, such as time-distance from potential customers, access, highway medians, and traffic signals
- Economic trends in the buying power of the contributing residential neighborhood
- Physical characteristics such as visibility, attractiveness, quality of construction, and property condition
- Direction of observable growth
- Character and location of existing or anticipated competition
- Retailers' inventory, investments, leasehold improvements, and enterprise
- Availability of land for expansion and customer parking
- Pedestrian or vehicular traffic count
- The 100% location or core of store groupings

When analyzing a group of local retail enterprises that are not located in a shopping center, an appraiser also examines the zoning policies that govern the supply of competing sites, the reasons for vacancy and business failure, and the level of rents compared with current rent levels in new buildings.

Central Business Districts

A central business district (CBD) is the core, or downtown area, of a city where the major retail, financial, governmental, professional, recreational, and service activities of the community are concentrated. CBDs have not experienced the same pattern of growth and development as other commercial areas. Business surveys conducted by the U.S. Department of Commerce show that CBDs have lost commercial establishments and have experienced smaller sales increases than other commercial districts.[2]

Although appraisers should be aware of the general trend for CBDs, they should also recognize that many of them are undergoing revitalization. Transportation facilities in most cities are oriented to the CBD. Through downtown development associations, many downtown merchants have attempted to revitalize CBDs with improved public transportation, larger parking areas, better access, and coordinated sales promotion programs.

The diverse operations located in CBDs usually reflect several types of land use—e.g., retail stores, offices, financial institutions, and entertainment facilities. Retail clothing stores serve office employees, and other retail establishments tend to locate where large numbers of people work, shop, and live. Financial institutions often locate in areas containing other financial institutions. Major entertainment and

---

2. *Survey of Current Business* (Washington, D.C.: U.S. Department of Commerce). *Business Statistics* is a biennial supplement to this monthly publication.

cultural facilities tend to be established in or near CBDs to serve the greatest number of residents and out-of-town visitors. Different parts of the CBD attract different uses, and the enterprises within the same general use category may be diverse. For example, office buildings in different parts of a CBD may house a wide variety of business and professional uses.

Appraisers should recognize that the shifting functions within CBDs can lead to changes in land uses and potential increases in real estate values. For example, a shift from commercial use to office and entertainment uses may attract more restaurants, art galleries, and specialty shops to a downtown area.

To assess the viability of a CBD, an appraiser must consider the sales potential of various commercial products and services and determine whether establishments in the CBD can attract a share of the market. To evaluate the viability of a particular location within a CBD, the appraiser considers which use—e.g., office, hotel, retail, or entertainment—is most appropriate to the subject property's location.

Regional Shopping Centers

A regional shopping center provides a variety of general merchandise, apparel, furniture, home furnishings, services, and recreational facilities built around one or more full department stores of at least 100,000 square feet each. Regional shopping centers contain a greater variety and number of the same type of stores found in neighborhood centers. A regional center may also have banks, service establishments, medical and business offices, and theaters.

A regional shopping center's trade area may include several neighborhood centers. Although neighborhood centers compete with a regional center for certain segments of economic support, neighborhood centers serve their immediate areas and may be seen as supplementing rather than competing with the major shopping services provided by a regional center.

The largest type of shopping centers is the super-regional center, which generally serves large metropolitan areas. *A super-regional shopping center provides an extensive variety of general merchandise, apparel, furniture, home furnishings, services, and recreational facilities built around at least three major department stores of at least 100,000 square feet each.* The amount of gross leasable area in a super-regional center may exceed 1,000,000 square feet.

In addition to major department stores and other features found in regional centers, super-regional centers contain specialty shops, arcades, and restaurants. Because a super-regional center offers an exceptionally broad variety of retail goods and services, its trade area is extensive. Trade areas are also extended by major transportation arteries and linkages, so the trade areas for some super-regional centers cross state boundaries.

The siting of a super-regional shopping center is a complex task, taking into account existing regional shopping centers, demographic trends, and transportation corridors. The land costs for super-regional centers are high, and a center can significantly affect the value of surrounding properties by creating a demand for uses that complement those found within the center.

Like super-regional shopping centers, regional centers generate substantial value for the land they occupy and significantly influence the values of surrounding sites and tracts. Generally, regional centers increase the value of adjacent or nearby land because they create a demand for satellite stores, office buildings, and other commercial uses. Moreover, these centers may stimulate demand for new single-family or multifamily residential development.

Community Shopping Centers

A community shopping center is a center of between 100,000 and 300,000 square feet that usually contains one junior department store, a variety store or discount department store, a supermarket, and specialty shops. Community shopping centers may also offer professional and financial services as well as recreational facilities. A community shopping center is part of the community or area it serves.

A community center's customers are usually from an area that is 10 to 20 minutes away by car. The viability of such a center depends on the sales potential for the various products and services it offers. The market allocates this potential among the various competing establishments in the service area. Sales potential may be estimated from surveys of consumer buying patterns, which are conducted by the U.S. Department of Commerce, certain universities, and private and trade organizations. Historical patterns and changes in the number and types of competing establishments may also be studied to determine the market share of a particular center.

Neighborhood Shopping Centers

A neighborhood shopping center is the smallest type of shopping center, with a gross leasable area of between 30,000 and 100,000 square feet. Neighborhood shopping centers provide for the sale of convenience goods (e.g., food, drugs, and sundries) and personal services (e.g., laundry, dry cleaning, shoe repair, and hair styling) to satisfy the daily needs of those residing in the immediate neighborhood. Neighborhood shopping centers must offer easy access and adequate parking and they must be situated in good locations, on or near public transportation routes.

Office Districts

Office districts consist of groups of office buildings, which can range in size from small to large multistory buildings. They may contain offices that primarily house members of one profession (e.g., medicine or law) or offices that serve a variety of tenants. The offices may be executive suites of multinational corporations or back offices for small service companies.

Office districts include planned office parks and strip developments on or near major traffic arteries. Office parks are popular with some industries because they offer these firms and their customers good locations, easy access, attractive surroundings, and utility without the congestion and higher rents of the CBD. Office parks are increasingly providing facilities for service industries as well.

Industrial Districts

Land and building values in an industrial district are influenced by the nature of the district, the labor supply, transportation facilities, the economics of bringing in raw material and distributing finished products, the political climate, the availability of utilities and energy, and the effect of environmental controls. To arrive at an informed conclusion about the value of an industrial property, the appraiser must obtain pertinent data on these influences.

Industrial districts range from those that contain heavy industry such as steel plants, foundries, and chemical companies, to those that house assembly and other "clean" operations. In most urban areas, heavy- and light-use districts are established by zoning ordinances, which may limit uses and place controls on air pollution, noise levels, and outdoor operations. In older manufacturing or warehouse districts, obsolete, multistory, elevator buildings are typical and parking and expansion areas are limited. Newer manufacturing districts and industrial parks usually contain one-story buildings. Each industrial district has a value pattern which reflects the market's reaction to its location and the characteristics of its sites and improvements.

Availability of labor.   A district is desirable only if it can be filled with an adequate and suitable work force, so an appraiser must ascertain whether there is an adequate and suitable labor supply. The characteristics and pay levels of the labor force are important, as is the recent history of local labor-management relations.

Because industry depends on a labor supply, many industrial districts are located near residential communities. Workers may be attracted to a particular plant by special inducements such as a company cafeteria, other employee facilities, or social activities; a plant's parklike appearance may also attract workers.

Availability of materials.   Manufacturing operations need a convenient and economical source of raw or semifinished materials, as well as facilities to distribute manufactured products conveniently and inexpensively. The desirability of a district or site greatly depends on its access to raw materials.

Distribution facilities.   The size, weight, and nature of a commodity and the distance to its destination determine how the commodity is shipped—by air, rail, truck, or water. Access to major highways, adequate ingress and egress, and onsite parking and maneuver areas are crucial considerations for most manufacturing and warehouse operations.

Agricultural Districts

Agricultural districts vary in size from a portion of a township to several counties. Most important value influences relate to individual properties rather than an entire agricultural district, because farms may be far apart. Nevertheless, the physical features of an agricultural district are usually representative of the individual farms and contribute to their desirability. To define an agricultural district, an appraiser considers soil types, the crops grown, typical land use, the average size of a farming operation in the district, and whether the operation is run by an owner or a tenant.

Grain farm districts are usually characterized by soil types and topography that are conducive to growing and harvesting crops such as corn and wheat. Orchards and groves make up another type of district in which the soil and climate combine to create a distinct economy.

Areas that cannot produce cash crops may be adapted to growing certain grasses. Generally, grasslands are used for livestock production and their boundaries are determined by altitude and climate.

Dairies are found where the soil is best for growing pasture grasses and hay. These areas are served by highways that lead to marketing centers where farm products are sold. Like an urban neighborhood, the farm community depends on government services such as roads and schools, the availability of utilities, and proximity to cultural institutions, markets, and shopping centers.

Specialty Neighborhoods and Districts

Some areas that contain specialized activities qualify as neighborhoods or districts. An area can be regarded as a district or a neighborhood if it has common functions or land uses. Although similar procedures are used to analyze all neighborhoods and districts, the specific characteristics that contribute to an area's desirability and value vary according to its function.

Medical Districts

A district may be composed entirely of hospitals, health care facilities, and physicians' offices. A medical district may comprise one or more hospitals with related facilities such as parking lots and patient services buildings, a number of physicians' offices, and several pharmacies. Medical districts can be found in densely populated urban areas and in spacious, parklike settings.

The desirability and value of a particular property, such as a doctors' office building, depend on its age and proximity to hospitals and other medical offices. The quality of professional personnel and the availability of modern equipment are also important considerations.

Research and Development Parks

Research and development parks may contain the research and development departments of large drug, chemical, or computer companies, or they may cater to firms that specialize in research activities. Research firms are usually small and specialize in identifying and developing new products, which are sold to other firms. Occasionally, a small research firm will create, develop, and market a new product with considerable success, but then the nature of the firm must shift from research to marketing.

Research and development parks are often sponsored and promoted by universities. Proximity to a university can provide a research operation with a convenient source of technical expertise and qualified employees. Universities may sponsor a park to sell excess land, provide employment for students and faculty, and raise an area's level of economic activity.

High Technology Parks

Firms engaged in high technology activities often locate near one another or in parks where technical expertise may be available from a nearby university or research park. Electronics and computer firms have dominated high technology parks, but firms involved with space equipment, drugs, cosmetics, and aviation may also have offices in these areas.

Education Districts

Local schools, colleges, and universities may constitute a district if they have several buildings or facilities and are considered an integral part of the surrounding residential neighborhood. Educational districts may contribute economically, as well as socially and culturally, to the surrounding community. Colleges and universities often attract students from far away who bring income to the community and thus contribute to its economic base. In some towns and smaller cities, universities and colleges may provide most of the economic base. An education district should be readily accessible to the surrounding residential neighborhood.

Historic Districts

Since 1931, when the first historic district zoning ordinance was passed in the United States,[3] interest in preserving historically and architecturally significant properties has grown and given rise to a unique type of district. The establishment of historic districts is one of the most widely applied and rapidly developing techniques used to preserve cultural heritage.

Historic districts may be informally perceived by observers, or they may be formally designated by local, state, or federal agencies. Historic districts are federally certified only after stringent criteria are satisfied, including substantial compliance with National Register criteria.[4] Once these criteria are met, developers, investors, and renovation specialists qualify for tax incentives such as the tax credits allowed

---

3. Russell V. Keune, ed., *The Historic Preservation Yearbook* (Bethesda, Md.: Adler & Adler, 1984), p. 461. See also William E. Lockard, Jr. and Dudley S. Hinds, "Historic Zoning Considerations in Neighborhood and District Analysis," *The Appraisal Journal*, October 1983.

4. Keune, p. 328.

under the Economic Recovery Tax Act of 1981. The tax credits for rehabilitating older buildings described in this legislation have been reduced in the Tax Reform Act of 1986.

Historic districts may include residential property, commercial property, industrial property, or other types of property alone or in combination with one another. Appraisers must become thoroughly familiar with the criteria applicable to each district's designation status and how these criteria are, or may be, applied to properties within its boundaries.

NEIGHBORHOOD AND DISTRICT ANALYSIS IN FORM REPORTS

Some organizations, businesses, and federal agencies have developed forms to standardize the reporting of appraisal data. The most widely used form is the Uniform Residential Appraisal Report form. (See Figure 8.2). Appraisal forms include spaces for recording many variables that are important to neighborhood analysis. However, written reports may provide a broader scope and content and may better serve the needs of the appraisal. The Appraisal Institute's Standards of Professional Practice require that any report communicating the results of an appraisal comply with specific reporting guidelines.[5]

SUMMARY

Through neighborhood and district analysis, an appraiser studies how value influences affect property. A *neighborhood* is defined as a group of complementary land uses; a *district* is a type of neighborhood that is characterized by homogeneous land use.

The relative uniformity of a neighborhood may result from similarities in 1) physical features, and physical barriers created by either the terrain or the location of major transportation arteries; 2) population characteristics, or 3) factors affecting land use and income-producing potential. The more limited boundaries of a district may depend on the subject property's proximity to an adjacent neighborhood where the land use is different or on the influence of the properties that are nearest to the subject.

To define the boundaries of a neighborhood or district, the appraiser should inspect the physical characteristics of the area in which the subject property is

---

5. Standard Rule 2-4 states, "Each written report or communication concerning the results of an appraisal must comply with the following specific reporting guidelines. An appraiser must...(f) set forth the appraisal procedures followed, the data considered, and the reasoning that supports the analyses, opinions, and conclusions....," American Institute of Real Estate Appraisers, *Standards of Professional Practice.*

Figure 8.2 Neighborhood Analysis Section of the URAR

NEIGHBORHOOD			Urban	Suburban	Rural
LOCATION			Urban ☐	Suburban ☐	Rural ☐
BUILT UP			Over 75% ☐	25-75% ☐	Under 25% ☐
GROWTH RATE			Rapid ☐	Stable ☐	Slow ☐
PROPERTY VALUES			Increasing ☐	Stable ☐	Declining ☐
DEMAND/SUPPLY			Shortage ☐	In Balance ☐	Over Supply ☐
MARKETING TIME			Under 3 Mos. ☐	3-6 Mos. ☐	Over 6 Mos. ☐

PRESENT LAND USE	%	LAND USE CHANGE	PREDOMINANT	SINGLE FAMILY HOUSING	
				PRICE $ (000)	AGE (yrs)
Single Family	___	Not Likely ☐	OCCUPANCY		
2-4 Family	___	Likely ☐	Owner ☐	Low	
Multi-family	___	In process ☐	Tenant ☐	High	
Commercial	___	To: _____	Vacant (0-5%) ☐	Predominant	
Industrial	___		Vacant (over 5%) ☐		
Vacant	___				

NEIGHBORHOOD ANALYSIS	Good	Avg.	Fair	Poor
Employment Stability	☐	☐	☐	☐
Convenience to Employment	☐	☐	☐	☐
Convenience to Shopping	☐	☐	☐	☐
Convenience to Schools	☐	☐	☐	☐
Adequacy of Public Transportation	☐	☐	☐	☐
Recreation Facilities	☐	☐	☐	☐
Adequacy of Utilities	☐	☐	☐	☐
Property Compatibility	☐	☐	☐	☐
Protection from Detrimental Cond.	☐	☐	☐	☐
Police & Fire Protection	☐	☐	☐	☐
General Appearance of Properties	☐	☐	☐	☐
Appeal to Market	☐	☐	☐	☐

Note: Race or the racial composition of the neighborhood are not considered reliable appraisal factors.

COMMENTS: _____

located, draw preliminary boundaries on a map by connecting the points where physical characteristics change, and test these boundaries against demographic data on the ages, occupations, and income and educational levels of the occupants. The appraiser must also determine whether changes in the neighborhood may exert an upward, stabilizing, or downward effect on the value of properties. Change may be evidenced by the level of maintenance in the neighborhood, the introduction of new land uses into the neighborhood, or the overall growth pattern of the larger metropolitan area in which the neighborhood is located.

Neighborhoods and districts often go through a four-stage life cycle, experiencing *growth*, *stability*, *decline*, and *revitalization*. Not all neighborhoods follow this cycle. The growth of a neighborhood may be interrupted, or a neighborhood may remain stable until it is revitalized, thus bypassing the decline stage.

Neighborhood analysis focuses on the four forces that influence value: social, economic, governmental, and environmental considerations. Social characterisitics relate to the occupants' motivations for living or working in a neighborhood. Social characterisitics include population density, occupant profile, safety and sanitation, the availability and quality of services, and the presence or absence of community organizations. An appraiser considers the social characteristics of a residential neighborhood only insofar as they relate to the buying public and can be objectively analyzed.

The economic characteristics of a neighborhood refer to the occupants' financial capacity to rent or own property and to maintain and rehabilitate it. An appraiser identifies general economic trends over a three- to five-year period, isolates the economic variables that affect values in different neighborhoods, and compares the economic characteristics of competing neighborhoods. Economic characteristics include occupant income levels, the extent of occupant ownership, rent levels, property values, vacancy rates, the extent of development and construction, the effective ages of properties, and changes in property use.

The governmental characteristics considered in neighborhood analysis pertain to the regulations and taxes imposed on property and the administrative machinery needed to enforce legal compliance. Governmental characteristics include the legal tax burden relative to the services provided; any special assessments; zoning, building, housing, and sanitary codes; private restrictions relating to lot or building size, architectural style, or property use; and the quality of fire and police protection, schools, and other government services.

Environmental characteristics identify any natural or man-made features that are contained in, or exert an effect on, a neighborhood. These features, which may contribute to or detract from the desirability of a neighborhood, can be measured in terms of the differences in the sale prices of comparable properties located in different neighborhoods. Environmental characteristics include land use patterns, lot size and shape, topography and vegetation, street patterns and width, building density and amount of open space, property maintenance, the adequacy of utilities, environmental nuisances and hazards, and time-distance *linkages*, which indicate the neighborhood's accessibility to public transportation, work areas, and other essential services and facilities.

To analyze special types of districts, appraisers must consider their unique features. Residential districts contain single-family homes or apartments of various types.

Commercial districts are characterized by a great diversity of business services and include central business districts as well as regional or super-regional shopping centers. Community shopping centers, which are often located along transportation corridors, and neighborhood shopping centers, which are frequently found along a strip or around a traffic intersection, generally provide a more limited scope of services.

In valuing commercial property, an appraiser should consider the size and purchasing power of the trade area, the location of the enterprise within the center, linkages with the firm's clientele, the volume of traffic through the area, the direction of present and future growth, the inventory and condition of the enterprise, and the existing or anticipated competition.

Office districts may house facilities for service industries, or they may contain professional and corporate offices. Heavy industry, assembly plants, and manufacturing factories and warehouses usually are found in older industrial districts. In valuing industrial districts, appraisers investigate the availability of a suitable labor supply, essential raw or semifinished materials, and distribution facilities. Medical districts, research and development parks, high technology parks, and education districts are all specialized districts. Agricultural districts are described by the predominant farming type and the soil and climatic conditions that foster this use. Historic districts are designated by government agencies to preserve properties that are historically and architecturally significant.

9 Land or Site Description

Appraisal assignments may be undertaken to estimate the value of land only or the value of both land and improvements. In either case, an appraiser must make a detailed description and analysis of the land. Land can be raw or improved; raw land can be undeveloped or in agricultural use. Land may be located in rural, suburban, or urban areas; and it may have the potential to be developed for residential, commercial, industrial, agricultural, or special-purpose use. *A site is land that is improved so that it is ready to be used for a specific purpose.* A site can have both onsite and offsite improvements which make it suitable for its intended use or development. Site improvements may include drainage systems, sewers, utility lines, grading, and access to roads.

In appraising any type of property, an appraiser describes and analyzes the land or site. *A land or site description is a detailed listing of factual data, including a legal description, other title and record data, and information on pertinent physical characteristics.* A land or site analysis goes further. *A land or site analysis is a careful study of factual data in relation to the neighborhood characteristics that create, enhance, or detract from the utility and marketability of the land or site as compared with competing comparable land or sites.*

To estimate the value of improved real estate, the appraiser analyzes two distinct entities—the land and the improvements. Although the two are joined physically, it is often desirable and sometimes necessary to value them separately. Separate valuations may be required by the appraisal procedure or for specific purposes, such as

- Local tax assessments
- Estimation of building depreciation
- Application of specific appraisal techniques
- Establishment of ground rent
- Eminent domain proceedings

- Estimation of casualty loss
- Valuation of agricultural land

One primary objective of land or site analysis is to gather data that will indicate the highest and best use of the land or site as though vacant so that land value can be estimated in terms of that use. (See Chapter 12 for a full discussion of highest and best use.) Whether a site or raw land is being valued, the appraiser must assess the highest and best use. When the highest and best use of land is for agriculture, an appraiser usually analyzes and values the land by applying the sales comparison and income capitalization approaches. If it seems likely that the land will be developed for urban residential use, commercial use, or some other use, an appraiser may use sales comparison analysis and special techniques of the income capitalization and cost approaches.

Land or site description and analysis are conducted to provide

- A description of the property being appraised
- A basis for analyzing of comparable sales
- A basis for allocating values to the land and the improvements
- An understanding of the property being appraised and its present use
- A foundation for determining the property's highest and best use

This chapter focuses on the description and analysis of the land component of real property. However, appraisers typically deal with land that has been improved to some degree, so the term *site* is used here except when raw land is specified. The information required for a full site description and analysis is noted and explained, and sources for obtaining this information are presented. Throughout this discussion, the property being appraised is the primary reference. However, the same type of detailed inspection and data collection are needed to analyze all comparable properties used in an appraisal.

LEGAL DESCRIPTIONS OF LAND

When land boundaries are created to differentiate separate ownerships, the land within one set of boundaries may be referred to as a *parcel, lot, plot*, or *tract*. These terms may be applied to all types of improved and unimproved land.

A parcel of land generally refers to a piece of land that may be identified by a common description in one ownership. Thus, every parcel of real estate is unique. To identify individual parcels appraisers use legal descriptions. A legal description identifies a property in such a way that it cannot be confused with any other property. Because it specifically identifies and locates a parcel of real property, a legal description may be included in an appraisal report. The legal description of a property is usually entered on a deed, which may be obtained from the owner of the property or from county records.

In the United States, three methods are commonly used to describe real property legally—the metes and bounds system, the rectangular survey system, and the lot and block system. An appraiser should be familiar with these forms of legal description and know which form or forms are accepted in the area where the appraisal is being conducted.

Metes and Bounds

The oldest known method of surveying land is the metes and bounds systems, which measures and identifies land by describing its boundaries. The system is centuries old, dating back to a time when property transfers were accomplished by a buyer and a seller walking the perimeter of a property and establishing landmarks along the way. Surveying tracts by metes and bounds was common in Western Europe and, when North America was colonized, the system was employed extensively both in transfers of property from crown governments to colonists and between colonists themselves.

Because this system was used for land transfers when the colonies were settled, it is the primary method of describing real property in the original 13 states. Eight other states have adopted the method as well. The states using metes and bounds descriptions are: Connecticut, Delaware, Georgia, Hawaii, Kentucky, Maine, Maryland, Massachusetts, New Hampshire, New Jersey, New York, North Carolina, Pennsylvania, Rhode Island, South Carolina, Tennessee, Texas, Vermont, Virginia, parts of Ohio, and the District of Columbia. Oregon uses metes and bounds along with other surveying methods.

A metes and bounds description of a parcel of real property describes the property's boundaries in terms of reference points. To follow a metes and bounds description, one starts at the point of beginning (POB), a primary survey reference point that is tied to adjoining surveys, and moves through several intermediate reference points before finally returning to the POB. The return is called *closing* and is necessary to ensure the survey's accuracy.

Bounds refer to the POB, which is also the point of return, and all intermediate points. Points, which are sometimes called monuments, are reference points such as marked stones, trees, a creek, the corner of another property, or simply a survey point. *Metes* describe the direction one moves from one reference point to another and the distances between points. One moves from point to point by knowing the courses of each point, which are identified in degrees, minutes, and seconds of an angle from the north or south. Thus, in moving from one point to another, one is moving from the vertex of one angle to the vertex of another.

Distances between angles are measured linearly in feet or meters. Sometimes, however, this measurement between angles is found to be inaccurate. When this happens, the actual distance between points or monuments is measured; actual distance takes precedence over angle measurement, especially in boundary disputes. Today, more accurate determinations of points, directions, and distances have been developed. Now permanent benchmarks, which are survey markers set in heavy concrete monuments, are used to eliminate possible confusion regarding points of beginning.

The metes and bounds system is the primary method of describing real property in 21 states, and it is often used in other states as a corollary to the rectangular survey system, especially in describing unusual or odd-shaped parcels of land. Metes and bounds descriptions frequently accompany historical land grants that authorized the transfer of property from crown governments to individuals, groups, or other political entities in the early years of the United States.

An example of a metes and bounds description is shown in Figure 9.1.

Figure 9.1   Metes and Bounds System

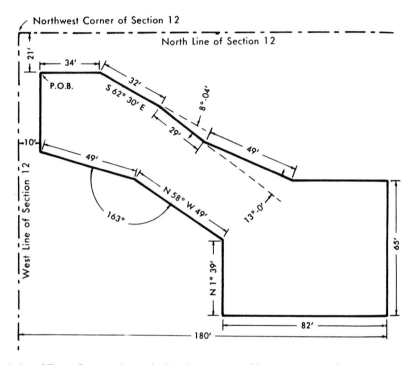

Description of Tract: Commencing at the Northwest corner of Section 12 thence South along the section line 21 feet; thence East 10 feet for a place of beginning; thence continuing East 34 feet; thence South 62 degrees, 30 minutes East 32 feet; thence Southeasterly along a line forming an angle of 8 degrees, 04 minutes to the right with a prolongation of the last described course 29 feet; thence South 13 degrees, 0 minutes to the left with a prolongation of the last described line a distance of 49 feet; thence East to a line parallel with the West line of said Section and 180 feet distant therefrom; thence South on the last described line a distance of 65 feet; thence due West a distance of 82 feet; thence North 1 degree West 39 feet; thence North 58 degrees West a distance of 49 feet; thence Northwesterly along a line forming an angle of 163 degrees as measured from right to left with the last described line a distance of 49 feet; thence North the place of beginning.

RECTANGULAR SURVEY SYSTEM

As the United States began to expand to the south and west, a more convenient system of land description was needed to facilitate the sale of large tracts of land that the federal government acquired through purchases, treaties, and war. Because the government needed to generate revenue by selling the land quickly in a simple and orderly fashion, the U.S. Rectangular Survey System was created.

The *rectangular survey system*, which is also known as the *government survey system*, was established by a land ordinance passed on May 20, 1785. In 1786 the first public land surveys in the United States were made in Ohio. The rectangular survey system became the principal method of land description for most land west of the Ohio and Mississippi rivers. Florida, Alabama, and Mississippi were also included in the system, but any land that was settled or colonized prior to the ordinance was not.

The initial reference points for government surveys were established by the commissioner of the U.S. General Land Office. From each point specified, true east-west and north-south lines were drawn. The east-west lines are called *base lines* and the north-south lines are called *principal meridians*. Each meridian has a unique name and is crossed by its own base line. Once these base lines and principal meridians were established, land could be located accurately.

The land surveyed under the rectangular survey system is divided by north-south lines six miles apart called *range lines*, and by east-west lines six miles apart called *township lines*. The rectangles created when the lines intersect are called *townships*. The standard township is six miles square and contains 36 square miles. When applied to surveying, the term *township* has two meanings: a location on a line north or south of a base line and a square of land that measures six miles by six miles. (In some states, *township* refers to a political subdivision similar to a county.)

The intersection of a base line and a principal meridian is the starting point from which the range lines and township lines are counted to locate a specific township in a legal description. Ranges are numbered east and west from the principal meridian; townships are numbered north and south from the base line.

In Figure 9.2, the shaded township is called Township 4 North, Range 3 East. It is four township rows north of the base line and three range lines east of the principal meridian. If this property were located in northern California, it would be called Township 4 North, Range 3 East, Mt. Diablo Base and Meridian, which would be abbreviated T.4N, R.3E., M.D.B.&M.

Townships are divided into 36 sections, each of which is one mile square and contains 640 acres. For a more specific description of a parcel, a section may be divided into quarter-sections and fractions of quarter-sections (see Figure 9.3). To accommodate the spherical shape of the earth, additional lines called *guide meridians* are drawn every 24 miles east and west of the principal meridian. Other lines, called *standard parallels*, are drawn every 24 miles north and south of the base line. These correction lines are used to adjust the rectangular townships to fit the curvature of the earth.

Sectioned land descriptions are commonly used and easily understood. A properly written legal description goes from the specific to the general—i.e., it begins with the exact site and ends with the base and meridian. The township illustrated in Figure 9.2 is the third one east and the fourth one north from the principal base and meridian; therefore, it is called Township 4 North, Range 3 East. Similarly, in Figure

9.3 the shaded 20-acre parcel located in the southeast part of the section is properly described as follows: The west half of the northeast quarter of the southeast quarter of Section 10, Township 4 North, Range 3 East, Mt. Diablo Base and Meridian.

Figure 9.2   Government Survey System

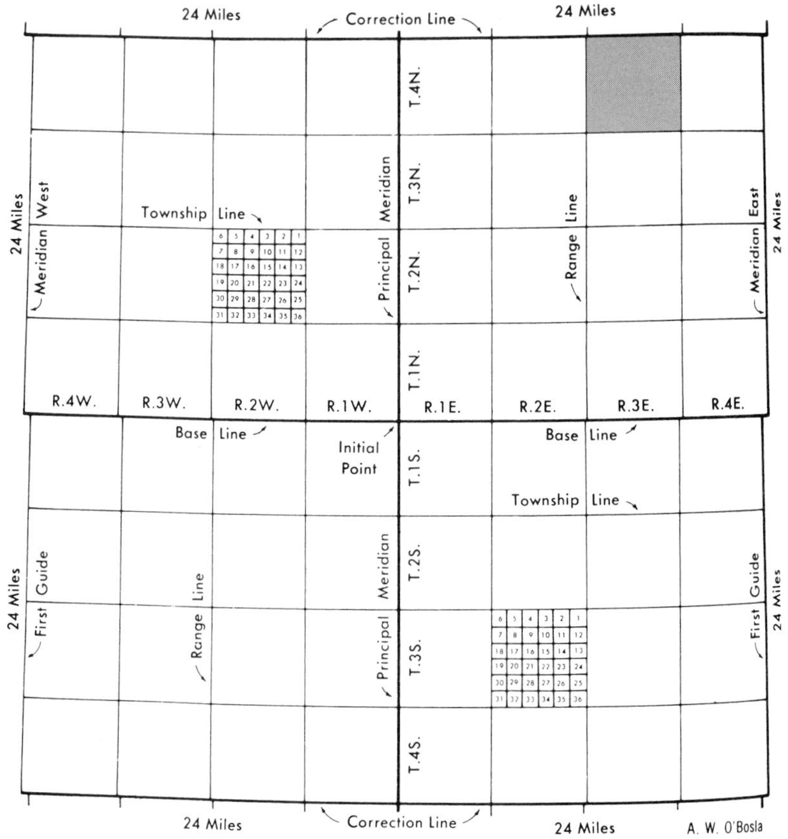

Source: John S. Hoag, *Fundamentals of Land Measurement* (Chicago: Chicago Title Insurance Company, 1976), p. 8. Reprinted through courtesy of Chicago Title Insurance Company.

If this were a full-sized section, the property described would contain 20 acres. However, townships are adjusted for the curvature of the earth and some do not contain precisely 640 acres, so this section may not contain exactly 20 acres. Furthermore, the township's northern boundary is not exactly six miles long, due to the curvature of the earth and to the convergence of the meridians. This discrepancy and any others caused by errors in measurement are allowed for in the most westerly half-mile of the township. Irregular townships may also be due to preexisting land grants and the boundaries of navigable waters.

Shortages and overages in the acreages of sections are usually found in the north and west corners of townships. Fractional sections and government lots may also be found where adjustments were necessary.

Figure 9.3   Division of a Section of Land

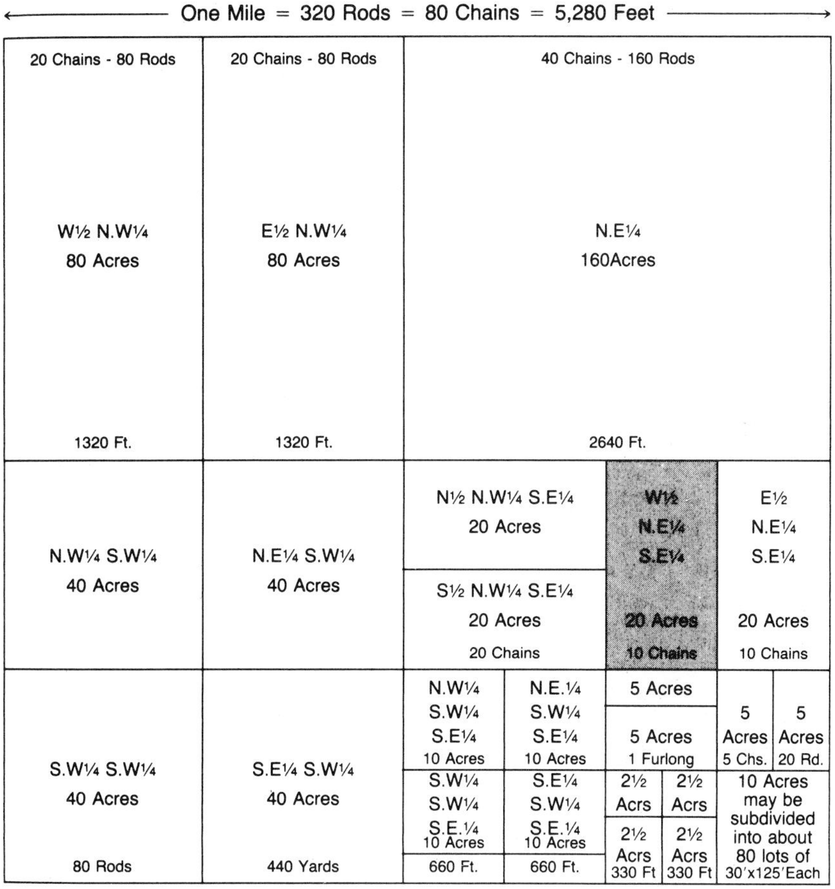

← One Mile = 320 Rods = 80 Chains = 5,280 Feet →		
20 Chains - 80 Rods	20 Chains - 80 Rods	40 Chains - 160 Rods

Division of a Section of Land diagram:

- **W½ N.W¼** — 80 Acres — 1320 Ft.
- **E½ N.W¼** — 80 Acres — 1320 Ft.
- **N.E¼** — 160 Acres — 2640 Ft.

- **N.W¼ S.W¼** — 40 Acres
- **N.E¼ S.W¼** — 40 Acres
- **N½ N.W¼ S.E¼** — 20 Acres
- **S½ N.W¼ S.E¼** — 20 Acres — 20 Chains
- **W½ N.E¼ S.E¼** — 20 Acres — 10 Chains
- **E½ N.E¼ S.E¼** — 20 Acres — 10 Chains

- **S.W¼ S.W¼** — 40 Acres — 80 Rods
- **S.E¼ S.W¼** — 40 Acres — 440 Yards
- **N.W¼ S.W¼ S.E¼** — 10 Acres — 660 Ft.
- **N.E¼ S.W¼ S.E¼** — 10 Acres — 660 Ft.
- 5 Acres
- 5 Acres — 1 Furlong
- **S.W¼ S.W¼** 2½ Acrs / **S.E¼ S.W¼** 2½ Acrs
- **S.E.¼** 10 Acres 2½ Acrs / **S.E.¼** 10 Acres 2½ Acrs — 330 Ft 330 Ft
- 5 Acres — 5 Chs. / 5 Acres — 20 Rd.
- 10 Acres may be subdivided into about 80 lots of 30'x125' Each

Geodetic Survey Program

As part of the rectangular survey system, the U.S. government also maintains an active geodetic survey program. Geodetic surveys are performed to map large land areas, taking into account the curvature of the earth's surface. These technically sophisticated surveys are performed for a number of purposes, including the compilation of land elevation data to create topographic maps. The nation's geodetic survey effort is conducted by both the U.S. Coast and Geodetic Survey and the U.S. Geological Survey.

Figure 9.4   U.S. Department of the Interior Geological Survey

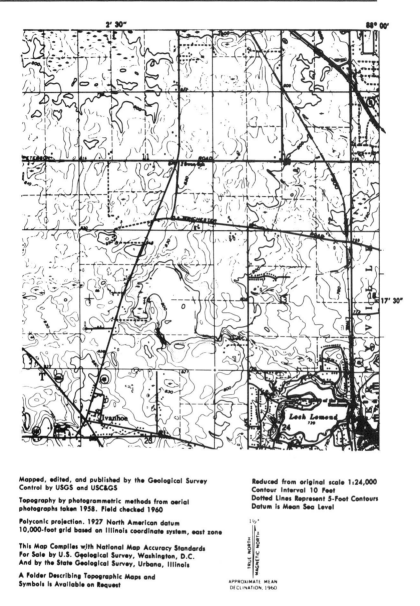

Mapped, edited, and published by the Geological Survey
Control by USGS and USC&GS

Topography by photogrammetric methods from aerial
photographs taken 1958. Field checked 1960

Polyconic projection. 1927 North American datum
10,000-foot grid based on Illinois coordinate system, east zone

This Map Complies with National Map Accuracy Standards
For Sale by U.S. Geological Survey, Washington, D.C.
And by the State Geological Survey, Urbana, Illinois

A Folder Describing Topographic Maps and
Symbols is Available on Request

Reduced from original scale 1:24,000
Contour Interval 10 Feet
Dotted Lines Represent 5-Foot Contours
Datum is Mean Sea Level

APPROXIMATE MEAN
DECLINATION, 1960

The topographic maps prepared under the direction of the U.S. Geological Survey, which are referred to as *quadrangles*, provide much information that is useful in land descriptions. Base lines, principal meridians, and township lines are shown along with topographic and cultural features. The topographic features commonly depicted on these maps include land elevations, which are represented by contour lines at specified intervals, rivers, lakes, intermittent streams and other bodies of water, poorly drained areas, and forest. The cultural features identified include improved and unimproved roads, highways, bridges, power transmission lines, levees, railroads, airports, and the locations of churches, schools, and other buildings.

Topographic maps are published in series, which refer to the number of minutes of longitude and latitude representing the boundary of a quadrangle. The two most popular series are 7.5 minute and 15 minute, representing scales of 1:24,000 (one inch = 2,000 ft.) and 1:62,500 (one inch = approx. 1 mile), respectively. Quadrangles published in the 7.5 minute series provide greater topographic and cultural detail, but, their applicability to land description depends on the nature of the appraisal assignment.[1]

Lot and Block System

The lot and block system was developed either as an outgrowth of the rectangular survey system or out of the need to simplify the locational descriptions of small parcels.

The system began when land developers subdivided land in the rectangular survey system and assigned lot numbers to identify individual sites within blocks. The numbering of lots and blocks is illustrated in Figure 9.5. The maps of these subdivisions were then filed with the local government to establish a public record of their precise locations. Each block was identified precisely using a ground survey or established monuments.

Applying the lot and block system to old, unsurveyed communities helped to identify each owner's site or parcel of land. Typically, a surveyor located the boundaries of streets on the ground and drew maps outlining the blocks. Then lot lines were established by agreement among property owners. A precise, measured description was established for each lot and each was given a number or letter that could be referred to in routine transactions. For example, a lot in a rectangular survey area might be described as follows: Lot 5 of Block 18 of Adam's Orangegrove Colony, a Subdivision of the southwest quarter of Section 10, Township 3 North, Range 3 East, Mt. Diablo Base and Meridian.

Tax parcels

Some government authorities use a variation of the lot and block system to lay out tax parcels. Typically, tax parcels are established using a numerical reference to coded map books, which are maintained by the assessing authority. These descriptions then become tax parcels, and the numbers refer to the map book, the page, the block, and

---

1. Indexes of U.S. Geological Survey quadrangles for states east of the Mississippi River are available from the Eastern Distribution Branch, U.S. Geological Survey, 1200 S. Eads Street, Arlington, VA 22202. To obtain quadrangles for states west of the Mississippi, contact the Western Distribution Branch, U.S. Geological Survey, Box 25286, Federal Center, Denver, CO 80225.

the parcel number. Few jurisdictions permit tax parcels to be used as legal descriptions of property for conveyance, but an appraiser can use a tax parcel as a description when gathering data.

Figure 9.5   Lot and Block System

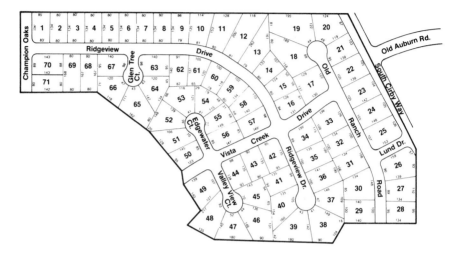

Woodridge Unit #1. Owner: Sunrise Properties, Sacramento, Calif.; engineer: Morton & Pitalo, Sacramento, Calif.

TITLE AND RECORD DATA

Before making an onsite inspection, an appraiser should obtain necessary property data from published sources and public documents. Most jurisdictions have a public office or depository for deeds where transactions are documented and made public. The accessibility of public records, which is legally known as *constructive notice*, ensures that interested individuals are able to research and, if necessary, contest deed transfers. Most county recorders' offices keep index books for land deeds and land mortgages, from which the book and page number of a recorded deed may be found. An appraiser might also find pertinent information in the property's *abstract of title*, which includes a summary of conveyances, transfers, and other facts used as evidence of title as well as any other public documents that may impair title. In addition, official county plat books may be examined in the county auditor's office.

Sometimes public records do not contain all relevant information about a particular property. Although official documents are the most dependable sources of information, they may be incomplete or not suited to an appraiser's purposes. Useful support data can be found in land registration systems, land data banks, and assessors' maps.

Ownership Information

A property's legal owner and type of ownership can be ascertained from the public records maintained by a county clerk and recorder. Local title or abstract companies may also provide information.

The most common form of property ownership is ownership in fee simple. If a property is not to be appraised in fee simple, the elements of title that are to be excluded should be indicated and carefully analyzed. If, for example, an appraiser is asked to estimate the value of a fractional ownership interest, he or she must understand the exact type of legal ownership to define the property rights to be appraised accurately.

An appraiser must also find out if the property has any outstanding rights that may affect its value. Current Appraisal Institute standards require that appraisers investigate any previous property ownership occurring within a specified number of years.[2] The appraiser must investigate the ownership of surface and subsurface rights. He or she may have access to a title report, an abstract of title, or other documentary evidence of the property rights to be appraised. Title data indicate easements and restrictions, which may limit the use of the property, as well as special rights and obligations such as air rights, water rights, mineral rights, obligations for lateral support, and easements for common walls.

Easements, rights-of-way, and private and public restrictions affect property value. Easements may provide for electrical transmission lines, underground sewers or tunnels, flowage, aviation routes, roads, walkways, and open space. Because some easements or rights-of-way acquired by utility companies or public agencies may not be used for many years, an appraiser's physical inspection of the property may not disclose any evidence of such use. The appraiser should search diligently for information pertaining to any limitations on ownership rights.

Restrictions cited in the deed may limit the type of building or the types of business that may be conducted on the property. A typical example is a restriction that prohibits the sale of liquor or gasoline in a certain place. Often a title report will not specify the details of private restrictions; a copy of the deed or other conveyance must be obtained to identify the limitations imposed on the property.

Zoning and Land Use Information

Land use and development may be regulated by city or county government, but they are often subject to regional, state, and federal controls. In analyzing zoning matters, an appraiser considers all current regulations and the likelihood of a change in zoning. Usually a zone calls for a general use, such as residential, commercial, or industrial, and then specifies a detailed type or density of use. Zoning regulations may control the height and size of buildings, lot coverage, the number of units

---

2. See Standards Rule 1-4 of the Standards of Professional Practice of the American Institute of Real Estate Appraisers.

allowed, parking requirements, sign requirements, building setbacks, plan lines for future street widenings, and other factors of importance to the highest and best use of the site.

Most zoning ordinances identify and define the uses to which a property may be put without reservation or recourse to legal intervention, and then describe the process for obtaining nonconforming use permits, variances, and zoning changes, if permitted. Although zoning ordinances and maps are public records that are available at zoning offices, an appraiser may need help from planning and zoning staff to understand the impact of zoning regulations. Often, the appraiser must contact several agencies. Many zoning and land-use restrictions are not listed in the recorded title to a property, so confirmation from controlling agencies may be necessary.

In areas subject to floods, earthquakes, and other natural hazards, special zoning regulations may impose restrictions on buildings. In coastal and historic districts, zoning restrictions may govern building location and design.

Probable changes in government regulations must also be considered. If, for example, a building moratorium or cessation of land-use applications is enforced for a stated period, achievement of a property's highest and best use may be delayed.

Public land use and government programs in an area can also affect land uses and values. The construction of public parking garages in an area, for example, may enhance or detract from property values. Requirements for the provision of mixed low- and high-cost housing can directly affect land use.

The reasonable probability of a zoning change must be considered. If the highest and best use of a site is predicated on a zoning change, an appraiser must investigate the probability that such a change will occur. The appraiser may interview planning and zoning staff or study patterns of zoning change to assess the likelihood of a change in a particular instance. The highest and best use recommendation may rely on the probability of a zoning change. The highest and best use conclusion must be supported by four elements—i.e., it must be physically possible, legally permissible, financially feasible, and maximally productive.

Assessment and Tax Information

Real property taxes in all jurisdictions are based on ad valorem assessments, and the records of the county assessor or tax collector can provide details concerning a property's assessed value and annual tax burden. Often, an appraiser obtains the property inventory on which the property assessment is based before conducting his or her own physical inspection and inventory of the property.

Taxation levels are significant in considering a property's potential uses. From the present assessment, the tax rate, and a short history of tax rates, the appraiser can form a conclusion about future trends in property taxation. Assessed values are not good indicators of market value because mass appraisals tend to equalize the application of taxes rather than produce realistic appraisals of market value.

PHYSICAL CHARACTERISTICS OF LAND

In site description and analysis, an appraiser describes and interprets the value influences of all physical characteristics of the site, including the physical relationship of the improvements to the land and to neighboring properties. Important physical characteristics include site size and shape, corner influence, plottage, excess land, topography, utilities, site improvements, location, and environment. Other physical characteristics are important in agricultural lands. These include soil, drainage, and irrigation.

Size and Shape

A size and shape description includes a site's dimensions, street frontage, width, and depth, and sets forth any advantages or disadvantages caused by these physical characteristics. The appraiser describes the site and analyzes how its size and shape affect property value. Special attention is given to any characteristics that are unusual for the neighborhood. The effects of the size and shape of a property vary with its probable use. For example, an odd-shaped parcel may be appropriate for a dwelling, but unacceptable for certain types of commercial or industrial use.

Land size is expressed in different units depending on local custom and land use. Land suitable for agriculture and large industrial tracts are described in acres. Other large tracts may be measured in miles and sometimes in rods and chains. Residential and commercial sites are usually described in square feet, although acreage may also be used. Dimensions are expressed in feet and tenths of feet for easy calculation; metric measurements such as square meters and hectares may also be used to describe land size.

Frontage is the measured footage of a site that abuts a street, stream, railroad, or other facility. The frontage may or may not be the same as the width of the rest of the property because a property may be irregularly shaped.

Often, a site that is larger or smaller than normal will not have the same square foot or acreage value as neighboring sites. Size differences can affect value and are considered in site analysis. Because the functional utility of a site often results from an ideal or optimum size and frontage-to-depth ratio, an appraiser should recognize value tendencies when appraising sites of unusual sizes or frontage-to-depth ratios. These value tendencies can be observed by studying market sales or leases of lots of various sizes.

Corner Influence

Properties with frontage on two or more streets may have a higher or lower unit value than neighboring properties with frontage on only one street. The advantage of easier access to corner sites may be diminished by a loss of privacy or a loss of utility due to setback requirements. An appraiser must determine whether the local market considers a corner location favorable or unfavorable.

Corner sites can have greater utility than interior properties because they allow more flexibility in the layout of building improvements and in the subdivision of large plots. A residence situated on a corner site may have a garage or carport at either the side or the rear of the property. Interior lots are likely to have only one entry for garages or carports. A corner location usually reduces the number of abutting owners from three to two. For commercial properties, a corner location provides both added exposure and a convenient rear service entrance. For a drive-in service, a corner site provides advantageous ingress and egress.

Corner sites can also have disadvantages. The original cost of constructing offsite improvements for corner sites is higher. Although part or all of side-street costs are apportioned to all the lots in a development, the developer frequently demands and receives higher prices for corner sites. Residences on corner sites are exposed to more traffic noise and danger and provide less security. Owners of corner sites may pay higher costs for front-footage sidewalks and assessments, and the side street setback may affect the permitted size of the building.

For mass appraisal work such as ad valorem taxation, assessors and others compile data and derive mathematical formulas to compute how the site affects a property's value. They use corner influence tables and size adjustments based on mathematical curves. However, if an appraiser uses the values derived with these formulas, unsound value estimates can result. More accurate adjustments for site depth, corner influence, and size can be made by carefully analyzing zoning restrictions, sales data, market attitudes, and preferences.

Plottage

Plottage is an increment of value that results when two or more sites are assembled or created to produce greater utility. In some situations, highest and best use results from assembling two or more parcels of land under one ownership. If the combined parcels have a greater unit value than they did separately, plottage value is created. Plottage value may also apply to an existing site of a special size or shape that has greater utility than more conventional, smaller lots. An analysis of neighboring land uses and values will indicate whether an appraised property has a plottage value.

Plottage is significant in appraising agricultural land. Properties of less-than-optimum size have lower unit values because they cannot support the modern equipment needed to produce maximum profits. In an urban area, plottage of commercial office and retail sites and of residential apartment sites may increase the unit values of the lots assembled.

Excess Land

The portion of a property's land area that represents a typical land-to-building ratio with the existing improvements may be considered an economic unit. *Excess land, in regard to an improved site, is the surplus land not needed to serve or support the existing improvement. In regard to a vacant site or a site considered as though vacant, excess land is the land not needed to accommodate the site's primary highest and best use. Such land may have its own highest and best use or may allow for future expansion of the existing or anticipated improvement.*

If the excess land is marketable or has value for a future use, its market value as vacant land is added to the estimated value of the economic entity.

Topography

Topographical studies provide information about land's contour, grades, natural drainage, soil conditions, view, and general physical usefulness. Sites may differ in value due to these physical characteristics. Steep slopes often preclude building construction. Natural drainage can be advantageous, or it can be disadvantageous if a site is downstream from other properties that have the right to direct excess flows onto it. However, adequate storm drainage systems may offset topographic and drainage problems that would otherwise inhibit the development of such a site.

In describing topography, an appraiser must employ the terminology used in the area. What is described as a steep hill in one part of the country may be considered a moderate slope in another. In some instances, descriptions of a property's topography may be taken from published sources such as contour maps.

Surface soil and subsoil conditions are important for improved properties and for agricultural land. The soil's suitability for building is important for all types of improved property, and it is a major consideration when the construction of large, heavy buildings is being contemplated. The need for special pilings or floating foundations has a major impact on the adaptability of a site for a particular use and, therefore, on its value.

Agronomists and soil scientists measure the agricultural qualities of soil; engineering qualities are tested by engineers trained in soil mechanics. Subsoil conditions are frequently known to local builders, developers, and others, but if there is doubt about the land's soil-bearing capacity, the client should be informed of the need for soil studies. All doubts must be resolved before the land's highest and best use can be successfully analyzed.

Utilities

An appraiser investigates all the utilities and services available to a site. Offsite utilities may be publicly or privately operated, or there may be a potential need for onsite utility systems such as septic tanks and private water wells. The major utilities to be considered are sanitary sewers; domestic water; types of raw water for commercial, industrial, and agricultural uses; natural gas; electricity; storm drainage; and telephone service.

Although neighborhood analysis describes in general the utility systems that are available in an area, a site description and analysis should provide a detailed description of the utilities that are available to the appraised site. Any limitations resulting from a lack of utilities are important in highest and best use analysis, and all possible alternative sources of utility service must be investigated.

The rates for utility services and the burden of any bonded indebtedness or other special utility costs should also be considered. For commercial and industrial users, the quality and quantity of water and its cost; the costs and dependability of energy sources; the adequacy of sewer facilities; and any special utility costs or surcharges that might apply to certain businesses are particularly significant.

Accurate information on public utilities can be obtained from local utility companies or agencies, local public works departments, and providers of onsite water and sewage disposal systems.

Site Improvements

In a site description, an appraiser describes offsite, as well as onsite, improvements that make the site ready for its intended use or development. Then the appraiser analyzes how the site improvements affect value. The quality, condition, and adequacy of sewers, curbs, utility hookups, and other improvements influence a site's use and value. The appraiser also describes and analyzes land improvements such as grading, landscaping, fences, curbs, gutters, paving, walks, roads, and other manmade land improvements. Site improvements are typically valued as part of site value.

The location of any existing buildings on a site must also be described and analyzed. Many appraisers make plot plans, which show all major buildings in relation to lot lines. Land-to-building ratios are usually quite significant. In a residential area where a typical building covers one-half of the lot, an 80 to 20 building-to-land ratio may diminish a property's value. The space allotted for parking influences a site's value for business and commercial use, so the parking space-to-building ratio in a commercial property must be analyzed.

The appraiser also notes any onsite improvements that add to or detract from a property's probable optimum use. For example, a commercial-zoned lot may be improved with an 18-unit apartment building that is too valuable to demolish. If the lot could accommodate a 24-unit building, but the present structure blocks access to the potential location of additional units, an appraiser may conclude that the site is underimproved and not being used at its highest and best use.

Location

The analysis of a site's location focuses on the time-distance relationships between the site and common origins and destinations. An appraiser describes and analyzes all forms of access to and from the property and the neighborhood. In most cases, private automobile parking and the location and condition of streets, alleys, connector roads, freeways, and highways are important to land use. Industrial properties are influenced by rail and freeway access and the proximity of docking facilities. Industrial, commercial, and residential areas are all affected by the location of airports, freeways, public transportation, and railroad service.

After noting the facilities available to the site and their conditions, the appraiser analyzes how these facilities affect the site and the uses to which it can be put. Residential sites, for instance, are influenced by their access to workplaces, schools, shopping areas, recreational facilities, and places of worship. The appraiser analyzes how well the transportation facilities serve the needs of property owners in the area.

Traffic volume may be either advantageous or disadvantageous to a site, depending on other conditions that affect its highest and best use. High-volume local traffic in commercial areas is usually an asset; heavy through traffic is deleterious to most retail stores, except those that serve travelers. The volume of traffic passing a property is determined by a traffic count, which can usually be obtained from a local or state road department. Traffic counts indicate average daily traffic, peak hours, and directional flows. Observing the speed and turning movements of actual vehicles helps an appraiser judge how traffic affects a property's highest and best use.

The noise, dust, and fumes that emanate from a heavily traveled artery or freeway are detrimental to most low-density, residential lots. On the other hand, the advertising value of these major arteries can benefit offices and shopping centers, unless congestion restricts the free flow of traffic. The visibility of a commercial property from the street is an advertising asset; it is most valuable when the driving customer can easily exit from traffic and directly approach the property.

Median strips, left-turn restrictions, one-way streets, and access restrictions can all limit the potential uses of a parcel. In site analysis, the appraiser should test any probable uses of the site in relation to the effects of traffic flows. Any planned changes in access should be verified with the appropriate authority and considered in the appraisal.

Environment

Appraisers should analyze climatic conditions in terms of land use. For instance, some sites are influenced by their exposure to the sun, the wind, or other environmental factors. A very windy location can be disastrous to a resort, but beneficial to a fossil-fuel power plant. The sunny side of the street is not always the most desirable for retail shops. In hot climates, the shady side of the street ordinarily gets more pedestrian traffic and greater sales, thus producing higher rents and higher land values.

Analysis of a site's environment focuses on the interrelationships between the appraised site and neighboring properties. The effects of any hazards or nuisances caused by neighboring properties must be considered. Of particular importance are safety matters—e.g., the safety of employees and customers, of occupants and visitors, and of children going to and from school.

A site's value is also influenced by important amenities created by developments on adjoining sites such as parks, fine buildings, and compatible commercial buildings. The types of structures surrounding the property being appraised and the activities of those who use them can greatly influence site value.

Special Characteristics of Agricultural Resource Land

The following are characteristics of agricultural resource lands.[3]

- *Soil.* Precise soil surveys that indicate the soils found on properties, appropriate crops, and expected production are often available. These surveys are useful in comparing agricultural properties.
- *Drainage and irrigation.* The long-term dependability and cost of adequate drainage and water supplies should be investigated and analyzed.
- *Climate.* General climatic conditions and growing seasons affect crop production and, therefore, land value.
- *Potential crops.* The crops grown on a property are related not only to climate, soil, and irrigation, but also to the availability of labor and transportation and access to markets that make, transport, and sell the products produced from crops.
- *Environmental controls.* Cropping patterns are influenced by regulations concerning herbicides, insecticides, special equipment, air and water pollution standards, and wildlife protection.
- *Other considerations.* The locations of minerals, wildlife habitats, and streams and lakes; the distances from populated areas; recreational land uses; and many other considerations must be analyzed in appraising agricultural land. Special tax provisions, such as reduced taxes on agricultural or resource properties should also be studied.

SUMMARY

An appraisal assignment may involve the valuation of *raw land* (i.e., land that is undeveloped, in agricultural use, or intended for development), land constituting a *site* (i.e., land so improved that it is ready to be used for a specific purpose), or the land component of an improved property. In each of these cases, the appraiser must describe and analyze the land or site. A land or site description is a detailed listing of data that includes a *legal description*, other title and record data, and information on the physical characteristics of the land. In land or site analysis, these data are carefully studied in relation to the neighborhood characteristics that affect the utility

---

3. For a thorough discussion of the methods used to describe and analyze the significant characteristics of land used for agricultural production, see *The Appraisal of Rural Property* (Chicago: American Institute of Real Estate Appraisers, 1983).

and marketability of the land or site and comparable land or sites. The data collected in land or site description are useful in determining the highest and best use of the land or site as vacant and in estimating land value.

The three principal methods used to describe real property in the United States are the *metes and bounds system*, the *rectangular survey system*, and the *lot and block system*. The metes and bounds system describes the boundaries of a property in terms of reference points. *Bounds* include the point of beginning (POB), which is also the point of return, and all intermediate points, which may be survey points, benchmarks, or monuments. *Metes* describe the course or angular direction in which one moves from one reference point to another. Distances are measured in terms of the metes and bounds described. The metes and bounds system is used primarily in the eastern part of the United States and to demarcate irregularly shaped parcels of land that cannot be adequately described with rectangular surveys.

The rectangular survey system was established to facilitate the surveying and sale of public lands west of the Mississippi River. Six-mile square *townships*, each of which contains 36 sections, are plotted along north-south meridians, called *range lines*, and east-west base lines, called *township lines*. Each section, which comprises 640 acres, is further divided into fractional sections. In support of the rectangular survey system, the U.S. Coast and Geodetic Survey and U.S. Geological Survey publish more elaborate maps, called *quadrangles*, which take into account the curvature of the earth.

The lot and block system simplifies the description of smaller parcels within the rectangular survey system. Subdivisions of sections are divided into blocks, which are further broken down into lots. Tax parcels used for assessment are often identified using this system.

Title information can be obtained from public records kept by the county clerk and recorder. Index books to land titles and land mortgages, abstracts of title, and plat books are all useful in locating data. Using this information, an appraiser identifies the property rights to be appraised and any restrictions or special rights associated with the property.

The appraiser also considers zoning regulations, probable zoning changes, building codes, physical limitations, public land use programs, and government policies in determining the highest and best use of a land or site. The assessment on a property is rarely a reliable indication of its value. When considered in conjunction with tax trends, however, data on the assessed value of a property may help suggest its potential uses.

To describe the physical characteristics of a land parcel or site, an appraiser must consider size and shape, corner influence, plottage, excess land, topography, utilities, site improvements, location, and environment. An appraiser describes the site's width and depth, regularity or irregularity of shape, and frontage or frontage-to-depth ratio. The advantages and disadvantages of corner influence must be weighed. For land under cultivation or land proposed for commercial and residential sites, the appraiser will recommend plottage if assemblage of the land with other parcels would produce a unit value greater than the unit value of the separate parcels. When typical land-to-building ratios for properties are observed, the combination of land and improvement components creates a functional economic unit.

An appraiser studies topographical characteristics in relation to land use. Surface soil and subsoil quality are important to agriculture, while grade, natural drainage, and soil-bearing capacity are essential to the construction of improvements. An estimate of the availability and cost of utilities helps the appraiser determine the highest and best use of a land parcel. Onsite and offsite improvements that make a site ready for its intended use or development must be described to analyze their effect on site value.

Location refers to time-distance linkages and the accessibility of a land parcel. An appraiser must consider the advantages or disadvantages of a site's proximity to major transportation arteries in terms of the intended use of the land. The appraiser also addresses any environmental conditions that affect the specific land parcel. Wind and sun exposure may affect an industrial or commercial property, and the hazards, nuisances, and amenities of adjoining properties may influence a residential or commercial property.

10 Building Description

An important part of every appraisal is the description of the building or buildings on the site. An appraiser describes each building's design, layout, and construction details, which include structural components, materials, and mechanical systems. The appraiser also determines building size and the condition of each element described. The building description provides the basis for making comparisons between the subject property's improvements and improvements that are considered typically in the subject property's market.

Accurate building descriptions are essential to all valuation assignments. Through them the appraiser obtains a thorough understanding of the physical characteristics of a subject property, which is needed to identify and select suitable comparables. Building descriptions also enable the appraiser to identify the extent and quality of building improvements, calculate their reproduction or replacement costs, and determine most forms of depreciation. Therefore, the quality of building descriptions directly affects the value estimate produced by applying the three approaches to value.

ELEMENTS OF BUILDING DESCRIPTION

An appraiser prepares a building description by considering a variety of specific information in sequence. Primary concerns are the type of use currently represented by the building, the codes and regulations affecting this use, and the building size, plan, and construction. The structural details of the building's exterior and interior, as well as its equipment and mechanical systems—both original construction and subsequent improvements—are also important. An appraiser must view a building objectively and analytically, paying careful attention to all components that ultimately contribute to the determination of the building's highest and best use as improved and any alternative highest and best uses required by the assignment.

Use Classification

Real estate is usually divided into five major use groups: residential, commercial, industrial, agricultural, and special purpose. The planning, construction, and use of buildings are directed by various laws, codes, and regulations, which are enacted at all levels of government to protect the health, safety, and welfare of the public.

Zoning regulations primarily control a property's use. Existing and potential property uses must be checked against zoning regulations to determine if they are conforming or nonconforming uses. When the present use does not conform to current zoning regulations, the appraiser should consider how this fact might affect property value.

Building design and construction are controlled by building, plumbing, electrical, and mechanical codes. When violations exist, the appraiser estimates the cost to correct the deficiency and judges how it will affect value.

Building Codes

Building codes are enacted at local, state, and federal levels. More than half of the states in the United States have codes that control various kinds of buildings constructed within their borders. Federal regulations are established to ensure occupational health and safety, environmental protection, pollution control, and consumer protection. Generally, building codes establish requirements for the construction and occupancy of buildings and contain specifications for building materials, methods of construction, and mechanical systems. These codes also establish standards of performance and address considerations such as structural strength, fire resistance, and adequate light and ventilation.

To describe a building adequately, an appraiser should be familiar with the codes in the area and examine whether the building complies with all applicable codes. A building that is not in compliance probably has less value than a similar building that is. Bringing a building up to code may produce additional expenses for its owners and may limit the building's future use.

Because building codes are not uniformly established and enforced, industrial and professional groups have developed model codes, which are gradually being accepted throughout the country, especially in large communities.

Size

For each building description, the appraiser must determine the building's size. This may be a formidable task because the methods and techniques used to calculate building size vary regionally, differ among property types, and may reflect biases that significantly affect value estimates. The appraiser must know which techniques of measurement are used in the area where the building is located, as well as those used to describe properties located elsewhere. An appraiser must also use, interpret, and report building size measurement techniques consistently within each assignment, because failure to do so can impair the quality of the appraisal report.

An appraiser uses the system of measurement commonly employed in the area and includes a description of the system in the appraisal report. One of the most common measurements, gross building area, is always calculated, but certain other building measurements can be ascertained from plans, when they are available. However, these measurements should be checked against actual building measurements because alterations and additions are often made after plans are prepared. The areas of attached porches, freestanding garages, and other minor buildings are always calculated separately.

Standards for measuring residential property have been developed by several federal agencies, including the FHA, the VA, the FNMA, and the FHLMC. Because there is a strong relationship between these agencies and the mortgage market industry, these standards have been used in millions of appraisals. The agencies use gross living area to measure single-family residences and gross building area (*GBA*) to measure multifamily buildings. *Gross living area is defined as the total area of finished, above-grade residential space.* It is calculated by measuring the outside perimeter of the structure and includes only finished and habitable above-grade living space. Finished basements and attic areas are not included in total gross living area. *Gross building area* (GBA) *is the total floor area of a building, excluding unenclosed areas, measured from the exterior of the walls.* It includes both the superstructure floor area and the substructure or basement area. Gross building area is also the standard of measurement for all industrial buildings.

Gross leaseable area (*GLA*) is commonly used to measure shopping centers. *Gross leaseable area is defined as the total floor area designed for the occupancy and exclusive use of tenants, including basements and mezzanines.* It is measured from the center of joint partitioning to outside wall surfaces.

Office buildings present special problems for appraisers because they are measured differently in different areas.[1] Office building descriptions should include gross, finished, and leaseable building areas. Once, most office buildings were measured in terms of net usable area, which is the area actually occupied by a tenant. Now, however, most measurement methods include the total area of the office floor in the leaseable area excluding vertical openings such as elevator shafts, stairwells, and air ducts. These methods allocate a pro rata portion of the restrooms, elevator lobbies, and corridors to each tenant; one method also includes a pro rata portion of the ground floor main lobby in each tenant's leased area. Office building management may measure for single-tenant and multiple-tenant floors in the same building

---

1. The Building Owners and Managers Association International (BOMA) in Washington, D.C., has established a methodology for measuring office building floor area. This widely used method is described in BOMA's "Standard Method for Measuring Floor Area in Office Buildings," which is periodically updated.

differently. Because these measurements vary with occupancies, an appraiser must apply a consistent method in calculating the floor-by-floor rentable area of the building.

An appraiser should never accept a statement about the size of a subject or comparable property without personally verifying the figure and clearly determining how it was calculated. If an unverified statement of size is used in an appraisal, the resulting value estimate could be erroneous and misleading.

Building measurement is further complicated by description practices in local and regional markets. For example, if condominiums are compared using a square foot standard, results may be skewed if the size of the subject property is expressed in terms of net living area, while all market data are expressed in terms of gross salable area. In both cases square footage is calculated, but the subject property's measurement must be adjusted to reflect the marketplace standard.

Accurate measurement of building size is essential in the sales comparison approach, especially when the subject and comparable properties vary in size. To adjust for size differences, identical units of comparison must be used. The selection of units of comparison is based on market analysis, experience, and judgment. The subject property's size measurement may be adjusted to reflect the system of measurement used in the marketplace, or all the properties under consideration can be reduced to a representative unit, such as square feet of gross living area or gross building area.

Building size is also important in estimating effective rent in the income capitalization approach to value. Comparable rentals rarely reflect buildings of exactly the same size. Therefore, size adjustments must be made to indicate the market rent of the appraised property. Often, comparable rental information is converted into rent per square foot. The rent for the subject property is estimated by multiplying the selected adjusted rent, based on the comparable data, by the number of square feet of leaseable area. Expense figures obtained from market data are also converted into square foot units, which may be used for income analysis as well.

The calculations used in the cost approach to value require measurements of the entire building and certain building components. Two similar buildings with the same square footage will have different costs if their exterior or interior walls are of different lengths. All significant differences must be considered when the cost of a comparable building is used to estimate the cost of the building being appraised.

BUILDING DESCRIPTION FORMAT

A complete building description includes information about the details and condition of a building's exterior, interior, and mechanical systems. Although there is no prescribed method for describing all buildings, the following outline may be used to establish a format for buidling descriptions.

    A. Exterior description
       1. Substructure
          a. Footings

        b. Slabs
        c. Piles
        d. Columns
        e. Piers
        f. Beams
        g. Foundation walls

2. Superstructure
    a. Framing
    b. Insulation
    c. Ventilation
    d. Exterior walls
    e. Exterior doors
    f. Windows, storm windows, and screens
    g. Facade
    h. Roof and drain system
    i. Chimneys, stacks, and vents
    j. Special features

B. Interior description
1. Interior walls
    a. Doors
2. Division of space
    a. Storage areas
    b. Stairs, ramps, elevators, escalators, and hoists
3. Interior supports
    a. Beams and columns
    b. Flooring system (subflooring)
    c. Ceilings
4. Painting, decorating, and finishing
    a. Basements
    b. Floor coverings
    c. Molding and baseboards
    d. Fireplaces
5. Protection against decay and insect damage
6. Miscellaneous and special features

C. Equipment and mechanical systems
1. Plumbing system
    a. Piping
    b. Fixtures
2. Systems that use energy
    a. Hot water system
    b. Heating systems
        (1) Warm or hot air
        (2) Hot water
        (3) Steam

        (4)   Electrical
    c. Heating fuels
        (1)   Coal
        (2)   Fuel oil
        (3)   Natural gas
        (4)   Electricity
    d. Air-conditioning and ventilation systems
    e. Electrical systems
  3. Miscellaneous equipment
    a. Fire protection
    b. Elevators, escalators, and speed ramps
    c. Signals, alarms, and call systems
    d. Unloading facilities
    e. Attached equipment—process related

EXTERIOR DESCRIPTION

In describing a building's exterior, an appraiser provides information about the details of the building's substructure and superstructure. When a group or complex of buildings is being described, the appraiser may also need to include information about the infrastructure. *The infrastructure is the core of development in a group of buildings or in a complex and serves as the common source of utilities or support services.* For example, the infrastructure of a building complex may provide a boiler and an electrical system that serve several structures.

Substructure

Substructure usually refers to a building's entire foundational structure, which is below grade, or ground, and includes such foundation supports as footings, slabs, piles, columns, piers, and beams. Piers do extend above ground, but in general, the substructure provides a support base on which the superstructure rests.

Footings

Footings are support parts that prevent excessive settlement or movement. The most common type of footing is a perimetric base of concrete that rests on undisturbed earth below the frost line. This base distributes the load of the walls over the subgrade. Other types of footings include plain footings, which are unreinforced and designed to carry light loads, and reinforced footings, which contain steel to increase their strength. Spread footings are frequently used where the soil has poor load-bearing capacity.

    Because footings are visible only when a building is under construction, an appraiser must obtain information about them from plans or by consulting architects, contractors, or builders. Footings that are improperly designed and constructed often

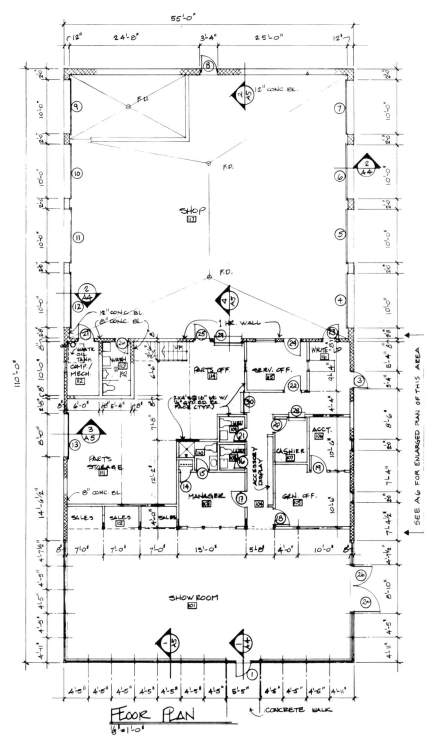

FLOOR PLAN
1/8"=1'-0"

Floor Plan of a Car Dealership

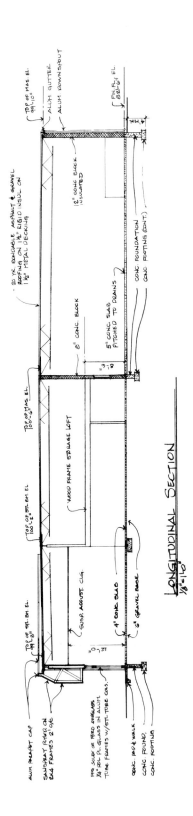

ALUM PARAPET CAP

SANDBLAST PANEL ON 2x4 FRAMES 2' O.C.

FRS SOLEX OR FRED ENVELOPE 1/4" DBL PL GLASS IN ALUM. TUBE FRAMES W/STL TUBE COLS.

CONC. PAV'T WALK
CONC. FOUND.
CONC. FOOTING.

TOP OF STL. BM. EL. 99'-8"

SUSP. ACOUST. CLG.

4" CONC. SLAB

6" GRAVEL BASE

12'-0"

TOP OF STL. BM. EL. 100'-2"

WOOD FRAME STORAGE LOFT

TOP OF MAS. EL. 100'-2"

8" CONC. BLOCK

5" CONC. SLAB PITCHED TO DRAINS

10'-3"

TOP OF MAS. EL. 99'-10"

20 YR. BONDABLE ASPHALT & GRAVEL ROOFING ON 1½" RIGID INSUL. ON 1½" METAL DECKING

ALUM GUTTER
ALUM DOWNSPOUT

12" CONC. BLOCK INSULATED

FIN. FLR. EL. 82'-0"

CONC. FOUNDATION
CONC. FOOTING (CONT.)

LONGITUDINAL SECTION
⅛"=1'-0"

Section of a Car Dealership

cause settling and wall cracks. An appraiser must observe any structural problems in the building and evaluate their effect on the property's value. If the problems can be corrected, the cost of correction is estimated. Some defects are ignored by the market and have little effect on a property's value, while others result in substantial value decreases.

A building's foundation is made of natural or prepared material. Today most foundations are made of poured concrete walls or of concrete or cinder block walls that rest on concrete footings. The foundations of many older buildings are made of cut stone or stone and brick. Mat and raft foundations, known as *floating foundations*, are used over soils that have low load-bearing capacity. They are made of concrete slabs that are heavily reinforced with steel so that the entire foundation functions as a unit. Pile foundations are made of columnar units of concrete, metal, or wood that transmit loads through soil with poor load-bearing capacity to lower levels where the soil's load-bearing capacity is adequate. The columnar units serve as substitutes for footings. Columns, piers, and grade beams are other types of foundation supports that can be used separately or combined with other foundation supports.

Superstructure

Superstructure usually refers to *the portion of the building above grade*. However, in multipurpose buildings, components such as parking garages that are above grade but not used for habitable space are often considered part of the substructure.

Framing

The structural frame is the load-bearing skeleton of a building to which the exterior and interior walls are attached. The structural frames of most houses in the United States are made of wood, although many have brick veneer siding. The three most common types of wooden frame construction are platform, balloon, and post and beam; of the three, platform framing is the most common.

In *platform construction*, one story of a building is constructed at a time and each story serves as a platform for the next. *Studs*, which are the vertical framing members, are cut at the ceiling height of the first story, then horizontal plates are laid on top, and more studs are cut for the second story.

In *balloon framing*, which is common in older, multistory, brick buildings, long studs run from the top of the foundation wall to the roof and are notched at each upper floor level to receive a horizontal framing member. Balloon framing is rarely used today because long studs cost a great deal and the framing has poor fire resistance.

Post and beam framing is composed of beams that are spaced up to eight feet apart and are supported on posts and exterior walls. The framing members used for this type of construction are much larger and heavier than those used in the other framing systems. The post and beam system was used in colonial houses and barns and it began to regain popularity in the mid-1970s.

One relatively new method of framing employs panels of framing members and siding or subflooring that are prefabricated at a mill or built at the site. Construction begins on the ground and materials are subsequently lifted as a unit and installed in place. Some buildings are constructed with solid masonry, exterior walls, which function as part of the framing system. Often, interior framing is made of steel beams or reinforced concrete; older masonry buildings have interior framing of wood beams and posts.

The form of industrial buildings has changed a great deal in the past century. At the turn of the century, the most popular type of industrial building was the multistory mill building, which had exterior masonry walls and large post and heavy beam framing systems that were often supported by solid interior masonry walls and columns. After 1900, steel began to replace timber framing, and by 1910, many multistory industrial buildings were built of reinforced concrete with rectangular columns and beams and heavy slab floors. By 1920, round, mushroom-capped columns were generally used under rectangular areas of heavier slab floors. Later, several other types of integral beam and slab construction (e.g., the tee-beam floor design with hollow tile between the tee-beams or the use of pans to form beams or waffle patterns) became common, especially in buildings that required lower live loads.

Today, large residential, commercial, and industrial buildings often have steel beams or reinforced or precast concrete framing systems. Precast units with prestressed, reinforced steel are widely employed. Tilt-up construction uses precast concrete slabs, which can be lifted into a vertical position to become exterior bearing or curtain walls. The interior frame may consist of precast and prestressed concrete beams and columns with lighter precast slabs used for the structural roof.

There has been a trend toward constructing more functional, single-story, horizontal buildings for industrial plants. The framing for these buildings is usually made of steel. *Bays*, which are the areas between columns, have become increasingly large. Bays of 30 to 50 feet are quite common, and some aircraft plants have been built with more than 100 feet between columns. When the frame must support heavy cranes, heavier and larger structural steel members are used.

When wood framing systems are defective, they can cause walls to crack, exterior walls to bulge, windows to stick, doors to open or close improperly, and the space between wall siding and masonry chimneys to be excessively wide. Steel framing is usually less expensive than precast or reinforced concrete, and it is easier and faster to erect. Steel framing does have one major disadvantage, however. Unless it is encased in heat-resistant, fireproof material such as plaster or concrete, the steel will buckle and bend in a fire, pulling adjacent members out of position and greatly increasing fire damage to the building. Reinforced and precast concrete framing is the most expensive and difficult to construct, but it is highly resistant to damage by fire.

Insulation

Insulation provides a number of benefits. It not only helps economize on fuel and ensures comfort in both warm and cold climates, but it also reduces noise transmission and impedes the spread of fire. The adequacy of building insulation and other energy conservation features are noted by an appraiser in a building description.

Before World War II, most buildings were constructed without added insulation, although the heavy building materials used then provided some insulation. Newer buildings are more energy efficient and many older buildings are being renovated to increase their energy efficiency by adding insulation. Insulation is classified by its form, which may be loose-fill, flexible, rigid, reflective, or foamed-in-place.

Loose-fill insulations, which are poured or blown by a machine into a building's structural cavities, are manufactured from mineral wool (e.g., rock, slag, or glass wool) or cellulosic fiber (e.g., recycled newsprint, wood chips, or other organic fibers).

Flexible insulations are manufactured in batt and blanket form from mineral wool or cellulosic fibers and are available in three forms. The insulation may be wrapped with kraft paper on the edges and a vapor barrier on one or both sides, faced with a vapor barrier on one side only, or friction-fit without any covering because the interlaced fibers are resilient enough to remain upright in the cavity. Flexible insulations are generally used where it is not practical to install loose-fill insulation or where the foil or kraft paper facing is needed as a vapor barrier.

Asbestos is a nonflammable, natural mineral fiber that was widely used in structures built between 1945 and 1970. Asbestos fiber poses a threat to human health when distributed in the air. Encapsulation or enclosure of asbestos is effective as a short-term solution. The Environmental Protection Agency has guidelines for the removal of asbestos when a building is being demolished or renovated. The EPA has had difficulty, however, in enforcing these regulations.

Legislation pending in the U.S. Senate (1987) would expand the role of the EPA in monitoring for asbestos and enforcing regulations on its removal. The Asbestos Hazard Abatement Act would include government and non-school buildings, owned or leased by the federal government, and possibly rental apartments and condominiums of more than nine residential units.

Opinion is divided on the effect of asbestos on the value of income-producing properties. While the presence of asbestos has hurt leasing, there is also little indication that investors are willing to sell properties at sharp discounts because of the problem.

Rigid insulations have become more popular and can be used in many parts of a building. They are available in four forms: structural wall insulation, fiberboard, structural deck insulation, and rigid board insulation.

Reflective insulation is made of foil to reflect heat that is transferred by radiation. It should be installed facing an air space of at least three-quarters of an inch and should remain free of dust or other materials that could reduce its reflective qualities.

There are two basic types of foamed-in-place insulation: urethane foam insulation and urea-formaldehyde foam insulation (UFFI). Both types are created by a chemical reaction that expands the mixture to approximately 30 times its original size and then solidifies it in about 24 hours.

In April of 1982, the Consumer Product Safety Commission banned urea-formaldehyde foam insulation in residences and schools. The ban resulted from the commission's investigation of the effects of formaldehyde gas, which can be released from the insulation at very high levels, especially immediately after installation. The ban took effect in August of 1982 and was lifted in April of 1983 by a federal court of appeals which held that the risks had not been proven. The ban was not retroactive, so it did not affect approximately 500,000 homes that have urea-formaldehyde foam insulation.

Appraisers must recognize any effects that the presence of urea-formaldehyde foam insulation may have on the market value of a structure.[2] They should be extremely cautious in valuing properties known to have or have had this type of insulation. Property sellers, real estate brokers, and salespersons representing sellers are obligated to disclose the presence of urea-formaldehyde foam insulation. Failure to fulfill this obligation could constitute a breach of a warranty of habitability and entitle the buyer to rescind his or her contract or to recover damages.

The ability of all insulation materials to resist the flow of heat is measured in R values. R value is the resistance to heat flow and is derived by measuring the British thermal units (Btus) that are transmitted in one hour through one thickness of the insulation.[3] The higher the R value, the better the insulation. There is no universal standard for the amount of insulation required because this varies with the climate and the type of building. For example, overceiling or underroof insulation with an R value of 13 might be satisfactory in a mild climate if there is gas or oil heat and no air-conditioning. In cold or hot climates, or in structures with electric heat or air-conditioning, insulation with an R value of 24 might be necessary. There has been a growing trend to superinsulate structures with insulation of much higher R values.

Ventilation

In many buildings, ventilation is needed to reduce heat in closed-off areas such as attics and spaces behind walls. It also prevents the condensation of water, which collects in unventilated spaces and causes building materials to rot and decay. When water condensation seeps into insulation, it reduces its R rating. Ventilation can be accomplished with holes that range in size from one inch to several feet in diameter; these holes should be covered with screening to keep out vermin. Ventilation can also be increased by using fans.

---

2. For further information, see "Urea-formaldehyde Ban Lifted by 5th United States Court of Appeals," *The Appraiser*, May 1983; John M. Housel, "UFFI: A Potential Hazard in Residential Housing," *The Real Estate Appraiser and Analyst*, Summer 1983; and B. J. Lansink, "UFFI and Value," *The Real Estate Appraiser and Analyst*, Summer 1984.

3. Heat is measured in British thermal units (Btus). A Btu is the quantity of heat required to raise the temperature of one pound of water at or near 39.2 degrees Fehrenheit by one degree.

Exterior Walls

The two basic types of exterior walls are load-bearing and nonload-bearing walls. Load-bearing walls are often made of solid masonry, such as cement block, brick, or a combination of these materials. Load-bearing walls can also be made of poured concrete, prestressed concrete, steel beams covered with siding material, or wood framing heavy enough to support the weight of the roof and the upper stories. Load-bearing walls can be strengthened with masonry pilasters, that are attached to the exterior of the wall.

Non-load-bearing walls, which are commonly used in larger buildings, are attached to the framing system. They can be made of porcelain enamel, steel, aluminum, precast aggregate concrete slabs, or glass. For industrial buildings, less attractive, but serviceable, materials such as corrugated iron, tilt-up precast concrete slabs, asbestos board, fiberglass, and metal sandwich panels are used. When the quality of the exterior walls is below the standard for buildings in the same market, the property may suffer a loss in value.

Exterior Doors

Exterior doors are usually made of solid wood, metal, or glass. Hollow exterior doors are a sign of poor-quality construction. Commercial and industrial buildings often have large steel truck doors. There are a variety of special-purpose doors and many have automatic door openers. Special automatic doors must be described in a building description. The presence or absence of energy-conserving material such as weatherstripping around doors is also noted. To prevent air leakage through cracks at the bottom of a door, door shoes, weatherproof thresholds, and sweeps can be attached.

Windows, Storm Windows, and Screens

Wood was the first material used for windows and is still commonly used in houses. It has good insulating properties, is readily available, can take either a natural or painted finish, and is easy to install and repair. Aluminum and steel are also used for windows in residential, commercial, and industrial buildings. In describing a building, an appraiser notes the type of window and its material or manufacture. Window types include single- and double-hung windows, casement windows, and horizontal sliding windows as well as clerestory, fixed, awning, hopper, center pivot, and jalousie windows.

Because windows are a major source of heat and cooling loss, their design and installation is important. There is a trend toward reducing the size of windows and placing them higher to conserve energy and increase security. Windows should be tightly sealed, with caulking at the joints and between the wall and the window. The use of insulated glass, multiple glazing, and storm sashes helps keep cold air out and heat in. An appraiser should describe these energy-saving features in a building description.

Storm doors and windows provide good insulation. They can save typical home owners 10% to 20% of their fuel costs and can produce similar fuel savings when used in office buildings. Storm doors and windows are used in commercial and industrial buildings in areas with extreme weather conditions. Modern storm doors and windows are often made of aluminum and permanently installed with screens. Wooden storm doors and windows that must be removed and stored during the summer are becoming obsolete. Appraisers may find it difficult to judge how much storm windows and doors add to the value of a building, but analyzing what is typical in the market can be helpful.

In most of the country, screens are needed for all windows that open. Most screens have aluminum frames and, in residences, screens are often combined with storm windows. An appraiser should count all removable window and door screens and note if any are missing.

Facade

Many houses, stores, office buildings, and industrial buildings have a facade, or front, that differs from the design and construction of the rest of the building. Frame houses may have extra masonry veneer on the facade or contrasting siding. Retail stores often have elaborate fronts of glass and other decorative materials; even some industrial buildings have facades that are more elaborate than their exteriors. An appraiser describes a special facade and considers its cost and effect on the property's value.

In modern industry and commerce, public image is important. An attractive store, warehouse, industrial plant, or office building has advertising and public relations value to the occupant. Ornamentation, identifying signs, lighting, and landscaping all contribute to a building's attractiveness.

Roof and Drain System

A roof is designed and constructed to support its own weight and the pressure of snow, ice, wind, and rain. There are many types of roofs. Flat roofs are used extensively in industrial and commercial buildings, but are less common in residences. Lean-to roofs are used on sheds and saltbox houses, and gambrel roofs are popular for barns and Cape Ann and Dutch colonial houses. Other types of roofs include gable, hip, and mansard roofs. In industrial construction, monitor and sawtooth roofs are sometimes used.

The most prevalant systems of roof construction for houses are trusses, joists or horizontal beams, joists and rafters, post and beams, and panels. In commercial and industrial construction, the roof structure may be of steel or wood trusses, glued wood beams, or a steel or concrete frame with wood joists or purlins or with steel bar joists. These systems support the roof sheathing, which may be plywood, steel roof deck, lightweight precast concrete slabs, reinforced concrete slabs, or insulated sheathing in large sheets.

The roof covering prevents moisture from entering the structure. In most regions, residential roofs are made of asphalt shingles, which are available in various weights and styles, including lock-tab and seal-tab varieties. Other common residential roof coverings are shingles and shakes made of wood (usually cedar), asbestos, and cement. Fiberglass shingles have recently been introduced and metal, clay tiles, slate, and built-up or membrane roofs are also found on houses.

Many of these residential roof coverings are also used for commercial and industrial buildings. The flat roofs of these buildings are made of built-up layers of felt or composition material that are nailed to the sheathing and covered with tar. Gravel or other surfacing material helps keep the roof from drying out and cracking. Membrane roof assemblies are becoming popular for commercial and industrial buildings.

Joints in roofs are created where two different roof slopes interact or where the roof meets adjoining walls or projections such as chimneys, pipes, and ventilation ducts. All joints must be flashed. Flashing is usually accomplished by nailing metal strips of galvanized iron or copper across or under the point, applying a waterproofing compound or cement, and securing the roofing material over the edges to hold it permanently in place.

An appraiser investigates the condition of a roof to determine its remaining useful life. Most roofs need to be replaced several times during a building's life, so a roof's condition and age are considered in the valuation process.

The water that falls on a roof must be directed to the ground or into a drain system. Gutters and downspouts channel water from roofs to prevent damage and protect the appearance of walls when roof overhangs are not provided. Gutters or eave troughs catch rainwater at the edge of the roof and carry it to downspouts or leaders, the vertical pipes that carry the water to the ground or into sewers, dry wells, drain tiles, or splash pans. In large buildings, storm water collects in roof drains, which are connected to storm drains by pipes in the building. Even so-called flat roofs may be slightly pitched to direct water to drains and gutters. Gutters and downspouts may be made of galvanized iron, aluminum, or copper.

Chimneys, Stacks, and Vents

Chimneys, stacks, and vents should be structurally safe, durable, and smoketight; they should also be able to withstand the action of flue gases. The efficiency of any fuel-burning heating system depends on its chimney, stack, or vent. Chimneys and stacks with cracked bricks, loose mortar joints, or other leaks may be serious fire and health hazards. Exhaust systems range from simple metal vents and flues to complex masonry fireplaces, industrial chimneys, and ventilation systems. A building's chimneys, stacks, and vents and their apparent condition are described in an appraisal report.

Special Features

Some buildings have special features that must be carefully described and considered in the valuation process. Special features might include artwork, ornamentation, exterior elevators, solar and wind equipment, unique fenestration, special masonry work and exterior materials, or other items required for the commercial or industrial use of buildings. When building features are unique, they present a difficult valuation problem. The appraiser must decide if the item or items add to the property's market value or if they are of value only to the current user. In the latter case, the item or items add use value, but they may add little or no market value. If such items are costly to remove, they can have a negative effect on value because they may not appeal to a future owner.

INTERIOR DESCRIPTION

The interior description of a building includes information about the interior walls and the spaces between them, including how the space is divided and finished.

Interior Walls

In residences, most interior walls are made of wood studs covered with drywall materials such as gypsum board, wood panels, ceramic tile, plywood, and hardboard. Plaster walls were once popular, but they are used less frequently now. Masonry houses often have masonry interior walls. The interior walls of commercial and industrial buildings may range from simple wire partitions to solid masonry walls that provide fire protection. Glass, wood, plywood, hardboard, metals, tiles, concrete, brick, and a number of other materials are used in wall construction. Interior walls can be painted, wallpapered, or decorated in other ways.

Doors

Types of interior doors include simple hollow-core doors, which are used in most residential construction; solid-core doors, which are found in older buildings; complex, self-closing, fire-resistant doors, which are found in commercial and industrial buildings; specialty, self-opening and closing doors, which are used in offices and commercial buildings; and special-purpose doors, such as those used in bank vaults. Hanging a door is complicated and often improperly done. Most poorly hung doors close improperly or fail to make contact with an edge of the frame when closed.

Division of Space

A building description provides a complete list of the number of rooms and their uses; room sizes may also be stated. The number of bedrooms and baths in a residential property usually influences the market for the property and its value. The number of units in an apartment building, as well as the types and sizes of the rooms within the units, significantly influence the property's income-producing potential. Similarly, the amount of office space in an industrial property and the partitioning in office suites may affect property value.

In certain parts of the United States, many types of buildings have basements. In these areas, buildings without basements may have substantially less value than similar buildings with basements. If basements are not common in the area, a basement may add little or no value to a building.

Storage Areas

An appraiser must describe and consider the adequacy of a building's storage areas. Homeowners often complain about a lack of adequate storage space, especially in kitchens. Good cabinets, closets, and other storage areas are important, particularly in homes without basements. Storage problems can also exist in commercial and industrial buildings.

Stairs, Ramps, Elevators, Escalators, and Hoists

Designing and constructing even the simplest staircase is a complicated task. In public buildings codes often regulate where stairs are located, how they are designed and constructed, and how they are enclosed for fire protection. In a residence, a well-planned stairway provides for safe ascent and descent, with adequate headroom and space for moving furniture and equipment. Railings should be installed on the sides of all interior stairwells, including stairwells in attics and basements where they are often omitted.

Elevators and escalators are mechanical systems that move people and freight and their adequacy must be considered by appraisers. The elevators and escalators in many multistory buildings are inadequate and do not meet current market standards. Curing these deficiencies is often extremely expensive or impossible.

Recent legislation provides handicapped persons with access to public buildings and requires that ramps be installed both inside and outside a building. An appraiser cannot assume that a building complies with these requirements, especially because the enforcement of these requirements can be triggered by a change in use or a title transfer.

Special elevators and hoists are often considered part of a building, although they may be studied under the category of equipment. These building components must be carefully described, and their contribution to the value of the building must be estimated.

Interior Supports

A building description includes consideration of the building's internal supports, which include beams and columns, the flooring system, and ceilings.

Beams and Columns

Many residential, commercial, and industrial buildings have basements or crawl spaces that are too large for the first floor joists or subfloor systems, and cannot be supported by the foundation walls alone. Therefore, foundation walls are an important part of the main framing system in large buildings, and they are designed to support heavy loads. Bearing beams that rest on columns of wood, masonry, or steel provide additional support. Cracked or sagging beams may be an early indication of more serious problems in the future. If an appraiser observes these signs, he or she should consider and report them.

Flooring System

Subflooring provides safe support for floor loads without excessive deflection and an adequate base for the support and attachment of finish floor material. Bridging stiffens the joists and prevents them from deflecting.

Ceilings

In residences with gypsum walls, ceilings are often made of the same material; in other buildings, tiles may be used. In some structures, the underside of the upper story is an adequate ceiling. Ceiling height must be measured and considered by an appraiser. Ceilings that are too low or high for the property's current highest and best use as improved may be an item of functional obsolescence and decrease the property's value.

Painting, Decorating, and Finishing

The primary purpose of interior painting and decorating is to give the building an attractive appearance. Most buildings are decorated many times during their useful lives. An appraiser reports the condition of the painting and decorating in a structure and notes when they will need to be redone.

The attractiveness of painting and decorating is subjective. Many new owners and tenants will redecorate to suit their personal tastes. Unusual decorations and colors may have limited appeal and, therefore, may detract from a building's value. The quality of decoration is sometimes an important consideration in valuing a restaurant, store, or other commercial building.

Basements

In residences and some commercial buildings, basements may be finished and used for purposes other than storage. If these uses are accepted and typical in the area, they can add significantly to the property value.

Dampness, which is often a problem in basements, may be caused by poor foundation wall construction, excess groundwater that is not properly drained by ground tiles, poorly fitted windows or hatches, poor venting of equipment, or poorly constructed or operating roof drains that allow water to enter. Signs that may indicate a wet basement include a powderly white mineral deposit a few inches off the floor, stains near the bottom of walls and columns or equipment that rests close to the floor, and the smell of mildew.

Flooring and Floor Coverings

A wide variety of flooring is available, and some flooring materials are selected primarily for their low cost and durability. Sand, compressed dirt, bituminous paving, brick, stone, gravel, concrete, and similar products are suitable for many industrial buildings, warehouses, garages, and basements. In many commercial and industrial buildings, floors must be especially thick or reinforced to support heavy equipment. Terrazzo flooring, which is made of colored marble chips that are mixed into cement and ground smooth, is used for high traffic areas such as the lobbies of public buildings.

Wood in various forms continues to be a popular material for floors. Planks and blocks are used for industrial floors, and many commercial buildings use wood floors to conform with their design and overall decoration. Wood planks and hardwood strips are found in many residences, although other types of flooring have become more popular. Resilient, ceramic, and quarry tiles are used in all types of buildings. Resilient flooring, which is usually a combination of vinyl and asphalt, is also produced as sheet goods.

Carpeting was once considered a luxury in residences, offices, stores, and commercial buildings, but today it is widely used in all types of buildings. An appraiser should consider whether floor coverings can endure wear and tear and how they conform to a building's design and decoration.

Molding and Baseboards

In the past, architects often designed unique moldings for buildings, but now moldings are of a standard size and shape and their use is decreasing. However, beautiful, restored molding can add value to older houses. Simple baseboards are used in many types of buildings to protect the walls from damage due to cleaning equipment or furniture.

Fireplaces

Fireplaces are popular in homes and commercial buildings such as restaurants, inns, and specialty stores. Most fireplaces do not provide a building's primary source of heat; in fact, because of their design, many have little heating power.

A typical fireplace has a single opening with a damper and a hearth. More complex designs feature two or more openings. Because fireplaces are difficult to construct, many are badly made and function poorly. One common problem is downdraft, whereby smoke is blown into the building by the wind outside. This can happen if the chimney does not extend at least two feet above any part of the roof within 10 feet of the chimney.

Many prefabricated fireplaces and flues are sold and installed in buildings that did not originally have fireplaces. Unless they are approved by Underwriters Laboratories and installed according to the manufacturer's instructions, these fireplaces can be potential fire hazards. To be safe, a fireplace should be supported with noncombustible material and have a noncombustible hearth that extends at least 16 inches in front of the opening and at least eight inches on each side. A carpet or rug that comes within a few inches of the front of a fireplace is a definite fire hazard.

Protection Against Decay and Insect Damage

All wood is susceptible to decay and insect damage. When wood is consistently exposed to moisture and water, destructive organisms propagate on or beneath its surface. The most prevalent of these organisms are aerobic fungi, which thrive where a proper combination of moisture, temperature, oxygen, and food exist. Sapwood of all species is subject to decay; heartwood varies in susceptibility from low to very high resistance, depending on the species.

Insects damage wood more rapidly and obviously than decay. Although several species of insects destroy wood, subterranean, dampwood, and drywood termites are by far the most destructive. Subterranean termites are very adaptable and are found across the United States. They colonize in moist soil and infest both damp and dry wood. Dampwood and drywood termites are more limited in their geographic distribution. Drywood termites colonize in wood and create infestations that are extremely difficult to eradicate.

To protect against decay and insect damage, builders may slope the ground away from foundations for good drainage and use vapor barriers on the interior sides of exposed walls; polyethylene as a soil cover in crawl spaces; flashing; gutters, downspouts, and splash blocks to carry water away from foundation walls; poured concrete foundation walls; concrete caps over unit masonry foundations; wood treatments; soil treatments; and metal termite shields. Using dry, naturally durable woods in construction and conducting regular maintenance inspections can also help prevent insect infestation and damage.

Miscellaneous and Special Features

Many industrial and commercial buildings are designed for special purposes. Steel mills, oil refineries, chemical plants, concrete factories, and mines are constructed for highly specialized functions. Commercial establishments often have unique design features (e.g., drive-in restaurants), or special facilities (e.g., the cooling room in a furrier's shop). Other properties with special purpose improvements include amusement parks, sports complexes, wharfs and docks, transportation terminals, and TV and radio transmission towers, studios, and theaters.

In valuing industrial and commercial properties, an appraiser may find it helpful to distinguish between two categories of equipment. The first category comprises equipment and mechanical systems that provide for human comfort. Plumbing, heating, air-conditioning, and lighting are human comfort items that will be discussed later in this chapter. The second category includes fixed building equipment that is process-related. Air hoses, process piping, craneways, bus ducts, heavy electrical lines, and freezer equipment are process-related items found in special-purpose industrial buildings. An appraiser must decide what contribution these special-purpose items make in terms of their use value, keeping in mind that their contribution may be different in terms of other types of value such as market or insurable value.

EQUIPMENT AND MECHANICAL SYSTEMS

Most buildings cannot perform the functions for which they were designed and constructed unless their equipment and mechanical systems are in good working order. Each item of equipment and each mechanical system should be inspected and described by the appraiser.

Major equipment and mechanical systems can be divided into two broad categories: those that do not consume a significant amount of energy and those that do. A plumbing system is not basically an energy consumer, although it may have pumps that use some electricity. The systems that consume energy are the hot water system, which is distinct from the plumbing system, the heating system, the air-conditioning and ventilation system, and the electrical system. Some buildings have other mechanical systems and equipment as well. Most of these systems use some electricity, but are not major energy consumers.

Plumbing System

Plumbing is an integral part of most buildings. It consists of piping, which is usually covered or hidden except in industrial buildings, and fixtures or equipment, which are visible. Laundries, laundromats, and certain industrial buildings have especially elaborate plumbing systems.

Piping

Much of the cost of a plumbing system may be due to piping, which consists of pipes that carry water (and occasionally other fluids) under pressure and waste pipes that depend on the flow of gravity. The quality of the materials used, the way the pipes were installed, and how easily they can be serviced are significant considerations in estimating how long the pipes will last and how much they will cost to maintain. Worn galvanized steel, lead, or brass water pipes may need to be replaced. Copper is an excellent pipe material with a long life; cast iron is good for below-grade waste lines. In many areas and many types of buildings, a high-quality piping system will last as long as the building. However, many buildings have pipes that do not last. An appraiser describes the conditions of the pipes and notes when they will probably need to be replaced.

Plastic pipes are widely used for waste, vent, and water lines. The durability and serviceability of plastic pipes should be checked. Water pipes must be strong enough to withstand the pressure needed to move water through them. Because there is no pressure in a waste drain line, these pipes must be slanted so that waste will flow from each fixture through the main line into the sewer or sewage disposal system. Building sewers should be installed to guard against sewer backup in heavy rains.

Fixtures

The plumbing fixtures used in bathrooms include lavatories, or washbasins; bathtubs; showers; toilets, which are known as water closets in the building trades; bidets; and urinals. High-quality fixtures are made of cast iron covered with acid-resistant vitreous enamel; fiberglass and other materials are also used.

The design of bathroom fixtures has changed substantially, and old fixtures may become obsolete during a building's economic life. An appraiser should report the need for modernization, but old fixtures of good quality, such as porcelain pedestal basins and footed tubs, are often rehabilitated.

Kitchen plumbing fixtures include single or double sinks, which should be installed in countertops and made of Monel metal, stainless steel, enameled steel, or cast iron covered with acid-resistant enamel. Other kitchen fixtures include garbage disposals, dishwashers, and instant hot water units. Some homes may have specialized plumbing fixtures such as laundry tubs, wet bars, swimming pools, or saunas.

Fittings, which are important parts of plumbing fixtures, include faucets, spigots, drains, shower heads, and spray tubes. The water in many areas is hard—i.e., it contains minerals such as calcium, magnesium, sulfates, bicarbonates, iron, and sulfur, which react unfavorably with soap and make it difficult to rinse from clothing, hair, and skin. Often hard water cannot be used until it is treated, either with simple equipment or with automatic, complex, multistage systems.

Commercial and industrial buildings have many of the same fixtures found in homes, and they also may have drinking fountains, janitor sinks, handwashing and eyewashing fountains, floor drains, and other special-purpose fixtures. An appraiser must decide which building fixtures are part of the real estate and which are personal property. Only those that are part of the real estate are included in the building's value.

Systems That Use Energy

As mentioned earlier, the systems that consume energy are the hot water system, the heating system, the air-conditioning and ventilation system, and the electrical system.[4] An appraiser must describe all these systems and indicate what type of fuel is used in the heating system.

Hot Water System

All homes and many commercial and industrial buildings need an adequate supply of hot water. A typical residential hot water system gets its heat from a furnace or self-standing water heater, which is powered by electricity, gas, or oil. Houses with inadequate hot water systems suffer from functional obsolescence. The size of the hot water tank needed in a residence is determined by the number of inhabitants and their water-using habits and by the recovery rate of the tank. Commercial and industrial buildings often require much more hot water than homes, so they often have large cast iron or steel boilers and storage tanks.

Heating Systems

Most heating systems use warm or hot air, hot water, steam, or electricity. The amount of heat a system can produce is rated in British thermal units (Btus). The heating-plant capacity required relates to the cubic content, exposure, design, and insulation level of the structure to be heated. An appraiser describes the heating system and analyzes whether it is appropriate in the local market area.

Warm or hot air heating systems. Heating systems based on warm or hot air depend on the natural force of gravity or use a pressure blower to push heated air through the ducts. The air is heated in a furnace that is fired by gas, oil, electricity, or coal and is distributed through one or more registers directly from the furnace or through ducts connected to registers throughout the building. Air circulation is maintained with a fan and a return duct system. Thermostats, filters, humidifiers, air cleaners, and air purification devices may be included in the heating system.

In some systems the central air-conditioning equipment uses the same ducts as the heating system. This is not always possible, however, because the air-conditioning may require ducts of a different size. Furthermore, heating registers should be placed low on the walls, while air-conditioning registers should be higher up or in the ceiling.

Some older heating systems relied on gravity and the use of larger ducts, with simple distribution patterns for circulation. Warm air systems are used in new apartment construction, especially for garden apartments and townhouse developments. When gas is used, the warm air system may function through unit heaters, radiant gas heaters, wall or floor furnaces, or individual gas furnaces. Gas-fired heating units need adequate ventilation. Indeed, all open-flame heating sources must have a sufficient air supply to support complete combustion.

4. Heating, ventilation, and air-conditioning systems are commonly referred to as HVAC systems.

Hot water heating systems. Heating systems based on hot water are called *hydronic systems*. In a hydronic system, water is heated in a cast iron or steel boiler and is moved by gravity (in older systems) or pumped by a circulator (in modern systems) through pipes and radiators where the heat is transferred by convection and radiation to the areas being heated. The colder water then returns to the boiler where it is reheated and the process is repeated.

Radiant heating is a type of hot water heating system in which hot water is circulated by a pump, called a *circulator*, through narrow pipes that are embedded in floors, walls, and ceilings. This system depends primarily on heat being transferred by radiation, rather than by convection, which characterizes a conventional system. In a conventional hot water heating system, air is warmed as it passes over the heated metal of a radiator and is then circulated in an area of colder air. Radiant heat can also be produced by electric heating elements embedded in floors, walls, and ceilings.

Steam heating systems. In these systems, steam is made in a boiler fueled by gas, oil, coal, or electricity and distributed through a piping system. In a simpler one-pipe gravity system, which may be used in small installations, radiators are served by a single riser from the main pipe. The condensate returns to the boiler through the same riser and is used again. More complex and expensive two-pipe systems are found in larger, high-quality installations.

At one time, vertical section, cast iron boilers were used in large installations. These units were fairly efficient when covered with insulated metal casings or jackets. Steel boilers were usually of a low-pressure, fire-tube type, in which combustion gases passed through tubes inserted into a cylindrical drum that contained water. Several types of two-pass or three-pass boilers were designed for better efficiency. Recently, small, efficient "package boilers" have become popular for heating and generating process steam.

Steam systems also use radiators to transfer heat by radiation and convection. The common cast iron radiator successfully transfers heat, but improvements are still being developed to operate steam heating more efficiently. Zone control is now widely used to stabilize the effects of different heating needs in different parts of a building. The amount of heat available for distribution can be controlled by separate temperature controls.

In many states, licenses are required for certain classes of steam boilers. Appraisers must be familiar with local boiler license laws and ascertain whether boilers have current, valid licenses.

Electrical heating systems. The equipment used in electrical heating systems includes heat pumps, wall heaters, baseboard units, duct heating units, and heating units installed in air-conditioning ducts. Such equipment gives an electrical heating system both heating and cooling capacity. Radiant floors, walls, and ceilings that have panels or cables under the surface; infrared units; and electric furnaces that use forced warm air or hot water can also be used in electrical heating systems. An electrical resistance system produces heat in the immediate area or room that is to be heated. It is the least expensive system to install because it requires no furnace, furnace room, ducts, flue, or plumbing. However, it does require a large electrical service and a great deal of wiring to each unit in the building.

Heat pumps that combine heating and cooling functions are increasing in popularity. A heat pump is actually a reverse refrigeration unit. In the winter, the pump takes heat from the outside air, the ground, or well water and distributes it inside the house. When the weather is very cold, the efficiency of the unit decreases and must be supplemented with resistance heating. In the summer, the pump cools by extracting heat from inside the house like a typical air-conditioning unit.

Convectors are finned heating elements that are installed in baseboards or concealed in walls or cabinets. A convector that is combined with a fan is a unit or room heater. Unit heaters are found in commercial and industrial buildings such as stores, warehouses, and garages, where large spaces must be heated. The units are usually placed near the ceiling in the space to be heated.

The automatic regulation of a heating system helps it operate efficiently. A multiple zone system with separate thermostats is more efficient than a single zone system with one thermostat. Complex systems provide an individual temperature control for each room. The efficiency of certain systems can be increased by putting a thermostat on the outside of the building. This helps building operators anticipate how much heat the system will need to produce.

Heating Fuels

The type of fuel used in a building's heating system should be explained in the building description. Depending on the area and the type of building, one type of fuel may be more desirable than another. Nevertheless, many building heating systems do not use the most economical fuel. For example, during the natural gas shortage in the 1970s, a moratorium was declared on the use of natural gas. Therefore, buildings were constructed in certain areas with heating systems that use other fuels even though gas is now more economical. For any specific use, different fuels have different advantages and disadvantages which are subject to change.

Coal. In the past, coal was the most popular fuel for heating; it is still used to generate power for some industrial and commercial uses. Coal is also used in residences for stoves and fireplaces, but the burning of certain types of coal creates environmental pollution.

Fuel oil. In spite of its high cost, fuel oil is a popular energy source which is easy to transport and store. Onsite tanks range from 275-gallon tanks, which are used in millions of houses, to tanks that hold thousands of gallons, which are buried on industrial and commercial sites.

Natural gas. This type of fuel is convenient because it is continuously delivered by pipelines and no storage tank is needed. In many parts of the country, natural gas is the most economical fuel. Liquid petroleum gas, such as butane and propane, is used in many rural areas. It requires onsite storage tanks and is usually more expensive, but in other respects it is similar to natural gas.

Electricity. Like oil, gas, or coal, electricity can be used to produce heat in a furnace or to heat water in a boiler. Electrical heating costs are high, except in a few areas. Good insulation and control can help to eliminate waste.

An appraiser cannot assume that a building's existing heating system contributes maximum value to the property. The heating system installed when the building was constructed may not be acceptable to current potential buyers.

New technology has continued to reduce energy consumption for large heating systems. Many industrial users who once depended on gas alone now install alternate, more efficient, oil or electric facilities to provide heat when the gas supply is curtailed. Electric heat has become so costly in some areas that buildings using it sell for substantially less than similar properties that use other types of fuel. *Cogeneration*, the simultaneous production of electrical energy and low-grade heat from the same fuel, is also being used in some parts of the country.

Buyers are sensitive to energy costs. Apartments in which the owner supplies heat and hot water often sell for less than similar properties in which tenants pay for utilities. Buildings that have high ceilings, many openings, and poor insulation may be at a disadvantage in the market.

Solar heating and domestic hot water systems have attracted much interest, and many such systems are on the market. Appraisers should keep up to date on solar development and its use in particular areas. A solar heating system should be carefully described and its contribution to the property's value should be estimated. When residential appraisals are reported on FHLMC-FNMA forms, solar heating and other special energy systems must be described and valued separately.

Air-Conditioning and Ventilation Systems

Before World War II, ducts, fans, and open windows were used to reduce heat and provide fresh air in most buildings. In many buildings, ducts and fans are still used to provide fresh air. In certain areas of the western United States, where the humidity is low even when it is very hot, air can be cooled with a simple system that blows air across wet excelsior or some other water-absorbing material. Package units using this process are still manufactured for home and commercial use. These units use less power and, therefore, are less expensive to operate than conventional air-conditioning systems.

The most common type of air-conditioning system consists of an electrically powered compressor that compresses Freon from gas into liquid outside the area being cooled. The heat released in this process is either blown away or carried away by water. The compressed Freon is then directed into thin tubes in the area being cooled, where it expands and absorbs heat from the air that is directed over the tubes by one or more fans. Another type of air-conditioning system is powered by gas, rather than electricity; and ammonia, not Freon, is used as the refrigerant. Air-conditioners range from small, portable units to units that provide many tons of cooling capacity. The capacity of an air-conditioning unit is rated in tons of refrigeration, which is equal to the amount of heat needed to melt a ton of ice in 24 hours, or 12,000 Btu/hr.

Commercial and industrial air-conditioning and ventilation systems are more complex. Some simply bring in fresh air from the outside and distribute it throughout the building; others merely remove foul air. Still others combine these two functions, but do not have any cooling or heating capacity. More complex systems wash, filter, and add or remove humidity from the air. The most complex systems perform all of these functions and also heat and cool air through a complex system of ducts and fans. In larger systems that use less electricity, water cools the pipes in which the gas has been compressed. The water is then conserved in towers that cool it for reuse.

An appraiser describes the air-conditioning and ventilation system in a building and decides whether it is appropriate to the geographic area. To do this, the appraiser may have to investigate whether the building's system meets current standards. If the appraiser concludes that the building has too much or too little air-conditioning, the appraisal report should include the data on which this decision is based.

Electrical Systems

A well-designed electrical system must be large enough to provide sufficient power for all the electrical uses in the building. Sometimes, one electrical service may supply power to more than one building.

The power in an electrical system is distributed from the electrical service by branch circuits, which are wires located throughout the building, to electrical outlets. Each branch circuit starts at a distribution box, where it is separated from the main service by a protection device such as a fuse or circuit breaker. When a short circuit or overload occurs on the branch circuit, the fuse or circuit breaker disconnects the circuit from the power supply to prevent a fire.

The wiring between the distribution boxes and the outlets may be a rigid or flexible conduit. This type of wiring is common in commercial and industrial buildings. In most houses, BX or armored cable is used. Plastic-coated wire is used in certain areas, and the old knob-and-tube wiring is still used in rural areas and older buildings, although it is considered obsolete.

Most electrical wire is copper. After World War II, aluminum wire became popular as the price of copper escalated, but its resistance to fire has been seriously questioned. In some sections of the country, aluminum wiring is prohibited by law.

A typical residential electrical system is a single-phase, three-wire system that provides a minimum of 100 amperes of electricity. The old 30-ampere systems are certainly obsolete and residences that have 60 amperes of service normally sell for less than those with larger services. Ampere services of 150, 200, 300, and 400 are needed when electric heating and air-conditioning is used. Most of these services can provide up to 220 volts by connecting three wires to the outlet.

Power wiring is used in commercial and industrial buildings to operate utility systems, appliances, and machinery. The electrical power is generally carried at higher voltages (e.g., 240, 480, 600 volts or more) and is usually three-phase or three-phase-four-wire, which allows both lighting and three-phase power loads to be delivered by the same supply.

Power wiring is carried in conduit or by means of plug-in bus ducts. Overhead bus ducts are frequently found in manufacturing plants where flexible service is needed. Large-capacity power wiring may contribute to the value of an industrial improvement; however, if it is an uncommon type and it adds to a building's operating costs or will be expensive to remove, it may result in functional obsolescence. Similarly, any building with insufficient electrical service or wiring suffers from functional obsolescence.

Switches and lighting fixtures are also part of the electrical system. Because lighting fixtures are stylized and styles change, they are often obsolete before they wear out. Fluorescent lighting, which may be suspended, surface-mounted, or recessed, is used extensively in commercial and industrial buildings. Often continuous rows are used in large spaces. Incandescent fixtures may be used for smaller rooms, accents, or special purposes.

In newer lighting design, the intensity and quality of light over working areas and display surfaces are important considerations. The degree of intensity will vary with the type of use. Sodium and mercury vapor lights are often installed in industrial buildings. Some installations are designed so that air moves past the lighting fixtures to augment the heating system.

Floor outlets or floor duct systems are extensively used in commercial and office buildings. These systems provide convenient electrical outlets for office machines and telephone outlets at desks using a minimum number of cords. Some houses and commercial buildings have low-voltage switching systems, in which many outlets and lights can be controlled from one place.

Miscellaneous Equipment

In building descriptions, appraisers also consider miscellaneous equipment, some of which is discussed below.

Fire Protection

Fire protection equipment includes fire escapes, standpipes and hose cabinets, alarm services, and automatic sprinklers. A wet sprinkler system must have adequate water pressure to ensure that the pipes are always filled. A dry system has pressurized air in the pipes. When a sprinkler head opens, the pressure is relieved and water enters. Dry systems are used on loading docks and in unheated buildings where there is a danger of water freezing.

Elevators, Escalators, and Speed Ramps

Elevators are usually classified as passenger or freight and may be either electric or hydraulic. Hydraulic elevators are suitable for low-speed, low-rise operations. Because attended passenger elevators need full-time operators, their costliness has made them practically obsolete. The type, speed, and capacity of an elevator, as well as the number of floors it serves, are related to the type of property and its utility.

Most modern elevators are high-speed and completely automatic. Control systems collect signals and distribute service among all the elevators in a system. Some elevators have auxiliary controls so that they can be manually operated if necessary.

The movement of large numbers of people up or down, or along horizontal or gradual slopes, can be accomplished with escalators and speed ramps. This equipment must be adequate to accommodate the number of persons who use the building.

Signals, Alarms, and Call Systems

Signals, alarms, call systems, and similar devices should not be overlooked by an appraiser. Smoke detectors are increasingly common in residential and multifamily structures and are required by law in many areas. Security alarm systems, which warn occupants of forced entry, fire, or both, are available for residential, commercial, and industrial use. Because fire and safety regulations change, systems that were adequate when they were installed may later be considered substandard.

Other items to be noted by an appraiser include clocks, pneumatic tube systems, mail chutes, incinerators, and telephone wiring. In small buildings, the telephone company supplies the wiring and equipment; larger buildings may have extensive systems of built-in cabinets, conduits, and floor ducts for telephone service. The telephone service in a building may be suitable for the current occupant, but unsuitable for a potential buyer.

Loading Facilities

Facilities for loading and unloading trucks and freight cars may be important in commercial and industrial buildings. Off-street loading docks are usually required by zoning ordinances. Many older buildings have only loading doors or substandard loading facilities. Loading docks may be open or covered. The floor of an efficient one-story industrial building may be built above grade at freight car or truck-bed level. In some buildings, docks are enclosed for trucks and freight cars, and leveling devices are provided to assist in loading or unloading. A properly designed industrial building has space in front of truck docks so that vehicles can maneuver.

Attached Equipment

Process-related fixed building equipment includes air hoses, process piping, industrial wiring for heavy electrical capacity, bus ducts, and freezer equipment. Although this equipment may be a part of other utility systems (e.g., plumbing or electrical), its contributory role in a specific industrial process warrants attention. The appraiser should consider attached equipment in terms of its use value.

QUALITY AND CONDITION SURVEY

In the quality and condition survey of a building description, an appraiser analyzes and explains the quality and condition of the items described. The character, quality, and appearance of building construction are reflected in each of the three approaches to value. The quality and condition of building components have a major influence on the cost estimate, the accrued depreciation estimate, the ability of the property to produce rental income, and the property's comparability with other properties in the sales comparison approach. Analysis of the quality of construction methods and materials complements the appraiser's analysis of the building's structural design and architecture.

A structure can have a good, functional layout and an attractive design but be built with inferior materials and poor workmanship. These deficiencies increase maintenance and utility costs and adversely affect the property's marketability. Conversely, a building can be built too well or at a cost that cannot be justified by its utility. Most purchasers will not pay for these excess costs and only part of the loss can be recaptured by the original owner through reduced maintenance expenses.

Practical or reasonable economy of construction results in an improvement that will produce a rental income commensurate with its cost. Maintenance and operating expenses for an economically constructed building may be slightly more than minimum, but this is preferable to a building of superior construction, which would have a higher level of taxes, interest, and amortization charges. To achieve the desired level of construction cost, building materials and construction methods must be chosen and used properly. An appraiser should recognize that an appropriate combination of elements results in a building that is adequate for its intended purpose.

The maintenance and age of a building affect its condition. In a quality and condition survey, an appraiser generally distinguishes between items in need of immediate repair and those that may be repaired or replaced at a later time.

Immediate Repair Items

An appraiser usually finds some items that need repair on the date of the appraisal, although some buildings may be in excellent condition. The following list indicates items that are commonly found to be in need of immediate attention.

- Touch-up paint on building interior and exterior and the removal of graffiti
- Minor carpentry repairs
- Leaky or noisy plumbing
- Stuck doors and windows
- Broken glass and torn screens
- Loose or damaged gutters and leaders
- Roof leaks and missing shingles, tiles, and slates
- Cracked sidewalks, driveways, and parking areas
- Infestation by vermin

- Cracked or loose tiles in bathrooms and kitchens
- Septic systems
- Safety hazards
- Fire hazards

Deteriorated Items

During building inspection, an appraiser usually encounters many items that show signs of wear and tear. However, it is not economical to repair or replace most of these items on the date of the appraisal. The appraiser must decide if an item needs immediate repair or replacement or whether this work can be done later. (The consideration of deteriorated items is discussed in Chapter 17.) If the cost of the repairs adds nothing to the value of the property, the maintenance can be delayed. For example, a building with a sound, 10-year-old roof may hold up well for at least another five years. Although the roof has suffered some depreciation, replacing it probably would not add any value to the property over the cost of a new roof.

The final step in a quality and condition survey is to report on the condition of those items that should last for the remaining estimated economic life of the building, assuming they are not subject to abnormal wear and tear or that they are not accidentally damaged. The appraiser focuses on items that are not in the same condition as the rest of the building.

SUMMARY

A building description includes specific information on the size, design or layout, structural components, materials, equipment, and mechanical systems of a building. The description of a structure's physical characteristics helps an appraiser to identify and select suitable comparables and to estimate building costs and depreciation. In preparing a building description, an appraiser considers the current use, zoning codes that affect use, the plan and construction of the structure, building codes that affect the plan and construction, and the building's size.

Although systems of measurement vary, *gross building area (GBA)* is always calculated. For residential properties, gross living area is also calculated. For shopping centers, *gross leaseable area (GLA)* is commonly measured. For office buildings, *GBA* and total leaseable area are measured and lobby, corridor, and restroom space is allocated on a pro rata basis. All statements of size should be verified, and the method of calculation should be ascertained by the appraiser. The units of comparison used in the sales comparison approach must be identical, and the rental and expense data used in the income capitalization approach must be based on equivalent units of area.

The building description format is divided into an exterior description, an interior description, and a description of equipment and mechanical systems. In the exterior description, the appraiser provides details on the *substructure* (i.e., the foundational structure located below grade that provides the support base or footings on which the superstructure rests), the *superstructure* (i.e., the portion of the building above grade), and the *infrastructure*, if the building is part of a complex that has a common source of utilities or support services.

In describing the substructure, the appraiser notes any problems that could cause settling or wall cracks. In examining the superstructure, the condition of the framing, insulation, ventilation, exterior walls, exterior doors, windows, facade, roof and drains, and chimneys and smoke stacks are observed.

Framing consists of vertical members called *studs*, and horizontal members called *joists*. Three forms of framing are used in wood construction: *platform*, which is the most common, *balloon*, and *post and beam*. In large industrial and commercial buildings, the framing consists of steel beams or heat-resistant beams of reinforced or precast concrete. Defective framing can cause wall cracks. In the heat of a fire, steel beams can buckle, and cause extensive damage.

Types of insulation include loose fill, which is poured or machine-blown into cavities; flexible, which is attached to a foil or facing and fitted in place; and rigid inboard and deck form. Reflective insulation is made of foil that is chemically treated to reflect heat, and foamed-in-place insulation may be of urethane or urea-formaldehyde foam. An insulation's R value is the measurement of its resistance to heat flow. In closed-off areas, ventilation reduces heat and prevents the condensation of water. Exterior walls may be load-bearing or nonload-bearing; this function determines the material of which they are built.

Exterior doors are made of wood, metal, or glass. An appraiser should note whether energy-saving materials such as weatherstripping are used. Windows may be made of wood, aluminum, or steel; common types include double hung, casement, horizontal sliding, central pivot, and jalousie. The appraiser should describe window design and any installation features that conserve energy. The appraiser also considers the special contribution of an elaborate or attractive facade.

Roofs may be flat, lean-to, gable, gambrel, hip, mansard, monitor, or sawtooth. Their structural elements include trusses, joists, rafters, beams, and purlins. Structural components and sheathing are made of wood, steel, or concrete; and coverings may be of asphalt, fiberglass shingle, slate, or tile. Flashing protects a roof's structural joints against water damage, and the drain system and pitch of the roof provide for the control and disposal of rainwater. Chimneys, stacks, and vents contribute to the efficiency of the building's heating system and ensure the safety of the occupants. Any special exterior features may enhance or diminish property value.

To describe the building interior, an appraiser investigates the condition of the interior walls and doors; space divisions; internal supports; painting, decorating, and finishing; and protection against decay and insect damage. Interior walls may be of wood, masonry, or concrete construction covered with drywall panels, plaster, tile, or brick. Doors may be hollow or solid core, fire-resistant, or self-opening and closing.

In describing the division of space, an appraiser considers the number, function, and size of all rooms and storage areas. The appraiser also investigates the adequacy and safety of stairways, ramps, and elevators. Internal supports and subflooring should be checked for loadbearing capacity, and the functionality of ceiling heights should be considered. Painting and decorating are often a matter of taste, but the appearance of basements and floors reflects upkeep. The appraiser should check basements for dryness and ventilation. Flooring in industrial and commercial buildings may be brick, stone block, pavement, concrete, or terrazzo mosaic. Wooden floors are common in all types of buildings. Fireplaces should be checked for potential hazards due to downdrafts and faulty flues. The appraiser must observe and describe any damage caused by fungi and termites.

Many industrial and commercial buildings have special-purpose improvements. An appraiser distinguishes between equipment and mechanical systems that provide for human comfort and fixed building equipment that is process-related. Equipment and mechanical systems can also be differentiated in terms of the amount of energy they consume. Hot water and heating systems consume energy, while plumbing is not basically energy consuming. Plumbing consists of piping and fixtures. Piping, which may be made of galvanized steel, cast iron, copper, or plastic, should be checked for durability. Fixtures and fittings may incur obsolescence.

Hot water heaters get their heat from a furnace or are independently powered by electricity, gas, or oil. Heating systems are classified by the type of heat they produce and the kind of fuel they consume. Heating systems include hot air, in which pressure-blown heated air is circulated through ducts; hot water or hydronic, in which boiler-heated water is pumped through radiators; steam, in which boiler-heated steam is piped to radiators; and electric, in which cable-generated heat is pumped through ducts that are also used for air conditioning. Heating systems are fueled with coal, fuel oil, natural gas, or electricity.

Fuel considerations are significant in an appraisal. The temperature control provided by a zone system contributes to greater energy efficiency. Technological developments such as cogeneration and solar heating promote energy conservation.

The most common type of air-conditioning system is an electrically powered Freon compressor. Complex ventilation systems distribute fresh air, filter foul air, and remove humidity. In an electrical system, power is distributed from the electrical service with power wiring using conduits and bus ducts, branch circuits using distribution boxes and circuit breakers, and outlets. In houses, BX, or armored, cable, single-phase wiring is common, while large-capacity, three-phase wiring is used in commercial and industrial buildings. Fluorescent lighting and sodium and mercury vapor lights are found in industrial buildings.

Miscellaneous building equipment includes fire protection systems, conveyance system, signal systems, unloading systems, and attached or fixed, process-related, building equipment.

The appraiser performs a quality and condition survey to determine how the building's functionality of design, economy of construction, and attractiveness relate to its quality of construction, economic utility, maintenance and operating expenses, and marketability. In this survey, the appraiser distinguishes among items in need of immediate repair, items that may be repaired or replaced at a later date, and items that are expected to last for the remaining economic life of the building.

11 Building Style and Function

Architectural style and functional utility are interrelated, and their combined effect on property value must be analyzed by appraisers. *Architectural style is the character of a building's form and ornamentation. Functional utility is the ability of a property or building to be useful and to perform the function for which it is intended, according to current market tastes and standards, as well as the efficiency of a building's use in terms of architectural style, design and layout, traffic patterns, and size and type of rooms.* Both architectural style and functional utility influence human lives by providing or withholding beauty, comfort, security, convenience, light, and air. They may also ensure reasonable maintenance expenditures, preserve valuable traditions, and indicate the need for change.

A building may have functional utility but lack architectural style, or it may have admirable style but little utility. Form and function work together to create successful architecture. Functional utility is not necessarily exemplified by minimal space or form; people's needs for comfort and pleasure must also be considered in the design of offices, stores, hospitals, and houses. An appraiser must recognize and rank all market preferences regarding style and functional utility and then relate these preferences to market value.

Considerations of style and functional utility are integral to an appraisal. They are noted along with other physical characteristics during property inspection. Using comparable data, an appraiser can analyze how style and function influence a property's market value. Style and functional utility are examined in relation to the function or use of a particular property—i.e., the use for which it was designed, its actual or contemplated use, and its most economic use. These three uses may be the same, or any or all of them may differ.

ARCHITECTURAL STYLE AND UTILITY

Architecture is the art or science of building design and construction. It is the formal organization of three-dimensional elements on a large scale to serve various human needs. Because architecture interprets human needs, it is a fundamental reflection of culture. Architectural style affects the market value of property, so an understanding of its nature is important to appraisers. Two basic types of styles are distinguished in American architecture: formal architecture and vernacular architecture.

Formal architecture refers to the art and science of designing and building structures that meet the aesthetic and functional criteria of those trained in architectural history. Formal architectural styles are identified by common attributes of expression and are frequently named in reference to a geographic region, cultural group, or time period. Italianate, Second Empire, and Prairie School are examples of formal architectural styles.[1]

Vernacular architecture is also concerned with the art and science of designing and building structures, but without reference to the aesthetic and functional criteria of academic architectural history. Vernacular architecture identifies structures that are designed and built by individuals according to custom and in response to the environment and contemporary life-styles. Vernacular styles share common attributes and may be technologically simple or sophisticated. However, these styles usually are unnamed because they are not formally studied by architectural historians. The sod houses built on the prairies of the American West and the mass-produced homes constructed in modern subdivisions are examples of vernacular styles. The traditional barn is another successful type of vernacular building.

Architectural style is influenced by market standards and tastes. Market standards are accepted norms, which reflect culturally shared attitudes and beliefs. They are established forms and methods of construction that have not yet been surpassed by advances in technology or perceived to be aesthetically undesirable.

Market tastes are preferences, which may be shared by groups or expressed individually. Commonly shared tastes characterize most of the market for real estate. In a free economy, tastes shift either in reaction to, or in accordance with, market standards.

Market tastes and standards are influenced in part by the desire to preserve tradition and by the desire for change, variety, and efficiency. Architectural trends respond to the market's desire to preserve tradition by including elements of past architectural styles; the market's desire for change provides the impetus for developing new elements of architectural design.

Changes in architectural trends are precipitated by the market's tolerance of current styles. When a style is too extreme, a shift to elements of past styles frequently occurs. Thus, extreme ornateness may be replaced by forms that are spare. A

---

1. Literature on American architectural history is abundant. For a description of styles in a real estate appraisal context, see Judith Reynolds, *Historic Properties: Preservation and the Valuation Process* (Chicago: American Institute of Real Estate Appraisers, 1982). Other helpful sources are cited in the bibliography of this text.

reactive shift, then, provides contrast to the preceding, dominant architectural style. Such changes also produce avant-garde or experimental building styles, which are ultimately tested in the market. An experimental style is eventually discarded or it becomes an accepted standard. However, design elements that are discarded in a reactive swing are not lost; old forms may disappear for a time and then reappear in a modified form.

Changes in architecture can also be generated by external forces. For example, rising energy costs have prompted new developments in the heating, ventilating, and air conditioning systems used in office buildings. These changes include the installation of solar energy panels, the trend toward stand-alone HVAC systems, and the use of new exterior materials that conserve energy.

Architectural styles are modified over periods that are loosely related to the economic life cycles of buildings; newly constructed buildings usually contrast in style with buildings of the previous period. Major revisions in architectural styles typically coincide with the end of a building life cycle, which normally occurs every 30 to 50 years.

Newly constructed buildings of all architectural styles enjoy broad market appeal, whether they are professionally designed or not. When a building is no longer new, however, it is compared with other buildings in terms of the quality and usefulness of its architectural style. Form and structure, the most basic components of architectural style, limit and define a building's potential uses (and changes of use); these factors become more influential as time passes.

Architectural styles reflect a complex relationship of cultural premises and human activity over time. Thus, descriptions of architectural styles provide appraisers with a record of architectural history and a catalog of social expression. Figures 11.1 and 11.2 illustrate formal and vernacular American architectural styles.

Materials, Structure, Equipment, and Siting

Architectural style is expressed in a number of building components. A building's materials, structure, equipment, and siting all shape and change its style. The availability of natural materials such as wood, stone, and clay and lime for making brick was primarily responsible for the different architectural styles that emerged and prevailed in various areas. When post-and-beam construction was developed, greater spaces could be spanned. This type of construction made it possible to build the large fabricating mills of the Industrial Revolution. The evolution of lightweight balloon framing and machines to mass produce nails changed the form of buildings in the nineteenth century. Furthermore, balloon framing allowed buildings to be constructed much more rapidly because precut components were used.

The development of the Franklin stove and central heating systems changed the shape and number of rooms in all structures because fireplaces were no longer needed to provide heat. The production of domestic equipment in the early twentieth century eliminated the need for root cellars, pantries, and large laundry rooms, which decreased the size of dwellings and changed room arrangements.

Figure 11.1   Formal Architecture

THE ITALIANATE STYLE

SECOND EMPIRE STYLE

Figure 11.2   Vernacular Architecture

Similarly, rapid advances in computers and semiconductors, wiring networks and switching devices, and satellite communications have affected building design. In modern business facilities, much attention is devoted to the installation, routing, and expansion capabilities of advanced communications systems.[2] Design considerations for contemporary office buildings include the capacities of feed conduit and electrical service to accommodate a wide variety of transmission linkages, the presence or absence of roof reinforcement to support satellite and microwave antennae, and the ability of HVAC systems to handle the increased heat output of office computers. These factors affect the size of conduit and risers, the amount and quality of electricity required, ceiling height, and other structural components.

In the mid-twentieth century, central air-conditioning and heating, made possible by modern technology, became widely used in residential, commercial, and industrial buildings. This resulted in a standardization of architectural styles, particularly housing styles, throughout the country and nearly obliterated the regional building styles developed in response to variations in climate.

For example, the thick, mud masonry walls and small windows of houses in the Southwest were well-suited to the hot, dry weather of the region. Houses in the rainy Northwest had overhanging roofs so that windows could be opened for ventilation without admitting the rain. The saltbox houses of New England were protected against the harsh northern wind because the windowless, steeped-roof side of the house faced north. Although regional building styles temporarily lost favor, structural defenses against climate were reincorporated into construction in the mid-1970s. Thus, because the market has become energy-conscious, climate-compatible design has re-emerged. Such design considerations are important in estimating market value because consumers increasingly desire energy-saving features.

The use of steel for framing and the invention of the elevator made the construction of taller buildings possible. Curtain walls of glass and metal are well-suited to the box-like forms of the international style. Curtain-wall construction separated the functions of support and enclosure, which were inseparable in heavy masonry multistory buildings. Curtain walls can be made of metal, masonry, precast concrete, or glass.

Steel bar joists have twice the load-bearing capacity of solid joists, so greater spaces can be spanned and pipes, ducts, and conduit can be threaded through open webbing. Lightweight, structural support systems and the use of lamination and plastic glues developed in the aircraft industry have facilitated the creation of new forms such as butterfly and arcaded roofs.

Due to technology developed since the 1940s, buildings can take new shapes because concrete can now be used in large slabs, building blocks, or beams. Reinforced concrete, elevator-building construction offers an alternative to steel framing

---

2. For further information, see Theodore H. Schell, "Developing Communications," *Buildings*, August 1983. Schell discusses the importance of planning for the installation of advanced communications systems in new commercial buildings. See also B.R. Jensen, "Building Efficiency: Cost and Value," *The Appraisal Journal*, January 1985; and Dean Schwanke, *Smart Buildings and Technology-Enhanced Real Estate, Vol. I* (Washington, D.C.: Urban Land Institute, 1985).

that is less vulnerable to fire. Building a structure with poured concrete is slow and must stop in cold weather, but precast concrete assembly can proceed nearly as quickly as steel construction. For additional strength, post-tensioning can be used to tighten reinforcing rods while the concrete hardens. Concrete-column reinforcement allows concrete buildings to be built as high as steel-framed towers. Lightweight aggregate can also be used in cement to reduce the load.

As materials, structural components, and equipment become more refined, architectural styles change. Technological advances are integrated into evolving architectural styles and may modify architectural trends.

Architectural design is also influenced by the possible placement of a building on its site. Every building has a physical setting that includes the space around it. In cities where buildings abut one another directly, there is little choice about placement. However, in some locations there is more flexibility, and a building's design, placement, and landscaping can provide a defense against the climate. High energy costs make siting an important element of compatibility, but appropriate placement on a site can also enhance a building's architectural design.

Architectural design can be adjusted to the climate and to an individual site. Trees can provide shade, act as windbreaks and sound barriers, and filter and add moisture to the air. Deciduous trees should be placed on the western side of a property, where they can provide shade from the afternoon sun in summer and allow the sun to shine through in winter. Conifers can be planted on the northern part of a property to act as windbreaks. Shade and sunlight can also be controlled by the angle and direction of overhanging roofs. These roofs deflect the high-angle rays of the summer sun and allow the low-angle rays of the winter sun to be admitted by the windows.

Because increasing fuel costs have created the need for alternate energy sources, active and passive solar features have been introduced into building design to a limited extent. Active solar heating systems use glass roof panels or glass attached to one side of the building. Warm air is stored in a medium such as water or pumped directly into the structure. Passive solar heating techniques include strategically placed windows or glass walls, insulation, heat-retaining walls and floors, and careful siting. Rooms, roofs, and windows can be situated to allow warm air to flow freely through the structure or to provide maximum ventilation and air cooling.

A house that is built underground takes advantage of the fact that below-grade temperatures are moderate year round. The heating and cooling equipment in such houses can operate with less power and significantly reduce energy costs. In the United States, underground housing is found primarily in the Central Plains region, where storm protection and reduced energy costs are primary concerns. These earth-covered dwellings of poured concrete and concrete block are usually located on grade and bermed—i.e., set into a site that is partly or completely excavated. Berming overcomes the constraints associated with high water tables, expansive clay soils, rock strata, and flat rural sites. Usually the site is partially excavated into a hillside; the house's sod-covered roof provides additional insulation.

Underground construction, solar heating techniques, climate-specific siting, and other energy-related building style adaptations should be considered by an appraiser in terms of their market acceptability and their influence on sale prices, rents, and other market value indicators.

FUNCTIONAL UTILITY

For something to be functional, it must work and be useful. The definition of functional utility, however, is subject to changing expectations and standards. Optimal functional utility implies that the design and engineering of a building are the best in terms of perceived needs at a given time.

Functional inutility is an impairment of the functional capacity of a property or building according to market tastes and standards. It becomes equivalent to functional obsolescence when ongoing change, caused by technological advances and economic and aesthetic trends, renders layouts and features obsolete. However, functional inutility must be judged in light of market standards of acceptability, specifically the standards of buyers who make up the market for a particular type of building.

As objectives of building design, functional utility and aesthetics are sometimes in conflict; market standards generally reflect a compromise between the two. Extremely utilitarian housing designs that omitted basements, entrance halls, and dining rooms were eventually rejected by much of the market and replaced with more flexible designs. Similarly, the trend toward ultimate efficiency in office building interiors produced "standard" space that had low ceilings, plain walls, and vinyl asbestos floors. Thereafter, this type of interior finish was considered substandard.

Functional utility represents more than practical utilitarianism. Overimprovements—i.e., superadequate structural components or space—are also items of functional obsolescence because their costs exceed their value. When an expensively finished retail space with high ceilings is included in an office building located where there is no market for retailing, the building incorporates functional obsolescence in the form of superadequacy.

Standards of functional utility vary with the type and use of property. Specific considerations for different property types are discussed in the remainder of this chapter. Some general standards of functional utility to be considered by appraisers include

- Suitability or appropriateness
- Comfort
- Efficiency
- Safety
- Security
- Accessibility
- Ease and cost of maintenance
- Market standards
- Attractiveness
- Profitability

One additional standard must be given special consideration. In determining the functional utility and appropriateness of an architectural style, an appraiser must consider compatibility.

Compatibility

Compatibility means that a building is in harmony with its use or uses and its environment. Harmony should extend to a building's form, materials, and scale. Styles of different periods frequently clash; a cubistic dwelling would not be in harmony with eighteenth-century colonial buildings. Similarly, monumental or ostentatious building is often out of place in a modest setting. Two-story structures tend to be overwhelmed in a row of skyscrapers, so their market value may be diminished by incompatibility of design. There are various types of incompatibility. A structure can be incompatible with its function, its various elements can be incompatible with one other, or the structure can be incompatible with its site or location in the neighborhood.

Compatibility is influenced by zoning, historical districts, construction and maintenance costs, land value, physical features, architectural trends, and technology. Sometimes these factors impose conformity. Usually, the predominant uses and building styles in an area are readily observable. However, a trend in development may be more difficult to observe; an architectural style that appears atypical may actually conform to the direction of the trend.

A building design that is typical in an area has less influence on value than a design that is atypical, so the impact of nonconformity must be considered carefully. A slightly unusual design that is attractive and generally in harmony with other, nearby buildings could command a higher price than its more typical neighbors. A building with an incongruous design, however, will probably be sold at a price below the general market level; if it is not, there may be offsetting qualities.

Isolated cases of nonconforming design may require an unsupported, but reasoned, appraisal judgment. If, however, international style office buildings in a particular location are regularly sold at lower prices per square foot than buildings of a different style, the loss in value can be determined from market data. Sometimes there may be sufficient demand for a detached dwelling in a row-house neighborhood or for an art nouveau movie theater in a retail shopping district dominated by nineteenth-century buildings. If demand exists, it may support a market value equal to or greater than that of more typical structures. Functional utility may override design as a primary market requirement. If the general proportions and scale of an atypical building are in harmony with the surroundings and functional utility demands are met, there may be no design penalty.

Building materials should be in harmony with one another and with a building's architectural style. A building that is designed to be constructed of one material will not necessarily be effective when constructed of another. Building materials should not be excessively varied nor should an architectural design have too many distracting features. The design and building materials used should be well-integrated and in harmony with the site. A frame building in a wooded, hilly area will probably be in better harmony with its setting than a brick building, assuming wood is not inappropriate for the structure's function. A frame building in an urban area dominated by masonry usually suffers a market value penalty; an office building with a metal facade may be penalized if stone facades are typical in the area.

DESIGN AND FUNCTIONAL UTILITY BY BUILDING TYPE

Marketability is the ultimate test of functional utility. Generally, a building is functional if it successfully serves the purpose for which it was designed or adapted. Specific design considerations that affect the functional utility of residential, commercial, industrial, agricultural, and special-purpose buildings are discussed below.

Residential

Trends in single-family houses and apartments change in regard to the inclusion or exclusion of items such as porches, balconies, fireplaces, dining rooms, large kitchens, entry halls, and family rooms. Standards for dwellings vary widely for different income levels and in different regions. Historic houses are often less functional, but they are in great demand due to their preservationist appeal. To judge the functional utility of residential buildings, appraisers should analyze standard expectations in the market. Nevertheless, the functional utility of a single-family or multifamily dwelling results primarily from its layout, accommodation of specific activities, adequacy, and ease and cost of maintenance.

Layout

The layout of an apartment or house relates to traffic patterns—i.e., where kitchens and bathrooms should be located for convenience and how private and public areas should be separated. A layout has functional inutility if it causes awkward traffic patterns. For example, inutility may result if people have to cross the living room to get to a bedroom, if the dining area is not adjacent to the kitchen, or if groceries have to be brought through the living room to the kitchen.

Full bathrooms, which include facilities for bathing, are most convenient, accessible, and private when they are near the bedrooms; they should be accessed directly or through a hall, not through a second bedroom. Powder rooms should be located off a hall and near, but not too near, the living room or dining room. Poor floor plans are easily recognized by those who make up the market for apartments and houses, but standards often vary with current trends in a region and neighborhood.

The location of various rooms in relation to the site can increase or diminish a dwelling's privacy, comfort, and serenity. In urban areas, master bedrooms and living rooms are increasingly found in the rear of residences. Often they have access to, and views of, a garden. This trend is relatively new. Formerly it was considered desirable for the living room and best bedroom to be at the front of the house and oriented to the street. Kitchens, which were once relegated to the rear, are now just as likely to be on one side of a hall in the middle or at the front of a residence.

The popularity of condominium ownership has produced versatility in apartment design. Clustered, duplex, and townhouse units are designed in interesting configurations that maximize their market appeal. Structures designed for other uses are now being converted to apartments. Silos, breweries, warehouses, and schools have been successfully converted into multiunit projects. Duplexes, which often have strong market appeal, maximize salable square footage because vertical access is included in the unit, rather than in public space. Multiunit housing is also built in stacked configurations with access at more than one level to minimize stair climbing. Low-rise, multiple housing projects can be designed in a great many ways. Elevator apartment buildings tend to have more standardized, predictable floor plans to make the best use of space within a simple rectangular configuration.

Accommodation of Specific Activities

In building design, the specific activities of occupants are accommodated with separate areas for food preparation, eating, conversation, sleeping, hygiene, hobbies, and relaxation. The trend in American housing throughout much of this century has been toward combining the functions of many rooms into fewer rooms. The combined living-dining room and the family room exemplify this trend.

Adequacy

Adequacy is a primary consideration in evaluating functional utility. The adequacy of building size, windows, doors, rooms, ceiling height, closets, security, privacy, and comfort are all considered in planning dwellings and in their appraisal.

Standards of adequacy vary. The one-bathroom apartment or house has, for the most part, become an anachronism. New kitchens and baths are larger, better equipped, and more expensively finished than the small, utilitarian kitchens and baths of the recent past. Dishwashers, garbage disposals, and wall ovens are usually standard in new construction and their absence may create a value penalty. Ceramic tile in baths and more elegant fixtures are becoming commonplace. The master bedroom frequently has its own compartmental bath and a separate dressing area. Closets are abundant in new apartments and houses, and ceiling heights have increased, especially in living rooms, despite high energy costs.

In general, more people have better housing today. Many amenities are now considered necessities and their inclusion is taken for granted. Even in periods of high construction and financing costs when average houses are smaller, the tendency is to retain extra bathrooms, labor-saving devices, and fireplaces.

Although an apartment is a dwelling unit within a larger structure, it must be seen as an integral part of the whole. Security, convenience, and ease of maintenance are primary considerations for apartments, whether they are rented or owned as cooperatives or condominiums. Amenities tend to be more important than space;

apartment buyers and sellers often prefer a fireplace or an extra bathroom to an additional 200 square feet of area. Because most apartments do not have gardens or yards, they should provide light, air, and an interesting view. Amenities such as convenient parking, swimming pools, tennis courts, and exercise facilities are important to apartment projects when these features are not available nearby.

Smaller kitchens and bathrooms tend to be more acceptable to the market for apartments than the market for houses. A dining area that is an ell or a part of the living room is generally acceptable. Living rooms may be spacious to offset the smallness of other rooms and closet space must be plentiful.

Kitchen and bath finishes and equipment that are designed in response to a passing fad can quickly make an apartment less desirable to the market. Pastel ceramic tile in bathrooms and dark-colored kitchen equipment may be undesirable where all white or neutral color schemes are the norm. Dishwashers, garbage disposals, and central air-conditioning have become standard for apartments, and laundry equipment is becoming common in more expensive units.

The mix of units in an apartment project should meet market demands; an improper unit mix may indicate functional inutility.

Ease and Cost of Maintenance

The ease and cost of maintenance in a single-family dwelling or condominium unit are increasingly important to its marketability. More family members have become wage earners and less time is available for home maintenance. Interior and exterior finishes that require extensive maintenance have become noncompetitive.

The efficiency of energy use is a primary consideration in the residential market because heating, cooling, lighting, and cooking fuels are expensive. As alternatives to electricity, natural gas, and oil, buyers have turned to insulation, fireplaces, wood stoves, ventilating fans, and passive solar techniques. In most markets, a house that wastes fuel and electricity suffers major functional obsolescence.

Because windows are a primary source of heat loss, energy-conservation features are particularly important for multifamily dwellings and often make the difference between a profitable operation and a nonprofitable one. A large part of the energy used in buildings is needed to offset heat lost through cracks and openings and through the building envelope. Insulation, tightly installed windows with double or triple glazing, caulking, and weatherstripping help reduce heat loss in the winter, and shade trees, blinds, and solar screens can help keep units cooler in the summer. Energy-efficient equipment and controls are also used to meet new standards of functional utility in multifamily buildings.

Commercial

Commercial buildings are used for offices, stores, banks, restaurants, and service outlets. Commercial hotels constitute an important subcategory. Frequently, two or more commercial uses are combined in a single building.

The structural and design features of commercial buildings are constantly changing. Developers want the most competitive building possible, within the cost constraints imposed by economic pressures, so they incorporate technological changes to meet the demand for innovation whenever possible.

The efficiency of commercial construction today is much greater than it was in the past. Greater utility is observed both in the portion of the total area enclosed by the structure, which produces direct income in the form of rent, and in the structural facilitation that has evolved out of new materials and construction methods. No single method of commercial building construction predominates; methods vie with one another, and one may surpass others in a given area at a particular time. Steel and reinforced concrete are commonly used structural materials.

An appraiser examines a number of specific elements of functional utility in commercial buildings. An additional concern—i.e., safety and security—may be affected by the treatment of any of the specific elements listed below.

- Column spacing
- Bay depth
- Live-load floor capacity
- Ceiling height
- Module width
- Elevator facilities
- The work letter
- HVAC adequacy
- Energy efficiency
- Public amenities
- Parking ratios

Column Spacing

Column placement relates to a building's total height, and greater spans are more expensive to construct. Closely spaced columns limit the possibilities for interior partitioning. In some areas columns are typically placed at 20 to 22 feet on center, but this placement is far more limiting than column placement of 28 to 30 feet on center. Tenants usually prefer the wider spacing, but the cost to construct it may prove prohibitive.

Bay Depth

Bay depth is the distance from the tenant side of the corridor wall to the exterior wall. Bay depth controls the layout of interior space and is dictated by the depth and width of the site, which prescribes the building's configuration. The box-like configuration of contemporary office buildings is cost efficient because the ratio of perimeter wall to enclosed area is optimized. A long, thin building is more expensive to construct than a square one with the same area. The shallower bays of older buildings are more adaptable to the needs of smaller tenancies, but greater bay depths are more profitable to build if they do not exceed market demand. Tenants are often more concerned with the configuration of the space and its ability to house staff and equipment than with the amount of square foot area.

Live-Load Floor Capacity

Floor loading capacity is measured in live-load pounds per square foot. Inadequate floor loading capacity is a type of functional obsolescence that often prohibits marketability and is expensive to cure. Live load includes everything that can be moved, excluding parts of the structure. A floor load capacity of 100 pounds per square foot, up from 70 pounds a generation ago, is generally considered adequate for commercial buildings. Microfilm and microfiche record storage and the use of small-frame computer equipment have reversed the trend toward ever-increasing live-load floor capacity.

Ceiling Height

New commercial buildings usually have finished ceilings. Finished ceiling heights depend on the building heights permitted by zoning and on market standards and preferences. Higher ceiling heights within a normal range are preferable for other types of office space.

Module Width

Building modules are based on the distance between window mullions, which determines the size of partitioned offices in a building. Ceiling tiles and other finish components also determine the dimensions of contemporary office space modules.

When older commercial buildings have architectural charm or other acceptable structural qualities, it may be cost effective to retrofit them with modern lighting, ventilation, and elevators, even if their design does not conform to contemporary standards. Structures with high ceilings, narrow bay depths, wide public corridors, tall doors, and elaborate woodwork may be successfully preserved and adapted to meet the demand of certain markets that do not require streamlined space.

Elevator Facilities

Elevators in multilevel office buildings should be adequate in terms of speed, load capacity, safety, and number, and they should be able to meet peak period demands. Appraisers judge the adequacy of elevators using certain standards. A building should have one elevator for every 25,000 to 40,000 square feet of leaseable area. The elevators should be able to transport from 10% to 30% of the building's occupants within five minutes at speeds of 300 to 350 feet per minute. The standards for elevators vary according to a building's tenants. For example, a building that houses a single organization may require more elevator service due to heavy interfloor traffic.

Many building codes require that elevators accommodate handicapped patrons, so control panels should be accessible and interiors and doors should be wide enough for wheelchairs.

Elevator capacity is expressed in weight and number of occupants. Electric elevators are faster than hydraulic ones and serve multistory buildings better; hydraulic elevators are sometimes used to connect two or more floors.

In assessing the functional utility in elevator service, an appraiser should consider the number of tenants, the number of floors, and the total building area served by the elevators, as well as the quality of elevator service in competing buildings.

The Work Letter

A work letter is an agreement, usually part of a lease, that specifies the level of interior finish and equipment that the landlord is to provide to the tenant, including lighting, partitioning, door allowance, and electrical capacity. The quality and dollar value of these standard installations vary. A typical work letter may include the following:

- One lineal foot of partitioning for every 12 to 15 square feet of office space
- One suite entrance door for every 5,000 square feet of office space and one interior door for every 200 to 300 square feet of space
- One 2-by-4-foot lighting fixture for every 80 square feet of office space
- One light switch for each room
- One duplex receptacle for every 125 square feet of space
- One telephone outlet for every 150 square feet of space
- One lineal foot of closet door for every 800 square feet of space and one bifold closet door for every 5,000 square feet of space

Inadequacies or superadequacies in the level of finish specified in a work letter can result in market value penalties; variations may result in a tenant payment or credit, or in a rental addition or concession.

HVAC Adequacy

To determine a building's functional utility, an appraiser must consider whether the heating, ventilation, and air-conditioning systems (HVAC) are adequate. It is particularly important that a building's principal use matches its mechanical equipment. For example, medical office buildings usually have substantially more plumbing lines and connections, ventilating diffusers, electrical wiring, and partitioning than typical office structures.

Energy Efficiency

Energy consumption is increasingly significant for commercial buildings. To remain competitive, office buildings must incorporate technological advances such as computer-programmed controls, zoned heating and cooling, and highly efficient mechanical equipment. Public pressure to economize on energy consumption has been building due to rising energy costs, peak load pricing policies, and the threat of energy allocation.

In inefficient commercial buildings, energy expenditures range from 125,000 to 150,000 Btus per square foot per year. In buildings that house computers, the costs are significantly higher. With improved building design, energy consumption can be reduced to 60,000 to 80,000 Btus per square foot per year; experimental buildings can operate on less than 50,000 Btus per square foot per year.

Most newer commercial buildings in urban areas have been constructed with fixed sash fenestration, but some are now being built with windows that open to admit fresh air and regulate temperatures. If energy allocation occurs and certain fuels are unavailable at times, fixed sash windows could become functionally obsolete.

Public Amenities in Retail Space

Amenities can contribute to a building's functional utility. Building amenities may include attractive public areas, well-kept grounds, and adequate, well-located restroom facilities. The type and use of a property may dictate building amenities. For example, a retail center must have good delivery access, suitable traffic patterns for shoppers, strong lighting, adequate column spacing, and a sufficient number of escalators. Surface and finish elements should be durable and easily maintained. A retail center must also have areas for shoppers and workers to rest, ample restroom facilities, and attractive, coordinated signs.

The specialty shopping center is the newest type of retail grouping; it houses a number of retailers, most of which offer nonessential goods and services. A specialty shopping center usually has no anchor tenants, so it must project a certain image with a central feature, integrated design elements, or attractive landscaping. Restaurants and entertainment facilities such as movie theaters are also included in this type of shopping center.

The quality and distribution of public amenities in shopping centers are important appraisal concerns. The need for adequately distributed amenities influences the design of shopping centers, which are as competitive in the market as office buildings. However, the configuration of the typical shopping center has changed even more drastically than the design of the typical office building.

Trends in shopping centers change so rapidly that many structures become functionally obsolete before they deteriorate physically. Because retail space is relatively easy to renovate, many centers can be streamlined and modernized when they lose their market appeal. Shopping centers have evolved from small strip centers, which were developed after World War II, to huge regional and super-regional centers, which may occupy up to 100 acres of land and include more than one million square feet of building area. Despite the trend toward greater size, however, most existing and newly built shopping centers have less than 200,000 square feet of space, and more than half have less than 100,000 square feet of area.

Supermarkets and drugstores were once the anchor stores of large suburban shopping centers, but they now tend to be free-standing structures located near, but not within, shopping centers. This phenomenon is the result of increased merchandising competition between supermarkets, department stores, drugstores, and smaller stores. Large suburban shopping centers are frequently town centers, where people go to shop, socialize, be entertained, and attend civic meetings.

Parking Ratios

Parking ratios are crucial to the success of retail centers, except those located in dense urban areas. The emergence of multiuse shopping centers and the trend toward smaller cars have increased the ratio between gross leaseable store area and parking spaces. One parking space for every 180 square feet of gross leaseable store area is usually adequate. Orientation to a means of access is crucial for all commercial buildings.

Commercial uses tend to occupy separate structures in areas of low-density development. These buildings are usually accessed by automobile, so sufficient, adjacent parking is essential. Pedestrian access from buildings to parking areas should also be accommodated. Access to both public transportation and automobile parking is important for commercial buildings located in densely developed urban areas.

Security and convenience govern the placement of parking facilities; the route between a commercial facility and its parking area must be direct and visible. The amount of parking provided is determined by the proximity and availabiliy of alternative sources of access, such as public transportation, and how much parking is provided by similar buildings. Some commercial buildings in urban areas do not include onsite parking because other forms of transportation are convenient or adequate parking facilities are located close by.

In efficient parking garage design, columns are placed every 28 feet, which permits three cars to be parked between columns. The popularity of small cars has given outdoor parking lots greater capacity; more cars can be accommodated by restriping spaces. Parking garage design has not changed fundamentally because columns are still needed, but, when possible, drive aisles have been reduced in width from 26 to 25 feet. The standard parking space has been reduced from 9 ft. by 18 ft. to 8¾ ft. by 17½ ft. in area. A compact car needs a space of approximately 8¼ ft. by 16½ ft. Most self-park garages allow 300 to 350 gross leaseable square feet per car, which includes aisles and ramps; garages with attendant parking allow substantially less than 300 square feet per car.

The most efficient configuration for a garage is 90-degree-angle parking. A typical parking ratio in an area without good public transit is one parking space for every 200 square feet of leaseable area.

Hotels

Hotels range from tiny inns, with fewer than a dozen rooms, to huge convention hotels, with more than a thousand rooms.[3] All hotels and motels were once measured against standard, up-to-date designs; this tendency continues, particularly for medium-priced hotels. For many older facilities and luxury hotels, however, variation in architectural styles and interior finish must be considered.

Many older hotels and apartment buildings that have been rehabilitated as hotels have unique architectural style and a quality of luxury that is difficult to replicate in newer structures. The desire to rehabilitate older buildings is widespread, affecting small inns in picturesque country areas.

All lodging facilities benefit from suitable fireproofing, soundproofing, and security systems. Beyond these basic considerations, the physical configuration of a hotel or motel is determined by the type of patrons it serves. A motor hotel, or motel, must be oriented to the needs of drivers who wish to spend a minimum amount of time on the premises; a resort hotel, on the other hand, must provide a variety of entertainment facilities for its guests. Although automobile parking is still necessary, it is usually situated away from direct view.

Functional inutility in hotel structures, like other types of buildings, can be categorized in terms of overimprovements, inadequacies, poor layout, inappropriate structural qualities or finishes, and inefficient equipment.

The amount of hotel space used for guest rooms varies. A hotel that is a major meeting and entertainment center has a much lower proportion of guest rooms to public areas than an apartment hotel. Many apartment hotels are successful transient operations, consisting entirely of suites with small equipped kitchens, living rooms, and separate bedrooms. These hotels have small lobbies and restaurants.

The layout of guest rooms also vary with the clientele. Larger rooms, separate dressing areas, and large closets are needed when most guests stay for several nights. Room size is usually geared to the necessary amount of furniture—i.e., the room should provide ample space around and between pieces of furniture. Business travelers need desks, while vacationers usually do not. The trend toward larger beds requires larger rooms, but rooms that are too large do not use space efficiently.

Support space for guest rooms includes hotel office and operations areas, restaurants, lounges, public meeting rooms, and often athletic facilities.

Industrial Properties

Like all properties, an industrial manufacturing property must have a site, buildings, and equipment that function as an operating unit. Inutility is measured against the standard of optimal efficiency for similar properties in the market.

Some industrial properties are designed and equipped to meet the needs of a specific occupant and have limited appeal to others. Buildings used for industries that

---

3. For a thorough discussion of hotels, see Stephen Rushmore, *Hotels, Motels, and Restaurants: Valuation and Market Studies* (Chicago: American Institute of Real Estate Appraisers, 1983).

involve bulky or volatile materials and products have specialized equipment and building designs, so they have few potential users. Buildings used for research and development or for light fabricating and processing are less limited in their appeal.

All industrial buildings are measured in terms of gross building area (GBA). For comparison and measurement in terms of market standards, the GBA can be divided into finished and unfinished categories. The most flexible design for industrial buildings, which will have the greatest appeal on the open market, is embodied in a one-story, square or nearly square structure that complies with all local building codes.

Industrial buildings can be constructed of many types of material, but concrete and steel are used most often. Tilt-up construction, which incorporates concrete walls that are cast horizontally and put in place vertically, is common. The walls are often designed to be load-bearing. Flat roofs supported by steel bar joists are also common. Prefabricated steel buildings are cheaper to build, and their appearance is now considered more acceptable than it was in the past. Plastic skylights can be installed for natural light in lieu of expensive monitor and sawtooth roofs.

Industrial properties must have land-to-building ratios that allow plenty of space for parking, truck maneuvering, yard storage, and expansion. Other locational considerations include reasonable real estate taxes, an available supply of labor, adequate utility service, beneficial zoning, and proximity to supply sources and customers.

Industrial parks are groups of industrial buildings that have similar uses. With landscaping, ample setbacks, building and lot size minimums, and professional architecture, engineering, and management, industrial parks provide an environment that is acceptable to occupants and government land-planning groups.

The combination of old and new industrial space has substantial functional obsolescence when the new construction contributes less than its cost to the value of the whole. The operating layout of industrial space should allow processes to be carried out with maximum efficiency. Typically, receiving functions are performed on one side of the building, shipping functions on the other, and processing or storage functions in the middle. Some industrial buildings include special features such as sprinkler systems, scales, loading dock levelers, refrigeration areas, conveyor systems, process piping (for compressed air, water, and gas), power wiring, and employee lockers and lunch rooms.

Storage Buildings

Storage structures range from simple cubicles, known as *miniwarehouses*, to huge regional warehouses with one million square feet of area. Functional utility and location have a major impact on the market value of storage buildings; obsolescence usually occurs before the structures deteriorate physically. The functions of warehouses are

- To store materials in a protected environment
- To organize materials so that they can be easily inventoried and removed
- To provide facilities for efficient delivery
- To provide facilities for efficient access and shipping

For optimal functional utility, warehouses should have adequate access, open areas, ceiling height, floor load capacity (often 300 pounds or more for heavy-duty industrial storage buildings), humidity and temperature controls, shipping and receiving facilities, fire protection, and protection from the elements.

The primary consideration in warehouse location is good access. Trucking is the most common means of transporting goods, but certain warehouse operations also need access to rail and water transportation. Operations that depend on trucks to transport goods should be near an arterial highway. The highway's access street or frontage road and the truck maneuvering area at the warehouse loading dock must allow for efficient use of loading facilities at all times. If a warehouse site slopes downward from a frontage road, the loading dock can be constructed at truck-bed level. For rail access, one portion of the site must be long and level.

Forklifts, conveyor belts, and automatically guided-vehicle conveyor systems are used to move materials inside warehouses. Truck docks must be wide enough to accommodate truck widths and the interior servomechanism used to move goods and materials. If electric trucks are used, a battery-charging area should be included. Most storage operations are palletized—i.e., pallets, or portable platforms, are used for moving and storing materials. Therefore, ceiling heights in warehouses should accommodate an ideal number of pallets. Because wide spans provide more flexibility, a square structure generally is the most cost effective.

Office space in warehouses may constitute as little as 1% of the total area, but generally approximately 5% of the total gross building area is used for offices. In distribution facilities, office space may comprise 35% to 50% of the total gross building area. Office space in warehouses should be adequately heated, cooled, and lighted, but its finish is generally utilitarian.

Sprinkler systems are needed in warehouses where flammable goods are stored. The nature of the stored material determines whether the system should be wet or dry, using water or chemicals.

Miniwarehouses are usually combined in one- or two-story rectangular structures located near those who will use them. They should be visible, accessible, and surrounded by enough land for parking and maneuvering. The sizes of individual units within miniwarehouses vary; they usually include small storage units, which have passage doors, and larger units, which have roll-up truck doors.

Buildings on Agricultural Properties

In most of the United States, there is a trend toward fewer, larger farms, and the contribution of farm buildings to the total value of farm real estate has been steadily decreasing. Statistics from the U.S. Department of Agriculture indicate that farm buildings contribute less than 20% of the total value of farm property. The number of farm buildings per acre of farmland has also decreased.

Farming is done by families and by large, specialized business operations. The equipment and management needed to run agricultural operations have become increasingly specialized.

Farming operations are conducted in fewer types of farm buildings because each operation is responsible for fewer functions. Farm buildings must accommodate the type of machinery and equipment used in farming today. More large machine sheds are needed to house tractors, combines, discs, plows, harrows, cultivators, pickers, trucks, and other equipment. Pipeline milking machines and overhead feed bins dictate the requirements for milking parlors and loafing sheds where livestock are sheltered. Changes in the care and feeding of poultry have substantially modified the design of poultry farm buildings.

The history of the United States has been shaped by certain types of buildings. Barns are second only to houses in their influence on American culture. Barns have successfully combined functional utility with picturesque design. Form, function, and materials have come together in a unique way to make the barn the most successful type of vernacular building. Some barns have traditionally been multifunctional, providing animal shelter, grain storage, and a threshing floor. Other barns, such as tobacco barns and modern farm buildings, fulfill a single, specialized function.

The typical American barn is 60 feet long and 30 feet wide, with two gable ends, a loft, and double doors on the wide sides. Most barns are built of wood, but some are made of stone, logs, or brick. Barns are suitable for modern, general-purpose farming if they are sufficiently adaptable. The use of baled, rather than loose, hay and the increased use of ensilage have lessened the need for barn storage. Silos, however, are more prevalent and larger.

Animal shelters should be dry and clean, provide protection from the wind and sun, and be adaptable to equipment storage. To be useful, each farm building must contribute to the operating efficiency of the entire farm. Each building's usefulness relates to the type and size of the farm. Functional inutility results from having too many farm buildings when fewer would be more efficient.

Special-Purpose Buildings

The architecture of special-purpose buildings tends to limit them to a single use. Although most buildings can be converted to other uses, the conversion of special-purpose buildings generally involves extra expense and design expertise. Special-purpose structures include churches, synagogues, theaters, sports arenas, and other types of auditoriums. Many automobile dealerships and gasoline service stations have been successfully converted to other uses.

The functional utility of a special purpose building depends on whether there is continued demand for the use for which the building was designed; when there is demand, functional utility depends on whether the building conforms to competitive standards. For example, there is a continued demand for movie theaters, but their design has changed due to high maintenance and utility costs. Ornate movie theaters have been replaced with simple, unembellished structures. However, there is a demand to convert older movie theaters into concert halls and legitimate theaters.

The design and materials used in new synagogues and churches are simple for the same reason. The functional utility of these structures, like sports and concert arenas, is primarily related to seating capacity. However, the structure's support facilities, general attractiveness, and appeal must also be considered.

The adaptive-use movement has generated public awareness of the conversion potential of special-purpose buildings. Buildings usually outlive their function, and energy shortages, the decline of modernism, and disproportionate construction costs have contributed to the preservation movement. Railroad stations, schools, firehouses, and grist mills are popular structures for conversion. The functional utility of these buildings is related to how much they deviate from building codes and to any cost of rehabilitation that exceeds the amount that provides an economic return. A typical cause of functional inutility in adaptive-use projects is an insufficient number of staircases to meet building codes. By contrast, a high ceiling in a specialty property does not indicate functional inutility if it is one of the unusual architectural qualities that contributes to net income.

Mixed-Use Buildings

Many buildings successfully combine two or more uses. The construction of mixed-use buildings, which began in the late 1950s and 1960s, reflects the influence of postwar developments such as the suburban shopping center and the planned business and residential units of urban environments. A prevalent example is the mixed-use development (MUD), which comprises at least three, significant, revenue-producing uses such as retail, office, and residential or hotel/motel facilities.

Mixed-use developments are characterized by the physical and functional integration of their components. They are megastructures built around centrally located shopping galleries or court areas of hotels. Walkways, plazas, escalators, and elevators provide an interconnecting pedestrian thoroughfare with easy access to parking facilities underground, at street level, or aboveground. Because mixed-use developments bring together diverse participants, they require extensive, extraordinarily coherent planning.[4]

In mixed-use buildings, each type of use creates a number of criteria, which must be analyzed separately. The structure should also be considered as a whole to determine its ability to combine uses. Combined uses should be compatible, but minor incompatibilities can be made more congruous with separate entrances, elevators, and equipment. Without separate entrances and elevators, the residential units in upper floors and the office units below would both suffer. Only in a rather large building can the extra expense of such features be justified. A hotel located in an

---

4. For a comprehensive analysis of mixed-use developments, see Robert E. Witherspoon, Jon P. Abbett, and Robert M. Gladstone, *Mixed-Use Developments: New Ways of Land Use* (Washington, D.C.: Urban Land Institute, 1976).

office building should have its own entrance and elevators. In general, security and privacy should characterize a building's residential area; professionalism and prestige should pervade the office portion of the structure.

Mixed-use buildings are an architectural challenge. Traditionally, residential and commercial buildings look different and are easily distinguished from one another. These differences have been diminished, however, by the eclecticism of postmodern architecture.

SUMMARY

Architectural style, which is the character of a building's form and ornamentation, and *functional utility*, a building's usefulness and ability to perform its intended function according to current market standards and the efficiency of layout, are interrelated. Both affect the attractiveness, comfort, and maintenance of buildings because form and function work together to create successful architecture.

Architecture is the art or science of building design and construction in which three-dimensional elements are organized on a large scale to serve human needs. American architectural style is divided into *formal architecture*, which conforms to the aesthetic and functional criteria of architectural historians, and *vernacular architecture*, which reflects conventional norms and adaptations made in response to the environment or contemporary life-styles.

Market tastes and preferences are influenced by the desire to preserve tradition and by desires for innovation, which precipitates a shift away from the predominant style, and improved efficiency, which motivates energy conservation. Major changes in architectural style generally occur at the end of building cycles, about every 30 to 50 years. As the economic life of a building progresses, utility and function become the principal factors affecting its value.

Architectural style depends on the availability of natural materials, the state of technology, and the versatility of the site. Innovations that have affected building design and construction include balloon and post and beam framing, the Franklin stove, central heating, computer and communications installations, air-conditioning, and elevators. The shape of buildings has also been influenced by the use of structural components such as steel bar joists with increased load-bearing capacity, and steel and reinforced concrete framing (post-tensioning and tube bundling), which facilitate the construction of curtain walls. Technological advances have resulted in the standardization of residential and office building styles.

Climate and physical setting also affect building design and placement. The placement of trees as windbreaks, the installation of solar heating systems and heat-retaining materials, and the use of underground construction and berming are examples of environmental adaptations.

Functional inutility is an impairment of the functional capacity of a building according to market standards. It corresponds to functional obsolescence brought on by technological advances, trends in style, or superadequacies in structural components.

Functional utility is not necessarily found in the most utilitarian or efficient design, although these features are important. Suitability, comfort, safety and security, ease and cost of maintenance, market standards, attractiveness, and profitability all contribute to functional utility. The *compatibility* of a building with its use and environment must also be considered. Building compatibility involves the integration of style, form, scale, design, material, function, site, and neighborhood. Marketability is the ultimate test of functional utility.

The functional utility of a single-family or multifamily residential property depends on its layout, accommodation of special activities, adequacy, and ease and cost of maintenance. Layout considerations focus on how effectively the location of rooms within a dwelling satisfies the occupants' desire for accessibility and seclusion. Versatility of configuration is particularly evident when townhouses, lofts, and duplex apartments are converted into condominiums.

In modern residential design, the functions of many rooms are combined into fewer rooms (e.g., the living-dining room and the family room). The adequacy of a dwelling is considered in terms of size, rooms, storage area, security, privacy, and comfort. Amenities such as well-equipped kitchens and bathrooms, parking, and recreational facilities are now often considered necessities. More family members have become wage earners, so less time is available for home maintenance. Due to rising energy costs, more attention is being focused on energy-conserving features.

In commercial buildings, functional utility is considered in terms of column spacing, bay depth, live-load capacity, ceiling height, module width, elevator facilities, HVAC adequacy, energy efficiency, public amenities, parking ratios, safety, and security. The *work letter* is an agreement, usually part of a lease, that specifies which equipment and installations the landlord is to provide the tenant.

Hotels, which are a special subcategory of commercial buildings, vary according to location, the clientele served, and design. In evaluating the functional utility of hotels, fire-and sound-proofing, security, the efficient use of space, adequate facilities, and possible overimprovements are important factors.

Some industrial buildings house technical processes that involve hazardous materials and specialized equipment; others accommodate more generalized uses such as research and development. To measure the functional utility of an industrial building, an appraiser applies the market standard of optimum efficiency for comparable buildings. Reinforced concrete and steel framing with steel bar joists for greater load-bearing capacity is common in industrial construction. All industrial buildings are measured in *gross building area* (GBA). The land-to-building ratios of industrial properties must allow space for parking and truck maneuvering. Operating layouts should facilitate efficient processing—i.e., receiving, fabricating, storage, and shipping operations.

Warehouses provide for the storage, organization, inventory, access, and delivery of materials. For functional utility, warehouses must have adequate loading facilities, ceiling height, floor load capacity, temperature and humidity control, and protection against fire and the elements.

Farm buildings include machinery sheds and barns, which provide for animal shelter, grain storage, and threshing. The mechanization of dairy and poultry farming has necessitated changes in the buildings where animals are sheltered. Farm buildings must contribute to the efficiency of the entire farm, although they generally account for less than 20% of the value of farm property.

The functional utility of special-purpose buildings depends on whether there is continued demand for their intended use and how well they conform to competitive standards for that use. Special-purpose buildings are limited because they are designed for a single use. The conversion of service stations, movie theaters, fire-houses, mills, and other special-purpose properties is costly, but feasible if the quality and design of the structures can assure enhanced property income.

Mixed-use developments (MUDs) accommodate at least three different types of income-producing uses and are usually located in a megastructure. The functional utility of MUDs depends both on the efficiency of the individual facilities and how well the stucture as a whole combines uses in a compatible manner.

12 Highest and Best Use Analysis

The economic principles of supply and demand, substitution, balance, and conformity are the basic tools for analyzing the relationships between economic behavior and appraisal. The interdependent factors that influence value—i.e., utility, scarcity, desire, and effective purchasing power—are also economic in origin because modern value and appraisal theory has evolved from neoclassical economic thought.

The relationships between economic behavior and appraisal are clearly evident in real estate markets. Here, where buyers and sellers of property rights interact, market value has great significance to debt and equity capital investors and to professional appraisers. In all types of property transactions, market value estimates based on careful analyses of market behavior shape financial decisions that affect individuals, neighborhoods, businesses, and governments.

An understanding of market behavior is essential to the concept of highest and best use. Market forces create market value, so the interaction between market forces and highest and best use is of crucial importance. When the purpose of an appraisal is to estimate market value, highest and best use analysis identifies the most profitable, competitive use to which the property can be put. Therefore, highest and best use is a market-driven concept.

DEFINITION

Highest and best use may be defined as

> The reasonably probable and legal use of vacant land or an improved property, which is physically possible, appropriately supported, financially feasible, and that results in the highest value.

To clarify the distinction between the highest and best use of 1) land or a site as though vacant, and 2) property as improved, consider a single-family residential property. If the property is located in an area zoned for commercial use, the maximum productivity of the land as though vacant will most likely be based on commercial use. If, however, there is adequate competition for a residential use, then the highest and best use of the property as improved will be for residential use. In this case, the value of the property as improved would exceed the value of the undeveloped commercial land.

The highest and best use of a specific parcel of land does not depend on subjective analysis by the property owner, the developer, or the appraiser; rather, highest and best use is shaped by the competitive forces within the market where the property is located. Therefore, the analysis and interpretation of highest and best use is an economic study of market forces focused on the subject property.[1]

Market forces also shape market value. The general data that are collected and analyzed to estimate property value are also used by the appraiser to formulate an opinion of the property's highest and best use as of the appraisal date. In all valuation assignments, value estimates are based on use. The highest and best use of a property to be appraised provides the foundation for a thorough investigation of the competitive positions of market participants. Consequently, highest and best use can be described as the foundation on which market value rests. Without interaction in the marketplace, highest and best use would not exist and market value estimations would be impossible.

When potential buyers contemplate purchasing real estate for personal use or occupancy, their principal motivations are the perceived benefits of enhanced enjoyment, prestige, and privacy. Purchasers of investment property are frequently motivated by the promise of net income or capital accumulation and certain tax advantages. Investors are more directly concerned with *feasibility, an indication that a project has a reasonable likelihood of satisfying explicit objectives.* These objectives may include assured occupancy, low management costs, and potential value enhancement.

Like highest and best use and market value, highest and best use and feasibility are interconnected. However, feasibility analyses may involve data and considerations that are not directly related to highest and best use determinations. A feasibility study can be based on highest and best use analysis, but it may be more detailed or have a somewhat different focus.

Traditionally, highest and best use analysis has been associated with land residual analysis, which is derived from classical economics. In classical land residual analysis, value is attributed to the income that remains after improvement costs are compensated. However, buildings can be changed while the essential characteristics of sites cannot, so the income to any particular site depends on a use decision. When an individual site can be substituted for another site in a particular market, the difference in value between the two sites is attributable to the superior features of one

---

1. The benefit that an amenity may contribute to the development of a community is not considered in the appraiser's analysis of highest and best use.

parcel of land. From a microeconomic point of view, therefore, land value is the driving force and property values in a specific market are a function of the income to the land.

The highest and best use of land as though vacant is an old concept derived from classical economic theory. The highest and best use of property as improved is a distinct concept elaborated by valuation theorists and practitioners. The concept was developed to answer two important questions that the older concept does not address. How should the property as improved be used? Should the existing improvement continue to be used, or should it be demolished so a new improvement can be constructed? Highest and best use of land as though vacant indicates only how the land should be used if it were vacant; it is primarily a tool for land valuation and is used by appraisers to measure a building's value contribution.

HIGHEST AND BEST USE OF LAND AS THOUGH VACANT

Highest and best use of land or a site as though vacant assumes that a parcel of land is vacant or can be made vacant by demolishing any improvements. With this assumption, uses that create value in the marketplace can be identified, and the appraiser can begin to select comparable properties and estimate land value. Land as though vacant is a fundamental concept of valuation theory and the basis for the cost approach. Because many appraisals include an allocation of value between the land and the buildings associated with it, a highest and best use analysis of the land as though vacant is frequently performed.

The questions to be answered in this analysis are: If the land is, or were, vacant, what use should be made of it? What type of building or other improvement, if any, should be constructed on the land, and when?

When a reasonable forecast of a property's highest and best use indicates a change in the near future, the present highest and best use is considered an interim use. For example, the highest and best use of a farm in the path of urban growth would be for *interim use* as a farm, with a potential future highest and best use as a residential subdivision. If the farm is ready for development at the time of the appraisal, there is no interim use. If the farm has no subdivision potential, its highest and best use is as a farm with no interim use.

In some cases, an appraiser may conclude that the highest and best use of a parcel of land is to be held for speculation—i.e., to remain vacant until its price appreciates. For many parcels of land, however, the highest and best use requires some change or improvement. The highest and best use of land as though vacant may call for its subdivision into smaller parcels of land or its assemblage with other land.

If an improvement is needed to realize the highest and best use of the land, the appraiser must determine the type and characteristics of the improvement to be constructed. For example, should the parcel of land be improved with an office building, a retail building, or a hotel? If an office building would be the highest and best use, how many stories should it have? How many offices should it contain? What size should the offices be? Which features should be included? What rental should be charged, and what level of operating expenses would be incurred? How much would such a building cost? In short, the conclusion of highest and best use for a parcel of land should be as specific as the marketplace suggests. General categories such as "an office building," "a commercial building," or "a single-family residence" may be adequate for the purpose in some situations; in other cases, the demand of market participants may be more specific.

Even when a site is not vacant, it is often analyzed as though it were. An appraiser considers whether a building with the same use, size, quality, and function as the existing building would be constructed on the site if it were vacant. If this new improvement were to be the highest and best use of the land as though vacant, it presumably would have no physical deterioration or functional obsolescence. The appraiser also must consider external obsolescence.

The present use of a site may not be its highest and best use. The land may be suitable for a much higher, or more intense, use. For instance, the highest and best use of a parcel of land as though vacant may be for a 10-story office building, while the office building that currently occupies the site has only three stories.

HIGHEST AND BEST USE OF PROPERTY AS IMPROVED

Highest and best use of a property as improved pertains to the use that should be made of an improved property in light of its improvements. For example, should a 30-year-old hotel building be maintained as it is, or be renovated, expanded, or partly demolished? Should it be replaced with a different type or intensity of use?

The use that maximizes an investment property's return on a long-term basis is its highest and best use as improved. If potential uses require no capital expenditures for remodeling, their estimated returns can be compared directly. If capital expenditures would be required to convert the structure from its existing use to other potential uses, rates of return must be calculated for these property uses, considering the total investment in the property and all capital expenditures. These rates of return can then be compared with rates of return for uses that do not require capital expenditures.

In analyzing the highest and best use of owner-occupied properties, appraisers must consider any rehabilitation or modernization that is consistent with market preferences. For example, the highest and best use of a luxury residence should reflect all rehabilitation that would be required for maximum enjoyment of the property.

PURPOSE OF HIGHEST AND BEST USE ANALYSIS

The purpose of highest and best use analysis is different for highest and best use as though vacant and highest and best use as improved. An appraiser should distinguish between the two types of highest and best use in the appraisal analysis, and the appraisal report should clearly identify, explain, and justify the purpose and conclusion for each type.

Highest and Best Use of Land as Though Vacant

The value of land is generally estimated as though vacant. (Land with legally nonconforming improvements is an exception to this rule.) When land is already vacant, the reasoning is obvious; an appraiser values the land as it exists. When land is not vacant, however, land value depends on the uses to which the land can be put. Therefore, the highest and best use of land as though vacant must be considered in relation to its existing use and all potential uses.

Land value can be determined by potential, rather than actual, use. For example, consider a valuable commercial site in an excellent location that is currently improved with a service station or other retail use. A purchaser who wants to build a high-rise office building on the site may pay a price for the property that includes no value, or even negative value, for the existing improvements. The potential use, not the existing use, usually governs the price that will be paid. Consider also a five-year-old, 120-unit apartment building that is purchased and demolished to make way for a hospital expansion program. The highest and best use of the site changed rapidly after hospital expansion was planned and put into effect.

Any building can be demolished; the fact that most buildings are not does not negate the possiblity. The possibility of removing existing improvements is the premise for the concept of highest and best use of land as though vacant. Land values are not penalized so long as the existing buildings have economic value. If the buildings no longer have value, demolition is appropriate. Buildings can be changed, but the basic physical characteristics of sites cannot.

Historic district zoning controls have made demolition permits difficult or impossible to obtain in some areas. Furthermore, special tax incentives for older buildings can substantially enhance their value and alter the highest and best use of property in many cases.

Several appraisal techniques require a separate estimate of land value; the identification of the land's highest and best use is necessary to estimate land value. The highest and best use of comparable properties should be the same or similar to that of the subject property. Therefore, there are two reasons to identify the highest and best use of land as though vacant in an appraisal: to estimate a separate land value and to identify comparable sales of vacant land.

Highest and Best Use of Property as Improved

There also are two reasons to analyze the highest and best use of a property as improved. The first is to identify the use of the property that can be expected to produce the highest overall return for each dollar of capital invested. If, for example, a property is currently being used as rental apartments, will this use continue to provide maximum benefits? Would the rate of return be increased by converting the property to an apartment hotel? The value of the property will differ under these two use assumptions, and the use providing the highest present value is the highest and best use.

The second reason to estimate the highest and best use of property as improved is to help identify comparable properties. The highest and best use of land as though vacant and property as improved should be the same for each comparable property as for the subject property. For example, it may be inappropriate to use a comparable property that has a highest and best use as offices in appraising a subject property that has a highest and best use as a hotel.

CRITERIA IN HIGHEST AND BEST USE ANALYSIS

The highest and best use of both land as though vacant and property as improved must meet four criteria. The highest and best use must be 1) physically possible, 2) legally permissible, 3) financially feasible, and 4) maximally productive. These criteria are usually considered sequentially; a use may be financially feasible, but this is irrelevant if it is physically impossible or legally prohibited. Only when there is a reasonable possibility that one of the prior, unacceptable conditions can be changed is it appropriate to proceed with the analysis. If, for example, current zoning does not permit a potential highest and best use, but there is a possibility that the zoning can be changed, the proposed use can be considered on that basis.

Physically Possible

The size, shape, area, and terrain of a parcel of land affect the uses to which it can be developed. The utility of a parcel may depend on its frontage and depth. Irregularly shaped parcels can cost more to develop and, after development, they may have less utility than regularly shaped parcels of the same area.

Certain parcels can achieve their highest and best use only as part of an assemblage. In such a case, an appraiser must either determine the feasibility and probability of assembly or make the highest and best use determination and other appraisal decisions conditioned on such an assembly. For example, a large petrochemical plant may be constructed on a site that has been created by assembling smaller tracts. The individual small tracts may not have had utility for industrial use and, thus, may have had a much lower unit value.

An appraiser also considers the capacity and availability of public utilities. If a sewer main located in front of a property cannot be tapped because of a lack of capacity at the disposal plant, the property does not have access to the public sewerage system and its use is limited.

When a site's topography or subsoil conditions make development restrictive or costly, its potential use is adversely affected. All sites available for a particular use compete with one another. If the cost of grading or constructing a foundation on the site being appraised is higher than for typical sites in the area, the subject site may be economically unusable for the highest and best use otherwise indicated.

The highest and best use of a property as improved also depends on physical considerations such as size, design, and condition. The condition of the property and its ability to continue in its current use may be relevant. If the property should be converted to another use, the cost of conversion must be analyzed in light of the returns to be generated by the new use. Obviously, the costs of conversion depend on the property's existing physical condition.

Legally Permissible

In all cases an appraiser must determine what uses are legally permissible. (Nonconforming uses are discussed later in this chapter). Private restrictions, zoning, building codes, historic district controls, and environmental regulations must be investigated because they may preclude many potential highest and best uses.

A long-term lease can also affect a property's highest and best use because, over the remaining term of the lease, property use may be limited by lease provisions. If a property is subject to a land lease that has 12 more years to run, it is probably not economically possible to construct a new building with a 40-year remaining economic life. In such a case, the appraisal report should state that the highest and best use determination is influenced by the lease's impact on future utility. A distinction, however, must be made between the highest and best use of property and a legal requirement to use property for a particular purpose beyond its economic life.

Private or deed restrictions relate to the covenants under which the property was acquired. These restrictions may prohibit certain uses or specify building setbacks, heights, and types of materials. If deed restrictions conflict with zoning laws or building codes, the most restrictive guidelines usually prevail.

If there are no private restrictions, the property uses allowed by the zoning typically constitute the available choices in most highest and best use determinations. However, the possiblity of a change in zoning should also be considered by the appraiser. If the highest and best use of the site or property is not allowed under current zoning, but there is a reasonable probability that a change in zoning could be obtained due to shifting economic and social patterns, these conditions can be considered in determining highest and best use. However, the appraiser must fully disclose all pertinent factors relating to a possible zoning change, including the time and expenses involved and the risk that the change will not be granted.

Building codes can prevent land from being developed to its highest and best use by imposing burdensome restrictions that increase the cost of construction. This is particularly common in metropolitan areas that include municipalities or jurisdictions with different building codes. Residential development in metropolitan areas has been greatly influenced by different offsite requirements in building codes. Less restrictive codes typically result in lower development costs and, therefore, attract developers; more restrictive codes tend to discourage development. Some areas limit growth by using building codes to retard new construction.

Increasing concern over the effects of land use has resulted in environmental regulations, which also must be considered in highest and best use analysis. Appraisers must be familiar with environmental regulations pertaining to clear air, clean water, and wetlands, and be sensitive to public reaction to proposed development projects. Adverse reactions from local residents and the general public have stopped many real estate developments.

Financially Feasible

In determining which uses are physically possible and legally permissible, an appraiser eliminates some uses from consideration. Then the uses that meet the first two criteria are analyzed further to determine which are likely to produce an income, or return, equal to or greater than the amount needed to satisfy operating expenses, financial obligations, and capital amortization. All uses that are expected to produce a positive return are regarded as financially feasible.

To determine financial feasibility, an appraiser estimates the future gross income that can be expected from each potential highest and best use. Vacancy and collection losses and operating expenses are then subtracted from each gross income to obtain the likely net operating income (*NOI*) from each use. A rate of return on the invested capital can then be calculated for each use. If the net revenue capable of being generated is enough to satisfy the required rate of return on investment and provide a return on the land, the use is financially feasible within some price limit.

Maximally Productive

Of the financially feasible uses, the use that produces the highest price, or value, consistent with the rate of return warranted by the market for that use is the highest and best use. To determine the highest and best use of land as though vacant, the same rate of return is often used to capitalize income streams from different uses into their respective values. This procedure is appropriate if all competing uses have similar risk characteristics. The use that produces the highest value is the highest and best use.

The land income that is capitalized into value is the residual income remaining after operating expenses and the return attributable to the other agents in production (i.e., labor, capital, and coordination) are allocated a market-determined portion of the property's income. Using an alternate land residual technique, the value of the improvements is multiplied by a building capitalization rate determined in the market. The income attributable to the improvements is then subtracted from the net operating income for the total property, and the remaining income is allocated to the land. This procedure is illustrated in the next section of this chapter.

The potential highest and best uses of land are *usually* long-term land uses, uses that are expected to remain on the site for the normal economic, or useful, life of the improvements. Depending on building type, quality of construction, and other factors, most buildings are expected to last at least 25 years, and some may last more than 100 years. Therefore, the stream of benefits, or income, produced by the buildings reflect a carefully considered, and usually very specific, land use program.

The capital investment required to convert a property to alternative uses may vary, but if the amount of invested capital remains constant, the total *NOI*s produced by various uses can be compared directly. The use that produces the highest *NOI* consistent with the risk incurred is the highest and best use. When the amount of invested capital varies among alternative uses, the income from each use is related to the capital investment required by calculating the rate of return. The use producing the highest rate of return is the highest and best use of the property as improved.

TESTING HIGHEST AND BEST USE

To test the highest and best use of land as though vacant or a property as improved, an appraiser analyzes all logical, feasible alternatives. The market usually limits the number of property uses to a few logical choices. Each alternative use must first meet the tests of physical possibility and legal permissibility. The uses that meet the first two tests are then analyzed to ascertain how many financially feasible alternatives must be considered.

For example, market analysis may indicate the need for a large office building in a community. If the subject site is surrounded by modern, single-family residential developments, however, a large, multistory office building would probably not be logical, even if it were legally permitted. Similarly, a housing development for the elderly might be a permissible use for a site, but if most residents of the area are under 40 years old, this use may be illogical and would probably not meet the criterion of financial feasibility.

An appraiser must exercise caution in performing market analysis to support an estimate of highest and best use. Although a given site may be particularly well suited for a specific use, there may be a number of other sites that are also well suited, and some may be better suited. Therefore, the appraiser must test the highest and best use conclusion to ensure that existing and potential competition from other sites has been fully recognized.

The examples that follow pertain to the highest and best use of property as though vacant and as improved. The techniques that are demonstrated may be used to refine a highest and best use analysis, but they are not necessarily the techniques required to determine highest and best use.

Highest and Best Use of Land as Though Vacant

Example 1. Single-Family Residence

Consider a site zoned to accommodate detached, single-family residences. A builder has narrowed the logical development alternatives to two types of houses, each compatible with other houses in the neighborhood. Use A calls for the construction of a large house with an estimated market value of $125,000, including the lot. Use B calls for the construction of a smaller house which would be worth approximately $100,000 with the lot. Similar sites in the area have been selling for about $30,000. The estimated costs of constructing the two houses and their respective value estimates can be used to select the highest and best use of the appraised land. The calculations are shown below.

	Use A	Use B
Market value	$125,000	$100,000
Cost to construct new	-80,000	-75,000
Land value	-30,000	-30,000
Anticipated profit (loss)	$ 15,000	($ 5,000)

The larger house, Use A, is the highest and best use of all the alternatives considered assuming other alternatives were eliminated earlier. The builder would incur a financial loss by constructing the smaller house, Use B. Furthermore, because the builder would invest time and effort in coordinating construction, be exposed to entrepreneurial risk, and invest funds or personal time in marketing the property, the loss from Use B would be even greater. Obviously, no knowledgeable builder or owner would construct Use B over Use A.

The investor's goal is to use the land to maximize total property value. In other words, the profit realized on the total property price must produce a surplus after deducting the full market value of the land. If the overall profit on the property is less than a market profit, the use is not highest and best. In this example, the overall profit of 12% ($15,000/$125,000) on the gross sale price of Use A must be competitive with profits on similar properties that have newly constructed improvements.

Example 2. Income-Producing Use

To estimate highest and best use among various income-producing uses, the available uses are generally considered in terms of their potential rates of return and perceived income stability. For example, consider a 150-ft. by 150-ft. site in a strip commercial area that has been valued at $160,000 using the sales comparison approach. Development trends in the area suggest that the site be developed as either a convenience retail store or a commercial office building. The development costs, potential net operating incomes, and overall rates of return for the two uses are shown below.

	Retail Use	Office Use
Land value	$ 160,000	$ 160,000
Development cost	+300,000	+400,000
Total investment	$ 460,000	$ 560,000
Potential *NOI*	$ 50,000	$ 55,000
Overall rate of return	10.9%	9.8%

Of the two alternatives, retail use requires a smaller investment for development and produces a greater rate of return. Thus, it appears to qualify as the highest and best use. Before a final opinion is reached, however, the appraiser must also consider the comparative risks, anticipated income stability, and foreseeable economic lives of the two improvements.

Example 3. Income-Producing Use When Land Value Is Unknown

In some cases, land value may not be known or readily indicated by the comparative sales data available. In such situations, a land residual technique may be used to identify the highest and best use of a site. Consider a 100-ft. by 200-ft. site that is zoned for apartment, office, or retail use. If the logical, alternative uses are an apartment building, an office building, and a retail building, the appraiser must assemble data on the construction costs, net operating income, and market rate of return that can be anticipated for each alternative use. Cost and income figures are shown below; the market capitalization rate for the improvements is 12%. (Market-derived land and building capitalization rates are discussed in depth in Chapters 18 and 20.)

	Apartment Building Use	Office Building Use	Retail Building Use
Cost to construct	$1,200,000	$950,000	$800,000
NOI	162,000	135,000	110,000
Return on improvement (12%)	−144,000	−114,000	−96,000
Return to land	$ 18,000	$ 21,000	$ 14,000

Assuming the alternative uses have comparable risks and similar time frames for the recovery of invested capital, the site's highest and best use would be represented by the office building, because this use produces the greatest income for the land. The land residual technique is useful in testing highest and best use alternatives, but it is rarely employed to measure land value.

As the examples indicate, highest and best use is not determined by a single item such as cost, size, total income, or rate of return. Highest and best use results when an optimal relationship among these items creates a maximum return to the land and the capital invested.

Highest and Best Use of a Property as Improved

An analysis of the highest and best use of a property as improved may indicate that little or no capital expenditure is required, or it may suggest that significant expenditures are required to convert the property to a different use or to rehabilitate or remodel the existing use.

Example 1. No Capital Expenditure

Consider a single-family residence that could be converted into a combination apartment-rooming house or could be used for single-family occupancy. The first use would require no capital expenditure. The first floor could be rented to a family, while the three upstairs bedrooms could be rented as is to college students.

The downstairs could be rented for $500 per month and each of the three upstairs rooms could be rented for $100 per month. Expenses for the property (e.g., heat, power, repairs and maintenance, real estate tax, insurance, and additional management cost) would be approximately $2,000 per year. These would be paid by the owner. Some vacancy or collection loss must be anticipated for both the downstairs and upstairs rentals.

As an alternative, the property could be rented for single-family occupancy for $575 per month net—i.e., the renters would pay all property-related expenses, including property taxes and insurance. For the use, some vacancy or collection loss must be anticipated.

The calculations for comparing these alternative uses are shown below.

	Combination Apartment-Rooming House Use	Single-Family Occupancy Use
Capital invested	$60,000	$60,000
Gross income	9,600	6,900
Vacancy or collection losses (5%)	−480	−345
Effective gross income	9,120	6,555
Expenses	−2,000	−0
NOI	$ 7,120	$ 6,555
Overall rate of return on investment	11.9%	10.9%

The figures suggest that the highest and best use of the property as improved would be a combination apartment-rooming house.

Example 2. Capital Expenditure Required

A warehouse property can be rented for $75,000 completely net to the owners. However, the owners are considering converting some of the warehouse space into office space to increase the rent. The conversion would cost approximately $125,000 and would probably add to the market value of the property, which is currently $600,000. An appraiser estimates that with the office space the annual rent could be increased to $85,000, even though the amount of warehouse space would be reduced. The highest and best use would be calculated as follows:

	Warehouse Use Only	Warehouse With Office Space
Capital invested	$600,000	$725,000
NOI	75,000	85,000
Overall rate of return	12.5%	11.7%

The warehouse without offices is the highest and best use of the property as improved, assuming that the income streams from both uses will be of equal length and that the market value estimate reflects the price for which the property could be sold in the market with or without the office construction. The appraiser must also consider how taxes may alter an investment's after-tax rate of return.

HIGHEST AND BEST USE STATEMENTS

All appraisal reports should contain summary statements that describe the analyses and conclusions pertaining to the highest and best use of land or a site as though vacant or of a property as improved; both must be described if a separate land valuation is included. When the highest and best use conclusion is the primary objective of an evaluation report, the income and return calculations and the reasoning employed should be included. If an appraiser concludes that the highest and best use of an improved property is different from its existing use, justification for this conclusion should be included in the market value appraisal report. When the highest and best use conclusions are based on techniques applied to identify the highest and best use among two or more potential uses, the analysis is usually included in the full appraisal report.

If land value is estimated separately in an appraisal, it is appropriate for the report to discuss the highest and best use of the land as though vacant as well as the highest and best use of the property as improved. If land value is not estimated separately and the appraisal is conditioned on continued use of the property as improved, the appraiser usually discusses only the highest and best use of the property as improved. In such cases, the existing improvements may not represent the highest and best use of the site, but they are expected to continue in use and, thus, add value to the site.

Each parcel of real estate may have a highest and best use of the land or site as though vacant and a different highest and best use of the property as improved. If an appraiser comments on both the highest and best use of the land as though vacant and the property as improved, each highest and best use must be identified separately in the highest and best use section of the appraisal report. The highest and best use of the land or site is presented first, with a statement that the determination was made under the theoretical presumption that the land is vacant and available for development. Then the highest and best use of the property as improved is given, with a statement that the determination was based on the future potential of the land and the existing improvements.

If the land is already improved to its highest and best use, the two statements may be combined. Nevertheless, the report should specifically state that the determination is the same for both the land as though vacant and the property as improved, or that the land is improved to its highest and best use.

An appraisal report should also identify the highest and best uses of the comparable sale properties both as though vacant and as improved. If the improved comparable properties have different highest and best uses of the land as though vacant and of the property as improved, this must also be explained. The difference could affect value, especially in the sales comparison approach.

The following examples illustrate highest and best use statements for single-family residences and income-producing properties. Obviously, the statements used in a particular appraisal report should be tailored to the situation.

Example 1. Single-Family Residence—Highest and Best Use of Land as Though Vacant

This type of highest and best use is analyzed to estimate the value of land separately. The appraiser recognizes that any significant elements of accrued depreciation would not be replicated if the land were vacant and a new building were constructed on the site. The highest and best use determination is being used in this appraisal to identify comparable properties.

The existing structure is not the highest and best use of the land as though vacant. The house was constructed approximately 10 years ago and, like most existing structures, it contains measurable elements of physical deterioration and functional obsolescence. If the site were vacant, a new single-family residence would be its highest and best use.

The architecture of the new house would be more compatible with other houses in the neighborhood. The house would contain approximately 2,000 square feet and have three bedrooms and two baths, a larger living room, and more electrical outlets. None of the elements of physical deterioration found in the existing structure would be present in the new structure. The cost of the new house, however, would include the expense of demolishing the existing structure.

Example 2. Single-Family Residence—Highest and Best Use of Property as Improved

In analyzing this type of highest and best use, an appraiser recognizes that existing improvements should continue to be used until it is financially advantageous to remodel the structure or demolish it and build a new one. The present use of the property as a single-family residence is its highest and best use as improved. No other use of the property would be as beneficial or profitable.

The existing structure is well maintained and in good repair. It has an effective age of about eight years and a remaining economic life of approximately 50 years. The structure is compatible with the neighborhood, which is zoned for single-family residential occupancy only. The structure was designed as a single-family residence, and no other use would be legally or financially feasible.

Example 3. Income-Producing Property—Highest and Best Use of Land as Though Vacant

The existing structure is not the highest and best use of the land as though vacant. To analyze this type of highest and best use, an appraiser recognizes that any significant elements of accrued depreciation would not be replicated if the site were vacant and a new building were constructed. The income attributable to the land under its highest and best use is capitalized to estimate the value of the land separate from the improvements. (At this point, the appraiser might state, "The valuation procedure is shown in the section entitled Land Valuation.")

If the present building were razed and the site were vacant, a new commercial building would be its highest and best use. The new building would contain 16 store units, the maximum permitted by the zoning, and each store would contain about 2,000 square feet. The building would be of concrete block construction with a poured concrete floor, a flat builtup roof, and an attractive facade. It would have adequate parking facilities. No physical deterioration would be evident in the new building, and its functional layout and design would be similar to other modern buildings of this type.

Example 4. Income-Producing Property—Highest and Best Use of Property as Improved

The existing property should be converted from office use to commercial use to maximize its productivity and value. The property currently contains 12 office units that have experienced high vacancy rates during the past two years. The units would have to be renovated and remodeled to regain a competitive position in the local office market. However, the surrounding area is in transition from residential and office uses to commercial and light industrial uses. Because substantial expenditures would be required to retain the present use or convert the structure to another use, it is recommended that the space be converted to commercial use as soon as possible.

The following calculations show the current capital investment, the additional capital investments required to retain the existing use and to convert to commercial use, and the estimated return for each use.

	Office Use	Commercial Use
Current capital investment	$250,000	$ 250,000
Additional capital investment	+50,000	+100,000
Total capital investment	300,000	350,000
NOI	30,000	50,000
Overall rate of return	10%	14.3%

The figures indicate that conversion would be profitable at this time. Conversion would provide a substantially higher return on both the current investment and new capital funds. Moreover, the income produced by the commercial use would probably be less risky and longer lasting; vacancy rates for the commercial space would probably be lower.

SPECIAL SITUATIONS IN HIGHEST AND BEST USE ANALYSIS

The premises of highest and best use analysis are fundamental to all studies of the uses to which vacant land or improved properties can be put. However, in identifying and testing highest and best uses, special considerations are required in situations involving single uses, interim uses, legally nonconforming uses, uses that are not highest and best, multiple uses, special-purpose uses, speculative uses, and excess land.

Single Uses

The highest and best use of land or sites as though vacant and property as improved are generally consistent with, and similar to, surrounding uses. For example, a single-family residential use is usually not appropriate in an industrial neighborhood.

However, a property's highest and best use may be unusual, or even unique. For example, market demand may be adequate to support one large, multistory office building in a community, but it may not support more than one. A special-purpose property such as a museum may be unique and highly beneficial to the site, but it may not be supported by surrounding land uses or comparable properties. Land value will be based on the highest and best use of property, regardless of its most likely use.

Interim Uses

In many instances, a property's highest and best use may change in the foreseeable future. A tract of land at the edge of a city might not be ready for immediate development, but current growth trends may suggest that the land should be developed in a few years. Similarly, there may not be enough demand for office space to justify the construction of a multistory office building at the present time, but increased demand may be expected within five years. In such situations, the immediate development of sites and improved properties to their future highest and best uses is usually financially unfeasible.

PARKING LOT AS INTERIM USE OF PROPERTY

(H. Armstrong Roberts, Inc.)

The use to which a site or improved property is put until it is ready for its future highest and best use is called an *interim use*. Thus, interim uses are current highest and best uses that are likely to change in a relatively short time. Interim uses may include farms, parking lots, old buildings, and temporary buildings.

An interim use may or may not contribute to the value of the site or improved property. Farming vacant land does not contribute to the site's value unless the income produced exceeds a typical return for similar vacant land that is not used for agricultural purposes. If old buildings or other uses cannot produce gross revenues that exceed reasonable operating expenses, they do not contribute to property value. If the net return is less than the amount that could be earned by the vacant land, the buildings do not have contributory value. Indeed, the value of such improved properties may be less than the value of their sites as though vacant when demolition costs are considered. The value of these sites is based entirely on their potential highest and best uses.

Many outmoded improvements clearly do not meet the tests of highest and best use, but they do create increments of value over the value of vacant land. These improvements may appear to violate the consistent use theory but, in fact, the market simply acknowledges that, during transition to new use, old improvements may make a property worth more than the vacant land.

Interim uses such as farming operations and parking lots may be contributory uses. In comparing a subject property with other properties, differences in their interim uses must be taken into account even though their future highest and best uses are identical. For example, consider two sites that are expected to be economically ready for high-rise office building construction in about five years. One property has a commercial interim use that produces $40,000 more in *NOI* per year than the other property, which has a parking lot as its interim use. The site with the commercial interim use might be worth $150,000 more than the other site ($40,000 for five years discounted at 10.5% with a factor of 3.743).

If the demolition costs for the two present uses are different, they must also be accounted for with an adjustment. If the present value of the future cost to demolish the commercial building is $50,000, and the parking lot will entail no demolition cost, the difference in values could be only $100,000 ($150,000 − $50,000). An appraiser must identify the interim use of the property being appraised and all comparable properties. Differences in the prices paid may be due to different return requirements and different anticipated demolition costs.

Legally Nonconforming Uses

A legally nonconforming use is a use that was lawfully established and maintained, but no longer conforms to the use regulations of the zone in which it is located. This kind of use frequently results from subsequent zoning or a change in the zoning ordinance. Zoning changes may create underimproved or overimproved properties.[2] A single-family residence located in an area that is subsequently zoned for commercial use is an underimproved property. In this case, the residence will most likely be removed so that the site can be improved to its highest and best use, or the house will be considered an interim use until converted to commercial use.

Nonconforming, overimproved property results when zoning changes reduce the permitted intensity of property use. For example, an old country store may be included in a neighborhood that is rezoned to low-density residential use. Nonconforming uses may also result from changes in the permitted density of development and changes in development standards that affect features such as landscaping, parking, setbacks, and access. Zoning ordinances vary with the jurisdiction; they usually permit a pre-existing use to continue, but prohibit expansion or major alterations that support the nonconforming use. When the nonconforming use is discontinued or terminated, it usually cannot be re-established.

When valuing land with a legally nonconforming use, an appraiser must recognize that the current use may be producing more income, and thus have more value, than the property could produce with a conforming use. It may also produce more income and have a higher value than comparable properties that conform to the zoning. Therefore, to estimate the value of a nonconforming-use property by comparing it with similar, competitive properties in the sales comparison approach, the appraiser should make an adjustment to reflect the higher intensity of use allowed for the subject property.

In most nonconforming use situations, the property value estimate reflects the nonconforming use. Land value, however, is based on the legally permissible use, assuming that the land is vacant and its value can be deducted from the total property value. The remaining value reflects the contribution of the existing improvements and a possible bonus for nonconforming use. The appraiser may find it helpful to allocate value separately to the nonconforming improvements and the bonus created by the nonconforming use.

Usually, any bonus resulting from a nonconforming improvement and use is directly related to the existing improvements. Therefore, the extra income or benefit should be capitalized over a time period that is consistent with the economic life of the improvements.

Often, legally nonconforming uses that correspond to the highest and best use of the property as improved are easily recognizable. Sometimes, however, it is not clear whether an existing nonconforming use is the site's highest and best use. The question can only be answered by carefully analyzing the income produced by the nonconforming use and the incomes that would be produced by alternative uses if the

---

2. J. Mark Quinlivan and Vance R. Johnson, "Nonconforming-Use Properties: The Concept of Positive Economic Obsolescence," *The Appraisal Journal*, January 1981. Other sources of information on highest and best use analysis are *Readings in Highest and Best Use Analysis* (Chicago: American Institute of Real Estate Appraisers, 1981); and Lincoln W. North, *The Concept of Highest and Best Use* (Winnipeg: Appraisal Institute of Canada, 1981).

property were brought into conformity with existing regulations. Some jurisdictions specify a time period for phasing out legally nonconforming uses. In most jurisdictions, a nonconforming use must be eliminated if the property suffers major damage.

Uses That Are Not Highest and Best

Many existing buildings and other improvements do not represent the highest and best use of their sites as though vacant. Nevertheless, the highest and best use is generally in the same category as the existing use. For example, the highest and best use of a site improved with a 10-year-old apartment building may be for a new, more functional apartment building. Similarly, the highest and best use of a residential site improved with a 20-year-old house may be for a new, more modern, single-family residence. In such cases, the improvement does not suffer from external obsolescence, so its value need not be discounted for inappropriate use of the site.

For certain sites, the general category of highest and best use may have changed—e.g., from apartment to industrial use, or from single-family residential to commercial use. The improvements on these sites suffer from external obsolescence, so they are worth less than similar improvements on more appropriate sites. It would be incorrect to value such an improvement as if it were located on an appropriate site. According to the concept of consistent use, an improvement must be valued on a basis that is consistent with the site's highest and best use.

To understand the importance of valuing a site and its improvements according to a consistent use, consider the following situation. An apartment building is located on a site that has an industrial use as its highest and best use. The site is worth approximately $1 million, considerably more than it would be worth if its highest and best use were for apartment use. The existing building on the site is worth $1.5 million. If the building were located on a site appropriate for apartment use, however, its value would be $2 million. Because both the site and the improvement must be valued according to the same highest and best use, the appraiser must consider the building's value to be $1.5 million. Consequently, the total value of the property would be $2.5 million. If the appraiser has used $2 million as the building value, an erroneous total property value of $3 million would have been indicated.

Multiple Uses

Highest and best use often includes more than one use for a parcel of land or a building. A large tract of land might be suitable for a planned unit development, with a shopping center in front, condominium units around a golf course, and single-family residential sites on the remainder of the land. Industrial parks often have sites for retail stores in front and warehouse or light manufacturing structures in the rear.

One parcel of land may also serve many functions. Timberland or pastureland may also be used for hunting, recreation, and mineral exploration. Land that serves as a right-of-way for power lines can double as open space or a park. Public streets with railroad siding are also considered multiple-use land.

A building can have multiple uses, too. A hotel may contain a restaurant, a bar, and retail shops in addition to its guest rooms. A multistory building may house offices, apartments, and retail stores. An office building may contain retail stores and a restaurant as well as offices; a single-family, owner-occupied home may have an apartment upstairs.

Appraisers can often estimate the contributory value of each use on a multiple-use site or in a multiple-use building. If, for example, the market value of a timber tract that can be leased for hunting is compared on a unit basis with the value of another timber tract that cannot, the difference should be the value of the hunting rights. In oil-producing areas, appraisers are often asked to segregate the value of mineral rights from the value of other land uses. Some properties may have mineral rights value; others may not. In such assignments, appraisers must make sure that the sum of the separate use values does not exceed the value of the total property.

Special-Purpose Uses

Because special-purpose properties are appropriate for only one use or for a very limited number of uses, appraisers may encounter practical problems in specifying their highest and best uses. The highest and best use of a special-purpose property as improved is probably the continuation of its current use, if that use remains viable. For example, the highest and best use of a plant now used for heavy manufacturing is probably continued use for heavy manufacturing, and the highest and best use of a grain elevator is probably continued use as a grain elevator.

ART MUSEUM

(H. Armstrong Roberts, Inc.)

If the current use of a special-purpose property is physically or functionally obsolete and no alternative uses are feasible, the highest and best use of the property as improved may be realized by demolishing the structure and selling the remains for their scrap or salvage value.

Sometimes a special-purpose property must be analyzed and appraised on the basis of two highest and best uses—i.e., continuation of the existing, special-purpose use (value in use), and conversion to an alternate use (value for an alternate use). For example, a church may first be analyzed on the basis of its highest and best use as a church; in this analysis, the contributory value of the improvements may be supported by cost or sales comparison data. If the demand for churches is low, the appraiser may also project a highest and best use as commercial office space; the estimated value of the improvements for conversion to this use would probably be derived from a detailed cost study or from sales data on churches converted to commercial uses.

Speculative Uses

Land that is held primarily for future sale may be regarded as a speculative investment. The purchaser or owner may believe that the value of the land will increase, but there may be considerable risk that the expected appreciation will not occur during the time the speculator holds the land. Nevertheless, the current value of the land is a function of its *future* highest and best use, so the appraiser should discuss its potential future highest and best use. The appraiser may not be able to predict the exact future highest and best use, but the general *type* of future use (e.g., as a shopping center or industrial park) is often known or indicated by the zoning or surrounding land-use patterns. Because there may be several types of potential highest and best uses (e.g., single-family or multifamily residential developments), appraisers usually cannot identify a specific future highest and best use; they can, however, discuss logical alternative uses and general levels of anticipated incomes and expenses.

Excess Land

Some parcels of land are too large for their principal highest and best uses. Improved sites may have excess land that does not support the existing improvements. Vacant sites or sites considered as though vacant may have land that is not needed to accommodate the site's primary highest and best use. In some cases, the highest and best use of such excess land is for open space or nondevelopment. In other situations, the highest and best use of excess land may be for future expansion of the existing or anticipated buildings or for future development as a separate entity.

The land required to support the property's primary use, such as a parking lot for an office building or a playground for a school, is not excess land. Only land beyond the normal needs of a particular use, as determined in the market, can be considered excess land. The appraiser should clearly identify the excess land and, if appropriate, indicate its unit value separately.

Some large sites are not considered to have excess land because the acreage that is not needed for the particular use cannot be used separately. For instance, an overly large lot in an area that is 100% built up and a site that cannot be divided because of the location of its buildings are not considered to have excess land.

SUMMARY

In highest and best use analysis, an appraiser identifies the most profitable, competitive use to which a property can be put. Like value, *highest and best use* is a market-driven concept which may be defined as the reasonably probable and legal use of vacant land or an improved property, which is physically possible, appropriately supported, financially feasible, and that results in the highest land value.

Highest and best use analysis is an economic study of market forces that is focused on the subject property. The general data collected and analyzed to estimate property value provide the evidence on which the highest and best use conclusion is based. Highest and best use is the basis for all valuation assignments and the foundation for analyzing feasibility, the reasonable likelihood that a project will satisfy specific objectives. Feasibility generally pertains to income-producing property and relates to investment objectives such as stabilized occupancy, budget management, and potential value enhancement must be considered. However, feasibility analyses often address considerations that are beyond the scope of highest and best use analysis.

Highest and best use is associated with the land residual concept of the classical economists—i.e., the idea that land value is equivalent to the portion of property income that remains after improvement costs are compensated. Land residual has been incorporated into current, macroeconomic theory. Buildings can be changed, but the characteristics of sites cannot, so the use decision is fundamental to determining how much income a site can produce. Thus, from a microeconomic perspective, income to the land is the driving force of property value. Classical economists addressed the highest and best use of land as though vacant; appraisal theorists and practitioners elaborated the highest and best use concept to address property as improved.

The highest and best use of land or a site as though vacant assumes that the land parcel is vacant or can be made vacant by demolishing the existing improvements. An appraiser considers what use should be made of the land, what type of improvement should be constructed, and when. The highest and best use of land or a site as though vacant forms the basis for the cost approach.

When a property's highest and best use is forecast to change in the near future, the present use is considered an *interim use*. The highest and best use of vacant land may be an exisiting use, a projected development, a subdivision, an assemblage, or a speculative holding. The highest and best use conclusion for a parcel of vacant land should be as specific as the marketplace suggests. The highest and best use of improved property considered as though vacant may be the existing improvement, a similar improvement, or demolition of the existing building to construct a different improvement.

The highest and best use of a property as improved may involve its continued maintenance, its renovation, its expansion, its partial or total demolition, or a combination of these uses. The appraiser's primary consideration is finding the use that maximizes the income to the property on a long-term basis. If some potential uses require capital expenditures for conversion or rehabilitation, the rate of return calculated for the entire property including the capital expenditure must be compared with rates of return for uses that do not require capital expenditures.

The purpose of determining the highest and best use of land as though vacant is to identify a site's potential use, which governs its value. The fact that any existing improvement can be demolished validates the assumption that underlies the concept of the highest and best use of land as though vacant. The highest and best use of land as though vacant must be determined when a separate estimate of land value is required, and when comparable parcels of vacant land that have been sold recently must be identified.

The purpose of determining the highest and best use of property as improved is to identify the use that is expected to produce the greatest overall return on the capital invested, and to help the appraiser select comparable properties.

A property's highest and best use must be 1) physically possible, 2) legally permissible, 3) financially feasible, and 4) maximally productive. These criteria should be considered sequentially and conditionally.

The size, shape, terrain, and soil conditions of a parcel of land affect its physical utility and adaptability. The size, design, and condition of an improved property may suggest that rehabilitation, conversion, or demolition are in order. Legal permissibility depends on public restrictions such as zoning, building codes, historic preservation regulations, and environmental controls as well as the private or contractual restrictions found in deeds and long-term leases. If there is reasonable probability of a zoning change, an appraiser may consider highest and best uses that are not now legally permitted, but all pertinent factors supporting the presumed zoning change must be disclosed.

Financially feasible uses should produce returns that exceed the income required to satisfy operating expenses and debt service (interest and amortization). To calculate the rate of return on invested capital, net operating income (*NOI*) is estimated by subtracting vacancy and collection losses and operating expenses from the property's gross income. Among financially feasible uses, the use that produces the highest price or value consistent with the rate of return warranted by the market is the maximally productive use.

Depending on the particular situation, various indicators may identify the highest and best use of land as though vacant. If, for example, the use decision is limited to one type of improvement, but the size of the improvement is in question, the *profits* produced by improvements of various sizes can indicate highest and best use. The highest and best use of income-producing property may depend solely on the *overall rate of return* on the investment, or it may depend on achieving an optimal relationship among investment, income, and rate of return to maximize the return to the land and the capital invested.

One rate of return can be used to capitalize income streams from different uses into values if the associated risks are similar. When land value cannot be determined by sales comparison, a *land residual* procedure may be used to estimate the income attributable to the land. The value of the improvements is capitalized at a market-determined building rate and then subtracted from the total property income.

In determining the highest and best use of property as improved, the appraiser may consider uses for which additional capital expenditures are and are not required. In all cases, the *rate of return* is calculated from the relationship between income and the capital investment. If the capital expenditure required to convert a property is the same for various alternative uses, the *NOIs* produced by these different uses can be compared directly.

The market usually limits the number of logical and feasible highest and best uses. The existing and potential competition from other properties suited to the same or similar uses should also be considered.

All appraisal reports should contain statements summarizing the highest and best use of land as though vacant, property as improved, or both if land value is estimated separately. In some situations, the highest and best use of land as though vacant may be different from the highest and best use of the property as improved. In these cases, each determination must be stated separately; when the land is already improved to its highest and best use, the two statements may be combined.

Statements of the highest and best use of land as though vacant, for both income-producing and non-income-producing property, often indicate that land value would be maximized by demolishing an existing improvement to eliminate accrued depreciation, and constructing a new improvement. Statements of the highest and best use of property as improved may recommend that the existing improvements be maintained for the same use or converted to a different use.

The determination of highest and best use involves special considerations in appraising single uses, interim uses, legally nonconforming uses, uses that are not highest and best, multiple uses, special-purpose uses, speculative uses, and excess land.

In *single-use* situations, the highest and best use may be unusual or unique. Land value should be based on this use, not the most likely use. *Interim uses* of sites or improved properties are highest and best uses that are anticipated to change within a short time. Interim uses may or may not contribute to value, and demolition costs must be considered for improvements with interim uses.

A *legally nonconforming use* is a use that was lawfully established and maintained, but no longer conforms to the use regulations of the zone in which it is located. Zoning changes often result in underimproved or overimproved properties with legally nonconforming uses. A nonconforming use may produce more income for the property than a conforming use, and more than comparable properties that conform with zoning. Both the economic life of the improvements and any regulations pertaining to nonconforming uses must be considered.

The existing use is not the highest and best use of a site when the use provided by the improvement is inconsistent with changes in neighborhood use patterns. In such cases, the appraiser should apply *consistent use* criteria when valuing the land and improvements. Highest and best use may indicate *multiple uses* for a parcel of land or a building. In multiple-use situations, the appraiser estimates the *contributory value* of each use, making sure that the sum of the individual values does not exceed the value of the total property.

Properties with *special-purpose uses* may sometimes be considered in terms of both their *value in use* and their potential *alternate use value*. A *speculative land* investment is created when a buyer holds land in anticipation of appreciation. Although the specific future highest and best use of such land may not be predictable, logical alternatives can usually be identified. *Excess land* may be land not needed to support the existing improvement, or to accommodate the primary highest and best use of a vacant site or site considered as though vacant. Excess land should be clearly identified.

13   Land or Site Valuation

The supply of land is relatively stable. Although vast changes have occurred in the earth's surface over the ages, and slight modifications in the supply and quality of land occur over the span of a lifetime, these natural events rarely affect the land with which appraisers are concerned.

There are, however, a few notable exceptions to the permanence of land, such as the accretion or erosion of land along a shoreline, the pollution of land with harmful wastes, the exhaustion of agricultural land through improper farming methods, and the transformation of arable land into desert due to ecological imbalances. Earthquakes may change the surface of the earth and faults beneath the surface can create vast sinkholes. Fortunately, these occurences are fairly rare.

Land has value because it provides potential utility as the site of a structure, recreational facility, agricultural tract, or right-of-way for transportation routes. If land has utility for a specific use and there is demand for that use, the land has value to a particular category of users. Beyond the basic utility of land, however, there are many principles and factors that must be considered in land valuation. Although it is sometimes considered the simplest of appraisal tasks, the valuation of land requires careful analysis of a complex variety of factors.

LAND VALUATION THEORY

Value Concepts and Principles

Anticipation, change, supply and demand, substitution, and balance are appraisal principles that influence land value. Anticipation means that value is created by the expectation of benefits to be derived in the future. Therefore, if buyers anticipate that sites in a certain location will be in demand for office use within the next five years, they may be motivated to acquire land for development even though the development of office space is not presently tenable. The competition among buyers who make up the market for these sites creates a price level for the land that may have little to do with its current use. In such circumstances, the highest and best use of the sites could be speculative holding for eventual office development.

The supply of, and demand for, sites in a particular location tend toward equilibrium. If supply declines and demand remains stable or increases, prices rise. Conversely, if the supply of sites for a particular use increases and demand remains stable or declines, prices fall. Temporary imbalances between supply and demand are usually resolved as equilibrium is re-established. The price of property reflects this relationship. When prices drop sufficiently, supply will contract because existing uses will be retained. When prices rise, a new supply may be created through rezoning, annexation, or abandonment of existing uses.

Although the supply of, and demand for, sites tend toward ultimate equilibrium, this principle may not apply in the short run. If one type of site is very scarce in a particular location, the pressure of intense market competition may increase the value of a site beyond the level indicated by its profitability. For example, the rents that can be obtained for office space in a particular location may not justify the high prices that are being paid for office sites. Similarly, the prices that can be obtained for improved residential properties may not justify the high prices paid for the last few lots in a popular location. Nevertheless, market value is generally the most probable price the market can sustain. Eventually, the equilibrium among rents, prices, and land values will be re-established; if all other factors remain constant, rents will rise or prices will fall.

Land value is substantially affected by the interplay of supply and demand, but it is the economic use of a site that determines its value in a particular market. For example, the price that a developer can afford to pay for a warehouse site is determined by the net income that the warehouse will earn and the cost of constructing it. Intense competition for choice sites or for the last remaining sites in a particular location can cause prospective owners or owner-occupants to pay more for a particular site than is indicated by the broad spectrum of market activity and the highest and best use of the site.

The principle of substitution, which holds that a buyer will not pay more for one site than for another that is similar or equal, affects land values by producing the greatest demand for the lowest priced sites. The principle of balance also influences land values. When the various elements of a particular economic mix or a specific environment are in a state of equilibrium, value is sustained; when the balance is upset, values change. If, for example, a district has too much industrially zoned land, property values will probably fall. (Because prices are usually quoted in inflated, not constant, dollars, prices appear to be increasing when they are actually falling or remaining level.)

Definition of the Appraisal Problem

At the start of a valuation assignment, an appraiser identifies the real estate and property rights to be valued, specifies the date and use of the appraisal, defines the type of value, and states the limiting conditions that govern the appraisal report. The next step is the selection and analysis of comparable data. The appraiser must identify all property rights, legal encumbrances, physical characteristics, and site improvements that pertain to the land in question.

Property Rights and Public Controls

The appraisal of land focuses on valuing the property rights attached to the land. These include the rights to develop the land within certain limits, to lease it to others, to farm it, to mine it, to alter its topography, to subdivide it, to assemble it, and to use it for waste disposal. Whenever possible, an appraiser should consult public records to identify easements, rights-of-way, and private or public restrictions that affect the property.

Because the supply of land cannot keep pace with the demand for it, governments regulate how land can be used and developed. Most municipalities and counties have some form of zoning that specifies what new development can take place on a parcel of land. In addition to zoning, many jurisdictions now have master plans that specify long-term development goals. Furthermore, developers frequently must provide public amenities such as open space, streets, and adjacent or offsite public improvements to acquire development rights. Sometimes, developers can proceed with development only after they submit approved site plans. In some areas, citizen groups may protest a development they do not like, and their wishes frequently influence the type of development that is finally approved.

Through the power of eminent domain, the government can remove land from private use to augment the supply of public land or to modify land use through urban renewal programs. In some rural jurisdictions, land use is influenced by government-sponsored transferable development rights (TDRs), which compensate farmers for retaining land in agricultural use and shift the cost of development to developers. Lower ad valorem taxes on agricultural land also affect rural land use; this form of tax subsidy tends to extend the duration of agricultural uses.

A significant amount of land in the United States has been encumbered with open space or conservation easements in perpetuity. These permanent encumbrances limit or prohibit the subdivision of land to prevent further development. Land subject to perpetual open space or conservation easements is usually restricted to its existing use, as specified in the deed of easement. These deeds are vested in preservation or conservation trusts. Other encumbrances prohibit the demolition or alteration of historic structures.

Physical Characteristics and Site Improvements

The physical characteristics, available utilities, and site improvements of land affect its use and value. The physical characteristics of a parcel of land that an appraiser must consider are size and shape, frontage, topography, location, and view. Topographical characteristics include the land's contour, grade, and drainage.

The availability of utilities such as water, sewers, electricity, natural gas, and telephone service also affects the use and development potential of a parcel of land. Utilities may be provided by offsite facilities such as public water mains, sewers, and power lines, or by onsite facilities such as spring basins, drilled domestic wells, and septic tanks.

A parcel of land becomes a *site* when it is improved and ready to be used for a specific purpose. A site may have both onsite and offsite improvements that make it suitable for its intended use or development. Necessary onsite improvements include grading, landscaping, paving, and utility hookups for water, gas, electricity, and telephone. Essential offsite improvements include streets, curbs, sidewalks, drains, and connecting utility lines. Site improvements are typically considered part of site value; only rarely are they valued with other property improvements. Like buildings and other structures, site improvements are subject to physical and functional obsolescence.

Highest and Best Use

Land value must always be considered in terms of highest and best use. Even if the site has improvements, the value of the site is based on its highest and best use as though vacant and available for development to its most economic use. Consideration of the land as though vacant is a commonly accepted procedure which facilitates the orderly analysis and solution of appraisal problems that require land to be valued as a separate component. Land has first claim to any income generated by the property and priority over any return on the improvements. Land value may be equal to, or even greater than, total property value, even when substantial improvements are located on the site.

Highest and best use is also affected by how much existing improvements contribute to property value. The contribution of the improvements is estimated by subtracting the value of the land from the value of the total property. Land is said to *have value*, while improvements *contribute to value*. When improvements do not contribute to property value, demolition is indicated. In this case, the cost of converting the property into a vacant site is a penalty, or negative building contribution, to be deducted from the value of the land.

Under certain circumstances, the appraisal of a property may require that the site be considered in terms other than its highest and best use. In appraisal to estimate the use value or legal, nonconforming use value of an improved site, an appraiser may often need to value the site according to its specified use or the existing improvements, not its highest and best use. In this case, the appraiser should value the site both in terms of its highest and best use and its conditional use.

LAND VALUATION TECHNIQUES

The six procedures used to value land are:

1. Sales comparison

2. Allocation

3. Extraction

4. Subdivision development

5. Land residual

6. Ground rent capitalization

All six procedures are derived from the three basic approaches to value. Sales comparison and income capitalization (i.e., ground rent capitalization) can be directly applied to land valuation. Allocation and extraction procedures reflect the influence of the sales comparison and cost approaches; the land residual technique is based on the income capitalization and cost approaches. Subdivision development draws on elements of all three approaches.

Sales Comparison

The sales comparison approach may be used to value land that is actually vacant or land that is being considered as though vacant for appraisal purposes. Sales comparison is the most common technique for valuing land and it is the preferred method when comparable sales are available. With this method, sales of similar parcels of land are analyzed, compared, and adjusted to provide a value indication for the land being appraised. The comparison process is based on an analysis of the similarity or dissimilarity of the parcels.

The appraiser gathers data on actual sales and ground leases as well as listings, offers, and renewal options; identifies the similarities and differences in the data; ranks the data according to their relevance; adjusts the sale prices of the comparables to account for the dissimilar characteristics of the land being appraised; and forms a conclusion as to the most reasonable and probable market value of the subject land.

The elements of comparison include property rights, legal encumbrances, financing terms, conditions of sale (motivation), market conditions (sale date), location, physical characteristics, available utilities, zoning, and highest and best use. The most variable elements of comparison are the site's physical characteristics, which include its size and shape, frontage, topography, location, and view. (A more complete discussion of elements of comparison appears in Chapter 14.) The units of comparison applied may be acres, square feet, front feet, lots, or any other unit used in the market. For example, land value may be expressed in dollars per apartment unit, per apartment room, or per square foot of net or gross building area. It is usually wise to correlate the results of two or more units of comparison in arriving at a land value estimate—e.g., dollar per acre and per lot, or dollars per unit and per square foot.

If sale prices have been changing rapidly over the past several years and an adequate amount of sales data are available, the sales selected for comparison should take place as close to the effective appraisal date as possible. If an appraiser must choose between transactions involving properties close to the subject property that occurred several years ago and recent transactions in more distant locations, a balance must be struck. The more recent sales will probably be most indicative.

Size is generally a less important element of comparison than date and location. Most types of development have an optimal site size; if the site is larger, the value of the excess land tends to decline at an accelerating rate. Because sales of different sizes may have different unit prices, appraisers ordinarily give more weight to comparables that are approximately the same size as the subject property.

Zoning is often the most basic criterion in selecting comparables. Sites zoned the same as the subject property are the most appropriate comparables. If sufficient sales in the same zoning category are not available, data from similar categories can be used after adjustments are made. As a general rule, the greater the dissimilarity between the subject and the comparables, the more potential there is for distortion and error in sales comparison.

In addition to recorded sales and signed contracts, appraisers should consider offers to sell, offers to purchase, and other incomplete transactions. Offers provide less reliable data than signed contracts and recorded sales. Usually, the final sale price is lower than the initial offer to sell, but higher than the initial offer to buy. Negotiation can take place in several stages.

Data on land sales are available from sources such as electronically transmitted and printed data services, newspapers, and records of deeds and assessments. Interviews with the parties involved in transactions—i.e., the buyers, sellers, lawyers, and brokers—can provide more direct information.

After comparable data are collected and categorized, and the comparable properties are examined and described, sales data can be assembled in an organized, logical manner. Sales are commonly arranged on a market data grid that has separate columns for important categories of property characteristics. Adjustments for dissimilarities between the subject property and the comparable properties are made to the sale prices of the comparables. Paired data set and patterned analyses may be used to isolate the effects of individual variables. (Paired data set analysis and valuing land with the sales comparison approach are discussed in Chapter 14.)

Generally, separate adjustments are made to the comparable sale prices for each unit of comparison. The magnitude of each adjustment is indicated by the data. Land parcels of different sizes sell at different unit prices because the optimal size of a parcel depends on its use. Unit prices also vary with the sale date and location. If the data selected are not sufficient to indicate the magnitude of the adjustments required, the appraiser must gather and analyze additional comparable data.

A sale price adjustment can be simply an acknowledgement of a property's superior or inferior quality, or it may be a precise dollar sum or percentage. Adjustments can also be totaled and factored into the comparable sale prices. Generally, adjustments are made in a particular order—i.e., adjustments for property rights, financing, and sale and market conditions are made before adjustments for location and physical characteristics. All adjustments should be presented in a logical and understandable manner in the appraisal report.

Allocation

Vacant sites in densely developed urban locations may be so rare that their values cannot be estimated by direct comparison. Similarly, sales of vacant sites in remote rural areas may occur so seldom that comparable data are inadequate. In such cases, land value can be estimated by allocation, or abstraction.

The allocation method is based on the principle of balance and the related concept of contribution, which affirm that there is a normal or typical ratio of land value to property value for specific categories of real estate in specific locations. This ratio is generally more reliable when the subject property includes relatively new improvements. With older improvements, the ratio of land value to total value increases. The allocation method does not produce conclusive value indications, but it can be used to establish land value when the number of vacant land sales is inadequate.

For example, allocation could be used in an appraisal assignment to value parcels of lakefront land used as sites for vacation homes. Assume that no sales of vacant land have occurred recently, but the appraiser has ascertained that houses on the lake have sold for $150,000 to $200,000. A developer of lakefront houses in a nearby area can purchase a lot of the same size for $60,000, build a house for $90,000, and make $30,000 in profit and overhead with a total improvement contribution of $120,000 and a total property value of $180,000, of which the land represents one third.

The appraiser must recognize that, in such an enterprise, the profit and overhead accrue from the developer's expertise and assumption of risk. No profit or overhead is imputable to the land, which is appraised as vacant, unimproved, and available for development. Therefore, none of the developer's profit or overhead can be allocated to the unimproved lot, and none can be attributed to the seller of the lot. In short, the lot price paid to the seller does not include profit or overhead.

The ratio of land value to total property value in the completed development is .333 to 1.0. The indicated land values for homes around the lake range from between $50,000 (.333 x $150,000) to $66,600 (.333 x $200,000). This is a rough estimate because more expensive and less expensive dwellings have been built on equally valuable lakefront lots.

Extraction

Extraction is a variant of the allocation method in which land value is extracted from the sale price of an improved property by deducting the contribution of the improvements, which is estimated from their depreciated costs. The remaining value represents the value of the land. Improved sales in rural areas are frequently analyzed in this way because the proportion of building contribution to total property value is generally small and relatively easy to identify. The land value estimates produced with the extraction method can be used with data gathered from vacant land sales in sales comparison. Sometimes, the extraction technique is applied to assessment ratios rather than specific numerical amounts. However, value indication derived in this way is generally unpersuasive because the assessment ratios may be unreliable and the extraction method does not reflect market considerations.

Subdivision Development

The subdivision development method is used to value land when subdivision and development represent the highest and best use of the appraised parcel and sales data on finished lots are available. Subdivision development analysis may involve industrial, residential, or recreational land. The subdivision of land is the normal pattern of real estate development. A landowner divides a large plot into smaller parcels to sell or lease them. A planned subdivision can create a higher, better, and more intense property use when zoning, the availability of utilities, community conditions, access, and a host of other elements combine favorably. Traditionally, subdivision developers divide large tracts into smaller plots and create roads, drainage, public utilities, and other improvements that are required by local law and zoning ordinances.

SUBDIVISION

(H. Armstrong Roberts, Inc.)

An appraiser begins to analyze a subdivision development by determining the number and size of lots that can be created from the appraised land physically, legally, and economically. The proposed lots must conform to legal requirements in the jurisdiction in terms of size, frontage, topography, soil quality, and land improvements—e.g., water facilities, drainage, sewage, streets and curbs. The lots must also meet the demands of the market in which the property is located. Without surveys and engineering studies, an appraiser cannot know exactly how many lots can be created from a particular parcel of land. However, a reasonable estimate of the number of potential lots can be deduced from zoning and subdivision ordinances or, preferably, from the number of lots created in similar subdivisions.

A sales comparison analysis of finished lots is then undertaken. After adjusting the comparable sales for differences, the appraiser estimates the most likely retail sale prices of the lots, the probable development period, and the absorption rate.

All direct and indirect costs associated with developing and marketing the lots must be deducted from the sum of their projected sale prices. These costs may include the engineering expenses to clear, grade, and finish the land; to build streets, roads, and sidewalks; and to install utilities. Carrying costs such as taxes, insurance premiums, overhead expenses, and inspection fees must be considered along with marketing costs for sales commissions and advertising. Further deductions must be made to provide an appropriate return on the total investment during the development period and an entrepreneurial profit for the developer.

Development and marketing costs and entrepreneurial profit are deducted from the projected gross sale price to arrive at the net sales proceeds. The periodic net sales proceeds are then discounted to present value at an appropriate yield rate over the estimated period required for project development and market absorption. The result is an indication of the value of the raw land. The discount rate selected should reflect the risk involved and be supportable in the market.

To illustrate the subdivision development procedure, consider a 10-acre tract of land that a developer wants to subdivide into 25 residential lots. The total projected gross sale price of the developed lots is $500,000. The following costs will be incurred in site development.

Development costs for grading, clearing, paving, and curbing; sewage and water lines; and design engineering	$150,000
Management and supervision	7,500
Contractor's overhead and profit*	50,000
Sales expenses	17,500
Taxes	10,000
Entrepreneurial profit**	30,000
Total	$265,000

* Developer's profit must be distinguished from contractor's profit. Contractor's profit is considered a direct cost in site development.

** Entrepreneurial profit is generally treated as a line item and may be estimated differently in different markets. In this example it is approximately 13% of total hard and soft costs ($30,000/$235,000).

If all sales and development costs occurred at one time, the indicated land value would be the difference between the projected gross sale price and all anticipated development costs, carrying and sales costs, and entrepreneurial profit ($500,000 − $265,000 = $235,000).

However, development is projected to take four years, so discounting must be employed. The discount rate selected should reflect the risk incurred during the anticipated selling period. In this example, a 10% discount rate was selected. The average, annual return on the net income is calculated as follows.

$$\$235,000/4 = \$58,750$$

The present value of $58,750 can be obtained by applying the present value of $1 per period factor for four years at 10%, which is 3.1699.

$$\$58,750 \times 3.1699 = \$186,230 \text{ (rounded)}$$

(The application of present value factors is covered in Chapter 20.)

So, the developer can afford to pay $186,230 for the land in view of antici- pated development costs, carrying and sales costs, and entrepreneurial profit. As an additional check, this land value can be compared with the prices being paid for similar parcels of raw land that have subdivision development as their highest and best use. There are several, more sophisticated variations of this procedure in which the timing of cost and income flows are itemized on a year-to-year basis. These techniques also involve the application of growth rates.

The subdivision development method of land valuation is used in feasibility studies and when comparable sales are scarce. Nevertheless, bona fide sales data provide a better indication of value than a subdivision development prospectus.

Land Residual

The land residual technique may also be used to estimate land value when sales data on similar parcels of vacant land are lacking. This technique is based on the principle of balance and the related concept of contribution, which are concerned with equilib- rium among the agents of production—i.e., labor, capital, coordination, and land.

The land residual technique can be used to estimate land value when 1) building value is known or can be accurately estimated, 2) stabilized, annual net operating income to the property is known or estimable, and 3) both building and land capitalization rates can be extracted from the market. Building value can be estimated for new or proposed buildings that represent the highest and best use of the property and have not yet incurred physical deterioration or functional obsolescence.

To apply the land residual technique, an appraiser first determines what actual or hypothetical improvements represent the highest and best use of the site. Then the stabilized, annual net operating income to the property is estimated from market rents and operating expenses as of the date of the appraisal. Next, the appraiser calculates how much of the income is attributable to the building and subtracts this amount from the total net operating income. The remainder is the residual income to the land, which is capitalized at a market-derived capitalization rate to provide an estimate of land value.

The following example illustrates the application of the land residual technique. A developer engages an appraiser to estimate the value of a site that he plans to purchase. The developer intends to use the site to construct a professional office building, which is considered the highest and best use of the site. The appraiser's investigation of the local market indicates that the total property can be expected to produce a net operating income of $100,000 per year. The market indicates a building capitalization rate of 8% and a land capitalization rate of 6%. The value of a new building with no depreciation is estimated to be $350,000.

NOI	$ 100,000
Less income to the building	
($I_B = V_B \times R_B$) = $350,000 x 0.08	= 28,000
Income attributable to the land	$ 72,000
Land value	
($V_L = I_L/R_L$) = $72,000/0.06	= $1,200,000

In this example, the property is considered free and clear of debt. If the purchase of the land or the construction of the improvement were to be financed, other items would have to be considered. With sufficient market data to indicate the value of the building, the property's anticipated net operating income, and the land and building capitalization rates, the value of the land can be calculated.

These are several variations of the land residual technique. In one alternate technique, the property is valued as improved and the cost of the improvements and any profit are deducted. The sum remainder is the residual value of the land. The land residual technique is useful when comparable sales are lacking and as a check on the sales comparison approach. It may be most useful in testing the feasibility of alternate uses of a particular site.

Ground Rent Capitalization

Ground rents can be capitalized at an appropriate rate to indicate the market value of a site. *Ground rent is paid for the right to use and occupy the land according to the terms of the ground lease*; it corresponds to the value of the landowner's interest in the land, the leased fee interest. Market-derived capitalization rates are used to convert ground rent into market value. This procedure is useful when an analysis of comparable sales of leased land indicates a range of rents and capitalization rates.

Ground leases can have different terms and escalation clauses. The appraiser should ascertain all lessor benefits during the term of the lease and the option periods, and determine when the reversion of the property will take place.

SUMMARY

The supply of land is relatively stable. Although physical and ecological changes may result in the accretion or destruction of land, these occurrences are rare. Land has value because it has specific utility and is in demand. Several appraisal concepts and principles contribute to the formation of land value. Anticipation, the expectation of increased demand for sites suitable to a particular use, motivates speculators to acquire land. The supply of, and demand for, sites tend toward equilibrium in the long run, but short-term imbalances do occur. Intense market competition can create land values that exceed profitability. The principle of substitution holds that the greatest demand is generated for the lowest priced sites. Balance implies that value is sustained when the various elements in an economic or environmental mix are in equilibrium.

The first steps in land valuation are identification of the real estate and property rights to be valued, specification of the date and use of the appraisal, and definition of the value and limiting conditions that govern the appraisal.

Encumbrances on property rights include easements, rights-of-way, and restrictions in private deeds and public zoning. Governments adopt master plans to direct development, sponsor transferable development rights to preserve agricultural or conservation uses, and take land for public use through the power of eminent domain.

An appraiser collects and analyzes data on the subject and comparable land parcels, identifying the property rights involved, any legal encumbrances, the physical characteristics of the site, and all available utilities and site improvements that may affect the site's development potential. The value of a site or parcel of land is based on its highest and best use as though vacant and available for development to its most economic use. Land is assumed to have *prior claim to the income* generated by the property before any return to the improvements. Land is said to have value, while improvements contribute to value. Improvements that make no contribution to property value constitute a value penalty equal to the cost of their demolition. A site's highest and best use may be the existing use or a different use. The statement of highest and best use should be as specific as the market warrants.

The six procedures used in land valuation all derive from the three approaches to value. *Sales comparison* is the most commonly used and preferred method to value land when comparable data are available. Using this technique, data on sales of similar parcels of land are analyzed, compared, and adjusted for dissimilarities with the subject property.

Elements of comparison include property rights, legal encumbrances, financing terms, sale and market conditions, location, physical characteristics, available utilities, zoning, and highest and best use. The units of comparison applied should correspond to those used in the market. Two or more units of comparison may be correlated. Generally, sale prices are adjusted for each unit of comparison and a market data grid is used to organize the data.

Data on land sales that are most similar to the subject are given the greatest weight. Appraisers analyze data on actual transactions and relevant transactions that did not reach completion.

The *allocation* procedure is based on the typical ratio of land value to improvement value for specific categories of real estate in specific locations. When the improvements are recent, the ratio is more dependable; as improvements age, the ratio of land value to total value increases. Allocation is less conclusive than other procedures, but it is useful when data on comparable transactions are not available.

Extraction is a similar procedure in which the contribution of the improvements is deducted from the total property value. The land value derived with this procedure should be compared with any available data on vacant land sales. Extraction is used to estimate the land value of improved properties in rural areas and in situations where the building contributes little to total property value.

The *subdivision development* procedure is used to value land when subdivision and development represents the highest and best use of the land being appraised and sales data on finished lots are available. The appraiser begins by determining the number and size of lots that can physically, legally, and economically be created from the parcel of land. Then finished lots are analyzed to estimate the likely sale price, development period, and absorption rate for the projected lots. From the anticipated gross sale price, the appraiser deducts all direct and indirect costs and an entrepreneurial profit. The net sales proceeds are discounted to present value with a market-derived yield rate for the period required for project development and market absorption. The resulting value indication should be compared with the prices being paid for similar parcels of raw land that have subdivision and development as their highest and best use. There are several, sophisticated variations of this procedure.

The *land residual* procedure is used when sales data on similar parcels of vacant land are not available. To apply this procedure, known or estimable building value, known or estimable property *NOI*, and market-extracted building and land capitalization rates are needed. The appraiser determines what actual or hypothetical improvements represent the highest and best use of the site and the stabilized annual *NOI* to the property is estimated. The portion of the NOI attributable to the building is deducted from total NOI and the remainder, the 'residual' income to the land, is capitalized at a market-derived rate to provide an estimate of land value. In another variant of the land residual procedure, the appraiser simply values the property as improved and deducts the cost of the improvements and an entrepreneurial profit from the total property value.

Ground rent capitalization is used to value land when the ground rent corresponds to the value of the landowner's interest in the property. Market-derived capitalization rates are used to convert ground rent into an indication of the market value of the land. This procedure is useful when comparable sales of leased land indicate a range of rents and capitalization rates.

14 The Sales Comparison Approach

In the sales comparison approach, market value is estimated by comparing the subject property to similar properties that have been sold recently or for which offers to purchase have been made. A major premise of the sales comparison approach is that the market value of a property is directly related to the prices of comparable, competitive properties.

The comparative analysis in the sales comparison approach focuses on differences in the legal, physical, locational, and economic characteristics of similar properties and the subject property and on differences in the real property rights conveyed, the dates of sale, the motivations of buyers and sellers, and the financing arrangements for each sales transaction, which can account for variations in prices.

RELATIONSHIP TO APPRAISAL PRINCIPLES

The principles of real estate appraisal are basic to the sales comparison approach. Guided by these principles, the appraiser ensures that all issues relevant to the valuation problem have been considered in a consistent manner.

Supply and Demand

Property prices are determined by the market. They result from negotiations between buyers and sellers; buyers constitute market demand and the properties offered for sale make up the supply. If the demand for a particular type of property is high, prices tend to increase; if demand is low, prices tend to decline. Shifts in the supply of improved properties frequently lag behind shifts in demand because supply is created by time-consuming construction, while demand can change rapidly. The analysis of real estate markets *at a specific time* may seem to focus on demand, but the supply of properties must also be considered. Proposed construction or demolition may change the supply-demand relationship and affect prices. To estimate demand, appraisers consider the number of potential users of a particular type of property, their purchasing power, and their tastes and preferences. To analyze supply, appraisers focus on existing properties that are unsold or vacant as well as properties that are being constructed or planned. Shifts in any of these elements may cause the prices of the subject property and comparable properties to vary.

Substitution

As applied in the sales comparison approach, the principle of substitution holds that the value of a property tends to be set by the price that would be paid to acquire a substitute property of similar utility and desirability. This principle implies that the reliability of the sales comparison approach is diminished if substitute properties are not available in the market.

Balance

The forces of supply and demand tend toward equilibrium, or balance, in the market, but absolute equilibrium is almost never attained. The balance between supply and demand changes continually. Due to shifts in population, purchasing power, and consumer tastes and preferences, demand varies greatly over time. The construction of new buildings and the demolition of old ones cause supply to vary as well.

Another aspect of this principle is that the relationship between land and improvements and the relationship between a property and its environment must both be in balance for a property to reflect its actual market value. If, for example, a property has too much land in relation to its improvements or too many expensive amenities for its location, an imbalance is created. Appraisers must watch for imbalances in the market and within properties because they can cause the market to impute different prices to otherwise comparable properties.

Externalities

Positive and negative external forces affect all types of property. A period of economic development or economic depression can often influence property values. An appraiser analyzes the neighborhood of a subject property to identify all significant external influences. To a great extent, these external forces are reflected in the adjustments made for property location. Two properties with identical physical characteristics may have quite different market values if one of the properties has less attractive surroundings. Factors such as the condition and lighting of streets, the convenience of transportation facilities, the adequacy of police protection, and the proximity to shopping and restaurant facilities vary with location. They must be considered by the appraiser to determine if they have a positive or negative effect on the value of the property being appraised.

APPLICABILITY AND LIMITATIONS

The sales comparison approach is applicable to all types of real property interests when there are sufficient recent reliable transactions to indicate value patterns in the market. For property types that are bought and sold regularly, the sales comparison approach often provides a reliable indication of market value. When data are available, this is the most direct and systematic approach to value.

When the number of market transactions is insufficient, the applicability of the sales comparison approach may be limited. For example, the sales comparison approach is rarely applied to special-purpose property because few similar properties may be sold in a given market. To value such properties, the cost or income capitalization approach may be more appropriate and reliable. Nevertheless, data on sales and offers for similar properties may establish broad limits for the value of the property being appraised.

When economic conditions are changing rapidly, the usefulness of the sales comparison approach may be limited. For example, changes in income tax laws and zoning regulations, the availability and cost of financing, or the supply of similar properties may cause the sale prices of comparable properties with similar uses to be unreliable indicators of the value of the subject property. If economic changes occur abruptly, an appraiser may have difficulty finding a reliable market basis on which to make adjustments for these changes. Rapid inflation or deflation can also jeopardize the reliability of an appraiser's adjustments and limit the usefulness of the sales comparison approach.

The sales comparison approach has broad applicability and is persuasive when sufficient data are available. It is usually used to appraise single-family residential property. The income capitalization approach is not relevant to most single-family houses because they either produce no income or they produce income that represents a noncompetitive return on the investment. Although the cost approach may be used to estimate the market value of relatively new single-family residences, it is not reliable for older residential properties that suffer from significant amounts of depreciation. Most single-family properties are amenable to direct comparison because many similar properties are bought and sold in the same market and many prospective buyers do not choose to rent or build.

The valuation of income-producing properties usually involves detailed analyses of income, expenses, rates, and factors which are part of the income capitalization approach to value. The sales comparison approach can also be useful in appraising these properties. If the appraiser can obtain reliable information on recent sales of similar properties, the sales comparison approach may provide a valid indication of value that can be used to test the reasonableness of the values derived in the cost and income capitalization approaches. Furthermore, sales comparison analysis may be used in conjunction with the income capitalization approach. Capitalization rates and factors extracted from market analysis of comparable properties may be applied to the income projection for the subject property to derive an indication of value in the income capitalization approach. (For more information on how rates and factors are extracted from market transactions and applied in the income capitalization approach, see Chapter 18.)

REQUIRED DATA AND SOURCES

To apply the sales comparison approach, an appraiser considers data on sales, contracts, offers, refusals, and listings of properties considered competitive with, and comparable to, the subject property. First, the appraiser thoroughly researches the prices, real property rights conveyed, financing terms, motivations of buyers and sellers, and transaction dates of the sale properties. Then details on each property's location, physical and functional condition, and income-producing characteristics must be examined.

Most appraisers maintain data files on the details of market transactions and add information when other transactions occur. Potential sources of sales data are many and varied. Primary sources of sales data include courthouse records, multiple listing services, and interviews with the parties to the transaction, their employees, lawyers, counselors, brokers, property managers, and lenders. In many cases, appraisers must contact other sources to obtain and verify information and to understand the motivation behind a transaction. Sales that are not arm's-length market transactions should be treated with caution. To verify sales data, an appraiser should confirm statements of fact with the principals to the transaction and with any brokers, closing agencies, and lending institutions involved. The owners and tenants of neighboring properties may also provide factual information.

The geographic limits of the appraiser's search for sales data depend on the nature and type of real estate being valued. If similar properties are commonly bought and sold in the same neighborhood or market area as the subject property, the search will probably be limited to the boundaries of the neighborhood or market area. Sometimes the appraiser must extend the search to similar neighborhoods or market areas. Certain types of properties have regional, national, and even international markets. To appraise major shopping centers, office buildings, resort hotels, multiuse complexes, and large industrial properties, appraisers may examine data from a wide geographic area within which the competitive properties are located.

After all sales information has been collected and analyzed, it can be organized on a market data grid. Each important difference between the subject property and the comparable properties that could affect property value is considered an element of comparison; each element is assigned a row on the grid and total property prices or unit prices are adjusted to reflect the value of these differences. (A sample market data grid and procedures for making adjustments on such a grid are presented later in this chapter.)

PROCEDURE

To apply the sales comparison approach, an appraiser follows a systematic procedure:

1. Research the market to obtain information on sales transactions, listings, and offerings to purchase properties similar to the subject property.
2. Verify the information by confirming that the data obtained are factually accurate and that the transactions reflect arm's-length market considerations.
3. Select relevant units of comparison (e.g., dollars per acre, per square foot, or per income multiplier) and develop a comparative analysis for each unit.
4. Compare the subject property and comparable sale properties using the elements of comparison and adjust the sale price of each comparable appropriately *or* eliminate the property as a comparable.
5. Reconcile the various value indications produced from the analysis of comparables into a single value indication or a range of values. An imprecise market may indicate a range of values.

Units of Comparison

After sales data have been gathered and verified, systematic analysis begins. Because like units must be compared, each sale price should be stated in terms of appropriate units of comparison—i.e., *the components into which a property may be divided for purposes of comparison.* The units of comparison selected depend on the appraisal problem. Apartment properties are often analyzed on the basis of price per apartment and price per room, but price per square foot of gross building or leasable building area is also widely used. Warehouses and industrial properties may be considered on the basis of price per square foot of gross building area or price per cubic foot of storage capacity. Hotels and motels are typically analyzed in terms of price per guest room; restaurants, theaters, churches, and auditoriums in price per seat; golf courses in price per acre and hole; mobile home parks in price per pad; tennis and racquetball facilities in price per court; automobile repair facilities in price per bay; and rights-of-way in price per mile, per square foot, or per acre.

Units of comparison are used to facilitate comparison of the subject and comparable properties. Because most properties can be analyzed with several units of comparison, the appraiser should apply all appropriate units of comparison, compare the results of each application, and examine the reasons for any wide variation in the results. This will help the appraiser choose the most appropriate and reliable unit(s) of comparison to use in the sales comparison approach. The unit(s) of comparison selected can have a significant bearing on the reconciliation of value indications in this approach.

Adjustments can be made either to total property prices or to units of comparison such as price per square foot of gross building area. Often adjustments for the property rights conveyed, financing, conditions of sale (motivation), and date of sale (market conditions) are made to the total sale price. The adjusted price is then converted into a unit price (e.g., per square foot, per apartment, or per acre), and adjusted for other elements of comparison such as location and physical characteristics.

Units of comparison such as income multipliers and income rates are not adjusted in sales comparison analysis, but the appraiser should consider why these units vary among the sale properties. The comparable sales are analyzed to extract these units of comparison, and the selection of appropriate unit(s) for the subject property is explained in the reconciliation of value. For example, an appraiser can analyze sales of income-producing properties to derive potential and effective gross income multipliers, overall and equity capitalization rates, and even total property and equity yield rates. These units of comparison are not adjusted. However, the appraiser considers the similarities and differences between the subject and comparable sale properties that cause the multipliers and rates to vary, and chooses the multiplier(s) and rate(s) that are appropriate to the property being appraised.

Income multipliers, capitalization rates, and yield rates are applied in the income capitalization approach to value, but it is entirely appropriate to extract rates and factors from comparable properties in sales comparison analysis.

Elements of Comparison

Elements of comparison are the characteristics of properties and transactions that cause the prices paid for real estate to vary. The appraiser considers and compares all differences between the comparable properties and the subject property that could affect their values. Adjustments for differences are made to the price of each comparable property to make the comparables equal to the subject on the date of the appraisal. Adjustments for differences in elements of comparison may be made to the total property price or to a common price unit, but the price units used must be consistently applied to the subject and comparable properties. For single-family residential property, the typical price units are total property price and price per square foot of gross living area. The amount of adjustment made for each element of comparison depends on the extent to which each comparable property differs from the subject property. Appraisers must be sure to consider all appropriate elements of comparison and avoid adjusting for the same difference more than once.

There are six common elements of comparison that should always be considered in sales comparison analysis.

1. Real property rights conveyed
2. Financing terms
3. Conditions of sale
4. Date of sale
5. Location
6. Physical characteristics

Other elements of comparison that may be relevant include income-producing characteristics such as tenant mix, the length of lease terms, escalation clauses in leases, and the history of the property's management as well as zoning and access to the property.

If, for example, an appraiser needs to estimate land value but can find no truly comparable properties with the same zoning as the subject, a very comparable parcel with slightly different zoning may be used in sales comparison analysis. An adjustment for zoning may be necessary if market data indicate a difference in value for similar properties located in different zones.

Similarly, an appraiser valuing an income-producing property may be asked to estimate the market value of the fee simple estate when the only sales available pertain to comparable properties that are 100% leased at contract rent. In this case, the appraiser must try to find sales data on comparable properties being rented at market rates and adjust the comparable sales prices accordingly.

Real Property Rights Conveyed

A transaction price is always predicated on the real property interest conveyed. Many types of real estate, particularly income-producing property, are sold subject to existing leases. The revenue-generating potential of a property is often fixed or limited by the terms of existing leases. In the valuation process, adjustments must be made to reflect the difference between contract rent and market rent and how this difference affects property price.

Market rent is used to estimate the value of a fee simple estate. When a property is considered free and clear of all leases, its value is normally based on the market rent that it can command. The transaction price of a property that is sold subject to existing leases reflects the contract rent that it will generate during the term of each lease and the market rent that will likely be achieved thereafter. In these situations, the real property interest that is sold or being appraised is the leased fee estate.

One of the initial steps in the valuation process is to determine the real property interest to be appraised. Once this is established, the appraiser can relate the market data to the subject property. The appraiser must precisely identify the real property rights conveyed in each comparable transaction selected for analysis.

The first adjustment to be considered is an adjustment for differences in real property rights. As an example, assume that the fee simple interest in an office building is being appraised. The subject building is being compared to a building that was fully leased at the time of sale; the leases were long term and the credit rating of the tenants was good. To compare a fee simple estate to a leased fee estate, the appraiser must determine if the contract rent of the sale property was above, below, or equal to market rent. If the market rent for office space is $20 per square foot, and the average rent for the sale property was $19 per square foot, the difference between market and contract rent is $1 per square foot.

For purposes of illustration, assume that the sale property is a 100,000-sq.-ft. building, and that the appropriate overall capitalization rate is 10%, the vacancy rate for the market in which the subject property is located is 5%, and 4% of effective gross income is a reasonable management expense. The effective difference between market and contract rent is estimated by deducting the vacancy allowance (5%) and management expenses (4%) from the actual difference between these rents ($1). Then this amount is multiplied by the total area of the sale property and the product is capitalized at the overall rate. The calculation of this adjustment is illustrated below.

$1.00 − $0.05 vacancy   = $0.95

$0.95 − $0.04 management   = $0.91 (rounded)

$0.91 × 100,000 sq. ft.   = $91,000

$91,000/10% (R_o) = $910,000

$910,000/100,000 sq. ft.   = $9.10 per square foot

The adjustment for the difference in real property rights is $9.10 per square foot of building area, or $910,000. If there were no difference between market rent and contract rent, the adjustment for real property rights would be zero. Similarly, if contract rent exceeded market rent, an appropriate adjustment would be required.

If no numerical adjustment is made in the sales comparison approach for differences in the real property rights conveyed in the subject and comparable properties, this subject must be addressed elsewhere in the appraisal report—e.g., in the reconciliation of value indications from the sales comparison approach or in the reconciliation and final value estimate section. The appraiser should also consider these differences in the income capitalization approach and estimate how they affect the value indication derived in this approach.

Financing Terms

The transaction price of one property may differ from that of an identical property due to different financing arrangements. For example, the purchaser of a comparable property may have assumed an existing mortgage at a favorable interest rate. In another case, a developer or seller may have arranged a buydown, paying cash to the lender so that a mortgage with a below-market interest rate could be offered. In both cases, the buyers probably paid higher prices for the properties to obtain below-market financing. Conversely, interest rates at above-market levels often result in lower sale prices.

Other nonmarket financing arrangements include installment sale contracts, in which the buyer pays periodic installments to the seller and obtains legal title only after the contract is fulfilled, and wraparound loans, which are superimposed on existing mortgages to preserve their lower interest rates. These loans offer below-market overall or blended interest rates to borrowers, but they yield market or above-market interest rates to lenders.

A financing adjustment may or may not include an adjustment for conditions of sale. A combined adjustment results when favorable financing is a function of the seller's need to sell the property quickly. Appraisers should recognize that, in some situations, these factors are interdependent.

Cash equivalency analysis is a procedure in which the sale prices of comparable properties that were sold with atypical financing terms are adjusted to reflect typical market terms. There are precise, mathematical calculations for analyzing cash equivalency, *but the financing adjustments derived with these calculations must be rigorously tested against market evidence.* More often than not, the cash discount indicated by the calculations is not specifically recognized by buyers and sellers. Furthermore, conditions of sale may reveal other noneconomic interests on the part of buyers or sellers. Therefore, appraisers must use cash equivalency calculations with caution and remember that the final adjustment is always derived from the market.

Cash equivalency calculations vary depending on the kind of financing arrangement that requires adjustment.[1] Two common situations involve points that the seller pays and loans that the seller finances. When the seller rather than the buyer pays points—i.e., the percentage of a loan that a lender charges for making the loan—the appraiser often deducts the full dollar amount from the sale price.

Appraisers may calculate adjustments for atypical financing by analyzing paired data sets or discounting the cash flows (e.g., payments and balloons) created by the mortgage contract at market interest rates. Discounting can be accomplished with present value factors from financial tables or it can be calculated directly with a financial function calculator or computer. One shortcoming of discounting is that it assumes that the buyer will hold the property for the life of the mortgage. Abundant market evidence indicates otherwise.

Estimating cash equivalency employs direct market evidence to make the appropriate adjustments. The appraiser tries to locate sales with and without atypical financing, makes adjustments for other items, and attributes the remaining differential to the financing terms. This method can be used as a guide if substantial data on transactions with and without special financing are available.

When paired data set analysis is used to derive a cash equivalency adjustment, the calculation for discounting and adjusting for any atypical conditions of sale are combined. In other words, when a cash equivalency adjustment is derived through paired data set analysis, the adjustments for financing and conditions of sale are represented by a single figure.

Calculating a cash equivalency adjustment by discounting cash flows can be accomplished in different ways. When a seller finances a mortgage at a below-market

---

1. For further discussion and examples of cash equivalency calculations, see Harold D. Albritton, "Use of Cash Equivalency in Valuation," *Controversies in Real Property Valuation: A Commentary* (Chicago: American Institute of Real Estate Appraisers, 1982), pp. 96-100; David C. Lennhoff, "Defining the Problem," *The Appraisal Journal*, April 1986; and Halbert C. Smith and John B. Corgel, "Adjusting for Nonmarket Financing: A Quick and Easy Method," *The Appraisal Journal*, January 1984.

interest rate, the appraiser can estimate the present value of the mortgage by applying a present value factor to the monthly mortgage payment at the market interest rate for the stated term of the mortgage. For example, an appraiser might find a comparable sale of a single-family residence that sold for $110,000 with a down payment of $25,000 and a seller-financed mortgage of $85,000 for a 20-year term at 10% interest. If the market rate is 13%, the sale can be adjusted to cash equivalency as follows.

Mortgage: $85,000, 20 years, 10%
Monthly payment: $820.27
Present value of $820.27 per month
for 20 years @ market rate of 13%
85.355132* × $820.27 = $70,014

PV of mortgage, rounded	$70,000
Plus down payment	25,000
Sale price adjusted for financing	$95,000

* PV of $1 per period factor, 20 years @ 13%

Another way to calculate the present value of the mortgage is to divide *the monthly payment or annual constant* at the contract interest rate by *the monthly payment or annual constant* at the market interest rate, and multiply the mortgage by the result. In this case, $0.00965/0.011715 = 0.82373$, × $85,000 = $70,017.

Discounting cash flows to calculate a cash equivalency adjustment may also take into account the expectation of a balloon payment. This example incorporates the same assumptions applied in the previous example, except that the buyer holds the mortgage for only seven years. The average mortgage life for loans on different types of properties can be ascertained from sales data on loans that were paid off rather than assumed by a buyer. In the following example, the same assumptions apply as in the preceding one. The buyer, however, holds the mortgage for only seven years. The present value of the mortgage is computed as the sum of two components: the present value of the mortgage payments at the market interest rate for the expected life of a mortgage, and the present value of the future mortgage balance at the market interest rate. To obtain the latter, the appraiser must first calculate the value in seven years of the remaining 13 years of monthly payments at the contract rate and then calculate the present value of that lump sum.

Although this method requires more calculation, it is preferable because it reflects the typical holding period more accurately.

Monthly payment: $820.27
Present value of $820.27 per month for 7 years @ 13%
   54.969328[a] × $820.27 = $45,090, rounded $ 45,000
Value of remaining mortgage payments in 7 years
   PV of $820.27 per month for 13 years @ 10%
   87.119542[b] × $820.27 = $71,462
PV of mortgage balance
   0.425061[c] × $71,462 = $30,376, rounded   30,000

PV of mortgage $ 75,000
Plus down payment   25,000

Sale price adjusted for financing $100,000

a. *PV* of $1 per period factor, 84 months @ 13%

b. *PV* of $1 per period factor, 156 months @ 10%

c. *PV* of $1 factor, 7 years @ 13%

Sometimes, this type of adjustment can convert a puzzling inconsistent sale into a usable comparable. Consider a shopping center that is sold for $2,580,000. Routine investigation of the sale indicates that the 10-year-old shopping center has a gross leasable area of 60,110 square feet, gross rents of $238,259, and a net income of $202,222. Thus, the property has a 15% expense ratio. The sale appears to reflect a price of $42.92 per square foot, a gross rent multiplier of 10.83, and an overall rate of 7.84%. Because these pricing units are inconsistent with the local market, the appraiser may be tempted to discard the sale as a comparable.

However, further inquiry reveals that the seller financed the entire transaction on a 39.5-year mortgage loan of $1,850,000 at a 9% interest rate. The current market interest rate for this type of property is 12%, and the typical mortgage life until prepayment is 15 years. The adjustment technique illustrated above is applied as follows.

Mortgage payments for 39.5 years @ 9%: $14,288.84.
Present value of mortgage payment for 15 years @ 12%
   83.321664[a] × $14,288.84 = $1,190,570, rounded $1,190,000
Mortgage balance in 15 years
   $14,288.84 for 24.5 years @ 9%
   $14,288.84 × 118.511817[b] = $1,693,396
PV of $1,693,396 in 15 years @ 12%
   0.182696[c] × $1,693,396 = $309,377, rounded $ 310,000

                                           $1,500,000
Down payment $ 730,000

Adjusted sale price $2,230,000

a. *PV* of $1 per period factor, 180 months @ 12%

b. *PV* of $1 per period factor, 294 months @ 9%

c. *PV* of $1 factor, 15 years @ 12%

After adjusting for financing, the units of comparison are: price per gross leasable square foot, $37.10; gross rent multiplier, 9.36; overall capitalization rate, 9.1%. Because these figures are reasonably consistent with other local market data, the appraiser can include the sale in the data file.

Transactions involving mortgage assumptions can be adjusted to cash equivalency with the same method applied to seller-financed transactions. However, the appraiser should be certain that the existing loan was assumed, not nullified by a due-on-sale clause. Other atypical mortgage terms include payments of interest only, followed by payments that include principal repayment. This type of mortgage can also be adjusted to its cash equivalent value using the adjustment procedure described here. The present values of the payments at the market rate, year by year, are derived using present value factors. If balloon mortgages are involved, present value factors may be applied to isolate the contributory market value of the unpaid balance of the mortgage.

The cash equivalency of any set of financing terms can be computed, but adjustments are needed to reflect the market conditions and financing terms under which the property is expected to be sold. These adjustments may indicate that the effect of the financing terms suggests a value that differs from the cash equivalency calculation.

Cash equivalency adjustments are based on precise mathematical calculations, but appraisers must make sure that they reflect market perceptions. *In choosing an appropriate adjustment to use in cash equivalency analysis, the appraiser gives greater emphasis to the market-derived adjustment than to the calculations.*

Conditions of Sale

Adjustments for conditions of sale usually reflect the motivations of the buyer and the seller. For example, a developer may pay more than market value for lots needed in a site assemblage because of acting under duress. A sale may be transacted at a below-market price if the seller needs cash in a hurry. A financial, business, or family relationship between the parties may also affect the price of property. Interlocking corporate entities may record a sale at a nonmarket price to serve their business interests. One member of a family may sell a property to another at a reduced price, or a buyer may pay a higher price for a property because it was built by his ancestors.

When nonmarket conditions of sale are detected in a transaction, the sale can be used as a comparable only with great care. The circumstances of the sale must be thoroughly researched before an adjustment is made.

Although conditions of sale are often perceived as applying only to sales that are not arm's-length transactions, some arm's-length sales may reflect atypical motivations or sale conditions due to unusual tax considerations, sale at legal auction, lack of exposure on the open market, or eminent domain proceedings. If the sales used in the sales comparison approach reflect such situations, an appropriate adjustment must be made for motivation or conditions of sale.

Market Conditions

Market conditions generally change over time, but the date of an appraisal is a specific time. Therefore, past sales must be examined in light of the direction of change between the sale date of the comparable and the valuation date of the subject property.

Changes in market conditions may be caused by inflation, deflation, fluctuations in supply and demand, or other factors. An economic recession tends to deflate all real estate prices. However, a decline in demand may sometimes affect only one category of real estate. If the demand for a specific type of property falls during a period of inflation, a reliable adjustment can be based on sales of that specific type of property during the period. Sales of other types of real estate during the same period may not reflect the market conditions for the specific property type.

Although the adjustment for market conditions is often referred to as a "time adjustment," time is not the cause of the adjustment. Market conditions shift over time; they create the need for an adjustment, not time itself. If market conditions have not changed, no adjustment is required even though considerable time may have elapsed.

Changes in market conditions are usually measured as a percentage of previous prices. If the size, condition, and environmental characteristics of a property remained unchanged, analysis of two or more sales of the same property over a period of time will indicate the rate of price change. The appraiser should examine several sets of sales to arrive at a reliable indication of the appropriate adjustment. An adjustment supported by just one matched data pair may be unreliable.

Sales and resales of the same properties provide the best indication of the change in market conditions over time, but if these sales are unavailable, sales of similar properties in the same market must be used. Even when data on the sale and resale of a property are available, these transactions must be examined very carefully because the rapid sale and resale of the same property may indicate that nonmarket sale conditions were involved in one or both transactions.

Location

An adjustment for location may be required when the locational characteristics of a comparable property are different from those of the subject property. Location adjustments are usually expressed as percentages that reflect the increase or decrease in value attributable to the property's location or neighborhood.

Most properties in the same neighborhood have similar locational characteristics, but variations may exist within neighborhoods. Consider, for example, the difference between a property with a pleasant view of a park and one located two blocks away with an unattractive view.

Adjustments for location may also be needed to reflect the difference in demand for various office suites within a single building, the retail advantage of a corner location, or the value contribution of an ocean view.

A property's location is analyzed in relation to the location of other properties. Although no location is inherently desirable or undesirable, an appraiser can
conclude that one location is better than, equal to, or worse than another.

To evaluate the desirability of one location relative to other locations,
appraisers must analyze sales of physically similar properties located in different
neighborhoods. Although the sale prices of properties in two different neighborhoods
may be similar, properties in one neighborhood may be sold more rapidly than
properties in the other.

Physical Characteristics

If the physical characteristics of a comparable property and the subject property
differ in many ways, each of these differences may require comparison and adjustment to the comparable. Physical differences may include building size, quality of
construction, architectural style, building materials, age, condition, functional utility, site size, attractiveness, and amenities.

The value added or lost by the presence or absence of a physical item in a
comparable property does not usually equal the cost of installing or removing the
item. Buyers may be unwilling to pay a higher sale price that includes the extra cost
of adding an amenity. Conversely, the addition of an amenity sometimes adds more
value to a property than the extra cost of its installation.

Characteristics of Income

Examples of characteristics that affect the income a property can produce include the
quality of management, the tenant mix, rent concessions, lease expiration dates,
renewal options, and lease provisions such as escalation and expense reimbursement
clauses that protect the property income from inflation.

Income-producing properties used in the sales comparison approach can be
analyzed in terms of their potential gross income (PGI), effective gross income
(EGI), operating expenses, capitalization and yield rates, and income multipliers.
(Formulas to derive multipliers for potential gross income, effective gross income,
and gross rent are presented in Chapter 20.) Income multipliers for certain categories
of properties show some conformity and predictably vary with the properties' expense
ratios. Rent multipliers will be higher if most of the below-market leases will soon
expire. Apartment buildings located in jurisdictions with legal rent controls tend to
have lower income multipliers. Income multipliers may also vary with the credit
rating of the tenants. Income multipliers should be arrayed and analyzed; deviations
from the recognizable pattern can usually be explained.

Paired Data Set Analyses

The adjustments used in comparable sales analysis must be market derived, but the
appraiser should also exercise judgment. Although a set of sales that are similar in all
but one respect can be analyzed to isolate how that one difference affects price, the

appraiser cannot expect the sales data to reveal the effect of a single characteristic in all situations. Frequently, a series of adjustments must be made to isolate the effect of a single characteristic. In some cases, this may be a relatively simple process. For example, if a property is sold twice within a limited period and no changes have occurred in the property or its environment within that period, an adjustment for market conditions can be derived from the prices of the two transactions. If two similar properties in different neighborhoods are sold within a limited time period, an adjustment for location can be computed. After these adjustments for market conditions and location have been applied, it may be possible to isolate the effects of other variables on price.

Although paired data set analysis is a theoretically sound method, *it is sometimes impractical because only a narrow sampling of sufficiently similar properties may be available and it is difficult to quantify the adjustments attributable to the other variables present.* However, even when only limited data are available, the appraiser should not discard paired data set analysis. Rather, the appraiser should determine the amount of adjustment indicated by the limited data and use other analytical procedures to test the reasonableness of the adjustment derived from the paired data sets. It is imperative that appraisers use all analytical tools pertinent to the appraisal problem.

TYPES OF ADJUSTMENTS

Adjustments can be applied to a comparable property in percentages or in dollars; the manner in which the adjustment is derived from the market determines whether it is expressed as a percentage or a dollar amount. Percentages are usually converted into dollar amounts that may be added to or subtracted from the price of the comparable on the market data grid.

Note that rigid statements on the *proper* way to make adjustments should be avoided. Adjustments can be made in several ways, depending on how the relationship between properties (i.e., subject and comparable, comparable and subject, or comparable and comparable) is expressed or perceived by the market. This relationship is converted into an algebraic expression, and the equation is solved to determine the amount of adjustment to be made for the differences between the properties.

The calculations that an appraiser uses to make an adjustment are based on a rationale, but the mathematics should not control the appraiser's judgment. A market value estimate is not determined by a set of precise calculations. Appraisal has an art aspect in that appraisers use their judgment to analyze and interpret quantitative data.

Percentage Adjustments

Adjustments for differences between a subject property and a comparable property are often expressed in percentages. An appraiser will usually use percentage adjustments to reflect changes in market conditions and differences in location. For example, the data may indicate that market conditions have resulted in a 5% increase in overall prices during the past year, or that prices for a particular category of property have recently increased 0.5% per month. Similarly, an appraiser may conclude from analysis of market data that properties in one location bring prices that are approximately 10% higher than the prices of similar properties in another location. These percentages may be converted into dollar amounts, which are added to or subtracted from the price of the comparable, or the percentages may be directly applied to the price or unit price of the comparable.

Five possible relationships may exist between the subject property and the comparable property in regard to any given property characteristic. If the subject and the comparable are equal for all practical purposes, no adjustment is necessary. The four other relationships between the properties, however, require adjustments. Algebraic statements that express these four relationships appear below. These statements indicate that, when the comparison is stated in terms of the subject (i.e., "the subject is ..."), the proper procedure is multiplication; when the comparison is stated in terms of the comparable (i.e., "the comparable is ..."), the proper procedure is division. In these equations, X equals the unknown value of the subject and 1.0 equals the known value of the comparable.

"*The subject is 10% superior to the comparable*" may be expressed as

$$
\begin{aligned}
X &= 1.0 + 10\% \times 1.0 \\
&= 1.0(1 + 0.1) \\
&= 1.1
\end{aligned}
$$

We multiply the price of the comparable by 1.1 to estimate the value of the subject. The percentage adjustment to the price of the comparable is plus 0.1, or 10%.

"*The subject is 10% inferior to the comparable*" may be expressed as

$$
\begin{aligned}
X &= 1.0 - 10\% \times 1.0 \\
&= 1.0(1 - 0.1) \\
&= 0.9
\end{aligned}
$$

We multiply the price of the comparable by 0.9 to estimate the value of the subject. The percentage adjustment to the price of the comparable is minus 0.1, or 10%.

"*The comparable is 10% superior to the subject*" may be expressed as

$$
\begin{aligned}
1.0 &= X + 10\% \times X \\
1.0 &= X(1 + 0.1) \\
1.0 &= X(1.1) \\
1/1.1 &= X \\
0.909 &= X, \text{ rounded } 0.91 = X
\end{aligned}
$$

We divide the price of the comparable by 1.1 to estimate the value of the subject. The percentage adjustment to the price of the comparable is minus 0.09, or 9%.

"*The comparable is 10% inferior to the subject*" may be expressed as

$$1.0 = X - 10\% \times X$$
$$1.0 = X(1 - 0.1)$$
$$1.0 = X(0.9)$$
$$1/0.9 = X$$
$$1.111 = X, \text{ rounded } 1.11 = X$$

We divide the price of the comparable by 0.9 to estimate the value of the subject. The percentage adjustment to the price of the comparable is plus 0.11, or 11%.

The appraiser must be consistent in stating the relationship between the subject and the comparable. Although percentage adjustments can be stated in terms of differences in the subject property in relation to the comparable property and in terms of differences in the comparable in relation to the subject, *only the value of the comparable is known, so the adjustment must be made to this figure.* When percentage adjustments are stated in terms of the differences in the subject in relation to the comparable (e.g., "the subject is a certain percentage superior or inferior to the comparable"), the appropriate percentages can be applied directly to the known value of the comparable. This relationship is expressed in the first two algebraic statements presented. If the appraiser finds it more convenient to state percentage adjustments in terms of the differences in the comparable in relation to the subject (e.g., "the comparable is a certain percentage superior or inferior to the subject"), the more oblique algebraic procedure expressed in the third and fourth algebraic statements must be followed. *The relationship between the subject property and the comparable property should be stated in a manner that corresponds to the way the market perceives it.*

Dollar Adjustments

Adjustments can also be computed in dollars. For example, an appraiser may conclude that the favorable financing terms employed in the sale of a comparable property resulted in a $100,000 premium paid by the buyer. In analyzing major investment properties, an appraiser can frequently use discounting to derive a dollar adjustment for financing terms. Adjustments for many physical characteristics may also be estimated in dollar amounts, which are added to or subtracted from the sale price of the comparable.

SEQUENCE OF ADJUSTMENTS

A sequence for making adjustments must be followed when percentage adjustments are calculated and added together.[2] The sequence also applies when percentage adjustments are used alone or in combination with dollar adjustments. It is recommended that appraisers adhere to a sequence of adjustments in all sales comparison analyses. Using the sequence, the appraiser obtains intermediate price figures and applies succeeding adjustments to each previously adjusted price. The sequence is illustrated in Table 14.1. The percentage adjustments applied in the illustration have been rounded. The percentage adjustments made to the price of a comparable property reflect the comparable's superiority or inferiority in regard to the real property rights conveyed, financing, conditions of sale, market conditions, location, and physical characteristics: "The comparable is a certain percentage superior or inferior to the subject." This treatment of the relationship between the comparable and the subject properties is used strictly for purposes of illustration.

Table 14.1   Sequence of Adjustments

Element of Comparison	Market-Derived Adjustments	Adjustment to Price of Comparable Sale
Sale price		$100,000
Adjustment for property rights conveyed	+5%	+5,000
Adjusted price		$105,000
Adjustment for financing terms	–2%	–2,100
Adjusted price		$102,900
Adjustment for conditions of sale*	+5%	+5,145
Adjusted price		$108,045
Adjustment for market conditions	+5%	+5,402
Adjusted price		$113,447
Adjustment for location	+3%	+3,403
Physical characteristics	–5%	–5,672
Indication of value of the subject property		$111,178

*The conditions of sale adjustment may be combined with another adjustment depending on how it is extracted from the market.

The first adjustment, which is made for the property rights conveyed, is applied to the transaction price. This adjustment takes into account differences in

---

2. This sequence of adjustments was first presented by Halbert C. Smith in *Real Estate Appraisal* (Columbus, Ohio: Grid, Inc., 1976).

legal estate between the subject property and the comparable property. The second adjustment converts the transaction price of the comparable into its cash equivalent or modifies it to match the financing terms of the subject property. The third adjustment is made for conditions of sale and reflects the difference between the actual sale price of the comparable and its probable sale price if it were currently sold in an arm's-length transaction. If the financing terms or conditions of sale for the comparable had been the same as those typical in the market for the subject property, zeros would have been shown on the chart. At this stage in the sequence, the resulting price figure is $108,045, which represents the amount for which the comparable property would have been sold under normal financing and sale conditions. This figure is approximately 108% of the actual transaction price.

The next adjustment is for market conditions. It reflects the change in the prices paid for real property due to changes in market conditions over time. The adjustment would be distorted if it were applied to the actual transaction price, which was influenced by non-market considerations such as atypical financing. The adjustment for market conditions results in a figure of $113,447, which represents the amount for which the comparable property would be sold as of the date of appraisal on an open-market basis. The adjusted price is approximately 113.4% of the transaction price.

The adjustments for location and physical characteristics take into consideration these differences between the comparable property and the subject property. In this particular example, no other adjustments are required. After all adjustments have been made to the sale price of the comparable, the resulting value indication for the subject property is $111,178.

The adjustment procedure discussed above relates to the addition of percentage adjustments. However, the multiplication of percentages may be appropriate under certain conditions. Cumulative percentage adjustments, which are obtained by multiplying percentage adjustments, are used when the base for one adjustment is the result of a previous adjustment. In other words, cumulative percentage adjustments are causally interrelated. Although a sequence is not required when the adjustments are multiplied, its use helps to clarify the procedure in this special application of the sales comparison approach. For example, consider a comparable property that was sold one year ago for $100,000. Current financing terms and conditions of sale are the same for the comparable and the subject property. A positive adjustment of 10% is made for the superior market conditions under which the subject is being sold, and a 10% negative adjustment is made to account for the inferior location of the subject property. The difference in market conditions affects the base to which the subsequent adjustment for location is applied. Thus, a cumulative percentage adjustment is appropriate. The calculation is

$$110\% \times 90\% = 99\%$$
$$0.99 \times \$100,000 = \$99,000$$

SAMPLE MARKET DATA GRID

The sample market data grid shown in Table 14.2 reflects the elements of comparison and the sequence of adjustments. The sample grid includes lines for all elements of comparison. If the subject and comparable sales are similar in regard to any element of comparison, no adjustment is required for that element. The grid may include separate lines for comparison and adjustment to ensure that adjustments are made in a consistent manner.

Table 14.2   Sample Market Data Grid
Comparison and Adjustment of Market Data

Element	Subject	Sale 1	Sale 2	Sale 3	Sale 4
Sale price	?				
Real property rights conveyed adjustment					
Adjusted price*					
Financing adjustment					
Conditions of sale adjustment					
Adjusted price**					
Date of sale adjustment					
Adjusted price***					
Final adjusted sale price					
For reconciliation purposes:					
Total adjustment					
Total adjustment as % of sale price					

*   Sale price adjusted for property rights conveyed
** Sale price adjusted for financing and conditions of sale
***Sale price further adjusted for market conditions

The section labeled "For reconciliation purposes" is provided to help the appraiser analyze the degree of comparability of each sale, which will indicate the relative reliability of the separate value indications derived in the sales comparsion approach. Each final adjusted sale price is a possible value indication for the subject property; together these sale prices constitute a range of value in which the value of the subject property will likely fall. Each of these prices can be analyzed to show the total, or absolute, adjustment to the sale price and the percentage of the sale price that is reflected by this total adjustment. With these figures, an appraiser can rank the sales' comparability to the subject and select an appropriate estimate of value, if the value conclusion is to be reported as a point estimate. The sale that requires the least total adjustment is often the most comparable and generally should be given more weight in reconciling the value indications from the sales comparison approach.

Although the calculations shown in the sample applications, which follow the grid, can be used as a guide in reconciling value indications, they must be carefully analyzed. In reconciling the value indications derived in the sales comparison approach, the appraiser must also consider the reliability of the data used in making adjustments.

SAMPLE APPLICATIONS

The following examples illustrate how the sales comparison approach is applied to the appraisal of an apartment building, a retail property, an industrial property, an office building, and a single-family residence.

Apartment Building

It is difficult to find an adequate number of sales of apartment buildings that are similar in terms of the number and size of units. Therefore, comparable transactions are usually analyzed in relevant units of comparison—e.g., price per apartment, price per room, price per square foot, and gross income or gross rent multiplier. To consider sales on the basis of price per room, an appraiser must adopt a standard system of room counting. If a potential gross income multiplier (*PGIM*) or an effective gross income multiplier (*EGIM*) is used with its respective operating expense ratio, it must be applied to the subject property's income in a manner consistent with the manner in which the multiplier and expense ratio were derived. An appraiser makes certain critical assumptions when using a *GIM* or *GRM*. One very important assumption is that only multipliers from properties with vacancy and operating expense ratios similar to the subject property's vacancy and operating expense ratio will be used for comparison.

The market data grid in Table 14.3 shows sales data pertaining to a subject apartment property and four comparable properties. In all the properties, the real property rights conveyed are leased fee estates and the rents are at market levels. The subject property has 177 apartments; the comparables have from 90 to 400 units. Stating the sale prices in units of comparison—i.e., price per room, per apartment, and per square foot—helps compensate for dissimilarities in the number of units. However, large apartment properties generally bring lower prices per room, per apartment, and per square foot than smaller properties, when all other factors are equal. Converting comparable sale prices into appropriate units of comparison does not entirely eliminate the need to make a separate adjustment for the size of the building (i.e., the number of apartments). The appraiser must relate the effect of the total building size to the prices per room, per apartment, and per square foot.

Table 14.3   Market Data Grid: Apartment Building Appraisal

	Subject	Comparables A	B	C	D
Real property rights conveyed	Leased Fee	Leased Fee	Leased Fee	Leased Fee	Leased Fee
Transaction price		$7,000,000	$2,050,000	$2,590,000	$5,600,000
Time of sale	Current	Current	Current	Current	Current
No. of apartments	177	400	90	114	384
No. of rooms	880	1,724	455	678	1,536
Area in sq. ft.	90,000	200,000	45,000	60,000	180,000
Rooms per apartment	4.97	4.31	5.06	5.95	4.00
Potential gross income (*PGI*)	$574,000	$1,070,650	$305,900	$435,625	$800,000
PGI per room per month	$54.36	$51.75	$56.03	$53.54	$43.40
Price per room		$4,060	$4,505	$3,820	$3,646
Price per apartment		$17,500	$22,778	$22,719	$14,583
Price per sq. ft.		$35.00	$45.56	$43.17	$31.11
Potential gross income multiplier (*PGIM*)		6.54	6.70	5.95	7.00

The sales data indicate that Comparable B has approximately the same average number of rooms per unit as the subject property. This fact might indicate that the price per unit from this sale is the best unit of comparison. Comparable D has a slightly lower rent per room than the subject and the other comparables, so this sale may need to be studied further. This property also has the highest *PGIM*, which may indicate that the purchasers felt they could raise rents significantly after the purchase. These factors suggest that Comparable D may not be in the same market as the other properties. If this sale is disregarded, the following value ranges are indicated by the units of comparison.

Unit	Indicated Value Range for Subject
Price per room	$3,361,600 to $3,964,400
Price per unit	$3,097,500 to $4,031,706
Price per sq. ft.	$3,150,000 to $4,100,400
PGIM	$3,415,300 to $3,845,800

Comparable B, which is the most similar to the subject in terms of the number of rooms per unit, gives the highest indication for rent and unit price comparisons. Because apartments in this building rent for more per room than apartments in the subject building, a value below the upper limit should be estimated. The indicated values range from approximately $3,100,000 to $4,100,000, which is a rather wide expanse. Comparable C is most similar to the subject in terms of the number of units, the number of rooms, and the number of square feet. Pertinent data from Comparable C indicate the following values for the subject property.

Price per unit	$4,021,263
Price per room	$3,361,600
Price per sq. ft.	$3,885,300
Gross income multiplier	$3,415,300

The values indicated by Comparable C fall within a narrower range, from approximately $3,360,000 to $4,020,000. A final value estimate of $3,700,000 would appear reasonable.

Retail Property

The most significant units of comparison in the appraisal of retail properties are the gross income multiplier and the price per square foot of gross leasable area. The summary grid in Table 14.4 shows data pertaining to a retail property and four comparable properties.

Table 14.4   Market Data Grid: Retail Property Appraisal

		Comparables			
	Subject	A	B	C	D
Real property rights conveyed	Leased Fee	Leased Fee	Leased Fee	Leased Fee	Leased Fee
Construction	Brick/steel	Brick/steel	Brick/steel	Brick/steel	Brick/steel
Age	10	5	3	12	8
Number of stores	4	3	5	5	3
Rental area in sq. ft.	6,000	6,000	8,000	6,000	5,400
Onsite parking in sq. ft.	3,500	3,000	5,000	1,000	6,000
Rental area-to-parking ratio	1.7:1	2:1	1.6:1	6:1	0.9:1
Gross income (at sale)	$18,600	$18,000	$27,200	$15,000	$16,200
Tenant credit rating	B	A	C	C	A
Average rent per sq. ft.	$3.10	$3.00	$3.40	$2.50	$3.00
Years since sale		0.5	1	2	1
Sale price		$165,500	$217,500	$124,500	$146,000
Gross income multiplier (GIM)		9.19	8.00	8.30	9.01
Price per sq. ft. of rentable bldg. area		$27.58	$27.19	$20.75	$27.04

The grid shows how the *GIM* and the price per square foot are abstracted from sales of comparable retail properties. A *GIM* is not usually adjusted because the relative desirability of the properties in the market is presumably reflected in both the rent the properties can command and the prices at which they are sold. The subject property is being leased and the appraisal is of the leased fee estate. Because all the comparable properties are leased fee estates, no property rights adjustment is needed.

The ratio of rental area to parking area in Comparable B is most similar to that of the subject property. Comparable A is also similar in this respect. Comparable C has relatively little parking, which may account for its lower rent. Comparables A and D are the most similar in terms of rental rates. These properties are both occupied by tenants with better credit ratings than the tenants in the subject property, which may indicate that these properties have higher *GIM*s than are applicable to the subject property.

The data indicate a *GIM* for the subject property between 8.3 and 9.0, probably from 8.5 to 8.8. The indicated price per square foot is between $27.00 and $27.50. These figures suggest the following ranges in value for the subject property.

Unit	Indicated Value Range for Subject
GIM	$158,100 to $163,680
Price per sq. ft.	$162,000 to $165,000

Industrial Property

Light industrial properties include warehouses used for storage and distribution, light manufacturing plants, and research and development facilities. The units of comparison used in appraising these properties are price per square foot of gross building area and price per square foot of building area exclusive of the land. The amount of finished office space must be estimated and treated separately if the comparables and the subject property differ in this respect.

Gross rent multipliers may also be used. Light industrial properties are frequently leased with the landlord paying only taxes, insurance, exterior maintenance, and management; in many cases, the landlord pays fewer expenses. This limited expense requirement results in fairly consistent expense ratios and facilitates the compilation of income multipliers.

Most light industrial buildings contain some finished office space, but the ratio of finished to unfinished space varies. Buildings designed with flexibility are the most marketable. Features such as additional floor load capacity, wide column spacing, docks and loading facilities, ceiling clearance, and enhanced mechanical and electrical systems make buildings adaptable when differing proportions of finished office space, semifinished light assembly space, and unfinished storage space are required.

Other types of industrial properties are compared with other units of comparison. Truck terminals are compared on the basis of price per door, and grain elevators are compared in terms of price per bushel of storage capacity. Processing facilities are compared based on the amount of goods that can be processed in a specific period of time.

The methods of storing, moving, and inventorying products have changed, so the design of industrial buildings has changed too. This has resulted in functional obsolescence in older buildings. Appraisers should become familiar with modern facilities to recognize the shortcomings of buildings that have functional obsolescence of one kind or another. Comparison of heavy industrial properties is more difficult because there are few sales of these properties available and many buildings of this type are quite specialized.

In valuing a small light industrial building built five years before the date of the appraisal, two sales of similar properties are analyzed. Table 14.5 shows data pertaining to the subject property and the two comparables. The subject property is owned in fee simple and the fee simple estate is being appraised. The subject building is 56 ft. x 90 ft. and it is situated on a 70-ft. x 198-ft. site. The office space in the building is 56 ft. x 25 ft. in area. It is of average quality and has paneled walls, an asphalt tile floor, an acoustical ceiling, and air-conditioning.

Table 14.5   Market Data Grid: Industrial Building Appraisal*

Item	Subject	Comparable A	Comparable B
Sale price	—	$145,000	$250,000
Real property rights conveyed	Fee simple	Fee simple	Fee simple
Adjusted price	—	$145,000	$250,000
Financing terms	Market	Market	Market
Conditions of sale	Market	Market	Market
Adjusted price	—	$145,000	$250,000
Date of sale	—	2 yrs ago	Current
Adjustment	—	+ 10%	0
Adjusted price	—	$159,500	$250,000
Location	Good	Similar	Inferior
Land value per sq. ft.	$3.00	$3.00	$2.50
Land area	13,860	11,600	18,000
Land value	$41,580	$34,800	$45,000
Building allocation	—	$124,700	$205,000
Building area in sq. ft.**	5,040	4,800	8,500
Building allocation per sq. ft.	—	$25.98	$24.12
Office premium per sq. ft.***	$15.00	$20.00	$15.00
Office area in sq. ft.	1,400	1,250	2,500
Office area premium	$21,000	$25,000	$37,500
Remainder (Basic bldg. contribution)	—	$99,700	$167,500
Price per sq. ft. of basic bldg.	—	$20.77	$19.71

*In industrial property appraisals, adjustments may also be based on price per unit of area.

**Includes office area.

***Reflects additional costs above basic building costs.

Office space of this type usually can command a sale price premium of $15 per square foot more than the warehouse space in the same building. The value of the site is estimated at $3 per square foot. Comparable A has a similar land value, but the quality of the office space is superior. Comparable B has less land value due to poor access, but the office space is of similar quality. Both comparables are owned in fee simple.

From the sales data, a value for the subject property can be calculated as follows.

Land value:	13,860 sq. ft. @ $ 3.00 =	$ 41,580	
Building:	5,040 sq. ft. @ $20.00 =	100,800	
Office premium:	1,400 sq. ft. @ $15.00 =	21,000	
Total		163,380	
	Rounded	$163,400	

Office Building

The primary units of comparison used in appraising office buildings are price per square foot of gross, usable, and leasable area, and the gross income multiplier. Price per square foot of leasable or rentable area is also useful because the percentage of usable area often varies considerably among competitive, otherwise comparable, properties.

Table 14.6 summarizes the comparative data used to analyze an office building. The four comparable office buildings are somewhat physically dissimilar from the subject property, but they were competitive with it. In this market, leasable (rentable) and usable areas are the same. This is not true in every market. The subject and all the comparables are leased properties and the leased fee estate is being appraised.

The subject and all of the comparable properties are rented at market levels and no adjustment is required for differences in the real property rights conveyed.

Comparable D is a significantly smaller building than the other comparables, and it has a different proportion of leasable area to gross building area. Due to its smaller size and higher proportion of leasable area, its square foot sale price units are higher. Comparable D may be considered least indicative of value, but its income multipliers are consistent with those of the other comparables.

Comparable B has the highest income multipliers and its rent per square foot is the lowest, which suggest that the buyer expects to be able to increase the rents in the near future. The *GBA* of Comparable B and its proportion of leasable area to *GBA* are most similar to those of the subject property. Comparable B may be considered quite indicative. The range of value indications produced by the comparables are

PGIM	$24,633,000 (C) to $25,668,300 (B)
EGIM	$24,893,610 (C) to $25,673,655 (B)
Price per sq. ft. of *GBA*	$25,340,000 (B)
Price per sq. ft. of leasable area	$25,588,680 (B)

A value of $25,500,000 can be estimated. This value conclusion can be broken down as follows:

$102.00 per sq. ft. of *GBA*
$136.00 per sq. ft. of leasable area (rounded)
with a *PGIM* of 7.14 and an *EGIM* of 7.54

Table 14.6   Market Data Grid: Office Building Appraisal

		Comparables			
	Subject	A	B	C	D
Sale price	—	$29,700,000	$20,000,000	$27,000,000	$12,000,000
Real property rights conveyed	Leased Fee	Leased Fee	Leased Fee	Leased Fee	Leased Fee
Adjusted price	—	$29,700,000	$20,000,000	$27,000,000	$12,000,000
Adjustment for financing terms	Market	Market	-$150,000	Market	+$100,000
Conditions of sale	Market	Market	Market	Market	Market
Adjusted price	—	$29,700,000	$19,850,000	$27,000,000	$12,100,000
Adjustment for market conditions	—	+10%	+20%	0	+10%
Adjusted price	—	$32,670,000	$23,820,000	$27,000,000	$13,310,000
Location	Good	Similar	Similar	Similar	Similar
Gross bldg. area (*GBA*) in sq. ft.	250,000	330,000	235,000	270,000	110,000
Leasable area in sq. ft.	188,000	230,000	175,000	191,700	88,000
Percentage of leasable area to GBA	75.2%	69.7%	74.5%	71.0%	80.0%
Potential gross income (*PGI*)	$3,570,000	$4,240,000	$2,760,000	$3,915,000	$1,690,000
Effective gross income (*EGI*)	$3,391,500	$3,985,600	$2,622,000	$3,680,100	$1,639,300
EGI/PGI (or vacancy and collection loss)	95% (5%)	94% (6%)	95% (5%)	94% (6%)	97% (3%)
Potential gross income multiplier (*PGIM*)	—	7.00	7.19	6.90	7.16
Effective gross income multiplier (*EGIM*)	—	7.45	7.57	7.34	7.38
Adjusted price per sq. ft. of *GBA*	—	$99.00	$101.36	$100.00	$121.00
Adjusted price per sq. ft. of leasable area	—	$142.04	$136.11	$140.85	$151.25
PGI per sq. ft. of leasable area	$18.99	$18.43	$15.77	$20.42	$19.20
EGI per sq. ft. of leasable area	$18.04	$17.33	$14.98	$19.20	$18.63

Single-Family Residence

Assume that the house being appraised is a 1,200-sq.-ft., frame ranch-style structure with a finished basement. It is situated on a 10,000-sq.-ft. lot and has six rooms, three bedrooms, one and one-half baths, and no garage. It is in average condition and is located in the same neighborhood as all the comparables. The comparable properties are described below.

Comparable A is a 1,200-sq.-ft., frame ranch house situated on a 10,000-sq.-ft. lot with an unfinished basement and an attached, two-car garage. It has six rooms, three bedrooms, and one and one-half baths. It was sold three weeks before the date of the appraisal for $67,000 at a below-market interest rate, which resulted in a price that was $5,000 higher than it would have been otherwise.

Comparable B is a 1,450-sq.-ft., frame ranch house situated on a 12,000-sq.-ft. lot with an unfinished basement and an attached, two-car garage. It has seven rooms, three bedrooms, and one and one-half baths. It was sold one month before the date of the appraisal for $75,000 at a below-market interest rate, which resulted in a price that was $5,000 higher than it would have been otherwise.

Comparable C is a 1,200-sq.-ft., frame ranch house situated on a 10,000-sq.-ft. lot with an unfinished basement and an attached, two-car garage. It has six rooms, three bedrooms, and one and one-half baths. It was sold one year before the date of the appraisal for $56,500 with market financing.

Comparable D is a 1,450-sq.-ft., frame ranch house situated on a 12,000-sq.-ft. lot with a finished basement and an attached, two-car garage. It has seven rooms, three bedrooms, and one and one-half baths. It was sold one year before the date of the appraisal for $70,000 with market financing.

Comparable E is a 1,200-sq.-ft., frame ranch house situated on a 10,000-sq.-ft. lot with an unfinished basement and no garage. It has six rooms, three bedrooms, and one and one-half baths. It was sold one year before the date of the appraisal for $53,200 with market financing.

The summary grid for comparative analysis is shown in Table 14.7. The comparable properties differ from the subject property in terms of financing, date of sale, size (i.e., livable area, number of rooms), and the presence or absence of a garage and a finished basement. To derive adjustments for these elements of comparison, paired data analysis is used.

Comparables A and C differ only in their financing terms and dates of sale. The adjustment for market conditions (date of sale) is calculated: ($62,000 − $56,500)/$56,500 = .097345. This 9.7% adjustment can be rounded to 10%.

The difference in size between Comparables A and B can be attributed to the additional room in Comparable B. A size adjustment is made after each price has been adjusted $5,000 downward for financing terms. The adjustment for size is calculated: $70,000 − $62,000 = $8,000.

Comparison of Comparables C and E indicates that the adjustment for the lack of a garage in Comparable E can be calculated: $62,150 − $58,520 = $3,630, rounded to $3,600.

In comparing Comparables B and D, the adjustment for the finished basement in Comparable D is calculated after adjusting Comparable D $7,000 upward for market conditions and adjusting Comparable B $5,000 downward for financing terms: $77,000 − $70,000 = $7,000.

Table 14.7   Market Data Grid: Single-Family Residence Appraisal

	Subject	Comparables				
		A	B	C	D	E
Sale price	—	$67,000	$75,000	$56,500	$70,000	$53,200
Real property rights conveyed	Fee simple	Fee simple	Fee simple	Fee simple	Fee simple	Fee simple
Adjusted price	—	$67,000	$75,000	$56,500	$70,000	$53,200
Financing terms	—	Nonmarket	Nonmarket	Market	Market	Market
Adjustment for financing	—	–$5,000	–$5,000	0	0	0
Conditions of sale	—	Arm's-length	Arm's-length	Arm's-length	Arm's-length	Arm's-length
Adjustment for conditions of sale	—	0	0	0	0	0
Adjusted price	—	$62,000	$70,000	$56,500	$70,000	$53,200
Date of sale	—	–3 weeks	–1 month	–1 year	–1 year	–1 year
Adjustment for date of sale	—	0	0	+10%	+10%	+10%
Adjusted price	—	$62,000	$70,000	$62,150	$77,000	$58,520
Location	—	Similar	Similar	Similar	Similar	Similar
Adjustment for location	—	0	0	0	0	0
Size in sq. ft.	1,200	1,200	1,450	1,200	1,450	1,200
Adjustment for size	—	0	–$8,000	0	–$8,000	0
Garage	None	2-car	2-car	2-car	2-car	None
Adjustment for garage	—	–$3,600	–$3,600	–$3,600	–$3,600	0
Finished basement	Yes	No	No	No	Yes	No
Adjustment for basement	—	+$7,000	+$7,000	+$7,000	0	+$7,000
Adjusted price	—	$65,400	$65,400	$65,550	$65,400	$65,520

All adjustments are made directly from market data. The financing adjustment is based on the actual price needed to recapture the seller's buydown payment to the lender. In this example, none of the comparables are given greater weight because none are considered better indicators than the others. No comparable was exactly like the subject and all required at least two adjustments. The range of adjusted sale prices is very narrow, so the value indication can be rounded to the nearest $100. The market value of the subject property is indicated to be between $65,400 and $65,550; $65,500 is a reasonable conclusion.

RECONCILIATION

When sales comparison analysis is completed, the appraiser often derives a single indication of value by reconciling the data. If a point estimate of value cannot be reached due to the scarcity or ambiguity of the data, a range of values may be appropriate. In reconciling the indications of market value, more reliance should be placed on sales that were transacted closest to the date of the appraisal and those that are most similar. Sales that require large adjustments are generally given less consideration.

SUMMARY

The sales comparison approach is based on the premise that the market value of a property is directly related to the prices of comparable, competitive properties. The value of a property in the market is set by the availability of substitute properties of similar utility and desirability. Value is sustained when the relationships between land and the improvements on land, and between property and its environment are in balance. Externalities such as the neighborhood and the economy can affect property value positively or negatively.

The sales comparison approach is applicable when there are sufficient data on recent market transactions to indicate value patterns; it is less useful when data are scarce. Abrupt changes in economic conditions, rates of inflation, zoning, property taxes, or supply may also limit the reliability of the approach. Sales comparison is usually used to value single-family residential properties. It may also provide information on income, expenses, and capitalization rates and factors that can be applied in the income capitalization approach.

To apply the sales comparison approach, the appraiser considers data from closed sales, contracts, offers, and listings of competitive properties. These data are used to establish the prices, real property rights conveyed, transaction dates, financing terms, motivations, locations, physical and functional conditions, and income-producing characteristics of the properties under consideration. Sources of information may include public records, sales data services, and interviews with the parties involved in a transaction. The geographic limits of the data search are set by the range of competitive properties.

A systematic, five-step procedure for applying the sales comparison approach involves: 1) researching the market for data on the prices of comparable properties, 2) verifying that the data are accurate and representative of arm's-length transactions, 3) determining relevant units of comparison, 4) comparing the subject with the comparables and adjusting the comparables for differences, and 5) reconciling the multiple value indications into a single value or a range of values.

Units of comparison, which are the components into which properties may be divided for purposes of comparison, vary with the appraisal problem. The use of units of comparison facilitates the comparative analysis of the subject and the comparables, but the units applied should be appropriate, reliable, and consistent. Some adjustments can be made to the total property price; others are made to the price per unit of comparison. Income multipliers and capitalization rates may also be used as units of comparison. Appraisers do not adjust these units; rather, they explain any similarities or differences in reconciling the separate value indications.

Elements of comparison are the characteristics of properties and transactions that cause prices paid for real estate to vary. They are used to help identify differences between the subject and comparable properties so that adjustments can be made. Appraisers must not adjust for the same difference more than once. The most common elements of comparison are property rights conveyed, financing terms, conditions of sale, date of sale, location, and physical characteristics. Other important elements of comparison are income-producing characteristics, zoning, and access.

An adjustment for the real property rights conveyed reflects the different income-generating potential of a property encumbered with leases and an unencumbered property. The adjustment is needed to account for the difference between the market rent that an unencumbered property is capable of commanding, and the contract rent that a property subject to existing leases will generate until the termination of each lease. If an adjustment is not made for such differences in the sales comparison approach, they must be addressed in the reconciliation of the separate value indications.

Financing arrangements such as mortgage assumptions, buydowns, installment sale contracts, and wraparound loans affect sale prices. Although cash equivalent prices can be computed mathematically, the financing adjustments derived with these calculations must be rigorously tested against market conditions and perceptions.

Cash equivalency calculations are commonly used to adjust sales in which the seller pays points or finances the loan. Cash equivalency adjustments for atypical financing may be calculated by analyzing paired data sets or by discounting the cash flows created by these mortgage contracts at market interest rates. The financing adjustment may or may not include an adjustment for conditions of sale; a combined adjustment results when favorable financing is a function of the seller's need to sell the property quickly.

An adjustment for conditions of sale is used to reflect the motivations of buyers or sellers in sales that are not arm's-length transactions due to duress or special relationships, and in arm's-length transactions influenced by unusual tax considerations, lack of market exposure, or eminent domain proceedings.

An adjustment for market conditions is derived by analyzing changes that have occurred over time and their effect on a specific type of property during that period. Analysis of two or more arm's-length sales of one property during a period in which no physical or neighborhood changes have occurred may indicate the rate of price change; several paired sets will provide a more reliable indication of the rate of price change.

An adjustment for location is required when the neighborhoods or environments of the subject and comparables differ significantly, creating variances in demand. Adjustments for physical characteristics account for differences in the size of improvements or sites, the quality and condition of the improvements, the construction material used, the functional utility of the improvements, and the amenities provided.

Adjustments for income-producing characteristics reflect differences in management quality, tenant mix, and contractual items such as rent concessions, lease expiration dates, renewal options, and special lease provisions to protect property income from inflation. The potential gross income, effective gross income, operating expenses, capitalization and yield rates, and income multipliers of comparable properties can be analyzed to identify such differences.

Paired data set analysis can be used to isolate the effect of a particular variable on price when sufficient data are available and other variables can be quantified. When sufficient data are not available, the technique may be employed to suggest the size of an adjustment, which can then be tested for reasonableness.

Adjustments are applied to a comparable property either as percentages or dollar amounts. The relationship between the subject and the comparable should be expressed as the market perceives it. The relationship between the subject and a comparable property is converted into an algebraic statement to determine the percentage adjustment to be applied to the comparable. The appraiser should express the relationship consistently.

When adjustments are calculated and added together, the appraiser follows this sequence: 1) property rights conveyed adjustment, adjusted price; 2) financing terms and conditions of sale adjustment(s), adjusted price; 3) market conditions adjustment, adjusted price; and 4) adjustments for location, physical characteristics, and other factors. The final adjusted price is an indication of the value of the subject property.

Use of a market data grid ensures that the adjustments are made in a consistent manner. The grid includes a section for reconciling the separate value indications derived in the sales comparison approach. Collectively, these indications constitute a range of value. The market data grid can be used to rank sales in terms of their comparability to the subject property and to find which sales require the least total adjustment. The sales that occurred nearest to the appraisal date and those that are most similar to the subject are given the most weight in the sales comparison approach.

15 The Cost Approach

The cost approach to value, like the sales comparison and income capitalization approaches, is based on comparison. In the cost approach, the cost to develop a property is compared with the value of the existing developed property. When applicable, the cost approach reflects market thinking by recognizing that market participants relate value to cost. Buyers tend to judge the value of an existing structure by considering the prices and rents of similar buildings and the cost to create a new building with optimal physical and functional utility. Moreover, buyers adjust the prices they are willing to pay by estimating the costs to bring an existing structure up to the level of physical and functional utility they desire.

Therefore, in applying the cost approach, an appraiser attempts to estimate the difference in worth to a buyer between the property being appraised and a newly constructed building with optimal utility. The appraiser estimates the cost to construct a reproduction of, or replacement for, the existing structure and then deducts all accrued depreciation in the property being appraised from the cost new of the reproduction or replacement structure. When the value of the land and an entrepreneurial profit, if appropriate, are added to this figure, the result is an indication of the value of the fee simple interest in the property.

The data used in the sales comparison approach often reflect the market's reaction to items of accrued depreciation. The total amount of accrued depreciation in a comparable property can be estimated by allocating its sale price between the land and the improvements and then deducting the contribution of the improvements from the estimated reproduction or replacement cost. If the price allocation is less than the current reproduction or replacement cost, there is accrued depreciation. In applying the cost approach, an appraiser attempts to identify and quantify the causes of accrued depriciation and relate them to the subject property.

RELATION TO APPRAISAL PRINCIPLES

Substitution

The principle of substitution is basic to the cost approach. This principle affirms that no prudent investor would pay more for a property than the cost to acquire the site and construct improvements of equal desirability and utility without undue delay. Older properties can also be substituted for the property being appraised, and their value is measured relative to the value of a new, optimal property. Consequently, the reproduction cost of a property on the date of the appraisal plus its site value provides a measure against which prices for improved properties may be judged.

Supply and Demand

Although markets tend toward equilibrium, market forces change and as they change, different points of equilibrium (i.e., prices) result. Shifts in supply and demand cause prices to increase or decrease. Thus, one property may have different values over time. If costs do not shift in proportion to price changes, the construction of buildings will be more or less profitable and the value of existing buildings will increase or decrease commensurately.

Balance

The principle of balance holds that the agents of production and the various property components must be properly apportioned if optimum value is to be achieved or sustained. An improper economic balance may result in an under- or overimprovement. An underimprovement is created by too little investment in the improvements relative to the value of the land; an overimprovement is created by too much investment.

Any excess or deficiency in the proportionate contributions of the land and the improvements results in a loss in value. An imbalance in the various components of the improvements also produces a loss in value. In the cost approach, the value penalty resulting from an excess or deficiency is measured by deducting depreciation from the estimated reproduction or replacement cost of the improvements on the date of the appraisal.

Externalities

When supply and demand are in balance and credit is available, the cost of new improvements minus depreciation plus the value of the land and an appropriate entrepreneurial profit tends to equal market value. However, properties can gain or lose value due to external conditions or events. Gains or losses in value from externalities may accrue to both land and buildings. Rising construction costs can significantly affect the market value of new construction and, in turn, the market value of older, substitute properties.

In the cost approach, a loss in building value due to external causes is ascribed to external obsolescence, which is one of the three major types of accrued depreciation. If, for example, an industrial plant that depends on trucks to transport its output is located a great distance from a recently completed highway, the property suffers from external obsolescence.

External conditions can cause a newly constructed building to be worth more or less than its cost. If a certain type of property is scarce or it is difficult to construct new competitive properties, the value of a newly constructed building may be higher than its reproduction or replacement cost. On the other hand, an economic recession might create an oversupply of a certain type of property, which would cause the value of a new property to be less than its reproduction or replacement cost. Externalities may have an especially strong effect on older properties.

Highest and Best Use

The concept of highest and best use is fundamental to real property value. In one application of the concept, land is valued as though vacant and available for its highest and best use; in the other application, the highest and best use of the property as improved is estimated. Thus, a site may have one highest and best use as though vacant, and the existing combination of site and improvements may have another highest and best use. Existing improvements have a value equal to the amount they contribute to the site or they penalize value by an amount equal to the cost to remove them from the site.

Existing improvements that do not develop the land to its highest and best use usually are worth less than their reproduction or replacement cost. A new building that is poorly designed may be worth less than its cost due to the functional obsolescence of its design. Thus, the improvement that constitutes highest and best use is the one that adds the greatest value to the site.

HISTORICAL BACKGROUND

The appraisal procedures that are now identified as the three approaches to value were developed after the stock market crash of 1929. The economic crisis that ensued had an immediate impact on the appraisal practices of the time. The collapse of the real estate market in the 1930s seemed to discredit the concept that market price is central to value. The role of cost in the formation of property value also came into question. There was not enough construction activity to derive accurate cost estimates for many types of property. Although the supply of capital and real estate was adequate, investors were wary of risking their money in new developments. The primary consideration was economic feasibility—i.e., whether effective demand could transform cost into value.

The depression era was characterized by a public backlash against the speculative excesses of the 1920s. Before the stock market crash in 1929, lending institutions competed to provide speculative real estate loans in a business environment devoid of government regulation. During the depression, however, the federal government entered the picture. The Federal Housing Administration (FHA) was established by the National Housing Act of 1934.

By insuring mortgages, the FHA created a more stable mortgage market. It also promoted better-quality, single-family housing by requiring builders to comply with government housing standards. As a precaution, the FHA required property appraisals before purchase so that it would not be left holding unsalable properties if the mortgagors defaulted.

Federal policy guidelines for appraisals specifically endorsed use of the replacement cost approach. By this means, the FHA intended to stimulate construction since the cost of building new dwellings was clearly greater than the value of these dwellings in the market at the time. The emphasis on quality construction in this period was reinforced by the background of many appraisers, whose appraisal skill was based on a direct knowledge of building costs and quality.

In the building boom that followed World War II, the real estate industry again became disillusioned with the cost approach. Some critics argued that it was not practical to estimate the replacement cost of an existing structure. Others found it difficult to keep up with increasingly complex construction costs. Nevertheless, the building costs services established before World War II helped maintain the validity of the cost approach throughout the 1940s, 1950s, and 1960s.

As investment analysis techniques became more sophisticated and the real estate industry grew more income oriented, the position of the cost approach was further jeopardized. In the 1980s, appraisal clients are mainly interested in the investment potential of properties, so replacement cost is not a major consideration for many real estate investors. Proponents of the cost approach rightly contend that this approach imparts a unique understanding of the economics of real estate. On the other hand, the usefulness of the cost approach in valuing existing improvements can be criticized on the grounds that replacement cost information is better computed by building professionals than by appraisers. Furthermore, due to technical and procedural developments, modern appraisal places far greater emphasis on the income and market characteristics of properties than on their replacement cost.[1]

---

1. Max J. Derbes, Jr., "Is the Cost Approach Obsolete?" *The Appraisal Journal*, October 1982; James E. Gibbons, *Appraising in A Changing Economy* (Chicago: American Institute of Real Estate Appraisers, 1982), pp. 3-6; Ralph E. Thayer, "Rethinking the Cost Approach to Valuation," *The Appraisal Journal*, April 1983; and Paul F. Wendt, *Real Estate Appraisal: Review and Outlook* (Athens: University of Georgia Press, 1974), pp. 2, 33, and 190.

APPLICABILITY AND LIMITATIONS

Because cost and market value are closely related when properties are new, the cost approach is important in estimating the market value of new or relatively new construction. The approach is especially persuasive when land value is well supported and the improvements are new or suffer only minor accrued depreciation and, therefore, represent a use that approximates the highest and best use of the land as though vacant.

The cost approach is also used to estimate the market value of proposed construction, special-purpose properties, and other properties that are not frequently exchanged in the market. Buyers of these properties often measure the price they will pay for an existing building against the cost to build a replacement, minus accrued depreciation, or the cost to purchase an existing structure and make any necessary modifications. If comparable sales are not available, they cannot be analyzed to estimate the market value of such properties. Therefore, the currently accepted market indications of depreciated cost, or the costs to acquire and refurbish an existing building, are the best reflections of market thinking and, thus, of market value.

In any market, building value can be related to the cost to reproduce or replace the building. The cost approach is particularly important when a lack of market activity limits the use of the sales comparison approach and when the properties to be appraised—e.g., single-family residences—are not amenable to valuation by the income capitalization approach. To estimate market value in these situations, an appraiser can calculate the cost of a replacement or reproduction of the building and then make a deduction for the amount of depreciation present in the existing improvement.

When the physical characteristics of comparable properties differ considerably, the relative values of these characteristics can sometimes be identified more precisely with the cost approach than with sales comparison. Because the cost approach starts with the cost to construct a substitute property with optimal physical and functional utility, it can help an appraiser determine accurate adjustments for physical differences in comparable sale properties. If, for example, an appraiser must make an adjustment for inadequate elevators in a comparable property, the cost to cure the deficiency can be used as a basis for this adjustment.

Because the cost approach requires that land and improvements be valued separately, it is also useful in appraisals for insurance purposes, when noninsurable items must be segregated from insurable items, and in appraisals for accounting purposes, when depreciation must be estimated for income taxes.

The cost approach is especially useful when building additions or renovations are being considered. The approach can be used to determine whether the cost of an improvement will be recovered through an increased income stream or anticipated sale price; therefore, its use can prevent the addition of overimprovements.

Finally, an estimate of probable building and development costs is an essential component of feasibility studies, which test the investment assumptions on which land use plans are based. Financial feasibility is indicated when a property's market value exceeds its total building and development costs, after deductions are made for entrepreneurial profit and risk.[2]

When improvements are older or do not represent the highest and best use of the land as though vacant, the physical deterioration, functional obsolescence, and external obsolescence of the structure are more difficult to estimate. Furthermore, relevant comparable data may be lacking or the data available may be too diverse to indicate an appropriate estimate of entrepreneurial profit.

In valuing investment properties, the persuasiveness of the cost approach is seriously diminished by the premise that improvements be constructed without "undue delay." Investment properties require from several months to several years to create; in the eyes of some investors, this constitutes an unacceptable delay.

When value estimates derived with the cost approach are not supported by market data, they must be regarded with caution. Because estimating accrued depreciation and entrepreneurial profit is difficult, the cost approach may be of limited effectiveness in valuing improved property. Moreover, the cost approach results in an indicated value for the fee simple interest in a property. In valuing real estate held in leased fee or property subject to other partial interests, appraisers must make adjustments to reflect the specific real property rights appraised.

PROCEDURE

After inspecting the neighborhood, the site, and the improvements and gathering all relevant data, an appraiser follows certain steps to derive a value indication by the cost approach. The appraiser will

1. Estimate the value of the land as though vacant and available to be developed to its highest and best use.
2. Estimate the reproduction or replacement cost of the improvements on the effective date of the appraisal. This includes direct (hard) and indirect (soft) costs.
3. Estimate other costs (indirect costs) incurred after construction to bring the new, vacant building up to market conditions and occupancy levels.
4. Estimate entrepreneurial profit, when appropriate, from an analysis of the market.
5. Add estimated replacement or reproduction cost, indirect costs, and entrepreneurial profit, often expressed as a percentage of total direct and indirect costs and sometimes land value, to arrive at the total replacement or reproduction cost of the primary structure(s).

---

2. Harold D. Albritton, "Distinction Among Appraisals, Marketability Studies, and Feasibility Studies," *Controversies in Real Property Valuation: A Commentary* (Chicago: American Institute of Real Estate Appraisers, 1982), pp. 19-22; and John Robert White, "Improving the Quality of Feasibility Studies," *Real Estate Valuing, Counseling, Forecasting* (Chicago: American Institute of Real Estate Appraisers, 1984), pp. 213-221.

6. Estimate the amount of accrued depreciation in the structure, which is divided into three major categories: physical deterioration, functional obsolescence, and external obsolescence.

7. Deduct the estimated depreciation from the total reproduction or replacement cost of the structure to derive an estimate of the structure's depreciated reproduction or replacement cost.

8. Estimate reproduction or replacement costs and depreciation for any accessory buildings and site improvements, and then deduct estimated depreciation from the reproduction or replacement costs of these improvements. Site improvements and minor buildings are often appraised at their net value—i.e., directly on a depreciated cost basis.

9. Add the depreciated reproduction or replacement costs of the structure, the accessory buildings, and the site improvements to obtain the estimated total depreciated reproduction or replacement cost of all improvements.

10. Add the land value to the total depreciated reproduction or replacement cost of all improvements to arrive at the indicated value of the fee simple interest in the property.

11. Adjust the indicated fee simple value to reflect the property interest being appraised, if necessary, to produce an indicated value for the interest in the subject property.

Land Value

In the cost approach, the estimated market value of the land is added to the depreciated cost of the improvements. The value of land is strongly influenced by its potential highest and best use. Land value can be estimated with sales comparison, allocation, extraction, subdivision development analysis, the land residual technique, or ground rent capitalization. (For a full discussion of the procedures used to estimate land value, see Chapter 13.)

Appraisers must remember that land value estimates produced with these techniques reflect the value of fee simple interests in land. If another interest is being appraised, the land value indication must be adjusted.

Reproduction or Replacement Cost of the Improvements

The cost to construct an improvement on the date of the appraisal may be developed as the cost to reproduce the improvement or the cost to replace it. The theoretical base for the cost approach is reproduction cost, but replacement cost may also be used. An important distinction must be made between the terms.

Reproduction cost is the estimated cost to construct, at current prices, an exact duplicate or replica of the building being appraised, using the same materials, construction standards, design, layout, and quality of workmanship, and embodying all the deficiencies, superadequacies, and obsolescence of the subject building.

Replacement cost is the estimated cost to construct, at current prices, a building with utility equivalent to the building being appraised, using modern materials and current standards, design, and layout.

The use of replacement cost eliminates the need to estimate *some* forms of functional obsolescence, but other forms of functional obsolescence, physical deterioration, and external obsolescence must still be measured.

Reproduction cost is sometimes difficult to estimate because identical materials may be unavailable and construction standards may have changed. Nevertheless, reproduction cost usually provides a basis for measuring depreciation from all causes.

Even a well-built, sound improvement with considerable remaining economic life may have a significant amount of functional obsolescence. Although the replacement cost estimate automatically eliminates some forms of functional obsolescence, an appraiser who uses a replacement cost estimate must consider the added costs of removing items of curable functional obsolescence (i.e., items that can be corrected at costs that do not exceed their value contributions) and any excess carrying costs associated with superadequate construction. However, estimating replacement cost simplifies the procedure for measuring accrued depreciation in instances of excessive or superadequate construction.

The decision to use replacement or reproduction cost is often related to the purpose of the appraisal. An appraiser using replacement cost should indicate that the estimate is based on substitute materials because they are functional and the structure's value would not be diminished by their use. If reproduction cost is used, the excess reproduction cost of a superadequacy such as unusually thick walls is considered an item of functional obsolescence.

In estimating reproduction cost, appraisers must ensure that their data sources are thorough and reliable. This function may be best delegated to an engineer or builder.

Types of Costs

To provide complete building cost estimates, appraisers must consider direct, or hard, costs and indirect, or soft, costs. Both types of costs are essential in reliable reproduction or replacement cost estimates. An entrepreneurial profit sufficient to induce a developer to undertake the risk associated with the building project must also be estimated.

Direct construction costs include the costs of material and labor as well as the contractor's profit required to construct the improvement new at the time of the appraisal. Other costs not included in the direct construction of improvements—e.g., professional fees, financing costs, taxes during construction, and carrying charges such as leasing commissions, sales commissions, and absorption expenses during the leaseup or sellout period—are indirect costs. Three methods may be used to estimate construction costs: the comparative unit method, the unit-in-place method, and the quantity survey method. These methods are discussed fully in Chapter 16.

An anticipated profit is often the primary motivation for developing property. The total cost of a project before entrepreneurial profit should be less than the market value of the completed property to reward investors for their risk. The difference between the cost of development and the value of a property after completion is the entrepreneurial profit or loss. This is also known as *developer's profit.* Whether a profit is actually realized depends on how successful the developers have been in selecting the site, constructing the improvements, obtaining the proper tenant mix, and designing the leases, and how well they have analyzed the market demand for the property.

Accrued Depreciation

Accrued depreciation is the difference between the reproduction or replacement cost of the improvements on the effective date of the appraisal and the market value of the improvements on the same date. Depreciation is caused by deterioration or obsolescence in the property. Deterioration is evidenced by the wear and tear on the structure. Functional obsolescence is caused by internal property characteristics such as a poor floor plan, inadequate mechanical equipment, or functional inadequacy or superadequacy due to size or other characteristics. External obsolescence is caused by conditions outside the property such as a lack of economic demand, changing property uses in the area, or national economic conditions. Some types of depreciation interact with one another, and the analysis of depreciation from all causes is cumulative.

Several methods may be used to estimate accrued depreciation: the economic age-life method, the modified economic age-life method, the breakdown method, the cost to cure estimate, sales comparison techniques, and income capitalization techniques. These procedures are discussed and illustrated in Chapter 17.

Final Value Indication

To complete the final steps in the cost approach, an appraiser uses the methods cited above to make current depreciated cost estimates for the improvements, including all site improvements and accessory buildings. The depreciated reproduction or replacement costs of all the improvements, including entrepreneurial profit, are added together to produce the estimated value of the improvements. Then the appraiser adds the land value estimate to this figure to obtain an indication of the total value of the fee simple estate. If another property interest is being appraised, the indicated property value must be adjusted accordingly.

SUMMARY

The cost approach is based on a comparison between the cost to develop a property and the value of the existing developed property. Because the market relates value to cost, the cost approach reflects market thinking. Buyers tend to compare the value of existing structures with the prices and rents obtained for similar buildings and with the cost to create new buildings with optimal physical and functional utility. Buyers adjust the prices they are willing to pay by estimating the cost to bring an existing structure up to desired levels of physical and functional utility.

To apply the cost approach, an appraiser estimates the cost to construct a new reproduction of, or replacment for, the existing structure and deducts all accrued depreciation in the property from that cost. When land value and an entrepreneurial profit are added to this figure, an indication of the value of the fee simple interest in the property is produced. Appraisers may use data from the sales comparison approach to determine the market's reaction to items of accrued depreciation. An appraiser estimates accrued depreciation by allocating the sale price of a comparable property between land and improvements and deducting the value contribution of the improvements from an estimate of their cost new. The appraiser can then relate this amount to the subject property.

The cost approach is applicable in valuing new or relatively new construction when improvements represent the highest and best use of the site, land value is well supported, and no functional or external obsolescence is evident. The cost approach is also used to estimate the value of proposed construction, additions, and renovations; special-purpose properties; and properties that are not frequently exchanged in the market.

The cost approach can be used to determine accurate adjustments for the physical differences of comparable properties in the sales comparison approach. The cost approach is also useful in appraisals that require separate valuations of land and improvements—e.g., when insurable items must be segregated from noninsurable items and when depreciation must be estimated for income taxes. The cost approach is essential in feasibility studies to ensure that market value will exceed improvement costs and allow a suitable margin for entrepreneurial profit.

The difficulty of estimating accrued depreciation in older improvements diminishes the reliability of the cost approach. It is also difficult to estimate how much entrepreneurial profit will be realized in a projected development. The value indication produced with the cost approach represents a fee simple interest; if the real estate being appraised is held in leased fee or involves partial interests, an adjustment must be made to reflect the specific property rights being appraised.

The procedure for valuing property with the cost approach includes 11 steps: 1) estimate the value of the land as though vacant and available for development to its highest and best use; 2) estimate the reproduction or replacement cost of the improvements as of the date of the appraisal, including direct and indirect costs; 3) estimate other costs (indirect costs) to bring the new, vacant building to market conditions and occupancy levels; 4) estimate entrepreneurial profit; 5) add reproduction or replacement costs, other costs, and entrepreneurial profit to arrive at the total cost of the primary structure(s); 6) estimate accrued depreciation in the categories of physical deterioration, functional obsolescence, and external obsolescence; 7) deduct estimated depreciation from the total cost of the structure to derive an estimate of its depreciated cost; 8) estimate the depreciated cost of accessory buildings and site improvements; 9) add the depreciated costs of the primary structure and the accessory buildings to obtain the total cost of the improvements; 10) add land value to the total depreciated cost of the improvements to obtain a value indication for the fee simple estate; and 11) adjust the fee simple value to reflect the interests being appraised, if necessary.

Six techniques can be used to estimate land value: sales comparison using paired data set and patterned analyses, allocation, extraction, subdivision development analysis, the land residual technique, and ground rent capitalization. The land value derived with these techniques is the fee simple value, which must be adjusted if other interests are being appraised.

The distinction between reproduction cost and replacement cost is important. *Reproduction cost* is the estimated current cost to construct an exact duplicate or replica of the building with the same materials, construction standards, layout, and quality of workmanship as the subject building. *Replacement cost* is the estimated current cost to construct a building with utility equivalent to the subject building, using modern materials, standards, and layout. Reproduction cost includes the cost of constructing superadequate features that may be functionally obsolete. The use of replacement cost eliminates the need to estimate *some* forms of functional obsolescence, but the cost of removing items of curable functional obsolescence and the excess carrying costs of superadequacies must still be considered. The use of replacement or reproduction cost estimates often depends on the purpose of the appraisal.

Costs are broken down into direct costs, indirect costs, and entrepreneurial profit. Direct costs include the costs of material and labor, and the contractor's profit. Indirect costs include professional fees, financing charges, taxes during construction, and carrying charges during the leaseup or sellout period. Entrepreneurial or developer's profit or loss is the difference between the cost of development and the value of the completed property.

Accrued depreciation can be broken down into physical deterioration, functional obsolescence attributable to a deficiency or superadequacy, and external obsolescence attributable to changes in the economy or neighborhood.

16 Building Cost Estimates

To derive an indication of property value through the cost approach, an appraiser adds the depreciated cost of the improvements to the value of the site as though vacant and available for its most profitable use. The depreciated cost of the improvements is calculated by deducting any accrued depreciation evident in the improvements from their estimated reproduction or replacement cost on the date of the appraisal. (Methods for estimating accrued depreciation are discussed in Chapter 17.) This chapter presents three methods an appraiser can use to estimate reproduction and replacement costs—the comparative-unit method, the unit-in-place method, and the quantity survey method.

To estimate costs competently, an appraiser must understand construction plans, specifications, and building techniques. In addition, the appraiser must perform a careful inspection and give a complete description of the improvements. If the appraisal assignment involves proposed improvements, the appraiser relies on the descriptions in plans and specifications to estimate costs.

REPRODUCTION AND REPLACEMENT COST ESTIMATES

Cost estimates can vary significantly depending on whether reproduction or replacement cost is used as the base. Therefore, an appraiser must use the same base when developing cost estimates for the subject property and for comparable properties.

When a reproduction cost estimate is sought, the appraiser ascertains the cost to construct a replica of the existing building using the same or similar materials at current prices. When the improvement contains superadequate features such as excessively high ceilings, the cost to reproduce these features is included in the reproduction cost estimate.

When a replacement cost estimate is to be made, the appraiser estimates the cost to construct an equally desirable, substitute improvement, which will not necessarily be constructed with similar materials or to the same specifications. Because

357

improved or more readily available materials would probably be substituted for outdated or more costly materials used in the existing structure, the appraiser estimates the cost of substitute materials. Furthermore, if the present structure contains superadequacies such as high ceilings, the cost of producing the extra space and other costs associated with the superadequacy are not included in the replacement cost estimate.

COSTS

To estimate reproduction or replacement cost, direct, or hard, and indirect, or soft, costs must be calculated. Both types of costs are necessary for construction and both must be measured accurately to ensure a reliable value indication.

Direct Costs

Direct costs are expenditures for labor and materials used in the construction of the improvement(s). A contractor's overhead and profit are treated as direct costs because a building contractor usually includes them in the construction contract. Although the contractor's overhead and profit should always be included among direct costs, a contractor who is also the developer may receive another type of profit. This entrepreneurial, or developer's, profit is not considered a direct cost, but it is added to the total direct and indirect costs. These two types of profit—i.e., contractor's and developer's, or entrepreneur's—should be carefully labeled and distinguished in calculations and in the appraisal report. Depending on the source of the cost data, the direct costs reported may or may not include the contractor's profit and overhead.

Direct costs generally include the cost of

- Labor used to construct buildings
- Materials, products, and equipment
- Contractor's profit and overhead, including job supervision, workers' compensation, fire and liability insurance, and unemployment insurance
- Performance bonds
- Use of equipment
- Watchmen
- Contractor's shack and temporary fencing
- Material storage facilities
- Powerline installation and utility costs

A building can cost substantially more if items such as insulated walls and windows and thicker slabs to accommodate more floor loads are used. Because the quality of materials and labor has a great influence on costs, the appraiser must be familiar with current costs for the materials used in the subject property. Competitive contractor bids may also affect final costs; building cost estimates based on the same set of specifications can vary substantially. A contractor who is working at capacity is inclined to make a high bid, but one who needs the work may submit a lower figure.

Indirect Costs

Indirect costs are expenditures for items other than labor and materials, such as administrative costs; professional fees; financing costs and interest paid on permanent and construction loans; taxes and insurance during construction; and marketing, sales, or leaseup costs incurred to achieve occupancy or sale. Indirect costs are usually calculated separately and are frequently based on a percentage of direct costs. The percentage is converted into a dollar amount and added to the direct costs of material, labor, and contractor's overhead and profit. However, some indirect costs are not related to the size and direct costs of the improvements; these are added as lump-sum dollar figures. Indirect costs include

- Architectural and engineering fees for plans, plan checks, surveys to establish building lines and grades, and environmental and building permits
- Appraisal, consulting, accounting, and legal fees
- The cost of permanent financing as well as interest on construction loans, interest on land costs, and processing fees or service charges
- Builder's (developer's) all-risk insurance and ad valorem taxes during construction
- Leaseup, marketing, and sales costs
- Administrative expenses of the developer
- Cost of title changes

Entrepreneurial Profit

If the cost approach is to provide a reliable indication of value, the appraiser must add to the direct and indirect costs a figure that represents the entrepreneurial or developer's profit that is reflected in the market. Some appraisers feel that entrepreneurial profit has no place in the cost approach. They contend that the existence or absence of developer's profit or loss is relevant only in the income capitalization and sales comparison approaches. Although a developer is motivated by the anticipation of profit, his or her efforts may not always be rewarded. Accordingly, it would be equally plausible to include a potential entrepreneurial loss in the cost estimate.[1] Essentially, entrepreneurial profit is a market-derived figure that reflects the amount that the entrepreneur, or developer, expects to receive in addition to costs. Depending on market practice, this type of profit may be measured as a percentage of 1) direct costs, 2) direct and indirect costs, 3) direct and indirect costs plus land value, or 4) the

---

1. George R. Acolia, "The Enigmatic Entrepreneurial Profit Factor," *Property Tax Journal*, March 1984.

value of the completed project. For example, if a structure costs $2 million to build (i.e., both direct and indirect costs), an appraiser may add 20%, or $400,000, to reflect the market's expectation of profit. Appraisers often derive an appropriate figure for profit expectation from market analysis. By analyzing recent sales of new properties in the same market, the appraiser can calculate entrepreneurial profit as the difference between the sale price and the sum of direct costs, indirect costs, and current market land value.

A cost approach analysis of a comparable sale might suggest the following calculation.

Improvements	
Direct costs	$300,000
+ Indirect costs	50,000
Total improvement costs	
(not including entrepreneur's profit)	$350,000
+ Land value	100,000
Total	$450,000

If the property's sale price was $500,000, the $50,000 difference represents the entrepreneur's profit, which is roughly 14.25% of total direct and indirect costs, approximately 11.10% of total direct and indirect costs plus land value, or 10% of the value of the completed project.

An appraiser can also survey developers to determine entrepreneurial profit. However, the amount of entrepreneurial profit varies with factors such as economic conditions and property type, so a typical relationship between this profit and other costs is difficult to establish. Nevertheless, entrepreneurial profit should not be omitted from the cost approach unless it is being applied to estimate economic feasibility. Entrepreneurial profit is a necessary element of cost because it motivates developers to construct improvements. Like direct and indirect costs, part or all of this profit may be deducted as functional or external obsolescence if the market indicates that the market value of the improvements is less than their current reproduction or replacement cost minus physical deterioration.

Although the prices of materials and cost of labor can usually be determined for a specific date, the cost of combining these elements in a completed building cannot be predicted with certainty. The entrepreneurial profit incentive, or lack of incentive, can raise or lower the building cost estimate.

Cost Data Sources

Construction contracts for buildings similar to the building being appraised are primary sources of comparable cost data, but local building contractors and professional cost estimators are often more reliable sources. Some appraisers maintain comprehensive files of current cost data that include current costs for completed houses, apartments, hotels, office buildings, retail buildings, and industrial buildings. These costs can provide the basis for calculating the cost to construct an existing or proposed building.

Many cost-estimating services publish data for estimating the current cost of improvements. A few of these services are Marshall and Swift Publication Company; Boeckh Publications, a division of American Appraisal Associates; and the F. W. Dodge Corporation. Computer-assisted cost-estimating services may also provide necessary data.

The cost manuals published by cost-estimating services usually include direct unit costs, but an appraiser must research the market to find which costs are most applicable to the appraisal. Quoted construction costs may include other necessary items; cost manuals almost always include some indirect costs such as escrow fees, legal fees, interest on construction loans, financing fees, carrying charges, and property taxes. However, discounts or bonuses paid for financing and leasing, sales, and marketing costs may not be included. The costs furnished by national cost services often do not include site or land improvement costs, such as the cost of demolition, roads, storm drains, rough grading, soil compaction, utilities, and jurisdictional utility hookup fees and assessments. Entrepreneurial profit is rarely, if ever, included in cost service data. The appraiser must estimate such costs separately and include them in the total reproduction or replacement cost estimate.

Cost-Index Trending

Cost services often include information on cost-index trending. Cost indexes are used to convert a known historical cost into a current cost estimate. In cost manuals base years are identified and regional multipliers are provided. To use cost-index trending, an appraiser looks for cost data on a building similar to the one being appraised. For example, consider an office building constructed and completed in January of 1980. At that time, the cost to construct the building was $500,000. Because the date of valuation is in January of 1986, the appraiser looks at the index for January 1986, which lists 1004.3, and the index for January 1980, which is 753.9. To bring the known historical cost up to the date of valuation, the appraiser divides the current cost index by the historical cost index for the period of construction, and multiplies the result by the historical cost.

$$1004.3/753.9 = 1.33$$

$$1.33 \times \$500,000 = \$665,000$$

Thus, the current cost is estimated to be $665,000.

Problems can arise when cost index data are used to estimate current reproduction or replacement cost. The accuracy of the figures cannot always be ascertained, especially when the data do not indicate which components are included in each figure (i.e., only direct costs, or direct costs and some indirect costs). Furthermore, historical costs may not be typical for the time period and the construction methods used at the time of the historical cost may differ from those used at the time of the appraisal. Appraisers who use cost-index trending should recognize that recent costs are more accurate than older costs adjusted with the index. Although cost-index trending may help an appraiser confirm a cost estimate, it is not a reliable substitute for the traditional cost-estimating methods.

COST-ESTIMATING METHODS

To prepare a comprehensive reproduction or replacement cost estimate, an appraiser can conduct a detailed inventory of the materials and equipment used in the subject improvements and determine the current costs of similar materials, equipment, labor, overhead, and fees needed to reproduce or replace the property on the date of the appraisal. This is the quantity survey method of cost estimating. In practice, most cost estimates are derived with the comparative-unit method or the unit-in-place method. Although these methods provide less detail, they are generally adequate for appraisal purposes.

Measurement

Buildings can be measured in several ways, but appraisers usually measure buildings in the manner that is customary in the subject area. To use a cost service effectively, the appraiser *must understand the measurement technique used by the service.*

The building's outside measurements are used to compute total gross area. For rectangular buildings, the width is multiplied by the depth. Then the area measurements of projections or cantilevers are added and the areas of insets or recesses are subtracted. The gross building area is the sum of the areas of all floor levels. In certain locations, however, dwellings are measured in terms of the area of ground floor coverage; in others, the gross area of living space is calculated. For example, a two-story house that measures 24 feet by 24 feet with an unfinished basement and attic has an area of 1,152 square feet ($24 \times 24 \times 2$). Guidelines established by the FNMA call for the measurement of total gross living area, which is defined to include finished and habitable above-grade living area only. On FNMA residential appraisal forms, finished basement or attic areas must be calculated and shown separately in the cost estimate.

To estimate the volume of space in a building, an appraiser multiplies the structure's width by its depth and mean height using outside measurements. The mean height is measured from six inches below the basement floor surface to the roof's mean height. Thus, the mean height of a gable roof is one-half the distance from the top of the ceiling joists to the ridge; the mean height of a hip roof is one-third of this distance. If the subject building does not have a basement, the method of determining volume is the same except that the height is measured from one foot below the surface of the first floor or from grade, whichever is lower.

Appraisers must judge the advantages and disadvantages of area and volume measurements in terms of local tradition, custom, and personal choice. Appraisers sometimes prefer to use area units, particularly for one-story structures. Generally, the unit measurement is less flexible, but not necessarily less accurate, because costs are substantially affected by ceiling heights, roof pitches, and similar building components. Although these elements are difficult to incorporate in area measurements, area measurement is widely used and applicable to warehouses, loft buildings, store buildings, and similar structures. Volume measurement may be applied to apartments, office buildings, and other structures that have considerable interior finish and partitioning, but area measurement is also used. Volume measurement is particularly relevant to places of worship because their ceiling heights vary considerably.

Comparative-Unit Method

The comparative-unit method is used to derive a cost estimate in terms of dollars per unit of area or unit of volume. It is based on known costs of similar structures adjusted for time and physical differences. Indirect costs may be included in the unit cost or computed separately. If the comparable properties and the subject property are in different construction markets, the appraiser may need to make an adjustment for location.

Unit costs vary with size; if a similar cost is applied to a larger area or volume, the unit cost is usually less. This reflects the fact that plumbing, heating units, elevators, doors, windows, and similar items do not usually cost proportionately more in a larger building than in a smaller one.

The comparative-unit method is a relatively uncomplicated, practical method of estimating costs and it is widely used. The unit-cost figures are usually expressed in terms of gross building dimensions. An appraiser estimates total cost by comparing the subject building with similar, recently constructed buildings for which cost data are available, either in the appraiser's files or from market research.

The appraiser should find and verify several sales of recently constructed buildings that are similar to the subject building. The value of the site is subtracted from the sale price of each comparable property to obtain the cost new of the improvements including entrepreneurial profit. Adjustments for physical differences among the comparables and the subject are then made to the cost new of the comparables. The appraiser divides the adjusted total cost new of each comparable building by the unit of area or unit of volume to arrive at the cost per unit of area or cost per unit of volume. It is also advisable to establish the trend of costs between the time of construction and the date of the appraisal. With these data, the appraiser can interpolate the cost new of the subject building.

In addition to the sales comparison method, a unit-cost figure can be developed with data from a recognized cost service. However, cost manuals rarely include entrepreneurial profit, so a unit cost computed with these data should be used to confirm the figures developed from specific market data adjusted for entrepreneurial profit.

Unit costs for the benchmark buildings found in cost-estimating manuals usually start with a base building of a certain size—i.e., a base area or volume—with additions or deductions according to the actual area or volume involved. If the subject building is larger than the benchmark building, the unit cost is usually less; if the building is smaller, it will probably cost more on a unit basis.

Because few buildings are exactly similar in terms of size, design, and grade of construction, the benchmark building is rarely identical to the building being estimated. Different roof designs and irregular perimeters and building shapes can affect comparative unit costs substantially. For example, the cost of walls per square foot of enclosed ground area may be different for a 100-ft. by 100-ft. building than for a building that is 40 feet × 250 feet, although each contains the same area. This example is illustrated in Table 16.1.

Table 16.1   Effect of Building Shape (Wall Ratio) on Cost

	Building A	Building B
Building size	100 ft. × 100 ft.	40 ft. × 250 ft.
Enclosed area	10,000 sq. ft.	10,000 sq. ft.
Linear feet of wall	400	580
Wall ratio*	25/1	17.24/1
Cost of wall		
Per linear foot	$50	$50
Total cost	$20,000	$29,000
Per square foot of enclosed area	$2	$2.90

* Ratio of the number of square feet of enclosed area to each linear foot of enclosing wall.

To develop a reliable conclusion with the comparative-unit method, an appraiser should calculate the unit cost from closely similar improvements or adjust it to reflect variations in size, shape, finish, and equipment. The unit cost should also reflect any changes in cost levels between the date of the benchmark unit cost and the date of valuation.

The ratio between the costs of equipment and the basic building shell has increased consistently through the years. Equipment tends to increase unit building costs and depreciate more rapidly than other building components.

To use area or volume cost estimates, an appraiser assembles, analyzes, and catalogs data on actual building costs. These costs should be divided into general construction categories and separate figures should be used to account for special finishes or equipment. The overall area or volume unit cost can then be broken down into its components, which may help the appraiser adjust a known cost for the presence or absence of items in later comparisons.

The apparent simplicity of the comparative-unit method can be misleading. To develop dependable unit-cost figures, an appraiser must exercise care and judgment when comparing the subject building with similar or standard structures for which actual costs are known. Inaccuracies can result if an appraiser selects a unit cost that is not comparable to the building being appraised. However, when it is correctly applied, the method provides an appraiser with reasonably accurate reproduction or replacement cost estimates.

The comparative-unit method, and later the other two methods of estimating costs, will be illustrated in reference to the warehouse structure shown in Figure 16.1. The details of the warehouse follow the figure.

Figure 16.1   Plan of a Warehouse

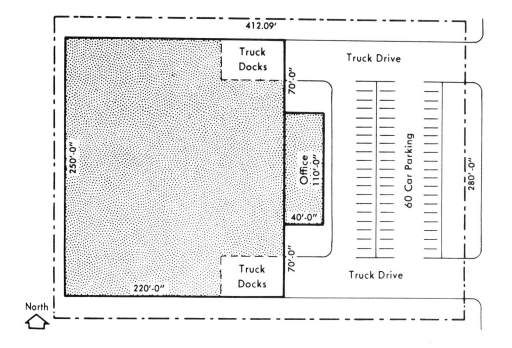

Area	Square Feet
Office	4,400
Warehouse	55,000
Total building	59,400

Office area. Heated, with air-conditioning equipment rated at 15 tons; ceiling height, 9 feet; flooring, asphalt tile over concrete slab; illumination, 60 foot, candle-intensity fluorescent lighting; ceiling, acoustic tile; partitions; stud and dry-wall; two washrooms that contain six fixtures.

Warehouse area. Heating to 65°F at −10°F outside temperature; clear ceiling height, 18 feet; bays, 41½ × 36½ feet; structural steel framing; insulated roof deck and slab over steel bar joists; 6-in. concrete floor slab at grade, waterproofed; electric service, 600 amperes, 120/240 volts. Four overhead wood truck doors; one washroom that contains three fixtures.

Exterior walls, block and brick facade; structural steel columns, steel deck; rigid insulation; built-up tar and gravel roofing. Structure has full sprinkler system. Other details are typical.

Table 16.2 illustrates how the comparative-unit method is applied on an area basis to the warehouse building. This procedure can be used to confirm a cost indication derived from available data on properties in the same construction market as the property being appraised. It may also be used independently when no local cost data are available.

Table 16.2   Warehouse Property—Comparative-Unit Method

Estimated costs*	
Comparative cost per sq. ft.	$18.98
Add for sprinkler system	+ 1.14
	$20.12
Adjustment for 18-ft. ceiling height	× 1.086
	$21.85
Adjustment for area/perimeter	× 0.895
	$19.56
Current cost multiplier (adjust benchmark cost to date of valuation)	× 1.12
	$21.91
Local cost multiplier (adjust standard manual cost to specific city)	× 0.98
Cost per sq. ft.	$21.47
Total cost: 59,400 sq. ft. @ $21.47	$1,275,318
Rounded	$1,275,300

* Contractor's overhead and profit are included in these base costs.

Source: *Marshall Valuation Service* (Los Angeles: Marshall and Swift Publication Co.), Section 14, August 1986, pp. 16, 24, and 25; Section 44, March 1986, p. 3; Section 99, January and February 1987, pp. 3 and 6.

In Table 16.2, an adjustment was made for a sprinkler system using a square-foot unit cost. Similar adjustments for the amount of office area, construction features, or equipment may also be necessary.

Actual costs for similar structures in the local market provide a base from which an appraiser may make adjustments to derive a cost indication for the subject property. Adjustments for observed physical differences are made by applying unit-in-place costs to property differences.

To use or compare building reproduction or replacement costs on a unit basis —e.g., dollars per unit of gross area—the appraiser should eliminate land improvements. Because these improvements vary widely, their inclusion distorts the overall unit cost and makes comparison more difficult. Separate estimates are needed for auxiliary building improvements such as garages and outbuildings and for land improvements such as driveways, pools, underground drainage facilities, rail sidings, fences, and landscaping. The cost of these improvements may be estimated individually from applicable unit prices on an area basis. Such comparative-unit costs may be developed and applied to any situation.

Consider a two-story, brick residence that cost $46,320 to build three years prior to the date of the appraisal, excluding the cost of the garage and other site improvements. The quality of construction is roughly comparable to that of an average mass-produced home. The house has asphalt shingle roofing, half-inch drywall, average finish and equipment, combination forced-air heat and air-conditioning, a dishwasher, a garbage disposal, and a fireplace. It has three bedrooms, two and one-half baths, and a full basement. The ground floor measurements are 22 feet × 34 feet. The residence contains 22,440 cubic feet, or 1,496 square feet, and costs approximately $2.06 per cubic foot, or $30.96 per square foot of gross area.

To prepare a cost estimate for a house that is roughly comparable to the house just described, the appraiser must adjust for several differences. The house being appraised contains 24,700 cubic feet and a gross area of 1,648 square feet. It has a concrete block foundation rather than poured concrete, no fireplace, and a good grade of wood siding instead of brick exterior walls. The downward adjustments to be made are $300 for the block foundation, $1,800 for no fireplace, and $2,800 for wood siding. The resulting unit costs are $1.85 per cubic foot, or $27.69 per square foot. If the contractor's overhead and profit are not included in the unit-cost adjustments, the totals may be increased by an additional 15% to 20%, or whatever is typical in the market.

Assume that the cost of construction has risen 12% in the last three years. The appraiser accounts for this change by increasing the $1.85 unit cost by 12% to $2.07 per cubic foot. The unit price of $27.69 per square foot becomes $31.01 per square foot.

Applying these current volume and area unit costs to the house being appraised results in current cost estimates of $51,129 and $51,104, respectively, which can be rounded to $51,100. This minor difference is probably due to a slight variation in size, ceiling height, roof pitch, roof design, or a similar feature that slightly altered the average building height. Note that volume and area measurements do not always produce identical estimates. Table 16.3 summarizes the procedure for making the comparison and time adjustment.

The application of the comparative-unit method to a residence in this example is no different in principle than its application to any other type of building. However, a substantial discrepancy may be produced if a warehouse with a 14-ft. ceiling height is compared with a warehouse with a 20-ft. height. Thus, it is essential that cubic- or square-foot unit costs be applied to very similar structures.

Table 16.3   Comparison and Time Adjustment

	Cost of Comparable House 3 Years Prior to Appraisal Date	Estimated Current Cost of Comparable House
Cost	$46,320.00	$46,320
Adjustments		
Wood siding		− 2,800
Block foundation		− 300
Fireplace		− 1,800
Estimated reproduction cost (as of 3 yrs. previous to appraisal date)		$41,420
Area in sq. ft.	1,496	1,648.00
Volume in cu. ft.	22,440	24,700.00
Per sq. ft.	30.96	$27.69*
Per cu. ft.	2.06	$1.85*
Time adjustment to present		+ 12%
Estimated present reproduction cost		
Per sq. ft.		$31.01
Per cu. ft.		$2.07
Total		$51,104**
Rounded		$51,100

* $41,420/1,496 sq. ft. = 27.69 sq. ft.; $41,420/24,700 cu. ft. = $1.85 per cu. ft.

**24,700 × $2.07 = $51,129; 1,648 × $31.01 = $51,104.

Unit-in-Place Method

The unit-in-place, or segregated-cost, method employs unit costs for various building components as installed and uses linear, area, volume, or other appropriate units of measurement. An appraiser may compute a unit cost based on the actual quantity of materials used plus the labor of assembly required for each square foot of wall. The cost may be applied on the basis of square or linear feet of wall of a certain height. The same procedure is applied for other structural components.

Unit-in-place cost estimates are made in terms of standardized costs for structural components as installed. Excavating costs are typically expressed in dollars per cubic yard; foundation costs may be expressed in dollars per linear foot or cubic yard of concrete. Floor construction may be reduced to dollars per square foot and interior partitions may be expressed in dollars per linear foot. The basic unit for roofing is a square of 100 square feet. The unit in place on which the cost is based may be one employed in a particular trade, such as the cost per ton of air-conditioning, or any basic unit of measurement may be selected. All constituent unit costs are totaled to provide the estimated direct cost of the entire improvement. Contractor's overhead and profit may be included in unit cost figures, such as those provided by some cost services, or they may be computed separately. The appraiser must ascertain exactly what is included in any unit price. Indirect costs are usually computed separately.

The unit-in-place method can be applied to estimate the cost of a brick veneer wall. Assume that a building's exterior walls above the foundation are composed of 4-in. face brick tied to impregnated 4-ft. × 8-ft., ½-in. sheathing on 2-in. × 4-in. studs, 16 inches on center, with insulation between. The stud wall has ½-in. drywall on the inside with two coats of paint. The wall is 17 feet high to the cornice line; for each square foot of wall surface, 7½ bricks are required. The following unit prices are developed for the wall. (Cost figures such as these vary with time and location.)

Face brick, installed; common bond, ½-in. struck joints, mortar, scaffolding, and cleaning included	$460 per 1,000 bricks
Dimension lumber in 2-in. × 4-in. wood stud framing, erected	$360 per 1,000 board ft.
Sheathing, erected	$0.42 per sq. ft.
Insulation, installed, 2½-in. foil backing, one side	$0.22 per sq. ft.
½-in. drywall with finished joints	$0.30 per sq. ft.
Painting, primer and one coat flat paint	$0.25 per sq. ft.

Thus, the cost per square foot of wall can be estimated as follows.

7½ bricks	$3.45
⅔ board feet of wood studding	.24
1 sq. ft. sheathing	.42
1 sq. ft. insulation	.22
1 sq. ft. drywall	.30
1 sq. ft. painting	.25
Total per sq. ft.	$4.88

Therefore, a wall 17 feet high would cost $83 per linear foot. The cost is estimated, without detailed quantities, for an above-ground, exterior wall including the interior finish. The base unit figure covers most of the cost of the total wall.

In actual practice, an estimator might refine the procedure by adding for waste and extra framing and by recognizing that windows and doors require wall openings, lintels, and facing corners, which will increase or decrease the basic unit cost. After the basic unit figures are established, the appraiser can estimate the cost of an entire building.

The unit-in-place method breaks down the cost of a building into the costs of its component parts. Such a cost estimate can be adapted to record the condition of components or compute the cost of a replacement. However, to assemble the basic costs of equipment, material, and labor and combine them into a final unit-in-place cost estimate, specialized knowledge may be required. When completely developed, this method substitutes for a complete quantity survey and produces an accurate reproduction or replacement cost estimate with considerably less effort.

Application of the unit-in-place method is not limited to cubic, linear, or area units. It may also be applied using the cost in place of complete components such as the cost of a roof truss that is fabricated offsite, delivered, and erected. Unit-in-place cost estimates may be based on an appraiser's compiled data or be obtained from a cost-estimating source that provides updated monthly figures.

Table 16.4 illustrates how the unit-in-place method can be used to estimate the reproduction cost of the warehouse shown in Figure 16.1.

The estimated cost of $1,257,930 must be adjusted from the cost on the date when the unit-in-place costs were estimated to current cost. The figure should also reflect the effect of location (e.g., city, community, or area) on the estimated unit prices. These adjustments can be calculated or derived from the cost service being used. For purposes of illustration, the factors of 1.00 and 0.98 are used to make adjustments for time and location.

Total (from estimated costs)	$1,257,930
Current cost multiplier	× 1.00
	$1,257,930
Local cost multiplier	× 0.98
Indicated reproduction cost	$1,232,771
59,400 sq. ft. @ $13.89 sq. ft., rounded	$1,232,800

Quantity Survey Method

The most comprehensive and accurate method of cost estimating is the quantity survey method. Strictly applied, it duplicates the contractor's method of developing a bid figure. A quantity survey is a computation of the quantity and quality of all materials used and all categories of labor hours required. Unit cost figures are applied to these figures to arrive at a total cost estimate for materials and labor. Then estimated soft costs for permits, insurance, equipment rental, field office, supervision, and other overhead are added along with a margin for the contractor's profit and an estimate of the developer's profit.

A contractor's cost breakdown for the warehouse shown in Figure 16.1 is summarized in Table 16.5. This summary is based on a breakdown of labor and materials, which is not included here.

Table 16.4   Warehouse Property—Unit-in-Place Method

Excavation	
59,400 cu. ft. @ $0.16	$9,500
Site	
115,385 sq. ft. @ $0.11	12,690
Foundation	
59,400 sq. ft. @ (60% × $1.22)	43,480
Framing	
59,400 sq. ft. @ ($3.08 × 1.2)	219,540
Floor—concrete	
59,400 sq. ft. @ ($2.07 + $0.39)	146,125
Floor—asphalt tile	
4,400 sq. ft. @ $0.80	3,520
Ceiling—acoustical tile, suspended	
4,400 sq. ft. @ $3.50	15,400
Plumbing (3 washrooms)	
9 fixtures @ $1,625	14,625
Drains @ $290 × 2	580
Sprinklers	
59,400 sq. ft. @ $1.14	67,720
Heating, cooling, and ventilating	
55,000 sq. ft. @ ($0.69 × 1.12)	42,500
4,400 sq. ft. @ $4.15	18,260
Electricity and lighting	
59,400 sq. ft. @ $1.06	62,960
Exterior wall—8-in. concrete block, brick facade	
15,180 sq. ft. @ $8.76	132,980
5,060 sq. ft. @ $10.21	51,660
Partitions—2-in. × 4-in. wood studs, 16 in. on center drywall, painted	
8,650 sq. ft. @ $3.12	26,990
10 doors @ $82	820
Overhead doors (4)	
10 ft. × 12 ft. × 4 = 480 sq. ft. @ $12.50	6,000
Roof joists and deck	
59,400 sq. ft. @ $4.59	272,650
Roof cover and insulation	
59,400 sq. ft. @ $1.45	86,130
Miscellaneous specified items	23,800
Total (59,400 sq. ft. @ $21.18 per sq. ft.)	$1,257,930

Figures are rounded.

Contractor's overhead and profit, insurance, taxes, and permits are included; architect's fees and indirect costs are not.

Source: *Marshall Valuation Service* (Los Angeles: Marshall and Swift Publication Co.), Segregated Cost Method, Section 44, March 1986.

Table 16.5   Warehouse Property—Contractor's Breakdown of Labor and Material

General conditions of contract	$6,622
Excavating and grading	20,895
Concrete	153,502
Carpentry	21,480
Masonry	163,770
Structural steel	236,377
Joists, deck, and deck slab	278,100
Roofing	48,480
Insulation	27,300
Sash	4,432
Glazing	9,552
Painting	6,417
Acoustical material	4,893
Flooring	2,812
Electric	63,519
Heating, ventilating, air-conditioning	54,435
Piping	5,445
Plumbing and sprinkler system	65,313
Contractor's overhead and profit	88,545
Total	$1,261,889
Rounded	$1,261,900

Based on the summary, an appraiser would estimate the contractor's cost at $1,261,900. This table is not a complete quantity survey breakdown; rather, it is a recapitulation of the contractor's and subcontractors' quantity survey analyses. The items shown are computed by the contractor based on an estimate of the required labor hours at prevailing wage levels and the required material quantities at current, delivered cost to the contractor.

In recent years, the percentage of a general contract that is subcontracted has increased. Subcontractors have become more efficient in their specialties; subcontractor unit-in-place costs compare favorably with the costs at which work can be done by the general contractor's own employees. Each contractor and subcontractor can provide a breakdown of materials, labor, indirect costs, overhead, and profit items, which are all part of the total estimated cost.

Overhead and profit may depend on the volume of work that the contractor has lined up. Contingencies are also available, particulary if renovation is involved. A contractor may allocate his or her anticipated profit among the various components of cost, rather than as a separate item, in the cost breakdown given to an appraiser.

The quantity survey method produces a complete cost breakdown, but it is time-consuming and costly. A detailed breakdown usually requires the services of an experienced cost estimator. However, quantity survey cost summaries for various types of improvements are available. When the cost figures are adjusted for physical differences and time, these summaries can give an appraiser a sound basis for estimating the reproduction or replacement cost of similar improvements through direct comparison. Due to the expertise, time, and cost required, the practical application of this method is limited.

The cost breakdown for the warehouse (Table 16.5) provides the basis for a general contract bid. Indirect costs such as leaseup, marketing, and carrying charges and commissions must be included in the final cost estimate and an appropriate allowance for developer's profit should also be made. Land improvements—e.g., parking facilities, landscaping, and signs—may or may not be included in the general contract. The costs for items that are not included are estimated separately and then added to the general contract figure to derive a final cost estimate for all improvements.

SUMMARY

To obtain an indication of the depreciated cost of property improvements, the appraiser estimates the reproduction or replacement cost of the improvements on the date of the appraisal and deducts any accrued depreciation evident in the property from this cost estimate. Because cost estimates vary significantly depending on whether reproduction or replacement cost is used, an appraiser must use one cost consistently.

Costs are divided into direct, or hard, costs and indirect, or soft, costs. *Direct costs* are expenditures for labor and materials used in the construction of improvement(s). Contractor's overhead and profit, and expenses for job supervision, workers' compensation, unemployment insurance, fire and liability insurance, performance bonds, security, equipment and facilities, utilities, and construction materials are all direct costs.

Indirect costs are expenditures for items other than labor and materials, such as administrative costs; professional fees; financing costs and the interest paid on permanent and construction loans; taxes and builder's (developer's) all-risk insurance during construction; and marketing, sales, or leaseup costs incurred to achieve occupancy or sale. Indirect costs include architectural and engineering fees; appraisal, consulting, accounting, and legal fees; charges and interest on permanent loans, construction loans, and land costs; insurance and ad valorem taxes; leaseup, marketing, and sales costs; administrative expenses of the developer; and the cost of title change.

Entrepreneurial or developer's profit is a market-derived figure that represents the amount the entrepreneur, who is actually the developer, expects to receive in addition to costs. Entrepreneurial profit can be estimated as a percentage of direct costs, direct and indirect costs, direct and indirect costs plus land value, or the value of the completed project. The estimate should be based on market analysis. Entrepreneurial profit varies with economic conditions and the property type, so it is difficult to establish a typical relationship between it and other costs.

Cost data can be obtained from construction contracts, building contractors, cost estimators, and cost-estimating service manuals, which list direct costs and some indirect costs. To use the data effectively, an appraiser must understand the measurement technique employed by the cost estimating service. Gross building area (*GBA*) and building volume are calculated from outside measurements; ground floor coverage and gross living area may be based on interior measurements. Area units of measurement are used for single-story structures, while volume units are applied to apartments and office buildings.

Cost-estimating services also provide data for cost-index trending, which is used to convert historical costs into current cost estimates. Cost manuals list base years and regional multipliers, but appraisers should recognize that recent costs are more accurate than historical costs adjusted with a cost-index.

Building costs can be estimated with *the comparative-unit method, the unit-in-place method,* or *the quantity survey method.* The comparative-unit and unit-in-place methods are less detailed than the quantity survey method, but they are generally adequate for appraisals in which greater reliance is placed on the sales comparison or income capitalization approaches.

The comparative-unit method is applied to derive a cost estimate in terms of dollars per unit of area or volume. It is based on known costs of similar structures that are adjusted for time and physical differences. Unit costs vary between buildings— i.e., when a similar cost is spread over a larger area or volume, the unit cost is usually less. Unit-cost figures are often expressed in gross building area units.

Total building cost may be estimated by comparing the subject building with similar, recently constructed buildings for which cost data are available. Adjustments for physical differences are made to the costs new of the comparable buildings. The adjusted cost new of each comparable is divided by the unit of area or volume to arrive at the cost per unit. If there is an interval between the completion of construction and the appraisal, the estimated cost new may be interpolated with cost trending data. The cost estimate must be adjusted for differences in building location.

A unit-cost estimate may also be calculated using cost manuals that provide data on benchmark buildings. A benchmark building is rarely identical to the building being appraised, so adjustments for size, design, grade of construction, finish, equipment, and other variables are required. The unit-cost estimate should also reflect changes in cost levels between the date of the benchmark unit cost and the date of the appraisal.

Unit costs should be classified by construction categories (e.g., warehouses or office buildings), and overall area or volume unit costs should be broken down by building components to facilitate adjusting for variables. The comparative-unit method appears simple, but care and judgment must be exercised in its application.

The unit-in-place, or segregated-cost, method employs unit costs for various building components as installed, and may use linear, area, or cubic measurements. Unit-in-place cost estimates are based on standardized costs for structural components as installed. The unit-in-place method breaks down the cost of a building into the costs of its component parts.

An appraiser adapts the standard cost estimate to the condition of the component, and the cost of its replacement. Adjustments are made to convert the cost on the date of completion into a current cost and to reflect differences in building location. Specialized knowledge may be needed to arrive at a final unit-in-place cost estimate, but when competently derived, a unit-in-place estimate can substitute for a complete quantity survey.

The quantity survey method is the most comprehensive and accurate way to estimate building cost. This method replicates the contractor's development of a bid. The appraiser calculates the costs of building materials of like quantity and quality and of all labor hours required. These estimates are used to calculate unit costs and total cost. Then an estimate of entrepreneurial profit is added to total hard and soft costs. Due to the expertise, time, and expense required to prepare a complete quantity survey cost breakdown, the practical application of this method is limited.

17   Accrued Depreciation

Accrued depreciation is a loss in value from the reproduction or replacement cost of improvements due to any cause as of the date of appraisal. It may also be defined as the difference between the reproduction or replacement cost of an improvement and its market value as of the date of appraisal. The value difference may emanate from physical deterioration, functional obsolescence, external obsolescence, or any combination of these sources. After separate elements of accrued depreciation are identified and measured, the appraiser deducts the dollar amounts of applicable types of depreciation from the reproduction or replacement cost of the improvements. The result is the estimated depreciated reproduction or replacement cost of the improvements.

Theoretically, depreciation can begin to accrue at the moment construction is completed, even in a functional building that is the highest and best use of its site. Although most forms of physical deterioration can be corrected or temporarily stabilized, physical deterioration tends to persist. As the building ages, functional obsolescence may occur. Even new buildings can have various forms of functional obsolescence such as those attributable to poor design.

In the cost approach, depreciation from all causes is subtracted from current replacement or reproduction cost. However, depreciation is a penalty only insofar as it is recognized by the market as a loss in value. For older buildings, the value loss may be offset by a temporary scarcity relative to demand or by a building's historical significance or architectural excellence.

If an appraiser uses replacement cost rather than reproduction cost to derive the current cost estimate, the estimate of accrued depreciation may be affected. Many forms of functional obsolescence are not calculated when replacement cost is used.

DEFINITIONS

To analyze accrued depreciation, an appraiser should understand these essential terms: depreciation, accrued depreciation, book depreciation, economic life, remaining economic life, effective age, and actual age.

Depreciation is a loss in property value from any cause. It may also be defined as *any difference between reproduction cost or replacement cost and market value.* Deterioration, or physical depreciation, is evidenced by wear and tear, decay, dry rot, cracks, encrustations, or structural defects in a building. Other types of depreciation are caused by obsolescence, which may be either functional or external. Functional obsolescence may be caused by the inadequacy or superadequacy of a building's size, style, or mechanical equipment. Physical deterioration and functional obsolescence can usually be observed in the improvement. External obsolescence is caused by factors outside the property such as changes in demand, general property uses in the area, zoning, financing, and government regulations.

Accrued depreciation is the difference between an improvement's reproduction or replacement cost and its market value as of the date of appraisal. To measure accrued depreciation, an appraiser identifies and measures the loss in value experienced by the subject structure in its present condition and compares this with the value it would have if it were new. Accrued depreciation is sometimes referred to as *diminished utility.*

Book depreciation is an accounting term that refers to the amount of capital recapture written off an owner's books. Generally, it is the amount that a particular owner can provide for the retirement or replacement of an asset under the tax laws. Book depreciation is not market-derived; traditionally, accountants have based depreciation on book value or original cost. In current cost accounting, however, assets are listed at current value, which is the same as market value measured by accepted appraisal methods.

Economic life is the period of time over which improvements to real estate contribute to property value. Economic life and physical life can differ widely; typically, physical life is expected to be longer than economic life. For example, improvements with varying degrees of physical integrity are ordinarily replaced with new structures. However, when some older properties are renewed or remodeled their economic lives are usually extended. At any given point in time a property's economic life cannot exceed its physical life. Rehabilitation can extend a property's physical life.

Remaining economic life is the estimated period during which improvements continue to contribute to property value. An appraiser determines remaining economic life in part by interpreting the attitudes and reactions of typical buyers of competitive properties.

Actual age, which is sometimes called historical or chronological age, is the number of years that have elapsed since construction was completed.

Effective age is the age indicated by the condition and utility of a structure. A building's effective age may be less than its actual age if it has had above-average maintenance, is of superior quality or design, or there is a scarcity of such buildings in the market. For example, a 40-year-old building may have an effective age of 20 years due to rehabilitation, modernization, or strong market demand. However, if the building has not been adequately maintained, its effective age may be greater than its actual age.

METHODS OF ESTIMATING ACCRUED DEPRECIATION

An appraiser identifies depreciation due to physical deterioration, functional obsolescence, and external obsolescence by analyzing similar improvements and the market's reaction to their observed condition. The amount of depreciation to be deducted from an improvement's current reproduction or replacement cost is typically indicated by the difference between the improvement's contribution to the current market value of the property and the market-value contribution of a similar improvement constructed new on the date of the appraisal.

Several methods can be applied to estimate accrued depreciation; each is acceptable if the appraiser applies it consistently and logically and if it reflects an informed, prudent buyer's reaction to the condition of the structure being appraised. To produce an accurate and supportable estimate of accrued depreciation with any method, the appraiser must consider all elements that may diminish value and account for each element only once. The methods for estimating accrued depreciation are the economic age-life method, the modified economic age-life method, the breakdown method, sales comparison techniques, and income capitalization techniques. An additional method, the physical age-life method, can be used to estimate physical deterioration *only*.

Accrued depreciation is applied to improvements only, because land is included in the value estimate at its current market value. External forces can cause land to lose value, but the effects of externalities on land or site value have already been reflected in estimating the current market value of the land or site.

Economic Age-Life Method

To estimate accrued depreciation with the economic age-life method, the ratio of a building's effective age to its total economic life is applied to the current cost of the improvements to obtain a lump-sum deduction for accrued depreciation. (See Table 17.1.)

$$\frac{\text{Effective age}}{\text{Total economic life}} \times \text{reproduction or replacement cost} = \text{accrued depreciation}$$

This method appears simple, but many items of accrued depreciation are obscured because they are all grouped together. One major weakness of the economic age-life method is that curable items are not treated separately. Furthermore, the

Table 17.1   Estimating Accrued Depreciation by the Economic Age-Life Method

	Replacement Cost	Reproduction Cost
Cost new	$213,560	$222,725
Total economic life	50 yrs.	50 yrs.
Remaining economic life	34 yrs.	32 yrs.
Effective age	16 yrs.	18 yrs.
Ratio applied to current cost	16/50 = 32%	18/50 = 36%
Less total accrued depreciation	$ 68,339	$ 80,181
Depreciated value of improvements	$145,221	$142,544
Plus land value	60,000	60,000
Indicated value by the cost approach	$205,221	$202,544
Rounded	$205,200	$202,500

method does not recognize that short-lived items may have a shorter remaining physical life than the total economic life of the structure. The economic age-life method should not be applied to derive a separate estimate of the incurable physical deterioration of short-lived or long-lived items in the breakdown method of estimating accrued depreciation. The economic age-life concept pertains only to overall depreciation. A distorted estimate will result if the economic age-life method is used to measure the incurable physical deterioration of short- or long-lived items separately. This method does consider functional and external obsolescence and physical deterioration, but it does not differentiate between the separate causes of accrued depreciation.

Modified Economic Age-Life Method

The effect of curable items of accrued depreciation is recognized in the modified economic age-life method. To apply the method, the appraiser estimates the cost to cure all curable items of physical deterioration due to deferred maintenance and functional obsolescence. This sum is deducted from the current cost of the improvements. The appraiser arrives at a percentage lump-sum deduction that covers all incurable elements by applying the ratio of effective age to total economic life to the current cost of improvements minus the estimate of curable physical and functional obsolescence. (See Table 17.2.) To apply the modified economic age-life method, the appraiser must recognize that when curable items are cured, the structure's remaining economic life may increase and the effective age may decrease.

Table 17.2 Estimating Accrued Depreciation by the Modified Economic Age-Life Method

	Replacement Cost	Reproduction Cost
Cost new	$213,560	$222,725
Less physical and functional curable items	1,975	$ 2,250
Depreciated cost	$211,585	$220,475
Total economic life	50 yrs.	50 yrs.
Remaining economic life*	35 yrs.	33 yrs.
Effective age*	15 yrs.	17 yrs.
Ratio applied to cost less physical and functional curable items	15/50 = 30%	17/50 = 34%
Less incurable items	$211,585	$220,475
from all causes	× 0.30	× 0.34
	$ 63,475	$ 74,962
Depreciated value of improvements	$148,110	$145,513
Land value	$ 60,000	$ 60,000
Indicated value by the cost approach	$208,110	$205,513
Rounded	$208,100	$205,500

* After curable physical deterioration and curable functional obsolescence have been accounted for, the remaining economic life of the structure may increase and its effective age may decrease depending on the magnitude of the changes.

Although immediately curable items are recognized in the modified economic age-life method, it does not allow for differences in the remaining economic lives of individual structural components, particularly short-lived items. The method is predicated on the assumption that a single age-life ratio can be applied to the entire structure.

The modified economic age-life method presumes that utility is reduced on a straight-line basis and, therefore, it has the advantage of being simple. Careful estimation of effective age often overcomes this weakness. The modified economic age-life method provides a convenient means for relating properties to one another and for making comparisons within a set of properties.

Breakdown Method

To apply the breakdown method of estimating accrued depreciation, an appraiser analyzes each cause of depreciation separately, measures the amount of each, and then totals the estimates to derive a lump-sum figure that is deducted from the estimated reproduction or replacement cost. If the appraiser is using replacement cost, certain types of functional obsolescence should not be deducted from the estimate of accrued depreciation.

The five basic types of accrued depreciation that affect structures are

1. Curable physical deterioration
2. Incurable physical deterioration
3. Curable functional obsolescence
4. Incurable functional obsolescence
5. External obsolescence

Table 17.3   Breakdown Method of Estimating Accrued Depreciation (Based on replacement cost)

Type	Category Curable	Category Incurable
Physical deterioration	Items of deferred maintenance	Classified according to short- and long-lived items
	Cost to cure	Physical age-life method
Functional Obsolescence		
A. Deficiency Requiring 1. Addition 2. Substitution or Modernization	1. Cost to cure over cost if installed new during construction 2. Cost to cure minus remaining value of existing components	1. Capitalization of net income loss due to deficiency 2. Capitalization of net income loss due to deficiency
B. Superadequacy	Not included when base is replacement cost*	Capitalization of added costs of ownership (taxes, insurance, maintenance, utilities)**
External obsolescence	Rarely curable on part of owner	Capitalization of property's net income loss due to external obsolescence; proportionate allocation to improvement

* When the base is reproduction cost, the estimate corresponds to the current reproduction cost of the superadequate component minus the physical deterioration already charged plus the cost to install a normally adequate component. Economic feasibility is the test of curability.

** When the base is reproduction cost, the estimate corresponds to the current reproduction cost of the superadequate component minus the physical deterioration already charged plus the present value of the added costs of ownership.

These items are discussed in this chapter in the order in which they are traditionally treated in appraisal reports. However, an appraiser may find it more convenient to measure all curable physical and functional items first and then analyze physical, functional, and external incurable items. Incurable items generally cannot be measured properly until all curable items have been measured due to the nature of curable and incurable deterioration. The replacement or reproduction cost of items of curable deterioration is offset by the amount they add to value; the replacement or reproduction cost of items of incurable deterioration exceeds the amount they add to value.

The valuation of single-family properties generally does not require the amount of detail used in the breakdown method. To estimate accrued depreciation for a single-family property, an appraiser may use a simple cost per square foot derived from a national cost service or a lump-sum accrued depreciation estimate from an age-life method, which are distillations of the method illustrated in the following pages. Although certain appraisal problems can be resolved with simple cost per square foot estimates, many appraisals require the use of the breakdown method. Appraisers should be familiar with the more exacting, detailed method to apply the simpler ones accurately.

The tables that follow illustrate applications of the breakdown method. The site value indicated in the tables is presumed to be supported by market analysis. The tables are based on a hypothetical two-story office building that has 4,667 square feet of gross building area and 3,770 square feet of net leasable area and is located on a 2,372-sq.-ft. site. The building contains most forms of accrued depreciation.

Table 17.4 is a summary of the reproduction and replacement cost estimates for the office building. In the subsequent tables, estimates of each category of depreciation are calculated using both reproduction and replacement cost to show the differences that result from different types of cost estimates.

Curable Physical Deterioration

Curable physical deterioration refers to items of deferred maintenance; the estimate of curable physical deterioration applies only to items in need of repair on the date of the appraisal. Thus, this element of accrued depreciation is measured as the cost of restoring an item to new or reasonably new condition—i.e., the cost to cure. Tables 17.5 and 17.6 show the calculations for estimating curable physical items of deterioration.

An observed condition in the improvements to be appraised is considered curable if the cost of correcting the condition would be offset by an equal or greater increase in value. Most structural defects, deficiencies, and superadequacies can be corrected with new construction technology, but the crucial consideration is *economic*. Will curing the condition restore function and is it prudent to cure it at this time?

Table 17.4   Difference between Reproduction and Replacement Cost by the Quantity Survey Method

	Reproduction Cost	Replacement Cost
Direct costs (including labor, materials, equipment, and contractor's overhead and profit)		
Excavation and site preparation	$ 395	$ 395
Foundation	4,685	4,685
Exterior walls	53,275	53,275
Roof structure	9,720	9,720
Roof cover	2,505	2,505
Frame*	19,590	12,690
Floor structure	12,925	12,925
Floor cover (carpeting)	5,995	5,995
Ceiling	5,505	5,505
Interior partitions	33,300	33,300
Painting (exterior and interior)	1,250	1,250
Plumbing system	5,675	5,675
Plumbing fixtures**	2,685	2,135
Electrical system	6,560	6,560
Electrical fixtures	3,415	3,415
HVAC	13,580	13,580
Total direct costs	$181,060	$173,610
Indirect costs (including architect's fees, survey, legal fees, permits and licenses, insurance, taxes, financing charges, selling expenses, leasing expenses, and holding expenses)***	$ 14,665	$ 12,950
Entrepreneurial profit	$ 27,000	$ 27,000
Total reproduction cost	$222,725	
Total replacement cost		$213,560
Cost per sq. ft. of gross building area	$ 47.72	$ 45.76

* The building was designed and built to accommodate three stories, not two. The difference in the reproduction and replacement cost estimates is due to additional framing cost.

** The original plumbing consisted of cast-iron fixtures. Steel fixtures are used now.

*** A portion of the indirect costs is based on a percentage of direct costs, so the indirect costs included in the reproduction and replacement cost estimates will differ slightly.

Table 17.5   Reproduction Cost
Curable Physical Deterioration (Deferred Maintenance)

	Reproduction Cost	Cost to Cure	Remainder
Roof cover (repair)	$2,505	$ 250*	$2,255
Painting	1,250	1,350**	0
Total curable physical deterioration		$1,600	

* The roof was damaged in a storm; the cost to cure the roof came to $250.

** The cost to cure the painting exceeds its current cost because additional labor and preparation not involved in new construction were required.

Table 17.6   Replacement Cost
Curable Physical Deterioration (Deferred Maintenance)

	Replacement Cost	Cost to Cure	Remainder
Roof cover (repair)	$2,505	$ 250*	$2,255
Painting	1,250	1,350**	0
Total curable physical deterioration		$1,600	

* The roof was damaged in a storm; the cost to cure the roof was $250.

** The cost to cure the painting exceeds its current cost because additional labor and preparation not involved in new construction were required.

Appraisers differ in how they categorize a curable item that is only partly worn. For example, a five-year-old roof that is expected to have a total physical life of 25 years obviously contributes less than it would if it were new. Some appraisers argue that the 20% loss in value cannot economically be cured as of the date of the appraisal; others believe that deteriorated roofs are indeed curable. The pro-rata loss in value due to such an item may be deducted as incurable or curable deterioration; the appraiser's choice of either category will not affect the market value opinion.

Incurable Physical Deterioration

Incurable physical deterioration identifies items of deterioration that cannot be practically or economically corrected at present. This type of depreciation is calculated for all structural elements that are not included in the curable physical category. Because the cost to cure curable physical items of deterioration has already been deducted from the total reproduction or replacement cost estimate, incurable physical deterioration does not apply to the total cost estimate. Incurable physical deterioration must be based on the reproduction or replacement cost of the entire structure that remains *after the cost to cure the components treated as physically curable has been deducted*. Otherwise, the cost of incurable physical deterioration would also be charged to curable items.

For purposes of analysis, items that have incurable physical deterioration are classified as long-lived and short-lived. A long-lived item is a building component that is expected to have a remaining economic life that is the same as the remaining economic life of the entire structure. A short-lived item is a component that is expected to have a remaining economic life that is shorter than the remaining economic life of the structure.

Whether items of physical deterioration, other than items of deferred maintenance, are classified as curable or incurable, the deterioration in short-lived items must be measured consistently and each element of the structure must be measured only once. Tables 17.7 through 17.10 show the calculations for estimating the physical deterioration evident in short- and long-lived items.

Table 17.7   Reproduction Cost
Incurable Physical Deterioration
Short-Lived Components

	Reproduction Cost Remaining	Effective Age	Total Physical Life	Ratio Applied to Cost	Incurable Physical Depreciation
Roof cover	$ 2,255*	10 yrs.	15 yrs.	$10/15$ (67%)	$ 1,511
Floor cover	5,995	7 yrs.	10 yrs.	$7/10$ (70%)	4,197
Ceiling	5,505	5 yrs.	15 yrs.	$5/15$ (33%)	1,817
Painting	0	New	5 yrs.	0	0
Plumbing fixtures	2,685	10 yrs.	20 yrs.	$10/20$ (50%)	1,343
Electrical fixtures	3,415	8 yrs.	10 yrs.	$8/10$ (80%)	2,732
HVAC	4,750**	10 yrs.	15 yrs.	$10/15$ (67%)	3,183
	$24,605				
Total incurable physical deterioration, short-lived components					$14,783
Rounded					$14,785

* Of the current reproduction cost of $2,505, $250 was "cured" in the treatment of physical curable deterioration, leaving a remainder of $2,255. The appraiser may choose to deduct the entire $2,505 if repairing the damaged item will not increase the remaining life of the building component.

** Of the current reproduction cost of $13,580 for the entire HVAC system, $4,750 is attributable to short-lived items such as fans, controls, and other mechanical components that will need repair or replacement before the end of the structure's estimated economic life.

In the tables, incurable physical deterioration for both short- and long-lived components is estimated with *the physical age-life method*. The mathematical procedure used to calculate the reproduction and replacement cost estimates is the same, but the remaining reproduction cost may differ from the remaining replacement cost for some items. (See Tables 17.7 and 17.9.)

To estimate the depreciation charged for incurable physical deterioration in short-lived components, the appraiser applies *the ratio of effective age to estimated total physical life* to the reproduction or replacement cost of each incurable physical short-lived component that remains after the cost to cure curable physical deterioration has been deducted from the total cost estimate. The depreciation evident in all the items is added to obtain an estimate of the total incurable physical deterioration in short-lived building components.

To calculate the amount of depreciation to be charged to incurable physical deterioration in long-lived components, the total remaining cost of curable physical components and incurable physical short-lived components must be deducted from the estimated reproduction or replacement cost. If this step is not completed, the charges for curable and incurable physical deterioration in short-lived components will be duplicated.

Table 17.8   Reproduction Cost
Incurable Physical Deterioration
Long-Lived Components

Reproduction cost		$222,725
Less reproduction cost of curable physical items	$ 1,500*	
and incurable physical short-lived items	$24,605	
		− 26,105
Reproduction cost of long-lived items		$196,620
Effective age—5 yrs.		
Total physical life (new)—75 yrs.		
Ratio applied to cost— 5/75		× 0.066666
Total incurable physical deterioration, long-lived components		$13,108
Rounded		$13,100

* This figure consists of the cost to cure the roof ($250) and the reproduction cost of the painting ($1,250). Reproduction cost of the painting is used because the cost to cure exceeds reproduction cost.

Table 17.9   Replacement Cost
Incurable Physical Deterioration
Short-Lived Components

	Replacement Cost Remaining	Effective Age	Total Physical Life	Ratio Applied to Cost	Incurable Physical Depreciation
Roof cover	$ 2,255*	10 yrs.	15 yrs.	$^{10}/_{15}$ (67%)	$ 1,511
Floor cover	5,995	7 yrs.	10 yrs.	$^{7}/_{10}$ (70%)	4,197
Ceiling	5,505	5 yrs.	15 yrs.	$^{5}/_{15}$ (33%)	1,817
Painting	0	New	5 yrs.	0	0
Plumbing fixtures	2,135	10 yrs.	20 yrs.	$^{10}/_{20}$ (50%)	1,068
Electrical fixtures	3,415	8 yrs.	10 yrs.	$^{8}/_{10}$ (80%)	2,732
HVAC	4,750**	10 yrs.	15 yrs.	$^{10}/_{15}$ (67%)	3,183
	$24,055				
Total incurable physical deterioration, short-lived components					$14,508
Rounded					$14,510

* Of the current replacement cost of $2,505, $250 was "cured" in the treatment of curable physical deterioration, leaving a remainder of $2,255.

** Of the current replacement cost of $13,580 for the entire HVAC system, $4,750 is attributable to short-lived items that will need replacement before the end of the structure's estimated economic life. The $8,830 remainder is included in the long-lived category.

Table 17.10   Replacement Cost
Incurable Physical Deterioration
Long-Lived Components

Replacement cost		$213,560
Less replacement cost of curable physical items	$ 1,500	
and incurable physical short-lived items	24,055	
		−25,555
Replacement cost of long-lived items		$188,005
Effective age—5 yrs.		
Total physical life (new)—75 yrs.		
Ratio applied to cost— $^{5}/_{75}$		× 0.0666
Total incurable physical deterioration, long-lived components		$ 12,521
Rounded		$ 12,520

After subtracting curable and incurable physical short-lived deterioration, *the ratio of effective age to estimated total physical life* is applied to the total replacement or reproduction cost of incurable physical long-lived building components.

The physical age-life method of estimating deterioration is particularly appropriate when the market does not provide reliable data for measuring economic life. An appraiser who applies this method to an entire structure assumes that deterioration occurs at a constant, average annual rate over the estimated life of the improvements. If, for example, the appraiser estimates a building's physical life at 75 years, he or she assumes that physical deterioration will accrue at a rate of 1.33% per year (1/75 = 1.33%). The appraiser then multiplies this percentage by the actual physical age of the structure and deducts this figure, multiplied by the reproduction cost less physical curable deterioration, from the current reproduction cost less physical curable deterioration to arrive at a cost estimate that reflects physical deterioration.

The physical age-life method can also be applied to structural components such as the foundation; walls; floors; plumbing; electrical, heating, and air-conditioning systems; elevators; and other mechanical equipment. For this application the appraiser must estimate the expected physical life of each component.[1]

Curable Functional Obsolescence

Functional obsolescence is a loss in value resulting from defects in design. It can also be caused by changes that, over time, have made some aspect of a structure, such as its materials or design, obsolete by current standards. The defect may be curable or incurable. *To be curable, the cost of replacing the outmoded or unacceptable aspect must be the same as or less than the anticipated increase in value.* Curable functional obsolescence is measured as the cost to cure the condition. Curable functional obsolescence may be divided into three subcategories.

1. *Deficiency requiring additions*, which is measured by how much the cost of the addition exceeds the cost if it were installed new during construction
2. *Deficiency requiring substitution or modernization*, which is measured as the cost of installing the modern component minus the remaining value, if any, of the existing component
3. *Superadequacy*, which is measured as the current reproduction cost of the item minus any physical deterioration already charged plus the cost to install a normally adequate or standard item. A superadequacy is curable if correcting it on the date of the appraisal is economically feasible; otherwise, it is considered incurable.

Tables 17.11, 17.12, and 17.13 show the calculations for measuring curable functional obsolescence when a reproduction cost is used.

The office building being appraised has no lavatory on the second floor, which has made it difficult to rent this space. Adequate space is available for the

---

1. Appraisers may consider the physical age life of the skeleton of a building in terms of double and triple physical lives. See Max J. Derbes, Jr., "Economic Life Concepts," *The Appraisal Journal*, April 1987.

addition. Although space allocation is included in the reproduction cost estimate, fixtures are not. The calculation is necessary because it would be improper to deduct a component from the reproduction cost that was not included in this cost.

Table 17.11   Reproduction Cost
Curable Functional Obsolescence Deficiency
Requiring Additions

Cost to install a lavatory in the existing structure	$1,200
Less cost to install a lavatory in the existing structure if the structure were being built new on the date of the appraisal	900
Loss in value	$ 300

The light fixtures in the subject office building were outdated. Table 17.12 shows the loss in value attributable to this item.

Table 17.12   Reproduction Cost
Curable Functional Obsolescence Deficiency Requiring
Substitution or Modernization

Cost of modern fixtures plus installation	$1,000
Less remaining value of existing fixtures	200
Loss in value	$ 800

Tenant space in the office building was formerly occupied by a law firm with a law library. The specially constructed library had built-in bookshelves along one wall of the space (16.67 linear feet). The bookshelves were structurally integrated as a part of the wall. This superadequacy is considered curable only if it is economically feasible to cure it on the date of the appraisal.

Table 17.13   Reproduction Cost
Curable Functional Obsolescence
Superadequacy

Determination of Feasibility

Cost to remove bookshelves	$ 50
Cost to restore wall	25
Less salvage value	0
Total cost to cure	$ 75
Potential gain in *NOI*	
(25 square feet × $6)*	$150
Less increased operating expenses	50
Plus reduced operating expenses	0
Gain in *NOI*	$100
Change in *NOI* capitalized at 10.5%**	$952

The capitalized gain in *NOI* that results from curing the superadequacy is greater than the cost to cure, so it is feasible to remove the bookshelves.

Depreciation Estimate

Current reproduction cost of the bookshelves	$550
Less physical deterioration already charged	275
Subtotal	$275
Plus net cost to cure	75
Loss in value	$350

* The market rent for office space is $6 per square foot. The built-in bookshelves occupy a 25-sq.-ft. area.

** The appraiser estimates a building capitalization rate of 10.5%.

Functional Obsolescence in Replacement Cost Estimates

If current cost is based on a replacement rather than a reproduction, the cost of excess or superadequate items is not included. Therefore, no expenditure to reproduce them and no charge for physical deterioration need be deducted. However, the cost to cure the superadequacy is still a valid charge. The $75 shown in Table 17.13 as the cost to cure the unwanted bookshelves represents the extent of curable functional obsolescence due to the superadequacy that must be applied to the replacement cost estimate. Tables 17.14, 17.15, and 17.16 illustrate appropriate calculations for measuring curable functional obsolescence when a replacement cost estimate is used. Like the preceding tables, these tables are based on the conditions observed in the subject office building.

**Table 17.14   Replacement Cost
Curable Functional Obsolescence
Deficiency Requiring Additions**

Cost to install a lavatory in the existing structure	$1,200
Less cost to install a lavatory in the existing structure if the structure were built new on the date of the appraisal	900
Loss in value	$ 300

As mentioned earlier, the curable functional obsolescence evidenced by the outdated light fixtures is measured by the cost to cure after the contributory value, if any, of the deteriorated items is deducted. If a structure contains an obsolete component that must be removed at a separate cost, the cost of removal would be added to the cost of the repairs.

**Table 17.15   Replacement Cost
Curable Functional Obsolescence
Deficiency Requiring Substitutions or Modernization**

Cost of modern fixtures plus installation	$800
Less remaining value of existing fixtures	200
Loss in value	$600

**Table 17.16   Replacement Cost
Curable Functional Obsolescence
Superadequacy**

Cost to remove the bookshelves and repair and refinish the wall less salvage value	$75*

* This is the only charge because the special bookshelves were not included in the replacement cost estimate.

Incurable Functional Obsolescence

Incurable functional obsolescence may be caused by a deficiency or a superadequacy. Incurable functional obsolescence due to a deficiency is measured as the net income

loss attributable to the deficiency in comparison with otherwise competitive properties. *The net income loss is divided by the building capitalization rate*, which is
developed in the income capitalization approach. For income-producing properties,
capitalizing the net income loss is a standard procedure.

The calculations for measuring incurable functional obsolescence due to a
deficiency are the same whether reproduction or replacement cost is used. (See Table
17.17.)

**Table 17.17   Reproduction and Replacement Cost
Incurable Functional Obsolescence
Deficiency**

Estimated *NOI* loss due to the deficiency	$ 1,274
Building capitalization rate applicable to subject property (developed in the income capitalization approach)	10.5%
NOI loss divided by building capitalization rate ($1,274/0.105)	$12,133
Estimated incurable functional obsolescence due to the deficiency (rounded)	$12,135

The office building being appraised has no parking facilities for the tenants
and street parking is not available. Market analysis indicates a differential of $0.75
per square foot of net leasable area between office buildings with adequate parking
and those without it. The subject property has 3,770 square feet of net leasable area,
which indicates an annual gross income loss of $2,830, minus vacancy loss and
expenses of $1,556, for a net operating income loss of $1,274 per year. In many cases,
the net income loss as a percentage of gross income loss attributable to functional
obsolescence differs from the general income and expense ratio for the property
because certain expenses, such as utilities and insurance, are not affected by the
deficiency, while other expenses, such as taxes and management, may be affected.

Incurable functional obsolescence due to a superadequacy is measured differently depending on whether a reproduction or replacement cost estimate is used. If
reproduction cost is the base, the appraiser must consider the cost to construct a
building that contains the same superadequacy. The superadequacy is measured as
the current reproduction cost of the superadequate component, minus any physical
deterioration already charged, plus the present value of any added cost of ownership
due to the presence of the superadequacy. The charge for this burden of ownership is
based on items such as additional taxes, insurance, maintenance, and utility charges.
The excess current reproduction cost of the item, over and above the cost that may be
supported by an increase in market rent as a result of the superadequacy, is added to
the capitalized net income loss to derive an indication of the total depreciation caused
by incurable functional obsolescence due to a superadequacy.

To estimate incurable functional obsolescence due to a superadequacy when
reproduction cost is the base, the appraiser must review the estimates of curable and
incurable physical deterioration. If the superadequate component has been included

in either of these categories, the reproduction cost of the superadequacy must be reduced by the amount of depreciation already charged. Such a charge is often made in estimating the incurable physical deterioration in long-lived components, but it could also be made in estimating curable or incurable physical deterioration in short-lived components. All charges made in estimating physical deterioration must be reviewed to ensure that charges for items of accrued depreciation are not made twice.

Replacement does not include the cost to construct a superadequacy, so no loss in the value of a superadequacy due to physical deterioration is considered when replacement cost is used. However, a charge is required if the superadequacy causes a monetary burden of ownership for items such as additional taxes, insurance, maintenance, and utility charges. The capitalized value of these additional expenses, over and above any increase in market rent resulting from the superadequacy, represents the loss in value caused by incurable functional obsolescence due to the superadequacy.

Occasionally a superadequacy that is incurable results in a rental value that is higher than that of an otherwise equivalent property, but not high enough to meet the capital requirements of the item's cost. In such a case, the incurable functional obsolescence due to the superadequacy is measured as the difference between the capitalized rent added by the superadequate item and the item's current cost minus physical deterioration plus the present value of the added cost of ownership. Incurable functional obsolescence caused by a superadequacy is calculated in Table 17.18.

Table 17.18   Reproduction Cost
Incurable Functional Obsolescence
Superadequacy

Current reproduction cost of the superadequacy	$6,900
Less physical deterioration already charged	690*
Subtotal	$6,210
Plus present value of added cost of ownership	0**
Estimated incurable functional obsolescence due to superadequacy	$6,210

* A 10% charge was made in incurable physical deterioration, long-lived. Therefore, 10% of the reproduction cost of the excess component must be deducted to avoid a double charge.

**No extra ownership expenses are incurred for this type of superadequacy.

The office building was designed and built to accommodate three stories, but only two stories were constructed. It is not economically feasible to add the additional floor. The framing cost new of a three-story building would be $19,590, while the framing cost new of a two-story building would be $12,690. Therefore, the cost of the superadequacy is $19,590 − $12,690, or $6,900.

Because replacement cost does not include the cost of the superadequacy, no loss in value for incurable functional obsolescence caused by a superadequacy is considered except a charge for any burden of ownership created by the superadequacy. This particular superadequacy does not cause additional expenses for the subject property, so there is no loss in value due to the superadequacy in this case.

External Obsolescence

External obsolescence, the diminished utility of a structure due to negative influences from outside the site, is incurable on part of the owner, landlord, or tenant. External obsolescence can be caused by a variety of factors—e.g., neighborhood decline; the property's location in a community, state, or region; or market conditions. An estimate of external obsolescence should be based on thorough neighborhood or district analysis. It must be justified in the neighborhood data section of the appraisal report.

External influences can cause any property to lose value. In the cost approach, the total loss in value due to external obsolescence is allocated between the land and the improvements. Therefore, an appraiser must first estimate the percentage of total value that is contributed by the improvements. Then the share of the loss that is applicable to the improvements is deducted from the current reproduction or replacement cost as external obsolescence.

The effect of external influences on land or site value is calculated, when appropriate, in land valuation analysis, especially in any adjustment made for location. If the income of the entire property were used to calculate the external obsolescence attributable to the building component, the loss in land value would be charged twice. Therefore, the appraiser may use the ratios of land and building values to total property value to isolate the external obsolescence in the building. Although the portion of total property value loss attributed to the land is calculated, this figure is *not* applied in deriving an estimate of external obsolescence. It is only used to segregate the amount of external obsolescence evident in the building component of the property. However, the information derived in calculating the ratios may be used to test the reasonableness of the loss in value charged to the land in the land value section of the appraisal report.

Two methods can be used to measure external obsolescence. The appraiser should select the procedure that is supported by the best market evidence. The appraiser can either 1) capitalize the income or rent loss attributable to the negative influence, or 2) compare sales of similar properties that are subject to the negative influence and others that are not. If pertinent sales data are abundant, the second procedure is preferable. However, an appraiser may encounter significant practical problems in attempting to account for other differences between the subject property and the comparable properties. Care should be exercised when this method is used.

To estimate external obsolescence by capitalizing the resulting loss in property income, the appraiser first estimates the loss to the entire property that is attributable to external forces. Then the loss is allocated between the land and the improvements. For example, if a ratio were appropriate and the improvements constitute approximately 80% of total property value, 80% of the total external obsolescence is allocated to the improvements. The ratio of improvement value to total property value is based on the value ratios for similar properties in the area. The effect of externalities on land may be corroborated by the land value estimate produced in the sales comparison approach.

An appraiser may apply the following procedure to estimate the income loss to the entire property due to external obsolescence. First, the total income loss is adjusted to reflect the curing of any physical and functional sources of depreciation. Then this figure is capitalized by applying appropriate capitalization rates to net operating income or by applying appropriate income multipliers to gross income or rent. The procedure tends to work best when net operating income and capitalization rates are used. Appraisers can often find market data to help break down an overall capitalization rate (R_O) into a building capitalization rate (R_B) and a land capitalization rate (R_L). It is much more difficult to find an income or rent multiplier that reflects the proportions of building and land.

When net operating income and appropriate capitalization rates are used, the net income loss can be capitalized at the overall capitalization rate developed in the income capitalization approach. To determine the capitalized income loss attributable to depreciation in the improvements and the loss in value attributable to the land, the ratio of component parts to total property value is applied to the capitalized income loss.

As an alternative, the appraiser can apply the ratio of component parts to total property value to the income loss before capitalization to determine the income loss attributable to the building and the land in dollar amounts. The market-derived building capitalization rate is then applied to the income loss attributable to the building. The resulting figure, which is an estimate of depreciation due to external obsolescence, can then be entered in the proper place in the cost approach format.

The appraiser may capitalize the remaining income at the market-derived land capitalization rate to derive an indication of the loss in value attributable to the land. If this percent of the loss in land value is close to the adjustment that was made for location in the sales comparison analysis of land value,[2] the appraiser can place greater reliability on both the location adjustment and the estimate of external obsolescence attributed to the building in the cost approach.

Table 17.19 illustrates one procedure for estimating external obsolescence. The procedure can be used with either a reproduction or a replacement cost estimate.

---

2. This procedure assumes that an adjustment for location has been made in the sales comparison approach. If a comparable property in proximity to the subject has recently been sold, there is no need for a location adjustment. Furthermore, the supply and demand for land must equal the supply and demand for buildings to relate a value loss due to external obsolescence to both.

**Table 17.19   Reproduction or Replacement Cost
External Obsolescence**

Estimated annual *NOI* not subject to external obsolescence after physical and functional accrued depreciation is cured	$10,180
Subject's current *NOI* after physical and functional accrued depreciation is cured	− 7,635
Estimated annual *NOI* loss due to external influences	$ 2,545
Overall rate (R_O) from income capitalization approach	10.0%
Capitalized net income loss to total property ($2,545/0.10)	$25,450
Proportion of overall loss attributable to building	73.5%
Amount of external obsolescence applicable to building	$18,705

The subject office building is adjacent to older apartments that are generally in poor condition. Office buildings in the same market area that are competitive with the subject and not subject to this detrimental influence rent for $1.50 more per square foot of net leasable area than the subject property. Therefore, the estimated annual net operating income loss is calculated as follows:

3,770 net leasable square feet × $6	$22,620
Less vacancy loss and expenses	−15,495
NOI	$ 7,125
3,770 net leasable square feet × $4.50	$16,965
Less vacancy loss and expenses	−12,385
NOI	$ 4,580

Net operating income loss
$7,125 − $4,580 = $2,545

TOTAL ESTIMATES OF ACCRUED DEPRECIATION

After each element of depreciation is accurately estimated, the results of the analysis are summarized. (See Tables 17.20 and 17.21.)

FINAL VALUE INDICATION

When accrued depreciation is measured by the breakdown method, the appraiser derives a final value indication in the cost approach by deducting the estimate of accrued depreciation from the reproduction or replacement cost of the improvements on the date of the appraisal and then adding the market value of the land on the same date. When appropriate, this total represents a fee simple value indication, which is adjusted to reflect the specific property rights being appraised. The final calculations are shown in Tables 17.22 and 17.23. Table 17.24 compares the value indications derived using replacement and reproduction cost estimates. In most appraisal assignments, either reproduction cost or replacement cost is used; it is rarely necessary to use both.

Table 17.20   Reproduction Cost
Total Estimate of Accrued Depreciation
Breakdown Method

Physical deterioration		
Curable, deferred maintenance	$ 1,600	
Incurable, short-lived items	14,785	
Incurable, long-lived items	13,100	
Total		$29,485
Functional obsolescence		
Curable ($800 + $350 + $300)	$ 1,450	
Incurable ($12,135 + $6,210)	18,345	
Total		$19,795
External obsolescence		18,705
Total accrued depreciation		$67,985

Table 17.21   Replacement Cost
Total Estimate of Accrued Depreciation
Breakdown Method

Physical deterioration		
Curable, deferred maintenance	$ 1,600	
Incurable, short-lived items	14,510	
Incurable, long-lived items	12,520	
Total		$28,630
Functional obsolescence		
Curable ($300 + $600 + $75)	$ 975	
Incurable	12,135	
Total		$13,110
External obsolescence		$18,705
Total accrued depreciation		$60,445

It is assumed that the office building being appraised is rented to a single tenant for six more years at a gross annual rent of $38,000. Market rent is $44,000 per year. The present value of the tenant's leasehold interest is $24,668, which was obtained by discounting the $6,000 difference between market rent and contract rent for the six-year term at the 12% discount rate currently sought by equity investors— i.e., $6,000 × 4.111407 (present value of $1 per period).

Table 17.22   Reproduction Cost
Summation and Final Value Indication
Cost Approach

Estimated current reproduction cost (including indirect costs and entrepreneurial profit)	$222,725
Estimated accrued depreciation	− 67,985
Estimated reproduction cost less accrued depreciation	$154,740
Estimated depreciated value of site improvements	0
Estimated land value	60,000
Fee simple value indication	$214,740
Adjustment for tenant's leasehold interest	− 24,668
Leased fee value indication	$190,072
Rounded	$190,000

Table 17.23   Replacement Cost
Summation and Final Value Indication
Cost Approach

Estimated replacement cost (including indirect costs and entrepreneurial profit)	$213,560
Estimated accrued depreciation	− 60,445
Estimated replacement cost less accrued depreciation	$153,115
Estimated depreciated value of site improvements	0
Estimated land value	$ 60,000
Fee simple value indication	$213,115
Adjustment for tenant's leasehold interest	− 24,668
Leased fee value indication	$188,447
Rounded	$188,400

Table 17.24   Comparison of Cost Approach Value Indications Using Replacement and Reproduction Costs

	Reproduction Cost	Difference in Dollars	Replacement Cost
Direct	$181,060	(7,450)	$173,610
Indirect	14,665	(1,715)	12,950
Entrepreneurial profit*	27,000		27,000
Total	$222,725	(9,165)	$213,560
Accrued depreciation			
Curable physical	$ 1,600	(0)	$ 1,600
Incurable physical, short-lived	14,785	(275)	14,510
Incurable physical, long-lived	13,100	(570)	12,530
Subtotal**	$ 29,485	(845)	$ 28,640
Curable functional, deficiency	800	(200)	600
Curable functional, deficiency	300	(0)	300
Curable, functional superadequacy	350	(275)	75
Subtotal	$ 1,450	(475)	$ 975
Incurable functional, deficiency	$ 12,135	(0)	$ 12,135
Incurable functional, superadequacy	6,210	(6,210)	0
Subtotal	$ 18,345	(6,210)	$ 12,135
External obsolescence	$ 18,705	(0)	$ 18,705
Total accrued depreciation	$ 67,985(30.5%)	(7,540)	$ 60,445(28.3%)
Depreciated value of improvements	$154,740	(1,625)	$153,115
Land value	$ 60,000		$ 60,000
Fee simple value indication	$214,740	(1,625)	$213,115
Adjustment for tenant's leasehold interest	−24,668	0	− 24,668
Leased fee value indicated by cost approach	$190,072	(1,625)	$188,447
Rounded	$190,100	(1,700)	$188,400

*This estimate is derived from market evidence of the profits accruing to speculative builders and developers.

**At this intermediate stage, some appraisers employ physical value, which is the value that would be calculated if the property had no functional or external obsolescence. Physical value is obtained by deducting all physical deterioration from the reproduction or replacement cost estimate.

ESTIMATING ACCRUED DEPRECIATION BY THE SALES COMPARISON APPROACH

In estimating accrued depreciation with sales comparison techniques, the reproduction or replacement cost of the property on the date of the appraisal minus the value contribution of the improvements on the same date should equal total accrued depreciation. Table 17.25 illustrates the procedure for estimating accrued depreciation through analysis of comparable sales.

Although this method is reliable, its accuracy depends on the availability of truly comparable sales of both improved properties and vacant sites. The real property interests conveyed in the improved properties used for comparison should be the same as the real property interests conveyed in the subject property. Sales of partial interests should be used with caution because vast differences can exist among leased fee or leasehold interests. Any adjustment for differences in real property interests must be supported with market data.

Table 17.25   Estimating Accrued Depreciation with Sales Comparison Techniques

(All sales are of fee simple interests.)

	Sale 1	Sale 2	Sale 3
Sale price	$215,000	$165,000	$365,000
Estimated land value	− 60,000	− 40,000	− 127,750
Value of improvements	$155,000	$125,000	$237,250
Estimated replacement cost on date of sale	$230,000	$195,000	$375,000
Less value of improvements	− 155,000	− 125,000	− 237,250
Indicated total accrued depreciation in dollars	$75,000	$70,000	$137,750
Indicated total accrued depreciation as % of current replacement cost (rounded)	33%	36%	37%

The sales used in Table 17.25 are current and similar to the subject property in terms of physical, functional, and external elements of accrued depreciation. Adjustments should be made for any dissimilarities. The sales indicate a narrow range for accrued depreciation of between 33% and 37% of total replacement cost. The total percentage of depreciation estimated by the other methods are shown below.

	Replacement Cost	Reproduction Cost
Economic age-life	32%	35%
Modified economic age-life	30%	33%
Breakdown	31%	33%

When sales comparison techniques are used to estimate depreciation, the type of depreciation—i.e., physical, functional, or external—is immaterial. If the sale is an open-market transaction involving a fee simple interest, site value is market-supported, and the estimate of current replacement or reproduction cost is accurate, the total will represent a reliable indication of accrued depreciation.

However, this method for measuring accrued depreciation has certain limitations. An adequate quantity of reliable comparable sales data is needed. Truly comparable sales are not always available and certain special-purpose properties are not frequently exchanged in the open market. When data are not available, the method is of little use. Furthermore, the allocation of comparable sale prices between site value and improvement value may be difficult to justify, particularly when the ratio of land value to building value varies.

SUMMARY

Depreciation is a loss in property value from any cause as of the date of the appraisal. In other words, it is the difference between reproduction or replacement cost and market value as of the date of the appraisal. Depreciation can emanate from three sources: physical deterioration, functional obsolescence attributable to a deficiency or a superadequacy, and external obsolescence caused by changes in the overall economy, demand patterns, or general property use in the neighborhood. Physical deterioration and functional obsolescence can usually be observed in an improvement. Depreciation represents a penalty because the market recognizes it as a value loss. A temporary undersupply of properties relative to demand may offsett the value loss older buildings generally experience. Historic or architectural significance may also compensate for the value penalty that time imposes.

Several important terms are associated with depreciation. To measure *accrued depreciation*, an appraiser estimates the amount of value loss incurred by the subject structure in its present condition, as compared with the value of the property if it were new. *Book depreciation*, the amount of capital recapture written off an owner's books, is based on original cost; it is not derived from the market. *Economic life* is the period over which improvements to real estate contribute to property value. Generally, the economic life of a property is shorter than its *physical life* if the property is not rehabilitated. *Remaining economic life* is an estimate of how long improvements will continue to contribute to property value.

Actual age (i.e., historical or chronological age) is the number of years that have elapsed since construction was completed. *Effective age* is the age indicated by the condition and utility of the structure. If a building has been well maintained, has an especially good design, or happens to be in an undersupplied market, its effective age may be less than its actual age.

To measure accrued depreciation, an appraiser considers all elements that may cause a loss in value and treats each element only once. Accrued depreciation can be estimated with *the economic age-life method, the modified economic age-life method, the breakdown method*, or sales comparison and income capitalization techniques. To estimate physical deterioration *only, the physical age-life method* may be used.

To apply *the economic age-life method*, the ratio of effective age to total economic life is applied to the current reproduction or replacement cost of the improvements. Although this is the simplest method, it does not distinguish between curable and incurable items of depreciation, or between short- and long-lived building components. The economic age-life method should not be used to derive separate estimates of the incurable physical deterioration of short- or long-lived items in the breakdown method.

The modified economic age-life method recognizes the effect of curable items of physical deterioration due to deferred maintenance and functional obsolescence. An appraiser estimates the curable depreciation in physical and functional items, and deducts this amount from the current reproduction or replacement cost of the improvements. To estimate incurable depreciation, the appraiser determines the ratio of effective age to total economic life and applies it to the current cost of the improvements minus the estimated curable depreciation. The appraiser must recognize that correcting curable items may increase the remaining economic life and decrease the effective age of the improvements. The modififed economic age-life method does not distinguish between short- and long-lived items of depreciation.

The breakdown method analyzes each cause of depreciation separately and measures its effect. The separate estimates are totaled to arrive at a lump-sum amount, which is deducted from the current reproduction or replacement cost of the improvements. When this method is applied to a replacement cost estimate, deductions for certain forms of functional obsolescence (i.e., superadequacies) in the improvements are not included. The five types of accrued depreciation that this method considers are 1) curable physical deterioration, 2) incurable physical deterioration, 3) curable functional obsolescence, 4) incurable functional obsolescence, and 5) external obsolescence.

An appraiser may choose to consider all curable physical and functional items before measuring incurable items. The depreciation in incurable items cannot be properly measured until the depreciation in curable items has been calculated. The cost to correct curable items is offset by a resulting increase in value; the cost to cure incurable items exceeds the resulting increase in value.

Curable physical deterioration applies to items of deferred maintenance that are in need of repair on the date of the appraisal. An item is curable if the cost of curing it is less than or equal to the increase in property value. Appraisers differ on how a partly worn item should be categorized. Some argue that the value loss cannot be cured as of the date of the appraisal, so the item is incurable; others contend that deterioration is curable. In any case, the pro-rata loss must be deducted as either curable or incurable physical deterioration.

Incurable physical deterioration refers to deterioration that cannot be practically or economically cured. The estimate of incurable physical deterioration is based on the reproduction or replacement cost of the entire structure *after* the cost to cure physically curable components has been deducted. Items of incurable physical deterioration are classified as long-lived and short-lived. A long-lived item is expected to have a remaining economic life equal to the life of the entire structure; a short-lived item is expected to have a remaining economic life that is shorter than the life of the structure. *The physical age-life method* can be used for both short- and long-lived items. The ratio of effective age to estimated total physical age is applied to the reproduction or replacement cost of the short- and long-lived items to derive an estimate of incurable physical deterioration.

Curable functional obsolescence is caused by defects in design or changes in structural standards and building materials. To be curable, the cost of replacing the outmoded or unacceptable aspect must be less than or equal to the anticipated increase in value. Curable functional obsolescence can result from a deficiency requiring additions, a deficiency requiring substitution or modernization, or a superadequacy. If the current cost is based on replacement rather than reproduction of the improvements, the cost of superadequate items is not included.

Incurable functional obsolescence may be caused by a deficiency or a superadequacy. When it is caused by a deficiency, incurable functional obsolescence is estimated by capitalizing the net income loss attributable to the deficiency—i.e. by dividing the net income loss by the building capitalization rate. When caused by a superadequacy, incurable functional obsolescence may be measured two different ways, depending on whether reproduction or replacement cost is used.

If reproduction cost is the base, the superadequacy is measured as the reproduction cost of the superadequate component, minus any physical deterioration already charged, plus the present value of the added costs of ownership (e.g., for taxes, insurance, maintenance, and utilities). If replacement cost is the base, the superadequacy is represented only by a charge for the extra monetary burden of ownership.

External obsolescence is caused by negative influences outside the site; it is incurable on the part of the owner. The total value loss due to external obsolescence must be allocated between the land and the improvements. The percentage of total property value contributed by the improvements is determined, and then the proportionate share of external obsolescence applicable to the improvements is deducted from the current reproduction or replacement cost. The effect of external obsolescence on land value is considered separately in land value analysis by the adjustment for location. The proportionate share of external obsolescence allocated to the land is *not* applied to the land value, but it may be used to test the reasonableness of the value loss charged to the property's location in the land value section of the appraisal report.

To estimate external obsolescence, the appraiser capitalizes the income or rent loss attributable to the negative influence. In one procedure, the current *NOI* is subtracted from the estimated *NOI* if the property were not subject to external obsolescence. Then this figure is divided by the overall capitalization rate and the value loss is allocated between the building and the land. With another procedure, gross income is simply multiplied by the gross income multiplier (*GIM*). Finally, an appraiser may apply sales comparison techniques, analyzing sales of similar properties that are subject to the negative influence and others that are not. With this method, practical problems may arise in isolating and quantifying other differences between the subject and the comparable properties.

To derive a final value indication, the appraiser totals the estimates for each form of accrued depreciation, subtracts the total from the reproduction or replacement cost of the improvements, and adjusts this figure to reflect the specific property rights being appraised.

18 The Income Capitalization Approach

Income-producing real estate is typically purchased as an investment, and from the investor's point of view earning power is the critical element affecting property value. One basic investment premise is that the higher the earnings, the higher the value. An investor who purchases income-producing real estate is essentially trading present dollars for the right to receive future dollars. The income capitalization approach to value consists of methods, techniques, and mathematical procedures that an appraiser uses to analyze a property's capacity to generate benefits (i.e., usually the monetary benefits of income and reversion) and convert these benefits into an indication of present value.

The income capitalization approach is one of three traditional approaches that an appraiser may use in the valuation process. However, it is not an independent system of valuation that is unrelated to the other approaches. The valuation process as a whole is composed of integrated, interrelated, and inseparable techniques and procedures designed to produce a convincing and reliable estimate of value, usually market value. The analysis of cost and sales data is often an integral part of the income capitalization approach, but capitalization techniques may be frequently employed in the cost and sales comparison approaches as well. For example, capitalization techniques are commonly used to analyze and adjust sales data in the sales comparison approach; in the cost approach, obsolescence is often measured by capitalizing an estimated rent loss. The income capitalization approach is described here as part of the systematic valuation process; however, the various methods, techniques, and procedures used in the approach are general purpose, analytical tools that are applicable in valuing and evaluating income-producing properties.

This chapter provides a broad overview of the income capitalization approach and discusses the rationale, methods, and history behind it. Chapters 19 through 22 continue this discussion with detailed explanations of the specific methods, techniques, and procedures used to project and capitalize future benefits.

RELATIONSHIP TO VALUE INFLUENCES AND APPRAISAL PRINCIPLES

The application of the income capitalization approach is based on, and consistent with, the operation of value influences and appraisal principles.

Anticipation and Change

The principle of anticipation is fundamental to the approach. Because value is created by the expectation of benefits to be derived in the future, value may be defined as the present worth of all rights to these future benefits. All income capitalization methods, techniques, and procedures attempt to forecast future benefits and estimate their present value.

The approach focuses on how change affects the value of income-producing properties. To provide sound value indications, investors' expectations of changes in income levels, the expenses required to ensure income, and probable increases or decreases in property value must be carefully addressed and forecast.

Supply and Demand

The principle of supply and demand and the related concept of competition are particularly relevant in forecasting future benefits and estimating rates of return in the income capitalization approach. Both income streams and rates of return are determined in the market. The rents charged by the owner of a motel, a shopping center, an office building, an apartment building, or any income-producing property usually do not vary greatly from those charged by owners of competing properties that offer the same quality of service. If the demand for a particular type of space is great, owners may be able to charge high rents that yield high returns. On the other hand, if demand is limited, rents may stabilize or even decline, which will decrease the rate of return. Therefore, to estimate rates of return and forecast future benefits, appraisers consider the demand for the particular type of property and how this demand affects supply.

Substitution

The prices, rents, and rates of property tend to be set by the prevailing prices, rents, and rates for equally desirable substitute properties. The principle of substitution is market-oriented and provides the basis for crucial tests which an appraiser applies in estimating market value. Although anticipation is the basic premise of value in the income capitalization approach, the principle of substitution may be used to test the validity of the approach and the reliability of the assumptions and data used in its application.

Balance

The principle of balance and all related concepts are especially significant in applying the income capitalization approach. A good balance between the types and locations of income-producing properties creates and sustains value; an imbalance in efficient land use may result in a decline in value. Efficient land use is facilitated by good planning and zoning laws.

The concept of contribution suggests that a reasonable balance among the four agents of production in an income-producing property creates and sustains maximum profitability. If a property is overimproved or underimproved, its rate of profit may be adversely affected.

Externalities

Positive and negative external forces affect the value of income-producing property. Apartments and office buildings are subject to the same types of external forces (e.g., the availability and quality of public transportation and shopping facilities) that affect single-family residences. Similarly, commercial establishments are enhanced by attractive, spacious, accessible surroundings and damaged by unattractive, poorly maintained, dirty surroundings. The negative externalities imposed by high crime rates have affected all types of income-producing property in recent years. External conditions such as pollution, unattractive surroundings, and high crime rates can even affect factories housing heavy industry.

INTERESTS TO BE VALUED

The rights of ownership in income-producing real estate are seldom held in fee simple by individual owners. An investor may hold title to real property rights as an individual, a corporate shareholder, or a general or limited partner. In addition, the interest in the real estate is often subject to mortgage financing, which further divides the real property rights into debt and equity interests. Finally, income-producing real estate is usually leased, which creates legal estates of the lessor's interest (i.e., the leased fee) and the lessee's interest (i.e., the leasehold).

As the flowchart in Figure 18.1 illustrates, the appraiser follows a logical sequence to identify the real property rights being appraised. The three main components of real property rights are ownership entities, financial interests, and legal estates. In a typical market value appraisal, the appraiser values an ownership entity's financial interest in a legal estate. The proper identification of all three categories of rights pinpoints the specific real property rights to be appraised.

Market valuation assignments relating to income-producing real estate often concern 100% ownerships of equity interests in a leased fee estate. A 100% ownership includes all shareholders or partners in a real estate venture. A typical example is the valuation of an existing multitenant office building for a prospective buyer. The real

Figure 18.1   Components of Real Property Rights

```
┌─────────────────────────────────────────────────────────────┐
│                     Ownership Entity                        │
└─────────────────────────────────────────────────────────────┘

┌──────────────────┐   ┌──────────────────┐   ┌──────────────────┐
│                  │   │    Corporate     │   │   Partnership    │
│    Individual    │   │   Shareholders   │   │    Interests     │
└──────────────────┘   └──────────────────┘   └──────────────────┘

┌─────────────────────────────────────────────────────────────┐
│                     Financial Interest                      │
└─────────────────────────────────────────────────────────────┘

          ┌──────────────────┐   ┌──────────────────┐
          │                  │   │       Debt       │
          │      Equity      │   │    (Mortgage)    │
          └──────────────────┘   └──────────────────┘

┌─────────────────────────────────────────────────────────────┐
│                       Legal Estate                          │
└─────────────────────────────────────────────────────────────┘

                   ┌──────────────────┐
                   │    Fee Simple    │
                   └──────────────────┘

          ┌──────────────────┐   ┌──────────────────┐
          │     Leased       │   │                  │
          │      Fee         │   │    Leasehold     │
          └──────────────────┘   └──────────────────┘
```

property rights to be valued may be free and clear of mortgage debt or they may be subject to specified financing terms. The scope of the assignment may require a value estimate of the equity interest alone or it may call for a total value including the mortgage. In the latter case, the final conclusion may be reported in cash, in terms equivalent to cash, or in other precisely revealed terms depending on the nature of the assignment and applicable professional standards.

Appraisers do not only value fee simple, leased fee, and leasehold estates. They are often called on to value real property rights complicated by other factors. For example, appraisers may value

- Minority shareholder or partnership interests
- Equity interests subject to various layers of debt, some of which may contribute to pre-tax cash flow and reversion
- Participation mortgages for lenders
- Master leasehold, sandwich leasehold, or subleasehold estates

Real property rights may be further affected by specific requirements of the client, who may ask an appraiser to value a property subject to anticipated rezoning, planned renovation or rehabilitation, the completion of construction, or management agreements (e.g., on hotels). It is essential that the client and the appraiser begin with a clear understanding of the fundamentals of the appraisal assignment—i.e., the valuation of specified real property rights as of a specific date expressed in clearly defined terms.

MARKET VALUE AND INVESTMENT VALUE

The income capitalization approach is typically used in market value appraisals of income-producing property. The approach may also be used to estimate investment value, which is the value of a property to a particular investor. Market value and investment value may coincide if the client's investment criteria are typical of investors in the market. In this case, the two value estimates may be the same number, but the two types of value are *not* interchangeable. Market value is objective, impersonal, and detached; investment value is based on subjective, personal parameters. To estimate market value with the income capitalization approach, the appraiser must be certain that all data and assumptions used are market-oriented.

In this text, the income capitalization approach is applied to estimate the market value of a fee simple or leased fee interest. The conclusions reached reflect the use and analysis of market data, and they should be consistent with the value indications reached with the other valuation approaches.

FUTURE BENEFITS

The benefits of owning specific rights in income-producing real estate include the right to receive all profits accruing to the real property during the holding period (i.e., the term of ownership) plus the proceeds from resale on reversion of the property at the termination of the investment. Various measures of future benefits are considered in the income capitalization approach. Commonly used measures include potential gross income, effective gross income, net operating income, pre-tax cash flow, and reversionary benefits.

Potential gross income (PGI) *is the total potential income attributable to the real property at full occupancy before operating expenses are deducted.* Potential gross income may refer to the level of rental income prevailing on the date of the appraisal or expected during the first full month or year of operation, or to the periodic income anticipated during a holding period.

Effective gross income (EGI) *is the anticipated income from all operations of the real property adjusted for vacancy and collection losses.* This adjustment includes losses incurred due to nonoccupancy, turnover, and nonpayment of rent by tenants.

Net operating income (NOI) *is the actual or anticipated net income remaining after all operating expenses are deducted from effective gross income, but before mortgage debt service and book depreciation are deducted.* Net operating income is customarily expressed as an annual amount. In certain income capitalization applications, a single year's net operating income may represent a steady stream of fixed income that is expected to continue for a number of years. In other applications, the income may represent the starting level for a stream of income that is expected to change in a prescribed pattern over the years. Still other applications may require that net operating income be measured for each year of the analysis.

Pre-tax cash flow is the portion of net operating income that remains after debt service is paid, but before ordinary income tax on operations is deducted. Like net operating income, a single year's pre-tax cash flow may represent a steady stream of fixed income, the starting level of a changing income stream, or the equity income for a particular year of the analysis. Pre-tax cash flow is also referred to as *equity dividend*.

After-tax cash flow is the portion of pre-tax cash flow that remains after ordinary income tax on operations has been deducted.

Reversion is a lump-sum benefit that an investor receives at the termination of an investment. The benefits may be calculated before or after taxes depending on the specific real property right being valued. For example, reversionary benefits for a fee simple estate are the expected proceeds from resale at the end of the investment holding period. Depending on the method adopted, this may be gross proceeds or some form of net proceeds; in either case, the type of proceeds must be identified and explained. For a mortgagee or lender, reversion consists of the balance of the mortgage when it is paid off. Reversionary benefits are measured either as an anticipated dollar amount or as a relative change in value over the presumed holding period. Reversionary benefits may or may not require separate measurement, depending on the purpose of the analysis and the method of capitalization employed.

RATES OF RETURN

In applying the income capitalization approach, an appraiser assumes that the investor's objective is a total, eventual return that exceeds the amount invested. Therefore, the investor's expected return consists of 1) full recovery of the amount invested (i.e., the return *of* capital), and 2) a profit or reward (i.e., a return *on* capital). Many rates, or measures of return, can be used in capitalization. Commonly used rates include the overall capitalization rate, equity capitalization rate, interest rate, discount rate, internal rate of return, and equity yield rate.

All rates of return can be categorized as either *income rates* (also referred to as *cash flow rates*) or *yield rates*. The overall capitalization rate and equity capitalization rate are income rates. The interest rate, discount rate, internal rate of return, and equity yield rate are yield rates.

Under certain conditions, the yield rate for a particular property may be numerically equivalent to the corresponding income rate; nevertheless, the rates are not conceptually the same nor are they interchangeable. An income rate is the ratio of one year's income, or an annual average of several years' income, to value; a yield rate is applied to a series of individual incomes to obtain the present value of each.

In the income capitalization approach, both income rates and yield rates can be derived for, and applied to, any component of real property rights or the underlying physical real estate. For example, an appraiser may analyze total property income in terms of income to the land and income to the building or in terms of income to the mortgage and equity interests in the property. Similarly, an appraiser may seek the total investment yield or may analyze the separate yields to the land and the building or to the mortgage and the equity interests. Finally, an appraiser may want to know the value of the unencumbered fee simple, the leased fee or the leasehold interest. (Practical examples of these applications and the relevant symbols, formulas, and procedures are presented in Chapters 19 through 21.)

Income Rates

A capitalization rate is any rate used to convert income into value. The rate reflects the relationship between one year's income or an annual average of several years' income and the corresponding capital value.

An overall capitalization rate (R_O) *is an income rate for a total property that reflects the relationship between a single year's net operating income expectancy or an annual average of several years' income expectancies and total price or value; it is used to convert net operating income into an indication of overall property value.* An overall capitalization rate is not a rate of return on capital or a full measure of investment performance. It may be more than, less than, or equal to the eventual equity yield on the capital invested, depending on future changes in income and value.

An equity capitalization rate (R_E) *is an income rate that reflects the relationship between a single year's pre-tax cash flow expectancy or an annual average of several years' pre-tax cash flow expectancies and the equity investment.* When used to capitalize the subject property's pre-tax cash flow into value, the equity capitalization rate is often referred to in the real estate market as the *cash on cash rate, cash flow rate,* or *equity dividend rate.* Like the overall capitalization rate, the equity capitalization rate is not a rate of return on capital; it may be more than, less than, or equal to the eventual equity yield rate, depending on future changes in income and value.

Yield Rates

An interest rate is a rate of return on capital; it is usually expressed as an annual percentage of the amount loaned or invested. An interest rate does not provide for the recovery or payment *of* capital. The term *interest rate* usually refers to debt capital, not equity capital.

A discount rate is a rate of return on capital used to convert future payments or receipts into present value. A mathematical correspondence or relationship exists between the discount rate used in a particular analysis and the interest rate, the internal rate of return, or the equity yield rate used.

An internal rate of return (IRR) *is an annualized rate of return on capital that is generated or capable of being generated within an investment or portfolio over the period of ownership.* Like an interest rate, an internal rate of return is usually expressed as an annual percentage of the amount invested. The internal rate of return for an investment may also be defined as a yield rate that is used to discount the future benefits of the investment to present value. The internal rate of return applies to all expected benefits, including the proceeds from resale at the termination of the investment. It can be used to measure the return on any capital investment, before or after income taxes.

An equity yield rate (Y_E) *is a rate of return on equity capital.* It may be distinguished from a rate of return on debt capital, which is usually referred to as an *interest rate.* The equity yield rate is the equity investor's internal rate of return.

Return on and Return of Capital

The notion that an investor is entitled to complete recovery of invested capital plus a payment for the use of capital prevails in the real estate market just as it does in other markets. Capitalization may apply to a rate of return of capital, to a rate of return on capital, or to both. The rate of return of capital is analogous to the rate at which an allowance for the recovery of investment capital is made; the rate of return on capital is analogous to an interest rate.

In direct capitalization, no mathematical distinction is made between the return on capital and the return of capital. Differences in risk levels and capital recovery periods are, of course, considered in selecting the capitalization rate. However, the multipliers and rates used in direct capitalization are not true measures of profitability. Although no explicit distinction is made in direct capitalization, implicit assumptions concerning the return on and return of capital can be analyzed in yield capitalization.

In real estate investments, capital may be recaptured in many ways. (The term *recapture* was coined at a time when property values were only thought to decline. Today appraisers use the term when some income provision must be made to compensate for the loss of invested capital.) Investment capital may be recaptured gradually in equal increments of annual income or it may be recaptured all or in part through resale of the property at the termination of the investment or through refinancing. Capital may also be recaptured in a real or hypothetical amortization program such as the gradual return of capital through an increasing proportion of periodic, level contributions to an interest-bearing sinking fund.

If an investor does not recapture all of the original investment at time of resale, some of the income stream must be used for repayment. In this case, the true rate of return on the investment will be somewhat less than the indicated income rate (i.e., the equity capitalization rate in direct capitalization). The difference between the rate of return on capital and the indicated capitalization rate will be the rate of return of capital. The recapture rate is considered positive. Amortization rates, rate surcharges, and sinking fund factors are types of recapture rates.

If, on the other hand, the investor ultimately recaptures the original investment, there is no need to repay the investor out of regular income and the true rate of return is equal to the indicated income rate, or the equity capitalization rate in direct capitalization. In this case, the recapture rate is zero. If the investor receives more than the original investment at resale, the true rate of return on capital is more than the indicated income rate; in this case, the recapture rate is considered to be negative.

In yield capitalization the distinction between return on and return of capital is always definite and precise. Every technique considers the effects of compound interest (i.e., interest on interest) over a specific period of time for a specified rate of interest. Therefore, the interest rate, or rate of return on capital, serves as a true measure of investment profitability. The rate of return on capital may be described as a discount rate, an equity yield rate, an internal rate of return, or a risk rate depending on the context.

In theory, the total rate of return on capital may be seen as a basic safe rate plus a premium to compensate for risk, the burden of management, and the illiquidity of the capital invested. Frequently, the rate is a combination of these elements with an additional allowance for anticipated inflation. Terms such as *discount rate* and *risk rate* are commonly used to refer to the total rate of return on capital, combining all rewards in a single rate.

As the various capitalization techniques and procedures are explained, one can see that each employs its own scheme or hypothesis to provide for a return on capital, over and above the return of capital.

Rate Selection

Whether it is an income rate or a yield rate, the rate of return used to convert income into property value should represent the annual rate of return necessary to attract investment capital. This rate is influenced by many factors, including the degree of apparent risk, market attitudes toward future inflation, the prospective rates of return for alternative investments, the rates of return earned by comparable properties in the past, the supply and demand of mortgage funds, and the availability of tax shelters. Because the rates of return used in the income capitalization approach represent *prospective* rates, not historical rates, the market's perception of risk and changes in purchasing power are particularly important.

The suitability of a particular rate of return cannot be proven with market evidence, but the rate selected should be consistent with the available data. Rate selection requires appraisal judgment and knowledge about prevailing market attitudes and economic indicators.

Risk

An appraiser must consider the element of risk in applying the income capitalization approach. The anticipation of receiving future benefits creates value, but the possibility of losing future benefits detracts from value. Higher rewards are required in return for accepting higher risk. This belief is fundamental in the real estate market and in the valuation of income-producing properties. It is generally accepted that all investments are predicated on the expectation of receiving a return on capital that represents the time value of money with an appropriate adjustment for perceived risk. The minimum rate of return for invested capital is sometimes referred to as the "safe," or "riskless," rate. Theoretically, the difference between the total rate of return on capital and the safe rate may be considered a premium to compensate the investor for risk, anticipated inflation, the burden of management, and the illiquidity of invested capital.

To a real estate investor, risk is the chance of financial loss and the uncertainty of realizing projected future benefits. Most investors avoid risk; they prefer certainty to uncertainty and expect a reward in return for assuming a risk. An appraiser recognizes investors' tendencies in analyzing market evidence, projecting future benefits, and applying capitalization procedures. The appraiser must be satisfied that the income or yield rate used in capitalization is consistent with market evidence and reflects the level of risk associated with receiving the anticipated benefits.

Inflation and Deflation

The amount of expected inflation or deflation affects the forecast of future benefits and the selection of an appropriate income or yield rate. If inflation, the erosion of the purchasing power of currency, is anticipated, the desired real rate of return (i.e., the rate of return unadjusted for inflation) on invested capital will tend to increase to compensate for lost purchasing power. It is the real rate of return that investors try to protect over time.

In theory, the total desired rate of return on capital includes any expected inflation rate. Therefore, the anticipated yield rate generally varies directly with the expected inflation rate. When discount rates that do not include a specific allowance for inflation are applied, the income streams and reversions calculated are expressed in constant, or uninflated, dollars.

Because the inflation rate and the yield rate tend to fluctuate together, there is no proof that a particular combination of rates provides the best reflection of current market attitudes. Nevertheless, the combination chosen must be consistent with general market expectations and the relationship or difference between the two rates must be plausible and supportable. In market value appraisals, the appraiser's objective is to simulate the expectations of a typical investor, not necessarily to make the most reliable prediction of yield and inflation rates.

Appraisers should be aware of the difference between inflation and appreciation. Inflation is an increase in the volume of money and credit, a rise in the general level of prices, and the consequent erosion of purchasing power. Appreciation results from an excess in demand over supply, which increases property values. Inflation and appreciation have a similar effect on future dollars, but different effects on discount rates. Inflation tends to increase discount rates while appreciation tends to decrease them. Although inflation does not create true value, certain properties are better hedges against inflation than others and the outlook for inflation may affect property value.

An appraiser can account for the effects of inflation in capitalization by expressing future benefits in terms of constant dollars that are adjusted to reflect constant purchasing power and by expressing the discount rate as a real, uninflated rate of return on capital. However, appraisers usually project income and expenses in terms of unadjusted, inflated dollars and express the discount rate as a nominal, or apparent, rate of return on capital that includes an allowance for inflation. It is convenient and customary to project income and expenses in dollars just as they are expected to occur, not to convert the amounts to constant dollar equivalents. Unadjusted discount rates rather than real rates of return are used so that these rates can be compared with other rates quoted in the open market—e.g., mortgage interest rates and bond yield rates. Above all, the appraiser must be consistent and not discount inflated dollars at real, uninflated rates.

INCOME CAPITALIZATION APPROACH METHODS

Two capitalization methods—direct capitalization and yield capitalization—are described below. These methods are based on different measures of expected earnings and include different assumptions concerning the relationship between expected earnings and value.

Direct Capitalization

Direct capitalization is a method used to convert an estimate of a single year's income expectancy, or an annual average of several years' income expectancies, into an indication of value in one direct step—either by dividing the income estimate by an appropriate income rate or by multiplying the income estimate by an appropriate factor. The income expectancy is frequently the anticipated income for the following year. The rate or factor selected represents the relationship between income and value observed in the market and is derived through comparable sales analysis. A property's income, usually annual net operating income or pre-tax cash flow, is divided by its sale or equity price to obtain the income rate. A factor or multiplier can be derived by dividing a property's sale price by its annual potential or effective gross income.

Direct capitalization is market-oriented; an appraiser analyzes market evidence and values property by inferring the assumptions of typical investors. Direct capitalization does not explicitly differentiate between the return on and return of capital because investor assumptions are not specified. However, it is implied that the selected multiplier or rate will satisfy a typical investor and that the prospects for future monetary benefits, over and above the amount originally invested, are sufficiently attractive.

Direct capitalization may be applied to potential gross income, effective gross income, net operating income, or pre-tax cash flow (i.e., equity dividend). The income selected for capitalization is determined by the purpose of the analysis and the data available.

Yield Capitalization

Yield capitalization is a method used to convert future benefits to present value by discounting each future benefit at an appropriate yield rate or by developing an overall rate that explicitly reflects the investment's income pattern, value change, and yield rate. Like direct capitalization, yield capitalization should be market-derived. The method is profit- or yield-oriented, simulating typical investor assumptions with formulas that calculate the present value of expected benefits assuming specified profit or yield requirements.

The procedure used to convert periodic income and reversion into present value is called *discounting;* the required yield rate of return is called the *discount rate.* The discounting procedure presumes that the investor will receive a satisfactory return on the investment and complete recovery of the capital invested. Yield capitalization is sometimes referred to as *annuity capitalization,* but because a particular level of profit or *yield* is required, *yield capitalization* is the preferred term.

The term *annuity* literally means an annual income, but it has come to mean a program of regular payments of specified amounts. Payments may be made more frequently, but the time interval between payments must be regular. An annuity can be level, increasing, or decreasing so long as the amounts are scheduled or can be forecast. Income that has the characteristics of an annuity is expected at regular intervals in specified amounts, so real estate income or rent may obviously be considered an annuity.

Appraisers distinguish between contract rent and market rent in analyzing annuity income, particularly if the market rent is considered speculative and could fluctuate. In contemporary usage, yield capitalization is not restricted to contract rent, although the appraiser must recognize that market rent may increase or decrease. The expected earnings of a property may be expressed as a stable income stream, an income stream that changes according to a prescribed pattern, an irregular income stream that changes in no particular pattern, one or more lump-sum payments, or any combination of these.

A number of analytical techniques and procedures can be used to value an entire property, specific property benefits, or partial interests in property. Present value can be calculated with or without considering the impact of financing and income taxes as long as the specific rights being appraised are clearly identified. The techniques and procedures selected are determined by the purpose of the analysis, the availability of data, and common practice in the marketplace.

Because yield capitalization always involves the analysis and discounting of incomes, the term *discounted cash flow (DCF) analysis* may be applied to any yield capitalization technique. Commonly, however, DCF analysis refers to a set of procedures in which an appraiser specifies the quantity, variability, timing, and duration of periodic incomes and the quantity and timing of reversions, discounting each to its present value at a specified yield rate. Because modern calculator and computer technology have removed the drudgery of repetitive calculations, DCF analysis is a practical appraisal tool. The various discouting procedures applied in contemporary DCF analysis are discussed in Chapters 21 and 22.

Direct Capitalization, Yield Capitalization, and Discounting

Direct capitalization is simple and easily understood. The capitalization rate or factor is derived directly from the market and no distinction is made between return on and return of capital. Direct capitalization does not explain value in terms of specific investor assumptions.

Yield capitalization, on the other hand, tends to be complex, requiring the use of special tables, calculators, or computer programs. To select a market-oriented discount rate, market attitudes and expectations must be interpreted. In yield capitalization, specific investment goals for the return on and of invested capital are considered and simulated with formulas and numerical multipliers or factors that reflect investment expectations. These formulas and factors are used to convert various income streams and reversions into present value by applying the investor's anticipated yield rate in the discounting procedure. Formulas and factors can be obtained from financial tables or calculated and used with hand-held financial calculators or programmable computers.

The income capitalization approach need not be limited to a single capitalization method. With adequate information and proper use, direct and yield capitalization methods should produce similar value indications. Both methods are market-derived and, therefore, should reflect a typical investor's view of market value.

Residual Techniques

Residual techniques are employed in the income capitalization approach so that physical value components (e.g., land and building), financial value components (e.g., mortgage and equity), or legal estates (e.g., leased fees and leaseholds) can be considered separately. Residual techniques presume that the value of a component or portion of the property is known or can be estimated. The income attributable to this component is then deducted from total property income to reveal the residual income, which is capitalized to ascertain the value of the unknown portion of the property. Residual techniques can be used in both direct and yield capitalization.

HISTORY OF THE APPROACH

To understand the development of the various methods, techniques, and procedures used in the income capitalization approach, it may be helpful to examine its history. The following discussion is divided into two time periods: the early years, when the theoretical bases for direct and yield capitalization were established, and the modern era, when specific techniques and procedures were developed and refined.[1]

Early Writings

The mathematical foundation for discounting can be traced to John Newton, who was among the first to provide a theory of compound interest, and Edmund Halley, the noted astronomer who published the first present value tables in 1693. John Smart is credited with providing the first comprehensive set of tables and the first partial payment table in 1726. His book, *Tables of Interest and Annuities*, included tables identical to the present value and compound interest tables found in modern appraisal texts.

In 1811 William Inwood published tables that had originally appeared in the works of others, such as John Smart. Of particular significance to appraisers, Inwood used real estate valuation examples to illustrate the use of Smart's tables. Inwood's examples postulated that the present value of an annuity was based on a single discount rate. Inwood's book also contained a table for calculating the present value of an income in perpetuity, which seems to mark the first time an author converted an interest rate into a coefficient. Inwood multiplied the coefficient by the investment's annual income, which was assumed to be perpetual, to calculate the current value of the investment. The Inwood premise has been used by real estate appraisers ever since.

In 1890 Alfred Marshall became the first economist to address valuation techniques specifically. He identified the interest rate as the link between income and value and offered the formula

$$\text{Value} = \frac{\text{Income}}{\text{Interest rate}}$$

With variations, this is the basic formula used in direct capitalization. In the early 1900s Irving Fisher contributed to capitalization theory by analyzing the proposition that value is the present worth of future benefits. This concept is fundamental to modern appraisal theory and is recognized directly in discounted cash flow analysis. Thus, by the early 1900s, the mathematical and conceptual foundations of

---

1. See James H. Burton, *The Evolution of the Income Approach* (Chicago: American Institute of Real Estate Appraisers, 1982).

direct and yield capitalization were established. In the years that followed, these concepts were applied in a manner consistent with prevailing investor attitudes and behavior.

Modern Era

Pre-1959

Two characteristics distinguish the application of the income capitalization approach before 1959 from the periods that followed. First, prior to 1959, property was usually valued by dividing it into its land and improvement components. During this period, the land and building residual techniques dominated appraisal practice. Their use reflected investors' concern with the physical components of property and the need to recapture the cost of depreciating improvements.

Second, before 1959 property value was estimated without considering financing. An "all cash" market value transaction was assumed without recognizing that a purchaser might use borrowed funds. Although band-of-investment techniques were available to synthesize an overall capitalization rate from the required returns of debt and equity investors, capitalization was dominated by physical residual techniques.

Real estate investors at this time were concerned with the productive economic life of the improvements, not with investment attributes such as financing. Prices were relatively stable and the effects of physical deterioration were not obscured by inflation. Capital gains were not seen as a significant source of equity return. Loan-to-value ratios and interest rates were relatively low, and creative financing, variable interest rates, and lender participation were not common. Because real estate financing was predictably regular, its effect on value was of little concern.

1959 to Mid-1970s

The year 1959 is especially significant to the income capitalization approach and serves as a transitional point in appraisal history. With the publication of *The Ellwood Tables*, L. W. Ellwood signaled the shift from reliance on physical residual techniques to techniques based on debt and equity components of real estate investment.

Ellwood's contribution to the income capitalization approach was monumental because his system allowed for the capitalization of a stream of cash flows and provided a basis for analyzing specific investment assumptions in the valuation process. Ellwood popularized the notion that financing affects value and included financing in his formula. He recognized that the property appreciation or depreciation reflected in the proceeds of resale or reversion was a potentially important benefit of real property investment. Ellwood's formula explicitly considered reversion and the effects of mortgage amortization. Ellwood also recognized that a finite, relatively short holding period was the proper framework for analysis and valuation.

He simplified the discounting procedure by publishing tables of precalculated rates that could be combined into a recognizable overall capitalization rate. These tables were particularly useful before electronic calculators became available.

In the 1960s, many appraisers began to use investment component, or band-of-investment, techniques to synthesize overall capitalization rates. (For further discussion of band-of-investment techniques, see Chapter 20.) Soon, the use of a band-of-investment technique that employed the loan constant and the equity capitalization rate as the appropriate returns to the lender and the equity investor became widespread. This technique, which is similar to one introduced by S. Edwin Kazdin in 1944, has been especially significant in the income capitalization approach during the past two decades.

Band-of-investment and Ellwood techniques came to dominate the income capitalization approach for several reasons. First, stable income streams became less common because inflation and real increases in property values began to overtake the effects of physical depreciation. Thus, capital gains became more significant. Second, investors were becoming increasingly sophisticated. They began to think in terms of tax shelters, leveraging, and shorter holding periods rather than the economic lives of properties, recapture rates, and long-term investments. During this period, major appraisal organizations first recognized the effect of financing in their definitions of market value.

Mid-1970s to the Present

Since the mid-1970s, capitalization theory and practice have been influenced by inflation and recurring national recessions. Recent developments in the real estate market include

- Marketing of partial interests, such as limited partnerships and joint ventures
- Rapid increases in market rent levels
- Use of complex participation mortgages, creative financing, and seller financing
- High mortgage interest rates, which have at times resulted in a preponderance of all-cash transactions
- More foreign investment in U.S. real estate
- Cycles of overbuilding, underbuilding, excess demand, and lack of sufficient demand.

In recent years, appraisers have focused on market participants' reactions to the dynamics of the market and relied on capitalization methods, techniques, and procedures to simulate investor decision making.

The methods that are most useful today include direct capitalization based on equity capitalization rates derived from comparable sales and yield capitalization that employs DCF analysis. In many circumstances, these methods best reflect the behavior of market participants. Computer-assisted analysis has also had a major effect on investment analysis and valuation. Computers process data quickly and can be used for statistical analysis, DCF analysis, business accounting, and the storage of comparable sales data.

Appraisers do not always agree on which income valuation techniques are appropriate. There is ongoing debate on the relevance of traditional capitalization techniques and the validity of DCF analysis. However, market participants use both traditional techniques and DCF analysis, so both are valid and relevant tools for the real property appraiser.

SUMMARY

From an investor's perspective, the earning power of a real estate investment is the critical element affecting its value. The fundamental investment premise is the higher the earnings, the higher the value. Investment in an income-producing property represents the exchange of present dollars for the right to receive future dollars.

In the income capitalization approach to value, an appraiser analyzes a property's capacity to generate benefits and converts these benefits into an indication of present value. The income capitalization approach is an integral part of the valuation process. Income capitalization techniques and procedures are employed to analyze and adjust sales data in the sales comparison approach and to measure functional and external obsolescence by capitalizing an estimated income loss in the cost approach.

The three main components of real property rights are ownership entities, financial interests, and legal estates. A market value appraisal of income-producing property most often involves 100% ownership of equity interests (either free of debt or subject to specified financing) in a leased fee estate.

Appraisers may be called on to value complex property rights such as minority shareholder or partnership interests; equity interests subject to various layers of debt; participation mortgages; and master leasehold, sandwich leasehold, and sub-leasehold estates. Property rights may also be valued subject to client requirements involving anticipated rezoning and rehabilitation, project completion, or management agreements.

The income capitalization approach is typically applied to derive an indication of market value, but it can also be employed to estimate investment value, which is the value of a property to a particular investor. Although the criteria of the investor and the market may coincide and the numerical estimates may be equivalent, market value and investment value are *not* interchangeable.

In the income capitalization approach, future benefits are commonly measured as *potential gross income* (*PGI*), the total potential income attributable to the real property at full occupancy before operating expenses are deducted; *effective gross income* (*EGI*), the anticipated income from all real property operations adjusted for vacancy and collection losses; *net operating income* (*NOI*), the actual or anticipated net income remaining after all operating expenses are deducted from effective gross income, but before mortgage debt service and book depreciation are deducted; *pre-tax cash flow*, the portion of net operating income that remains after debt service is paid, but before ordinary income tax on operations is deducted; *after-tax cash flow*, the portion of pre-tax cash flow that remains after ordinary income tax on operations is deducted; and *reversion*, the lump-sum benefit that an investor receives at the termination of an investment.

An investor's total expected return includes full recovery of the amount invested, the *return of capital*, and a profit, the *return on capital*. Rates of return can be categorized as either *income rates* or *yield rates*. An income rate is the ratio of one year's income or an annual average of several years' income to value. It may be used as a capitalization rate to convert income into value. A yield rate is applied to a series of individual incomes to obtain the present value of each. Both income and yield rates can be used to analyze components of real property rights and the physical real estate by applying residual techniques in the capitalization procedure.

Overall capitalization and equity capitalization rates are income rates. They are not rates of return on capital and do not reflect the eventual equity yield rate. *An overall capitalization rate* (R_O) is an income rate for a total property that reflects the relationship between annual net income expectancy and total property value; it is used to convert net operating income into an indication of overall property value. An *equity capitalization rate* (R_E) is an income rate that reflects the relationship between annual pre-tax cash flow expectancy and the equity investment. It is also referred to as a *cash on cash rate, cash flow rate*, and *equity dividend rate*.

Interest rates, discount rates, internal rates of return, and equity yield rates are all yield rates. An *interest rate* is a rate of return on capital, usually expressed as an annual percentage of the amount loaned or invested. A *discount rate* is a rate of return on capital used to convert future payments into present value.

An *internal rate of return* (*IRR*) is an annualized rate of return on capital that is generated or capable of being generated within an investment (including both debt and equity capital) over the period of ownership. The *IRR* is typically expressed as an annual percentage of the amount invested and used to discount the future benefits of the cumulative invested capital to present value. An *equity yield rate* (Y_E) is the rate of return on equity capital, as distinguished from the rate of return on debt capital.

Capitalization may apply to one or both rates of return—the rate of return of the capital recovered or recaptured and the rate of return on capital, the interest rate. Capital may be recaptured through equal increments of an annual income, resale of the property, refinancing, or an amortization program involving periodic contributions to a sinking fund. *Direct capitalization*, which converts an estimate of a single year's income expectancy into an indication of value directly by dividing the income estimate by an appropriate rate or multiplying it by an appropriate factor, makes no distinction between the return on and the return of capital. The multipliers or factors used are not true measures of investment profitability, and they do not explain value in terms of specific investor assumptions.

Yield capitalization, which converts future benefits into present value by discounting each future benefit at an appropriate yield rate or by developing an overall rate that explicitly reflects the investment's income pattern, value change, and yield rate, analyzes the return of and the return on capital. Each yield capitalization technique considers the effects of compound interest at a specified rate over a specific period. The interest rate, the rate of return on capital, is a true measure of investment profitability. Because risk is one of the elements that the return on capital compensates, the term *risk rate* is commonly used to refer to the total return on capital.

The capitalization rate selected for valuation may be an income rate or a yield rate, but it should represent the annual rate of return necessary to attract investment capital. Because rates of return are prospective, market perceptions of risk and changes in purchasing power due to inflation or deflation are important considerations. The capitalization rates chosen should simulate market expectations.

All investments are predicated on the expectation of receiving a return on capital that represents the time value of money plus an appropriate adjustment for risk. Risk reflects the chance of financial loss and the uncertainty of realizing future benefits. Investors expect a reward for assuming risk. The rate of return on capital thus combines a safe "riskless" rate with a premium to compensate the investor for risk, anticipated inflation, the burden of management, and the illiquidity of invested capital.

Inflation erodes purchasing power and jeopardizes the rate of return that an investor anticipates. Appraisers usually project income and expenses in terms of inflated, unadjusted dollars and express the discount rate as a nominal, apparent rate of return on capital that includes an allowance for inflation. When discount rates are applied without an allowance for inflation, the income streams and reversions calculated are expressed in constant, uninflated dollars. Appraisers should discount consistently, using inflated, unadjusted dollars at inflated, unadjusted rates, or constant, adjusted dollars at real, adjusted rates.

Appreciation results from an excess of demand over supply and increases property values. Inflation and appreciation have a similar effect on future dollars, but different effects on discount rates.

Discounting is the procedure used to convert periodic income and reversion into present value; the required rate of return applied in this procedure is called the *discount rate*. The procedure presumes that the investor will receive a satisfactory return on the investment plus complete recovery of the capital invested.

Yield capitalization is sometimes referred to as *annuity capitalization* because real estate income or rent has many of the characteristics of an *annuity*. An annuity is literally an annual income, but the term is used to refer to any program of regular payments of level, increasing, or decreasing amounts. *Yield capitalization* is the preferred term because it acknowledges that a particular level of profit or yield is required.

Appraisers should distinguish between contract rent and market rent, which can fluctuate. The expected earnings analyzed in yield capitalization may be one or more lump-sum payments, a stable income stream, an income stream that changes according to a prescribed pattern, or an income stream that changes in no particular pattern.

Discounted cash flow (DCF) analysis describes any yield capitalization technique, but it usually refers to a set of procedures in which an appraiser specifies the quantity, variability, timing, and duration of periodic incomes and the quantity and timing of reversions, discounting each to its present value at a specified yield rate. Yield capitalization lends itself to DCF analysis because investment goals are specified and simulated with formulas and mathematical multipliers or factors. Direct capitalization, however, is still applicable in many situations. With adequate data and proper use, direct and yield capitalization should provide similar value indications.

Since the mid-1970s, the income capitalization approach has been influenced by macroeconomic conditions and specific developments within the real estate market. Current valuation methods draw on equity capitalization using rates derived from comparable sales and yield capitalization with computer-assisted DCF analysis.

19 Income Estimates

To apply any capitalization procedure, a reliable estimate of income expectancy must be developed. Although some capitalization procedures are based on the actual level of income at the time of the appraisal rather than a projection of future income, an appraiser must still consider the future outlook. Failure to consider future income would contradict the principle of anticipation, which holds that value is the present worth of future benefits. Historical income is significant, so is current income, but the ultimate concern is the future. The earning history of a property is important only insofar as it is accepted by buyers as an indication of the future. Current income is a good starting point, but the direction of income and the expected rate of change are critical to the capitalization process.

Four types of income can be converted into value in the income capitalization approach: potential gross income (*PGI*), effective gross income (*EGI*), net operating income (*NOI*), and pre-tax cash flow. Reliable projections of income are important because large valuation differences can result when the same rate or factor is used to convert different income estimates into value. If, for example, a potential gross income multiplier of 6.0 is applied to potential gross income estimates of $50,000 and $55,000, values of $300,000 and $330,000 result. A $5,000 difference in potential gross income produces a $30,000 difference in value. Similarly, when an overall capitalization rate of 10.0% is applied to net operating income estimates of $35,000 and $40,000, values of $350,000 and $400,000 result. In this example a $5,000 difference in net operating income results in a value difference of $50,000. Thus, income forecasting is a sensitive and crucial part of income capitalization.

An appraiser may estimate income for a single year or series of years depending on the data available and the capitalization method employed. The analysis can be based on the actual level of income at the time of the appraisal, a forecast of income for the first year of investment, a forecast of income over a specified holding period, or a stabilized, average annual income over a specific holding period. If a market value estimate is sought, the income forecast should reflect the expectations of market participants. In an assignment to estimate investment value, an appraiser may base the income forecasts on the specific ownership or management requirements of the investor.

If an investment in a partial interest—e.g., an equity interest in a fee simple or leased fee estate—is being valued, pre-tax cash flow is usually capitalized. Therefore, the appraiser must deduct mortgage debt service from net operating income to calculate pre-tax cash flow. In some cases, debt service is based on an existing mortgage and the amount is specified; in other cases, debt service must be estimated based on typical mortgage terms indicated by current market activity.

LEASE ANALYSIS

The income to various lease interests is generally derived through the conveyance and operation of leases. *A lease is a written document in which the rights to use and occupy land or structures are transferred by the owner to another for a specified period of time in return for a specified rent.* An appraiser begins to develop an income and expense forecast for investment real estate by studying all existing and proposed leases that apply to the subject property. These leases provide information on rent and other income and on the division of expenses between the landlord and the tenant.

If leases exist and the income estimate is based on the continuation of lease income, the appraiser examines lease provisions that could affect the quantity, quality, and durability of property income. The appraiser must either read the leases or rely on the client or another authorized party to disclose all pertinent lease provisions. The appraiser also analyzes the leases of competitive properties to estimate contract rent, market rent, and other forms of income. Because lease analysis is important, the characteristics of leases must be fully understood.

Lease Types

Although a lease can be drawn to fit any situation, most leases fall into one of several broad classifications: flat rental, graduated rental, revaluation, index, and percentage. Within these classifications, a lease may be applied on a *gross rental basis*, with the lessor paying all the operating expenses of the real estate, or a *net rental basis*, with the tenant paying all these expenses. Lease terms frequently fall between these extremes, with a specified division of expenses between the lessor and the lessee.

Leases can also be categorized by their terms of occupancy—e.g., month-to-month, short-term (of five years or less), or long-term (of more than five years).

Flat Rental

A flat rental lease specifies a level of rent that continues throughout the duration of the lease. In a stable economy, this type of lease is typical and acceptable. In a changing economy, however, leases that are more responsive to fluctuating market conditions are preferred. When flat rental leases are used in inflationary periods, they tend to be short-term.

Graduated Rental

Graduated rental leases provide for specified changes in the amount of rent at one or more points during the lease term. A step-up lease, which allows for smaller rent payments in the early years, can be advantageous to a tenant establishing a business in a new location. This type of lease can also be used to recognize tenant expenditures on a property that are effectively amortized during the early years of the lease. Long-term ground leases may include provisions for increasing rent to reflect the expectation of future increases in property value and protect the purchasing power of the landlord's investment. Because property value is usually expected to increase, tenants are expected to pay commensurately increasing rents.

Step-down leases are less common than step-up leases and are generally used to reflect unusual circumstances particular to a property such as the likelihood of reduced tenant appeal in the future or the recognition of capital recapture of interior improvements during the early years of a long-term lease.

Revaluation

Revaluation leases provide for periodic rent adjustments based on revaluation of the real estate under prevailing market conditions. Although revaluation leases tend to be long-term, some are short-term with renewal option rents based on revaluation of the real estate when the option is exercised. When the parties to a lease cannot agree on the revaluation, appraisal revaluation or arbitration may be stipulated in the terms of the lease.

Index

Index leases are generally long-term leases that provide for periodic rent adjustment based on the change in a specific index such as a nationally published, cost of living index.

Percentage

In percentage leases, some or all of the rent is based on a specified percentage of the volume of business, productivity, or use achieved by the tenant. Percentage leases may be short- or long-term and are most frequently used for retail properties. A straight percentage lease may have no minimum rent, but most specify a guaranteed minimum rent with the percentage, or graduated percentage, rent payable on sales that exceed a specified level.

Lease Data

The data contained in a typical lease include

- Date of the lease
- Reference information, if lease is recorded
- Legal description or other identification of the leased premises
- Name of lessor—i.e., owner or landlord
- Name of lessee—i.e., tenant
- Lease term
- Occupancy date
- Commencement date for rent payment
- Rent amount, including any percentage clause, graduation, escalation provisions, and payment terms
- Rent concessions, including any discounts or benefits
- Landlord's covenants—i.e., items such as taxes, insurance, and maintenance for which the owner or landlord is responsible
- Tenant's covenants—i.e., items such as taxes, insurance, maintenance, utilities, and cleaning expenses for which the tenant is responsible
- Right of assignment or right to sublet, i.e., whether the leasehold, or tenant's interest, may be assigned or sublet under what conditions, and whether assignment relieves initial tenant of future liability
- Option to renew, including date of required notice, term of renewal, rent, and other renewal provisions
- Options to purchase
- Escape clauses
- Security deposits, including advance rent, bond or expenditures by tenant for leasehold improvements, etc.
- Casualty loss—i.e., whether lease continues after a fire or other disaster and on what basis
- Lessee's improvements, including whether they can be removed when lease expires and to whom they belong
- Condemnation, including the respective rights of the lessor and lessee if all or any part of property is appropriated by a public agency
- Revaluation clauses
- Special provisions

A sample form for analyzing a typical office lease is shown in Figure 19.1. Special attention should be paid to lease data on rent, rent concessions, the division of expenses, renewal options, escalation clauses, purchase options, escape clauses, and tenant improvements.

Figure 19.1   Office Space Rental Worksheet

Building: _____

_____

Lessor: _____

Lessee: _____

Premises: Floor _____ Rentable area _____ Usable area _____ Loss factor _____

Term: Commencement _____ Expiration _____

Base rent: _____ CPI _____

Graduations: _____

_____

Escalations: _____

    Real estate taxes _____

    Porter wage _____

    Operating expenses _____

    Energy _____

Work letter (cost): _____

Special Provisions (e.g., repainting, etc.): _____

Who pays:	Lessor	Lessee	Stop	Base Amount per Square Foot
Tenant electric	( )	( )	( )	( )
Building electric	( )	( )	( )	( )
Tenant HVAC	( )	( )	( )	( )
Buidling HVAC	( )	( )	( )	( )
Tenant space cleaning	( )	( )	( )	( )
Public space cleaning	( )	( )	( )	( )
Fuel	( )	( )	( )	( )
Repairs and maintenance				
Exterior	( )	( )	( )	( )
Interior	( )	( )	( )	( )
Fire insurance (building)	( )	( )	( )	( )

Renewal options:

How many: _____ Years each _____

New rent: _____

_____

New escalation (and base year): _____

New rentable area or loss factor: _____

New work letter: _____

Occupancy (or status) of building when lease originally signed: _____

_____

Comments: _____

_____

_____

_____

Rent

The quantity of income to be paid by the tenant is basic lease data. An appraiser considers rent from all sources, which may include base, or minimum, contract rent, percentage rent, and escalation rent. The source of rental income should be clearly identified.

Rent Concessions

In some instances, when real estate markets are oversupplied, landlords give tenants concessions such as free rent for a specified period of time or extra tenant improvements. In shopping center leases, retail store tenants are sometimes given rent credit for interior store improvements. All rent concessions result from market conditions and the relative negotiating strengths of the landlord and the tenant.

Lessor/Lessee Division of Expenses

Most leases outline the obligations of the lessor and the lessee to pay for taxes, utilities, heat, repairs, and other expenses required to maintain and operate the leased property. An appraiser should identify the division of expenses in each lease analyzed and compare rents or estimated rental value to a known lease for comparable space.

Renewal Options

Renewal options that allow a tenant to extend the lease term for one or more prescribed periods of time are frequently included in short- and long-term leases. A typical renewal option requires that the tenant provide advance notice of the intention to exercise the option and identifies the length of the renewal period or periods as well as the rent or method of determining the rent to be paid. The option rent may be set at the original rent or at a level determined when the lease was negotiated, or it may be calculated with some established procedure or formula when the option is exercised. Renewal options are binding on the lessor, but allow the tenant to reach a decision in light of the circumstances prevailing at the time of renewal. Thus, they are generally considered favorable to the tenant, not the lessor.

Escalation Clauses

Tax- and expense-stop clauses are often added to traditional gross or flat rental leases. Tax-stop clauses provide that any increases in taxes over a specified level be passed on to the tenant.

Expense-stop clauses provide that all increases in operating expenses become obligations of the lessee. In multitenanted properties retail or office buildings, increased expenses are usually prorated among the tenants in proportion to the area occupied or on some other equitable basis. The prorated shares are then added to the tenants' rents and the expenses allocated to vacant space are normally paid by the owner. In certain areas, escalation payments are based on changes in a local wage rate or another index. In New York City, for example, the porter wage escalation formula is used. Each one cent increase in the porter wage rate, the hourly wage paid to office workers who are members of the porters' union, produces a one to one-and-one-half cent increase in expense charges per square foot of space. Some escalation clauses are drawn so broadly that the lease is almost applied on a net rental basis.

Purchase Options

Certain leases may include a clause granting the lessee an option to purchase the leased property. In some cases, this option must be exercised on the lease termination date or at some point or points during the lease term; in other cases, this option may be available at any time. The option price may be fixed or it may change periodically based on an empirical formula or a depreciated book value. A purchase option may only give the lessee the right to purchase the property if an offer to purchase is made by a third party. This provision is referred to as a *right of first refusal.*

In any case, a purchase option restricts marketability and, unless the property is being appraised in fee simple, the option price may represent a limit on the market value of the leased fee estate.

Escape Clauses

An escape clause permits a tenant to cancel a lease under circumstances that would not ordinarily be considered justification for lease cancellation. For example, a condemnation or casualty clause might permit the tenant to cancel the lease if the condemnation or casualty loss creates a serious obstacle to continued operations. A casualty clause may stipulate that the lessor be allowed a reasonable time to make necessary repairs with appropriate abatement of rent during the interim. A landlord might include a demolition clause in a lease to preserve the prospects for sale or redevelopment of the site. This type of escape clause can affect rent levels and market value.

Tenant Improvements

Extensive tenant improvements can influence lease rent. When capital expenditures are made by the lessor, reimbursement may be accomplished through rent increases that amortize the lessor's expenditures over all or part of the lease period. If capital expenditures are made by the tenant, the lessor may lower the tenant's rent below market levels for all or part of the lease term.

RENT ANALYSIS

The income to investment properties consists primarily of rent. Different types of rent affect the quality of the income studied in the income capitalization approach to value. The five types of rent are contract rent, market rent, excess rent, percentage rent, and overage rent.

Contract rent is the actual rental income specified in a lease. It is the rent agreed on by the landlord and the tenant and it may be higher, lower, or the same as market rent.

Market rent is the rental income that a property would most probably command in the open market; it is indicated by the current rents paid and asked for comparable space as of the date of the appraisal. Market rent is sometimes referred to as *economic rent.*

Excess rent is the amount by which contract rent exceeds market rent at the time of the appraisal. Excess rent is created by a lease that is favorable to the lessor and may reflect an advantageous location, unusual management, or a lease negotiated in a stronger rental market. Excess rent can be expected to continue for the remainder of the lease but, due to the higher risk associated with the receipt of excess rent, it is often calculated separately and capitalized at a higher rate.

Percentage rent is rental income received in accordance with the terms of a percentage clause in a lease. Percentage rent is typically derived from retail store tenants on the basis of a certain percentage of their retail sales.

Overage rent is percentage rent paid over and above the guaranteed minimum rent. This type of rent should not be confused with excess rent. Overage rent is a contract rent; it may be market rent, part market and part excess rent, or excess rent only.

To a certain extent, the interest being appraised determines how rents are analyzed and estimated. The valuation of fee simple interests in income-producing real estate is based on the market rent the property is capable of generating. However, to value proposed projects without actual leases, properties leased at market rent, and owner-occupied properties, only market rent estimates are used in the income capitalization approach.

To value a lessor's marketable interest in real estate, the leased fee, the appraiser generally must consider existing contract rent for leased space, which may or may not be at market levels, and market rent for vacant and owner-occupied space. When discounted cash flow analysis is used, future market rent estimates are also required.

Appraisers usually estimate market value in one of two ways. An appraiser can value a fee simple property at the market rent the property is capable of generating and deduct the present value of the rent loss, calculated as market rent less contract rent. To use this technique, the appraiser may extract capitalization rates or factors from comparable sales of fee simple real property interests; however, such sales of multitenant buildings are rare. Therefore, the appraiser may need to analyze a number of property sales subject to leases to find properties that were sold with market rents or with rent structures that can be easily adjusted for market rent equivalency.

Using the second technique, an appraiser values a leased fee property subject to existing contract rent for leased space and market rent for vacant and owner-occupied space. Because most real estate transactions reflect similar income characteristics, market-derived capitalization rates and factors may adequately reflect reasonable value estimates of lessors' marketable interests. If adequate comparable data exist, rent loss analysis is unnecessary.

Rent analysis begins with a study of the subject property's present rent schedule. By examining audits and leases and interviewing selected tenants during property inspection, an appraiser can verify the rent schedule. Further verification may be necessary if the owner's or manager's representation of the schedule is in doubt.

The sum of the scheduled, current rents may be compared with previous totals using operating statements for the past several years. Statements of rents, including the rent paid under percentage leases or escalation clauses, should be examined for all the tenants on the premises. After analyzing the existing rent schedule for the subject property, the appraiser reduces all rents to a unit basis for comparison. All differences in rents within the property are described and explained. Then rental data for comparable space in the market are assembled so that market rents can be adjusted to an equivalent rent basis if necessary and reduced to a unit of comparison.

When a market rent estimate is required, the appraiser gathers, compares, and adjusts market data to form a sound conclusion as to market rent for the subject property. The parties to a lease should be identified to ensure that the party held responsible for rent payments is actually a party to the lease or, by endorsement, the guarantor. It is also important to ascertain that the lease represents a freely negotiated, arm's-length transaction. Leases that do not meet these criteria do not provide reliable indications of the rental terms typical in the market.

The rents of comparable properties can provide a basis for estimating market rent for a subject property once they have been reduced to a unit basis equivalent to the unit applied to the subject property. The appraiser may need to adjust comparable rents just as the transaction prices of comparable properties are adjusted in the sales comparison approach.

The elements of comparison are the legal rights being appraised, conditions of rental (i.e., arm's-length lease terms), market conditions, location, physical characteristics, and the income-producing characteristics stipulated in the lease. An appraiser may also consider the positive effect on value created by vacancies that are likely to be rented at market rates against the negative effect on value of a long-term tenant who has a low rent. Rents for comparable properties are analyzed and adjusted for differences in these elements of comparison to develop a market rent estimate for the subject property.

The amount of data to support a market rent estimate for a subject property depends on the complexity of the appraisal problem, the availability of comparable rentals, and the extent to which the pattern of adjusted rent indications derived from the comparables varies from the income pattern of the subject property.

When sufficient, closely comparable rental data are not available, the appraiser should include data that require adjustment. First, the legal rights and other conditions that affect the rent paid must be analyzed and adjustments must be made. If rentals do not reflect arm's-length negotiations, they might have to be eliminated as comparables. Each rental is then analyzed individually for a possible adjustment for market conditions. Economic conditions change, and leases negotiated in the past may not reflect prevailing rents. After the market adjustment is made, all other adjustment categories are analyzed.

The stability of the location or trends in the market's attitude toward property location might also affect income potential and require adjustment. Then physical differences are analyzed and adjustments are made for these differences. Finally, the appraiser examines income-producing characteristics pertaining to who pays operating expenses and makes adjustments to reflect any differences. If an appraiser uses proper judgment in making adjustments, a reasonably clear pattern of market rents should emerge.

DEVELOPING INCOME ESTIMATES

To determine the earning power of a property, an appraiser must first analyze its net operating income expectancy. The appraiser estimates income and expenses after researching and analyzing 1) the income and expense history of the subject property; 2) income and expense histories of competitive properties; 3) recently signed leases, proposed leases, and asking rents for the subject and competitive properties; 4) actual vacancy levels for the subject and competitive properties; 5) management expenses for the subject and competitive properties; 6) published operating data; 7) market expectations; and 8) tax assessment policies and projected changes in utility rates.

Appraisers often present this information in tabular form to assist the reader of the report. Income and expenses are generally reported in annual or monthly dollar amounts and analyzed in terms of total dollar amounts, dollars and cents per rentable area, or dollar and cents per other unit of comparison. Table 19.1 summarizes a subject property's operating expense history, Table 19.2 presents comparable rental data, and Table 19.3 analyzes the operating expenses of comparable properties.

Table 19.1 Subject Property Operating Expense History (Based on 435,146 rentable square feet)

	1985 Actual		1986 Actual		1987 Actual		1988 Budget	
	Dollars	Per Square Foot	Dollars	Per Square Foot	Dollars	Per Square Foot	Dollars	Per Square Foot
Fixed expenses								
Real estate taxes	$1,689,600	$ 3.88	$1,973,722	$ 4.54	$2,279,860	$ 5.24	$2,347,500	$ 5.39
Insurance	18,948	.04	17,956	.04	46,861	.11	50,000	.11
Variable expenses								
Electricity	$1,453,482	$ 3.34	$1,569,948	$ 3.61	$1,534,296	$ 3.53	$1,800,000	$ 4.14
Steam heat	575,599	1.32	519,203	1.19	525,646	1.21	619,190	1.42
Cleaning	848,260	1.95	797,455	1.83	935,544	2.15	990,000	2.28
Payroll	62,441	.14	73,553	.17	82,350	.19	90,000	.21
Repairs and maintenance	125,417	.29	222,074	.51	283,215	.65	381,996	.88
Water and sewer	19,638	.05	23,444	.05	16,958	.04	33,600	.08
Administrative, legal, and accounting	8,603	.02	13,712	.03	77,397	.18	77,400	.18
Management fees	33,240	.08	36,105	.08	36,643	.08	38,400	.09
Miscellaneous	22,492	.05	511	.001	3,862	.01	3,600	.01
Total operating expenses	$4,857,720	$11.16	$5,247,683	$12.05	$5,822,632	$13.39	$6,431,686	$14.79

Note. Figures have been rounded.

Table 19.2 Actual Rentals of Competitive Office Buildings in Downtown CBD of Major U.S. City

I.D. Number	Location	Tenant	Commencement Date	Rentable Area in Square Feet	Term (in Years)	Rent per Square Foot	Escalation	Work Letter/ Miscellaneous
1	180 Main Street	Law firm	7/1/86	11,600	15	$22.00[a]	Pro rata share of operating expenses and real estate taxes in excess of base year	$20.00 work letter; 4 months free rent; one 5-year renewal option at $5.00 below market rent
		Oil company	8/15/86	15,600	10	23.00 (5 years) 26.50 (5 years)	Pro rata share of operating expenses and real estate taxes in excess of base year	Building standard; 6 months free rent; one 5-year renewal option
		Stock brokerage company	9/1/87	15,600	10	29.00 (5 years) 41.50 (5 years)	Pro rata share of operating expenses and real estate taxes in excess of base year	Building standard; three 5-year renewal options
		Accounting firm	7/1/87	31,200	10	28.00	Pro rata share of operating expenses and real estate taxes in excess of base year	Not available
2	33 Broad Street	Bank	7/1/86	25,000	10	8.00[b] 35.00[c]	Pro rata share of operating expenses and real estate tax increases in excess of a $4.00 base for each	Building standard; 3 months free rent
		Computer services firm	7/1/87	10,000	10	22.00[d] 25.00[e]	Pro rata share of operating expenses and real estate tax increases in excess of a $5.00 base for each	$20.00 work letter
		Stock brokerage firm	7/1/86	10,200	10	26.50	Pro rata share of operating expenses and real estate tax increases in excess of a $4.00 base for each	$22.00 work letter plus $6.00 work letter for computer room; 3 months free rent; one 5-year renewal option

(continued)

Table 19.2 Actual Rentals of Competitive Office Buildings in Downtown CBD of Major U.S. City (continued)

I.D. Number	Location	Tenant	Commencement Date	Rentable Area in Square Feet	Term (in Years)	Rent per Square Foot	Escalation	Work Letter/ Miscellaneous
3	One Exchange Place	Law firm	7/1/87	15,000	10	26.00	Pro rata share of operating expenses and real estate tax increases in excess of a $4.00 base for each	$22.00 work letter
4	101 Front Street	Accounting firm	1/1/87	25,000	3	22.00	Pro rata share of real estate taxes in excess of first full assessment; $.01 per square foot for each $.01 increase in the porter wage	Building standard
5	One Commercial Plaza	Bank	7/1/87	88,823[f]	20	27.10 (5 years) 30.81 (5 years) 35.65 (5 years) 40.93 (5 years)	25.0% of real estate taxes in excess of $2.85 per square foot[g]; 25.0% of operating expenses in excess of $3.42 per square foot	$25.00 work letter

a. For 10 years, then $2.00 below market rent for 5 years; minimum rent set at $29.00

b. Basement

c. Ground floor

d. Floors 2 through 4

e. For 7 years, then market rent for 3 years

f. Includes 4,600 square feet of retail space

g. Tenant's contribution to real estate escalations is reduced 50% in Year 1, 40% in Year 2, 30% in Year 3, 20% in Year 4, and 10% in Year 5

Note. Base year is year of lease commencement.

Table 19.3 Analysis of Operating Expense Comparables (Per Square Foot)

Property I.D.	Subject Property Pro Forma	Comparable A 130 Main Street	Comparable B 110 Second Avenue	Comparable C 717 Fourth Avenue	Comparable D 133 Third Avenue	Comparable E One Commerce Plaza
Operating year	1988	1987	1987	1987	1987	1987
Year built	1986	1986	1975	1968	1971	1985
Rentable area in square feet	60,000	75,000	49,411	56,411	52,000	66,000
Operating Expenses						
Fixed expenses						
Real estate taxes	$ 3.50	$ 3.51	$ 3.48	$ 3.01	$ 3.47	$3.35
Insurance	.11	.06	.09	.10	.17	.09
Variable expenses						
Cleaning	$ 1.40	$ 1.61	$ 1.38	$ 1.27	$ 1.28	$1.30
Payroll, payroll taxes, and benefits	.60	.45	.52	.98	.93	.41
Electricity	2.50	3.03	2.47	2.31	2.25	2.45
HVAC	1.50	1.25	1.60	1.35	1.75	1.55
Repairs and maintenance	.25	.25	.43	.78	.79	.18
Water and sewer	.04	.02	.02	.02	.03	.04
Administrative and general	.27	.19	.19	.26	.08	.11
Management	.30	.25	.20	.40	.35	.30
Total operating expenses	$10.47	$10.62	$10.38	$10.48	$11.10	$9.78

After thoroughly analyzing property and lease data for the subject and comparable properties, the appraiser develops a net operating income estimate for the subject property. If the appraiser is focusing on the benefits accruing to the investment before taxes, he or she also estimates the pre-tax cash flow. A sample outline for estimating net operating income and pre-tax cash flow is presented in Table 19.4. Both these estimates are developed from the gross income estimate.

Table 19.4   Income Estimate

Potential gross income		
Scheduled rent*	$XXXX	
Escalation income	XXXX	
Market rent**	XXXX	
Other income	XXXX	
Total potential gross income		$XXXX
Vacancy and collection loss		−XXXX
Effective gross income		$XXXX
Operating expenses		
Fixed	$XXXX	
Variable	XXXX	
Replacement allowance	XXXX	
Total operating expenses		−XXXX
Net operating income		$XXXX
Total mortgage debt service		−XXXX
Pre-tax cash flow (equity dividend)		$XXXX

* Rent from existing leases, adjusted for rental concessions if appropriate

** Rent attributed to vacant and owner-occupied space; in fee simple valuation, rent attributable to the whole property

Potential Gross Income

Potential gross income is the total income attributable to a real property at 100% occupancy before operating expenses are deducted. Appraisers usually analyze potential gross income on an annual basis. Potential gross income comprises rent for all space in the property, rent from escalation clauses, and all other income to the real estate.

Scheduled Rent

Scheduled rent is the portion of potential gross income derived from the rent levels stipulated in the leases in effect on the date of the appraisal. Some appraisers refer to this income as *existing lease* or *contract income or rent*. Scheduled rent may or may not coincide with the rent that could currently be obtained in the local market if the space were vacant and available for leasing.

To calculate scheduled rent, an appraiser must adjust for rent concessions, discounts, or other benefits that may induce a prospective tenant to enter into a lease. These concessions, or offsets, usually take the form of rent-free months at the beginning of the lease term, but they may also be reflected in extra services or benefits to the tenants. These benefits might include higher tenant improvement allowances, reduced expense or base rent escalations, below-market renewal options, tenant cancellation clauses, or building naming rights.[1]

Escalation Income

Escalation income is derived from lease escalation clauses. Escalation income consists of additional charges to tenants for part or all of the increases in operating expenses or charges that result from exercising a specific escalation formula contained in an existing lease.

Market Rent

Rent for vacant or owner-occupied space is usually estimated at market rent levels and distinguished from scheduled rent in the income estimate. In fee simple valuations, all rentable space is assumed to be leased at market rent so no rent attributable to specific leases is included in the income estimate. In developing market rent estimates, an appraiser assumes that property management is competent.

Other Income

Other income covers all income generated by the operation of the real property that is not derived directly from space rental. It includes income from services supplied to the tenants such as switchboard service, antenna connections, and garage space; income from coin-operated equipment and parking fees is also included. Because service-derived income may or may not be attributable to the real property, an appraiser might find it inappropriate to include this income in the property's gross potential income. The appraiser may treat other income as business income or real property income, depending on how the market perceives it.

Vacancy and Collection Loss

Vacancy and collection loss is an allowance for reductions in potential income attributable to vacancies, tenant turnover, and nonpayment of rent.

---

1. Kenneth Barnes, "Rental Concessions and Value," *The Appraisal Journal*, April 1986.

Annual rent collections are typically less than annual potential gross income, so an allowance for vacancy and collection loss is usually included in the appraisal of income-producing property. The allowance is usually estimated as a percentage of potential gross income, which varies depending on the type and characteristics of the physical property, the quality of its tenants, current and projected supply and demand relationships, and general and local economic conditions.

Published surveys of similar properties under similar conditions may indicate an appropriate percentage allowance for vacancy and collection loss. An appraiser should survey the local market to support the vacancy estimate, but his or her conclusion may differ from the current level indicated by primary or secondary research because it reflects typical investor expectations over the specific holding period assumed or projected in the income capitalization approach.

Effective Gross Income

Effective gross income is the anticipated income from all operations of the real property after allowance for vacancy and collection losses.

Operating Expenses

In the income capitalization approach, a comprehensive analysis of the annual expenses of property operation is essential whether the value indication is derived from estimated net operating income or pre-tax cash flow. *Operating expenses are the periodic expenditures necessary to maintain the real property and continue the production of the effective gross income.*

An operating statement that conforms to this definition of operating expenses is used for appraisal purposes and may differ from statements prepared for an owner or an accountant. Operating statements are prepared either on a cash or accrual basis, and the appraiser must know the accounting basis used in operating statements for the property being appraised. Operating statements provide valuable factual data and can be used to identify trends in operating expenses.

Expenses may be recorded in categories selected by the property owner or the records may follow a standard system of accounting established by an association of owners or by accounting firms that serve a particular segment of the management market. In any case, an appraiser analyzes and reconstructs expense statements to develop a typical expense expectancy for the property on an annual accrual basis.

Operating expense estimates usually list fixed expenses, variable expenses, and a replacement allowance. These classifications have long been in use, but there are other valid systems that an appraiser can employ.

Fixed Expenses

Fixed expenses are operating expenses that generally do not vary with occupancy and have to be paid whether the property is occupied or vacant. Real estate taxes and building insurance costs are typically considered fixed expenses. Although these expenses rarely remain constant, they generally do not fluctuate widely from year to year, do not vary in response to changing occupancy levels, and are not subject to management control. Therefore, an appraiser can usually identify a trend and legitimately estimate these expense items.

Tax data can be found in public records and the assessor's office may provide information about projected changes in assessments or rates and their probable effect on future taxes. If a property is unfairly assessed, operating expense may need to be adjusted for the reconstructed operating statement used in the appraisal. If the subject property is subject to an unusually low assessment or appears to deviate from the standard pattern in the jurisdiction, the most probable amount and trend of future taxes may be thoroughly analyzed. Any past changes in the assessment of the subject property should be studied. If the assessment is low, the assessor may raise it sooner or later; if the figure is high, however, a reduction may not be easily obtained. In projecting real estate taxes, an appraiser tries to anticipate tax assessments based on past tax trends, present taxes, the municipality's future expenditures, and the perceptions of market participants.

For proposed properties or properties that are not currently assessed, appraisers can develop operating statement projections without including real estate taxes. The resulting estimate is net operating income before real estate taxes, but a provision for real estate taxes is included in the capitalization rate used to convert net income into property value. For example, if real estate taxes are typically 2% of market value and net operating income after real estate taxes would normally be capitalized at 11% to derive a market value estimate for the property, the estimated net operating income before real estate taxes could be capitalized at 13% (i.e., 11% + 2%) to derive the property value indication. Alternately, the appraiser may choose to estimate real estate taxes for a proposed project based on building cost or the taxes paid by recently constructed, competitive properties.

An owner's operating expense statement may show the insurance premiums paid on a cash basis. If the premiums are not paid annually, they must be adjusted to an annual accrual basis before they are included in the reconstructed operating statement. Fire, extended coverage, and owner's liability insurance are typical insurance items, but depending on property type, elevators, boilers, plate glass, or other items may also be insured. The appraiser must determine the amount of insurance and, if it is inadequate, adjust the annual cost to indicate appropriate coverage for the property.

Insurance on business inventory and other personal property is the occupant's responsibility and, therefore, cannot be charged to the operation of the real estate. When questions concerning co-insurance or terms of coverage arise, an appraiser might need to obtain professional insurance counsel.

Variable Expenses

Variable expenses are all operating expenses that generally vary with the level of occupancy or the extent of services provided. Individual variable expense items may vary greatly from year to year, but specific types of property may reflect a reasonably consistent pattern of variable expenses in relation to gross income. Because fewer services are provided to the tenants of retail and industrial properties, these properties usually have a much lower ratio of expenses to gross income than apartments and office buildings.

Operating statements for large properties frequently list many types of variable expenses, but typical categories include

- Management charges
- Leasing fees
- Utilities—e.g., electricity, gas, water, and sewer
- Heat
- Air-conditioning
- General payroll
- Cleaning
- Maintenance and repair
- Decorating
- Grounds and parking area maintenance
- Miscellaneous—e.g., security, supplies, rubbish removal, and exterminating

Management charges. Management charges are proper expenses of operation, whether management services are contracted or provided by the property owner. The expense of management is usually expressed as a percentage of effective gross income and reflects the local pattern for such charges.

The operation of multitenant properties requires a considerable amount of supervision, accounting, and other services. Larger properties may have onsite offices or apartments for resident managers and corresponding expenses for their maintenance and operation. Other management expenses may include the cost of telephone service, clerical help, legal or accounting services, printing and postage, and advertising.

Leasing fees. Leasing fees are commissions paid to agents for negotiating and securing property leases. When these fees are spread over the term of a lease or a lease renewal, they are included in the operating statement. However, initial leasing fees, which may be extensive in a new shopping center or other large development, are usually treated as part of the capital expenditure for developing the project. In these cases, initial leasing fees are not included as periodic expenses. When a net income or pre-tax cash flow forecast is developed, leasing fees can be deducted in the year they are payable or spread over the lease term, depending on local practice.

Utilities. Utility expenses for an existing property are usually projected based on an analysis of past charges and current trends. The subject property's utility requirements can be compared with known unit utility expenses for similar properties to estimate probable future utility expenses. Hours of tenant operation may prove to be significant in the analysis. For example, the number of nights per week that a shopping center is open and the hours of after-dark operation will directly affect electricity consumption, and may indirectly affect expenses for maintenance and garbage removal. In analyzing utility expenses, appraisers recognize local circumstances and the increasing cost of all types of energy.

Although the cost of *electricity* for leased space is frequently a tenant expense, and therefore not included in the operating expense statement, the owner may be responsible for lighting public areas and for the power needed to run elevators and other building equipment.

Gas. When used for heating and air-conditioning, gas can be a major expense item that is frequently paid by the tenant or reflected in the rent.

Water. The cost of water is generally not a major consideration except for laundries, restaurants, taverns, hotels, or similar operations. Leases for these properties may stipulate that the tenant pay this expense. If the owner typically pays for gas and water, these charges should be included in the expense statement.

Sewer. In municipalities with sewerage systems, a separate charge for use of the system may be paid by the tenant or the owner of the real estate.

When the property owner is responsible for all utility charges, the total expense may be substantial, particularly for hotels, motels, recreation facilities, apartments, and office buildings.

Heat. The cost of heat is generally a tenant expense in single-tenant properties, industrial or retail properties, and apartment projects with individual heating units. It is a major expense item in operating statements for office buildings and many apartment properties. The fuel consumed may be coal, oil, gas, electricity, or public steam. Heating supplies, maintenance, and applicable wages are included in this expense category under certain accounting methods. Public steam suppliers and gas companies maintain records of fuel consumption in terms of degree days from year to year. An appraiser can use these records and fuel cost data to compare the property's heating expense for the most recent year or years with a typical year. Probable changes in the cost of the fuel used should be reflected in the appraiser's projection.

Air-conditioning. Air-conditioning expenses may be charged under the individual categories of electricity, water, payroll, and repairs, or heating and air-conditioning may be combined under the category of heating, ventilating, and air-conditioning (HVAC). The cost of air-conditioning varies substantially with local climatic conditions and the type of installation. A projection of this expense may be based on typical unit charges for the community or the property type. Most office buildings and many apartment buildings have central HVAC systems and operating expenses are included in their annual statements. Most commercial properties and many apartment buildings have individual heating and air-conditioning units that are operated by the tenants. However, the maintenance and repair of these units, particularly for apartments, may continue to be obligations of the property owner.

General payroll. General payroll expenses include payments to all employees whose services are essential to property operation and management, but whose salaries are not included in other specific expense categories. In some areas, the cost of custodial or janitorial service is based on union wage schedules; in others, the charge is negotiated based on local custom and practice. If a custodian or manager occupies an apartment as partial payment for his or her services, the apartment's rental value may be included as income and an identical amount deducted as an expense. In certain properties, additional expenses are incurred for the salaries of watchmen, doormen, porters, and elevator operators. Unemployment and social security taxes for employees may be included under general payroll expenses or listed in a separate expense category.

Cleaning. In office buildings the cost of cleaning is a major expense which is usually estimated in terms of cents per square foot of rentable area, whether the work is done by payroll personnel or by an outside cleaning firm. This expense is equivalent to maid service or housekeeping in hotels and furnished apartments. In hotels and motels, cleaning expenses are attributed to the rooms department and may be based on a percentage of the department's gross income that reflects previous experience and industry standards. Cleaning may be an owner or tenant expense, depending on the property type and lease provisions.

Maintenance and repair. Maintenance and repair expenses may cover roof repair, window caulking, tuckpointing, exterior painting, and the repair of heating, lighting, and plumbing equipment. There may be a contract for elevator maintenance and repair, but because these contracts vary, an appraiser must determine how much additional operating expense may not be covered by the maintenance contract. A contract that covers air-conditioning equipment would probably be included in the air-conditioning expense category.

Alterations may be considered capital expenditures and, therefore, are not included as a periodic expense under repair and maintenance. If the lessor makes alterations in the rented space, the expense may or may not be amortized by additional rental; in some cases, the tenant may pay for alterations.

The total expense for property maintenance and repair is affected by the extent to which building component and equipment replacements are covered in the replacement allowance. If extensive replacement allowances are included in the reconstructed operating statement, annual maintenance and repair expenses will be reduced. However, maintenance and repair expenses for the main portion of the building should always be listed in the maintenance and repair category.

Decorating. Decorating expenses may include the cost of interior painting, wallpapering, or wall cleaning in tenant or public areas. Lease provisions may stipulate that the owner is only responsible for decorating vacant space to attract new tenants. Decorating expenditures may vary with local practice and the supply and demand for space.

Grounds and parking area maintenance. The cost of maintaining grounds and parking areas can vary widely depending on the property type and total area. Hard-surfaced public parking areas with drains, lights, and marked car spaces are subject to intensive wear and can be costly to maintain. These expenses may be entirely or partly compensated with an increment added to the rents of tenants served by the facility. In this case, both the added income and the added expenses are included in the appraiser's reconstructed operating statement.

Miscellaneous. Expenses for miscellaneous items vary according to the property type. If this expense category is more than a minor percentage of effective gross income, however, it may be wise to explain individual expense items or reallocate them to specific categories.

Security. Certain types of buildings in some areas may require security provisions, the cost of which will vary according to the number of employees needed to control entry and exit and to circulate through the property. Maintenance and energy expenses may also be incurred if security provisions include electric alarm systems, closed circuit television, or flood lighting.

Supplies. The cost of cleaning materials and miscellaneous items not covered elsewhere may be included under supplies.

Rubbish removal and exterminating. Garbage and pest control services are usually contracted and their cost is included in the expense statement. The cost of snow removal may be substantial in northern states, particularly if properties have outdoor parking in addition to sidewalks and driveways.

Replacement Allowance

A replacement allowance provides for the periodic replacement of building components that wear out more rapidly than the building itself and must be replaced periodically during the building's economic life. These components may include

- Roof covering
- Carpeting
- Kitchen, bath, or laundry equipment
- Compressors, elevators, and boilers
- Specific structural items and equipment that have limited economic life expectancies
- Interior improvements to tenant space that are made periodically by the landlord, usually at lease renewal
- Sidewalks
- Driveways
- Parking areas
- Exterior painting

The annual allowance for each component is usually estimated as the anticipated cost of its replacement prorated over its anticipated remaining economic life, provided this does not exceed the remaining economic life of the structure. Some appraisers use simple averaging, while others prefer to show the actual cost and timing of these replacements. New elevators or other components that are expected to have economic lives that equal or exceed the remaining economic life of the structure do not require an allowance for replacement.

If an appraiser is using a short projection period in the income capitalization approach, items that will not require replacement during this period need not be considered in the replacement allowance, particularly if market evidence indicates that market participants follow a similar practice. Rather, the effect of these items is reflected in the anticipated resale price. When a long-term projection is being considered, however, the appraiser may need to identify future expenditures for replacements. In any case, appraisers should attempt to reflect market practice in the use of replacement allowances.

The scope of items to be covered in a replacement allowance is a matter of appraisal judgment based on market evidence; however, the extent of the replacement allowance is based on annual repair and maintenance expenses of the property. Historical operating statements prepared on a cash basis may include periodic replacement expenses under repair and maintenance. If extensive provisions for replacement are made in the reconstructed operating statement, these charges may be duplicated unless the annual maintenance expense estimate is reduced.

In certain real estate markets, space is rented to a new tenant only after substantial interior improvements are made. If this work is performed at the landlord's expense and is required to achieve market rent, the expense of these improvements should be included in the reconstructed operating statement as part of the replacement allowance.

A total expense estimate that provides for all items of repair and replacement may exceed the actual expenditures shown in the owner's operating statements for recent years. This is particularly common when the building being appraised is relatively new and the owner has not set up a replacement allowance. In preparing a reconstructed operating statement for a typical year, an appraiser recognizes that replacements must be made eventually and that replacement costs affect operating expenses, which can be reflected in increased annual maintenance costs or, on an accrual basis, as an annual replacement allowance.

An appraiser must understand whether or not a replacement allowance is included in an operating statement to derive a market capitalization rate for use in the income capitalization approach. A capitalization rate derived from a comparable sale property is valid only if it is applied to the subject property on the same basis. Consequently, a rate derived from a sale with an expense estimate that does not provide for a replacement allowance cannot be applied to an income estimate for the subject property that includes such an allowance.

Total Operating Expenses

Total operating expenses are the sum of fixed and variable expenses and the replacement allowance cited in an appraiser's operating expense estimate.

Net Operating Income

Net operating income is the anticipated net income remaining after all operating expenses are deducted from effective gross income but before mortgage debt service and book depreciation are deducted.

Total Mortgage Debt Service

Total mortgage debt service is the periodic payment for interest on and retirement of the mortgage loan (principal). Mortgage debt service is deducted from net operating income to derive pre-tax cash flow, which is used in certain capitalization procedures. If the definition of value used in the appraisal assumes existing financing, the mortgage debt service to be deducted from the net operating income is specified in the existing mortgage. If the definition of value assumes market financing, the amount of mortgage debt service to be deducted is based on market terms.

Pre-Tax Cash Flow

Pre-tax cash flow (equity dividend) is the income that remains after total mortgage debt service is deducted from net operating income.

Expense and Income Ratios

The ratio of total operating expense to effective gross income is the *operating expense ratio*. The complement of this ratio is the *net income ratio*—i.e., net operating income to effective gross income. These ratios tend to fall within limited ranges for specific categories of property. Experienced appraisers recognize approximately correct ratios, so they can identify statements that deviate from typical patterns and require further analysis.

Nationwide studies of apartment and office building properties conducted by the Institute of Real Estate Management (IREM) and the Building Owners and Managers Association (BOMA) can often be used as general guides in selecting operating expense ratios. Sometimes local BOMA or IREM chapters, or real estate appraisal organizations and their chapters, conduct and publish studies of operating expenses that can be used as market indicators. Published studies are useful, but the appraiser must still develop operating expense ratios from comparable properties in the subject property's market or verify the applicability of published ratios in this market.

Exclusions from Reconstructed Operating Statements

The operating statements prepared for real estate owners typically list all expenditures made during a specific year. However, they may include nonrecurring items that should not be included in an expense estimate intended to reflect typical annual expenses. They may also include business expense items or specific circumstances of ownership.

A reconstructed operating statement or pro forma statement represents an opinion of the probable future net operating income of an investment. Certain items included in operating statements prepared for property owners should be omitted in reconstructed operating statements prepared for appraisal purposes. These items include book depreciation, income tax, special corporation costs, and additions to capital.

Book Depreciation

The *book depreciation* for improvements on a parcel of real estate is based on historical cost or another previously established figure that may have no relation to current market value. Moreover, book depreciation may be based on a formula designed for tax purposes. The capitalization method and procedure selected provide for the recapture of invested capital, so including depreciation in the operating expense statement would be redundant.

Income Tax

The amount of income tax varies with the type of property ownership; the property may be held by a corporation, a partnership, a public utility, or an individual. The income tax obligation of the owner is not an operating expense of the property.

Special Corporation Costs

The expenses attributable to corporate operation also pertain to the type of ownership. Corporate expenses are not part of a reconstructed operating statement developed for appraisal purposes.

Additions to Capital

Expenditures for capital improvements do not recur annually and, therefore, should not be included in an estimate reflecting the typical annual expenses of operation. Capital improvements may enhance value by increasing the annual net operating income or economic life of the property, but the capital expenditure is not a periodic operating expense.

SAMPLE ONE-YEAR INCOME FORECAST

The property being appraised, ABC Apartments, is a 55-unit apartment project with a potential annual rent of $147,600 at 100% occupancy. Open parking is included in the rent. Additional income from coin-operated equipment averages about $1,150 per year, so total potential gross income at 100% occupancy is $148,750. Annual vacancy and collection loss is estimated at 4% and local management services are available for 5% of rent collections. The building superintendent receives an annual salary of $4,200, including fringe benefits.

Last year's tax bill was $16,250, but taxes are expected to be $17,000 by the end of this year. The owner carries $1 million in fire and extended coverage insurance and pays a three-year premium of $4,300. The appraiser believes that this coverage should be increased to $1,200,000. An additional expense for other insurance coverage is $700 per year.

The payroll to cover site maintenance and snow removal averages $5,400 per year. Trash removal costs $40 per month and miscellaneous supplies are estimated at $300 per year. Pest control costs are $60 per month and other miscellaneous expenditures are projected at $300 per year.

Building tenants pay their own utilities, including the gas and electricity for individual apartment heating and air-conditioning units. Based on experience and anticipated rate changes, the electricity for public space is expected to total $2,000 in the coming year. Other utility expenses, including water, consistently come to about $900 each year.

Repair and maintenance expenses are $12,000 to $13,000 per year, including replacement expenditures. The appraiser anticipates that replacement expenses will increase, and the reconstructed operating statement should include a separate replacement allowance in addition to normal repair and maintenance expenses. Exterior painting, which is estimated to cost $4,200 in the present market, is scheduled to be done every three years.

Most of the apartments are rented on three-year leases, with a typical redecorating cost of $200 per apartment at lease renewal. Public space is minimal, and redecorating this space costs about $240 every third year. All the apartments have stoves, refrigerators, dishwashers, disposals, and exhaust fans, so a replacement allowance of $1,300 per apartment is required. The economic lives of these items vary, but they are estimated to average 10 years. Carpeting replacement by the owner costs about $900 per unit, and the average economic life of carpeting is six years. The roof is considered to have a 20-year life and a replacement cost of $18,000.

The operating statement shown in Table 19.5 reflects these data. The precision of each entry is set by the appraiser, but rounding to the closest $5 or $10 is well within the estimated accuracy of the entries.

SAMPLE MULTIYEAR INCOME FORECAST

In certain appraisals, such as those in which discounted cash flow analysis is used, the appraiser forecasts the expected future monetary benefits of the investment over the total projected holding period. The anticipated benefits may include the net operating income and the pre-tax cash flow for each year of the expected holding period plus the reversion—i.e., the resale price after the expenses of sale and any mortgage balance are deducted. The following example is based on a 10-year forecast of the future

Table 19.5   ABC Apartments: Reconstructed Operating Statement

Potential gross annual income

Rents	11 units @ $2,400/yr.	$ 26,400
	12 units @ $2,580/yr.	30,960
	16 units @ $2,760/yr.	44,160
	16 units @ $2,880/yr.	46,080

		$147,600
Other income		+ 1,150

Total potential gross income @ 100% occupancy		$148,750
Less vacancy and collection loss @ 4%		− 5,950
Effective gross income		$142,800

Operating expenses

Fixed

Real estate taxes		$ 17,000
Insurance		
Fire and extended coverage ($4,300 × 1.2)/3		1,720
Other		+ 700
Subtotal		$ 19,420

Variable

Management ($142,800 × .05)		$ 7,140
Superintendent		4,200
Payroll		5,400
Electricity		2,000
Other utilities		900
Repair and maintenance		6,500
Exterior paint ($4,200/3)		1,400
Interior decorating		3,750*
Miscellaneous		
Trash removal ($40 × 12)		480
Pest control ($60 × 12)		720
Supplies		300
Other		300
Subtotal		$ 33,090

(continued)

Table 19.5   ABC Apartments: Reconstructed Operating Statement (continued)

Replacement allowance	
Kitchen and bath equipment	
($1,300 × 55)/10	$ 7,150
Carpeting	
($900 × 55)/6	8,250
Roof	
$18,000/20 yrs.	900
Subtotal	$ 16,300
Total operating expenses	−$68,810
Operating expense ratio	
($68,810/$142,800) = 48.2%	
Net operating income	$73,990
Net operating income ratio	
($73,990/$142,800) = 51.8%	

*55 units × $200 = $11,000; $11,000 + $240 = $11,240; $11,240/3 = $3,750 (rounded). This entry could be included under *replacement allowance.*

benefits from an office building investment. Both net operating income and pre-tax cash flow are estimated for each year. The proceeds from resale of the property at the end of the tenth year are also estimated.[2]

All the techniques discussed in this chapter are used to develop a net operating and pre-tax cash flow estimate for the first year of the forecast. Estimates for the other years are based on existing lease provisions and assumptions regarding lease renewals and growth rates applied to other income and operating expenses.

PROPERTY ANALYSIS

The subject property is a 50,000-sq. ft. site improved with a 50-year-old, 25-story office building in a secondary location north of the downtown commercial district. The rentable area totals 951,049 square feet of office and retail space. The retail space is small; it includes 13,293 square feet of space covered by five leases. The building is fully occupied by 19 tenants under 21 leases. Many of the leases are old and will expire soon. The leases for approximately 58.4% of the building's rentable area will expire and be available for renewal or releasing in 1990 and 1991. The last

---

2. This example has been adapted from an article by Peter F. Korpacz and Mark I. Roth entitled "Changing Emphasis in Appraisal Techniques: The Transition to Discounted Cash Flow," *The Appraisal Journal,* January 1983.

existing lease will expire in 2009. Hence, all of the leases will roll over in 22 years. (Lease expiration and subsequent re-leasing is referred to as lease rollover.) The property's lease expiration profile is summarized in Table 19.6.

Table 19.6 Lease Expiration Profile

Year	No. of Expiring Leases	Rentable Area in Sq. Ft.	Percent of Total Area (Cumulative)
1988	0	0	
1989	0	0	
1990	7	268,458	28.2
1991	6	286,706	58.4
1992	2	51,302	63.8
1993	2	22,730	66.2
1994	1	7,930	67.0
1995	1	45,979	71.8
1996-1997	0	0	71.8
1998	1	924	71.9
1999-2008	0	0	71.9
2009	1	267,020	100.0
Total	21	951,049	

The current average gross rent per square foot of rentable area is $8.57. Appraisers estimate current average market rents at $18 per square foot for office space and $25 per square foot for retail space. The weighted-average market rent is estimated to be $18.10 per square foot. Therefore, the market differential (i.e., the difference between potential gross income at market rent and existing contract rent) is $9.53 per square foot ($18.10 − $8.57), and the total actual rent is 47.35% of market rent. The market for office space is in balance and there is above-average demand for space in this building. Although the building is old, it has been remodeled with extensive capital expenditures to improve its mechanical systems and maintain its competitive position. It is located in a good secondary area and is ideally suited to back office, computer, bookkeeping, or storage operations that require a large, contiguous space.

Rationale Regarding the Forecast

The appraiser determines that investors in office buildings similar to the subject property typically forecast net operating incomes or pre-tax cash flows over a 10-year projected holding period. To establish a purchase price that will justify the risk inherent in the proposed investment, the forecast net operating incomes or pre-tax cash flows and the reversion are discounted at an appropriate yield rate.

To simulate typical investor analysis, an appraiser

1. Analyzes current income, establishes the market rent level for each tenant space, and forecasts future income for each year of a 10-year period based on existing leases, probable renewal at market rent, and expected vacancy experience
2. Forecasts other income, including income from escalation clauses contained in existing leases and assumed escalation provisions in new leases
3. Forecasts future property expenses after analyzing historical operating expenses, the experience of competitive properties, and the current budget for the property
4. Forecasts mortgage debt service based on existing or proposed financing terms
5. Estimates the net operating incomes or pre-tax cash flows to be generated by the property in each year of the forecast holding period
6. Estimates the reversionary benefits to be received at the end of the forecast holding period

In a market value appraisal, these steps must be applied to reflect the thinking of market participants. In the sample case, the appraiser begins by assembling pertinent information on recent sales of office buildings in the same market as the subject property. To verify each sale, the appraiser reviews with the participants, usually the buyer, the net operating income or pre-tax cash flow forecast assumptions used in connection with each sale. Table 19.7, which lists information on Comparable Sale 1, illustrates the type of detailed information that must be gathered for each comparable sale.

Assumptions for the Subject Property

After gathering and analyzing data on local market conditions and the income and expense expectations of comparable properties, the appraiser develops assumptions about the subject property.

Forecast Period

The forecasts are based on an assumed 10-year holding period commencing on the date of valuation. A 10-year forecast is typical in this market. This forecast considers the effects of re-leasing 71.9% of the building space; a lease for the other 28.1% of the building is held by one major space user and does not expire until the year 2009. Income for Year 11 is forecast to estimate the resale price of the property at the end of the 10-year projection period.

Existing Rents

Contract rents and rent adjustments are forecast in light of existing leases and escalation provisions.

Table 19.7   Comparable Sales Data

Sale No.	1
Address	110 Main St.
	Subject city, subject state
Date of sale	June 1987
Sale price	$60 million
Seller	XYZ Investment Co.
Purchaser	110 Main Street Co.
Description	A 32-story, multitenant office building that was built in 1966 and contains 748,701 sq. ft. of area on floors that range from 8,100 sq. ft. to 30,600 sq. ft.; situated on a 32,609-sq.-ft. plot
Comments	The property was sold on an all-cash basis; the buyer expects above-average increases in net income.
Sale price per sq. ft.	$80.14
Average scheduled rent per sq. ft. at sale date	$12.44

Anticipated financial data for Year 1 (buyer's estimate)	
Average market rent per sq. ft.	$27.50
Average scheduled rent per sq. ft.	$12.44
Fixed expenses per sq. ft.	$ 2.67
Variable expenses per sq. ft.	$ 4.79
Replacement allowance	$ 0.00
Net operating income per sq. ft.	$ 4.98
Overall capitalization rate*	6.2%
Equity capitalization rate	6.2%
Anticipated 10-year yield (*IRR*)	13.5%
Purchaser's assumptions	
Market rent rate	Averages $27.50 per sq. ft. in Years 1 and 2, increasing 8% per year thereafter
Escalation income	Typical total rent will closely approximate market rent rates
Expense increases	Real estate taxes assumed to increase 2% per year; energy expenses assumed to increase 5% per year; other operating expenses assumed to increase 4% per year

(continued)

Table 19.7   Comparable Sales Data (continued)

Re-leasing	All space assumed to be re-leased for successive 5-year terms
Vacancy	75% of space being re-leased assumed to be vacant for 3 months
Leasing fees	Standard commission schedule payable in first year of lease
Interior improvements to tenant space	$20.00 per square foot for new leases; $7.50 per square foot for renewal of existing leases
Resale	Computed by applying a 10% overall capitalization rate to the net operating income in Year 11 after deducting 2.5% for selling expenses

*Because the property is not mortgaged, the equity capitalization rate is the same as the overall capitalization rate.

Escalation Income

Escalation income is calculated in accordance with the specific terms of existing leases. For anticipated new leases, escalation income is based on a pro rata share of the increases in operating expenses and real estate taxes that exceed the base year. The base year is defined as the year of lease commencement. By local custom, escalation income is assumed to be collected in the year after it accrues.

Although specific escalation provisions vary, the appraiser's analysis reveals that prospective investors use a combination of escalation provisions which, taken together, increase tenant collections annually so that total collections in any given year do not lag far behind market rents.

Renewal Options

It is assumed that the renewal options contained in existing leases, which specify new contract rents or escalation provisions, will be exercised, and the income specified under these renewals is incorporated into the forecast. One lease has a seven-year renewal option, beginning in 1989 at a specified annual rent that is less than the expected market rent for that year ($18.00 market rent compared with $13.00 contract rent). Other renewal options that do not specify contract rent or escalation provisions are also assumed to be exercised; in these cases, market rental rates and new escalation provisions are applied.

Tenant Turnover

Approximately 35% of the space in the building is occupied by three major corporations that are likely to remain. It is assumed that this space will be re-leased to the existing tenants. Another 50% of the building is assumed to be re-leased to existing tenants, and it is assumed that 15% will be leased to new tenants. These assumptions are consistent with comparable sales data, given the character of the property and its tenants.

New Lease Terms

When the existing leases and any renewal options expire, all space is assumed to be re-leased for successive 10-year terms. In this market, 10-year leases are customary for this type of space.

Market Rental Rates

The market rental rates applied to leasing activity are set forth below.

Office space: For two years beginning January 1, 1988, an average of $18 per square foot; market rate assumed to increase 5% per year thereafter

Retail space: For the year beginning January 1, 1988, an average of $25 per square foot; market rate assumed to increase 5% per year

The office rental rate assumptions are supported by an analysis of actual leases for office space in competitive buildings. Rate increase assumptions are consistent with the assumptions made by the buyers of all but one of the comparable sales (see Table 19.8).

Table 19.8   Analysis of Growth Rate Assumptions Derived from Office Building Sales

| | | Market Rent Growth Rates | | | | | Expense Growth Rates | | |
| | | 1st Period | | 2nd Period | | | | | Real Estate |
Sale No.	Date	%	No. of Years	%	No. of Years	Thereafter	Variable Operating	Energy	Taxes and Insurance
1	9/87	0.0	2	—	—	5.0%	4.0%	5.0%	2.0%
2	9/87	4.0	—	—	—	4.0	4.5	4.5	3.0
3	6/87	0.0	2	4.0	2	5.0	4.5	5.0	3.0
4	7/86	0.0	3	—	—	5.0	4.0	4.0	4.0
5	3/87	0.0	2	4.0	2	5.0	4.0	5.0	4.0
6	3/87	0.0	3	—	—	5.0	4.0	4.0	4.0
7	4/86	5.0	—	—	—	5.0	5.0	5.0	4.0
8	4/86	0.0	2	—	—	5.0	4.5	4.5	4.0
9	7/86	5.0	—	—	—	5.0	5.0	6.0	5.0
10	10/86	0.0	3	—	—	5.0	4.0	5.0	4.0
11	8/87	0.0	2	4.0	2	5.0	4.0	4.0	5.0

Vacancy and Collection Loss

Fifteen percent of the building space is being leased to new tenants and is assumed to remain vacant for an average of four months. The other 85% is assumed to be re-leased by existing tenants, so no vacancy is assumed. The appraiser has considered the rent loss associated with vacancies by not accruing contract rent or escalation income for the space for a four-month period beginning at the expiration of each lease. Furthermore, an additional allowance for the underlying level of vacancy and collection loss inherent in any multitenant office building is estimated at 0.5% of total gross revenue, as indicated by comparable sales data.

Real Estate Taxes and Insurance

Real estate taxes and insurance are estimated at $998,000, or $1.03 per square foot of rentable area, for the year ending in December 1988. The combined real estate tax and insurance expense is assumed to increase at a rate of 4% per year thereafter.

Management

Management fees are estimated at $75,000 for 1988 and expected to increase 4.5% each subsequent year. Although the building is large, the small number of tenants and the significant leasing activity scheduled for the near term should attract competent management at this rate.

Leasing Fees

To estimate leasing fees, the appraiser applies a weighted-average, leasing commission rate of 17.15% of the first year's base rent to all re-leasing activities. This estimate reflects that 35% of the space will be re-leased to the three major corporations at a commission rate of 14% of the first year's contract rent, 50% of the space will be re-leased to existing tenants at a commission rate of 14% of the first year's contract rent, and 15% of the space will be leased to new tenants at a commission rate of 35% of the first year's contract rent. Commissions are assumed to be paid in full upon occupancy and are deducted from income. This commission schedule is consistent with the typical rates obtained by local real estate brokers.

Variable Operating Expenses

Variable operating expenses, excluding leasing fees and management which are treated separately in this case, are estimated to be $2,161,000 in 1982, or $2.23 per square foot of rentable area (see Table 19.9). The expense estimates are supported by an analysis of the recent operating histories of competitive buildings. The HVAC estimate is decreased from 1987 to 1988 because the building is being converted from steam to oil heat. Expenses for energy-related items are expected to increase 4.5% per year, and other expenses are estimated to increase 4% per year. These rate increases are based on the expense rate increase assumptions indicated by comparable sales. Expenses for tenant electricity and the cleaning of tenant space are not included because existing tenants pay for their own cleaning and electricity. This is not unusual in leasing back office space and the market rent estimate of $18 per square foot is based on the assumption that future tenants will continue this practice.

Table 19.9   Estimate of Variable Operating Expenses for Subject Property*

	1987 Budget	1988 Estimate
HVAC	$ 500,000	$ 400,000**
Payroll	154,000	175,000
Repairs and maintenance	385,000	440,000
Building electricity	600,000	660,000
Security	175,000	200,000
Cleaning public areas	25,000	30,000
Garbage collection	5,000	6,000
Administrative and general	185,000	200,000
Water and sewer	44,000	50,000
Total	$2,073,000	$ 2,161,000
Total per rentable sq. ft.	$2.18	$2.27

* Excluding management expenses and leasing fees, which are estimated separately

** Reflects conversion to oil heat for part of year

Replacement Allowance

The replacement allowance consists of the cost of preparing tenant space and the cost of replacing building components that wear out over time. All space being leased to new tenants is assumed to require decorating costs of $20.00 per square foot. Space being re-leased to existing tenants is assumed to incur decorating costs of $7.50 per square foot. The cost per square foot is expected to increase 5% per year.

In addition, the cost to replace building improvements (e.g., roof, HVAC equipment, and structural components) is forecast at $100,000 for Year 1, increasing 5% each year thereafter.

Mortgage Debt Service

One existing mortgage is included in the forecast. The amount of principal at the beginning of the forecast is $28,500,000, the interest rate is 12%, and annual debt service is $3,654,475 based on monthly payments. The loan is self-amortizing over a remaining term of 23 years.

Reversion

There are several ways to estimate a resale price. A market-derived capitalization rate can be applied to the appropriate income for the last year of the forecast or the year following the end of the forecast. In this case, the resale price is forecast by applying a 10% overall capitalization rate to the net operating income for the year after the projection period (Year 11). Sales expenses of 2.5% are deducted to arrive at the net resale price; the balance of the mortgage is deducted to calculate the owner's net sale proceeds, or equity reversion.

Forecast Results

Mathematical calculations based on the assumptions set forth above result in the forecast shown in Table 19.10. The future benefits are converted into a value indication for the subject property using an appropriate capitalization procedure.

This example demonstrates one way of forecasting future benefits, but it is not intended to represent the only acceptable forecasting procedure. The rent levels, growth rates, expense levels, and other economic and financial information described here are particular to the specific property being appraised and real estate market under consideration. In market value appraisals, the forecasting of future benefits should be based on market-derived information. In assignments to estimate investment value, the appraiser has more latitude in interpreting market attitudes and specific investor preferences.

SUMMARY

An estimate or scheduled projection of future income is fundamental to the income capitalization approach. Historic and current income are relevant to the forecast, but the future direction of income is the critical concern. An appraiser can estimate and capitalize four levels of income: *potential gross income (PGI)*, *effective gross income (EGI)*, *net operating income (NOI)*, and *pre-tax cash flow*. Depending on the data available and the capitalization method to be used, income analysis may be based on the actual income level at the time of the appraisal, a forecast of the first year's income, a forecast of property income over a specified holding period, or the stabilized, or average, annual income over a holding period. To value investments in partial interests, pre-tax cash flow is usually capitalized.

An income and expense forecast begins with lease analysis. *Gross rental* describes leases in which the lessor pays all operating expenses of the real estate. *Net rental* identifies leases in which the tenant pays all such expenses. Leases can be classified as flat rental, with a specific level of rent that continues for the duration of the lease; graduated rental, in which the rent undergoes specified changes at one or more points during the lease term (e.g., step-up and step-down); revaluation, in which rent is adjusted at periodic intervals based on a revaluation of the real estate; index, in which periodic rent adjustments are tied to a specific index, and percentage, in which

Table 19.10 Income Estimates

	1988	1989	1990	1991	1992	1993	1994	1995	1996	1997	1998**
Income											
Contract and market rents*	$8,149,802	$8,149,802	$8,986,591	$12,645,178	$15,241,645	$16,035,714	$16,485,322	$17,432,668	$19,487,680	$20,291,478	$20,291,478
Escalation income	153,078	283,867	360,523	528,617	625,906	772,808	1,074,136	1,455,791	1,816,841	2,061,857	2,336,857
Vacancy and collection loss	(40,749)	(40,749)	(44,933)	(63,226)	(76,208)	(80,179)	(82,427)	(87,163)	(97,438)	(101,457)	(101,457)
Effective gross income	$8,262,131	$8,392,920	$9,302,181	$13,110,569	$15,791,343	$16,728,343	$17,477,031	$18,801,296	$21,207,083	$22,251,878	$22,526,878
Operating expenses											
Fixed expenses											
Real estate taxes	926,671	963,738	1,002,287	1,042,379	1,084,074	1,127,437	1,172,534	1,219,436	1,268,213	1,318,942	1,371,699
Insurance	71,329	74,182	77,149	80,235	83,445	86,783	90,254	93,864	97,619	101,523	105,584
Variable expenses											
HVAC	400,000	420,000	441,000	463,050	486,203	510,513	536,038	562,840	590,982	620,531	651,558
Payroll	175,000	182,875	191,104	199,704	208,691	218,082	227,896	238,151	248,868	260,067	271,770
Repair and maintenance	440,000	459,800	480,491	502,113	524,708	548,320	572,994	598,779	625,724	653,882	683,307
Electricity	660,000	693,000	727,650	764,033	802,234	842,346	884,463	928,686	975,121	1,023,877	1,075,070
Security	200,000	209,000	218,405	228,233	238,504	249,236	260,452	272,172	284,420	297,219	310,594
Cleaning	30,000	31,350	32,761	34,235	35,776	37,385	39,068	40,826	42,663	44,583	46,589
Garbage removal	6,000	6,270	6,552	6,847	7,155	7,477	7,814	8,165	8,533	8,917	9,318
Water	50,000	52,250	54,601	57,058	59,626	62,309	65,113	68,043	71,105	74,305	77,648
Administrative and general	200,000	209,000	218,405	228,233	238,504	249,236	260,452	272,172	284,420	297,219	310,594
Management	75,000	78,375	81,902	85,587	89,439	93,464	97,670	102,065	106,658	111,457	116,473
Leasing fees	0	0	870,166	976,026	183,326	85,293	31,239	190,196	0	0	4,424
Replacement allowance	100,000	104,500	1,508,943	1,676,378	411,366	259,884	179,535	434,857	454,426	474,875	162,148
Total operating expenses	$3,334,000	$3,484,340	$5,911,416	$6,344,111	$4,453,081	$4,377,765	$4,425,522	$5,030,252	$5,058,752	$5,287,397	$5,196,776
Net operating income	$4,928,131	$4,908,580	$3,390,765	$6,766,458	$11,338,262	$12,350,578	$13,051,509	$13,771,044	$16,148,331	$16,964,481	$17,330,102
Mortgage debt service	($3,654,475)	($3,654,475)	($3,654,475)	($3,654,475)	($3,654,475)	($3,654,475)	($3,654,475)	($3,654,475)	($3,654,475)	($3,654,475)	($3,654,475)
Pre-tax cash flow	$1,273,656	$1,254,105	($ 263,710)	$3,111,983	$7,683,787	$8,696,103	$9,397,034	$10,116,569	$12,493,856	$13,310,006	$13,675,627
Resale price										$173,301,020	
Less sale expenses										(4,332,526)	
Net resale price										$168,968,494	
Less mortgage balance										($ 24,005,550)	
Equity reversion										$144,962,944	

* Also reflects added vacancy associated with lease rollovers, as discussed under vacancy and collection loss

** For calculation of residual price in 1997

a portion of the rent is based on a specified percentage of the volume of business or productivity.

Typical lease data include the lease date, a legal description of the leased property, the names of the lessor and the lessee, the lease term, the dates of occupancy and the commencement of payments, the amount and source of the rent, escalation clauses (e.g., tax- and expense-stop clauses), rent concessions, landlord and tenant convenants regarding the division of expenses, the right of assignment or right to sublet, renewal options, purchase options (e.g., the right of first refusal), escape clauses, stipulated advance rent or bonding, provisions for casualty or condemnation loss, specifications concerning tenant improvements, and revaluation clauses.

Five different types of rent can affect income: *contract rent*, the actual rental income specified in a lease; *market rent* or economic rent, the rental income a property would most probably command in the open market; *excess rent*, the amount by which contract rent exceeds market rent at the time of the appraisal; *percentage rent*, rental income received in accordance with the terms of a percentage clause in a lease; and *overage rent*, rent paid over and above the guaranteed minimum rent.

The valuation of a fee simple interest such as an owner-occupied property is based on the market rent the property is capable of generating. However, most income-producing properties are leased. To value a leased fee interest, the appraiser must examine existing contract rent for leased space and market rent for vacant or owner-occupied space. If discounted cash flow analysis is used, future market rents are estimated.

Appraisers can estimate market value either by valuing the fee simple property at market rent and deducting the present value of the rent loss (i.e., market rent less contract rent), or by valuing the leased fee property subject to existing contract rent for leased space and market rent for vacant and owner-occupied space.

Scheduled current rent for the subject property is reduced to a unit basis so that it can be compared with the rent for similar properties. When the market rents of comparable properties are adjusted to an equivalent rent basis and reduced to the same unit of comparison, a clear inidication of market rent should result. Rents are adjusted in the same way the transaction price of a comparable property is adjusted in the sales comparison approach. Comparable rent must reflect similar terms of lessor/lessee obligation, conditions of rental, time of renting, property location, and physical and income-producing characteristics as the subject rent.

Net operating income and pre-tax cash flow expectancy are analyzed to determine a property's earning power. The appraiser examines the income and expense history of the subject property; the income and expense histories of competitive properties; recently signed leases, proposed leases, and asking rents for the subject and competitive properties; actual vacancy levels for the subject and competitive properties; management expense budgets for the subject and competitive properties; published operating data; market expectations; and tax assessment policies and utility company projections for rate changes. This information is often presented in tabular form when income and expenses per rentable area are analyzed on a monthly or annual basis.

To develop a net operating income estimate for the subject property, the appraiser begins by computing the potential gross income from scheduled rent in existing leases, rent from escalation clauses, market rent attributable to vacant and owner-occupied space, and other income. Income generated by the operation of the real property but not directly attributable to rent is considered other income; depending on market practice, this income may also be treated as business income. *Vacancy and collection loss*, which allows for reductions in potential income due to vacancies, tenant turnover, and nonpayment of rent, is deducted from potential gross income to obtain effective gross income.

Next the appraiser undertakes a comprehensive analysis of *operating expenses*, the periodic expenditures necessary to maintain the real property and continue the production of income. The appraiser should know whether the operating statements examined were prepared on a cash or accrual basis. An operating expense estimate includes *fixed expenses*, which generally do not vary with occupancy and must be paid whether the property is occupied or not; *variable expenses*, which generally do vary with the level of occupancy or the extent of services provided; and a replacement allowance, which provides for the periodic replacement of building components during the economic life of the building.

Fixed expenses include taxes and premiums for fire and owner's liability insurance. Variable expenses include charges for management services that are contracted or provided by the owner; leasing fees or commissions to agents who negotiate and secure property leases; utility expenses incurred by the owner for electricity, gas, water, and sewerage; heat charges; air-conditioning costs; general payroll for all employees whose services are essential to property operation and management but whose salaries are not included in other specific categories; cleaning charges; maintenance and repair costs; decorating expenses; charges for grounds and parking area maintenance; and miscellaneous expenses for security, supplies, and rubbish and snow removal.

A replacement allowance provides for items that wear out, including roofing; carpeting; kitchen, bath, and laundry equipment; elevators and boilers; interior improvements in tenant space at lease renewal; sidewalks; driveways; parking lots; and exterior painting. The annual allowance for each item is calculated as its anticipated replacement cost prorated over its remaining economic life. Discounted cash flow analysis may also be applied to the actual costs of these items and the timing of payment.

Fixed expenses, variable expenses, and the replacement allowance cited in the operating expense estimate are added together to calculate *total operating expenses*. The anticipated net income remaining after all operating expenses are deducted from effective gross income, but before mortgage debt service and book depreciation are deducted, is net operating income.

The appraiser deducts *mortgage debt service*, the periodic payment for interest on and retirement of the mortgage loan principal, from net operating income to derive *pre-tax cash flow*, or equity dividend, which is used in certain capitalization procedures. The value definition used in the appraisal may assume existing financing or market financing; the mortgage debt service deducted should be consistent with the value definition applied.

The appraiser may use an *operating expense ratio*, the ratio of total operating expenses to effective gross income, or a *net income ratio*, the ratio of net operating income to effective gross income, to identify income or expense statements that do not conform to typical patterns and require further analysis.

A reconstructed operating statement, or pro forma statement, represents an opinion of the probable future net operating income of the investment. The following items are often included in operating statements for property owners, but should be omitted from reconstructed operating statements for appraisal purposes: book depreciation, which may have little relation to market value and could be redundant in light of provisions for capital recapture; income tax, which varies with the type of property ownership and is not considered an operating expense; special corporation costs; and additions to capital, which are one-time expenditures for capital improvements.

Once the future net operating income or pre-tax cash flows and the reversion are estimated, they may be discounted to obtain an indication of the present value of the investment.

20 Direct Capitalization

Direct capitalization is a method used to convert a single year's income estimate into a value indication in the income capitalization approach. This conversion is accomplished in one step, either by dividing the income estimate by an appropriate income rate or by multiplying it by an appropriate income factor.

In direct capitalization, no precise allocation is made between the return on and the return of capital because the method does not simulate investor assumptions or forecasts concerning the holding period, the pattern of income, or changes in the value of the original investment. However, a satisfactory rate of return for the investor and recapture of the capital invested are implicit in the rates or factors used in direct capitalization because they are derived from similar investment properties.

Direct capitalization may be based on potential gross income, effective gross income, net operating income, equity income, mortgage income, land income, or building income. Therefore, the income rates used in direct capitalization include the overall (property) capitalization rate (R_O), the mortgage capitalization rate (R_M), the equity capitalization, or equity dividend, rate (R_E), the land capitalization rate (R_L), and the building capitalization rate (R_B). Income factors include the potential gross income multiplier $(PGIM)$, the gross rent multiplier (GRM), and the effective gross income multiplier $(EGIM)$.

The income rates and factors reflect the relationship between income and value and are derived from market data. It is essential that the properties used as comparables reflect risk, income, expense, and physical and locational characteristics that are similar to the property being appraised. Hence, income multipliers and rates must be extracted from properties with similar income-expense ratios, land-building ratios, and risk characteristics.

In addition to direct capitalization procedures in which a rate or factor is directly applied to the income estimate, physical, financial, economic, and legal residual techniques may also be used.

DERIVATION OF OVERALL CAPITALIZATION RATES

Any interest in real estate that has an income stream can be valued by direct capitalization, but the interest most commonly appraised is the fee simple estate, which include all property rights in the real estate. The direct capitalization formula that applies to this type of valuation is

$$\text{Value} = \frac{\text{Net operating income}}{\text{Overall capitalization rate}}$$

An appraiser can estimate an overall capitalization rate with various techniques; the techniques used depend on the quantity and quality of data available. Accepted techniques include 1) derivation from comparable sales, 2) derivation from effective gross income multipliers, 3) band of investment—mortgage and equity components, 4) band of investment—land and building components, and 5) the debt coverage formula.

Derivation from Comparable Sales

Deriving capitalization rates from comparable sales is preferred when sufficient data on sales of similar, competitive properties are available. Data on each property's sale price, income, expenses, financing terms, and market conditions at the time of sale are needed. In addition, the appraiser must be certain that the net operating income of each comparable property is calculated and estimated in the same way that the income of the subject property is estimated and that neither nonmarket financing terms nor different market conditions have affected the prices of the comparables. When these requirements are met, the appraiser can estimate an overall rate by dividing each property's net operating income by its sale price. Table 20.1 illustrates this procedure using data from four comparable sales.

Table 20.1   Derivation of Overall Capitalization Rates From Comparable Sales

	Comparables			
	A	B	C	D
Price	$368,500	$425,000	$310,000	$500,000
Net operating income	50,000	56,100	42,718	68,600
Indicated R_O	0.1357	0.1320	0.1378	0.1372

If all four transactions are equally reliable and comparable, the appraiser might conclude that an overall rate of 0.1320 to 0.1378 be applied to the subject property. The final rate selection depends on the appraiser's judgment as to how comparable each sale is to the subject property.

If there are differences between a comparable property and the subject property that could affect the overall capitalization rate selected, the appraiser must account for these differences. In such cases, the appraiser must decide whether the rate chosen for the subject property should be higher or lower than the rate in a specific sale. Appraisal judgment is also needed to determine whether the rate selected for the subject should fall within the range established by the sales or, in certain cases, be set above or below the range.

When rates derived from comparable sales are used, the overall capitalization rate is applied to the subject property in a manner consistent with rate derivation. In other words, if the market-derived capitalization rates are based on the properties' net operating income expectancies for the first year, the capitalization rate for the subject property should be applied to its anticipated net operating income for the first year of operation.

The net income to be capitalized may be estimated before or after an annual allowance for replacements is considered. Again, it is imperative that the appraiser analyze comparable sales and derive their capitalization rates in the same manner used to analyze the subject property and capitalize its income.

The examples that follow illustrate the importance of deriving and applying rates consistently. In the first example, the replacement allowance for the subject property is estimated at $2,500. The overall rate indicated by comparable sales in which a replacement allowance was not deducted as an operating expense was 0.0850. If the replacement allowance were deducted as an operating expense, the indicated overall rate would be 0.0825. In the first calculation, the allowance is included as an expense item to be deducted from effective gross income. Therefore, the net operating income here is $2,500 more than in the second calculation. The valuation conclusions produced by the two calculations are identical.

Before Deducting Allowance for Replacements

Net operating income	$ 85,000
Overall rate	0.0850
Capitalization: $85,000/0.0850 =	$1,000,000

After Deducting Allowance for Replacements

Net operating income	$ 82,500
Overall rate	0.0825
Capitalization: $82,500/0.0825 =	$1,000,000

This technique for estimating overall capitalization rates is preferred and will produce a reliable indication of value by the income capitalization approach if three conditions are met.

1. Income and expenses must be estimated on the same basis for the subject property and all comparable properties.

2. Market expectations concerning resale prices, tax benefits, and holding periods must be similar for all the properties.

3. Financing terms and market conditions that affect the comparables must be similar to those affecting the subject property or an adjustment must be made for any dissimilarities.

Derivation from Effective Gross Income Multipliers

Sometimes an overall capitalization rate cannot be derived directly because the stringent data requirements cannot be met, but reliable sales transaction and *gross* income data can be obtained from several comparable transactions. In such cases, an effective gross income multiplier can be derived and used in conjunction with an operating expense ratio (OER) to produce an overall capitalization rate. (The derivation of income multipliers is discussed later in this chapter.)

The operating expense ratio is the ratio of operating expenses to effective gross income. Although effective gross income multipliers can be based on annual or monthly income, annual income is used unless otherwise specified. Monthly income is primarily used for single-family or small multifamily residential properties. Frequently, an appraiser can obtain marketwide averages of operating expense ratios as well as the effective gross income multipliers indicated by comparable sales.

The formula for deriving an overall rate from the effective gross income multiplier and the operating expense ratio is

$$R_O = \frac{1 - OER}{EGIM}$$

According to Table 20.1, Comparable A was recently sold for $368,500. The property's potential gross income is $85,106, its effective gross income is $80,000, and its operating expenses are $30,000. Thus, the effective gross income multiplier is 4.6063 ($368,500/$80,000) and the operating expense ratio is 0.3750 ($30,000/$80,000). The overall capitalization rate extracted from the effective gross income multiplier of Comparable A is

$$R_O = \frac{1 - 0.3750}{4.6063}$$

$$= 0.1357$$

This calculation is performed for all comparables and an estimated overall capitalization rate is reconciled from the overall capitalization rate indications derived. The effective gross income multiplier is supportable if the property comparability requirements that apply to the direct derivation of an overall rate are met.

Band of Investment—Mortgage and Equity Components

Because most properties are purchased with debt and equity capital, the overall capitalization rate must satisfy the market return requirements of both investment positions. Lenders must anticipate receiving a competitive interest rate commensurate with the perceived risk of the investment or they will not make funds available. Lenders also require that the principal amount of the loan be repaid through periodic amortization payments. Similarly, equity investors must anticipate receiving a competitive equity cash return commensurate with the perceived risk or they will invest their funds elsewhere.

The capitalization rate for debt is called the *mortgage constant* (R_M). It is the ratio of the annual debt service to the principal amount of the mortgage loan. If the loan is paid off more frequently (e.g., with monthly payments), the mortgage constant is calculated by multiplying each period's payment by the frequency of payment and then dividing this amount by the amount of the loan. For example, the annual constant for a monthly payment loan is obtained by multiplying the monthly payment by 12 and dividing the result by the amount of the loan. Of course, the same result can be obtained by multiplying the ratio of monthly payments to the mortgage amount (i.e., the monthly constant) by 12.

The mortgage constant is a function of the interest rate, the frequency of amortization, and the term of the loan. It is the sum of the interest rate and sinking fund factor; when the loan terms are known, the mortgage constant can be found in financial tables. (Appendix C contains financial function tables for selected rates.) An appraiser must take care to use a table that corresponds to the frequency of amortization (e.g., monthly, quarterly, or annually).

The equity investor also seeks a systematic cash return. The rate used to capitalize equity income is called the *equity capitalization rate* (R_E). It is the ratio of annual pre-tax cash flow to the amount of equity investment. This rate is not simply a rate of return on capital, rather it is a rate of return both on and of capital. The equity capitalization rate may be more or less than the eventual equity yield rate. For appraisal purposes, a property's equity capitalization rate is the anticipated return to the investor, usually for the first year of the holding period.

The overall capitalization rate must satisfy both the mortgage constant requirement of the lender and the pre-tax cash flow requirement of the equity investor. It is a composite rate, weighted in proportion to the total property investment represented by debt and equity. The loan-to-value ratio (M) represents the loan or debt portion of the property investment; the equity ratio is expressed as $(1 - M)$. Typical mortgage terms and conditions may be obtained by surveying lenders active in the market area. Equity capitalization rates are derived from comparable sales by dividing the pre-tax cash flow of each sale by the equity investment. The equity capitalization rate used to capitalize the subject property's pre-tax cash flow ultimately depends on the appraiser's judgment.

When the mortgage constant and equity capitalization rates are known, an overall rate may be derived with the band-of-investment, or weighted-average, technique.

Mortgage component $\quad\quad M \times R_M \ =$
Equity component $\quad\quad (1 - M) \times R_E \ = \ \underline{\quad + \quad}$
$$R_O \ =$$

To illustrate how the overall capitalization rate is calculated with the band-of-investment technique, assume that the following characteristics describe the subject property.

Available loan   75% ratio, 13.5% interest, 25-year
                                  amortization period, 0.1399 constant (R_M)
Equity capitalization rate   12.0% (derived from comparable sales)

The overall rate is calculated as follows:

$$R_O \ = \ (0.75 \times 0.1399) + (1-0.75) \ (0.1200)$$
$$= \ 0.1049 + 0.0300$$
$$= \ 0.1349$$

Although this technique is frequently used to derive overall capitalization rates, appraisers should be careful when using it for this purpose. The technique is particularly applicable in real estate markets where sufficient market data are available and it can be demonstrated that the equity capitalization rate is the primary investment criterion used by buyers and sellers. A capitalization rate used to estimate market value should be justified and supported by market data, but such data often are not available to derive information for mortgage-equity analysis. Therefore, survey and opinion data about equity capitalization rates, available loan terms, and loan-to-value ratios are often substituted for market data. When survey and opinion data or other data not derived from market transactions are used, mortgage-equity techniques are more appropriately used to test market-derived capitalization rates.

Band of Investment—Land and Building Components

A band-of-investment formula can also be applied to the physical components of property—i.e., the land or site and the buildings. Just as weighted rates are developed for mortgage and equity in mortgage-equity analysis, weighted rates for the land and buildings can be developed if accurate rates for these components can be estimated independently and the proportion of total property value represented by each component can be identified. The formula is

$$R_O = L \times R_L + B \times R_B$$

where L = land value as a percentage of total property value, R_L = land capitalization rate, B = building value as a percentage of total property value, and R_B = building capitalization rate.

Assume that the land represents 45% of the value of the property and the building represents the other 55%. The land capitalization rate derived from comparable sales data is 0.1025; the building capitalization rate is 0.1600. The indicated R_O is calculated as follows:

$$R_O = (0.45 \times 0.1025) + (0.55 \times 0.1600)$$
$$= 0.0461 + 0.0880$$
$$= 0.1341$$

Debt Coverage Formula

In addition to the traditional terms of lending (i.e., the interest rate, loan-to-value ratio, amortization term, maturity, and payment period), real estate lenders sometimes use another constraining factor—the debt coverage ratio (DCR). This is the ratio of net operating income to annual debt service, the payment that covers interest on and retirement of the outstanding principal of the mortgage loan (I_M).

$$DCR = \frac{NOI}{I_M}$$

This measure of constraint is frequently used by institutional lenders, who are generally fiduciaries. They manage and lend the money of others, including depositors and policyholders. Due to their fiduciary responsibility, institutional lenders are particularly sensitive to the safety of loan investments, especially the safety of principal. They are concerned with safety and profit and are anxious to avoid default and possible foreclosure. Consequently, when they underwrite income property loans, institutional lenders try to provide a cushion so that the borrower will be able to meet the debt service obligations on the loan even if building income declines.

To estimate an overall rate, the debt coverage ratio can be multiplied by the mortgage constant and the loan-to-value ratio.[1] The formula is

$$R_O = DCR \times R_M \times M$$

Assuming that net operating income is $50,000 and annual debt service is $43,264, the debt coverage ratio is calculated as follows.

$$DCR = \frac{\$50,000}{\$43,264}$$

$$= 1.1557$$

---

1. See Ronald E. Gettel, "Good Grief, *Another* Method of Selecting Capitalization Rates?!" *The Appraisal Journal*, January 1978.

If R_M equals 0.1565 and M is 0.75, R_O is estimated as

$$R_O = 1.1557 \times 0.1565 \times 0.75$$
$$= 0.1357$$

RESIDUAL TECHNIQUES

Residual techniques allow an appraiser to capitalize the income allocated to an investment component of unknown value once all investment components of known value have been satisfied. The physical, or land and building, residual techniques and the financial, or mortgage and equity, residual techniques are the primary residual techniques used in direct capitalization.

Regardless of which known and unknown, or residual, components of the property are being analyzed, the appraiser starts with the value of the known item(s) and the net operating income. The appraiser

1. Applies an appropriate capitalization rate to the value of the known component to derive the annual income needed to support the investment in that component

2. Deducts the annual income needed to support the investment in the known component from the net operating income to derive the residual income available to support the investment in the unknown component

3. Capitalizes the residual income at a capitalization rate appropriate to the investment in the residual component to derive the present value of this component

4. Adds the values of the known component and the residual component to derive a value indication for the total property

Building Residual Technique

An appraiser using this technique assumes that land or site value can be estimated independently. The appraiser applies the land capitalization rate to the known land value to obtain the amount of annual net income needed to support land value. Then this amount is deducted from the net operating income to derive the residual income available to support the investment in the building(s). The appraiser capitalizes this residual income at the building capitalization rate to derive an indication of the present value of the building(s). Finally, the land value and the building value are added to derive an indication of total property value. The land and building capitalization rates derived from the market are applied to the subject property with the calculations shown below.

Estimated land value		$ 200,000
Net operating income	$ 85,500	
Land value × R_L ($200,000 × 0.09)	−18,000	
Residual income to building	$ 67,500	
Building value (capitalized: $67,500/0.15)		+450,000
Indicated property value		$ 650,000

To apply the building residual technique, the appraiser must obtain information on present land value, current net operating income, and land and building capitalization rates. This technique is simple, but its applicability and usefulness are extremely limited.

When the required data are available, the building residual technique can be used in valuing properties with improvements that have suffered substantial accrued depreciation. In fact, current reproduction or replacement cost minus the present value of the improvements provides an estimate of total accrued depreciation. In addition, the building residual technique directly measures the contribution of the improvements to total property value, so it can help an appraiser determine when demolition or major renovation of property improvements is economically feasible.

Land Residual Technique

The land residual technique assumes that the value of the building(s) can be estimated separately. In land residual applications, an appraiser will often consider a new, highest and best use building that does not exist. Thus, building value is usually estimated as the current cost to construct a new building that represents the highest and best use of the land or site.

The building capitalization rate is applied to the building value to obtain the amount of annual net income needed to support the value of the building. This amount is then deducted from net operating income to indicate the residual income available to support the investment in the land. The residual income is capitalized at the land capitalization rate to derive an indication of the value of the land. Finally, the building value is added to the land value to derive a total property value indication. As in the building residual technique, the land and building capitalization rates derived from the market are applied to the subject property with the calculations shown below.

Estimated building value		$ 450,000
Net operating income	$ 85,500	
Building value $\times R_B$ ($450,000 $\times$ 0.15)	$-67,500$	
Residual income to land	$ 18,000	
Land value (capitalized: $18,000/0.09)		$+200,000$
Indicated property value		$ 650,000

The land residual technique allows appraisers to estimate land values when recent data on land sales are not available. The technique can be applied to proposed construction to test the highest and best use of the land or site or to new structures that do not suffer from accrued depreciation. However, the land residual technique is not applicable when the cost to produce a new building is inconsistent with the market contribution of such a new building to property value.

Equity Residual Technique

To apply the equity residual technique, an appraiser deducts annual debt service from net operating income to obtain the residual income for the equity interest. The appraiser who uses this technique assumes that mortgage loan terms can be obtained from the market and that the dollar amount of the debt can be estimated. The residual equity income is then capitalized into value with a market-derived equity capitalization rate as shown below. This technique is especially useful for appraising the fee simple interest in a newly constructed property or the equity interest in a property subject to a specific mortgage.

Mortgage amount		$ 375,000
Mortgage interest rate	12.0%	
Mortgage amortization term	25 yrs.	
Monthly amortization payment		
($375,000 $\times$ 0.0105322)	$3,950	
Net operating income	$ 60,000	
Mortgage $\times R_M$		
($375,000 $\times$ 0.12639)	$-47,400$	
Residual income to equity	$ 12,600	
Equity value capitalized:		
($12,600/0.09)		$+140,000$
Indicated property value		$ 515,000

Mortgage Residual Technique

In the mortgage residual technique, the amount of available equity is the known component and the mortgage amount or value is unknown. The income needed to satisfy the equity component at the equity capitalization rate is deducted from the net operating income to obtain the residual income to the mortgage component. The residual mortgage income is then capitalized into value at the mortgage capitalization rate.

Available equity		$ 140,000
Net operating income	$ 60,000	
Equity $\times R_E$ ($140,000 $\times$ 0.09)	$-12,600$	
Residual income to mortgage	$ 47,400	
Mortgage value (capitalized: $47,400/0.1264)		+375,000
Indicated property value		$ 515,000

GROSS INCOME MULTIPLIERS

Gross income multipliers are used to compare the income-producing characteristics of properties in the sales comparison approach. Nevertheless, converting a potential or effective gross income stream into a lump-sum capital value by applying a gross income multiplier is capitalization. Therefore, the derivation and use of multipliers are discussed in direct capitalization.

To derive a gross income multiplier from market data, sales of properties that were rented at the time of sale or were anticipated to be rented within a short time must be available. The ratio of sale price to annual gross income *at the time of sale* or projected over the first year or several years of ownership is the gross income multiplier.

Appraisers who attempt to derive and apply gross income multipliers for valuation purposes must be careful for several reasons. First, the properties analyzed must be comparable to the subject property and to one another in terms of physical, locational, and investment characteristics. Properties with similar or even identical multipliers can have very different operating expense ratios and, therefore, not be comparable for valuation purposes.

Second, the term *gross income multiplier* is used because some of the gross income from a property or type of property may come from sources other than rental. A *gross rent multiplier* applies to rental income only.

Third, the appraiser must use similar income data to derive the multiplier for each transaction. The sale price can be divided by either the potential or effective gross income, but the data and measure must be used consistently throughout the analysis to produce reliable results. Different income measures may be used in different valuation studies and appraisals, however. The income measure selected is dictated by the availability of market data and the purpose of the analysis.

To illustrate the difference between different gross income multipliers, data from Comparable A in Table 20.1 are used in the following calculations:

$$\text{Potential gross income multiplier} = \frac{\text{sale price}}{\text{potential gross income}}$$

$$= \frac{\$368,500}{\$\ 85,106} = 4.3299^*$$

$$\text{Effective gross income multiplier} = \frac{\text{sale price}}{\text{effective gross income}}$$

$$= \frac{\$368,500}{\$\ 80,000} = 4.6063$$

*In actual practice, multipliers are typically rounded to two decimal places.

After the gross income multiplier is derived from comparable market data, it must be applied on the same basis it was derived. In other words, an income multiplier based on effective gross income can only be applied to the effective gross income of the subject property; an income multiplier based on potential gross income can only be applied to the potential gross income of the subject property. The timing of income also must be comparable. If sales are analyzed using the next year's income expectation, the multiplier derived must be applied to next year's income expectation for the subject property.

SUMMARY

Direct capitalization is used to convert an estimate of a single year's income expectancy into an indication of value in one step, either by dividing the income estimate by an appropriate rate or multiplying it by an appropriate factor. The method does not distinguish between the return on and the return of capital because investor assumptions are not simulated. Because the rates or factors used in direct capitalization are derived from similar investment properties, a satisfactory rate of return on and of capital may be assumed.

In addition to *PGI*, *EGI*, and *NOI*, direct capitalization may be based on equity income, mortgage income, land income, or building income. Thus, the income rates that may be used include the overall property capitalization rate (R_O), the equity capitalization rate (R_E), the mortgage capitalization rate (R_M), the land capitalization rate (R_L), and the building capitalization rate (R_B). The income factors include the potential gross income multiplier (*PGIM*), the gross rent multiplier (*GRM*), and the effective gross income multiplier (*EGIM*). The income rates and factors are derived from data on comparable properties that have similar income-expense ratios, land-building ratios, investment risk, and physical and locational characteristics.

The direct capitalization formula is

$$\text{Value} = \frac{\text{Net operating income}}{\text{Overall capitalization rate}}$$

The techniques that can be used to estimate an overall capitalization rate include derivation from comparable sales, derivation from effective gross income multipliers, band of investment—mortgage and equity components, band of investment—land and building components, and the debt coverage formula.

When reliable data on similar, competitive properties are available, an appraiser can derive overall capitalization rates by dividing the *NOI* of each property by its sale price. If a comparable sale and the subject property differ, the appraiser must decide whether the rate for the subject property should be higher or lower. The overall rate should be applied to the subject property in a manner consistent with the way the rates were dervied from comparable sales. Deriving rates from comparable sales is the preferred technique when income and expenses of the subject and comparable properties are estimated on the same basis, market expectations for all the properties are similar, and the market conditions affecting the comparables are similar to those affecting the subject.

If adequate data to derive an overall capitalization rate are not available, but reliable data on sales transactions and gross incomes are, an *effective gross income multiplier* can be used with the operating expense ratio (*OER*) to estimate an overall capitalization rate. The formula for this procedure is

$$R_O = \frac{1 - OER}{EGIM}$$

This calculation is performed for all the comparable properties and an overall capitalization rate is reconciled from the different rate indications.

Lenders of mortgage funds expect both a return on capital, in the form of interest, and a return of capital through amortization of the principal. Similarly, equity investors expect a return on equity commensurate with the investment risk. Accordingly, one band-of-investment technique considers the overall capitalization rate as a composite rate, weighted by the proportions of debt and equity in the property investment.

The mortgage constant (R_M), which is the capitalization rate for debt, represents the ratio of annual debt service to the principal amount of the mortgage loan. The mortgage constant is a function of the interest rate, the frequency of amortization, and the term of the loan. Given the interest rate and the loan terms, the mortgage constant can be found in published financial tables.

The equity capitalization rate is the ratio of annual pre-tax cash flow to the amount of equity investment. The equity capitalization rate reflects the anticipated return to the investor, usually for the first year of the holding period.

The overall rate must satisfy the requirements of both the mortgage constant and the pre-tax cash flow. In addition to R_M and R_E, the loan-to-value ratio (*M*) and the equity ratio $(1 - M)$ are needed to weight the mortgage components. The formula for this band-of-investment, or weighted average, technique is

$$R_O = M \times R_M + [(1 - M) \times R_E]$$

This technique can only be used when reliable, market-derived data on equity capitalization rates, available loan terms, and loan-to-value ratios are available.

A second band-of-investment technique considers the overall capitalization rate as a composite rate weighted by the proportions of land and building components in the property. The formula is

$$R_O = L \times R_L + B \times R_B$$

where L represents the percentage that land contributes to the overall property, and B is the percentage contribution represented by the building.

Institutional lenders use the *debt coverage ratio* (*DCR*), which is the ratio of *NOI* to annual debt service (I_M). The *DCR* may also be used to estimate the overall capitalization rate with the formula

$$R_O = DCR \times R_M \times M$$

where M represents the percentage of the mortgage component.

Residual techniques allow an appraiser to capitalize the income allocated to an investment component of unknown value after all investment components of known value have been satisfied. There are both physical (i.e., land and building) and financial (i.e., mortgage and equity) residual techniques.

Four procedures are common to all residual techniques. The appraiser 1) applies an appropriate capitalization rate to the value of a known component to obtain the annual income needed to support the investment in that component, 2) deducts this amount from the *NOI* to derive the residual income available to support the unknown, or residual, component, 3) capitalizes the residual income at a capitalization rate appropriate to the investment in the residual component to derive the present value of this component, and 4) adds the values of the known and residual components to derive a value indication for the total property.

In the building and land residual techniques, either land or building value is estimated independently and converted into the annual net income required to support this component by applying an appropriate capitalization rate. This income is deducted from *NOI* to derive the residual income available to support the investment in the unknown component. The residual income is then capitalized and added to the value of the known component to obtain an indication of overall property value. The building residual technique is limited in its applicability. The land residual technique may be applied to proposed construction to test the highest and best use of the land or to new construction that shows little accrued depreciation.

In the equity and mortgage residual techniques, either the mortgage or the equity amount is converted into net annual income by applying an appropriate capitalization rate. This income is deducted from *NOI* to derive the residual income available to support the investment in the unknown component. The residual income is then capitalized and added to the value of the known component to obtain an indication of overall property value. The equity residual technique is especially useful in valuing a newly constructed property or an equity interest subject to a specific mortgage.

Gross income multipliers may be used to compare the income-producing characteristics of properties in the sales comparison approach and to convert gross income streams into property value in direct capitalization. The ratio of the sale price of a property to its annual gross income at the time of sale or projected over the first year or several years of ownership is the gross income multiplier. The appraiser must be sure that the properties used to derive gross income multipliers are comparable, that the gross income multipliers obtained apply only to rental income, that similar income data on either potential or effective gross income are used to derive the multipliers, and that the gross income multiplier obtained is applied to the same income base from which it was derived.

21 Yield Capitalization —Theory and Basic Applications

Yield capitalization is used to convert future benefits into present value by applying an appropriate yield rate. To select an appropriate yield rate for a market value appraisal, an appraiser analyzes market evidence of the yields anticipated by typical investors. When investment value is sought, the yield rate used should reflect the individual investor's requirements, which may differ from requirements that are typical in the market.

To perform yield capitalization, an appraiser 1) selects a holding period, 2) forecasts all future cash flows or cash flow patterns and analyzes the relationship between present and future cash flows, 3) chooses an appropriate yield, or discount, rate, and 4) converts future benefits into present value by discounting each annual future benefit or by developing an overall rate that reflects the income pattern, value change, and yield rate. The application of capitalization rates that reflect an appropriate yield rate, the use of present value factors, and discounted cash flow analysis are all yield capitalization procedures. Mortgage-equity formulas and yield rate or value change formulas may be used to derive overall capitalization rates. Like direct capitalization, yield capitalization may also employ residual techniques. To apply the discounting process, the appraiser must be familiar with income patterns, capital return concepts, the mathematics of discounting, and the appropriateness of discount rates.

THE NATURE OF ANNUITIES

Literally, the word *annuity* means an annual income, but it is used to refer to a program or contract of regular payments of stipulated amounts. Payments need not be annual, but the interval between payments must be regular. An annuity can be level, increasing, or decreasing so long as the amounts are scheduled and predictable.

Income that has the characteristics of an annuity is expected at regular intervals in predictable amounts. Obviously, real estate income or rental income can have the characteristics of an annuity.

Some appraisers make a distinction between contract rent and fair market rent in describing annuity income, particularly when the market rent is considered speculative and could decline. In modern practice, however, yield capitalization is not restricted to contract income, and unassured income could increase rather than decline.

The income expected from a real estate investment may be in the form of a regular or irregular pattern. Various capitalization techniques can be applied to different patterns of income streams.

RETURN ON AND RETURN OF CAPITAL

In the real estate market, and in other markets, it is assumed that an investor is entitled to complete recovery of the invested capital and an additional payment for the use of capital. In yield capitalization the distinction between the return on and the return of capital is always definite and precise. Each technique considers the effects of compound interest, or interest on interest, over a specific period of time at a specified rate of interest. Therefore, the interest rate, which is the rate of return on capital, is a true measure of the investment's profitability. The rate of return on capital may be called the discount rate, the equity yield rate, the internal rate of return, or the risk rate depending on the context.

In theory, the total rate of return on capital may be seen as a basic safe rate plus a premium to compensate the investor for risk, the burden of management, and a lack of liquidity. However, the terms *discount rate*, *risk rate*, and *yield rate* are commonly used to refer to a total rate of return on capital, which combines all the rewards of investment in a single rate.

In a real estate investment, capital may be recaptured gradually as a part of regular income or it may be recaptured completely or partially through resale, or reversion, of the property at the termination of the investment. If the investor does not recapture all of the original investment at the time of resale, at least part of the income stream must be used to repay the investor. Therefore, the true rate of return on the investment will be somewhat less than the income rate or overall capitalization rate indicated. In this case, the difference between the rate of return on capital and the indicated capitalization rate would be the rate of return of capital. The recapture rate is considered positive. Amortization rates, rate surcharges, and sinking fund factors are all types of recapture rates.

If, at the termination of the investment, the investor recaptures the original capital, there is no need to repay the investor out of regular income; in this case, the true rate of return on the investment may be equal to the indicated income rate or overall capitalization rate and the recapture rate is zero. If the investor receives more than the original investment at resale, the true rate of return on capital would be more than the indicated income rate; in this case, the recapture rate is considered negative. Each capitalization technique and procedure has its own scheme or hypothesis to provide for a return on capital over and above the return of capital.

DISCOUNTING

Periodic income and reversions are converted into present value through discounting, a procedure based on the assumption that benefits received in the future are worth less than the same benefits received today. A return on the investment compensates an investor for foregoing present benefits (i.e., the immediate use of capital) and accepting future benefits. This payment is usually called *interest* by lenders and *yield* by equity investors. The discounting procedure includes the assumption that the return of capital will be accomplished through periodic income, the reversion, or a combination of both.

Because an investor seeks a total return that exceeds the amount invested, the present value of a prospective benefit must be less than its expected future value. A future payment is discounted to present value by calculating the amount that, if invested today, would grow with compound interest at a satisfactory rate to equal the future payment. The standard formula for discounting future value to present value is

$$\text{Present value} = \frac{\text{Future value}}{(1 + i)^n}$$

where i is the rate of return on capital per period that will satisfy the investor and n is the number of periods that the payment will be deferred. The two examples that follow illustrate applications of the discounting formula.

Problem 1. *What is the present value of $115 due one year hence discounted at 15% per year?* To solve this problem, the amount that should be invested now to grow to $115 with compound interest at the rate of 15% per year must be calculated.

$$\text{Present value} = \$115/1.15^1 = \$100$$

Problem 2. *What is the present value of $1,000 due in three years discounted at 10% per year?* This problem can be solved by calculating the amount that should be invested now to grow to $1,000 in three years with compound interest at 10% per year.

$$\text{Present value} = \$1,000/1.10^3 = \$751.31$$

If a series of future payments is expected, each payment is discounted with the standard formula and the total present value of the payments is the sum of all the present values. This standard discounting procedure is the foundation for all the discounting formulas discussed here and nearly all the discounting routines used with modern computer programs and preprogrammed electronic calculators. Elaborate systems and tables have been built on this simple relationship, but the standard formula can be used to solve some very complex appraisal problems. The various discounting tables and systems available are simply convenient extensions of this basic formula.

The amount deposited or received can be in the form of a single lump sum, a series of periodic installments such as rent, or a combination of both. When amounts are compounded or discounted, the rate used is the effective interest rate which, on an annual basis, is identical to the *nominal interest rate*. If amounts are compounded or discounted more often than annually (e.g., semiannually or monthly), the effective interest rate is derived by dividing the nominal annual rate by the number of compounding or discounting periods. For example, a nominal rate of 12% is an effective rate of 6% for semiannual conversion periods, or an effective rate of 1% for monthly conversions. Standard tables of factors or preprogrammed financial calculators can be used to facilitate the application of factors, but the user must select the appropriate conversion frequency (i.e., monthly, quarterly, or annually).

Each precomputed factor and yield capitalization formula have specific built-in investment assumptions that are implied when the table is used or the factor is calculated. Therefore, the appraiser must identify the assumptions applicable to the subject property and use the factor table and capitalization formula that correspond to the assumptions. Thus, to do compounding or discounting, the appraiser must know the basic formulas, how the various factors relate to one another, and how they may be used or combined to simplify income capitalization.[1]

The tables and factors allow appraisers to solve many arithmetic problems that are fundamental to the valuation process, thus they are useful in applying capitalization techniques. However, in the final analysis, a value estimate reflects the appraiser's judgment based on appropriate research and market data.

Discounted Cash Flow Analysis

Discounted cash flow (DCF) analysis can be used both to estimate present value and to extract a discount rate from a sale. In DCF analysis the quantity, variability, timing, and duration of cash flows are specified. (Here *cash flow* is used to refer to the periodic income attributable to the interests in real property. The terms *cash flow* and *income flow* are often used synonymously.) Each cash flow is discounted to present value and then all the present values are totaled to obtain the total value of the income to the real property interest being appraised. The future value of that interest, the reversion, is forecast at the end of the projection period (i.e., the holding period or remaining economic life) and is also discounted. The cash flows discounted with the DCF formula may be the net operating income to the entire property or the cash flows to specific interests—e.g., the pre-tax cash flow to the equity interest (equity dividend), the after-tax cash flow to the equity interest, or the debt service for the mortgage interest.

---

1. See Appendix C for a discussion of financial tables.

The DCF formula is a yield formula expressed as

$$PV = \frac{CF_1}{1+Y} + \frac{CF_2}{(1+Y)^2} + \frac{CF_3}{(1+Y)^3} + \ldots + \frac{CF_n}{(1+Y)^n}$$

where PV = present value; CF = the cash flow for the period specified; Y = the appropriate periodic yield, or discount, rate; and n = the number of periods in the projection.

With the DCF formula, an appraiser can discount each payment of income separately and add all present values together to obtain the present value of the property interest being appraised. The formula treats the reversion as a cash flow that can be valued separately from the income stream. The formula can be used to estimate total property value (V_O), loan value (V_M), equity value (V_E), leased fee value (V_{LF}), leasehold value (V_{LH}), or any other interest in real property.

When a series of periodic incomes varies in an irregular pattern, the basic DCF formula is used in its analysis and valuation. Any series of periodic incomes, with or without a reversion, can be valued with the basic formula. Formulas for valuing level annuities, increasing and decreasing annuities, deferred annuities, and step-up or step-down annuities are merely shortcuts to be used in these special situations.

Selection of a Yield Rate for Discounting

The selection of the yield rate is critical to DCF analysis. To select an appropriate rate an appraiser must verify and interpret the attitudes and expectations of market participants, including buyers, sellers, advisers, and brokers. Although the actual yield on an investment cannot be calculated until the investment is sold, an investor may set a target yield for the investment before or during ownership. Historical yield rates derived from comparable sales may be relevant, but they reflect past, not future, benefits in the mind of the investor and are not reliable indicators of current yield. Therefore, the selection of yield rates for discounting cash flows should focus on the prospective or forecast yield rates anticipated by typical buyers and sellers. An appraiser can verify investor assumptions directly by interviewing the parties to comparable sales transactions or indirectly by estimating the income expectancy and likely reversion to a comparable property and deriving a prospective yield rate.

The appraiser narrows the range of indicated yield rates and selects an appropriate rate by comparing the physical, economic, and financial characteristics of the comparable properties with the property being appraised and gauging the competition for capital in other financial markets. In some situations, there may be reason to select a yield rate above or below the indicated range. The final selection of a yield rate requires judgment just as the appraiser uses judgment to select an overall rate or equity capitalization rate from the range indicated by comparable sales. In selecting the yield rate, the appraiser should analyze current conditions in capital and real estate markets and the actions and perceptions of real estate investors.

Different Rates

Yield rates are partially a function of perceived risks. Different portions of forecast future income may have different levels of risk and, thus, different yield rates. In lease valuation, for example, one rate might be used to discount the series of net rental incomes stipulated in the lease and a different rate might be used to discount the reversion. One rate reflects the benefits, constraints, and limitations of a contract, while the other is subject to free, open-market conditions. The decision to apply a single yield rate to all benefits or different rates to different benefits should be based on investors' actions in the market.

INCOME STREAM PATTERNS

After specifying the amount, timing, and duration of the cash flows to the property interest being appraised, the appraiser should identify the pattern that the income stream is expected to follow during the projection period. These patterns may be grouped into three basic categories—variable annuity, level annuity, and increasing or decreasing annuity.

Variable Annuity: Nonsystematic Change

A variable annuity is a determinable income stream in which payment amounts vary per period. To value a variable annuity, the present value of each income payment is calculated separately and these values are totaled to obtain the present value of the entire income stream. This procedure is discounted cash flow analysis.

Any income stream can be valued as if it were a variable annuity. Level annuities and annuities that change systematically are special cases which can be handled with special formulas that reflect the systematic pattern of the income stream. These shortcut formulas can save time and effort in certain cases, but valuing an income stream as a variable annuity with a hand-held calculator may be just as easy.

Level Annuity

A level annuity is an income stream in which the amount of each payment is the same; it is a level, unchanging flow of income over time. The payments in a level annuity are equally spaced and there are no irregularities in timing. There are two types of level annuities: ordinary annuities and annuities payable in advance.

Ordinary Annuity

An ordinary annuity, which is probably the most common type of level annuity, is distinguished by income payments that are received at the *end* of each period. Standard fixed-payment mortgage loans, many corporate and government bonds, endowment policies, and certain lease arrangements are ordinary annuities.

Annuity Payable in Advance

An annuity payable in advance is a level annuity in which the payments are received at the *beginning* of each period. A lease that requires payments at the beginning of each month creates an annuity payable in advance.

Increasing or Decreasing Annuity

An income stream that is expected to change in a systematic pattern is either an increasing annuity or a decreasing annuity. Three basic patterns of systematic change are reflected in step-up and step-down annuities, straight-line (constant dollar) change per period annuities, and exponential-curve (constant ratio) change per period annuities.

Step-Up and Step-Down Annuities

A step-up or step-down annuity is usually created by a lease contract that calls for a succession of level annuities set at different levels for different periods within the lease term. For example, a lease might call for monthly payments of $500 for the first three years, $750 for the next four years, and $1,200 for the next six years. Over the 13-year term of the lease, there are three successive level annuities—one for three years, one for four years, and one for six years.

Straight-Line (Constant-Amount) Change per Period Annuity

An income stream that increases or decreases by a fixed amount each period fits the pattern of a straight-line (constant-amount) change per period annuity. These income streams are also called *straight-line increasing* or *straight-line decreasing annuities*. For example, a property may have an estimated first-year net operating income of $100,000 that is forecast to increase $7,000 per year. Thus, the second year's net operating income will be $107,000, the third year's net operating income will be $114,000, and so forth. Similarly, the income stream of a straight-line decreasing annuity is expected to decrease by a constant amount each period.

Exponential-Curve (Constant-Ratio) Change per Period Annuity

An income stream with an exponential-curve (constant-ratio) change per period is also referred to as an *exponential annuity*. This type of income stream increases or decreases at a constant ratio and, therefore, the increases or decreases are compounded. For example, a property with an estimated first-year pre-cash tax flow of $100,000 that is forecast to increase 7% per year over each preceding year's cash flow will have a pre-tax cash flow in the second year of $107,000 ($100,000 × 1.07). However, the third year's pre-tax cash flow will be $114,490 ($107,000 × 1.07) and the fourth year's cash flow will be $122,504 ($114,490 × 1.07).

REVERSION

As mentioned previously, income-producing properties typically provide two types of financial benefits—periodic income and the future value obtained from sale of the property or reversion of the property interest at the end of the holding period. This future cash flow is called a *reversion* because it represents the return of capital at the end of the investment.

A single property may include one or more property interests that have their own streams of periodic benefits and reversions. For example, a property may have an equity interest with equity capitalization, or equity dividend, as the periodic benefit and the equity reversion (i.e., property reversion minus the mortgage balance at loan maturity or property resale) as the reversionary benefit. The same property could have a mortgage with debt service as the periodic benefit and the mortgage balance as the reversionary interest. Table 21.1 shows the possible investment positions in an income-producing property and identifies the income streams and reversions associated with each interest.

Table 21.1   Summary of Incomes and Reversions Associated with Various Real Property Interests in Income-Producing Property

Real Property Interest	Income	Reversion
Property: fee simple	Net operating income	Property value or proceeds of resale
Lender (mortgagee)	Mortgage debt service	Balance if paid prior to maturity
Equity	Cash flow (equity dividend)	Equity proceeds of resale
Leased fee	Net operating income based on contract rent	Property reversion or proceeds of resale of leased fee estate
Leasehold	Rental advantage when contract rent is below market rent	None if held to end of lease or proceeds of resale of leasehold estate

Note. Incomes and reversions may be calculated before or after income taxes.

The reversion is often a major portion of the total benefits to be received from an investment in income-producing property. If the investor's capital is not recaptured, the effective rate of return *on* the investment will always be negative or zero. For certain investments, *all* capital recapture is accomplished through the reversion; for other investment properties, part of the recapture is provided by the reversion and part is provided by the investment's income stream.

To judge how much of the return of an investment will be provided by the reversion, an appraiser acknowledges that three general situations could result from the original investment. First, the property may increase in value over the holding period. Second, the property's value may not change—i.e., the value of the property at the end of the holding period or remaining economic life may be equal to its value at the beginning of the period. Third, the property may decline in value over the period being analyzed. Because these possible outcomes affect the potential yield of investment and the amount of income considered acceptable, the appraiser must estimate the change, if any, that will occur in the original investment or the property value over the holding period.

The appraiser usually projects the reversion to the property as property value or the proceeds of resale. The term *proceeds of resale* refers to the net difference between the transaction price and any selling expenses, which may include brokerage commissions, legal fees, fix-up costs, and possibly penalties for the prepayment of debt.

An appraiser judges the likely value of the reversion in light of the expectations of investors in the market for the type of property being appraised. The appraiser may ask: Do investors expect a change in the value of this type of property in this particular locale? By how much will values change and in which direction? The appraiser analyzes and interprets the market and estimates the value of the future reversion based on the direction and the amount or percentage of change that investors expect.

DISCOUNTING MODELS

Clearly, the present value of any pattern of increasing, level, or decreasing income or of any irregular income can be calculated with DCF analysis. Specific valuation models, or formulas, categorized as either income models or property models have been developed for application to the corresponding pattern of projected benefits. Income models can be applied only to a stream of income. The present value of an expected reversion or any other benefit not included in the income stream must be added to obtain total present value. With the property models, an income stream and a reversion can be valued in one operation. Other present value models employ mortgage-equity concepts and discounted cash flow analysis; these are covered in Chapter 22.

Income Models

Valuation models can be applied to the following patterns of income: variable or irregular income, level income, straight-line (constant-amount) change per period income, and exponential-curve (constant-ratio) change per period income.

Variable or Irregular Income

As mentioned previously, the present value of an uneven stream of income is the sum of the discounted benefits treated as a series of separate reversions. This model simply totals all present values using the standard discounting formula. The routine can be applied as a property valuation model as well as an income valuation model because it can be adapted to include the final reversion as part of the final cash flow expected at the end of the last, or *n*th, period.

Level Income

When a lease provides for a level stream of net operating income or when net operating income can be projected at a stabilized level, one or more capitalization procedures may be appropriate depending on the investor's assumptions with respect to capital recovery. Capitalization can be accomplished using capitalization in perpetuity, the Inwood premise, or the Hoskold premise.

Capitalization in perpetuity. Capitalization in perpetuity can be considered a property valuation model or an income valuation model. If, for example, a property is expected to generate stable net operating income for a finite period of time and then be resold for the original purchase price, the property could be valued with capitalization in perpetuity simply by dividing the expected periodic income by an appropriate discount rate. In this model the discount rate and the overall capitalization rate are the same, either because the income is expected to last forever or because the original investment is presumed to be recovered at the termination of the investment.

The Inwood premise. The Inwood premise holds that the present value of a stream of income is based on a single discount rate. Each installment of income is discounted as a reversion with a single discount rate, and the total discounted values of the installments are accumulated to obtain the present value of the income stream. The present value of a series of $1 payments can be found in compound interest tables for a given rate and a given period of time. It is assumed that the income will be sufficient to return all investment capital to the investor and to pay the specified return on the investment.

Usually interest is assumed to decline gradually and is calculated as a specified percentage of the unrecaptured capital. Any excess over the required interest payment is considered a return of capital and reduces the amount remaining in the investment. Because the installments are always the same amount, the principal portion of the payments increases by the same amounts that the interest portion of the payments decreases. It is also valid, but not customary, to see the interest payments as constant, always amounting to the specified return on the original investment, with any excess over the required, fixed-interest payments credited to a hypothetical sinking fund that grows with interest at the same rate. These two concepts produce identical results in capitalization as long as a single rate of return is used and the amount and duration of the income are the same. The Inwood premise is widely accepted and is the basis for compound interest tables.

The Inwood premise applies only to a stream of income. Therefore, the present value of an expected reversion or any other benefit not included in the income stream must be added to obtain the total present value of the investment.

The Hoskold premise. The Hoskold premise differs from the Inwood premise in that it employs two separate interest rates: a speculative rate, representing a fair rate of return on capital commensurate with the risks involved, and a safe rate for a sinking fund designed to return all the invested capital in a lump sum at the termination of the investment. It is assumed that the stream of income is of limited duration and is sufficient to 1) pay a fair return on capital at the speculative rate, and 2) contribute necessary installments to a conservative, minimum-risk sinking fund, which will grow with interest at a safe rate and repay the investor in full at the termination of the investment.

The return on capital is always the same; the contributions to the sinking fund are always the same. The sinking-fund contributions are sometimes thought of as a return of capital, but technically they are payments that provide for the future return of capital, which will not occur until the end of the investment. The Hoskold premise was designed to value investments in wasting assets such as mineral deposits because it was considered unrealistic to discount an entire stream of income with a single speculative rate that would necessitate a piecemeal reinvestment or the establishment of a hypothetical sinking fund at an unachievable rate of return. The system has merit, but it is not generally accepted.

At one time special tables of Hoskold factors were used by many real estate appraisers. The Hoskold premise has become less popular and is now considered appropriate only for certain types of investments or in geographic areas where it is an accurate reflection of the behavior of buyers and sellers in the open market. A Hoskold capitalization rate can be easily constructed by adding the speculative rate to the sinking fund factor for the safe rate. Generally, the prevailing rate for insured savings accounts or government bonds is considered an appropriate safe rate. The Hoskold factor for valuing an income stream is, of course, the reciprocal of the Hoskold capitalization rate.

Like the Inwood premise, the Hoskold premise is applicable only to the valuation of an income stream. The present value of an expected reversion or any other expected benefit not included in the income stream must be added to obtain the total present value.

The incompatibility of Inwood and Hoskold applications. It is inappropriate to apply the two premises to the same income stream. It is difficult to compare single-rate and dual-rate systems fairly. The single rate of return used to value an investment under the Inwood premise is not necessarily the same as the speculative rate used under the Hoskold premise.

Assume, for example, an investment has an annual income of $1,000 that will last for 20 years. This income could be discounted with the Inwood premise at 10% to obtain a present worth of, roughly, $8,500—i.e., $1,000 × 8.514 (the present value factor of $1 per period at 10% for 20 years). The Hoskold premise could also be employed with a speculative rate of 8.75% and a safe rate of 5% to obtain approximately the same result. It is pointless to compare the 10% Inwood rate with the 8.75% Hoskold rate. They do not mean the same thing and are not interchangeable. In solving this and other capitalization problems, the appraiser must be satisfied that the data are compatible with the chosen technique and properly related to the market.

Straight-Line (Constant-Amount) Change per Period in Income

When income is expected to increase or decrease by a fixed amount per period, the periodic income with respect to time can be graphically portrayed as a straight line. Hence the term *straight-line* is used to describe this type of income pattern.

To obtain the present value of an annuity that has a starting income of d at the end of the first period and increases or decreases h dollars per period for n periods, the following equation is used.

$$\text{Present value} = (d + hn)\, a_{\overline{n}|} - \frac{h(n - a_{\overline{n}|})}{i}$$

where $a_{\overline{n}|}$ is the present value of $1 per period at a rate of i for n periods. In the formula, h is positive for increase and negative for decrease.

This formula for valuing straight-line income patterns should not be confused with straight capitalization with straight-line recapture. Although straight capitalization with straight-line recapture may be seen as a model for valuing a particular income stream, the procedure can also be applied to properties in which the expected change in value is commensurate with expected changes in income. Therefore, straight capitalization with straight-line recapture and related concepts are discussed with property models later in this chapter. Again, the preceding formula applies to income streams only. Special tables of present value factors based on this formula are available.[2]

---

2. See James J. Mason, MAI, ed. and comp., *American Institute of Real Estate Appraisers Financial Tables*, rev. ed. (Chicago: American Institute of Real Estate Appraisers, 1982), Table No. 5, Ordinary Annuities Changing in Constant Amount.

Exponential-Curve (Constant-Ratio) Change per Period in Income

Projecting that income will change at a constant rate often provides the best reflection of market expectations. Portrayed graphically, this type of income stream follows an exponential curve rather than a straight line. To obtain the present value of an annuity that starts at $1 at the end of the first period and increases or decreases each period thereafter at a rate of x for n periods, the following equation is used.

$$\text{Present value} = \frac{1 - (1 + x)^n/(1 + i)^n}{i-x}$$

where i is the annual discount rate and x is the ratio of the increase or decrease in income for any period to the income for the previous period. In the formula, x is positive for increase and negative for decrease.

Property Models

When both value and income changes can be expected to follow a regular or predictable pattern, one of the yield capitalization models for property valuation may be applicable. The common yield capitalization models employ a capitalization rate (R) in the same way that R is used in direct capitalization. There is a difference, however, between direct capitalization, as discussed in the previous chapter, and yield capitalization as discussed here. In direct capitalization, R is derived directly from market data without considering the expected rate of return on capital or the means of recapture; in yield capitalization, R cannot be determined without taking into account the prospective rate of return on capital and the timing of recapture. However, this does not mean that yield capitalization procedures are not market-oriented. On the contrary, yield capitalization procedures may well represent the most realistic simulation of decision making in the marketplace.

Real estate investors are greatly influenced by the prospects for capital appreciation as a hedge against inflation. When an investor looks forward to property appreciation as a part of the eventual yield, he or she is obviously anticipating that the total yield rate will be higher than the expected rate of income—i.e., the overall capitalization rate. The total yield rate is a complete measure of profitability that includes any property appreciation. Therefore, the capitalization rate for an appreciating property equals the total yield rate minus an adjustment for expected growth. Similarly, the capitalization rate for a depreciating property can be seen as the yield rate plus an adjustment for expected loss.

If the adjustment for growth is treated as a positive change and the adjustment for loss is treated as a negative change, the capitalization rate (R) can be expressed in terms of the yield rate (Y) and an adjustment rate (A) with a simple formula.

$$R = Y - A$$

Note that when A is deducted from Y, a gain is indicated, and when A is added to Y, a loss is indicated. Because A is often expressed as a function of the relative change in property value, the Greek letter delta (Δ) is used to denote relative change in value. To calculate A it is usually necessary to multiply Δ by a conversion factor such as an annual sinking fund factor or an annual recapture rate to convert the total relative change in value into an appropriate periodic rate of change. If we call the conversion factor a, the general formula for R may be expressed as

$$R = Y - \Delta a$$

where R is the capitalization rate, Y is the yield rate, and Δ is the relative change in value. This general formula for the capitalization rate can be adapted for use with typical income/value patterns for the property as a whole or for any property components. In the general formula, R, Y, and Δ apply to the total property and are expressed without subscripts. However, if there is a possibility of confusing the total property with any of its components, subscripts should be used for clarification, e.g., R_O, R_E, etc. Once the appropriate capitalization rate has been determined, an indication of property value can be obtained by applying the universal valuation formula

$$\text{Value} = \frac{\text{Income}}{\text{Cap rate}}$$

Level Income

Level income with no change in value. When both income and value are expected to remain unchanged, a property may be valued by capitalization in perpetuity, as explained in the discussion of income models. According to the general formula $R = Y - \Delta a$, the capitalization rate (R) becomes the yield rate (Y) when there is no change in value because Δ equals zero.

Level income with change in value. When level income with a change in value is projected over a period of n years, the general formula for R can be adapted by using the sinking fund factor for rate Y over n years for the conversion factor (a).

For example, consider a commercial property that will generate a stable *NOI* of \$25,000 per year for the next 10 years. Total property appreciation of 50% is expected during this 10-year period. The appraiser is asked to value the property to yield 15%. To solve this problem, the formula $R = Y - \Delta a$ is used with the sinking fund factor for 15%, 10 years, as a. According to the tables, the sinking fund factor is .049252, so R is calculated as follows.

$$R = 0.15 - (0.50 \times 0.049252) = 0.125374$$

Value $= NOI/R$

Value $= \$25{,}000/0.125374 = \$199{,}403$

Straight-Line (Constant-Amount) Changes in Income and Value

When income and value are expected to increase or decrease by fixed amounts per period according to the standard straight-line pattern, property value can be estimated with straight capitalization with straight-line recapture.

The general formula for the capitalization rate (R) can be adapted for use with the standard, straight-line income/value pattern by using the straight-line recapture rate as the conversion factor (a). The straight-line recapture rate is simply the reciprocal of the projection period. For example, if income is projected over a period of 25 years, the annual straight-line recapture rate is $1/25$, or 4%. Depreciation of 100% would indicate that the projection period is equal to the property's remaining economic life. The concept of a limited remaining economic life does not apply to appreciating properties, but 100% appreciation would indicate a projection period equal to the amount of time required for the property to double in value.

Classic straight-line recapture. Straight-line capitalization has long been used to value wasting assets. This classic procedure has limited applicability due to its underlying assumptions, but it should be thoroughly understood to ensure its proper use. The classic straight-line procedure presumes that capital is recaptured in equal amounts during the economic life of the investment and that net income always consists of a fixed amount that represents the return of capital, plus a declining return on the capital remaining in the investment. Total income, therefore, diminishes until the asset is worthless and all capital has been recovered.

The steady decline in value and income presumed in this procedure is not always consistent with market behavior, but it has important uses. Straight-line recapture is used to compute depreciation in all kinds of income-producing properties for income-tax purposes. It is also an acceptable premise for valuing assets in some corporate mergers and property exchanges. Straight-line recapture is appropriate whenever the projection of income and value in an investment corresponds with the assumptions implicit in the procedure.

Classic straight-line recapture is most easily understood when it is applied to an investment in a wasting asset such as a perishable structure, a stand of timber, or a mineral deposit. The procedure is not appropriate for valuing an investment in land or any other asset that can sustain value indefinitely.

For example, consider an investment in a partial interest in real estate such as a leasehold in which all improvements must be written off during the term of the lease. Assume that $50,000 is invested in a 10-year leasehold to earn 8% per year as a yield on capital. What flow of income to the investor would be required to return the entire amount of the investment on a straight-line basis during the 10-year period and, in addition, yield 8% per year to the investor?

Yearly recapture would, of course, be one tenth of $50,000, or $5,000. The investor is entitled to a return on unrecaptured capital amounting to 8% of $50,000 in the first year, 8% of $45,000 in the second year, 8% of $40,000 in the third year, and so forth. In other words, the income flow starts at $9,000 the first year and drops $400 each year after that. The total income payable at the end of the tenth and final year would be $5,400, of which $5,000 would be the last installment of the return of capital and the other $400 would be the interest due on the capital remaining in the investment during the tenth year. Thus the investor achieves 100% capital recovery plus an 8% return on the outstanding capital.

Note that the recapture rate amounts to 10% of the original investment and is simply the reciprocal of the economic life. Also, all income was presumed to be payable at the end of each year and the yields were always computed at the end of the year on the amount of capital outstanding during the year.

Based on the starting income, the capitalization rate in this example would be $9,000/$50,000, or 18%. The 18% capitalization rate could also be calculated by adding the 10% recapture rate to the 8% yield rate.

The straight-line capitalization procedure reflects some useful mathematical relationships.

First period return on investment = original value × yield rate
Periodic change in value = original value × periodic rate of change
Periodic change in income = periodic change in value × yield rate

When income and value decline according to these relationships, the periodic rate of change is the recapture rate and the reciprocal of the recapture rate is the economic life.

Expanded straight-line concept. The traditional concept of straight-line capitalization can be expanded to remove some of its theoretical constraints and facilitate a broader range of practical applications. The assumption of a predictable decline in income can be expanded to include any predictable change, which allows the appraiser to consider growing assets as well as wasting assets. Presuming a predictable rate of change within the foreseeable future can also eliminate the need to consider the full economic life of a property. Although there are significant theoretical differences, the expanded straight-line concept corresponds mathematically to classic straight-line recapture.

Under both the expanded and classic straight-line concepts, changes in value and income are presumed to occur on a straight-line basis. The basic requirements for a satisfactory return on, and complete recovery of, invested capital are also preserved. The expanded concept does not presume, however, that capital is recaptured in annual installments throughout the economic life of a property. Rather, the property could be resold for a predictable amount at some point during its economic life, thereby providing for partial or complete return of the invested capital at the time of resale.

For example, assume that $50,000 is invested in a property that is expected to be worth $65,000 in 10 years and that this 30% increase will occur at an average rate of 3% per year. How much first-year income would be required to yield 12% per year on the invested capital? A 12% return on the $50,000 investment would be $6,000, of which $1,500 (3% of $50,000) is provided by the increase in property value. The required first-year income would therefore be $6,000 minus $1,500, or $4,500.

Property income would then increase at a rate of $180 per year, which reflects a 12% return on the $1,500 average annual increase in capital value. The overall capitalization rate based on the starting income would be $4,500/$50,000, or 9%. This rate could also be calculated by subtracting the 3% appreciation rate from the 12% interest rate.

The straight-line capitalization rate is simply a combination of the yield rate and the straight-line rate of change, which is expressed in the general formula $R = Y - \Delta a$, where Δ is the relative change in value in n periods and a is $1/n$.

For example, consider a leasehold that will produce NOI of $19,000 the first year. This NOI is expected to decline thereafter according to the standard straight-line pattern and value is expected to fall 25% in 10 years. To appraise the leasehold to yield 12%, use the formula $R_{LH} = Y_{LH} - \Delta_{LH} a$, where the subscript LH denotes leasehold.

$$R_{LH} = 0.12 - (-0.25 \times 0.1) = 0.145$$
$$\text{Value} = NOI/R$$
$$\text{Value} = \$19,000/0.145 = \$131,034$$

The classic and expanded straight-line concepts are popular because they are simple and do not require the use of compound interest tables. However, straight-line concepts have theoretical and practical limitations. Experimentation and further study will reveal that the straight-line premise does not always present a realistic pattern of changing income and changing value.

Exponential-Curve (Constant-Ratio) Changes in Income and Value

When both income and value are expected to change at a constant ratio, the capitalization rate can be determined without tables using the general formula

$$R = Y - \Delta a$$

where Δa is the relative change in value and income for one period. Thus, Δa can be replaced with the periodic compound rate of change (CR). The formula then becomes

$$R = Y - CR$$

where Y is the yield rate per period and CR is the rate of change per period. An expected loss is treated as a negative rate of change, and the formula becomes

$$R = Y - (- CR)$$

or

$$R = Y + CR$$

If both income and value are expected to change at the same rate, the capitalization rate is expected to remain constant. Therefore, this pattern of growth or decline is sometimes referred to as the *frozen cap rate* pattern.

For example, assume an income-producing property is expected to produce NOI of $50,000 for the first year. Then both NOI and value are expected to grow at a constant ratio of 2% per year. In other words, 2% is the expected ratio of the increase in income for any year to the income for the previous year and the ratio of the increase in value for any year to the value for the previous year is also 2%. To appraise the property to yield 11%, the formula is $R_O = Y_O - CR_O$

$$R_O = .11 - .02 = .09$$

$$\text{Value} = \$50,000/0.09 = \$555,556$$

Variable or Irregular Income and Value Changes

When income and value are not expected to follow a regular pattern of change, the present value of a property can be obtained by applying the standard discounting formula separately to each projected benefit, including the final reversion.

However, the absence of a regular income pattern does not necessarily mean that detailed DCF analysis is the only method that should be considered. The appraiser may discover that one of the typical valuation models can be adjusted to compensate for a deviation from the regular pattern or that a special valuation model can be devised to solve the problem at hand.

MORTGAGE INTERESTS

The purchase and ownership of real property nearly always involves debt secured with the real estate as collateral. Appraisers use mortgage information in the form of dollar amounts and rates or factors, depending on the data available, to value income-producing properties. Mortgage information may include 1) the monthly or periodic payments and annual debt service on a level-payment, fully amortized loan, 2) their accompanying partial payment factors and annual constants (R_M), and 3) the balance outstanding (B) on an amortized loan at any time before it is fully amortized, expressed as a dollar amount or a percentage of the original loan amount. The percentage or proportion of any principal amount paid off before full amortization (P) must also be calculated, especially if mortgage-equity analysis is used.

Mortgage investments have a great impact on real property value and equity yield rates. Because yield is a significant consideration in the lender's decision to invest in a mortgage interest in real estate, the lender's yield must be understood and often must be calculated.

Types of Mortgage Loans

A mortgage is a legal document pledging a described property as security or collateral for the repayment of a loan under certain terms and conditions. There are various types of mortgage loans and many are identified by their repayment characteristics—e.g., interest only, direct reduction, variable rate, wraparound, equity participation mortgages, and others.

An interest-only mortgage is a nonamortizing loan in which the lender receives only interest during the term of the loan and recovers the principal in a lump sum at the time of maturity.

A direct reduction mortgage is a mortgage loan that is repaid in periodic, usually equal, installments that include a repayment of part of the principal and the interest due on the unpaid balance.

A variable-rate mortgage is a mortgage with an interest rate that may move up or down following a specified schedule or the movements of a standard or index to which the interest rate is tied.

A wraparound mortgage is a mortgage that is subordinate to, but inclusive of, any existing mortgage(s) on a property. Usually, a third-party lender refinances the property, assuming the existing mortgage and its debt service which are wrapped around a new, junior mortgage. A wraparound lender gives the borrower the difference between the outstanding balance on the existing mortgage(s) and the face amount of the new mortgage.

An equity participation mortgage is a mortgage in which the lender receives a share of the income and sometimes the reversion from a property on which it has made a loan.

A shared appreciation mortgage is a mortgage in which the borrower receives assistance in buying the real property in return for a portion of the property's future appreciation in value.

A convertible mortgage is a mortgage in which the lender may choose to take an equity interest in the real estate in lieu of cash amortization payments by the borrower. In this way, the mortgage interests of the lender may be converted into equity ownership over the life of the mortgage.

A graduated-payment mortgage is a mortgage designed to aid borrowers by matching mortgage payments to projected increases in income; the periodic payments start out low and gradually increase. Because the borrower's payments in the early years of the loan are not sufficient to pay the entire interest due or to amortize the mortgage, the borrower is actually borrowing the difference between the payments and the current interest due.

A zero-interest mortgage is a debt secured by real estate with no interest; in some circumstances, a rate of interest may be imputed—e.g., for income taxation.

Mortgage Components

Periodic (Monthly) Payment

The monthly payment factor for a fully amortized, monthly payment loan with equal payments is the direct reduction loan factor, or monthly constant, for the given loan interest rate and amortization term. Thus, the monthly payment factor for a 30-year, fully amortized, level monthly payment loan at 10.5% interest is .009147. This number can be obtained from a direct reduction loan table or by solving for the monthly payment (PMT) on a preprogrammed financial calculator given the number of periods (n), the interest (i), and the present value (PV).

Assume that the loan described above had an initial principal amount of $160,000. The monthly payment required to amortize the principal over 30 years and provide interest at the nominal rate of 15.5% on the outstanding balance each month would be

$$\$160,000 \times 0.013045 = \$2,087.20$$

Annual Debt Service and Loan Constant

Cash flows are typically converted to an annual basis for real property valuation, so it is useful to calculate the amount of annual debt service as well as the monthly payments. For a 30-year, fully amortized, level monthly payment loan of $160,000 at a 15.5% interest rate, the annual debt service is

$$\$2,087.20 \times 12 = \$25,046.40$$

The annual loan constant is simply the ratio of annual debt service to the loan principal. (The annual loan constant is often called the *mortgage constant* although it is actually the annual debt service per dollar of mortgage loan outstanding.) The annual loan constant is expressed as R_M to signify that it is a capitalization rate for the loan or debt portion of the real estate investment. For the loan mentioned, the annual loan constant can be calculated as follows:

$$R_M = \frac{\text{Annual debt service}}{\text{Loan principal}}$$
$$= \frac{\$\ 25,046.40}{\$160,000.00}$$
$$= 0.156540$$

The annual loan constant can also be obtained when the amount of the loan principal is not known. In this case, the monthly payment factor is simply multiplied by 12.

$$R_M = \text{monthly payment factor} \times 12$$
$$= 0.013045 \times 12$$
$$= 0.156540$$

Although these figures are rounded to the nearest cent, in actual practice loan constants are rounded up to make sure that the loan will be repaid during the stated amortization period.

Outstanding Balance

Properties are frequently sold, or loans may be refinanced, before the loan on the property is fully amortized. Furthermore, loan contracts often mature before the completion of loan amortization. In such cases, there is an outstanding balance on the note; from the lender's point of view, this is the loan or debt reversion.

The outstanding balance (B) on any level-payment amortized loan is the present value of the debt service over the *remaining* amortization period discounted at the interest rate. Thus, at the end of 10 years, the balance for the 30-year note discussed above would be the present value of 20 years of remaining payments. The balance is calculated by multiplying the monthly payment by the present value of $1 per period factor (monthly) for 20 years at the interest rate.

$$B = \$2,087.20 \times 73.861752$$
$$= \$154,164.25$$

Similarly, the outstanding balance at the end of 18 years would be equal to the monthly payment times the present value of $1 per period factor (monthly) for 12 years at the interest rate.

$$B = \$2,087.20 \times 65.222881$$
$$= \$136,133.20$$

The outstanding balance on a loan can also be expressed as a percentage of the original principal. This is useful, and sometimes necessary, if dollar amounts are not given or unavailable.

For a 10-year projection with 20 years remaining on the note,

$$B = \frac{\$154,164.25}{\$160,000.00}$$
$$= 0.963527$$

For an 18-year projection with 12 years remaining on the note,

$$B = \frac{\$136,133.20}{\$160,000.00}$$

$$= 0.850833$$

A percentage balance can also be calculated as the *ratio* of the present value of $1 per period factor for the remaining term of the loan at the specified interest rate, divided by the present value of $1 per period factor for the full term of the loan at the interest rate. This can be expressed as

$$B = \frac{PV\ 1/P\ \text{remaining term}}{PV\ 1/P\ \text{full term}}$$

In the case of the 30-year, 15.5% loan, the balance for a 10-year projection with 20 years remaining is calculated as

$$B = \frac{73.861752}{76.656729}$$

$$= 0.963539$$

For a 18-year projection with 12 years remaining, the balance would be

$$B = \frac{65.222881}{76.656729}$$

$$= 0.850844$$

These results are similar to the results obtained using dollar amounts. The differences are due to rounding.

Percentage of Loan Paid Off

It is often necessary to calculate the percentage of the loan paid off before full amortization over the projection period, especially in Ellwood mortgage-equity analysis. The percentage of the loan paid off is represented by the symbol P and is most readily calculated as the complement of B.

$$P = 1 - B$$

For the 30-year note, P is calculated as follows:

$$P_{10} = 1 - 0.963539$$
$$= 0.036461$$

$$P_{18} = 1 - 0.850844$$
$$= 0.149156$$

The percentage of the loan paid off prior to full amortization over the projection period (P) can also be calculated directly. There are many different procedures for this operation although they are not all presented here. The simplest and most direct procedure is to calculate P as the *ratio* of the sinking fund factor for the full term (monthly or whatever term the mortgage calls for) divided by the sinking fund factor for the projection period (monthly).

$$P = \frac{1/S_n}{1/S_{nP}}$$

For the 30-year monthly payment note at 15.5%, the calculations are

$$P_{10} = \frac{0.000129}{0.003524}$$

$$= 0.036606$$

$$P_{18} = \frac{0.000129}{0.000862}$$

$$= 0.149652$$

Any differences are due to rounding.

Lender's Yield

The monetary benefits that accrue to the lender are similar to the benefits received by the equity owner—i.e., periodic income from debt service and the reversion represented by the outstanding principal paid off prior to or at maturity. In calculating the lender's yield, discounting formulas must be applied.

To illustrate how the lender's yield on a mortgage loan investment is calculated, consider a mortgage loan with the following characteristics.

Loan amount	$100,000
Balance in five years	$96,544
Interest rate	13.5%
Term	25 years
Payment	Monthly
Points	3
Other	Borrower to pay all other costs

If the mortgage runs full term, the yield can be obtained using a calculator.

n = 300
PMT = $1,165.65
PV = $97,000 ($100,000 less 3 points, or $3,000)*
i = 13.97%

*Each point is equal to 1% of the loan amount; 100,000 × 0.01 = $1,000.

If the mortgage is paid off in five years, the lender's yield is calculated

n = 60
PMT = $1,165.65
PV = $97,000
FV = $96,544
i = 14.36%

If there were no points in either of these examples, the yield to the lender would be 13.5% in each case. Points or any other monetary payments that reduce the lender's investment are important considerations in calculating a lender's yield.

EQUITY INTERESTS

Equity in real property is an owner's interest after all claims and liens have been satisfied. Therefore, an equity interest, like a mortgage loan, represents a financial interest in real property.

Equity ownership in real property is legally accomplished in many ways—e.g., as an individual owner, joint owner, partner, or shareholder in a corporation. The legal form of equity ownership does not affect property value in most appraisal assignments. However, in some instances an appraiser is called upon to estimate the value of a specific legal form of equity interest. For example, an appraiser may be asked to value a limited partner's equity interest in a partnership created solely to be the legal owner of the real property. This type of assignment may be undertaken to value assets for estate tax purposes or for sale or purchase decisions.

Because the equity side of the real estate market dominates sales activity, appraisers must thoroughly understand the benefits that accrue to equity owners and know how equity yield is calculated.

Benefits of Equity Ownership

Equity owners essentially look for two kinds of benefits: income, usually on an annual basis, and reversion at the end of the ownership period. The income is the annual cash flow before or after taxes and the reversion is the pre- or after-tax equity proceeds of resale after any outstanding mortgage balance and all selling expenses have been paid. Any refinancing benefits taken during the ownership period are usually viewed as a form of early reversion. In investment analysis assignments, the sum of all benefits over the ownership period is analyzed in comparison to the equity invested to reveal the equity yield rate. In valuation assignments, an equity yield rate is applied to the forecast benefits to produce a present value conclusion. If market value is sought, the equity yield rate is derived from the market.

Equity Yield Rate

For the investor, the equity yield rate is a prime measure of investment performance. An investor may compare the expected equity yield of a real property investment with the yields on alternative investments (e.g., stocks and bonds) and with a lender's yield on mortgages secured by similar real property. Usually the equity investor will seek a higher yield than the lender because the lender has a more secure position. The lender can foreclose the mortgage and take clear title to the real property if the mortgage terms are not fulfilled.

The equity yield rate must be distinguished conceptually from the equity capitalization rate. The equity yield rate (Y_E) is a rate of return *on* equity capital; the equity capitalization rate is simply the relationship between one year's equity income or cash flow and equity capital. The equity yield rate is a full measure of investment performance, but the equity capitalization rate is not. The equity yield rate is *not* a rate of return on capital. It may be more or less than the eventual equity yield on the capital invested, depending on future changes in equity income and equity value. Although it cannot be considered a full measure of performance, the equity capitalization rate is useful and important. In certain markets and at certain times, it is the preferred measure of investment performance.

Derivation of the Equity Yield Rate

To estimate equity yield rates, appraisers must do market research. This research can take many forms and may include one or more of the following analyses.

- Direct comparison with equity yield rates abstracted from recent comparable sales (For an example, see the two-variable algebraic method of rate abstraction described in Chapter 22.)
- Verification of the prospective equity yields used by market participants, particularly buyers, in recent or anticipated sales
- Comparison with the equity yield rates achieved in alternative investments such as stocks and bonds.

To develop an equity yield rate from recent comparable sales, an appraiser analyzes the forecast benefits of equity ownership in relation to the equity capital invested. This process will be covered in the next chapter.

Leverage

The term *leverage* is often used to show how borrowed funds increase or decrease the amount that, free and clear, would be considered the equity return. In the recent past, leverage has been used almost exclusively to analyze equity capitalization rates in relation to overall and mortgage capitalization rates. However, leverage may also be considered in the analysis of equity yield rates. Leverage in capitalization rates can be analyzed for any individual year of the forecast or for the average forecast year. Leverage in yield rates, however, can only be analyzed for the entire forecast period. The underlying principles are the same in both cases. (See Table 21.2 and the example that follows.)

Table 21.2   Leverage Analysis

Type of Leverage	Equity Capitalization Rate (R_E)	Equity Yield Rate (Y_E)
Positive	R_O greater than R_M	Y_O greater than Y_M
Zero	R_O equals R_M	Y_O equals Y_M
Negative	R_O less than R_M	Y_O less than Y_M

In analyzing cash flows, positive leverage is indicated when the overall capitalization rate is greater than the mortgage capitalization rate. The difference between the two rates directly benefits the equity owner, so the equity capitalization rate is higher than it would be if there were no mortgage. For example, assume a property was sold for $100,000 and analysis of the transaction indicates a net operating income of $10,000, an equity price of $25,000, and a mortgage of $75,000 payable in annual installments of $7,125.00. The indicated capitalization rates are:

Overall (R_O)	10.0%
Mortgage (R_M)	9.5%
Equity (R_E)	11.5%

Because the mortgage capitalization rate is less than the overall capitalization rate, the equity interest receives a benefit that is reflected in the equity capitalization rate. If there were no mortgage, the equity capitalization rate would be 10.0%, the same as the overall capitalization rate. When the overall capitalization rate exceeds the mortgage capitalization rate, positive leverage results. Similarly, when the overall yield rate exceeds the mortgage yield rate, positive leverage is indicated and the equity yield rate must exceed the overall yield rate. However, if the overall capitalization rate is less than the mortgage capitalization rate or the overall yield rate is less than the mortgage yield rate, negative leverage results. The leverage is zero when the overall and mortgage capitalization and yield rates are equal.

The analysis of leverage is important because positive or negative leverage can affect the level of risk associated with a real property investment and the yield required to satisfy an investor willing to assume the risk. Often, negative leverage on early cash flows may suggest the need to achieve a greater yield rate. Conversely, positive leverage on early cash flows may reduce the yield rate required. On a yield basis, positive equity yield leverage is expected due to the greater risk associated with equity interest as compared to the more secure mortgage interest. If negative equity yield leverage is anticipated, the equity buyer may consider the investment to be inappropriate.

SUMMARY

Yield capitalization is used to convert future benefits into present value by discounting each future benefit at an appropriate yield rate or by applying an overall rate that explicitly reflects the investment's income pattern, change in value, and yield rate. For market value appraisals, the analysis focuses on the yield anticipated by typical investors. In yield capitalization, an appraiser 1) selects a holding period, 2) forecasts all future cash flows or the patterns and relationships of present and future cash flows, 3) selects the appropriate yield, or discount, rate, and 4) converts the future benefits into present value by discounting each annual future benefit or applying an overall rate.

The application of rates that reflect an appropriate yield, the use of present value factors, and discounted cash flow analysis are yield capitalization procedures. To derive overall capitalization rates, mortgage-equity formulas and yield rate/value change formulas may be applied; residual techniques may also be used in yield capitalization.

A knowledge of *income patterns* and *capital return concepts* is fundamental to the discounting process. An *annuity* is literally an annual income, but it has come to mean a program or contract of regular payments in stipulated amounts. An annuity can be level, increasing, or decreasing, but it must be scheduled at regular intervals in predictable amounts. Real estate or rental income may have the characteristics of an annuity. Yield capitalization can be applied to both stable contract rent and speculative market rent.

Yield capitalization distinguishes between the *return on* capital (i.e., interest and compound interest) and the *return of* capital (i.e., income and reversion). If an investor does not recapture all the original investment at the time of resale, part of the income must be used to repay the investor. In this case, the true rate of return on the investment is less than the indicated income rate or overall capitalization rate. The rate of return of capital equals the difference between the rate of return on capital and the indicated capitalization rate and the *recapture rate* is considered positive. If, on the other hand, the investor recaptures the original capital at the termination of the investment, the true rate of return on the investment will equal the indicated capitalization rate and the *recapture rate* will be zero. If the investor receives more than the original investment upon resale, the true rate of return on capital is greater than the indicated capitalization rate and the recapture rate is negative.

The *return on* an investment induces investors to forego the present benefits of the immediate use of capital for future benefits. To a lender this return is interest, to equity investors it is the yield. The investor's objective is a total return that exceeds the amount invested. The discounting procedure assumes that the *return of the investment* is accomplished through periodic income, the reversion, or a combination of both.

An appraiser converts periodic income and reversion into present value through the discounting procedure. The present value of a prospective benefit is obviously less than the future value of that benefit. A future payment is discounted to present value by calculating the amount that should be invested today to grow with compound interest to equal the future payment. The standard discounting formula is:

$$\text{Present value} = \frac{\text{Future value}}{(1 + i)^n}$$

where i is the rate of return on capital per period and n is the number of periods that the payment will be deferred. If a series of future payments is expected, the total present value of the series is the sum of all the present values.

When amounts are compounded or discounted, the *effective interest rate* is used. On an annual basis, this rate is identical to the *nominal interest rate*. When amounts are compounded or discounted more often than annually, the effective interest rate can be derived by dividing the nominal annual rate by the number of compounding or discounting periods.

In *discounted cash flow (DCF) analysis*, the quantity, variability, timing, and duration of cash flows are specified. The cash flows that constitute the periodic income (i.e., the *NOI* for the entire property or the cash flows to a specific property interest) and the reversion are discounted with the DCF formula:

$$PV = \frac{CF_1}{1+Y} + \frac{CF_2}{(1+Y)^2} + \frac{CF_3}{(1+Y)^3} + \ldots + \frac{CF_n}{(1+Y)^n}$$

where Y represents the appropriate periodic yield, or discount, rate and n is the number of periods in the projection. The formula can be used to estimate total property value (V_O), loan value (V_M), equity value (V_E), leased fee value (V_{LF}), or leasehold value (V_{LH}). Any series of periodic incomes, with or without a reversion, can be valued with this basic formula.

The actual yield on an investment cannot be calculated until the investment is sold, but investors do consider target yields. Although historical yield rates are relevant, they are not reliable indicators of current yield. The appraiser should select a *yield rate* that reflects the rates currently anticipated by typical market buyers and sellers. Rates can be chosen directly by analyzing comparable sales transactions, or indirectly by estimating the income expectancy and likely reversion of comparable properties. To select an appropriate yield rate, the appraiser should also assess the competition for capital in other financial markets. The yield rates applied to discount net rental incomes subject to lease contracts differ from those applied to the reversion because the resale value is subject to open-market conditions and different risks.

Once the appraiser has specified the amount, timing, and duration of all cash flows, the *income stream pattern* over the projection period can be forecast. There are three major types of annuities. A *variable annuity* is a determinable income stream in which the payment amounts vary per period; a *level annuity* is an income stream in which the payment amounts are equal and unchanging; and an *increasing or decreasing annuity* is an income stream that is expected to change in a systematic pattern. There are two types of level annuities—ordinary annuities and annuities payable in advance—and three types of increasing or decreasing annuities—step-up or step-down annuities, straight-line (constant-amount) change per period annuities, and exponential-curve (constant-ratio) change per period annuities.

Periodic income and the *reversion*, the future value obtained by selling the property at the end of the holding period, are the financial benefits of income-producing property. The reversion may be considered a future cash flow because it is the return of capital upon termination of the investment. The number of periodic income streams and reversions for a property varies according to the property interests involved (e.g., fee simple, lender, equity investor, leased fee, and leasehold).

The reversion often represents a major portion of the benefits provided by income-producing property. In deciding what portion of the return of the investment the reversion provides, the investor considers three possible outcomes. The property may increase in value over the holding period, it may not change in value, or it may decline in value.

An appraiser projects the reversion to a property when the property is expected to be sold. The projected property value or *proceeds of resale* are equal to the net difference between the transaction price and any selling expenses such as brokerage commissions, legal fees, fix-up costs, and possible penalties for the prepayment of debt.

Specific valuation models, or formulas, categorized as income or property models have been developed to project patterns of benefits. Income models are applied only to income streams, not to anticipated reversions. Property models can be used to value an income stream and the reversion in one operation.

Income models describe patterns of *variable or irregular income*, in which each benefit is separately discounted, *level income, straight-line (constant-amount) change per period income*, and *exponential-curve (constant-ratio) change per period income*. The present value of level income can be estimated by capitalization in perpetuity, in which the discount rate equals the overall capitalization rate; capitalization under the Inwood premise, which employs a single discount rate and is the basis of compound interest tables; or in capitzalization under the Hoskold premise, which employs the sum of two separate rates—a speculative rate for risk and a safe rate for the sinking fund. The Hoskold premise is not generally accepted. Applying both the Inwood premise and the Hoskold premise to the same income stream is inappropriate because it is difficult to compare single-rate and dual-rate systems.

The formula used to calculate the present value of an income pattern characterized by a straight-line (constant-amount) increase or decrease per period is:

$$\text{Present value} = (d + hn)a_{\overline{n}|} - \frac{h\,(n - a_{\overline{n}|})}{i}$$

where d is the starting income at the end of the first period, h is the dollar increase or decrease per period, n is the number of periods, and $a_{\overline{n}|}$ is the present value of $1 per period at rate i for n periods. In the formula, h is positive for increase and negative for decrease. This formula for straight-line income patterns should *not* be confused with straight capitalization with straight-line recapture, which is a property model formula.

To obtain the present value of an annuity with an income pattern subject to exponential-curve (constant-ratio) increases or decreases per period, this formula is used

$$\text{Present value} = \frac{1 - (1 + x)^n/(1 + i)^n}{i - x}$$

where the annuity starts at $1 at the end of the first period, increases or decreases at the rate of x per n periods, and is discounted at the annual rate of i. In the formula, x is positive for increase and negative for decrease.

Property models can be used when changes in both property value and income can be projected according to a regular or predictable pattern. In yield capitalization, a capitalization rate (R) is determined by considering the prospective rate of return on capital and the timing of capital recapture. Because capital appreciation can be a hedge against inflation, real estate investors consider property appreciation as part of the eventual yield. An investor anticipates that the eventual total yield rate, which is a complete measure of profit, will be higher than the expected income rate (R_o).

The capitalization rate for an appreciating property equals the total yield rate minus an adjustment for expected value growth $(R = Y - A)$. The capitalization rate for a depreciating property equals the yield rate plus an adjustment for expected value loss $(R = Y + A)$. The symbol A is expressed as a function of the relative change in property value, which is represented by the Greek letter delta (Δ). To calculate the adjustment, Δ must be multiplied by a conversion factor (e.g., an annual sinking fund factor or an annual recapture rate) expressed as a. Thus, $R = Y - \Delta a$ and $R = Y + \Delta a$. Once the appropriate capitalization rate is obtained, it can be used in the general formula $V = I/R$.

Property models describe *properties with level income and unchanging value with capitalization in perpetuity* $(R = Y)$; *properties with level income and changing value* (*a* = sinking fund); *properties in which income and value are increasing or decreasing in straight-line, constant amounts* with straight capitalization with straight-line recapture (*a* = straight-line recapture rate); *properties in which income and value are increasing or decreasing at an exponential-curve, constant ratio* (Δ*a* = periodic compound rate of change, or *CR*); and *properties with income and value changes that do not follow a regular pattern*, so that each benefit must be separately discounted.

The mortgage information needed to value income-producing properties includes the *periodic (monthly) payment factor*, or direct reduction loan factor, for the given loan interest rate and amortization term; the *annual debt service* which is used to compute the partial payment factor or annual constant (R_M = annual debt service/loan principal and R_M = monthly payment factor × 12); the *outstanding balance* (*B*) at any time prior to full amortization (*B* = *PV* of the debt service over the remaining amortization period discounted at the interest rate and *B* = monthly payment × *PV* of $1 per period factor for the remaining years at the interest rate), and the *percentage of the principal amount paid off* (*P*) prior to full amortization (*P* = 1 − *B* and *P* = the sinking fund factor for the full term/the sinking fund factor for the projection period

$$P = \frac{1/S_{\overline{n}|}}{1/S_{\overline{nP}|}}$$

Mortgages affect real property values and equity yield rates. *Lender's yield* influences a lenders' decision to invest in a real estate mortgage.

A *mortgage* is a legal document in which a described property is pledged as security or collateral for the repayment of a loan under certain terms and conditions. Many types of mortgages are identified by their significant repayment characteristic —e.g., *interest-only, direct reduction, variable-rate, wraparound, equity participation, shared appreciation, convertible, graduated-payment*, and *zero-interest* mortgages.

In real estate *equity* is an owner's interest after all claims and liens are satisfied. Equity ownership can be held by an individual owner, joint owner, partnerships, or corporate shareholders. Two benefits are received by equity owners: income in the form of annual pre- or after-tax cash flow and reversion, the equity proceeds of resale. When an equity yield rate is applied to forecast benefits, a present value conclusion results.

An *equity yield rate* (Y_E) is a rate of return *on* equity capital and, thus, it is a full measure of investment performance. It should not be confused with an equity capitalization rate, which is simply the relationship between one year's equity income and equity capital. Equity yield rates can be derived directly by comparing the equity yield rates of recent comparable sales, by verifying prospective equity yields with the participants in recent or anticipated sales, or by comparing the equity yield rates achieved in alternative investments such as stocks and bonds.

Leverage refers how borrowed funds increase or decrease the equity return. Leverage is analyzed in conjunction with equity capitalization rates and equity yield rates. Leverage in capitalization rates can be analyzed for any individual year of the forecast or for the average forecast year. Leverage in yield rates can only be analyzed for the entire forecast period. The characteristic relationships between R_O and R_M and Y_O and Y_M, and the indicated leverage of R_E and Y_E are stated below:

Type of Leverage	Equity Capitalization Rate (R_E)	Equity Yield Rate (Y_E)
Positive	R_O greater than R_M	Y_O greater than Y_M
Zero	R_O equals R_M	Y_O equals Y_M
Negative	R_O less than R_M	Y_O less than Y_M

The analysis of leverage is important because positive or negative leverage can affect the risk of an investment and the yield required to satisfy an investor willing to assume that risk.

22 Yield Capitalization —Advanced Applications

MORTGAGE-EQUITY ANALYSIS

L. W. Ellwood was the first to organize, develop, and promulgate the use of mortgage-equity analysis in yield capitalization for real property valuation. His contribution, which became known as the "Ellwood formula," is based on the theory that mortgage money plays a major role in real property prices and values. The effect of mortgage financing is evident in his formula. Ellwood saw real property investments as a combination of two components—debt and equity—and held that the return requirements of both components must be satisfied through income and/or reversion. The original formula has been refined and simplified, but the concepts introduced, which include the analysis of mortgage terms, value changes, and forecasting periods remain fundamental to mortgage-equity analysis today.

Determining an overall capitalization rate with mortgage-equity analysis is a yield capitalization procedure that is accomplished by applying formulas. The modified Ellwood formula in use today is analogous to the yield and change formula covered in Chapter 21. However, these formulas differ insofar as the yield and change formula uses a property yield rate and does not consider how a mortgage may affect the investor's equity yield. In applying this formula, an appraiser assumes that the property interest being appraised is free and clear of financing; however, this situation is very rare. The mortgage-equity formula, on the other hand, includes a mortgage component and addresses the yield requirements of both the lender's interest and the investor's equity interest.

Mortgage-equity analysis can be applied in both market value and investment value analyses. If all the components used in the mortgage-equity formula are market-derived, the value indication should be market value; if some of the components are oriented to a specific investor, the value derived will be investment value.

Recently, appraisers have been criticized for using mortgage-equity techniques, which are often referred collectively to as *the Ellwood technique*, in market value appraisals. The formula is not unsuitable for market value appraisals, but some analysts fail to use market-derived information in applying the formula. Both mortgage-equity analysis and discounted cash flow analysis, which is discussed later in this chapter, have been misused, but the fault lies with the users, not with these analytical tools.

Applications

Mortgage-equity analysis can facilitate the valuation process in many ways. It may be used 1) to compose overall rates, 2) to derive building and land capitalization rates for residual techniques, 3) to analyze and test capitalization rates obtained with other capitalization techniques, 4) as an investment analysis tool to test the values indicated by the sales comparison and cost approaches, and 5) to analyze a capitalization rate graphically.

Mortgage-Equity Formula

The general mortgage-equity formula is:

$$R_O = \frac{Y_E - M\,(Y_E + P1/S_{\overline{n|}} - R_M) - \Delta_O\,1/S_{\overline{n|}}}{1 + \Delta_I J}$$

where:

R_O = overall capitalization rate
Y_E = equity yield rate
M = loan-to-value ratio
P = percentage of loan paid off
$1/S_{\overline{n|}}$ = sinking fund factor at the equity yield rate
R_M = mortgage capitalization rate or mortgage constant
Δ_O = change in total property value
Δ_I = total ratio change in income
J = J factor (This symbol is discussed later in this chapter.)

The part of the formula represented as $Y_E - M\,(Y_E + P1/S_{\overline{n|}} - R_M)$ can be referred to as the *basic capitalization rate* (r), which satisfies the lender's requirement and adjusts for amortization. It also satisfies the investor's equity yield requirement before any adjustment is made for income and value changes. Therefore, the basic rate starts with an investor's yield requirement and adjusts it to reflect the effect of financing. The resulting basic capitalization rate is a building block from which an overall capitalization rate can be developed with additional assumptions. If level income and no change in property value are expected, the basic rate will be identical to the overall capitalization rate. The last part of the numerator, $\Delta_o \, 1/S_{\overline{n}|}$, allows the appraiser to adjust the basic rate to reflect a change in overall property value. If the value change is positive, the overall capitalization rate is reduced to reflect this anticipated monetary benefit; if the change is negative, the overall capitalization rate is increased.

Finally, the denominator, $1 + \Delta_I J$, accounts for any change in income. The J factor is always positive. Thus, if the change in income is positive, the denominator will be greater than one and the overall rate will be reduced. If the change in income is negative, the overall rate will be increased. For level-income applications, $\Delta = 0$, so the denominator is $1 + 0$, or 1.

Akerson Format

The mortgage-equity procedure developed by Charles B. Akerson substitutes an arithmetic format for the algebraic equation in the Ellwood formula.[1] This format is applicable to level-income situations; when modified with the J factor, it can also be applied to changing-income situations.

The Akerson format is

Loan ratio $\times$ annual constant	$= \underline{\hspace{2cm}}$
Equity ratio $\times$ equity yield rate	$= +\underline{\hspace{2cm}}$
Loan ratio $\times$ part paid off $\times$ $1/S_{\overline{n}|}$	$= -\underline{\hspace{2cm}}$
Basic rate (r)	$= \underline{\hspace{2cm}}$
$+$ Dep or $-$ App $\times$ $1/S_{\overline{n}|}$	$= +\underline{\hspace{2cm}}$
Overall capitalization rate	$= \underline{\hspace{2cm}}$

where $1/S_{\overline{n}|}$ is the sinking fund factor at the equity yield rate for the projection period and Dep/App denotes the change in value from property depreciation or appreciation during the projection period.

Level-Income Applications

Mortgage-equity analysis can be used to value real property investments with level income streams, or variable income streams converted to level equivalents, using overall capitalization rates and residual techniques.

Use of Overall Capitalization Rates

In the simplest application of the mortgage-equity formula and the Akerson format, a level income and a stable or changing overall property value are assumed.

---

1. The format was first presented by Charles B. Akerson in "Ellwood without Algebra," *The Appraisal Journal*, July 1970.

The following example illustrates the application of the mortgage-equity formula using an overall capitalization rate applied to a level flow of income.

NOI (level)	$25,000
Projection period	10 years
Loan terms	
Interest rate	9%
Amortization term (monthly payments)	25 years
Loan-to-value ratio	75%
Property value change	10% loss
Equity yield rate	15%

An overall rate is calculated as follows:

$$R_O = \frac{Y_E - M\,(Y_E + P1/S_{\overline{n}} - R_M) - \Delta_O\,1/S_{\overline{n}}}{1 + \Delta_I J}$$

$$R_O = \frac{0.15 - 0.75\,(0.15 + 0.1726 \times 0.04925 - 0.1007) - (-0.10 \times 0.04925)}{1 + 0 \times J}$$

$$R_O = \frac{0.15 - 0.75\,(0.057801) + 0.004925}{1}$$

$$R_O = 0.15 - 0.043350 + 0.004925$$

$$R_O = \frac{0.111575}{1}$$

$$R_O = 0.111575$$

The capitalized value of the investment is $25,000/0.1116 = $224,014.

Using the same data and assumptions, an identical value can be derived by applying the Akerson format and overall capitalization.

0.75 × 0.100704	=	0.075528
0.25 × 0.15	=	+0.037500
−0.75 × 0.172608 × 0.049252	=	−0.006376
Basic rate (*r*)	=	0.106652
0.10 × 0.049252	=	+0.004925
R_O	=	0.111577
The capitalized value is $25,000/0.1116 =		$224,014

Use of Residual Techniques

The land and building residual techniques can be applied with land and building capitalization rates based on mortgage-equity procedures. The general mortgage-equity formula or the Akerson format is applied to derive a basic rate, which is used to develop land and building capitalization rates.

For example, assume that a commercial property is expected to produce level annual income of $15,000 per year over a 10-year term. Mortgage financing is available at a 75% loan-to-value ratio, and monthly payments at 11% interest are made over an amortization term of 25 years. The land is currently valued at $65,000 and is forecast to have a value of $78,000 at the end of the projection period, indicating a 20% positive change in land value. The building is expected to have no value at the end of the projection period and the equity yield rate is 15%.

The first step in valuing this property is to derive the basic rate (r). The Ellwood formula is applied to derive the basic rate.

$$r = Y_E - \dot{M}\,(Y_E + P1/S_{\overline{n}|} - R_M)$$
$$= 0.15 - 0.75\,(0.15 + 0.137678 \times 0.049252 - 0.117614)$$
$$= 0.15 - 0.029375$$
$$= 0.120625$$

The Akerson format can also be used to derive the basic rate.

0.75×0.117614	=	0.088211
0.25×0.15	=	0.037500
$0.75 \times 0.137678 \times 0.049252$	=	-0.005086
Basic capitalization rate (r)	=	0.120625

Next, land and building capitalization rates are calculated. The formulas and procedures are shown below. To solve for land appreciation, Δ_L

$$R_L = r - \Delta_L 1/S_{\overline{n}|}$$
$$= 0.120625 - (0.20 \times 0.049252)$$
$$= 0.120625 - 0.009850$$
$$= 0.110775$$

To calculate building depreciation, Δ_B

$$R_B = r - \Delta_B 1/S_{\overline{n}|}$$
$$= 0.120625 - (-1.0 \times 0.049252)$$
$$= 0.120625 + 0.049252$$
$$= 0.169877$$

These rates can be used to value the property with the building residual technique.

NOI	$15,000
Land income	
$(V_L \times R_L) = \$65,000 \times 0.110775$	7,200
Residual income attributable to building	$ 7,800
Capitalized value of building	
$(I - R) = \$7,800/0.169877$	$ 45,916
Plus land value	+ 65,000
Indicated property value	$110,916

When the rates are used in the land residual technique, a similar property value is indicated.

NOI	$15,000
Building income	
$(V_B \times R_B) = \$46,000 \times 0.169877$	7,814
Residual income attributable to land	$ 7,186
Capitalized value of land	
$(I_L - R_L) = \$7,186/0.110775$	$ 64,870
Plus building value	+ 46,000
Indicated total property value	$110,870

Changing-Income Applications

The general mortgage-equity formula can be applied to income streams that are forecast to change on a curvilinear or exponential-curve (constant-ratio) basis by using a J factor for curvilinear change or a K factor for constant-ratio change. The J factor, which is used in the stabilizer $(1+\Delta_I J)$, may be obtained from precomputed tables[2] or calculated with the J-factor formula. The K factor, which is an income adjuster or stabilizer used to convert an income stream changing at a constant ratio into its level equivalent, can be obtained from precomputed tables[3] or calculated with the K-factor formula.

Use of the J Factor

The J-factor formula for curvilinear income reflects an income stream that changes from time zero in relation to a sinking fund accumulation curve. The formula is

2. James J. Mason, ed., comp., *American Institute of Real Estate Appraisers Financial Tables*, rev. ed. (Chicago: American Institute of Real Estate Appraisers, with tables computed by Financial Publishing Company, 1982.)

3. Charles B. Akerson, *Capitalization Theory and Techniques Study Guide*, rev. ed. (Chicago: American Institute of Real Estate Appraisers, with tables computed by Financial Publishing Company, 1980) and *The Appraiser's Workbook* (Chicago: American Institute of Real Estate Appraisers, with tables computed by Financial Publishing Company, 1985).

$$J = 1/S_{\overline{n}|} \times \frac{n}{1-1/(1 + Y)^n} - \frac{1}{Y}$$

where:

$1/S_{\overline{n}|}$ = sinking fund factor at equity yield rate
n = projection period
Y = equity yield rate

Consider the facts set forth in the level annuity example, but substitute a 20% overall property value gain for the 10% loss and assume a 20% increase in income. Note that the J factor is applied to the income in *the year prior to the first year* of the holding period.

$$R_O = \frac{0.15-0.75\,(0.15+0.172608 \times 0.049252-0.100704) -(0.20 \times 0.049252)}{1 + (0.20 \times 0.3259)}$$

$$= \frac{0.15 - 0.043348 - 0.009850}{1 + (0.20 \times 0.0652)}$$

$$= \frac{0.096802}{1.0652}$$

$$= 0.09088$$

The capitalized value is $25,000/0.09088 = 275,088$

The net operating incomes for the projection period that are implied by the curvilinear J-factor premise are calculated below.

Period	1st Year Adjustment	×	$S_{\overline{n}|}$	=	Periodic Adjustment	+	Base NOI*	=	NOI
1	$246.26	×	1/1.000000	=	$ 246	+	$25,000	=	$25,246
2	246.26	×	1/0.465116	=	529	+	25,000	=	25,529
3	246.26	×	1/0.287977	=	855	+	25,000	=	25,855
4	246.26	×	1/0.200265	=	1,230	+	25,000	=	26,230
5	246.26	×	1/0.148316	=	1,660	+	25,000	=	26,660
6	246.26	×	1/0.114237	=	2,156	+	25,000	=	27,156
7	246.26	×	1/0.090360	=	2,725	+	25,000	=	27,725
8	246.26	×	1/0.072850	=	3,380	+	25,000	=	28,380
9	246.26	×	1/0.059574	=	4,134	+	25,000	=	29,134
10	246.26	×	1/0.049252	=	5,000	+	25,000	=	30,000

*The base *NOI* is the income for the year prior to the beginning of the projection period.

The mathematical proof of the example is shown below.

Valuation of Equity

Period	NOI	−	Debt Service	=	Cash to Equity	×	PVF at 15%	=	PV
1	$25,246	−	$20,772	=	$4,474	×	0.869565	=	$ 3,890
2	25,529	−	20,772	=	4,757	×	0.756144	=	3,597
3	25,855	−	20,772	=	5,083	×	0.657516	=	3,342
4	26,230	−	20,772	=	5,458	×	0.571753	=	3,121
5	26,660	−	20,772	=	5,888	×	0.497177	=	2,927
6	27,156	−	20,772	=	6,384	×	0.432328	=	2,760
7	27,725	−	20,772	=	6,953	×	0.375937	=	2,614
8	28,380	−	20,772	=	7,608	×	0.326902	=	2,487
9	29,134	−	20,772	=	8,362	×	0.284262	=	2,377
10	30,000	−	20,772	=	9,228	×	0.247185	=	2,281
10*					$159,365 × 0.247185			=	39,393

Value of equity at 15% = $68,789

Check $275,028 × 0.25 = $68,757

*Reversion

Resale ($275,028 × 1.20)	$330,034
Loan balance ($275,028 × 0.75)(1 − 0.1726)	170,669
Equity proceeds	$159,365

Use of the K Factor

The K-factor formula is applied to income that changes on an exponential-curve (constant-ratio) basis and is expressed as

$$K = \frac{1 - (1 + C)^n/S^n}{(Y - C)a_{\overline{n}|}}$$

where:

K = factor
C = constant-ratio change in income
S = future value factor
Y = equity yield rate
$a_{\overline{n}|}$ = present value factor for ordinary level annuity

When the general mortgage-equity formula is used to derive an overall capitalization rate applicable to an income expected to change on a constant-ratio basis, K is substituted for the denominator $(1 + \Delta_I J)$. The following example is based on a property with a 70% mortgage at 11% interest, a 20-year amortization period, and monthly mortgage payments. The property has a starting net operating income of $50,000 that will increase at 3% per year. A 10% increase in property value and a 14% equity yield are assumed.

This property can be valued using the K factor in the mortgage-equity formula.

$$R_O = \frac{Y_E - M (Y_E + P\, 1/S_{\overline{n}|} - R_M) - \Delta_O 1/S_{\overline{n}|}}{K}$$

$$= \frac{0.14 - 0.70 \,(0.14 + 0.0919 \times 0.1513 - 0.1239) - (0.1 \times 0.1513)}{1.0537}$$

$$= 0.098573$$

The capitalized value of the investment is

$$\$50,000/0.098573 = \$507,238$$

Proof:

Year	Property	Mortgage	Equity
0	−$507,238	−$355,067	−$152,171
1	50,000	43,980	6,020
2	51,500	43,980	7,520
3	53,045	43,980	9,065
4	54,636	43,980	10,656
5	56,275 + 557,959	43,980 + 322,450	12,295 + 234,512

$$Y_E = 14.0\%$$

Solving for Equity Yield

Given an actual or proposed equity sale price and a forecast of equity benefits, an equity yield rate may be estimated. When level income is forecast, a formula is used. The calculations can be performed by iteration or with the financial functions of a calculator. When income is expected to change on a curvilinear basis or a constant-ratio basis, formulas must be used to solve for the yield. A calculator cannot be used to solve the problem conveniently, and the iteration technique is too time-consuming.

Level-Income Example

Consider a property that is purchased for $250,000. The net operating income is forecast to remain level at $35,000 per year and the buyer believes that property value will decline 15% over a five-year ownership period. The mortgage amount is $200,000 and monthly payments are at 10% interest with an amortization term of 20 years. The investment forecast is outlined below.

Purchase		Holding Period	
Sale price	$250,000	*NOI*	$35,000
Mortgage	200,000	Debt service	23,161*
Equity	$ 50,000	Pre-tax cash flow	$11,839

Resale After 5 Years	
Sale price	$212,500
Mortgage balance	179,605**
Equity reversion	32,895
Original equity	50,000
Equity change	−$17,105

* $200,000 × 0.115803 mortgage constant
** Unamortized portion of $200,000 mortgage at end of 5-year projection period.

$$R_E \text{ (equity capitalization rate)} = \frac{\$11,839}{\$50,000} = 0.236780$$

$$E \text{ (equity change)} = \frac{-\$17,105}{\$50,000} = -0.342100$$

The equity yield rate may now be computed through iteration or by using the formula and interpolation. Iteration is performed using the formula

$$Y_E = R_E + \Delta_E \ 1/S_{\overline{n}|}$$

Because the sinking fund factor for 10 years at the Y_E rate cannot be identified without knowing Y_E, a trial-and-error procedure must be used to develop Y_E. Without discounting, the 34.21% equity decline over the five-year holding period would subtract 6.84% each year from the equity capitalization rate of 23.67%. Consequently, Y_E will be less than 23.87% and more than 16.83% (23.67% − 6.84%).

The first computation is performed with a Y_E of 18%. When the correct equity yield rate is applied, the equation will balance.

Estimated Y_E	R_E +	Δ_E ×	$1/S_{\overline{n}|}$ =	Indicated Y_E
0.1800	0.2368 +	(−0.3425) ×	0.139778 =	0.1889
0.2000	0.2368 +	(−0.3425) ×	0.134380 =	0.1908
0.1900	0.2368 +	(−0.3425) ×	0.137050 =	0.1899

Therefore, $Y_E = .1900$, or 19.0%

This procedure for computing Y_E is correct because Y_E is defined as the rate that makes the present value of the future equity benefits equal to the original equity. The future benefits in this case are the pre-tax cash flow of 11,839 per year for five years and the equity reversion of $32,895 at the end of the five-year period.

If Y_E is 19%, the present value of the two benefits can be computed.

$$\$11,839 \times 3.057635 = \$36,199$$
$$\$32,895 \times 0.419049 = \underline{13,785}$$
$$\$49,984$$

Thus, the equity yield rate has been proven to be 19.0%. Precision to 0.03% represents a level of accuracy in keeping with the normal requirements of the calculation and current practice. This example is based on level income, but the same procedure can be applied to changing income streams by incorporating J and K factors into the formula.

J-Factor Premise Example

Consider the information set forth in the previous example, but assume that income is expected to decline 15% according to the J-factor premise.

$$R_O = \$35,000/\$250,000 = 0.14, \quad M = \$200,000/\$250,000 = 0.80$$

$$Y_E = R_E + \frac{\Delta^E}{S_{\overline{n}|}} + \frac{R_O \Delta_I}{1-M} J$$

Try 15%,

$$0.2368 + -0.3421 \times 0.1483 + \frac{0.14 \times -0.15}{0.2} \times 0.4861 = 0.135$$

Try 12%,

$$0.2368 + -0.3421 \times 0.1574 + \frac{0.14 \times -0.15}{0.2} \times 0.5077 = 0.130$$

Try 13%,

$$0.2368 + -0.3421 \times 0.1543 + \frac{0.14 \times -0.15}{0.2} \times 0.5004 = 0.131$$

Therefore, $Y_E = 13.2\%$

K-Factor Premise Example

Consider the same information, but assume that income is expected to decrease at a compound rate of 3% per year, indicating a constant-ratio change in income.

$$Y_E = R_E + \Delta_E 1/S\Delta n + \frac{R_O(K-1)}{1-M}$$

Try 13%,

$$0.2368 + -0.3421 \times 0.1543 + \frac{0.14 \times 0.9487 - 1}{0.2} = 0.148$$

Try 15%,

$$0.2368 + -0.3421 \times 0.1483 + \frac{0.14 \times 0.9497 - 1}{0.2} = 0.151$$

Therefore, $Y_E = 15.1\%$

Rate Analysis

Rate analysis allows an appraiser to test the reasonableness of the valuation conclusions derived through application of overall capitalization rates. Once an overall capitalization rate has been determined, with mortgage-equity analysis or another technique, its reliability and consistency with market expectations of equity yield and value change can be tested using Ellwood graphic analysis.

To create a graph for rate analysis, the appraiser chooses equity yield rates that cover a realistic range of the equity yield rates expected and demanded by investors. It is often wise to include a rate that is lower than the market would accept as well as a rate that is higher. For the analysis to be useful to the client, the range of yield rates chosen should be in line with investors' perceptions of the market.

In most real estate investments, there is no assurance that the investment can be liquidated at the convenience of the equity investor or on the terms dictated by the investor. Moreover, in negotiating a purchase price, the prospects for profit within a plausible range of possibilities may be more impressive than the slim chance of achieving a specific equity yield rate. The appraiser's own value judgments can easily be subjected to the same realistic test. The appraiser should ask the following questions.

- What resale prices correspond to various yield levels?
- Can the property suffer some loss in value and still produce an acceptable profit?
- How sensitive is the equity yield rate to possible fluctuations in value?

- What prospective equity yield rates can be inferred from the overall capitalization rates found in the marketplace?

Many of these questions focus on the relationship between change in property value and the equity yield rate.

The unknown variable in rate analysis is the change in property value (Δ_O). The formula for the required change in property value in a level-income application is

$$\Delta_O = \frac{r - R_O}{1/S_{\overline{n}|}}$$

Level-Income Example

Consider an investment that will generate stable income and has an overall capitalization rate of 10%. It can be financed with a 75% loan at 10% interest amortized over 25 years with level monthly payments. If the investment is held for 10 years, what levels of depreciation or appreciation should be expected with equity yield rates of 9%, 12%, and 15%?

To solve this problem, the appraiser must first find the basic rate (r) and the sinking fund factor for each equity yield rate. The Ellwood Tables show the figures listed below.

Y_E	r	$1/S_{\overline{n}|}$
9%	0.096658	0.065820
12%	0.105185	0.056984
15%	0.113584	0.049252

When the difference between r and the overall rate (R_O) is divided by the corresponding sinking fund factor, the result is the expected change in property value. If r is greater than R_O, a value increase is indicated; if r is less than R_O, value loss is indicated. Analysis of the 10% overall rate is shown below.

Y_E	$\dfrac{r - R_O}{1/S_{\overline{n}|}}$
9%	− 0.0508 (5.1% depreciation)
12%	0.0910 (9.1% appreciation)
15%	0.2758 (27.6% appreciation)

The formula produces answers consistent with the notion that a loss is negative and a gain is positive. In some texts the numerator in this formula is expressed as $R_O - r$. Use of this formula results in a change of sign—i.e., positive answers indicate depreciation and negative answers indicate appreciation.

J-Factor Premise

A similar analysis can be performed when income is presumed to change commensurately with value according to the J-factor premise. In this case the expected change in overall property value is calculated by dividing $(r - R_O)$ by $(R_O J + 1/S_{\overline{n}})$.

Graphic Rate Analysis

Various systems have been developed to employ mortgage-equity concepts in graphic rate analysis. The graphic analysis of capitalization rates is a helpful analytical tool used by practicing appraisers and investment analysts. Rate analysis in graphic or tabular form is particularly useful in interpreting market data. Although analyzing a market-oriented overall capitalization rate cannot possibly reveal a property's eventual equity yield rate or resale price, the analysis can reveal combinations of Y_E and Δ_O that are implicit in the overall rate. Thus, an appraiser can use rate analysis to decide whether a particular combination of Y_E and Δ_O is consistent with market evidence.

The figures that follow illustrate two types of graphic analysis. Figure 22.1 shows Ellwood-style graphic analysis, with time on the horizontal axis and the percentage of change in property value on the vertical axis. Figure 22.2 shows another style of graphic analysis with the equity yield rate on the horizontal axis and the percentage of change in value on the vertical axis. Graphs like these can be constructed manually by plotting three or more key points and connecting the points with a smooth curve; they can also be constructed automatically by computer.

The graph in Figure 22.1 shows change in value and income under the J-factor premise with respect to time for equity yield rates of 5%, 10%, 15%, 20%, and 25%. It is assumed that $R_O = 0.11$, $I = 0.125$, $R_M = 0.135$, $M = 0.7$, and $\Delta_O = \Delta_I$. The graph in Figure 22.2 shows the change in value and income under the J-factor premise for equity yield rates ranging from 5% to 25% over a 10-year holding period.

It is assumed that $R_O = 0.11$, $I = 0.125$, $R_M = 0.135$, $M = 0.7$, and $\Delta_O = \Delta_I$. After a graph is created, it must be interpreted by the appraiser. Usually the appraiser determines whether the range of property value changes (Δ_O) is reasonable for the market and then forms an opinion as to the reasonableness of the overall capitalization rate. If the value changes are in line with the expectations of market participants, the overall rate being tested is probably reasonable. If the value changes are not within the range expected by the marketplace, the overall capitalization rate is considered unreasonable and further analysis is needed.

Rate Extraction

A two-variable algebraic technique allows an appraiser to infer the market's expectation of yield and change in property value and extract a market-oriented overall capitalization rate. Traditional techniques for extracting market data employ an equation with one variable that provides a unique answer, but the two-variable

Figure 22.1   Ellwood-style Graphic Analysis

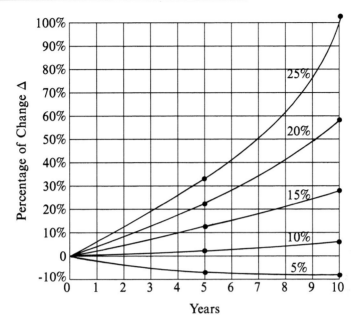

Figure 22.2   Alternative Graphic Analysis

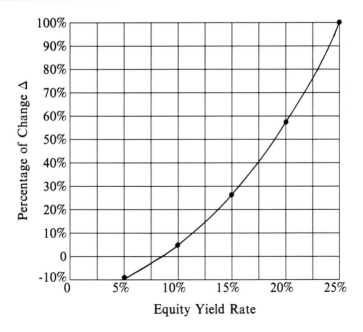

technique has no single solution. Instead, an infinite number of matched pairs (Y_E, Δ_O) is produced and each set is mathematically correct according to the market. The following example illustrates this technique.

Factual Data on Three Apartment Complexes

	Sale 1	Sale 2	Sale 3
Number of units	240	48	148
Sale price	$4,678,000	$811,000	$3,467,000
Cash down payment	$1,300,000	$462,145	$1,370,000
Gross income	$ 594,540	$126,240	$ 507,120
NOI	$ 368,600	$ 71,500	$ 293,400

Comparative Factors

	Sale 1	Sale 2	Sale 3
Price per unit	$19,492	$16,896	$ 23,426
Gross income per unit			
Yearly	$ 2,477	$ 2,638	$ 3,426
Monthly	$ 206	$ 219	$ 285
Gross income multiplier (GIM)	7.870	6.420	6.830
Overall capitalization rate (R_O)	0.079	0.088	0.085
Loan-to-value ratio (M)	0.722	0.430	0.605
Mortgage constant (R_M)	0.107	0.127	0.136
Percent paid off (P)	−0.125	0.016	0.032
Equity capitalization rate (R_E)	0.006	0.059	0.006
Debt coverage ratio (DCR)	1.021	1.610	1.030

Using the mortgage-equity J-factor formula, pairs of Y_E and Δ_O can be extracted. The formula for change in income and value is

$$\Delta_{O=1} = \frac{Y_E - M\ (Y_E + P\ 1/S_{\overline{n}|} - R_M) - R_O}{R_O J + 1/S_{\overline{n}|}}$$

**Calculated Required Changes for the Three Sales
(Five-Year Projection)**

	$\%\Delta_{O=1}$		
$\%Y_E$	Sale 1	Sale 2	Sale 3
10	19.9	10.7	16.1
12	23.2	16.8	20.8
14	26.7	23.3	25.7
16	30.5	30.3	31.0
18	34.5	37.8	36.6
20	38.8	45.8	42.7
22	43.4	54.3	49.1
24	48.3	63.4	55.9
26	53.7	73.2	63.2
28	59.0	83.4	70.9
30	64.9	94.6	79.2

Note that the rate of change in propety value is assumed to equal the rate of change in income. This reflects the appraiser's belief that this assumption is consistent with market perceptions. The relationship between equity yield and change in value and income can now be graphed. Once the graph is completed, the appraiser can draw certain conclusions. If the sales used reflect market perceptions completely, every pair of equity yield rate and change in property value is a perfect pair. When the figures are put into the mortgage-equity formula to derive an overall capitalization rate, the resulting value estimate will be market-oriented. In this case, any pair of Y_E + Δ_O that does not coincide with the lines on the graph is not market-oriented. The graph can also be used to reflect the most likely pair of Y_E and Δ_O for developing an overall capitalization rate. By verifying current investor perceptions of the yield anticipated for the type of property being appraised, the appraiser can determine the necessary property value change. Then, with the mortgage-equity formula, the overall capitalization rate can be calculated. This overall rate will reflect typical investor assumptions for both yield and change in property value.

Discounted Cash Flow Analysis

The mortgage-equity analysis discussed here is applicable only to properties with stable or stabilized income streams and properties with uneven income streams that are expected to change according to the J- or K-factor pattern. Discounted cash flow

Figure 22.3   Graphic Illustration of the Relationship between Equity Yield and Total Change in Value and Income

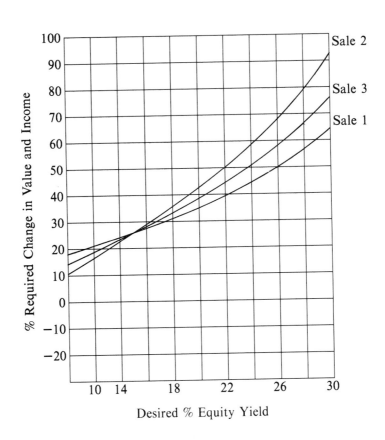

(DCF) analysis does not have these constraints; it is appropriate for any pattern of regular or irregular income. In many markets DCF is the technique that is preferred and used by most investors. Advanced computer technology makes DCF analysis a practical tool for everyday appraisal work.

Like mortgage-equity techniques, DCF analysis is used to solve for present value given the rate of return, or to solve for the rate of return given the purchase price. In typical appraisal work, the appraiser begins by developing detailed spreadsheets, either manually or with computer software. These spreadsheets show itemized incomes, expenses, and cash flows year by year or month by month over the presumed period of ownership. The cash flows, including the net resale price, are then discounted at a required rate of return to derive an indication of present value. In this way the appraiser can account for all cash flows in and out of the real property interest being appraised with respect to time, so that the time value of money is properly recognized in the analysis.

Critics point out that projections not warranted by market evidence can result in unsupported market values and that the results can be subtly affected by minor leaning. These problems, like problems with the mortgage-equity technique, reflect misuse by individual appraisers; they do not affect the soundness of the technique. Other critics object to the risk of projecting financial results five or 10 years into the future and cite this as a reason for not using or relying on the DCF technique. However, this argument ignores the reality of the real estate marketplace. Investors do make forecasts and they do rely on DCF analysis, particularly in regard to investment-grade, multitenanted properties such as shopping centers and office buildings. In keeping with the principle of anticipation, forecasting is the essence of valuation. Hence, forecasting must be approached in the same way that all market data extractions are accomplished—i.e., with diligent research and careful verification. Discounted cash flow analysis can only provide accurate results if the forecasts are based on accurate, reliable information.

Forecasting

In making forecasts, an appraiser follows the same steps taken by investors who use DCF analysis in their decision making. These steps typically include forecasting income, vacancy, operating expenses, and pre-tax cash flow over ownership periods of five to 15 years. (Ten years is often cited as an average or standard period of ownership). When appropriate, debt service and after-tax cash flow may also be forecast. In addition, the residual income from the sale of the property at the end of the forecast period is estimated.

Typical forecast categories to be addressed in DCF analysis include:

- Current market rental rates and expected rate changes
- Existing base rents and contractual base rent adjustments
- Renewal options and existing escalation provisions
- Re-leasing assumptions including new lease terms; vacancy and sometimes free rent at existing lease expirations; tenant space preparation costs; and leasing commissions
- Tenant turnover
- Operating expenses
- Residual value and any selling or transaction costs
- Changes in Consumer Price Index
- Discount rate(s)
- Business cycle—i.e., the state of the economy and economic trends
- Monetary cycle—i.e., the expansion or contraction of the money supply

Applications

The two DCF analyses that follow concern a shopping center and an office building. The first example provides an overview of the procedures for forecasting and discounting income flows into value. The second example presents more detailed market research of cash flow assumptions and a more complicated valuation procedure.

Shopping Center Example

The property being appraised is a five-unit strip store in which each unit contains 2,000 square feet. Market rents are currently $8.00 per square foot per year and the landlord is responsible for real estate taxes and exterior maintenance. Rents are increasing at a compound rate of 4% per year.

STRIP SHOPPING CENTER

(H. Armstrong Roberts, Inc.)

Taxes are currently $7,000 per year. The tax assessor reviews and reassesses each property every three years. The subject property was reviewed one year ago and taxes are expected to increase by about $800 with each subsequent review.

General exterior maintenance including cleanup and landscaping costs $100 per month; this expense is expected to increase each year by $10 per month. The roof should be replaced during the second year at a cost of $12,500, but no other exterior repairs or replacements are expected during the projection period.

Management fees, which include lease-up costs, are 5% of the rents collected plus 5% of the repair and maintenance expense negotiated. No vacancy or collection loss is anticipated.

The lease on Unit A will run for two more years at a rent of $825 per month. The tenant will re-lease at market rent when the lease expires. Unit B has a 10-year lease with five years remaining. The rent is currently $1,223 per month and will increase at a rate of 5% per year or one-half the change in the Consumer Price Index (CPI), whichever is greater. The CPI is expected to increase 7% per year over the next five years. Units C, D, and E were just leased for 10 years. These leases and all new leases are set at market rent with provisions to keep the rents at market rates throughout the projection period.

The property is expected to be worth $485,000 net to the seller in five years. The appraiser has determined that a discount rate of 15% is proper and is using a five-year discounted cash flow analysis to estimate the value of the owner's interest—i.e., the leased fee estate.

Five Year DCF Analysis

	Year 1	Year 2	Year 3	Year 4	Year 5
Income					
Unit A	$ 9,900	$ 9,900	$17,306	$17,999	$18,718
Unit B	14,676	15,410	16,180	16,989	17,839
Unit C	16,000	16,640	17,306	17,999	18,718
Unit D	16,000	16,640	17,306	17,999	18,718
Unit E	16,000	16,640	17,306	17,999	18,718
Total	$72,576	$75,230	$85,404	$88,985	$92,711
Expenses					
Taxes	$ 7,000	$ 7,000	$ 7,800	$ 7,800	$ 7,800
Maintenance	1,200	1,320	1,440	1,560	1,680
Management	3,689	4,453	4,342	4,527	4,720
Repairs	0	12,500	0	0	0
Total	$11,889	$25,273	$13,582	$13,887	$14,200
NOI	$60,687	$49,957	$71,822	$75,098	$78,511

Present Value of Income Stream

Cash Flow   *PV* of $1

$60,687 × 0.869565 = $ 52,771.29
$49,957 × 0.756144 =   37,774.68
$71,822 × 0.657516 =   47,224.11
$75,098 × 0.571753 =   42,937.51
$78,511 × 0.497177 =   39,033.86

Subtotal   = $219,741.45

Present Value of Reversion

$485,000× 0.497177 = 241,130.84

Total Present Value $460,872.29
$460,872   (rounded)

Office Building Example

An appraiser has been engaged to estimate the current market value of the leased fee interest in a property on an all-cash basis as if free and clear of existing financing and as subject to the existing mortgages. The property being appraised is a 45,000-sq. ft. site improved with a four-year-old, three-story suburban office building in a desirable location several miles away from a major city. The property has 11,000 square feet of rentable office space and 4,000 square feet of retail space. Leases are held by three tenants: RKM Insurance Corporation, ABC Appraisal Company, and BMI Computer Center.

Leases. The insurance corporation's lease, which covers 5,000 square feet of rentable area, was signed four years ago and expires June 30, 1993. The base rent is set at $18.00 per square foot through December 31, 1990 and $20.00 per square foot thereafter. There are no renewal options. The tenant also pays:

- A pro rata share of any increases in real estate taxes that exceed $1.50 per square foot
- A pro rata share of total energy-related expenses
- A pro rata share of all other operating expenses that exceed $1.50 per square foot plus a 15% administrative charge

The lease held by ABC Appraisal Company covers 6,000 square feet of rentable area. It was signed recently and expires March 31, 1994. The base rent is $24.50 per square foot and there are no renewal options. In addition to base rent, the tenant pays:

- A pro rata share of any increases in real estate taxes that exceed $2.05 per square foot
- A pro rata share of all energy expenses that exceed $2.50 per square foot
- A pro rata share of all increases in other operating expenses that exceed $2.60 per square foot

BMI Computer Center leases 4,000 square feet of ground floor retail space. The lease is one year old and expires December 31, 1995. Base rent is $23.00 per square foot until December 31, 1991; thereafter it is $26.00 per square foot. This tenant pays a percentage rent based on 6% of sales in excess of $600,000. Sales in 1987 totaled $468,000 and are forecast to increase 7% per year. In addition, the tenant pays:

- A pro rata share of all increases in real estate taxes that exceed $1.75 per square foot
- Thirty percent of all increases in energy expenses that exceed $2.20 per square foot
- Thirty percent of all increases in other operating expenses that exceed $2.35 per square foot

Other revenue. Parking revenue is expected to total $15,000 per year for the next two years, increasing 5% per year thereafter.

Property expenses. Property expenses for 1988 are forecast as follows:

Real estate taxes	$2.05 per square foot
Energy-related expenses	$2.50 per square foot
Other operating expenses	$2.60 per square foot
Replacement reserves	$0.10 per square foot
Management expenses	2.5% of effective gross revenue

In this market management expenses are not reimbursed in whole or in part by the tenants.

Mortgage information. The two mortgages on the property are summarized below.

First Mortgage

Outstanding balance	$1,100,000
Annual interest rate	11.25%, payable monthly
Amortization term	32 years
Payments	Level payment, self-amortizing

Second Mortgage

Outstanding balance	$250,000
Annual interest rate	13.5% for 1988 and 1989, 14% thereafter; payable quarterly
Amortization term	25 years
Payments	Interest only for 1988 and 1989; level payment, self-amortizing for balance of term

Miscellaneous Assumptions

Leasing commissions	For a new tenant, 3% per year payable in the first year of the lease; for a renewal tenant, 1.5% per year
Tenant turnover	The RKM Insurance Corporation is expected to move out when its lease expires; the other tenants are expected to release their space.
Lease terms	Average of four years
Tenant improvement costs	For a new tenant, $15.00 per square foot; for an existing tenant, $5.00 per square foot in 1988 dollars
Selling expense at resale	2.5%

Market research. Eight recent sales of competitive office buildings have been researched and verified. The information derived from each sale is summarized in Tables 22.1 and 22.2.

Table 22.1 Comparable Office Building Sales

Sale	Rentable Area (Sq. Ft.)	Sale Price	Sale Price per Sq. Ft.	Equity Price	Mortgage Amount	Mortgage Interest Rate	NOI Ratio	EGRM	First Year Cash Flow Rate	First Year Overall Rate	Forecast Equity IRR	Forecast Period (Years)
1	16,000	$2,464,000	$154.00	$1,000,000	$2,464,000	10.50%	45.5%	6.0	6.50%	7.58%	13.8%	10
2	23,000	3,500,000	152.17	1,250,000	1,500,000-1st 750,000-2nd	12.00 13.25	52.5	7.5	2.10	7.00	14.0	11
3	12,500	1,950,000	156.00	1,500,000	450,000	9.00	60.0	8.0	5.50	7.50	13.8	10
4	25,000	4,050,000	162.00	1,500,000	1,500,000-1st 1,050,000-2nd	11.50 13.50	50.5	7.0	4.30	7.21	14.5	10
5	16,000	2,550,000	159.38	2,550,000	0	—	55.0	7.7	7.14	7.14	13.0	5
6	15,000	2,265,000	151.00	1,500,000	765,000	9.50	48.0	7.5	6.20	6.40	14.0	10
7	9,000	1,575,000	175.00	1,575,000	0	—	43.0	5.0	8.60	8.60	13.0	10
8	35,000	5,075,000	145.00	1,600,000	3,000,000-1st 475,000-2nd	12.50 14.0	65.0	7.5	3.00	8.67	14.0	10

NOI ratio = net operating income/effective gross revenue
EGRM = effective gross revenue multiplier; sale price/effective gross revenue
IRR = prospective internal rate of return or discount rate

Table 22.2 Analysis of Cash Flow Assumptions for Comparable Office Building Sales

Sale	Market Rent Growth Rate	Expense Growth Rate			Resale Price OAR	Vacancy	Re-Leasing Terms (Years)	Re-Leasing Escalation Provisions		
		R. E. Taxes	Energy Items	Other Operating Expenses				R. E. Taxes	Energy Items	Other Operating Expenses
1	6.0%	5.0%	8.0%	8.0%	11.0%	3 months plus 2.0%	3	*	*	*
2	5.5	5.0	10.0	6.0	11.0	3 months plus 3.0%	5	*	*	*
3	6.0	4.5	7.5	6.0	12.0	5.0%	5	*	*	*
4	6.0	5.0	8.0	7.0	10.5	3 months plus 3.0%	3	*	*	*
5	5.5	5.0	8.0	6.0	12.0	4 months plus 2.0%	3	*	*	*
6	6.5	6.0	8.5	6.0	10.5	3 months plus 3.0%	3	*	*	*
7	6.0	5.0	7.5	5.0	11.0	3 months plus 3.0%	5	*	*	*
8	6.0	4.5	9.0	6.0	11.0	2 months plus 2.5%	5	*	*	*

*Pro rata share of increases over base year—i.e., year in which lease commences.

The comparable sales are used to extract capitalization rates, discount rates, growth rates, and other pertinent information. The appraiser has formed the following conclusions.

Forecast period	10 years
Market rent	$24.50
Market rent growth rate	6% per year
Vacancy	3.0% + 3 months vacancy at rollover
Expense growth rates	
Real estate taxes	5.0%
Energy costs	8.0%
Other operating expenses	6.0%
Overall capitalization rate	
for calculating reversion	11.0%
Discount rates	
Free and clear of financing	13.0%
Subject to existing financing	14.0%

Based on these investment assumptions, a 10-year cash-flow forecast is made for the subject property (see Table 22.3). The values indicated by DCF analysis are shown below.

Free and Clear of Financing (All Cash)

Equity discount rate	13.0%
Present value of equity	$2,393,094
Mortgage	0
Total real property value	$2,393,094

Subject to Existing Financing (Cash and Terms)

Equity discount rate	14.0%
Present value of equity	$1,160,196
First mortgage balance	1,100,000
Second mortgage balance	250,000
Total real property value	$2,510,196

Table 22.3 Cash Flow Forecast

	1988	1989	1990	1991	1992	1993	1994	1995	1996	1997	1998*
Revenue											
Base rent	$329,000	$329,000	$329,000	$339,000	$351,000	$369,305	$443,698	$476,455	$515,636	$529,334	$586,231
Real estate tax escalation	3,950	5,487	7,102	8,797	10,577	9,655	5,689	6,703	3,752	4,848	3,221
Energy escalation	13,850	16,950	20,298	23,914	27,819	22,853	11,622	14,341	8,731	11,525	7,939
Other operating escalation	7,450	9,985	12,672	15,520	18,540	16,049	8,698	10,495	6,058	7,885	5,303
Percentage rent	0	0	0	807	3,384	6,141	9,090	12,247	0	0	0
Parking	15,000	15,750	16,537	17,364	18,233	19,144	20,101	21,107	22,162	23,270	24,433
Total revenue	369,250	377,172	385,609	405,402	429,553	443,147	498,897	541,348	556,339	576,862	627,127
Less vacancy	11,077	11,315	11,568	12,162	12,887	13,294	14,967	16,240	16,690	17,306	18,814
Effective Gross Revenue	358,173	365,857	374,041	393,240	416,666	429,853	483,930	525,108	539,649	559,556	608,313
Property Expenses											
Real estate taxes	30,750	32,287	33,902	35,597	37,377	39,246	41,208	43,268	45,432	47,703	50,089
Energy	37,500	40,500	43,740	47,239	51,018	55,100	59,508	64,268	69,410	74,963	80,960
Other operating	39,000	41,340	43,820	46,450	49,237	52,191	55,322	58,642	62,160	65,890	69,843
Replacement reserve	1,500	1,590	1,685	1,787	1,894	2,007	2,128	2,255	2,391	2,534	2,686
Management	8,954	9,146	9,351	9,831	10,417	10,746	12,098	13,128	13,491	13,989	15,208
Total expenses	117,704	124,863	132,498	140,904	149,943	159,290	170,264	181,561	192,884	205,079	218,786
Net operating income	240,469	240,994	241,543	252,336	266,723	270,563	313,666	343,547	346,765	354,477	389,527

Table 22.3 Cash Flow Forecast (continued)

	1988	1989	1990	1991	1992	1993	1994	1995	1996	1997	1998*
Other Deductions:											
Tenant improvements	0	0	0	0	0	55,737	70,898	0	53,107	70,367	
Leasing commissions	0	0	0	0	0	13,115	16,682	0	12,496	16,557	
Total other deductions						68,852	87,580		65,603	86,924	
Cash from operations	240,469	240,994	241,543	252,336	266,723	201,711	226,086	343,547	288,874	302,603	
Debt service:											
Interest	157,246	156,616	126,039	125,358	124,609	123,786	122,878	121,878	120,773	119,551	
Amortization	5,057	5,688	13,835	14,516	15,264	16,088	16,995	17,996	19,101	20,322	
Total debt service	162,303	162,304	139,874	139,874	139,873	139,874	139,873	139,874	139,874	139,873	
Pre-tax cash flow	78,166	78,690	101,669	112,462	126,850	61,837	86,213	203,673	149,000	162,730	
Resale price											3,541,164
Selling expenses											88,529
Loan balance											1,205,137
Proceeds of resale (pre-tax)											2,247,498

*For calculating the resale price in 1997

Critique of the Internal Rate of Return

Limitations and Pitfalls

Without question, the internal rate of return (*IRR*) is a very significant measure of investment performance. It is widely used and its popularity is well deserved. The *IRR* can be simply defined as *that rate of discount that makes the net present value of an investment equal to zero*. The IRR *discounts all returns from an investment, including returns from its termination, to equal the original investment*. The *IRR* does have limitations and appraisers may encounter pitfalls in its use. By understanding these shortcomings, practitioners can avoid wasted effort and false conclusions. The search for a single *IRR* within a plausible range is not always fruitful. Unusual combinations of cash flows may produce more than one *IRR* or no *IRR* may be indicated.

   More than one *IRR*. Consider a real estate investment with the cash flows set forth below. Assume that the investor borrows $10,000 and pays 10% interest only, with the principal to be repaid in a lump sum at the end of 10 years. The investor's net cash flows are tabulated as follows:

Year	Cash Flow Before Loan	Loan	Interest	Net Cash Flow
0	$-12,300	$ 10,000	$ 0	$-2,300
1	2,000	0	-1,000	1,000
2	2,000	0	-1,000	1,000
3	2,000	0	-1,000	1,000
4	2,000	0	-1,000	1,000
5	1,000	0	-1,000	0
6	1,000	0	-1,000	0
7	1,000	0	-1,000	0
8	1,000	0	-1,000	0
9	1,000	0	-1,000	0
10	9,000	-10,000	-1,000	-2,000

The *IRR* for the net cash flows after financing can be obtained through graphic analysis. Net present values are calculated for even discount rates between 0% and 24% and plotted on a graph.

   The table and graph that follow indicate not one, but two, *IRR*s. With a computer, the two *IRR*s are calculated as 4.50839% and 18.3931%.

Table of Net Present Values

Discount Rate	Net Present Value
0	$-300
2	-133
4	- 21
6	48
8	86
10	99
12	93
14	74
16	45
18	8
20	- 34
22	- 80
24	-128

Graphic Solution to Example

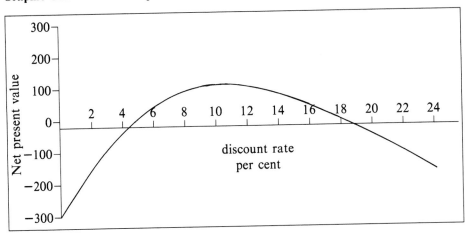

Multiple rates like these are interesting from a theoretical point of view, but it is difficult to accept more than one *IRR* as a useful measure of performance. In real estate investment analysis, the presence of more than one *IRR* usually suggests that some other measure of performance would be more appropriate or that the cash flows or time frame should be adjusted to permit a more meaningful analysis. Close examination of the example presented here reveals some characteristics of the *IRR* that may not be apparent in ordinary examples.

Negative net present value at zero rate of return. The cumulative value of the net cash flows in the example is negative. Negative income totals $4,300 while positive income totals $4,000. Therefore, the net present value—i.e., the difference between the present value of expected benefits, or positive cash flows, and the present value of capital outlays, or negative cash flows—with no discounting, or at a zero discount rate, is −$300 (see graph). This should be a warning sign to the analyst. Whenever the total outgo over a period of time is equal to, or more than, the total income for the same period of time, the *IRR* should be viewed with suspicion.

Under these conditions, the *IRR* cannot be positive unless the mixture of positive and negative cash flows over time is such that the net present value increases with increases in the discount rate until the net present value reaches zero. This phenomenon can be seen in the example. This kind of reverse discounting is mathematically valid, but it is contrary to the practical notion of reducing net present value by increasing the discount rate. It is not surprising that the *IRR* in such cases is difficult to comprehend and of questionable practical value.

Negative *IRR*. If the net present value at 0% rate of return is negative, a negative *IRR* may be indicated. A negative *IRR* may be interpreted as a rate of loss, but the *IRR* is generally understood to be a positive rate of return. Any prospective loss rate will normally discourage capital investment.

The concept of a negative *IRR* has theoretical, as well as practical, limitations. A glance at the *IRR* equation reveals that a negative *IRR* of 100% or more has no meaning because it involves division by zero or powers of negative numbers.

Little or no equity. Because the *IRR* is a measure of the return on invested capital, it cannot be used to measure the performance of opportunities that require no investment of capital. Some investments can be "financed out" or financed with loans that cover 100% or more of the capital required. If the projected net cash flows are all positive, there is no *IRR*. Obviously, no discount rate can make a series of positive benefits equal to zero.

The same rationale can be applied to investments that call for very low equity or a very small down payment in relation to the expected returns. For example, a profit of $1 on an investment of $1 amounts to a 100% rate of return; a return of $100 on an investment of $1 indicates a 10,000% rate of return. When the investment is very small, slight changes in income can cause astronomical changes in the rate of return or rate of loss. The *IRR* is an impractical yardstick for such investments.

However, the *IRR* can be a valuable indicator in analyzing investments that are financed out at the start and then expected to operate at a loss for a period of time. In these arrangements, the early negative cash flows may represent a significant investment of equity capital and the prospective *IRR* may be the best measure of performance. It may also be useful to compare the prospective *IRR* before financing with an interest rate that reflects the cost of capital. The difference can be used as a measure of prospective leverage.

Reinvestment Concepts

The *IRR* is an *internal* rate of return on capital *within* an investment. No consideration is given to the rate of return on reinvested capital after it has been withdrawn from the investment. Obviously, the income from a real estate investment may be reinvested in another project at another rate of return, stored in a vault, or spent, but the *IRR* is not affected. Thus, no assumptions regarding a reinvestment rate are needed to understand and use the *IRR*.

Although investment rates are not relevant to the *IRR*, some analysts choose to envision the reinvestment of income at a rate equal to the *IRR*. This assumption is implied if the objective is to measure the total return on a fixed capital sum over a fixed period of time and the fruits of reinvestment are not otherwise taken into account. This is a popular premise, but it can be misleading.

It is correct to assume that if all the dollars withdrawn from a project are reinvested at the same *IRR*, the final composite rate of return will be equal to the *IRR* of the investment. It is also correct to assume that if all the dollars withdrawn from a project are reinvested at a rate of return that is not equal to the *IRR*, the final composite rate of return will not be equal to the *IRR* of the investment. It does not follow, however, that the final composite rate of return on invested and reinvested dollars must equal the original *IRR* of the investment.

If an investor wants to find the *IRR* associated with a *capital sum* at work over a period of time, the reinvestment of income must be considered. If, on the other hand, the objective is to find the *IRR* associated with a *particular property*, the reinvestment of income may be irrelevant.

The *IRR* is an independent, informative statistic that reflects the amount of earnings for each dollar invested over a specific unit of time for a particular set of cash flows. It can be applied to a single property or an entire investment portfolio. If an overall *IRR* that reflects the combined results of project earnings and reinvestment is sought, the reinvestment cash flows can be incorporated into the analysis. In short, there is no automatic or implicit assumption in the *IRR* regarding reinvestment. The *IRR* can, however, accommodate reinvestment assumptions by including the expected costs and benefits of reinvestment in the projection of cash flows.

Reinvestment assumptions are sometimes made to prevent multiple *IRR*s such as those found in the preceding example. If it is assumed that all income is reinvested to grow at a known rate and withdrawn in a lump sum at the termination of the investment, there can be only one overall IRR that represents the combined results of project earnings and reinvestment.

IRR Before Taxes Versus *IRR* After Taxes

The *IRR* is generally seen as a measure of an investment's ultimate net financial performance after all expenses, including income taxes, have been paid. The *IRR* can, however, be used to measure profit before income taxes as well. In fact, the *IRR* is applicable to any level of financial return; it is a general-purpose yardstick of comparison with no arbitrary restrictions. Comparing the after-tax performance of one investment opportunity to the after-tax performance of another is only one of its many applications. As mentioned earlier, the *IRR* before financing for a particular investment can be compared with the *IRR* after financing to assess the effects of leverage produced by borrowing. Similarly, the *IRR* before taxes can be compared with the *IRR* after taxes to determine the impact of taxation and any tax-shelter benefits.

Although the *IRR* is not restricted to a particular use, there is considerable debate regarding its proper use in the analysis of real estate investments.

Arguments in favor of the *IRR* before income taxes. Income taxes depend on the tax bracket of the investor as well as the earning power of the real estate. Therefore, some analysts feel that the *IRR* before taxes is a better measure of intrinsic performance because it is not dependent on outside influences. This argument is often raised when market value is sought and the tax bracket of the investor is not known.

The market for real estate investments is influenced, to some extent, by decision makers who are tax-exempt or do not pay income taxes directly (e.g., charitable foundations and real estate investment trusts). Consequently, the *IRR* before taxes is more meaningful in comparisons that involve this segment of the market.

The *IRR* before taxes also has the advantage of simplicity. Projecting cash flow before taxes is less complicated and less subject to error because many calculations are eliminated. Including assumptions regarding tax brackets and allowable deductions introduces more uncertainties and weakens the forecast. Furthermore, yields on stocks, bonds, and mortgages are reported in terms of a rate of return before income taxes. Real estate must compete for capital with alternative investment opportunities, so the *IRR* before income taxes provides a logical basis of comparison.

Arguments in favor of the *IRR* after income taxes. Tax shelter is a major attraction for real estate investors. Some analysts argue that any yardstick that does not reflect the full effect of taxes and tax-shelter benefits is deficient. (For a discussion of how the Tax Reform Act of 1986 affects tax shelters, see Chapter 25.)

The fact that income taxes vary with the tax bracket of the investor may be seen to encourage, rather than discourage, the use of the *IRR* after taxes. The tax bracket of the investor is an important variable that cannot be ignored in any complete analysis. If an estimate of market value is sought and the investor's tax bracket is unknown, the analyst can simulate the decision-making process of a typical investor by using a typical tax rate.

Computer models are readily available and can be used to produce detailed after-tax cash flow anlaysis. The required calculations can be automated without too much effort or expense. Similarly, the reported yields on stocks, bonds, and mortgages can easily be converted to reveal equivalent yields after taxes for purposes of comparison. The yields reported for tax-exempt municipal bonds need not be converted at all, but can be compared directly to the *IRR* after taxes.

Clearly, there are valid arguments for using either the *IRR* before taxes or the *IRR* after taxes. The *IRR* selected depends on the application and the objective of the analysis.

Conclusion

The *IRR* can be as important to the real estate investor as the interest rate is to the mortgage lender; in fact, the two measures are equivalent. The *IRR* is not a meaningful measure of all investments and, when it is meaningful, it is not the only possible criterion. It is, however, a fundamental and pure measure of financial performance within a particular investment. In general, the *IRR* is an extremely valuable analytical tool if the decision maker understands its limitations and has access to complementary or alternative analytical techniques.

OTHER MEASURES OF PERFORMANCE

The *IRR* is not the only measure of financial performance or profitability. Other popular alternatives such as the payback period, the profitability index or benefit/cost ratio, the net present value or dollar reward, and the time-weighted rate are discussed in Chapter 25. *These yardsticks do not measure performance or profit on the same scale or under the same assumptions.* The usefulness of any of these measures depends on the situation and the preferences of the user. Neither the *IRR* nor any alternative measure is superior in all situations. The two measures described below represent specific modifications of the *IRR*.

IRR with Reinvestment

This variation on the *IRR* was mentioned in the discussion of reinvestment concepts. The assumption underlying this concept is that all income from a project can be immediately reinvested at a specified rate and left to grow at that rate, with compound interest, until the end of the investment holding period. The combined results of the investment's earnings and reinvestment are then reflected in one overall rate of return. This measure traces the presumed total performance of a capital sum at work in more than one investment, rather than the performance of a single project. This measure can also be used to prevent multiple solutions to the *IRR* equation. The *IRR* with reinvestment is often called the adjusted *IRR*.

IRR with a Specified Borrowing Rate

The *IRR* with a specified borrowing rate is another variation on the *IRR* that can be used to prevent multiple rates. It is sometimes called *the* IRR *for investment*. The *IRR* for investment specifies an interest rate for borrowing funds during the period when the investment is producing negative cash flows; thus it prevents the use of the *IRR* as a borrowing rate. Stipulating a fixed borrowing rate modifies the cash flows as well as the *IRR* and prevents the possibility of more than one *IRR*.

SUMMARY

The mortgage-equity analysis developed by L. W. Ellwood is based on the theory that mortgage financing strongly influences real property prices and values. Ellwood believed that both the debt and equity components of an investment have return requirements that must be satisfied through income and reversion. In mortgage-equity analysis, an overall capitalization rate is derived with a yield capitalization procedure based on formulas. The yield and change formula, $R = Y - A$, uses a property yield rate and does not consider the effects of a mortgage on the investor's equity yield. Ellwood's mortgage-equity formula, on the other hand, includes a mortgage component and clearly defines the yield requirements of both the lender's interest and the investor's equity interest.

Mortgage-equity analysis can be applied to derive market value or investment value. Use of mortgage-equity techniques in market value appraisals has been criticized. Problems arise because analysts fail to use market-derived data in applying the formula; the formula is appropriate for use in market value appraisal.

Mortgage-equity analysis can be used to derive overall capitalization rates, to calculate land and building capitalization rates for use in residual techniques, to test the rates obtained with other capitalization techniques, to test the values indicated by other approaches, and to examine capitalization rates with graphic analysis.

The general mortgage-equity formula is:

$$R_O = \frac{Y_E - M (Y_E + P1/S_{\overline{n}} - R_M) - \Delta_O 1/S_{\overline{n}}}{1 + \Delta_I J}$$

The first part of the numerator, $Y_E - M (Y_E + P1/S_{\overline{n}} - R_M)$, is the basic capitalization rate (r), which satisfies the requirements of both the lender and the equity investor. The last part of the numerator, $\Delta_O 1/S_{\overline{n}}$, allows the basic rate to be adjusted for a change in overall property value. The denominator, $1 + \Delta_I J$, adjusts for a change in income.

An arithmetic format developed by Charles B. Akerson can be substituted for the algebraic equation in the Ellwood formula. This format is directly applied to level-income situations and, when modified with the J factor, can be applied to changing-income situations as well.

The Akerson format is

Loan ratio × annual constant	=	_____
Equity ratio × equity yield rate	=	+_____
Loan ratio × part paid off × $1/S_{\overline{n}}$	=	−_____
Basic rate (r)	=	_____
+ Dep or − App × $1/S_{\overline{n}}$	=	+_____
Overall capitalization rate	=	_____

Mortgage-equity analysis is applied to real property investments with level income streams through the use of overall capitalization rates and residual techniques. The general mortgage-equity formula can be used to value income streams that are anticipated to change on a curvilinear basis by incorporating the J factor into the formula. Exponential-curve (constant-ratio) change can be handled with the K factor. The J factor is used in the stabilizer $(1 + \Delta_I J)$ and can be obtained from precomputed tables or calculated with the formula

$$J = 1/S_{\overline{n}|} \times \frac{n}{1-1/(1 + Y)^n} - \frac{1}{Y}$$

The K factor is an income adjuster or stabilizer that is used to convert an income stream changing at constant ratio into its level equivalent. The K factor can be obtained from precomputed tables or calculated with the formula

$$K = \frac{1 - (1 + C)^n/S^n}{(Y - C)a_n}$$

where C is the constant-ratio change in income. When the general mortgage-equity formula is applied to an income expected to change on a constant-ratio basis, the K factor is substituted for the denominator $(1 + \Delta_I J)$.

Given an actual or proposed equity sale price and a forecast of equity benefits, an equity yield rate can be estimated. The computations are accomplished through iteration or with a calculator. When income is forecast to be level, the formula for Y_E is

$$Y_E = R_E + \Delta_E \, 1/S_{\overline{n}|}$$

When income is forecast to change on a curvilinear basis,

$$Y_E = R_E + \Delta_E 1/S_{\overline{n}|} + \frac{R_O I}{1-M} J$$

If income is forecast to change on an exponential-curve (constant-ratio) basis,

$$Y_E = R_E + \Delta_E 1/S_{\overline{n}|} + \frac{R_O(K-1)}{1-M}$$

An appraiser can test the reasonableness of value conclusions derived with overall capitalization rates by analyzing the rates graphically. For this analysis, the appraiser selects equity yield rates that cover the full range of realistic expectations.

There is no assurance that a real estate investment can be liquidated on the initiative of the equity investor. Furthermore, in negotiating a purchase price, the prospects for a reasonable profit may be more impressive than the chance of achieving a specific equity yield rate. The relationship between the equity yield rate and the change in property value is highly significant. Rate analysis is used to determine the change in property value (Δ_O). The formula for calculating the required property value change in a level-income application is:

$$\Delta_O = \frac{r - R_O}{1/S_{\overline{n}|}}$$

When level income is forecast, the difference between the basic rate (r) and the overall rate (R_o) divided by the sinking fund factor is the anticipated change in property value. If r is greater than R_o, appreciation is indicated; if r is less than R_o, depreciation is indicated.

When value and income are presumed to change at the same rate, the J factor is used. In this situation the formula for anticipated change in overall property value is:

$$\Delta_o = \frac{r - R_o}{R_o J + 1/S_{\overline{n}|}}$$

Graphic rate analysis reveals combinations of Y_E and Δ_o that are implicit in the market capitalization rate. With this type of analysis, an appraiser can test whether a particular combination of Y_E and Δ_o is consistent with market evidence. The reasonableness of overall capitalization rates is scrutinized against the range of property value changes anticipated by market participants.

A two-variable algebraic technique can be used in developing market-oriented overall capitalization rates. This technique produces an infinite number of pairs of Y_E and Δ_o and each pair is mathematically correct according to the market. When the anticipated rate of change in property value equals the anticipated rate of change in income, the formula used to determine Δ_o is

$$\Delta_{o=I} = \frac{Y_E - M\,(Y_E + P\,1/S_{\overline{n}|} - R_M) - R_o}{R_o J + 1/S_{\overline{n}|}}$$

By graphically analyzing the relationship between equity yield and the change in property value, an appraiser can identify pairs that are market-oriented. Any pair not suggested by the lines on the graph is not market-oriented and should not be used to derive an overall capitalization rate with the mortgage-equity formula.

Mortgage-equity analysis can only be applied to stable or stabilized income streams, but *discounted cash flow* (DCF) analysis is appropriate for any pattern of regular or irregular income. Discounted cash flow analysis can be used to solve for present value given the rate of return or for the rate of return given the purchase price. This type of analysis accounts for all cash flowing in and out of the real property interest over time so the time value of money is recognized. Discounted cash flow analysis is commonly used for investment forecasts in the real estate market. Appraisers must always use market-extracted data in its applications.

In making forecasts, appraisers follow the steps taken by investors using DCF analysis. Forecasts typically include data on income, vacancy, operating expenses, debt service when appropriate, pre- or after-tax cash flow over the ownership period, and the residual income from sale of the property at the end of the forecast period. The average ownership period is 10 years.

The *internal rate of return* (IRR) is the rate of return that makes the net present value of an investment equal to zero. It is a highly significant measure of investment performance, but it has limitations. In some situations a single *IRR* cannot be found because unusual combinations of cash flows can produce multiple *IRR*s or no *IRR* at all. If more than one *IRR* is found, some other measure of performance may be more appropriate or the cash flows or time frame should be adjusted to permit more meaningful analysis.

An investment's net cash flows may have a negative cumulative value. When the total outgo over a period is equal to, or more than, the total income for the same period, the *IRR* should be viewed with suspicion. A negative net present value at a 0% rate of return may indicate a negative *IRR*, which suggests a loss and would discourage investors.

The *IRR* measures the return on invested capital, but it cannot measure the performance of investments that are 100% financed by loans or investments that call for very low equity in relation to the expected returns. The *IRR* can, however, be a valuable indicator for investments that are initially "financed out" and expected to operate at a loss for a period of time. Comparing a project's *IRR* before financing with its *IRR* after financing is useful in assessing the effects of leverage produced by borrowing.

The *IRR* can be used to forecast the investment performance of a single property or an entire investment portfolio. Cash flows that are reinvested can be incorporated into the analysis to reflect the combined results of earnings and reinvestment. However, the *IRR* includes no automatic or implicit assumption regarding reinvestment. When all income from a project is reinvested to grow at a known rate and then withdrawn in a lump sum at the end of the holding period, only one *IRR* can represent the combined results of project earnings and reinvestment.

By comparing the *IRR* before taxes with the *IRR* after taxes, an investor can assess how taxation and tax shelters affect the profitability of an investment. Some practitioners favor the *IRR* before taxes because it is simpler, less prone to error, independent of outside influence, and can be compared with investment yields that are reported on a pre-tax basis. Those who favor the *IRR* after taxes argue that the income-tax bracket of the investor is an important variable that must be included so that the analysis simulates the decision-making process of the typical investor.

Other, more popular yardsticks of investment performance measure profitability under different assumptions. Two of these measures are specific modifications of the *IRR*: the IRR *with reinvestment*, also called the *adjusted* IRR, and the IRR *with a specified borrowing rate*, or the *IRR* for investment, which specifies a fixed borrowing rate.

23 Reconciling Value Indications

An appraisal is performed to answer a client's question about real estate. To answer the question, an appraiser follows the valuation process. In the course of this process, the appraiser identifies, gathers, and analyzes general and specific data; determines the property's highest and best use; and applies the sales comparison, income capitalization, and/or cost approaches as warranted by the question and suggested by the available data.

Usually more than one approach is used, and each approach results in a different indication of value. Therefore, if two or three approaches are used, the appraiser will have at least two or three value indications. Moreover, several value indications may be derived in a single approach. In the sales comparison approach, for example, the analysis of each comparable sale produces an adjusted sale price, which is an indication of value. In the income capitalization approach, different indications of value may result from direct capitalization, yield capitalization, and the application of gross income multipliers to income streams.

When multiple value indications are derived in a single approach, the appraiser often resolves any differences as part of the application of the approach. In certain cases, however, an appraiser may choose to resolve these differences after reviewing the entire appraisal so that all pertinent information can be used to derive a single value indication from each approach. Resolving the differences among various value indications is called reconciliation. *Reconciliation is the analysis of alternative conclusions to arrive at a final value estimate.*

REVIEW

To prepare for reconciliation, the appraiser reviews the entire appraisal to make sure that the data and analytical techniques used and the logic followed are valid, realistic, and consistent. Data are checked to ensure that they are authentic and reflect pertinent market activity. The appraiser should also make certain that sufficient, meaningful market evidence has been considered.

The legal estate appraised, the value definition applied, and the qualifying conditions imposed are also reviewed to ascertain that the methods and techniques used in the analysis address each of these items specifically. *The appraiser should examine the differences in the analyses and conclusions derived in the various approaches and resolve any inconsistencies.* For example, is the effective age of the property used in the cost approach consistent with the property condition stated when adjustments are made in the sales comparison approach? Are all the approaches based on the same conclusions of highest and best use? Do the results of all the approaches confirm the determination of highest and best use?

Finally, the logic employed throughout the valuation process should be scrutinized. Do the approaches and methods applied efficiently and systematically lead to meaningful conclusions that are directly related to the purpose and use of the appraisal? Will the final value opinion help solve the client's problem? For example, if the client wants to establish a basis for making depreciation deductions in computing his or her federal income tax, does the appraisal give separate values for the improvements and the land? If the client needs a valuation as a basis for insurance coverage, does the appraisal contain a well-supported estimate of the reproduction or replacement cost of the insured improvements? If the client wants to know what use should be made of a parcel of land, have all reasonable and realistic potential uses been examined?

All mathematical calculations should be checked, preferably by someone other than the person who did them originally. Errors can lead to incorrect value indications and destroy the credibility of the entire appraisal. An independent check of all calculations is an important part of the review.

RELATIONSHIP TO THE VALUATION PROCESS

The resolution of differences among valuation procedures may depend on subtle differences in the objectives of the appraisal or in the interests being appraised. For example, if an appraiser is estimating the market value of a proposed office tower both as completed and occupied and as completed but unoccupied, the cost of achieving occupancy must be carefully handled in the cost approach.

In all appraisals, and particularly in appraisals required for litigation, the definition of the appraised value should be reexamined in the reconciliation. The appraiser should consider the use of the appraisal. Should the value be commensurate with the current highest and best use or with all of the uses to which the property could be put or to which it could be physically, legally, and economically adapted?

Appraisers may also need to answer questions that relate to the potential users of property. Can the investment value of a property to a plot assembler be reasonably reconciled with an estimate of the property's market value to a purchaser? Can the intrinsic value of a new office building—i.e., the value of the building as a separate tangible asset—be reasonably reconciled with an estimate of the market value of the building for a mortgagee who is contemplating foreclosure? Must an opinion of the insurable value of a property be reconciled with estimates of its cost less insurance exclusions before and after any deductions for deterioration?

RELATIONSHIP TO THE MARKET

An appraiser should always keep in mind that a client seeks his or her professional opinion and often wants to know the basis for that opinion as well. The final value estimate represents the statistical or mathematical result of the three approaches and application of the appraiser's judgment as well. An appraiser should employ the amount of data that market participants would consider appropriate to solve the appraisal problem at hand. These data should be applied consistently in each approach that is relevant to the appraisal problem. The valuation process is a collection of tools from which an appraiser selects appropriate procedures.

Approaches that are not of primary importance in a specific assignment may be extremely useful in reconciliation. For example, the cost approach may be omitted, but deducting the final value estimate from the sum of the reproduction cost new and the land value may produce a depreciation estimate that should be discussed in the reconciliation.

In market value appraisals, all the estimates used in each approach to value must be consistent with market perceptions. The conclusion should reflect market value, not the appraiser's value. Although the data analyzed should support the appraiser's final value opinion, the data alone do not produce the value estimate. Professional training and experience give an appraiser the ability to exercise good judgment and form a sound value opinion. Sometimes an appraiser must offer substantive, albeit subjective, judgments when precise market information is not available. The effect of these judgments must be evaluated in the reconciliation process. If the appraisal assignment calls for an estimate of market value, but market data are scarce, a disinterested appraiser with practical training and experience is the best judge of value.

RECONCILIATION CRITERIA

Reviewing an appraisal helps substantiate its accuracy, its consistency, and the logic leading to the value indications. However, an appraiser relies more on professional experience, expertise, and judgment in reconciliation than in any other part of the valuation process.

In reconciliation an appraiser considers and evaluates alternate value indications to arrive at a final value estimate. The appraiser weighs the relative significance, applicability, and defensibility of each value indication and relies most heavily on the approach that is most appropriate to the purpose of the appraisal. All factors that influence the assignment are brought into focus and related to the client's question, which ultimately guides the appraiser's deliberations.

Reconciliation necessarily involves appraisal judgment based on a careful, logical analysis of the procedures that lead to each value indication. Appropriateness, accuracy, and quantity of evidence are the criteria with which an appraiser forms a meaningful, defensible final value estimate. These criteria are used to analyze multiple value indications within each approach and to reconcile the indications produced by the different approaches into a final estimate of defined value.

Appropriateness

Using the criterion of appropriateness, an appraiser judges how pertinent each approach is to the purpose and use of the appraisal. The appropriateness of an approach is usually most directly related to property type and market viability. For example, an appraisal to estimate the market value of a 30-year-old community shopping center will ordinarily employ procedures associated with the income capitalization approach—e.g., the derivation of a gross rent multiplier, net income capitalization, and the discounting of cash flows. The cost approach might not be useful in valuing obsolete improvements, but it may be applied to estimate land value and determine, through an analysis of highest and best use, whether demolition of the property is appropriate. The sales comparison approach could be used to obtain a value indication in terms of price per unit of area; this approach may be of secondary importance because of the age of the improvements and the importance of income expectations.

Although the final value estimate is based on the approach that is most applicable, the final value estimate may not be identical to the value produced by the most applicable approach. If two approaches are significant, the final estimate of value may be closer to one value indication than to the other. For example, assume that the value indication derived with the income capitalization approach is lower than the value derived with the sales comparison approach. If market participants are primarily interested in income-earning potential, the final estimate may be closer to the value indicated by the income capitalization approach than the value derived with sales comparison.

The criterion of appropriateness is also used to judge the relevance of each comparable property and each significant adjustment made in an approach. The appraiser asks, Is this comparable property a valid and reliable indicator of the value of the subject property? Is it similar in terms of physical characteristics and location? Was it bought and sold in the same market? Are the characteristics of the transaction similar to those expected for the subject property? If the subject property produces income, are the income and expenses of this comparable property good indicators of the income and expenses of the subject property? Are the cost data appropriate and are the estimates of accrued depreciation justified by market analysis?

Accuracy

The accuracy of an appraisal is measured by the appraiser's confidence in the correctness of the data, the calculations performed in each approach, and the adjustments made to the sale price of each comparable property. For example, are the cost data and estimates of accrued depreciation used in the cost approach as accurate as the adjustments made in the sales comparison approach, or the income, expenses, and capitalization rates applied in the income capitalization approach? An appraiser may have more confidence in the accuracy of the data and calculations used in one approach than in the others.

The number of comparable properties, the number of adjustments, and the gross and net dollar amounts of adjustments may suggest the relative accuracy of a particular approach. If a large number of comparable properties are available for one approach, greater accuracy may be indicated and the appraiser may place more reliance on this approach than on the others. For example, if there are many properties competitive with the subject property from which an appraiser can extract income and expense data and capitalization rates, the appraiser might attribute greater accuracy and confidence to the income capitalization and sales comparison approaches and less to the cost approach.

If fewer total adjustments must be made to one or two comparable properties than to other comparables within an approach, an appraiser may attribute greater accuracy and weight to the value indications obtained with fewer adjustments. However, such a conclusion would normally be valid only if the size of the adjustments is relatively equal. Although the number of adjustments among comparable properties may be similar, the gross or net dollar amount of the total adjustments might vary considerably. For example, in the sales comparison approach an appraiser may analyze five comparable properties that each require nine adjustments. However, the gross dollar amount of adjustments for one comparable property may total 15% of the sale price, while the gross dollar amount of the adjustments for the other four properties may be less than 5% of each sale price. If other considerations are similar, less accuracy will probably be attributed to the comparable property that requires the largest percentage of dollar adjustments.

In some cases, however, the gross amount of dollar adjustments may not be a good indicator of accuracy, particularly if fewer total adjustments are required. One large adjustment may be more accurate and supportable with market evidence than many smaller adjustments. For example, an appraiser may find abundant market evidence in a community to indicate the amount of value added by a swimming pool, a garage, or an extra bedroom. Although an adjustment for the presence or absence of one of these items may result in a larger gross adjustment for one comparable than for other comparables, greater accuracy might be attributed to this sale because there is reliable market evidence to support the value contribution.

Usually, the net dollar amount of adjustments is a less reliable indicator of accuracy. This figure is obtained by adding all positive and negative adjustments to a sale and then subtracting the smaller amount from the larger amount. However, the figure may be misleading because one cannot assume that any inaccuracies in the positive and negative adjustments will cancel out each other. Several adjustments that are all positive (or all negative) may be more accurate and produce a smaller total gross adjustment than a combination of positive and negative adjustments.

Furthermore, inaccuracies may be compounded when the adjustments are added together. The net dollar amount of adjustments should not be regarded as an indicator of accuracy unless the appraiser is confident of each adjustment.

Quantity of Evidence

Appropriateness and accuracy produce *quality* and determine how relevant and correct the value indication derived from a comparable or an approach may be. Although these criteria are considered separately in reconciliation, both must be studied in relation to the *quantity* of evidence provided by a particular comparable or approach. Even data that meet the criteria of appropriateness and accuracy can be weakened by a lack of sufficient evidence.

To illustrate the importance of the quantity of evidence, assume that an appraiser is attempting to extract an overall capitalization rate from three comparable sales. The properties are considered appropriate in terms of their physical and locational characteristics and the similarity of the transactions. The available data for each sale are verified and considered reliable and each comparable could produce an accurate indication of value. However, the available data for one comparable include an income and expense forecast for a 10-year holding period, but the data for the other comparables are less detailed. No income and expense data could be obtained for one comparable and for another only income and expense data for the first year of the holding period could be found. Because more data are available for the first comparable, the appraiser will have greater confidence in the value indication obtained from this sale than those obtained from the other comparables. In statistical terms, the confidence interval in which the true value lies is narrowed by additional data which add precision to accuracy.

Regardless of the quantity of evidence available, the responsibility of the appraiser goes beyond the manipulation of numerical data. It is the appraiser's duty to provide a value estimate that fits the definition of value used in the assignment.

Finally, although the evidence from comparable sales may be accurate and appropriate, these data relate to events that took place before the effective date of the appraisal. Reported building sales, land sales, rentals, expenses, development costs, and vacancy and absorption rates all reflect the *past*. These data are relevant only insofar as they help the appraiser estimate the *future* anticipated benefits of the property and the *present* value of these benefits. Market data are important, but they should not restrict the appraiser's analyses.

FINAL VALUE ESTIMATE

In an appraisal report, the final value estimate may be stated as a single figure or as a range of values. Or an appraiser may choose to show the range and then cite the final value as a single figure within the range. Traditionally, a value estimate is reported as a single dollar amount called a *point estimate*. This figure is the appraiser's best estimate of the value of the property. A point estimate is required for many purposes —e.g., real estate taxation, calculating depreciation deductions for federal income tax, estimating compensation in condemnation cases, determining lease terms that are based on value, and making certain property transfer decisions. Furthermore, because a single figure is typically used by appraisers to report value estimates, many clients expect a point estimate of value.

A point estimate may be rounded to reflect the lack of precision associated with the value estimate, but even a rounded number may imply greater precision than is warranted. Because an appraised value is an estimate, it implies a range in which the property value may fall. For example, an appraiser may report a value estimate of $9,400,000 to represent a result drawn from two approaches with preliminary conclusions of $9,390,000 and $9,380,000. In this case the conclusion of $9,400,000 is not statistically derived. It is outside the range indicated by the two approaches, but it reflects the market value of the property based on the two approaches.

An appraisal is an opinion of value. Although it is an impartial, expert, and reasoned conclusion formed by a trained professional based on an analysis of all relevant evidence, it is still an opinion. It represents the appraiser's perception of the most likely, most probable dollar value of the appraised interest subject to the qualifying conditions imposed. The opinion may, in fact, be too high or too low, but the appraiser does not think so.

On occasion, an appraiser may deliberately avoid stating a single point estimate and report a range of value. By reporting a range, the appraiser indicates that the value lies somewhere within the range—i.e., that the value is no lower than the low end and no higher than the high end of the range. A wide range is of no use to a client; a narrow range implies a guarantee that can only be arbitrary. When provided with a value range, a client is likely to see the extreme that suits his or her purpose as a virtual guarantee. Accordingly, most appraisers report their final value conclusions as single figures.

Rounding

Customarily, appraisal conclusions are rounded to reflect the lack of precision associated with value opinions. The more confidence the appraiser has in the opinion, the less need there is for rounding. For example, a value opinion of $404,000 might be rounded to $400,000 if the appraiser has moderate confidence in the estimate. If, on the other hand, the appraiser has a great deal of confidence in the accuracy of the estimate, this opinion might be rounded to $405,000.

Rounding generally reflects market pricing. However, the prices of non-luxury dwellings are often misleading. A price of $129,000 may be listed, but an appraiser would generally prefer a rounded conclusion of $130,000.

SUMMARY

Reconciliation is the analysis of alternative conclusions to arrive at a final value estimate. Reconciliation is required because different value indications result from the use of more than one approach and within the application of a single approach.

To prepare for reconciliation, an appraiser *reviews* the entire appraisal to ascertain that the data, techniques, and logic used are valid and consistent. Data must be based on market evidence and inconsistencies among the approaches should be reconciled. For example, the effective age of a property estimated in the cost approach should be consistent with the property's condition as stated in the sales comparison approach when adjustments are made. All the approaches applied must be based on the same highest and best use determination.

The appraiser should make sure that the approaches and methods used relate to the real property interests being appraised, the definition of value under consideration, and the purpose and use of the appraisal. An independent check of all mathematical calculations is advisable.

Subtle differences in the appraisal objectives or the real property interests being appraised may account for differences in value indications. For example, different values will result if a rental property is appraised as if completed but empty and as completed and occupied. The definition of the appraised value should be re-examined during reconciliation, especially if the appraisal is required for litigation.

The final value estimate is not derived simply by applying technical and quantitative procedures; rather, it involves the exercise of judgment. The value conclusion reached must be consistent with market thinking, and the quantity of data used should correspond to the amount of data the market considers relevant to the problem. Approaches that are not primarily important in a specific case may be useful in reconciliation.

An appraiser produces a meaningful, defensible value estimate by considering three criteria: appropriateness, accuracy, and quantity of evidence. *Appropriateness* relates to the use of certain approaches in specific assignments, the pertinence of the value indications derived to the specific market, and the choice of properties to be used as comparables. All data, calculations, estimates, and adjustments are examined for *accuracy*. The *quantity of evidence* is analyzed to determine if the conclusion reached is sufficiently supported in the market. Market data reflect past phenomena, but an appraiser must rely on data to estimate future benefits and the present value of these benefits. Nevertheless, the data available should not dictate the range of future possibilities under consideration.

The final value estimate may be stated as a single figure, a range, or a single figure within a range.

24 The Appraisal Report

$\mathbf{A}$n appraisal report leads the reader from the definition of the appraisal problem through reasoning and relevant descriptive data to a specific conclusion. The appraiser must present all facts, reasoning, and conclusions clearly and succinctly. The length, type, and content of appraisal reports are dictated by the client, regulatory requirements, the courts, the type of property being appraised, and the nature of the problem.

Every appraisal report is prepared to answer a particular question and provide the information needed by a client. Some common appraisal questions are: What is the market value of the property? What is the highest and best use of the land as though vacant or the property as improved? What is the value of the part taken in condemnation? What is the damage or benefit to the remainder of the property as a result of the taking?

INSTITUTE STANDARDS FOR WRITTEN REPORTS

Each analysis, opinion, or conclusion that results from an appraisal must be communicated in a manner that is meaningful to the client and will not be misleading to concerned parties or the public. To ensure the quality of appraisal reports, professional appraisal organizations have set minimum standards for the facts, descriptions, and statements of work and purpose to be included in all types of appraisal reports. To comply with the requirements adopted by the American Institute of Real Estate Appraisers,[1] an appraiser will

---

1. See Standards Rule 2 of the Institute's Standards of Professional Practice for greater detail and the precise wording of the specific requirements that apply to appraisal reports signed by Institute members or candidates.

- Identify and describe the real estate being appraised
- Specify the real property interest(s) being appraised by analyzing the owner-ship, financial, and legal interests in the property
- Define the opinion that is the purpose of the appraisal and describe the use of the appraisal
- Specify the date of the valuation and the date when the report was completed
- Determine the highest and best use of the real estate being appraised when this is necessary and appropriate
- Describe the appraisal procedures used
- Provide supporting data and the reasoning behind the analyses, opinions, and conclusions in the report
- Explain all assumptions and limiting conditions that affect the analyses, opinions, and conclusions set forth in the report and disclose any extraordi-nary assumptions and limiting conditions in the relevant sections of the report
- Identify personal property or other items that are not real property
- Discuss the history of the property including prior recorded sales and current offers
- Discuss the effects of leases and existing or assumed financing

Appraisal reports prepared by members or candidates of the Appraisal Institute must contain a certification that includes the following items:

- A statement that, to the best of the appraiser's knowledge and belief, the facts in the report are true and correct and all assumptions and limiting conditions that affect the appraiser's analyses, opinions, and conclusions are set forth in the report
- A statement disclaiming or acknowledging any personal interest in the sub-ject property
- A statement disavowing or disclosing any personal bias on the part of the appraiser with respect to the parties involved
- A statement that the appraiser's compensation is not contingent on any action or event resulting from the analyses, opinions, or conclusions in, or the use of, the report
- A statement that the analyses, opinions, and conclusions in the report have been developed in conformity with the requirements of the Code of Profes-sional Ethics and the Standards of Professional Practice of the American Institute of Real Estate Appraisers
- A statement that the use of the report is subject to the requirements of the Institute regarding review by its duly authorized representatives
- A statement that the appraiser is or is not currently certified under the Institute's voluntary continuing education program (This item is not required for candidates.)
- A statement confirming that a personal inspection of the subject property was or was not made and identifying the individual(s) who carried out the inspection

- An acknowledgment of any significant professional assistance that the appraiser received in preparing the report

TYPES OF REPORTS

An appraisal report may be oral or written. Written communications include letter, form, and narrative reports. Usually a report is presented in the manner requested by the client. However, when a client asks for only the appraiser's opinion without detailed documentation, the appraiser must still perform the analysis required for a complete appraisal. In this case, all material, data, and working papers used to prepare the report are kept in the appraiser's permanent file. Although the appraiser may never need to provide written substantiation for the opinion submitted in abbreviated form, he or she may be asked to explain or defend the opinion at a later time.

Oral Reports

An appraiser may make an oral report when the circumstances or the needs of the client do not permit or warrant a written report. Each oral report should include a property description and the facts, assumptions, conditions, and reasoning on which the conclusion is based. After communicating an oral report, the appraiser should keep on file all notes and data relating to the assignment and a complete memorandum of the analysis, conclusion, and opinion.

Letter Reports

Sometimes, by prior agreement with the client, an appraiser submits the results of an appraisal in a letter report. A typical letter report sets forth only the conclusions of the appraiser's investigations and analyses. Much data and reasoning are omitted from a letter report, but certain items must be included for the report to be meaningful. A letter report must

- Adequately identify the property and the property rights being appraised
- State the purpose of the appraisal
- Describe the analysis or analyses performed
- Set forth the date of valuation, the date of the report, and all limiting conditions
- Include a certification statement.[2]

If appropriate, a statement regarding the limited nature of the report and analysis should also be included.

---

2. Members and candidates of the Appraisal Institute must include a certification that complies with Standards Rule 2-5.

Although the usefulness of a letter report is limited, a client may desire and specifically request that the appraiser communicate his or her opinion in a letter without detailed documentation. As in the case of an oral report, the appraiser must keep all notes and data on file with a complete summary of the analysis, conclusion, and opinion. In addition, the client should be informed that many regulatory agencies and third-party users of appraisal reports do not accept letter or short narrative reports.

Form Reports

In many instances, form reports meet the needs of financial institutions, insurance companies, and government agencies. In the secondary mortgage market created by government agencies and private organizations, form reports are required for the purchase and sale of most existing mortgages on residential properties. Because these clients review many appraisals, using a standard report form is more efficient and convenient. With such a form, those responsible for reviewing the appraisal know exactly where to find each category or item of data in the report. By completing the form, an appraiser ensures that no item required by the reviewer is overlooked. Figure 24.1 is a completed uniform residential appraisal report form.

The Institute's Standards of Professional Practice apply to the use of form reports.[3] The standards establish guidelines for a proper valuation. The methodology of valuation is determined by the nature of the specific appraisal problem. If a report form seems too rigid and does not provide for the inclusion of all data that the appraiser believes to be pertinent, the relevant information and comments should be added as a supplement.

The appraiser should make sure that the completed report is consistent in its description of the property and provides all the data indicated by the categories listed. If the highest and best use of the property does not conform to the use for which the form is appropriate, the form cannot be used. The properties and neighborhoods compared should be as similar as possible and all appropriate adjustments should be made. Data must be presented in a clear and comprehensible manner and all form reports should include a proper certification and statement of limiting conditions.

A form appraisal report is unacceptable if the appraiser fails to 1) consider the purpose of the report, the value definition, and the assumptions and conditions inherent in the report; 2) question the client about any underwriting criteria that conflict with proper appraisal practice; and 3) conduct an appropriate review before signing the report.

---

3. See Guide Note 3 to the Institute's Standards of Professional Practice, The Use of Form Appraisal Reports for Residential Property.

Narrative Reports

A narrative appraisal report gives an appraiser the opportunity to support and explain the opinions and conclusions presented and to convince the reader of the soundness of the final conclusion or value estimate. Because a narrative report is the most common and complete type of appraisal report, this chapter focuses primarily on the narrative report.

The objectives of a narrative appraisal report are to answer, in writing, the questions asked by a client and to substantiate those answers with facts, reasoning, and conclusions. To achieve these objectives and be most useful to the client, an appraisal report must guide the reader to the appraiser's conclusions by presenting adequate pertinent supporting data and logical analysis.

A narrative report summarizes the facts and appraisal methods and techniques that an appraiser has applied within the framework of the valuation process to arrive at a value estimate or another conclusion. This type of report reflects the appraiser's ability to interpret relevant data and select appropriate valuation methods and techniques to estimate a specifically defined value.

In preparing an appraisal report, the appraiser should keep descriptions separate from analysis and interpretation. If factual and descriptive data are presented in early sections of the report, subsequent analysis and interpretation may refer to these facts and indicate how they influence the final value estimate. Repetition and unnecessary duplication are undesirable, but the presentation of data may depend on the nature and length of the report.

Because the appraiser may not be present when a narrative report is reviewed or examined, the report is the appraiser's representative; a good report creates a favorable impression of the appraiser's professional competence. The following suggestions may help an appraiser improve the impression created by a report.

- The paper, cover, and binding used should be of good quality.
- The report may be typed or professionally printed. In either case, the size and style of the type should be attractive and readable. Graphic illustrations such as photographs and charts should be well prepared. The style of headings and subheadings should be appropriate to the subject matter.
- In many reports, illustrations are presented on the pages that face the material being discussed. For example, a photograph of the subject property may be placed on the page facing the identification of the property. An area map could face the regional and area data to show the location of the neighborhood. A neighborhood map could be included on a page facing the neighborhood description to show the location of the subject property.

Figure 24.1   Residential Appraisal Form

Property Description & Analysis   **UNIFORM RESIDENTIAL APPRAISAL REPORT**   File No. 18060A-87

SUBJECT

Property Address 849 BERKSHIRE DRIVE	Census Tract 4077
City OLD TOWN County FREEPORT State MD Zip Code 11905	LENDER DISCRETIONARY USE
Legal Description SECTION 45, BLOCK 540, LOT 17	Sale Price $ 228,500
Owner/Occupant SMITH/OWNER Map Reference 0-9-11	Date N/A
Sale Price $ 228,500 Date of Sale N/A PROPERTY RIGHTS APPRAISED	Mortgage Amount $
Loan charges/concessions to be paid by seller $ N/A X Fee Simple	Mortgage Type
R.E. Taxes $ 5,945.80 Tax Year 87 HOA S/Mo. N/A Leasehold	Discount Points and Other Concessions
Lender/Client COLONIAL MTG. CO. Condominium (HUD/VA)	Paid by Seller $
APPLICANT/JONES De Minimis PUD	Source

NEIGHBORHOOD

LOCATION: Urban / X Suburban / Rural
BUILT UP: X Over 75% / 25-75% / Under 25%
GROWTH RATE: Rapid / X Stable / Slow
PROPERTY VALUES: X Increasing / Stable / Declining
DEMAND/SUPPLY: Shortage / X In Balance / Over Supply
MARKETING TIME: Under 3 Mos / X 3-6 Mos / Over 6 Mos

PRESENT LAND USE %: Single Family 96, 2-4 Family 4
LAND USE CHANGE: Not Likely / X Likely / In process / To
PREDOMINANT OCCUPANCY: X Owner / Tenant / Vacant (0-5%) X / Vacant (over 5%)

SINGLE FAMILY HOUSING PRICE $(000): Low 180, High 280, Predominant 240
AGE (yrs): Low 10, High 50, Predominant 30

NEIGHBORHOOD ANALYSIS (Good Avg Fair Poor):
Employment Stability X
Convenience to Employment X
Convenience to Shopping X
Convenience to Schools X
Adequacy of Public Transportation X
Recreation Facilities X
Adequacy of Utilities X
Property Compatibility X
Protection from Detrimental Cond. X
Police & Fire Protection X
General Appearance of Properties X
Appeal to Market X

Note: Race or the racial composition of the neighborhood are not considered reliable appraisal factors. THE SUBJECT IS LOCATED IN A
COMMENTS: RESIDENTIAL NEIGHBORHOOD CONSISTING OF HOMES OF SIMILAR STYLES, SIZE AND AGE. HOMES ARE IN WELL MAINTAINED CONDITION WITH GOOD, CARED FOR LAND- SCAPING. NO CONDITIONS OBSERVED THAT WOULD ADVERSELY AFFECT MARKETABILITY.

SITE

Dimensions 70.86 X 130.35 X 88.83 X 136.30
Site Area 10,408 SQ. FT.
Corner Lot YES
Zoning Classification RES. -R40   Zoning Compliance YES
HIGHEST & BEST USE: Present Use YES   Other Use

Topography LEVEL
Size TYPICAL FOR AREA
Shape IRREGULAR
Drainage APPEARS ADEQUATE
View AVERAGE
Landscaping GOOD
Driveway CONCRETE
Apparent Easements NONE
FEMA Flood Hazard Yes* No X
FEMA* Map/Zone PNL:14, ZN:C5/16/83

UTILITIES: Electricity X Other 100 AMP/CB; Gas NONE; Water X; Sanitary Sewer X; Storm Sewer X
SITE IMPROVEMENTS: Street MACADAM Public X; Curb/Gutter CONCRETE/MACA. X; Sidewalk CONCRETE X; Street Lights POLES X; Alley NONE

COMMENTS (Apparent adverse easements, encroachments, special assessments, slide areas, etc.): THERE WERE NO ADVERSE EASEMENTS, ENCROACHMENTS OR OTHER CONDITIONS EVIDENT AT TIME OF INSPECTION.

IMPROVEMENTS

GENERAL DESCRIPTION: Units 1; Stories 3; Type (Det./Att.) DETACHED; Design (Style) SPLIT; Existing YES; Proposed NO; Under Construction NO; Age (Yrs.) 30; Effective Age (Yrs.) 5-10

EXTERIOR DESCRIPTION: Foundation F.CONCR.; Exterior Walls BRICK; Roof Surface ASPHALT; Gutters & Dwnspts ALUMINUM; Window Type D.HUNG; Storm Sash COMBO; Screens COMBO; Manufactured House NO

FOUNDATION: Slab 25%; Crawl Space 25%; Basement 50%; Sump Pump NONE; Dampness ‡; Settlement ‡; Infestation ‡ ‡NONE EVIDENT

BASEMENT: Area Sq. Ft. 644; % Finished 0; Ceiling; Walls; Floor; Outside Entry NONE

INSULATION: Roof; Ceiling X; Walls X; Floor; None; Adequacy; Energy Efficient Items: NONE

ROOM LIST

ROOMS	Foyer	Living	Dining	Kitchen	Den	Family Rm.	Rec. Rm.	Bedrooms	# Baths	Laundry	Other	Area Sq. Ft.
Basement												644
Level 1				1					.5			330
Level 2		1	1	1		1						974
3RD												770

Finished area above grade contains: 8 Rooms; 3 Bedroom(s); 2.5 Bath(s); 2,074 Square Feet of Gross Living Area

INTERIOR

SURFACES Materials/Condition:
Floors HARDWOOD/GOOD
Walls SHEETROCK/GD
Trim/Finish WOOD/GOOD
Bath Floor CER/GOOD
Bath Wainscot CER/GOOD
Doors HOLLOW WOOD
PANEL/GOOD
Fireplace(s) # 1

HEATING: Type HA; Fuel OIL; Condition GOOD; Adequacy GOOD
COOLING: Central CAC; Other NONE; Condition GOOD; Adequacy GOOD

KITCHEN EQUIP: Refrigerator X; Range/Oven X; Disposal X; Dishwasher X; Fan/Hood X; Compactor; Washer/Dryer X; Microwave X; Intercom

ATTIC: None; Stairs; Drop Stair; Scuttle X; Floor; Heated; Finished

IMPROVEMENT ANALYSIS (Good Avg Fair Poor):
Quality of Construction X
Condition of Improvements X
Room Sizes/Layout X
Closets and Storage X
Energy Efficiency X
Plumbing-Adequacy & Condition X
Electrical-Adequacy & Condition X
Kitchen Cabinets-Adequacy & Cond. X
Compatibility to Neighborhood X
Appeal & Marketability X
Estimated Remaining Economic Life 50-55 Yrs.
Estimated Remaining Physical Life 70 Yrs.

AUTOS

CAR STORAGE: Garage X; Carport; None
No. Cars 2; Condition AVG.
Adequate X; Inadequate; Built-In
House Entry X; Outside Entry X; Electric Door; Basement Entry

Additional features: CEMENT PATIO 17 X 28, WOOD DECK 13 X 10.

COMMENTS

Depreciation (Physical, functional and external inadequacies, repairs needed, modernization, etc.): NO INADEQUACIES OR NEEDED REPAIRS OBSER

General market conditions and prevalence and impact in subject market area regarding loan discounts, interest buydowns and concessions: THE CURRENT MORTGAGE MARKET OFFERS A WIDE VARIETY OF CONVENTIONAL LOANS WITH COMPETITIVE ANNUAL PERCENTAGE RATES. AS A RESULT, THE TERMS OF FINANCING HAVE HAD LITTLE OR ANY IMPACT ON SALES PRICES IN THE MARKET AREA.

Freddie Mac Form 70 10/86 **12Ch** O.T.   Forms and Worms Inc. * 315 Whitney Ave. New Haven, CT 06511 1(800) 243-4545   Item #110960   Fannie Mae Form 1004 10/86

Figure 24.1   Residential Appraisal Form (continued)

Valuation Section

UNIFORM RESIDENTIAL APPRAISAL REPORT

File No. 18060A-87

Purpose of Appraisal is to estimate Market Value as defined in the Certification & Statement of Limiting Conditions.

BUILDING SKETCH (SHOW GROSS LIVING AREA ABOVE GRADE)

If for Freddie Mac or Fannie Mae, show only square foot calculations and cost approach comments in this space.

```
22  X  15  X  1  =  330
22  X  15  X  1  =  330
28  X  23  X  1  =  644
22  X  35  X  1  =  770
TOTAL GROSS LIVING AREA 2074 SQ. FT.

NO OBSOLESCENCE NOTED.
```

ESTIMATED REPRODUCTION COST - NEW - OF IMPROVEMENTS

Dwelling	2,074 Sq Ft @ $	60	= $	124,440
	BSMT: 644 Sq Ft @ $	10	=	6,440
Extras FIREPLACE			=	3,000
Special Energy Efficient Items			=	
Porches, Patios, etc. PATIO/DECK			=	4,000
Garage/Carport 440 Sq Ft @ $	17	=	7,480
Total Estimated Cost New			= $	145,360

	Physical	Functional	External	
Less				
Depreciation 21360			= $	21,360
Depreciated Value of Improvements			= $	124,000
Site Imp. "as is" (driveway, landscaping, etc.)			= $	20,000
ESTIMATED SITE VALUE			= $	100,000
(If leasehold, show only leasehold value.)				
INDICATED VALUE BY COST APPROACH			= $	244,000

(Not Required by Freddie Mac and Fannie Mae)

Does property conform to applicable HUD/VA property standards? ☐ Yes ☐ No

If No, explain:

Construction Warranty ☐ Yes ☒ No

Name of Warranty Program

Warranty Coverage Expires

The undersigned has recited three recent sales of properties most similar and proximate to subject and has considered these in the market analysis. The description includes a dollar adjustment, reflecting market reaction to those items of significant variation between the subject and comparable properties. If a significant item in the comparable property is superior to, or more favorable than, the subject property, a minus (−) adjustment is made, thus reducing the indicated value of subject. If a significant item in the comparable property is inferior to or less favorable than, the subject property, a plus (+) adjustment is made, thus increasing the indicated value of the subject.

ITEM	SUBJECT	COMPARABLE NO. 1		COMPARABLE NO. 2		COMPARABLE NO. 3	
Address	849 BERKSHIR E DROLD TWN	928 ROXBURY DR. OLD TOWN		989 GLOUCESTER CT. OLD TOWN		1112 HOWARD DR. OLD TOWN	
Proximity to Subject		1 BLOCK NORTH		1/4 MILE NORTHWEST		1/2 MILE EAST	
Sales Price	$ 228,500	$ 233,000		$ 199,000		$ 245,000	
Price/Gross Liv. Area	$ 110.17 ☑	$ 112.34 ☑		$ 95.95 ☑		$ 118.13 ☑	
Data Source	INSPECTION	MLS/CLOSED		MLS/CLOSED		MLS/CLOSED	
VALUE ADJUSTMENTS	DESCRIPTION	DESCRIPTION	+(−)$ Adjustment	DESCRIPTION	+(−)$ Adjustment	DESCRIPTION	+(−)$ Adjustment
Sales or Financing Concessions		CONV.		CONV.		CONV.	
Date of Sale/Time	3/87	1/87	+9000	12/86	+10000	4/87	+2000
Location	GOOD	GOOD		AVERAGE	+7000	GOOD	
Site/View	10408/AVG.	9000/AVG.		7200/AVG.	+2000	8200/AVG.	+1000
Design and Appeal	SPLIT/AVG.	SPLIT/AVG.		SPLIT/AVG.		SPLIT/AVG.	
Quality of Construction	GOOD	GOOD		GOOD		GOOD	
Age	30	29		28		29	
Condition	GOOD	GOOD		GOOD		GOOD	
Above Grade	Total Bdrms Baths	Total Bdrms Baths		Total Bdrms Baths		Total Bdrms Baths	
Room Count	8 · 3 · 2.5	7 · 3 · 2.5		7 · 3 · 2.5		7 · 3 · 2.5	
Gross Living Area	2,074 Sq Ft	2074 Sq Ft	0	2074 Sq Ft	0	2074 Sq Ft	0
Basement & Finished Rooms Below Grade	PT. UNFIN.	PT. FIN.	−2000	PT. FIN.	−2000	PT. FIN.	−2000
Functional Utility	AVERAGE	AVERAGE		AVERAGE		AVERAGE	
Heating/Cooling	AVG/CAC	AVG/CAC		AVG/NONE	+3000	AVG/CAC	
Garage/Carport	2 CAR	2 CAR		2 CAR		2 CAR	
Porches, Patio, Pools, etc.	WOOD DECK PATIO	PATIO	+1500	NONE	+4000	IGP, PATIO	−6000
Special Energy Efficient Items	NONE	NONE		NONE		NONE	
Fireplace(s)	1	1		NONE	+3000	NONE	+3000
Other (e.g. kitchen equip., remodeling)	NONE	NONE		NONE		NONE	
Net Adj. (total)		☒ + ☐ − $	8,500	☒ + ☐ − $	27,000	☐ + ☒ − $	2,000
Indicated Value of Subject		$ 241,500		$ 226,000		$ 243,000	

Comments on Sales Comparison: BASED ON PAIRED SALES AND MLS DATA, TIME ADJ. IS 12% PER ANNUM, LIVING AREA ADJ. IS $18/SQ. FT. + OR − BTHRM. FACILITIES. COMP. #3'S LOC. ADJ. IS DUE TO THE CLOSE PROXIMITY TO AND IT BEING SUBJECT TO NOISE FROM OLD COUNTRY ROAD.

INDICATED VALUE BY SALES COMPARISON APPROACH .... $ 240,000

INDICATED VALUE BY INCOME APPROACH (If Applicable) Estimated Market Rent $ N/A /Mo. x Gross Rent Multiplier N/A = $ N/A

This appraisal is made ☒ "as is" ☐ subject to the repairs, alterations, inspections or conditions listed below ☐ completion per plans and specifications.

Comments and Conditions of Appraisal: APPRAISAL DONE IN CURRENT CONDITION. THIS APPR. ASSUMES A CERTIFICATE OF OCCUPANCY OR COMPLIANCE EXISTS FOR THE SUBJ. DWELLING AS DESCRIBED HEREIN. *SEE ATTACHED

Final Reconciliation: BASED ON THE ANALYSIS OF THE ABOVE DATA, PLACING THE MOST EMPHASIS ON THE MARKET DATA APPROACH, THE ESTIMATE OF MARKET VALUE IS: $240,000.

This appraisal is based upon the above requirements, the certification, contingent and limiting conditions, and Market Value definition that are stated in

☐ FmHA, HUD &/or VA instructions.

☐ Freddie Mac Form 439 (Rev. 7/86)/Fannie Mae Form 1004B (Rev. 7/86) filed with client _____ 19____ ☒ attached

I (WE) ESTIMATE THE MARKET VALUE, AS DEFINED, OF THE SUBJECT PROPERTY AS OF MAY 29, 19 87 **to be $** 240,000

I (We) certify: that to the best of my (our) knowledge and belief the facts and data used herein are true and correct; that I (we) personally inspected the subject property, both inside and out, and have made an exterior inspection of all comparable sales cited in this report; and that I (we) have no undisclosed interest, present or prospective therein.

Appraiser(s) SIGNATURE	Review Appraiser SIGNATURE (if applicable)	
NAME	NAME	☐ Did ☒ Did Not Inspect Property

Freddie Mac Form 70 10/86 **12Ch** DT   Forms and Worms Inc.' 315 Whitney Ave. New Haven, CT 06511 1(800) 243-4545 Item # (10960) Fannie Mae Form 1004 10/86

Charts and graphs may be presented on facing pages when they relate to the narrative discussion. Comparable sales can be shown next to the narrative discussion of how the sales were adjusted to reflect the value of the subject property. Illustrations that are not directly related to the report should be placed in the addenda.

• The contents of a report should be presented in clearly labeled sections that are identified in the table of contents.

NARRATIVE REPORT FORMAT

A narrative appraisal report should be designed for maximum communication with the reader, who may be the client or another person to whom the report is submitted. Readers may scan rather than study a narrative report, so it is wise to organize a report in a manner that readily discloses the property description, the essential analysis of the problem, and the value conclusion.

A well-prepared report has more than thorough research, logical organization, and sound reasoning. These basic attributes are enhanced by good composition, a fluid writing style, and clear expression. The use of technical jargon and slang should be avoided. To communicate with the reader effectively, the contents of the report should be set forth as succinctly as possible.

Outline of a Narrative Report

Narrative appraisal reports may vary in content and arrangement, but they all contain certain elements. Essentially, a narrative report follows the order of the valuation process.

Most narrative reports have four major parts. The contents of each section may be formally divided with subheadings or presented so that the information flows continuously. In either case, the major divisions should have individual headings and be separated from one another. The four parts of a report are the introduction, the premises of the appraisal, the presentation of data, and the analysis of data and conclusions. Many reports have a fifth section, the addenda, which includes supplemental information and illustrative material that would interrupt the text. The organization of narrative reports varies, but the following outline can be used as a general guide.

Part One—Introduction

Title page
Letter of transmittal
Table of contents
Certification of value
Summary of important conclusions

Part Two—Premises of the Appraisal

Assumptions and limiting conditions
Purpose and use of the appraisal
Definition of value and date of value estimate
Statement as to whether the value estimate is in terms of cash, terms
   equivalent to cash, or other precisely defined terms
Property rights appraised

Part Three—Presentation of Data

Identification of the property
Identification of any personal property or other items that are not real
   property
Area, city, neighborhood, and location data
Zoning, taxes, and assessment data
Site data
Description of improvements
History, including prior sales and current offers or listings
Marketability study, if appropriate

Part Four—Analysis of Data and Conclusions

Highest and best use of the land as though vacant
Highest and best use of the property as improved
Land value
Sales comparison approach
Cost approach, including feasibility study, if appropriate
Income capitalization approach
Reconciliation of the value indications into a final value estimate
Qualifications of the appraiser

Addenda

Detailed legal description, if not included in Part Three
Detailed statistical data
Leases or lease summaries
Other appropriate items

The arrangement of items in this outline is flexible and can be adapted to almost all appraisal assignments and classifications of real property. In practice, an appraiser would adapt this outline to the particular requirements of the assignment and to his or her personal preference. Some types of property may require unique treatment within or in addition to the basic framework presented here.

Part One—Introduction

Title page. The title page lists the property address, the date of valuation, and the name and address of the appraiser. The name of the client and the name and address of the person authorizing the report may also be included.

Letter of transmittal. The letter of transmittal formally presents the appraisal report to the person for whom the appraisal was prepared. It should be drafted in proper business style and be as brief as the character and nature of the assignment permit. A suitable letter of transmittal may include these elements:

- Date of letter and salutation
- Street address of the property and a brief description, if necessary
- Statement identifying the interest in the property being appraised
- Statement that the property inspection and all necessary investigation and analyses were made by the appraiser
- Reference that the letter is accompanied by a complete appraisal report or supported by material in the appraiser's file
- Effective date of the appraisal
- Value estimate
- Any extraordinary assumptions or limiting conditions
- Appraiser's signature

Table of contents. The various sections of the report are customarily listed in sequence in the table of contents. The major divisions of the report and any subheadings used in the report should be listed here.

Certification of value. The certification of value may follow the final value estimate or be combined with it. The signature of the appraiser, the date, and a seal, if appropriate, may then be added. The certification states that the appraiser has personally conducted the appraisal in an objective manner. In all certifications of value, members and candidates of the Appraisal Institute must include statements certifying that

- The statements of fact contained in the report are true and correct to the best of the appraiser's knowledge.
- The analyses, opinions, and conclusions in the report are limited only by the assumptions and limiting conditions set forth, and are the personal, unbiased, professional analyses, opinions, and conclusions of the appraiser.
- The appraiser has no (or the specified) present or prospective interest in the subject property and has no (or the specified) personal bias with respect to the parties involved.
- The appraiser's compensation is not contingent on an action or event resulting from the analyses, opinions, or conclusions in the report or on the use of the report.
- The appraiser's analyses, opinions, and conclusions have been developed, and the report has been prepared, in conformity with the requirements of the Code of Professional Ethics and the Standards of Professional Practice of the American Institute of Real Estate Appraisers.
- Use of the report is subject to the professional requirements of the Institute regarding review by its duly authorized representatives.
- The appraiser is (or is not) currently certified under the voluntary continuing education program of the Institute. (This item is not required for candidates.)

- The appraiser has (or has not) made a personal inspection of the subject property.
- No one (or the specified individuals) provided significant professional assistance in preparing the report.

Whether the certificate is included in the transmittal letter or presented on a separate, signed page, it is important because it establishes the appraiser's position, thereby protecting both the appraiser's integrity and the validity of the appraisal.

The following certification is frequently used by members of the Appraisal Institute.

I, the undersigned, do hereby certify that I have personally inspected the property located at:

Property address
County, City, State

To the best of my knowledge and belief, the statements of fact contained in this report and upon which the opinions herein are based are true and correct, subject to the assumptions and limiting conditions explained in the report.

Employment in and compensation for making this appraisal are in no way contingent upon the value reported, and I certify that I have no interest (or the stated interest), either present or contemplated, in the subject property. I have no personal interest or bias with respect to the subject matter of the appraisal report or the parties involved.

This appraisal report identifies all of the limiting conditions (imposed by the terms of my assignment or by the undersigned) affecting the analyses, opinions, and conclusions contained in this report.

The analyses, opinions, and conclusions contained in this report have been developed in accordance with the *Code of Professional Ethics and Standards of Professional Practice* of the American Institute of Real Estate Appraisers. (For members and candidates of the Appraisal Institute.)

The use of this report is subject to the requirements of the American Institute of Real Estate Appraisers relating to review by its duly authorized representatives.

No one other than the undersigned prepared the analysis, opinions, or conclusions concerning real estate that are set forth in this appraisal report. I am (or am not) currently certified under the voluntary continuing education program of the American Institute of Real Estate Appraisers.

In my opinion, the subject property has a value representative of market conditions on (date) of: (Dollar amount)

_____
(Signature)

Summary of important conclusions. When an appraisal report is long and complicated, a summary of the major points and important conclusions in the report may be useful. Such a statement is convenient for readers of the report and allows the appraiser to stress the major points considered in reaching the final estimate. The following list indicates the type of material that is frequently included in a summary; however, all of the items do not apply to each appraisal assignment.

- Brief identification of the property
- Determinations of the highest and best use of the land as though vacant and the property as improved
- Age of improvements
- Estimate of land value
- Value indication from the sales comparison approach
- Value indication from the cost approach
- Value indication from the income capitalization approach
- Final estimate of defined value
- Allocation of value between the land and the improvements, between the leased fee and the leasehold estates, or between real and personal property
- Special assumptions and conclusions

An appraiser may use a different type of summary for longer or more complex reports. In many appraisal reports a summary is omitted particularly if the letter of transmittal briefly discusses the major conclusions set forth in the report.

Part Two—Premises of the Appraisal

Assumptions and limiting conditions. Assumptions and limiting conditions may be stated in the letter of transmittal, but they are usually included as separate pages in the report. These statements are used to protect the appraiser and to inform and protect the client and other users of the report. Appropriate standard conditions are an important part of a report and should be stated clearly. Some typical general assumptions and limiting conditions are listed below as they might appear in an appraisal report.

This appraisal report has been made with the following general assumptions:

1. No responsibility is assumed for the legal description or for matters including legal or title considerations. Title to the property is assumed to be good and marketable unless otherwise stated.
2. The property is appraised free and clear of any or all liens or encumbrances unless otherwise stated.
3. Responsible ownership and competent property management are assumed.
4. The information furnished by others is believed to be reliable. However, no warranty is given for its accuracy.
5. All engineering is assumed to be correct. The plot plans and illustrative material in this report are included only to assist the reader in visualizing the property.

6. It is assumed that there are no hidden or unapparent conditions of the property, subsoil, or structures that render it more or less valuable. No responsibility is assumed for such conditions or for arranging for engineering studies that may be required to discover them.

7. It is assumed that there is full compliance with all applicable federal, state, and local environmental regulations and laws unless noncompliance is stated, defined, and considered in the appraisal report.

8. It is assumed that all applicable zoning and use regulations and restrictions have been complied with, unless a nonconformity has been stated, defined, and considered in the appraisal report.

9. It is assumed that all required licenses, certificates of occupancy, consents, or other legislative or administrative authority from any local, state, or national government or private entity or organization have been or can be obtained or renewed for any use on which the value estimate contained in this report is based.

10. It is assumed that the utilization of the land and improvements is within the boundaries or property lines of the property described and that there is no encroachment or trespass unless noted in the report.

This appraisal report has been made with the following general limiting conditions:

1. The distribution, if any, of the total valuation in this report between land and improvements applies only under the stated program of utilization. The separate allocations for land and buildings must not be used in conjunction with any other appraisal and are invalid if so used.

2. Possession of this report, or a copy thereof, does not carry with it the right of publication.

3. The appraiser, by reason of this appraisal, is not required to give further consultation, testimony, or be in attendance in court with reference to the property in question unless arrangements have been previously made.

4. Neither all nor any part of the contents of this report (especially any conclusions as to value, the identity of the appraiser, or the firm with which the appraiser is connected) shall be disseminated to the public through advertising, public relations, news, sales, or other media without the prior written consent and approval of the appraiser.

An appraisal report might contain the following items as additional assumptions and limiting conditions.

1. Any value estimates provided in the report apply to the entire property, and any proration or division of the total into fractional interests will invalidate the value estimate, unless such proration or division of interests has been set forth in the report.

2. Only preliminary plans and specifications were available in the preparation of this appraisal; the analysis, therefore, is subject to a review of the final plans and specifications when available.

3. Any proposed improvements are assumed to have been completed unless otherwise stipulated; any construction is assumed to conform with the building plans referenced in the report.

4. The appraiser assumes that the reader or user of this report has been provided with copies of available building plans and all leases and amendments, if any, encumbering the property.

5. No legal description or survey was furnished so the appraiser utilized the county tax plat to ascertain the physical dimensions and acreage of the property. Should a survey prove these characteristics inaccurate, it may be necessary for this appraisal to be adjusted.

6. The forecasts, projections, or operating estimates contained herein are based upon current market conditions, anticipated short-term supply and demand factors, and a continued stable economy. These forecasts are, therefore, subject to changes in future conditions.

7. This report should be considered a limited analysis in that the appraiser did not perform all of the requirements for an appraisal as set forth by the American Institute of Real Estate Appraisers (for members and candidates).

8. This limited assignment is not an appraisal in that a value estimate of the subject property has not been provided.

Purpose and use of the appraisal. The purpose of an appraisal report is the question for which the client seeks an answer. This section can be combined with the property identification section of the report or the appraiser may simply state

> The purpose of this report is to estimate market value on (a given date).

Definition of value and date of value estimate. An acceptable definition of the value being appraised is included in the report to eliminate any confusion in the mind of the client or another reader of the report. (Acceptable definitions of various types of value are cited in Chapter 2.)

An appraisal assignment may call for an estimate of current value or an estimate of value as of some point in the past. The date as of which the value conclusion is applicable is essential. When an estimate of value as of a future date is requested by a client, special care and analysis are required. In this case, the report must clearly identify the date of the future value estimate. The appraiser should also include a statement of qualifying assumptions and limiting conditions that are appropriate to, and imposed by, the terms of the assignment.

Statement as to whether the value estimate is in terms of cash, terms equivalent to cash, or other precisely defined terms. When market value is estimated, the report must clearly state whether the estimate is expressed in terms of cash, terms equivalent to cash, or other precisely specified terms.

Property rights appraised. In identifying the subject property, the appraiser must define the particular rights or interests being valued. This is particularly important in assignments that involve a partial interest in a property, limited rights such as surface or mineral rights, a fee simple estate subject to a long-term lease, or a leasehold interest. Other encumbrances such as easements, mortgages, or special occupancy or use requirements should also be identified and explained in relation to the defined value to be estimated.

Part Three—Presentation of Data

Identification of the property. The subject property is identified so that it cannot be confused with any other parcel of real estate. This can be achieved by including a full legal description of the property in the report. When a copy of the official plat or an assessment map is used, the appraiser may refer to it at this point and present it on a facing or following page. If the official plat is unavailable, the appraiser can describe the property by name, specifying the side of the street on which the property fronts, the street address, and the lot and block number. A photograph of the subject property on a facing page can enhance this section of the report. *Personal property and other items that are not real property should be identified.*

Area, city, neighborhood, and location data. All facts about a city and its surroundings that the appraiser considers pertinent to the appraisal problem should be included in the area data. (Different types of data, their appropriate uses in relation to various classifications of property and specific appraisal problems, and their degrees of influence are discussed in Chapters 7 and 8.) An appraiser weighs and considers all pertinent factors in data analysis, but the report should discuss only data that are found to be significant to the problem at hand. Both positive and negative aspects of the area should be discussed; if only data in support of either positive or negative factors are included, the report will be misleading.

If a considerable amount of supporting statistical data—e.g., population figures, cost of living indexes, or family income figures—is needed, the appraiser may incorporate these data into the body of the report or present them on facing pages and refer to them in the discussion. A separate section is not needed for area data in many reports; area data are often combined with neighborhood data.

Area data that may be significant to an appraisal report include

- Distance and direction from employment centers
- Public transportation
- Road patterns, road layout, and street widths
- Adequacy of utilities and street improvements
- Proximity to shopping
- Proximity to schools
- Proximity to parks and recreational areas
- Proximity to sources of nuisances
- Police and fire protection; rubbish collection
- Trends in the neighborhood or district

- Population trends
- Percentage of home ownership
- Types of employment and wage levels
- Conformity of development
- Vacancy and rent levels
- Restrictions and zoning
- New construction activity
- Percentage of vacant land
- Changing land use
- Level of taxes
- Adequacy of street and off-street parking
- Type and amount of street traffic
- Type and amount of pedestrian traffic
- Proximity to expressways, tollroads, and airports
- Rail connections and service for freight
- Concentration of advertising by retail merchants
- Other beneficial or detrimental influences

The amount of neighborhood and location data depends on the appraisal assignment and the client. For example, when an appraiser is retained by an out-of-town client who is unfamiliar with the property and the community, it may be wise to include more community and neighborhood data than would be needed by a local client. If the appraisal concerns an important business property that derives its income from the purchasing power of the surrounding area, the appraiser should provide a detailed description of the neighborhood and discuss how the population and its purchasing power affect the value of the subject property.

An appraiser must also note the presence of special amenities or detrimental conditions and give reasons or data to support any conclusion about these items. For example, if an appraiser states that an area is growing, actual growth figures or building projections should be included in the report. If a report states that a neighborhood is in decline due to abnormal deterioration or poor maintenance, the appraiser might refer to specific properties that exhibit these detrimental conditions or use photographs to illustrate this conclusion.

Area and neighborhood data are the background against which a property is considered. The data are significant to the extent that they affect property value. Therefore, this section of an appraisal is incomplete when the trends indicated by the data are not analyzed. The appraiser applies professional experience and judgment to interpret relevant data in terms of how they affect the marketability of the subject property. Without this interpretation, city and neighborhood data lose significance; proper analysis of data is needed to establish the potential of the property being appraised.

In studying neighborhood trends, appraisers must avoid stereotyped or biased assumptions relating to race, age, color, religion, gender, or national origin and not presume that racial, ethnic, or religious homogeneity is necessary to maximize value in a neighborhood. Moreover, appraisers must not make assumptions or use unsupported premises about neighborhood decline or a property's effective age or remaining economic life.

Zoning, taxes, and assessment data. Zoning data are either included in the land description section of the appraisal report or presented in a separate section. When they are significant, zoning and private restrictions should be discussed in detail. The actual text of the specific zoning ordinance may be incorporated into the body of the report or reproduced in the addenda. If the specific ordinance is not included, the appraiser should provide sufficient data to help the reader understand the limitations that zoning regulations place on the use or development of the site. When vacant land is being valued, the appraiser may explore the possibility of a zoning change or point out existing public and private restrictions and describe their effect on the utility and value of the property. In addition, current assessed values and ad valorem tax rates should be reported and existing assessment trends or prospective changes in tax rates should be analyzed.

Site data. Pertinent facts about the subject site belong in the site data section. Site data may include descriptions of the property's frontage, depth, site area, and shape; soil and subsoil conditions; floodplain; easements and restrictions; utilities; and any improvements that benefit the site. The appraiser should offer a conclusion as to the utility or adaptability of the site for existing or proposed improvements.

Description of improvements. In the description of improvements section, all building and improvement data relevant to the appraisal problem are presented and discussed. Although an appraiser considers and processes much data in the course of an appraisal, only significant elements that influence the value conclusion are set forth in the report. These elements may include

- Actual and effective building age and building size
- Number and size of units
- Structural and construction details
- Mechanical equipment
- Physical condition
- Functional utility or inutility

This information may be supported with drawings, photographs, floor plans, and elevations. If the description of structural details and mechanical equipment is long, an outline may be used in the body of the report with emphasis on the important items.

History. Historical property data may include information on original assemblage, acquisition, or construction costs; expenditures for capital additions or modernization; financial data or transfers of ownership; casualty loss experience; history and type of occupancy; reputation or prestige; current offers or listings; and any other facts that may pertain to or affect the computations, estimates, or conclusions presented in the report.

Marketability study. In the appraisal of income-producing properties such as office buildings, shopping centers, and apartment buildings, a marketability study may be performed to find out how the subject property fits into the overall market in terms of rent levels and absorption rates. A marketability study is usually directly related to the conclusions presented in the appraisal report. Such a study may identify the specific real estate market or submarket, the supply of existing properties (e.g., inventory of space, construction trends, vacancy patterns, and absorption rates), the demand forecast (e.g., projected expansion or shrinkage), the current balance of supply and demand, and competitive rent levels.

Part Four—Analysis of Data and Conclusions

Highest and best use should be expressed in terms of the property's most probable and profitable use. Land use patterns in the area, zoning regulations, and the profitability of existing or proposed improvements should be discussed. (A complete discussion of how an appraiser determines highest and best use is provided in Chapter 12.)

Highest and best use of the land as though vacant. Land is generally appraised as though vacant and available for development to its highest and best use. If an appraiser's estimate of the value of the land as though vacant is based on a particular highest and best use, the report should clearly state this fact and specify that the value estimate does not apply unless the future property use is in accordance with the program proposed. If, for some reason, the property cannot be adapted to its highest and best use, the report should indicate this fact and identify the use that underlies the appraiser's value estimate. The character and amount of data presented and analyzed in this section are dictated by the purpose of the appraisal.

Highest and best use of the property as improved. To determine the highest and best use of a property as improved, an appraiser considers whether or not the removal and replacement of the existing improvements are economically warranted on the date of the appraisal. If an existing improvement is to be retained, the property's highest and best use is based on how the entire property should be used to maximize its benefits or the income it produces. An appraiser may suggest a possible course of action such as rehabilitation, improved maintenance, or better property management.

Land value. In the land value section of an appraisal report, market data and other information pertaining to land value are presented along with an analysis of the data and reasoning that lead to the value conclusion. Data identifying the factors that affect land value should be presented in a clear and precise manner. The location, size, zoning, utilities, floodplain, and other characteristics of the land may be described. The narrative should lead the reader to the land value estimate.

Approaches to value. An appraiser develops the approaches applicable to the assignment and derives indications of value. For each approach used, factual data and the analysis and reasoning leading to the value indication are presented.

Many clients are not familiar with the mechanics of the three approaches to value, so the appraiser may want to explain the procedures in the development of the data. The extent of the explanation depends on the circumstances of the appraisal.

Simple statements that describe what is included in each of the three approaches can help the reader understand the report. For example, the approaches could be described as follows.

> In the sales comparison approach, the subject property is compared to similar properties that have been sold recently or for which listing prices or offering figures are known. Data for generally comparable properties are used, and comparisons are made to demonstrate a probable price at which the subject property would be sold if offered on the market.
>
> In the cost approach, an estimated reproduction or replacement cost of the building and land improvements as of the date of appraisal is developed, together with an estimate of the losses in value that have taken place due to wear and tear, design and plan, or neighborhood influences. To the depreciated building cost estimate, entrepreneurial profit and the estimated value of the land are added. The total represents the value indicated by the cost approach.
>
> In the income capitalization approach, the current rental income to the property is shown with deductions for vacancy and collection loss and expenses. The prospective net operating income of the property is estimated. To support this estimate, operating statements for previous years and comparable properties may be reviewed along with available operating cost estimates. An applicable capitalization method and appropriate capitalization rates are developed and used in computations that lead to an indication of value.

The three approaches are seldom completely independent. An appraisal is composed of a number of integrated, interrelated, and inseparable procedures that have a common objective—a convincing, reliable estimate of value. At times, the three approaches are so intertwined that some appraisers use a "one-approach" concept and do not make separate presentations.

Reconciliation of value indications. Reconciliation of the value indications should lead the reader logically to the final estimate of value. The final estimate of defined value may be stated in many ways. The following is a simple example.

> As a result of my investigation and analysis, it is my opinion that the market value of the identified interest in the property, on July 20, 19____ [4] is:

FOUR HUNDRED THOUSAND DOLLARS

($400,000)

When the appraiser chooses to allocate the value conclusion among property components, this breakdown may be added after the final value estimate.

---

4. The date on which the value opinion is applicable may differ from the date of the letter of transmittal.

. . . that may be allocated as follows:

Land	$ 80,000
Improvements	300,000
Personal property and other items	+ 20,000
Total	$ 400,000

Qualifications of the appraiser. The appraiser's qualifications are usually included in the appraisal report as evidence of his or her competence to make such an appraisal. These qualifications may include facts concerning

- Professional experience
- Educational background and training
- Business, professional, and academic affiliations and activities
- Clients for whom the appraiser has rendered professional services, the types of properties appraised, and the nature of the appraisal assignments

The use of these statements is so widespread that many appraisers find it expedient to insert a printed statement of their qualifications in each appraisal report. Of course, the appraiser's qualifications must be presented accurately and in a manner that is not misleading.

Addenda

Depending on the size and complexity of the appraisal assignment, an addenda may be used to avoid interrupting the narrative portions of the report. The following items may be included in the addenda.

- Plot plan
- Plans and elevations of buildings
- Photographs of properties referred to in the report
- City, neighborhood, and other maps
- Charts and graphs
- Abstracts of leases
- Historical income and expense data
- Specifications of buildings
- Detailed estimates of reproduction or replacement costs of buildings
- Sales and listing data
- Tax and assessment data
- Marketability analysis data (e.g., construction trends, vacancy trends, and competitive rent levels)

SUMMARY

The function of an appraisal report is to lead a reader from the definition of an appraisal problem through reasoning and analysis of relevant data to a specific conclusion. An appraisal should be communicated in a meaningful and straightforward manner. The American Institute of Real Estate Appraisers has specific requirements for the contents of an appraisal report and for the appraiser's certification of value.

Appraisal reports may be oral or written; written reports may be letter, form, or narrative reports. Regardless of how the report is conveyed, all data and notes as well as a summary of the analysis and conclusions should be kept in the appraiser's permanent file.

An *oral report* must include a property description and the facts, assumptions, conditions, and reasoning on which the conclusion is based. A *letter report* identifies the property and the property rights appraised, states the purpose of the appraisal, describes the analysis performed, cites the date of the valuation and the date of the report, sets forth all limiting conditions, and includes the required certification. *Form reports*, which are often used by financial institutions, insurance companies, and government agencies, offer a standard, comprehensive format for recording data and may be supplemented with other relevant information.

A *narrative report* illustrates an appraiser's ability to interpret pertinent data and to select appropriate methods to estimate a specifically defined value. Appraisers are advised to keep factual and descriptive data separate from analysis and interpretation, and not to repeat or unnecessarily duplicate material in their reports.

Narrative reports follow the steps in the valuation process. Most reports have four major divisions: the *introduction*, the *premises of the appraisal*, the *presentation of data*, and the *analysis of data and conclusions. Addenda* may include supplemental information and illustrative material.

The introduction to the report contains a *title page, letter of transmittal, table of contents, certification of value*, and *summary of important conclusions*. The title page lists the property address, the date of valuation, the name of the appraiser, and sometimes the name of the client. The letter of transmittal identifies the property and the real property interests appraised, states that an inspection and investigation has been carried out by the appraiser, cites the effective date of the appraisal, sets forth the value estimate, and lists any extraordinary assumptions or limiting conditions. The table of contents outlines the four major divisions of the report, any subheadings, and the addenda if applicable.

In the certification of value, the appraiser *must* certify that the statements of fact are correct to the best of his or her knowledge; that the analysis and conclusions are limited only by the reported assumptions and conditions; that the appraiser has no interest in the subject property; that the appraiser's compensation is not contingent upon any aspect of the report; that the appraisal was performed in accordance with the *Code of Professional Ethics and Standards of Professional Practice* of the American Institute of Real Estate Appraisers, which may review the report; that the appraiser is (or, is not) certified; that the appraiser has (or has not) made a personal inspection of the property; and that no one, except as specified, has provided assistance in preparing the report.

The summary of important conclusions provides information on the highest and best use of the land and the property, the age of the improvements, land value, the property value indications derived from each approach, the final estimate of defined value, the allocation of value between the land and the improvements, and any special assumptions or conclusions.

The premises of the appraisal section includes all *assumptions and limiting conditions*, the *purpose and use of the appraisal*, the *definition of value and the date of the value estimate*, a *statement as to how value is estimated*, and the *property rights appraised*.

Assumptions and limiting conditions are used to protect the appraiser and to inform the client and others using the report. Assumptions may concern the credibility of the legal description and title, the absence of liens or encumbrances, the nature of the ownership and management, engineering and structural conditions, compliance with zoning and environmental regulations, and the legality of the property use. Limiting conditions may restrict the appraisal to the stated program of property use or current market conditions, disavow any proration or division of value according to fractional interests, repudiate subsequent demands on the appraiser, or prohibit the dissemination or publication of the report.

The presentation of data section contains an *identification of the property*; *identification of any personal property*; *neighborhood and location data*; *zoning, taxes, and assessment data*; *site data*; *a description of the improvements*; *history*; and possibly a *marketability study* to examine rent levels, vacancy patterns, construction trends, and absorption rates for income-producing property.

The final section contains data analysis and conclusions and addresses *highest and best use of the land as though vacant*, with qualifications when the value conclusion is contingent on this determination; *highest and best use of the property as improved*, with suggestions on how to maximize income through rehabilitation, better maintenance, or management; *land value*, with an analysis of market data and the reasoning behind the conclusion; the *approaches to value*, with explanations of the procedures applied in the three approaches; *reconciliation of value indications*, which is a logical transition to the appraiser's final value estimate; and the *appraiser's qualifications*, a printed statement on the training, experience, and professional affiliations of the appraiser and a record of his or her professional services.

The addenda contains material that might interrupt the narrative if it were included in the body of the report. These items could include plans, photographs, maps, charts, abstracts of leases, building specifications, income and expense data, cost estimates, sales and listings, tax assessments, and marketability analysis data.

25 Evaluation

Real estate appraisals may involve valuation activities, evaluation activities, or both. In valuation assignments a specific type of value is sought; in evaluation assignments the values estimated with valuation techniques or other methods are used in making real estate decisions. Evaluation activities may be either general or specific in nature. Both the valuation and evaluation services of professional appraisers are covered by the Appraisal Institute's Code of Professional Ethics and Standards of Professional Practice.

Specific evaluation assignments include highest and best use studies, market studies, marketability studies, rent studies, absorption analyses, feasibility studies, and other studies that have a specific analytical objective. In more general assignments, practitioners provide clients with unbiased advice regarding real estate decisions. This advice may be of assistance in setting goals, establishing an analytical framework for real estate decision making, or finalizing real estate decisions.

Many real estate valuation assignments call for evaluation services. In conducting a market value appraisal required for mortgage loan purposes, an appraiser may also provide data and evaluation advice that can be used to structure the specific terms of the mortgage.

Buyers and sellers who wish to know market value for transaction purposes are usually interested in other market facts as well—e.g., high and low market price indicators, the frequency of offers and sales, and the average market exposure of properties before sale. This information can help investors finalize their decisions.

RELATIONSHIP OF EVALUATION TO VALUATION

Valuation studies are primarily microeconomic analyses because they focus on valuing identified interests in specified real estate as of a given date. Broad economic trends and forces are considered, but the analyst concentrates on a specific parcel or parcels of real estate.

Evaluation studies may be macroeconomic analyses, microeconomic analyses, or a combination of both. They may relate to broad market categories or to a given parcel or parcels of real estate. Valuation assignments always include the identification and definition of one or more types of value. In evaluation assignments the nature and scope of the services being performed must be explained, but a particular type of value may not be specified because value *per se* may not be being estimated. Appraisers must clearly distinguish between valuation and evaluation assignments to avoid confusion and possible misunderstanding.

Market Value and Investment Value

The word *value* is commonly understood, but when this term is applied to real estate it is subject to misunderstanding. The term must be qualified before it can be used effectively. The statement "The value of your property is $150,000" has no specific meaning to real estate professionals and could lead to serious misunderstanding. If, however, an appraiser says that "Your property is estimated to have a market value of $150,000," an explicit meaning is conveyed. By necessity, appraisers refer to market value, insurable value, liquidation value, and other precisely identified and defined types of value.

Evaluation assignments frequently call for estimates of market value or investment value as well as associated analyses that will enable a client to make one or more real estate decisions. Just as appraisers must distinguish between the valuation and evaluation aspects of assignments, they must also distinguish between market value and investment value.

Market value can be called "the value of the marketplace"; *investment value is the specific value of goods or services to a particular investor (or class of investors) for individual investment reasons.* Market value and investment value are different concepts, although the values estimated for each may or may not be numerically equal depending on the circumstances. In addition, market value estimates are commonly made without reference to investment value, but investment value estimates are frequently accompanied by a market value estimate to facilitate decision making.

Market value estimates assume no specific buyer or seller. Rather, the appraiser considers a hypothetical transaction in which both the buyer and the seller have the understanding, perceptions, and motivations that are typical of the market for the property or interests being valued. Appraisers must distinguish between their own knowledge, perceptions, and attitudes and those of the market or markets for the property in question. The special considerations of a given client are irrelevant to a market value estimate.

On the other hand, the goals of a specific investor are directly related to investment value, as are the advantages or disadvantages of a particular property or real estate situation to that investor. An appraiser may be asked to analyze a series of investment opportunities or possible decisions and evaluate them in light of their benefits to a given client. Even decisions involving a single parcel of real estate will normally require the evaluation of other possible decisions and an analysis of how each possibility may affect the decision being considered.

For example, an appraiser may be asked to consider whether a parcel of land that is adjacent to the client's industrial property is worth $500,000, the price being asked by its owner. Market analysis indicates that the property is overpriced in comparison with other properties and that its market value is $400,000. However, the client's successful business must be expanded and it will have to be relocated if the additional land is not acquired. If the existing operation is moved, disruption of business and other factors will create a loss of more than $100,000. Because this loss exceeds the difference between the property's market value and its asking price, it might be concluded that the property has an investment value of $500,000 or more to the client in question.

Each voluntary purchase or sale of real estate is based on an investment value decision made by the parties to the transaction. Thus, the market is made up of transactions in which willing participants make investment decisions.

The transaction price of a property varies with the bargaining strength and motivation of buyers and sellers and with the number of opportunities available to these market participants. Ultimately a property's market price reflects the interaction of those who create market supply and demand. Depending on the circumstances of the buyer and the seller in each case, the transaction price at a given moment can be expected to fluctuate above or below the property's value at perfect market equilibrium. Sellers are normally expected to accept a price that equals or exceeds investment value, while buyers will pay a price that does not exceed investment value. Market value estimates synthesize these transactions without considering any particular buyer or seller.

The field of real estate evaluation is diverse, so the remainder of this chapter focuses on the techniques used by investors, developers, lenders, and real estate professionals to estimate investment value. Although these techniques can be applied in various types of valuation assignments, they are especially useful in providing clients with specific advice for real estate decision making.

COMMON MEASURES OF INVESTMENT PERFORMANCE

Great strides have been made in the field of real estate evaluation since the 1950s. In general, the analytical tools used in evaluation now parallel the techniques used in other investment fields. However, some measures of investment performance are particularly applicable to real estate. These measures are not individually perfect, but as a body of tools they have proven effectiveness. They reflect a common market understanding and are useful in typical real estate applications.

It is beyond the scope of this text to explore all evaluation analysis techniques, but a basic understanding of the most common measures of investment performance is considered fundamental to both valuation and evaluation practice.

Simple Ratios

For many years investors have used simple ratio relationships to compare and evaluate the returns from investment properties. One of the most common relationships is the overall rate of return, which is the ratio between the net earnings of a given parcel of investment real estate and the price or value of that parcel. It is expressed as R in the formula

$$R = \frac{I}{V}$$

Other formulas employ simple gross income or net income multipliers. In these formulas, the price or value of a property is expressed as a multiple of its potential gross or effective gross earnings, or as a multiple of its net earnings. This multiple is the reciprocal of the overall rate.

Each of these measures can be an effective comparative tool when applied to very similar properties. Comparisons of investment performance that employ gross incomes reflect differences among properties to a degree, but measures that relate to net income produce better results.

Unfortunately, simple measures of investment performance incorporate many factors that may require specific analysis in a given evaluation assignment. For example, if an overall rate is used alone, future changes in net incomes, terminal investment values, financing structures, the effects of income taxes, and other elements that may be crucial to a particular property decision are not considered. The overall rate may reflect a blend of the effects of these and other factors but, in its simple form, it does not consider these factors individually. Therefore, it is possible that the overall rate and related simple measures of comparison may be misunderstood or misapplied in some situations.

Payback Period

As a measure of investment return, the *payback period* is seldom used alone, but it is commonly employed in conjunction with other measures. It is defined as *the length of time required for the stream of cash flows produced by an investment to equal the original cash outlay*. The *breakeven point* is reached when the investment's cumulative income is equal to its cumulative loss. The payback period can be calculated from either before- or after-tax cash flows, so the type of cash flow selected should be identified. The equation for payback period may be expressed as:

$$PB = \frac{\text{Equity capital outlay}}{\text{Annual net equity cash flows}} \qquad PB = \frac{1}{R_E}$$

This measure of performance is used by investors who simply want to know how long it will take them to recapture the dollars they have in an investment. In theory, an investment with a payback period of three years would be preferable to one of five years, all else being equal. Similarly, an investment that will return the investor's capital in six years would be unacceptable to an investor who seeks investment payback within four years.

For an equity investment that is expected to produce equal cash flows, the payback period is simply the reciprocal of the equity capitalization, or equity dividend, rate.

If annual equity cash flows are not expected to be equal over the payback period, the equity cash flows for each year must be added until they equal or exceed the equity capital outlay; this point indicates the year in which payback occurs.

Although the payback period is simple and easily understood, it has a number of drawbacks. First, it measures the amount of time over which invested money will be returned to the investor, but it does *not* consider the *time value of the money invested*. A five-year investment payback for a $100,000 investment that pays $10,000 in Year One and $90,000 in Year Five is not distinguished from the payback for a $100,000 investment that pays $90,000 in Year One and $10,000 in Year Five. The time value of money allows the first investment to use an additional $80,000 (i.e., the difference between the $90,000 paid in the second investment and the $10,000 paid in the first investment) from the second year through the fifth.[1]

Furthermore, the payback period does not consider the effect of any gain or loss beyond the breakeven point and does not specifically account for investment risks. An investment with a three-year payback may be far riskier than one with a five-year payback, but the shorter period generally appears preferable. Thus, this measure of performance should only be used to compare investments with similar investment characteristics or in conjunction with other performance measures in carefully weighted applications.

Investment Proceeds per Dollar Invested

Investment proceeds per dollar invested is calculated as a simple relationship between the anticipated total proceeds as a return to the investment position divided by the amount invested. The resulting index or multiple provides a crude measure that is not time-weighted. It is sometimes used to compare very similar investments over similar time periods.

Profitability Index

Although measuring the investment proceeds per dollar invested is too imprecise for general use, a refinement of this technique is much more powerful and more

---

1. A more sophisticated, but less popular, measure is the discounted payback period, which recognizes the time value of money at a stipulated rate of return. In this context the payback period is the amount of time required for the discounted benefits to equal the discounted costs.

commonly applied. The *profitability index* (*PI*), or *benefit/cost ratio*, is defined as the present value of the anticipated investment returns (benefit) divided by the present value of the capital outlay (cost). The formula is

$$PI = \frac{\text{Present value of anticipated investment returns}}{\text{Present value of capital outlay}}$$

This measure is based on a desired minimum rate of return or a satisfactory yield rate. The present value of the anticipated investment returns and the present value of the capital outlay are calculated using the desired rate as the discount rate. If, for example, the present value of the capital outlay discounted at 10% is $12,300 and the present value of the benefits is $12,399, the profitability index, based on a satisfactory yield rate of 10%, is $12,399/$12,300 = 1.008.

A profitability index greater than 1.0 indicates that the investment is profitable and acceptable in light of the chosen discount rate. A profitability index of less than 1.0 indicates that the investment cannot generate the desired rate of return and is not acceptable. A profitability index of exactly 1.0 indicates that the opportunity is just satisfactory in terms of the desired rate of return and, coincidentally, the chosen discount rate is equal to the *IRR*. The discount rate used to compute the profitability index may represent a minimum desired rate, the cost of capital, or a rate that is considered acceptable in light of the risks involved.

This refined measure overcomes the difficulties with the time value of money that are encountered in calculating the proceeds per dollar invested. A profitability index is particularly useful in comparing investments that have different capital outlay requirements, different time frames for receiving income or other investment returns, and different general risk characteristics.

The profitability index is commonly used in conjunction with other measures, particularly net present value. In this application it contributes special insights into the investments under consideration. Like all other measures of investment performance, it is *not* generally used alone in making investment decisions. A common decision rule for investors is that the profitability index of an investment should be at least 1.0—i.e., the present value of the benefits divided by the capital outlay should be equal to or greater than one.

Net Present Value

Net present value (*dollar reward*) is defined as the difference between the present value of all expected benefits, or positive cash flows, and the present value of capital outlays, or negative cash flows. Net present value (*NPV*) is simply the present value of anticipated investment returns *minus* the present value of the capital outlay. This measure, like a profitability index, is based on a desired rate of return. It is computed using the desired rate as a discount rate and the result is viewed as an absolute dollar reward. The reward (or penalty) is expressed in total dollars, not as a ratio. The formula is

$$NPV = CF_0 + \frac{CF_1}{(1 + i)} + \frac{CF_2}{(1 + i)^2} + \ldots + \frac{CF_n}{(1 + i)^n} - CO$$

where i is the applicable discount rate and n is the number of periods in the analysis. This formula solves for the difference between the present value of all investment returns and the amount of the original capital investment. The dollar reward is simply NPV at a stipulated discount rate. A positive NPV indicates a reward; a negative NPV indicates a penalty. An NPV of zero indicates that the chosen discount rate coincides with the IRR.

A number of decision rules can be established for applying the NPV. As an example, assume that a property with an anticipated present value of $1,100,000 for all investment returns over a 10-year holding period can be purchased for $1,000,000. If one investor's NPV goal is zero, this investment exceeds that criterion. It also meets another investor's goal for an NPV of $100,000, but it would not qualify if the goal were $150,000.

Net present value does consider the time value of money and different discount rates can be applied to different investments to account for general risk differences. However, this method cannot handle different required capital outlays. It cannot differentiate between an NPV of $100,000 on a $1,000,000 capital outlay and the same NPV on a $500,000 capital outlay. Therefore, this technique is best used in conjunction with other measures.

Time-Weighted Rate

A *time-weighted rate* is technically an average of all actual, instantaneous rates over a period of time. It is similar to the rate of growth for capital invested in a mutual fund in which all dividend income is automatically reinvested. The time-weighted rate, which is also known as the *unit-method rate* or the *share-accounting rate*, is used primarily to measure the performance of a portfolio manager, not the performance of the portfolio itself.

Discounted Cash Flow

Discounted cash flow (DCF) analysis provides appraisers and other investment analysts with the most detailed, precise means of considering the amounts and timing of investment cash inflows and outflows over the life of an investment. With this procedure, any series of cash inflows and outflows over any specified time frame at any rate of return can be analyzed and the present value of the investment's anticipated performance can be measured.

Discounted cash flow analysis relies on compound interest measurements to convert future dollars into their present value equivalents. Because dollars to be received in the future are worth less than current dollars, successive cash inflows and outflows are discounted at a selected rate to their present value as of a given date. The sum of the present values for each future positive or negative cash flow represents the DCF value indication at a given discount rate. Different rates may be used to reflect differences in investment risks.

Given similar data, DCF calculations produce the same results as other income comparison methods. However, methods that are less precise may produce different results because they are less able to handle the explicit details considered in DCF analysis. Discounted cash flow techniques may be applied to cash flows before or after income taxes. The results of DCF analysis can then be used as the present value component (PV) in comparisons made with profitability indexes or net present value methods.

Discounted cash flow techniques can be applied on either a constant-dollar or nominal-dollar basis. If constant dollars are used, they are discounted with rates that do not include an allowance for inflation. Consequently, investment performance is measured without considering the effects of inflation. More often, nominal or actual dollars are measured for the cash inflows and outflows anticipated. In this case, the discount rate applied contains a component that accounts for inflation. However, because the rate of inflation is an element of risk, a specific analysis of future inflation rates or components of inflation is not usually included in the discount rate, although this may be done in more detailed analyses.

For income streams that extend over many years, such as those stipulated in long-term leases, DCF is commonly performed for terms of five, 10, or 15 years. Although these terms may be shorter than the term of a given property lease, they offer two principal advantages. First, buyers and sellers in many markets develop their expectations of future price changes over short or medium terms. Therefore, the appraiser can establish market expectations regarding the terminal values of the investment and factor these expectations into income analysis time frames that are consistent with market thinking and behavior.

Second, the mathematics of compound interest are data-specific and precise, but they sometimes lead to conclusions that are difficult to accept. Consider, for example, the following table which shows the amounts to which $100,000 will grow at 10% interest compounded annually over various investment periods.

Years	Future Value
10	$ 259,374
20	$ 672,750
30	$ 1,744,940
40	$ 4,525,926
50	$ 11,739,085
75	$127,189,537

Although these figures are accurate and a 10% rate of growth may well represent market thinking for a given property, many people cannot accept the implication that the property *must* have a value of more than $127 million in 75 years. Therefore, an appraiser may determine that the market is acting as though it considers a 10% growth rate appropriate over the income projection period, but he or she should not necessarily conclude that the market is actually considering the effect produced by that growth rate over an extremely long time frame.

Although DCF analysis can be applied to historical investment results, it is usually applied to future expectations. Therefore, DCF analysis frequently involves forecasting cash inflows and outflows. In valuation assignments, the analyst applies the anticipations of the marketplace; in performing DCF analysis for evaluation assignments, different investment scenarios are presumed to test the subjective judgments of the appraiser or others.

Discounted cash flow techniques are precise, persuasive, and time-sensitive. They can be applied to different income patterns and can deal with various risk situations. They reduce the number of assumptions required for a given analysis and explicitly consider both advantageous and disadvantageous investment expectations.

Discounted cash flow techniques have some disadvantages. They must rely on forecast estimates and the analyst must consider and have access to historical data. The precision of DCF techniques can be misinterpreted as accuracy and the rates applied in discounting may be highly subjective.

Internal Rate of Return

The internal rate of return (*IRR*), which is discussed in Chapter 22 in the context of yield analysis, expands on present value calculations and techniques; it represents a special case among investment performance measures. The *IRR* is simply defined as *that rate of discount that produces a profitability index of one and a net present value of zero.* Measured separately, the *IRR* is the discount rate at which the present value of all net investment returns, including any return of capital from the disposal of the investment, exactly equals the capital outlay for the investment.

In other words, the *IRR* calculation is a DCF analysis solved backwards— i.e., all cash inflows and outflows are analyzed to find what discount rate can be applied to make them exactly equivalent to the original capital outlay. Thus, the *IRR* considers all positive and negative cash flows from the inception of the investment to its termination and reflects the indicated return *on* investment in addition to the return *of* investment.

The *IRR* concept and method are also referred to as *yield analysis.* Although the term is imprecise and appears in different contexts, the *IRR* is considered a prominent example of yield analysis.

As mentioned in Chapter 22, the reinvestment presumption is a controversial aspect of *IRR* analysis. The presumption that money received from the investment before its termination are actually reinvested is not essential to the *IRR* concept. Nevertheless, mathematical consistency can be demonstrated between the results of such an analysis and the presumption that these funds are reinvested at the same rate of interest as the *IRR*. This controversy, and other weaknesses in the *IRR*, have led to the development of alternative measures such as the financial management rate of return (*FMRR*), the adjusted internal rate of return, and the modified internal rate of return. These methods were created to address other factors or to compensate for the reinvestment consideration.

Calculating an *IRR* is an iterative process. A successive series of calculations are made to establish a range for the *IRR* and this range is refined to the required degree of precision. These calculations can be facilitated with financial calculators and computers, but they can also be done manually. Because many variables are usually involved, no formula can calculate the *IRR* in a single step.

The *IRR* is one of the most important performance measures for real estate investments. Real estate has historically produced higher returns than many other forms of capital investments, and *IRR* methods have the advantage of producing marginally higher results than those produced for other investments. They can also provide a limited measure of advantage or disadvantage to the real estate investment under consideration.

Despite its precision and persuasiveness, the *IRR* has many weaknesses, which are analyzed in Chapter 22. These weaknesses are reviewed below.

More than one *IRR*. In some situations it is possible that more than one number will mathematically satisfy the *IRR* definition. Although this is somewhat unusual, appraisers are cautioned against the unqualified use of *IRR* measures and concepts.

Discounting of negative cash flows. Standard *IRR* and DCF methods discount both positive and negative cash flows at the applicable discount rate. Some investors argue that different risks are attributable to these cash flows and that this methodology does not make financial sense.

Conflict with *NPV*. The *IRR* of an investment may vary considerably from the *NPV* for that investment. To illustrate, consider the following data for a one-year investment.

	Required Capital	Net Receipt At Year End
Investment A	$20,000	$24,000
Investment B	30,000	35,100

The *IRR* calculated for Investment A is 20% and the *IRR* for Investment B is 17%. For an investor who requires a 10% yield, the net present values for each investment are calculated as follows:

$$\text{Investment A: } \$24,000 \times 0.909091 - 20,000 = \$1,818$$

$$\text{Investment B: } \$35,100 \times 0.909091 - 30,000 = \$1,909$$

Both techniques are based on compound interest, but these calculations reveal that Investment B produces a higher *NPV*, while Investment A has a higher *IRR*.

No recognition of differences in capital outlays. A primary weakness of the *IRR* is that it does not provide for differences in the amount of capital outlay required for the various properties under consideration. It presumes that all capital differences have both the opportunity *and the obligation* to earn a return at the same rate as the calculated *IRR*. Consequently, the *IRR* is less effective when it is applied to investments that have widely different capital requirements. In these cases, the profitability index is used in conjunction with the *IRR*. In the example presented above, the *PI* for Investment A is 1.09, while the *PI* for Investment B is 1.06. Although the *PI* supports the *IRR* indication in this case, it is possible that the higher the *IRR* becomes, the lower the corresponding *PI*.

Despite its weaknesses, the *IRR* is commonly given substantial weight in the analysis of investment properties. The *IRR* is particularly applicable in evaluating investment portfolios. Like other investment performance measures, it frequently must be used in conjunction with other techniques and considerations.

The "Correct" Investment Performance Measure

No single investment performance measure is the best or most appropriate in all situations; each has its advantages and disadvantages and all are more effective when used in conjunction with other measures. Under certain circumstances one or more of these measures should be given greater weight, but the analyst must always recognize the individual limitations of each measure.

Omitting one or more of these measures in making a given real estate decision does not indicate the likely failure of that investment; similarly, applying appropriate measures is no guarantee of success. All decisions are made under conditions of uncertainty, but the measures of investment performance discussed here represent valuable tools that allow appraisers and investors to weigh the facts, exercise sound judgment, and make reasoned decisions. They also provide a framework for implementing an investment program and monitoring investment decisions once they are made.

Judgment is the ability to draw on information and individual experience to make better decisions. As used in valuation and evaluation assignments, investment performance measures are not panaceas, but aids that can be useful in developing, considering, and explaining investment decisions and judgments.

EVALUATION SERVICES

Appraisers are called upon to perform evaluation services because they have the market knowledge and experience needed to help clients solve real estate problems. Just as the valuation process is a time-honored approach to conducting real estate valuations, an appropriate problem-solving process is needed to perform evaluation assignments.

Most, if not all, of the techniques used in valuation studies are also applicable to evaluation analyses. However, an evaluation may not require any valuation or it may use one or more valuations as part of a broader analysis. In addition, an evaluation frequently involves consideration of the specific needs and objectives of the client, not the generalized, composite market perspective that characterizes market value assignments.

Although the tools common to valuation and evaluation may be used differently in each type of assignment, appraisers must at all times maintain their objectivity and support their findings with facts extracted from competent research. By their nature, evaluation assignments are often more subjective than valuation assignments. Therefore, a practitioner who undertakes an evaluation assignment must identify and evaluate both facts and judgments and then relate the findings to the financial decisions under consideration.

In the remainder of this chapter, essential evaluation services and common elements in typical evaluation assignments are reviewed. Risk analysis is a fundamental part of any type of decision making. Evaluation analysis tools include the investment performance measures previously discussed and other techniques. Evaluation studies commonly focus on specific analyses of the income tax consequences of investments, but there are many other types of studies that an appraiser may be asked to perform. Appraisers may be retained to provide real estate counseling services in conjunction with their valuations or evaluations. Each of these activities is briefly discussed in the following pages.

Risk Analysis

The concepts of risk and uncertainty are fundamental to real estate evaluation and any other form of investment analysis. Frequently, valuation analyses and many of the investment performance measures used in evaluation are viewed as point estimates—i.e., single parameter estimates. Real estate professionals typically regard point estimates as the *most probable* numbers, not the only possible numbers. Recognizing and dealing with other possibilities is a major function of risk analysis.

Risk is defined as *the probability that foreseen events will not occur.* An appraiser may identify the most probable amounts and timing of cash flows and then analyze both the probability that the cash flow forecasts are correct as stated and the risk that they are not. If the appraiser is absolutely certain that the exact amounts forecast will be realized, there is no risk.

Uncertainty, on the other hand, is defined as *the probability that unforeseen events will occur.* With the supplementary concept of uncertainty, an appraiser can analyze the range of probabilities that certain events will happen and also allow for the possibility that unforeseen events will occur. These two considerations form the basis for risk analysis.

Most analysts who consider the investment implications of future cash flow opportunities do not expect their forecasts to be realized exactly as they have anticipated. Appraisers avoid predictions, even in valuation assignments; instead, they make forecasts. Thus, when a single figure is used in an analysis, it is usually considered the point of central tendency or the most probable number within a range of possible numbers.

In some situations, however, appraisers deal with exact figures—e.g., contract rents, purchase prices, mortgage terms, calculated units of comparison, and other historical data. A distinction must be made between a number that represents a fact and a number that reflects a future estimate. If a practitioner does not understand an estimated or forecast number in terms of its range of possibilities and associated probabilities, he or she may seriously misjudge investment risks or fail to consider other uncertainties.

A number of methods have been developed to analyze the risk and uncertainty of real estate investments directly. None of these methods offers any special insight into the future, but each provides an opportunity to analyze the factors upon which the success or failure of an investment is contingent and to deal with the expected consequences.

Probability Analysis

Probability is defined as *the relative likelihood that a specified event will occur.* Although the concept is usually associated with games of chance, the concept of probability is basic to life. As people grow and learn, they translate their experiences into intuitive probabilities. Thus, people carry umbrellas on cloudy days, stop at red lights, avoid harmful foods, and generally act in accordance with the probability of possible future outcomes.

The same processes are applicable to real estate evaluations. Based on past experience and other factors, judgments can be made about the foreseeable future. Various possibilities are identified and their relative probabilities are assessed. Therefore, probability, the relative frequency of an expected occurrence, is linked to risk, the identification of events that are unlikely to occur, in the framework of risk analysis.

Ranges of probability can be determined with at least four methods. First, observation and analysis of past events may indicate patterns or measures of relative frequency. Second, probability may be determined through controlled experiment and observation, which is the method applied in scientific experiments. In real estate applications survey research methods may be employed. Third, theoretical distributions may be used to establish probability. For example, an appraiser may infer that the rates of return on a particular type of real estate investment will fall within a given range because of a theoretical relationship between these rates and rates of return in other capital markets. Fourth, probability ranges can be based on subjective judgment. When ranges of probability are determined in this way, they should be tested and all judgments should be evaluated.

Some analysts avoid identifying several possible outcomes (e.g., for cash flow amounts or resale prices) and the probabilities associated with each because the process seems too indefinite. However, when this process is done properly, the limitations of a single point estimate are overcome. In fact, risk analysis facilitates judgments and investment decision making.

Some prominent risk analysis methods are briefly described here. These methods may not be applied in every evaluation assignment, but each is applicable in specific circumstances. Occasionally two or more of these methods are used together to confirm or contrast their conclusions and provide another basis for making investment decisions.

Utility Functions

Utility functions are subjective weights that are assigned to possible investment outcomes to reflect a particular investor's relative preference for each. According to this concept, an investor who is a strong risk-taker would give a higher ranking of personal utility to a riskier investment than would an investor with a more conservative investment outlook.

Although utility functions are very subjective, they do offer a quantitative means of analyzing differences between investment options. For example, assume that an investor has two real estate investment alternatives. The first is a relatively conservative investment that is judged to have a 60% chance of developing an *NPV* of $20,000 and a 40% chance of producing an *NPV* of $10,000. The second investment has an 80% chance of earning a $40,000 *NPV* for the same capital outlay, but a 20% chance of suffering a $10,000 loss.

Different investors may view these outcomes and probabilities in different ways. If an investor is particularly interested in the opportunity to earn a $40,000 *NPV*, he or she may be willing to accept the risk of loss associated with the second investment. In this case, the investor may assign the utility functions shown below to calculate the total utility of each investment.

	Possible Outcomes	Utility Function	Probability	Utility × Probability
First investment	$ 20,000	125	0.60	75
	10,000	90	0.40	36
Total utility				111
Second investment	$ 40,000	200	0.80	160
	−10,000	−30	0.20	− 6
Total utility				154

The second investment, with a total utility measure of 154, would be selected over the first investment, which has a total utility measure of 111. However, another investor may be unable or unwilling to deal with the possibility of loss. This investor would assign a different set of utility functions to the risks associated with each investment and would probably prefer the first investment.

Debt Coverage Ratio

The debt coverage ratio (DCR) is a risk measure that is commonly used in mortgage loan situations. It can be useful in structuring a mortgage or deed of trust and in testing the relative degree of safety associated with a given set of loan terms.

A debt coverage ratio is measured as the ratio of a property's net operating income to its annual debt service. The DCR for a property with debt service of $800,000 and a net operating income of $1,000,000 would be calculated as

$$DCR = \frac{\text{Net Operating Income}}{\text{Annual Debt Service}} = \frac{\$1,000,000}{\$800,000} = 1.25$$

If the lender's risk measurement criterion precluded any loan with a DCR of less than 1.25 as being too risky, the property in this example would be marginally acceptable.

The DCR is commonly used in simple feasibility analyses. If a builder or developer knows that a DCR of 1.25 would probably apply to the project being undertaken, he or she might develop an estimate of the most probable NOI that the property could produce and calculate the amount of debt service required to obtain a ratio of 1.25. Then the allowable mortgage could be determined on the basis of that debt service. If the amount were sufficient, the developer could proceed with the proposed project.

To illustrate another use of the DCR, assume that an 80% mortgage is available for a particular type of development and that the applicable mortgage constant is 0.12. If the required DCR is 1.3, the overall rate necessary to warrant the loan would be

$$R_O = M \times R_M \times DCR$$
$$= 0.80 \times 0.12 \times 1.3$$
$$= 0.1248$$

With further calculations, the pre-tax cash flow rate can be found

Overall rate:	1.00	0.1248
Mortgage portion:	0.80 × 0.12 =	0.0960
Equity portion:	0.20	0.0288

Indicated pre-tax cash flow rate is $0.0288/0.20 = 0.1440$

Thus, given the details and requirements of the loan, the equity position must be capable of producing income at a pre-tax cash flow rate of 14.4% to make the investment's risk acceptable to the lender.

Debt service coverage requirements vary for different lenders at different times. To use the ratio effectively, a reasonably accurate estimate of net operating income must be presumed. Although the DCR is simple to use, it does not measure the amount of risk associated with the borrower. However, because *DCR*s establish a standard ratio of risk between property income and debt service, they are commonly used for mortgage underwriting purposes.

Payback Period

The payback period discussed previously can also be used as a simple risk measurement. Its use varies in different situations, but in any application the payback period indicates the amount of time that investment money will be exposed to the risks inherent in a given investment.

If the economy is moving from a recession into a period of anticipated continuous growth, investors may be more willing to expose their real estate investments to longer periods of risk because they anticipate that longer terms will allow them to take advantage of the growth cycle. Conversely, when economic problems are expected, investors may desire shorter payback periods to avoid the adverse conditions of a downward business cycle.

In managing investment portfolios that may include real estate, it is possible to commit funds for discrete time periods. Thus, the payback period may also be used to help determine exactly when to enter into and exit from a given investment.

Upside/Downside Potential

Considering the upside and downside potentials of an investment is a general evaluation tool that offers an opportunity to compare investment risk. To apply this method to alternative properties or investment concepts, the analyst first quantifies the best and worst anticipations for the investments being analyzed and then forms general conclusions regarding the risks associated with each.

There is no single analytical procedure that characterizes this method of risk analysis. Commonly a series of possible DCF outcomes under alternative hypotheses or situations are presumed; then the best outcomes are compared with one another and the worst outcomes are compared with one another. This method also identifies the factors that create downside situations and recommends possible steps to avoid these factors or mitigate their effect.

An analysis of upside/downside potential does not provide any absolute measure of risk, but it does avoid the pitfalls of single point estimates and can be especially useful in developing hypothetical outcomes for risk analysis and investment planning.

Expected Values

The use of expected values, which are determined with probabilities, was illustrated in the example of utility functions. The concept is simple. A series of possibilities is defined for each investment decision under consideration and the probability of each is assessed. Every investment outcome is multiplied by a weighted probability and the sum of these figures indicates the expected value of that investment. This procedure is shown below.

	Investment A			Investment B		
	NPV	*P*	Expected Value	*NPV*	*P*	Expected Value
Best case	$600,000	0.30	$180,000	$500,000	0.40	$200,000
Most probable case	500,000	0.60	300,000	450,000	0.40	180,000
Worst case	200,000	0.10	20,000	400,000	0.20	80,000
		1.00	$500,000		1.00	$460,000

P indicates the probability of various investment outcomes.

Given these data, Investment A has a higher expected value than Investment B. Note, however, that the method also allows the analyst to identify other important risk factors, such as the possibility that Investment A may realize an *NPV* of only $200,000. If the investor has established a target *NPV* of at least $350,000, the risk of Investment A would be considered higher than the risk of Investment B because there is no probability of a lower *NPV* in the latter investment.

Monte Carlo Simulation

To perform a Monte Carlo simulation, the practitioner constructs an analytical model in which all the elements of the investment are assigned probabilities. These various elements are then integrated into a larger theoretical population. By repeatedly sampling from this group, the range of possible outcomes and the "values" that each of the underlying assumptions produces can be determined.

For example, a simple DCF model can be used to identify high, low, and best case possibilities for each income and expense item and the associated probabilities. Monte Carlo simulation can then be applied to sample the possibilities repeatedly as though they existed in a very large population of occurrences. The expected values are totaled and a probability distribution for the outcomes is indicated.

This method enhances the utility of risk analysis becasue it lets the practitioner see the range of consequences associated with different combinations of possible outcomes and weigh their expected values. The method is particularly valuable because it can be used to identify extreme possible outcomes so that extremes of risk can be properly considered.

As its name suggests, Monte Carlo simulation is based on gaming studies. It is frequently used in development analysis and other large-scale real estate decision-making situations. It is especially effective in evaluation situations because the consequences of various alternatives can be tested against their expected outcomes and the associated probabilities.

Risk-Adjusted Discount Rates

Risk-adjusted discount rates are frequently used in financial analysis; they are also applicable in some real estate valuations and evaluations. Generally an analyst capitalizes income with a discount rate that reflects all the elements of risk associated with the income stream. However, in some situations the specific analysis of one or more risk factors may warrant a special adjustment to the discount rate used.

As an example, consider a real estate developer who seeks a return of 18% on development activities. This developer generally rejects projects that extend beyond five years to avoid the risk of a future downswing in the business cycle. Accordingly, if the developer were attracted to an opportunity that extended beyond five years, the additional *term risk*—i.e., the risk associated with the extra time—would be offset by adjusting the discount rate applied to the periods after the fifth year.

It is mathematically possible to develop a single discount rate to cover multiple-term, multiple-risk situations. However, when direct market evidence is available to support risk-adjusted rates in each individual situation, these rates are more representative of direct market behavior and their application is more appropriate than the use of an indirect, synthesized discount rate.

Risk-adjusted discount rates may be used in at least two ways. When market research indicates that they are supportable and produce reliable results, risk-adjusted discount rates are used in valuation applications to incorporate market information directly into risk analysis. In evaluation applications, these rates help adjust financial analyses for perceived risks by identifying outcomes that directly reflect the risk factors used in adjusting the discount rate.

Other Evaluation Analysis Methods

So far, this chapter has focused on measures of real estate investment performance and ancillary risk analysis methods. Like the broader field of financial analysis, real estate evaluation abounds with analytical tools and methods. A survey of some important techniques follows.

Sampling

Appraisers rarely have access to all available information for use in their analyses. Even when an appraiser has conducted an extensive research program, sample information frequently must be used. Therefore, the principles and implications of sampling should be understood by all appraisers.

Although "all of the data" is preferable to "some of the data," appraisers frequently deal with an incomplete census of information due to time and cost limitations. Consequently, research involves conducting censuses and obtaining sample data for analytical purposes.

The use of sample data has both strengths and weaknesses, as does the use of complete census data. Samples are generally cheaper and more readily obtained and selected samples are sometimes more indicative than the results of a broader survey.

They are easily tabulated, lend themselves to cross-referencing, and provide a foundation for statistical inference, including probability studies. Moreover, samples may represent the only source of data available. However, sampling must be well-conducted and the data must be properly interpreted. If not, the results may be inaccurate and misleading, more expensive than they are worth, or less reliable than they appear. Sampling requires special training and understanding; many people misunderstand or mistrust samples for a variety of justified and unjustified reasons.

Whether or not the appraiser conducts formal sampling, the extent to which sample data have been used should be considered in the analytical process. The risks associated with identified sample data and the uncertainties associated with other potential data must be considered.

Samples may be particularly important when other data are scarce or when the available data are less applicable due to market changes. Sampling may be the only way to obtain some types of data. Samples are particularly important in quantifying market demand; defining market characteristics; identifying market attitudes, perceptions, motivation, and understanding; analyzing market behavior; and interpreting market activities and intentions.

Sensitivity Analysis

Sensitivity analysis, which is applied in both valuations and evaluations, is performed by entering one or more variables at a time into an analytical model to determine the model's sensitivity to each change. Factors that cause greater changes in the results are considered more sensitive and, therefore, pose greater risk to the expected outcome.

For example, assume that a property has an estimated NOI expectancy of $200,000. It is possible that the NOI could be as much as 10% less, or only $180,000. A 75% mortgage is available for the property with a debt service constant of 13%. The equity capitalization, or equity dividend, rate is most probably 10%, but it may range higher to 11%. The analyst wants to know which item is more sensitive, a 10% change in the NOI or a 10% change in the equity capitalization rate. The calculations are shown below.

	$ 200,000 NOI	$ 180,000 NOI
0.75 mortgage × 0.13 constant	0.0975	0.0975
0.25 equity × 0.10 cap rate	0.0250	0.0250
Indicated overall rate	0.1225	0.1225
Indicated value (NOI/R_o)	$1,632,653	$1,469,388

	$ 200,000 NOI	$ 180,000 NOI
0.75 mortgage × 0.13 constant	0.0975	0.0975
0.25 equity × 0.11 cap rate	0.0275	0.0275
Indicated overall rate	0.1250	0.1250
Indicated value (NOI/R_o)	$1,600,000	$1,440,000

This sensitivity test indicates that a 10% change in the *NOI* is substantially more significant than a 10% change in the equity capitalization rate. The largest resulting change for the discount rate was approximately $32,500, $1,632,653 — $1,600,000, compared with a maximum change of more than $163,000, $1,637,653 — $1,469,388 for the *NOI*.

Sensitivity tests can be applied to virtually any element of the analysis that is subject to change. The results of sensitivity analysis facilitate decisions regarding the need for further data, the ranges and consequences of risk factors, and the steps that should be taken to implement these decisions.

Network Analysis

Network analysis is commonly used as a management tool to schedule and conduct project activities. In real estate evaluation, network analysis allows an appraiser to outline the steps used in implementing real estate decisions, to identify critical variables and contingencies, and to deal with the risks and uncertainties associated with given decisions.

Project Evaluation and Review Technique (PERT) charts illustrate how network analyses are conducted. Simple flow charts can also be used to show the orderly processing of decisions and to indicate the critical timing aspects involved. Large-scale analyses may rely on computer programs, which are available even for small computers, but network analysis can also be applied with manual computations.

Rating Grids

Rating grids have many applications and can be used in many different ways. A "most appropriate" investment alternative is selected by assigning arbitrary weights to the factors considered in a given decision and then totaling the weights for each alternative.

As an example, assume that three people are given the responsibility to select a site for a new building. They consult an appraiser who identifies seven factors that are important to the decision and locates three properties from which the choice must be made. Each factor is to be judged on a scale of one to 10; a rating of 10 is extremely good and a rating of one is unacceptable. The analysis is represented by the following grid.

Factor	Alternative 1			Alternative 2			Alternative 3		
	Joe	Sam	Art	Joe	Sam	Art	Joe	Sam	Art
Lot size	8	7	7	5	4	6	6	5	4
Exposure	3	3	4	9	7	7	5	6	7
Quality of area	6	7	6	8	6	7	5	6	4
Traffic conditions	8	6	8	7	5	6	3	5	4
Price	4	7	5	7	6	6	9	9	8
Utilities	6	6	7	6	7	6	8	9	8
Distance to homes	3	8	8	9	6	3	6	5	4
Totals	38	44	45	51	41	41	42	45	39

A grid such as this can be very helpful to those who must reach a specific real estate decision. In an actual application, decision makers may center their discussion on individual preferences, the various weights assigned to individual factors, and the adequacy of the original list of factors. As the grid shows, each individual favors a different alternative, so it is unlikely that any choice can be made without further discussion.

Linear Programming

Linear programming is a complex type of mathematical analysis that is concerned with optimizing the allocation of resources. The equation is in a linear form and subjects the various resources to linear inequality constraints.

The optimization model designates certain values as constants and then tests for one or more investment-decision variables. For example, one application may identify dollar returns and capital outlay requirements at varying times as constants and test for the present value of the investment in dollars. Another model could be constructed to solve for the minimum cost of an annuity to produce a desired minimum result.

Linear programming offers an opportunity to deal with two or more projects simultaneously; thus, it is especially effective in making portfolio investment decisions. The optimization technique represents a unique way to consider risk-return relationships and analyze the diversification of opportunities. Due to the complexity of linear programming, however, the use of a computer is required.

Regression Analysis

With the increased capability and accessibility of small computers, regression analysis has become an important tool for all types of financial analyses. It is particularly useful and applicable to real estate studies.

Regression analysis may be used for explanatory purposes, to make predictions or forecasts, or for a combination of these activities. Regression identifies the possible relationships between or among variables to provide a better understanding of the underlying data.

Simple regression analysis measures the relationship between an independent variable and a dependent variable with the equation

$$Y_C = a + bX$$

where Y_C is the forecast value, a is a constant, b is a multiplier or coefficient, and X is the value of an independent variable. Thus, the equation states that for an independent variable, X, the expected value of the Y variable to which it is being related is Y_C.

Regression analysis does not necessarily imply or attempt to quantify causative relationships. Rather, it reveals the apparent relationships between the values of different variables and their tendency to vary regularly with one another. When strong relationships are found, measuring these relationships can help explain one or more of the variables and forecast their values.

When more than one independent variable is involved in the analysis, multiple regression is used. For multiple regression analysis, the simple regression equation is expanded by adding terms for subsequent independent variables. The equation becomes

$$Y_C = a + b_1X_1 + b_2X_2 + \ldots + b_nX_n$$

This equation uses the same symbols used in the sample equation, but each independent variable and its associated multiplier or coefficient are identified with an appropriate numerical subscript.

Regression analysis takes a number of mathematical forms, but it is relatively simple to perform even with a small computer. Care should be exercised in entering the data and interpreting the results; both require special consideration. Computer applications also allow practitioners to analyze situations in which the relationships among variables are best expressed graphically with some type of curved line.

Regression is an important tool in real estate valuation, particularly when a large number of properties or a large quantity of data is being considered. It is equally applicable to a broad range of market and property analyses in real estate evaluations. Regression analysis is often used for its forecasting capabilities, but its explanatory powers should not be overlooked. It may, for example, be used to identify the factors of analysis, explain their significance, and avoid duplication in weighting two variables that are closely associated.

Evaluation Studies

Real estate appraisers are frequently asked to provide both valuation and evaluation services for use in real estate decision making. The decisions being contemplated may involve the acquisition or disposition of real estate, the development or redevelopment potential of a property, or financial management and planning alternatives.

The specific services performed for each client must be tailored to the individual circumstances and meet established professional standards. The range of possible services is nearly infinite, but some typical evaluation studies are discussed below. Each study may be conducted independently or it may be a component of a more detailed investment analysis.

Feasibility Studies

Feasibility studies are undertaken to test the ability of various investment scenarios to meet explicit investment objectives. Scenarios that meet the objectives are "feasible;" those that do not are infeasible.

Feasibility studies are frequently confused with highest and best use studies. Highest and best use studies, which are another common type of evaluation study, seek to determine the optimum use(s) for specified real estate. The use or uses that produce the highest net return are considered the "highest and best." Feasibility studies focus on specific investment objectives and analyze all contributing and limiting factors to determine whether a given combination of factors meets the minimum objectives established by the decision makers.

Highest and best use studies center on a property and its use. Feasibility studies are concerned not only with property and selected use(s), but also with an investment alternative and the objectives of a given client. The business interests or motivations of a particular client may lead to real estate decisions that appear to defy highest and best use determinations but meet the standards established by the feasibility criteria. Even when common uses are being considered, a given investment alternative may be feasible to one investor and impracticable to another.

These distinctions demonstrate that feasibility studies involve both objective analysis and the subjective application of findings to a particular client's circumstances. By combining these services, appraisers help clients distinguish among facts, estimates, and subjective factors and weigh the results of evaluation analyses— including the anticipated consequences of the real estate decision.

Virtually any analytical tool may be used in feasibility studies, but DCF analysis is the technique most commonly applied. A proper feasibility analysis provides for evaluation at several points to test the internal consistency and findings of the analysis and to facilitate the application of the decision-making guidelines established to determine feasibility.

For example, an appraiser who is testing the feasibility of a developer's plans for a subdivision could devise a test to monitor cumulative positive and negative cash flow. If the developer has established a decision-making guideline that the development must at no time have a negative cash flow of more than $200,000, the appraiser can determine the possibility and associated probability of the negative cash flow exceeding this limit and report that the plan is infeasible if an excess appears likely. Feasibility analysis may also identify crucial variables which by themselves indicate that a planned investment is impracticable.

Market Studies

Market studies relate to the general market conditions of supply, demand, and pricing or to the demographics of specific areas or property types. Market studies are generally considered macroeconomic studies. They often focus on housing conditions in a given sector of a community, in a region, or in the nation as a whole. Market studies may include analyses of construction and absorption trends, pricing and price changes, construction types and locations, or other factors relating to housing.

The studies may reveal or explain facts and behavior regarding property types, investor activities, or other matters of market concern. Market studies involving the activities of mortgage lenders and borrowers, the construction of various types of buildings, and the preferences of investors are particularly common.

Marketability Studies

Marketability studies are microeconomic studies that focus on the marketability of a given property or class of properties. Usually, the appraiser must identify one or more market segments in which the property would generate market demand and all the factors related to that demand.

Marketability studies are especially useful in determining highest and best use and testing specific development proposals. In either case, a marketability study can provide a client with the information needed to judge the source(s) of most likely demand, the timing for this demand, the amount of money that would most likely be spent by each demand component, and the property's ability to capture the available demand.

Marketability studies are commonly undertaken to project the tenant composition of planned retail facilities or to improve the tenant mix in existing facilities. They are fundamental to an economic understanding of how potential demand is translated into effective demand and the risks involved in achieving cash flow objectives.

Marketability studies often provide the basis for development decisions on single-family subdivisions, multifamily projects, and residential condominiums. In fact, these studies are useful wherever time and money are available to conduct a detailed analysis of demand factors and to adapt the proposed plans to the findings.

Cost-Benefit Studies

Cost-benefit studies can be done on a macroeconomic or microeconomic basis. For example, a community may require a cost-benefit study to determine the economic benefits that would most likely result from a new public project such as an expressway or a sewage treatment plant. The cost-benefit study would focus on the relationship between the benefits created and the costs associated with the project to determine whether the benefits warrant the costs.

Developers also use cost-benefit studies. They are frequently called on to install major items that properly belong to the infrastructure. This clearly goes beyond the direct needs of developers, who must look to the future to recapture the extra dollars invested. A cost-benefit study can establish the relative worth of such expenditures in relation to the benefits.

Pricing and Rent Projection Studies

Pricing and rent projection studies may be components of marketability studies or the subject of separate studies. These analyses are frequently conducted to establish sales and marketing strategies for real estate products and to facilitate decisions involving property management and investment.

Other Evaluation Studies

Other types of real estate evaluation studies include economic base studies, consumer profile studies, absorption studies, land-use strategy studies, and studies of other economic characteristics. Many call for special skills and training on the part of the real estate appraiser and some require the services of other professionals. Most real estate appraisers possess special skills and are uniquely qualified by their experience and training to provide a diverse range of evaluation studies.

INCOME TAXES AND REAL ESTATE EVALUATION

Federal and state income taxation affects all types of investments. Real estate has long been the subject of special provisions under various income tax codes and rulings and these provisions have influenced investors' decisions regarding different real estate types and locations, the prices they will pay, and the structuring of legal ownership to obtain every available advantage.

Income tax codes have historically provided real estate investors with the advantages of tax shelter, the deduction of expenses, income tax deferral, leverage, and the conversion of ordinary income into capital gains.

Tax shelter. Income tax laws have allowed some investors to shelter all or part of the income produced by a real etate investment from income taxes. Moreover, surplus benefits that exceed the income produced by a given investment could be credited toward the income produced by other investments, thereby multiplying the benefits produced by the tax-sheltered real estate.

The Tax Reform Act of 1986, which does not allow passive activity losses to be deducted, will have a substantial impact on this type of tax-sheltered investment. Passive activity is an arrangement in which the individual who receives the income has no material participation in the enterprise—i.e., no regular, continuous, or substantial involvement in the business operation. Under the new tax law, passive activity losses may only be written off against passive gains.

The Tax Reform Act of 1986 permits the deduction of losses only to the extent that the financial resources of the operation are at risk. In other words, the deduction cannot be greater than the amount of the investment. Deductions are also limited to a maximum of $25,000 per year for any investor with a taxable income of less than $100,000. Individuals earning $100,000 to $150,000 may deduct lesser amounts determined according to a sliding scale. With this scale, deductions are reduced and ultimately eliminated as the size of the investor's income increases. Any individual with a taxable income of $150,000 or more is not entitled to any deduction for losses.

Deduction of expenses. Certain types of operating expenses and other special costs have traditionally qualified as deductions from taxable income, which reduce the income tax liability of a given real estate investment. These costs may include specified operating expenses and depreciation allowances.

Income tax deferral. Tax laws have long provided a means to shift the time frames in which income taxes must be filed and paid. This provision has allowed investors to structure investment plans to take advantage of special timing and reduce their total income tax liability. The Tax Reform Act of 1986 strongly recommends that investors adhere to the calendar year for income tax purposes.

Leverage. Leverage is important to virtually all types of investors. In real estate investments, leverage has been available both before and after income taxes. Some cash flow situations that look particularly onerous before income taxes could be structured under the old tax laws to provide attractive after-tax cash flows.

Conversion of ordinary income into capital gains. The treatment of capital gains as qualifying income items has permitted taxpayers in high income brackets to state the returns from profits on real estate investments at the time of sale and obtain lower marginal tax rates for these returns. Due to the differences among tax brackets, this provision has been a major consideration of the income tax structure and its effects on investors. The Tax Reform Act of 1986 has eliminated this treatment of the capital gains from real estate and other investments. Accordingly, capital gains will be taxed like income, but filed under a separate classification.

In the 1980s, federal income taxes have undergone frequent and sweeping changes. There is strong public support for income tax simplification and the revision of federal and state income taxes as a means to reduce the public debt. It is likely that this impetus for reform will produce even greater changes in the foreseeable future.

In real estate evaluation, the fundamental economics of real estate operations must be distinguished from the marginal benefits that may accrue as the result of income tax advantages, investment structuring schemes, favored financing plans, or other programs that manipulate the specific circumstances of a given investment. Fundamental economic laws and relationships remain operative in all types of business cycles and special investment situations. Although the marginal benefits associated with specific investment circumstances are important, the accrual of these benefits depends on the underlying economics of the real estate operation to which they pertain. Therefore, the importance of these marginal benefits to the investment should not be overstated.

Real estate appraisers must understand and address the effects of federal and state income taxes in conducting real estate evaluations. Such an understanding is useful in situations where specific client needs are involved and where general market data reflect the effects of income tax provisions.

COUNSELING AS AN EXTENSION OF REAL ESTATE EVALUATION

Real estate counseling is defined by the American Society of Real Estate Counselors of the NATIONAL ASSOCIATION OF REALTORS® (ASREC) as

> Providing competent, disinterested, and unbiased advice, professional guidance, and sound judgment on diversified problems in the broad field of real estate involving any or all segments of the business such as merchandising, leasing, management, planning, financing, appraising, court testimony, and other similar services. Counseling may involve the utilization of any or all of these functions.

Unlike appraisers, counselors may go beyond evaluation and offering advice to a client and directly represent the client's interests. The Code of Professional Ethics and Standards of Professional Practice of the American Institute of Real Estate Appraisers distinguish between appraisal assignments and the ancillary services that go beyond appraising; these documents set forth procedures to be followed by appraisers in such situations. Similarly, ASREC has ethical and performance standards to guide practitioners in the field of real estate counseling.

Counseling assignments cover a variety of real estate situations; counseling services can be provided in all real estate fields and the range of situations covered is unlimited. Counseling services may include appraising just as appraisers may counsel clients within the scope of evaluation assignments. Appraisers may offer advice on real estate economics and the components and consequences of the economic decisions a client must make.

When counseling clients as part of real estate evaluations, appraisers base their advice on supportable facts and conclusions. The typical result of an evaluation assignment is a letter or report that summarizes the appraiser's facts, data, analyses, and conclusions and confirms any advice that has been rendered orally. An evaluation report not only establishes the appraiser's services on a professional basis, but also constitutes a direct communication that can prevent misunderstandings and give the client a framework in which to apply the appraiser's findings and advice.

SUMMARY

Real estate appraisals may involve valuation services, evaluation services, or both. Evaluations are usually conducted to provide assistance in real estate decision making. Many valuation assignments include evaluation services because market participants who need to know market value may also be interested in other data that characterize the market. Both evaluation and valuation assignments are covered by the *Code of Professional Ethics and Standards of Professional Practice* of the American Institute of Real Estate Appraisers.

Evaluation assignments may call for general market analysis or the analysis of specific real estate. In valuation assignments real property interests are identified and particular categories of value are defined; by contrast, the nature and scope of evaluation assignments must be specified in each individual case.

The distinction between market value and investment value is important. *Investment value* is the specific value of goods or services to a particular investor. Market value does not relate to a specific buyer or seller; rather, a hypothetical or typical market participant is assumed. Every voluntary transaction is based on individual investment-value decisions. Thus, the market is made up of a multitude of transactions that involve willing parties who make individual investment decisions. The *transaction price* of a property varies with the strength of the participants' motivation and with the availability of opportunities. Depending on the specific circumstances, the transaction price of a property at any given moment may fluctuate above or below its exact value at *perfect market equilibrium*. Market value estimates are a synthesis of these transactions.

Certain *measures of investment performance* are particularly applicable to real estate. Simple ratios ($R = I/V$) may be used, but they do not reflect the effect of specific factors. The *payback period* or *breakeven point* (PB = equity capital outlay/annual net equity cash flows) does not consider the time value of money or specific investment risks. A *profitability index* or *benefit/cost ratio* ($PI = PV$ of anticipated investment returns/PV of capital outlay) is commonly used in conjunction with *net present value* (NPV) or *dollar reward*

$$NPV = CF_0 + \frac{CF_1}{(1 + i)} + \frac{CF_2}{(1 + i)^2} + \ldots + \frac{CF_n}{(1 + i)^n} - CO$$

which does consider the time value of money. *Time-weighted rates*, which may also be called *unit-method rates* or *share-accounting rates*, are used primarily to measure portfolio management.

Discounted cash flow (DCF) analysis is the most detailed and precise way to measure cash inflows and outflows over the life of an investment. The sum of the present values of all future positive and negative cash flows represents the DCF value indication at a given discount rate. Discounted cash flow analysis can be performed on a before- or after-tax basis. It can be used in conjunction with other measures and applied on a constant, noninflated or nominal, actual dollar basis. The techniques of DCF analysis can deal with varying risk situations and explicitly consider investment advantages and disadvantages. This type of analysis relies on forecast estimates and very subjective discount rates may be applied.

The *internal rate of return* (IRR), which is the rate of discount that produces a profitability index of one and a NPV of zero, may be regarded as a DCF analysis that is solved backward. All cash inflows and outflows are analyzed to find the discount rate that renders them equivalent to the original capital outlay. Thus, the IRR reflects the indicated return *on* and *of* the investment. The IRR does have some disadvantages. Controversy over the reinvestment presumption and weaknesses such as the possibility of more than one IRR, the discounting of negative cash flows, conflict with the *NPV*, and a lack of recognition for differences in capital outlays have led to modifications of the *IRR*. Nevertheless, the *IRR* is a prominent example of yield analysis and a very important measure of investment performance.

No single measure of investment performance is always the best or most appropriate. Each has its limitations and all are more effective when used in conjunction with other measures. Measures of performance are tools that can help an appraiser exercise his or her professional judgment.

To complete an evaluation assignment, an appropriate problem-solving process must be identified for the specific situation. An evaluation usually focuses on the subjective goals of a specific client, rather than a general composite of the market. Because evaluation relates the appraiser's findings to a specific decision-making situation, *risk analysis* is a fundamental component.

Probability is the relative likelihood that a specified event will occur. Recognizing the range of probability, appraisers regard point estimates as the most probable numbers, not the only possible numbers. *Risk* is the probability that unforeseen events will not occur, while *uncertainty* is the probability that unforeseen events will occur. When the future is involved, appraisers use forecasts but avoid predictions.

Within the framework of risk analysis, probabilities are linked with risks. Ranges of probability are determined in four different ways: analysis of past events, controlled experiment and observation, theoretical distribution, and individual judgment. By identifying several possible outcomes, the limitations of a single point estimate are overcome.

To analyze risk, appraisers may assign *utility functions*, which are subjective weights given to each possible investment outcome to reflect the investor's relative preferences. A *debt coverage ratio* (*DCR*) is calculated by dividing *NOI* by annual debt service; this measure is commonly used in structuring or underwriting mortgages and in feasibility analysis. Investors may consider an investment's *payback period* or its *upside/downside potential*. The latter is measured by analyzing best and worst case anticipations in conjunction with DCF analysis. *Expected values* are weighted probabilities similar to utility functions. Using *Monte Carlo simulation*, specific investment elements are assigned probabilities and integrated into a larger theoretical population; sampling from this larger group provides a range of possible outcomes. *Risk-adjusted discount rates* reflect all the risk elements associated with an income stream for a specified period and are adjusted to offset additional term risk.

In addition to investment performance measures and risk analysis methods, real estate evaluation may draw on other analytical tools. These techniques include *sampling*, the application of statistical inference to sample data for use in forecasting market demand; *sensitivity analysis*, which isolates how changes in variables such as the *NOI* or R_L affect risk; *network analysis*, which diagrams the flow of processes and the critical timing aspects involved; *rating grids*, which assign arbitrary weights to the different factors involved in a decision to be made by several individuals; and *linear programming*, which employs a linear equation that subjects the variables to inequality constraints and is used to optimize the allocation of resources. *Regression analysis* examines the relationship between one or more independent variables and a dependent variable by plotting lines on graphs. It is used to identify and weight analytical factors and to make forecasts. Simple linear regression is based on the equation $Y_c = a + bX$; multiple regression uses the equation

$$Y_c = a + b_1X_1 + b_2X_2 + \ldots + b_nX_n$$

The range of evaluation services is extremely wide. *Feasibility studies* test the ability of given investment alternatives to meet explicit objectives (e.g., cash flow expectations) by analyzing all contributing and limiting factors and determining which combination(s) meet the investor's criteria. Feasibility studies begin with a highest and best use determination and an investment scenario. *Market studies* are macroeconomic studies that relate to supply and demand, demographics, pricing, and construction and absorption trends. *Marketability studies* are microeconomic studies that focus on the marketability of a given property or a class of properties to determine a specific highest and best use, test development proposals, or project an appropriate tenant mix. *Cost-benefit studies* examine the probable economic benefits that will result from proposed public projects, and *pricing and rent projection studies* are conducted to determine marketing strategies.

In the 1980s federal income tax laws have undergone extensive change. Tax reform has redirected the attention of investors toward the fundamental economics of real estate and away from the marginal benefits that result from tax advantages. Many traditional tax advantages have been curtailed by the Tax Reform Act of 1986. The tax shelter benefits of real estate are diminished because passive activity losses may only be written off against passive gains. The "at risk" rule provides that the losses deducted cannot exceed the amount of the investment. Deductions are also limited according to the taxable income of the investor. Income tax deferral is threatened because adherence to the calendar year is recommended for income tax purposes. The conversion of ordinary income into capital gains is no longer advantageous because the special treatment of capital gains has been eliminated.

Real estate counseling is defined by the American Society of Real Estate Counselors of the NATIONAL ASSOCIATION OF REALTORS* and recognized in the Appraisal Institute's Code of Professional Ethics and Standards of Professional Practice. Counseling involves services that are often associated with evaluation, but are beyond the scope of appraising. To prevent misunderstandings and establish counseling services on a professional basis, appraisers are advised to prepare a letter or report for the client summarizing the data, analyses, and conclusions applied and confirming any oral advice rendered.

Appendix A
Professional
Practice

The body of knowledge that comprises the discipline of appraisal is the foundation of professional practice. In solving most appraisal problems, however, the final conclusions depend to a great extent on the ability, judgment, and integrity of individual appraisers. To form a sound conclusion, relevant data must be available and the appraiser must be committed to finding and analyzing the data; a valid analysis also depends on the skillful application of appraisal techniques. Because appraisal is an inexact science, appraisers must reach their conclusions in an impartial, objective manner, without bias or any desire to accommodate their own interests or the interests of their clients. Professional appraisers have the requisite knowledge and the ability to apply it capably and objectively.

A profession is distinguished from a trade or service industry by a combination of the following factors:

1. High standards of competence in a specialized field
2. A distinct body of knowledge that is continually augmented by the contributions of members and can be imparted to future generations
3. A code of ethics or standards of practice and members who are willing to be regulated by peer review

These criteria guided the individuals who founded the American Institute of Real Estate Appraisers in 1932. At that time, the United States was in a period of unparalleled economic chaos and a sound basis was needed to establish the value and utility of real estate. The Appraisal Institute was formed for three purposes.

1. To establish criteria for selecting and recognizing individuals with real estate valuation skills who were committed to competent and ethical practice
2. To develop a system of education to train new appraisers and sharpen the skills of practicing appraisers

3.   To formulate a code of professional ethics and standards of professional conduct to guide real estate appraisers and serve as a model for other practitioners

The first act of the new organization was to publish a code of ethics and standards of professional practice to protect the public and its members. Through the years these guidelines were refined and in 1984 the Code of Professional Ethics and the Standards of Professional Practice were separated into two discrete documents. The heart of these documents is contained in the six canons of the Code of Professional Ethics and two Standards of Professional Practice.

- **Canon 1**
  A Member or Candidate of the Appraisal Institute must refrain from conduct that is detrimental to the Appraisal Institute, the real estate appraisal profession and the public.
- **Canon 2**
  A Member or Candidate must assist the Appraisal Institute in carrying out its responsibilities to the users of appraisal services and the public.
- **Canon 3**
  In the performance of an appraisal assignment, each analysis and opinion of a Member or Candidate must be developed and communicated without bias and without the accommodation of the Member's or Candidate's personal interests.
- **Canon 4**
  A Member or Candidate must not violate the confidential nature of the appraiser-client relationship.
- **Canon 5**
  In promoting an appraisal practice and soliciting appraisal assignments, a Member or Candidate must use care to avoid advertising or solicitation that is misleading or otherwise contrary to the public interest.
- **Canon 6**
  A Member or Candidate must comply with the requirements of the Appraisal Institute's Standards of Professional Practice.
- **Standard 1**
  In developing a real estate appraisal, an appraiser must be aware of, understand, and correctly employ those recognized methods and techniques that are necessary to produce a credible appraisal.
- **Standard 2**
  In reporting the results of a real estate appraisal, an appraiser must communicate each analysis, opinion, and conclusion in a manner that is not misleading.

Appendix B
Mathematics
in Appraising

$\mathbf{A}$ppraisers use a wide variety of mathematical techniques ranging from simple arithmetic and algebraic formulas to the statistical techniques of multiple regression analysis. Addition, subtraction, multiplication, and division can be done manually or with a simple calculator, but more sophisticated calculators may be needed to solve algebraic formulas and to perform linear regression analyses. Computers are required for nearly all stepwise multiple regression analyses.

With the greater availability of calculators and computers, the use of sophisticated techniques is increasing in appraisal practice. This section provides a review of the mathematical procedures and terminology used by appraisers. Familiar processes are illustrated and the rules that apply to each process are discussed.

BASIC ARITHMETIC FOR DATA PROCESSING

Data collected in the market are analyzed in the valuation process to derive an estimate of value. These data may include building dimensions, population figures, reproduction and replacement costs, rents, and sale prices. Processing these numbers ultimately leads to final conclusions and value estimates, which are also expressed numerically. The mathematical relationships represented by rates and factors are usually stated as decimals rather than fractions.

Rates

Rates are percentages expressed in terms of a specific time period. For example,

$8 interest per year on $100 principal = 8% interest per year

$0.50 interest per month on $100 = 0.005 or 0.5% interest per month

A rate reflects the relationship between one quantity and another. In the first example, the 8% rate relates the $8 of interest returned to the $100 of principal invested. In appraising, an unknown capital amount can be determined when only the rate and the amount of annual return are known.

Reciprocals

The reciprocal of a number is 1 divided by that number. For example, the reciprocal of 4 is 1/4, which may be expressed as 0.25.

When two numbers have a reciprocal relationship, 1 divided by either number equals the other number. Reciprocal relationships exist between some financial factors. For example, the present value of $1 per period factor and the partial payment factor are reciprocals. These annual factors in the 10% tables for 10 periods are 6.144567 and 0.162745, respectively. Because they are reciprocals,

$$\frac{1}{6.144567} = 0.162745$$

and

$$\frac{1}{0.162745} = 6.144567$$

When a reciprocal relationship exists, multiplication by one of the numbers is equivalent to division by the other.

Factors

Factors are the reciprocals of rates and may be used to express relationships between income and capital value. Using I, R, and V to represent income, rate, and value, and F to represent a factor, the relationships may be expressed as

$$I = V \times R \qquad I = \frac{V}{F}$$

$$R = \frac{I}{V} \qquad F = \frac{V}{I}$$

$$V = \frac{I}{R} \qquad V = I \times F$$

These relationships, which are commonly referred to as *IRV* and *VIF*, may be shown as follows.

$$\frac{I}{R \mid V} \qquad \text{and} \qquad \frac{V}{I \mid F}$$

The formula for any single component is represented by the horizontal or vertical relationship of the remaining two components as one multiplied by, or divided by, the other.

The financial tables included in Appendix C reflect various rates that are applicable for specific numbers of compounding, or discounting, periods.

BASIC STATISTICS

Statistics can be applied to interpret available data and to support a value conclusion. In the language of statistics, a *population* is defined as all the items in a specific category. If, for example, the category is houses in Chicago, the population consists of all the houses in Chicago. However, data pertaining to an entire population are rarely available and conclusions often must be developed from incomplete data.

Using statistical concepts, conclusions about a population can be derived and evaluated from sample data. A *sample* is part of a population; the quality of conclusions based on a sample will vary with the quality and extent of the sample.

One item in a population is called a *variate*. In appraising, statistics can be used to identify the attributes of the typical variate in a population. When observations about a population can be measured, the analysis may be quantitative; when these observations cannot be measured, the analysis is qualitative—i.e., it reflects the attributes of the population.

A variate is *discrete* when it can assume a limited number of values on a measuring scale and *continuous* when it can assume an infinite number of values. A typical population of attributes for house types might include one-story, two-story, and split-level houses. It is usually impractical to display or identify a population of variates because there are many.

One common problem in statistics is how to describe a population in universally understandable terms. For example, how does one describe all the houses in a community that have sold in the past year without describing each sale individually?

One possible solution is to use a single number called a *parameter* to describe the whole population. When one parameter is used to describe a population, it is called an *aggregate*, which is the sum of all the variates. For example, all the house sales in a community in a given year can be described by the total dollar amount of all the sales. In statistical language this is written as

Σ = sigma = sum of
X = variate
ΣX = aggregate (summation of the variates)

Measures of Central Tendency

Three common statistical measures are the mean, the median, and the mode. All three measure central tendency and are used to identify the typical variate in a population or sample. Measures that refer to a population are called *parameters*, while similar measures in a sample are called *statistics*.

The *mean*, which is commonly called the *average*, is by far the most commonly used parameter. It is obtained by dividing the sum of all the variates in a population by the number of variates. In real estate appraising, the mean may represent an average sale price, an average number of days for sale, an average apartment rent, or an average cost per square foot.

When the mean is used to describe a population, it can be distorted by extreme variates. Consider the following list of 36 house sales in a neighborhood. From these figures, the mean of the population can be calculated. (The list also indicates the median and the mode of the population, which are discussed next.)

$72,000
74,600
76,000
77,200
78,000
79,000
79,800
79,800
82,000
82,000
84,000
85,600
85,800
86,000
87,000
87,200
87,400
87,800
87,800   ← median (Md.) = $87,800
87,800
88,000
89,800
90,000 ⎫
90,000 ⎪
90,000 ⎬ mode (Mo.) = $90,000
90,000 ⎭
90,600
91,000
91,000
93,800
93,800
96,600
97,000

```
              97,200
              97,200
              98,800
          ───────────
          $3,131,600
```

$$\text{Mean} = \overline{X} = \frac{\Sigma X}{N} = \frac{\$3,131,600}{36} = \$86,989$$

where ΣX = sum of the variates and N = number of variates.

The same procedure can be performed with grouped data. To group the data, the frequency (f) with which a given sale price occurs must be identified and its contribution must be effectively weighted. Given the same data, identical results are produced.

X	f	fX
$72,000	1	$ 72,000
74,600	1	74,600
76,000	1	76,000
77,200	1	77,200
78,000	1	78,000
79,000	1	79,000
79,800	2	159,600
82,000	2	164,000
84,000	1	84,000
85,600	1	85,600
85,800	1	85,800
86,000	1	86,000
87,000	1	87,000
87,200	1	87,200
87,400	1	87,400
87,800	3	263,400
88,000	1	88,000
89,800	1	89,800
90,000	4	360,000
90,600	1	90,600
91,000	2	182,000
93,800	2	187,600
96,600	1	96,600
97,000	1	97,000
97,200	2	194,400
98,800	1	98,800
	$N = 36$	$fX = \$3,131,600$

$$\text{Mean} = \overline{X} = \frac{fX}{N} = \frac{\$3,131,600}{36} = \$86,989$$

The average, or mean, price in this example might not accurately represent the population of houses that have been sold at prices outside the indicated range.

The *median* is another measure used to describe a population, a sample, or an average variate. The median divides the variates of a population or sample into equal halves. To find the median, the variates are arranged in numerical order like the list of sale prices in the example. If the total number of variates is odd, the median is the middle variate. If the total number of variates is even, as in the example, the median is the arithmetic mean of the two middle variates.

In the list of 36 house sales, the middle two variates are $87,800 and $87,800. The mean of these two variates is $87,800, which is the median of the 36 sales. The same number of sales occur above the median as below it.

Like the median and the mean, the *mode* is a parameter used to describe the typical variate of a population. The mode is the variate or attribute that appears most frequently in a population. Of the 36 house sales, four were sold at $90,000. No other sale price occurs with this frequency, so the mode in this sample is $90,000. If two variates occur with equal frequency, both are modes and the sample is bimodal.

To illustrate, consider the following population of the types of condominium apartments available in a nine-unit complex.

> efficiency
> efficiency
> efficiency
> town house ⎫
> town house ⎪
> town house ⎬   mode (the most frequent attribute)
> town house ⎪
> town house ⎭
> multibedroom

One of the problems in using statistics is selecting the appropriate measure of central tendency to describe a population. The following numbers could be used to describe the 36 variates in the group of house sales.

$$\overline{X} = \$86,989 \text{ (the mean of all the sales)}$$
$$\text{Md.} = \$87,800 \text{ (the median of the sales)}$$
$$\text{Mo.} = \$90,000 \text{ (the mode of the sales)}$$

The mean is often used to describe a sample or population because this measure is widely understood and amenable to further statistical analysis.

Measures of Variation

The parameters of mean, median, and mode, are used to describe the central tendencies of a population. Other sets of parameters can provide more information about the population being described. *Measures of variation*, or *measures of dispersion*, describe the disparity among the values of the variates that make up the population. They indicate the degree of uniformity among the variates and reflect the quality of the data as a basis for a conclusion.

Range

One way to measure the disparity between the variates is with a *range* (R). The range is the difference between the highest and the lowest variates.

R = maximum variate minus minimum variate

The range for the 36 house sales is calculated as

$R = \$98,800 - \$72,000 = \$26,800$

As a measure of variation, the range has limited usefulness because it considers only the variation between the highest and lowest values, not the variation in the remaining values. Furthermore, a range does not lend itself to further statistical analysis.

Average Deviation

Another parameter used to measure the variation in a population is the average deviation, which is also known as the *average absolute deviation* because positive and negative signs are ignored. The average deviation is a measure of how much the actual values of a population or sample deviate from the mean. It is the mean of the sum of the absolute differences of each of the variates from the mean of the variates.

The average deviation of the 36 sales can be calculated from ungrouped or grouped data.

Ungrouped Data

X Sale Price		$\lvert X - \overline{X} \rvert$ Absolute Deviation between Each Variate and the Mean Sale Price of $86,989
$ 72,000		$ 14,989
74,600		12,389
76,000		10,989
77,200		9,789
78,000		8,989
79,000		7,989
79,800		7,189
79,800		7,189
82,000		4,989
82,000		4,989
84,000		2,989
85,600		1,389
85,800		1,189
86,000		989
87,000		11
87,200		211
87,400		411
87,800		811
87,800		811
87,800		811
88,000		1,011
89,800		2,811
90,000		3,011
90,000		3,011
90,000		3,011
90,000		3,011
90,600		3,611
91,000		4,011
91,000		4,011
93,800		6,811
93,800		6,811
96,600		9,611
97,000		10,011
97,200		10,211
97,200		10,211
98,800		11,811
$3,131,600	Total of sale prices	$192,088 Total deviation from mean $\Sigma \lvert X - \overline{X} \rvert$

Grouped Data

X	$\lvert X - \overline{X} \rvert$	f	$f\lvert X - \overline{X} \rvert$
$72,000	$ 14,989	1	$ 14,989
74,600	12,389	1	12,389
76,000	10,989	1	10,989
77,200	9,789	1	9,789
78,000	8,989	1	8,989
79,000	7,989	1	7,989
79,800	7,189	2	14,378
82,000	4,989	2	9,978
84,000	2,989	1	2,989
85,600	1,389	1	1,389
85,800	1,189	1	1,189
86,000	989	1	989
87,000	11	1	11
87,200	211	1	211
87,400	411	1	411
87,800	811	3	2,433
88,000	1,011	1	1,011
89,800	2,811	1	2,811
90,000	3,011	4	12,044
90,600	3,611	1	3,611
91,000	4,011	2	8,022
93,800	6,811	2	13,622
96,600	9,611	1	9,611
97,000	10,011	1	10,011
97,200	10,211	2	20,422
98,800	11,811	1	11,811
		36	$192,088

Total deviation from the mean $\Sigma f\lvert X - \overline{X} \rvert$

$$A.D. \text{ (ungrouped data)} = \frac{\Sigma\lvert X - \overline{X}\rvert}{n} = \frac{\$192,088}{36} = \$5,336$$

$$A.D. \text{ (grouped data)} = \frac{\Sigma\lvert X - \overline{X}\rvert}{n} = \frac{\$192,088}{36} = \$5,336$$

A.D. = average deviation

Σ = sum of

f = frequency

X = observed value

$|\ \ |$ = aggregation (ignore whether the difference is positive or negative)

n = number of observations in sample (N = population)

$\overline{X}$ = mean of sample (μ = population)

These calculations indicate that the average deviation of the individual values in the population from the mean is $5,336, or about 6%. This relatively small variation suggests that the mean is an acceptable representation of the population.

Like the range, the average deviation does not lend itself to further statistical calculations.

Standard Deviation

The standard deviation is a way to describe a sample or a population that lends itself to further mathematical treatment. When this measure is used, the rules of probability can be applied to draw inferences from samples concerning the attributes of the population. The square of the difference between each observation and the mean of the observations is used in lieu of the absolute deviation. In this way the effects of extreme variance from the mean are magnified.

In the example the mean house sale price is $86,989; for an $82,000 sale, the standard deviation is $4,989 squared, or $24,890,121.

When the standard deviation of an entire population is being calculated, it is symbolized by the lowercase sigma (σ). The formula may be expressed verbally as follows. *The standard deviation of a population is the square root of the sum of the squared differences between each observation and the mean of all the observations in the population, divided by the number of observations in the population.*

When the standard deviation of a sample of a population is being calculated, it is symbolized by the lowercase letter s. Expressed verbally, the formula is: *The standard deviation of a sample is the square root of the sum of the squared differences between each observation and the mean of all the observations in the sample, divided by the number of observations in the sample minus one.*

One is subtracted from the number of observations in a sample to adjust for the one degree of freedom that is lost when the mean is calculated. (See the discussion of simple linear regression analysis that is presented later in this appendix.) A set of data starts with as many degrees of freedom as there are observations; each time a statistic is calculated directly from the data, one degree of freedom is lost.

Formulas for calculating the standard deviations follow.

For a population:

Ungrouped   Grouped

$$\sigma = \sqrt{\frac{\Sigma(X - \overline{X})^2}{N}} \qquad \sigma = \sqrt{\frac{\Sigma f(X - \overline{X})^2}{N}}$$

For a sample:

Ungrouped   Grouped

$$s = \sqrt{\frac{\Sigma(X - \overline{X})^2}{n - 1}} \qquad s = \sqrt{\frac{\Sigma f(X - \overline{X})^2}{n - 1}}$$

Samples are typically used in real estate appraising, so the second formula is more applicable. The standard deviation for the 36 house sales as grouped data is calculated in Table B.1.

The standard deviation is an important way to describe the dispersion of a population or sample. It indicates how well the mean represents the whole sample or population by describing a standard measure of variation. The standard deviation is used and understood in many disciplines and it can be calculated easily with an electronic calculator. It will undoubtedly be more widely used by appraisers in the future.

The standard deviation can also indicate what percentage of the sample of a population may be expected to fall within selected ranges of *confidence intervals*. (Confidence levels are discussed later in this appendix.)

Approximately 68.26% of the sample or population will generally fall within plus or minus one standard deviation from the mean, provided the data meet the tests of normal distribution, which are explained later. Many types of real estate data conform to the pattern of a normal distribution when they are developed with appropriate sampling techniques.

Assuming this is a normal distribution, 68.26% of the house sales in the population will fall between $80,161 ($86,989 − $6,828) and $93,817 ($86,989 + $6,828). Approximately 95.44% of the sales should fall within two standard deviations from the mean and approximately 99.74% should fall within three standard deviations from the mean.

Because the standard deviation lends itself to further mathematical calculations, it can be used for analytical purposes as well as to describe a population.

Table B.1   Standard Deviation for 36 House Sales

X	f	$(X - \overline{X})$	$(X - \overline{X})$	$f(X - \overline{X})^2$
$72,000	1	$14,989	$224,670,000	$ 224,670,000
74,600	1	12,389	153,487,000	153,487,000
76,000	1	10,989	120,758,000	120,758,000
77,200	1	9,789	95,824,500	95,824,500
78,000	1	8,989	80,802,100	80,802,100
79,000	1	7,989	63,824,100	63,824,100
79,800	2	7,189	51,681,700	103,363,000
82,000	2	4,989	24,890,100	49,780,200
84,000	1	2,989	8,934,120	8,934,120
85,600	1	1,389	1,929,320	1,929,320
85,800	1	1,189	1,413,720	1,413,720
86,000	1	989	978,121	978,121
87,000	1	11	121	121
87,200	1	211	44,521	44,521
87,400	1	411	168,921	168,921
87,800	3	811	657,721	1,973,160
88,000	1	1,011	1,022,120	1,022,120
89,800	1	2,811	7,901,720	7,901,720
90,000	4	3,011	9,066,120	36,264,500
90,600	1	3,611	13,039,300	13,039,300
91,000	2	4,011	16,088,100	32,176,200
93,800	2	6,811	46,389,700	92,779,400
96,600	1	9,611	92,371,300	92,371,300
97,000	1	10,011	100,220,000	100,220,000
97,200	2	10,211	104,265,000	208,530,000
98,800	1	11,811	139,500,000	139,500,000
				$1,631,755,444
Rounded				$1,631,760,000

$$s = \sqrt{\frac{\Sigma f(X - \overline{X})^2}{n - 1}}$$

Mean: $86,989

$$s = \sqrt{\frac{\$1,631,760,000}{36 - 1}}$$

$$s = \sqrt{\$46,621,714}$$

$$s = \quad \$6,828$$

Statistical Inference

Statistical inference is based on the assumption that past market actions provide a valid basis for forecasting present or future market actions. In the example, past sale prices are used to estimate current sale prices. The same technique can be used to forecast rents, costs, depreciation, and other amounts using the rules of probability.

A normal curve is produced when a normal distribution is plotted on a graph to illustrate a distribution of data. Although the original data may not be normally distributed, the results of repeated random samples may approximate a normal distribution. Sales are often treated as though they were normally distributed in competitive, open-market situations. A normal curve often takes the form of a bell curve.

One major characteristic of a bell curve is its symmetry. Both halves of the curve have the same shape and contain the same number of observations. The mean, median, and mode are the same value and fall at the midpoint, or apex, of the curve.

Figure B.1 is a bell curve that illustrates the 36 house sales. It shows that 68.26% of the observations will fall within the range of the mean, plus or minus one standard deviation; 95.44% will fall within plus or minus two standard deviations; and 99.74% will fall within plus or minus three standard deviations. The figure depicts an analysis of the probable population distribution for the 36 sales, assuming a normal distribution.

Under the bell curve, the ranges for one, two, and three standard deviations are shown. The percentage of the population that will fall within a given distance from the mean or within any specified range can be calculated. For example, the percentage of sales included within a range of $91,989 to $81,989 (i.e., the mean of $86,989 plus or minus $5,000) may be estimated by calculating the Z value for this range with the formula presented below and then consulting a table of areas under the normal curve for the calculated value of Z.

Z = the deviation of X from the mean measured in standard deviations

$$Z = \frac{X - \text{mean}}{\text{standard deviation}}$$

$$Z = \frac{\$91,989 - \$86,989}{\$6,828} = 0.73$$

This formula shows that $91,989 and $81,989 each deviate from the mean of $86,989 by 0.73 standard deviations.

The percentage of sales within this Z range of plus or minus 0.73 standard deviations can be found by locating 0.7 in the Z column of Table B.2 and then looking across the top of the table for the next digit—i.e., 0.03. The table indicates that 26.73% of the sales fall between $86,989 and $91,989 or between $86,989 and $81,989; therefore, 53.46% of the sales will fall between $91,989 and $81,989.

Figure B.1   Area Under the Normal Curve for 36 House Sales

50% of sales under $86,989
50% of sales over $86,989
68.26% of the sales between
  $80,161 and $93,817
95.44% of the sales between
  $73,333 and $100,645
99.74% of the sales between
  $66,505 and $107,473

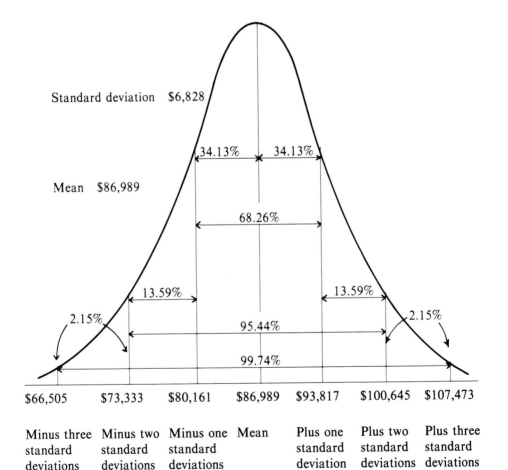

Frequency

Standard deviation $6,828

34.13%   34.13%

Mean $86,989

68.26%

13.59%   13.59%

2.15%   2.15%

95.44%

99.74%

| $66,505 | $73,333 | $80,161 | $86,989 | $93,817 | $100,645 | $107,473 |

| Minus three standard deviations | Minus two standard deviations | Minus one standard deviations | Mean | Plus one standard deviation | Plus two standard deviations | Plus three standard deviations |

Sale Price

Source: Joseph Lambert, Ph.D.

Table B.2   Areas under the Normal Curve

Z	.00	.01	.02	.03	.04	.05	.06	.07	.08	.09
0.0	0.0000	0.0040	0.0080	0.0120	0.0160	0.0199	0.0239	0.0279	0.0319	0.0359
0.1	0.0398	0.0438	0.0478	0.0517	0.0557	0.0596	0.0636	0.0675	0.0714	0.0753
0.2	0.0793	0.0832	0.0871	0.0910	0.0948	0.0987	0.1026	0.1064	0.1103	0.1141
0.3	0.1179	0.1217	0.1255	0.1293	0.1331	0.1368	0.1406	0.1443	0.1480	0.1517
0.4	0.1554	0.1591	0.1628	0.1664	0.1700	0.1736	0.1772	0.1808	0.1844	0.1879
0.5	0.1915	0.1950	0.1985	0.2019	0.2054	0.2088	0.2123	0.2157	0.2190	0.2224
0.6	0.2257	0.2291	0.2324	0.2357	0.2389	0.2422	0.2454	0.2486	0.2517	0.2549
0.7	0.2580	0.2611	0.2642	0.2673	0.2704	0.2734	0.2764	0.2794	0.2823	0.2852
0.8	0.2881	0.2910	0.2939	0.2967	0.2995	0.3023	0.3051	0.3078	0.3106	0.3133
0.9	0.3159	0.3186	0.3212	0.3238	0.3264	0.3289	0.3315	0.3340	0.3365	0.3389
1.0	0.3413	0.3438	0.3461	0.3485	0.3508	0.3531	0.3554	0.3577	0.3599	0.3621
1.1	0.3643	0.3665	0.3686	0.3708	0.3729	0.3749	0.3770	0.3790	0.3810	0.3830
1.2	0.3849	0.3869	0.3888	0.3907	0.3925	0.3944	0.3962	0.3980	0.3997	0.4015
1.3	0.4032	0.4049	0.4066	0.4082	0.4099	0.4115	0.4131	0.4147	0.4162	0.4177
1.4	0.4192	0.4207	0.4222	0.4236	0.4251	0.4265	0.4279	0.4292	0.4306	0.4319
1.5	0.4332	0.4345	0.4357	0.4370	0.4382	0.4394	0.4406	0.4418	0.4429	0.4441
1.6	0.4452	0.4463	0.4474	0.4484	0.4495	0.4505	0.4515	0.4525	0.4535	0.4545
1.7	0.4554	0.4564	0.4573	0.4582	0.4591	0.4599	0.4608	0.4616	0.4625	0.4633
1.8	0.4641	0.4649	0.4656	0.4664	0.4671	0.4678	0.4686	0.4693	0.4699	0.4706
1.9	0.4713	0.4719	0.4726	0.4732	0.4738	0.4744	0.4750	0.4756	0.4761	0.4767
2.0	0.4772	0.4778	0.4783	0.4788	0.4793	0.4798	0.4803	0.4808	0.4812	0.4817
2.1	0.4821	0.4826	0.4830	0.4834	0.4838	0.4842	0.4846	0.4850	0.4854	0.4857
2.2	0.4861	0.4864	0.4868	0.4871	0.4875	0.4878	0.4881	0.4884	0.4887	0.4890
2.3	0.4893	0.4896	0.4898	0.4901	0.4904	0.4906	0.4909	0.4911	0.4913	0.4916
2.4	0.4918	0.4920	0.4922	0.4925	0.4927	0.4929	0.4931	0.4932	0.4934	0.4936
2.5	0.4938	0.4940	0.4941	0.4943	0.4945	0.4946	0.4948	0.4949	0.4951	0.4952
2.6	0.4953	0.4955	0.4956	0.4957	0.4959	0.4960	0.4961	0.4962	0.4963	0.4964
2.7	0.4965	0.4966	0.4967	0.4968	0.4969	0.4970	0.4971	0.4972	0.4973	0.4974
2.8	0.4974	0.4975	0.4976	0.4977	0.4977	0.4978	0.4979	0.4979	0.4980	0.4981
2.9	0.4981	0.4982	0.4982	0.4983	0.4984	0.4984	0.4985	0.4985	0.4986	0.4986
3.0	0.4987	0.4987	0.4987	0.4988	0.4988	0.4989	0.4989	0.4989	0.4990	0.4990

The probability of a randomly selected sale falling within a given range can also be determined with the Z value. Using the sample of 36 house sales, which has a mean of \$86,989 and a standard deviation of \$6,828, the probability of a randomly selected sale falling between \$86,989 and \$88,989 is calculated as follows:

$$Z = \frac{X - \text{mean}}{\text{standard deviation}} = \frac{\$88,989 - \$86,989}{\$6,828} = 0.29$$

The table of areas under the normal curve, Table B.2, shows that a Z value of 0.29 corresponds to 0.1141. This indicates that there is an 11.41% chance that the sale will fall within \$2,000 above the mean. Because the curve of normal distribution is symmetrical, there is the same probability that a sale will fall within \$2,000 below the mean.

Probability a sale will fall between
$88,989 and $86,989   11.41%
Probability a sale will fall between
$84,989 and $86,989   11.41%

Probability a sale will fall between
$84,989 and $88,989   22.82%

If the range in this example is expanded to $4,000 plus or minus the mean of $86,989—i.e., between $82,989 and $90,989—the probability of a randomly selected sale falling within this range is increased.

$$Z = \frac{X - \text{mean}}{\text{standard deviation}} = \frac{\$90,989 - \$86,989}{\$6,828} = 0.59$$

According to Table B.2, 0.59 = 0.2224.

Probability a sale will fall between
$90,989 and $86,989   22.24%
Probability a sale will fall between
$82,989 and $86,989   22.24%

Probability a sale will fall between
$82,989 and $90,989   44.48%

In these examples the range being tested has been equally distributed above and below the mean sale price. However, the probability of a randomly selected sale falling within any selected range in the population can also be tested. For example, the probability of a sale falling between $80,000 and $100,000 can be calculated as follows.

$$Z \text{ area}^1 = \frac{X^1 - \text{mean}}{\text{standard deviation}} = \frac{\$80,000 - \$86,989}{\$6,828} = 1.02$$

$$Z \text{ area}^2 = \frac{X^2 - \text{mean}}{\text{standard deviation}} = \frac{\$100,000 - \$86,989}{\$6,828} = 1.91$$

A Z value of 1.02 in Table B.2
indicates a probability of   0.3461
A Z value of 1.91 in Table B.2
indicates a probability of   0.4719

Probability   0.8180

There is an 81.8% chance that a randomly selected sale in this sample will fall between $80,000 and $100,000.

Confidence Level

Using statistical inference and the laws of probability for a normal distribution, the previous examples have shown how confidence intervals can be constructed for a sample when normally distributed data have been assumed or approximated. These calculations may be valuable in loan administration, housing development, appraising, and other decision-making situations involving real estate.

The examples have illustrated that, with 36 sales as a sample, an appraiser can state with a 95% degree of confidence that any sale randomly selected from the population will fall between $73,333 and $100,645. Similarly, there is a 68% level of confidence that a given sale will fall between $80,161 and $93,817.

These measures may be meaningful when used in conjunction with other statistical conclusions. However, they depend on how accurately the estimated mean represents the true population mean, so some confidence in the reliability of the mean must be established. Regardless of the size of the population, there is a specific sample size that will permit a certain level of confidence in the estimated mean.

For the 36 house sales, the standard deviation for price has been calculated as $6,828. The arithmetic mean is $86,989, or approximately $87,000. If an appraiser wants to be 95% certain that the true mean is within $1,000 of the estimated mean of $86,989—i.e., between $86,000 and $88,000—the necessary sample size can be calculated with the following formula.

$$n = \frac{z^2 s^2}{e^2}$$

$$n = \frac{(1.96)^2 \, (\$6,828)^2}{(\$1,000)^2} = 179 \text{ sales}$$

where n = sample size required

z = Z statistic at 95% confidence level

s = standard deviation of the sample

e = required maximum difference in the mean

Thus, with a sample of 179 sales, the required level of confidence could be met. Similarly, for a confidence interval of not more than $1,500, the calculations would be

$$n = \frac{(1.96)^2 \, (\$6,828)^2}{(\$1,500)^2} = 80 \text{ sales}$$

Using the original sample of 36 sales, an appraiser may want to know the limits within which the true population mean may fall at a 95% confidence level. By substitution

$$e^2 = \frac{z^2 s^2}{n}$$

and

$$e^2 = \frac{(1.96)^2 \, (\$6,828)^2}{36} = \$4,975,041$$

$$e = \$4,975,041 = \$2,230$$

Thus, the appraiser can be 95% certain that the true population mean falls between $84,759 and $89,219.

Although calculations such as these may not seem to be directly related to day-to-day appraising, professional appraisers have a continuing interest in obtaining adequate data and understanding the markets in which they appraise. Statistical calculations can be useful in quantifying change and performing the neighborhood analyses that are essential to value estimation. Many appraisers routinely analyze the inferences that can be drawn from measures such as the standard deviations of raw and adjusted sale or rental data. These calculations are also applied in appraisal review, loan underwriting, and other analyses.

REGRESSION ANALYSIS

Regression analysis is another technique used by appraisers to analyze market data. It can be applied to estimate value and to isolate and test the significance of specific value determinants.

Simple Linear Regression Analysis

To estimate a probable sale price in the market, it is seldom sufficient to develop a sample of sales, calculate the standard deviation, and base an estimate on this evidence. In most cases the range of values at the confidence level required is too broad to be useful. However, the accuracy of an estimate can be substantially increased by considering one or more characteristics of the sale properties in addition to their sale prices.

In simple linear regression analysis, one independent variable, or property characteristic, is used to reflect a relationship that changes on a straight-line basis. In other words, a change in the independent variable is reflected in the same proportion in the dependent variable, which is unknown. The basic regression equation is

$$Y_c = a + bX,$$

where Y_c is the predicted value of the dependent variable; a is the constant; b is the coefficient, or multiplier, for the independent variable; and X is the value of the variable. If, for example, the independent variable is the square foot area of a building and the dependent variable is its sale price, the simple linear regression equation $Y_c = 10,000 + 45X$ means that the sale price of the building is predicted to be $10,000 plus $45 times its square foot area.

To find the constant (a) the data for this regression must be graphed. Increasing square foot areas are indicated along the horizontal axis of the graph and increasing sale prices are indicated along the vertical axis. Then a number of sales are plotted on the graph and a line that evenly divides these points is drawn. This is the regression line, and its slope is the b coefficient. The point on the vertical axis of the graph at which the regression begins is the intercept, or the constant symbolized as a. In other words, this is a base value that represents all positive and negative factors that are *not* explained by the equation and to which the coefficients, or adjustment factors, are added.

Another important statistic that results from a simple linear regression is the coefficient of determination (r^2). This statistic represents the approximate percentage of variation in the dependent variable, which is explained by the equation and is one measure of the efficacy of the regression. When a regression is performed on an electronic, hand-held calculator, the coefficient of determination given is unadjusted for degrees of freedom (i.e., the number of observations minus the number of variables). This adjustment should be applied to the resulting coefficient of determination:

$$r^2 = 1 - (1-r^2) \ (n-1/n-2)$$

The standard error of the estimate is another measure of how well the regression fits. It is expressed as S_{yx} and represents the remaining dispersion in the data after the regression equation is applied. The b coefficient also has a t value. The t value is the coefficient expressed as a ratio to its standard deviation; it is a measure of the significance of the coefficient. The precise degree of significance represented by a particular t value depends on several factors and must be calculated. As a general rule, however, coefficients with t values greater than 2 are usually significant at a reasonably high confidence level.

Simple regression analysis is particularly useful when one element is overwhelmingly important in determining a property's sale price. Furthermore, this technique allows appraisers to analyze the relationships between real estate values and the significance of their various components.

Example of Simple Linear Regression

Using the 36 house sales analyzed earlier, simple linear regression can be used to demonstrate the apparent relationship between the sale price of a property and its living area in square feet. The gross living area (*GLA*) of each of the 36 houses is shown in Table B.3. Most appraisers would only analyze properties with the same approximate square foot area as the subject property and disregard the other sales.

Table B.3   Comparable Sales Data Set for Simple Regression Analysis

Sale	*GLA* in Square Feet	Sale Price	Price per Square Foot *GLA*
1	1,321	$76,000	$57.53
2	1,372	88,000	64.14
3	1,394	78,000	55.95
4	1,403	74,600	53.17
5	1,457	85,800	58.89
6	1,472	87,400	59.38
7	1,475	84,000	56.95
8	1,479	85,600	57.88
9	1,503	72,000	47.90
10	1,512	77,200	51.06
11	1,515	82,000	54.13
12	1,535	79,000	51.47
13	1,535	87,800	57.20
14	1,577	91,000	57.70
15	1,613	90,000	55.80
16	1,640	79,800	48.66
17	1,666	91,000	54.62
18	1,681	79,800	47.47
19	1,697	87,200	51.38
20	1,703	87,000	51.09
21	1,706	89,800	52.64
22	1,709	90,600	53.01
23	1,709	93,800	54.89
24	1,720	93,800	54.53
25	1,732	82,000	47.34
26	1,749	97,200	55.57
27	1,771	97,200	54.88
28	1,777	86,000	48.40
29	1,939	87,800	45.28
30	1,939	90,000	46.42
31	1,939	90,000	46.42
32	1,939	90,000	46.42
33	1,939	96,600	49.82
34	1,940	87,800	45.26
35	2,014	98,800	49.06
36	2,065	97,000	46.97

The appraiser is valuing a 1,375-sq.-ft. dwelling, so sales 1, 2, and 3 are most similar in terms of size. Their prices are reported as $57.53, $64.14, and $55.95 per square foot, respectively. The other sales may provide a clue to the "right answer," but they do little to resolve the discrepancy between these figures. Adjustments could be made for other differences in the properties, but complications would develop if multiple adjustments produced overlapping effects.

Sales 1, 2, and 3 indicate a price range of $55.95 to $64.14 per square foot; when these figures are applied to the 1,375-sq.-ft. area of the subject property, a value range of $76,931 to $88,192 is indicated. (These figures would be rounded in the appraiser's report.) The remaining market information cannot be used effectively in traditional appraisal analysis except perhaps to reinforce the appraiser's judgment.

With simple linear regression, however, more of the market data can be analyzed. To apply the formula $Y_c = a + bX$, the 36 sales were analyzed with a calculator and produced the following figures.

a = $49,261
b = $22.59
r = 0.6599 (simple correlation coefficient)
r^2 = 0.4354 (adjusted coefficient of determination)

Thus, for the 1,375-sq.-ft. property being appraised,

Y_c = $49,261 + $22.59 × 1,375
Y_c = $80,322, or $58.42 per square foot

The 36 sales are plotted on the graph shown in Figure B.2 and the calculated regression line is indicated. The graph also shows the standard error of the estimate, which allows the appraiser to construct confidence intervals around the regression line. The calculations in this example produce a standard error estimate of $5,205. When this figure is applied to the property being appraised, the appraiser can state that 36 sales in the market support an estimate of $80,300 for the appraised property, based only on a comparison of their square foot area. Moreover, at a 68% confidence level, the market price should fall between $80,300 + $5,205—i.e., from $75,095 to $85,505. At a 95% confidence level, the price should fall between $80,300 + 2 × $5,205, or from $69,890 to $90,710.

Although other statistical measures such as the standard error of the forecast (sf) may be used, most appraisers would consider this analysis to be sufficient and reasonably representative of most single-family market situations. Although a more refined analysis of these data could be performed, this example illustrates a simple application of a regression technique. The standard error of the forecast for the appraised property could be calculated as follows:

$$Sf = S_{yx} \sqrt{1 + \frac{1}{n} + \frac{(X_K - \bar{X})^2}{(X - X)^2}}$$

$$Sf = 5,205 \sqrt{1 + \frac{1}{36} + \frac{(1720-1670)^2}{1,469,045}}$$

$$Sf = 5,281$$

Applying this adjustment to the standard error makes only a small change because the measure of value (i.e., square footage) of the subject property is quite close to the mean square footage of the sample data. The greater the difference between the appraised property and the mean of the sample in regard to any property attribute, the more this distortion affects the standard error as a measure of variation in the regression prediction.

Multiple Regression Analysis

Multiple regression analysis is performed with the same basic methods as simple linear regression, but the analysis is expanded to include more than one independent variable. Some hand-held calculators are preprogrammed or can be programmed to perform regressions using two or three independent variables, but multiple regressions are generally performed on a computer. Stepwise regression is an improvement on the standard regression procedure because variables can be added or removed from the regression equation depending on their degree of explanatory power. This type of regression produces an optimum combination of variables by retaining only the most significant.

Example of Stepwise Multiple Regression Analysis[1]

Assume that an appraiser is asked to appraise a 7,575-sq.-ft. lot improved with a recently constructed residence. The house contains 1,720 square feet of living area, and has three bedrooms and two full baths. This house has no porch or swimming pool, but some swimming pools are found in the neighborhood. The dwelling has central air conditioning and its physical characteristics are similar to those of other properties in the neighborhood. There is an attached, two-car garage.

After inspection of the property and the collection and verification of comparable sales data, stepwise multiple regression analysis is selected for use in the sales comparison approach to value.

Figure B.3 shows a computer printout of the 36 sales selected for the initial analysis. These sales were randomly selected from the total data file after the

---

1. Figures B.3 through B.13 were adapted by Realty Researchers of Birmingham, Alabama from a model developed by Valuation Systems Company, Tulsa, Oklahoma. They are used with permission.

Figure B.2   Plot of Sales, Regression Line, and Standard Error for 36 Sales

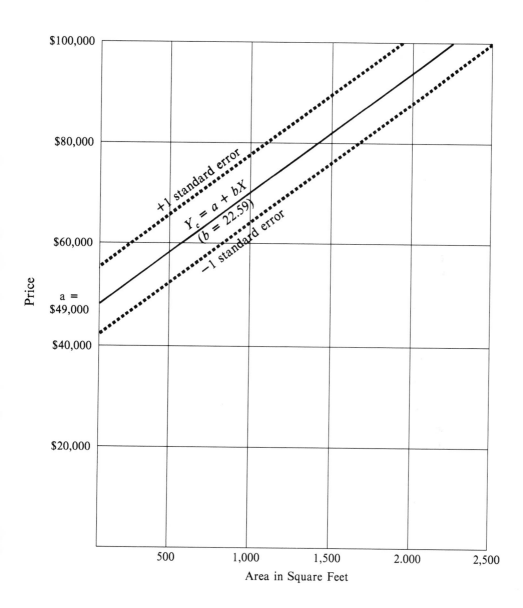

appraiser identified the independent variables; the presence of a porch, number of bedrooms, lot size, garage size, living area, and any time parameters were considered to be the essential elements of the search. As indicated in the last column of the printout, sale price was selected as the dependent variable for multiple regression analysis.

Figure B.4 is a summary of the arithmetic means of each of the variables and their standard deviations. A simple correlation matrix of the calculated interaction among each of the variables is also shown.

Each step of the multiple regression analysis applied to the comparable sales data is summarized in Figure B.5. After the initial regression equation is calculated by computer, as shown in Step 5 of the figure, the equation is used to calculate the expected prices of the 36 comparable sale properties. Actual sale prices are compared with estimated sale prices for each comparable and the differences are shown in Figure B.6 as the "residuals." The calculated percentages of error in the estimate are indicated and the magnitude of the error is expressed in the number of standard deviations of the dependent variable. In this projection of actual comparable sales information, only two sales were found to have more than a 10% error and most have less than 5%.

The percentage of error in the residuals is shown in Figure B.7, which is a dynamic plot of residual error. The lowest amount of error is shown on the left side of the plot and the highest error is indicated on the right.

Next the regression equation is run again, deleting the sales that produced the highest amount of error and those that were not arm's-length transactions or involved unconventional financing terms. Appraisers should use extreme caution in discarding any observation in a regression. The basic objective of regression analysis is to account for price variations, and this objective can be thwarted if too many observations are discarded in an effort to retain only the most comparable sales. The results of the second run of the equation are shown in Figures B.8 through B.12. After the least comparable sales are deleted, the second run produces a maximum residual error of 3.44% of the actual price.

The appraiser recognizes and accepts the validity and statistical reliability of the analysis, so the computer can now be used to produce a final indication of value using the stepwise multiple regression analysis procedure. The final results of the projection for the property being appraised are shown in Figure B.13. The final projection indicates an estimated price that is essentially equal to the actual price of the property in a recent sale and establishes, at a 95% confidence interval, a range of approximately + $4,000 as a reasonable price for the property appraised.

Nonlinear Regression Analysis

Most appraisal data do not reflect straight-line relationships, but appraisers often deal with short segments of a curve so tools such as linear regression and correlation can be used. However, inferences can be distorted when linearity is assumed for data that are clearly nonlinear. Fortunately, many sets of curvilinear data can be transformed rather easily and processed as if they were linear.

Figure B.3   Selected Sales—First Analysis

```
STEPWISE MULTIPLE REGRESSION ANALYSIS


OBSERVATIONS
```

OBS NUM ***	PROPERTY I.D. # *************	1 PORCH *****	2 BDRMS *****	3 LT SZ *****	4 GAR A *****	5 LIV A *****	DEP VAR. PRICE *****
				INDEPENDENT VARIABLE			
1	6358500000230	1	3	8100	468	1666	91000
2	6358500000290	1	3	8100	484	1457	35800
3	6358500000110	1	3	7575	520	1720	93300
4	6358500000270	3	3	9936	448	1749	97200
5	6358500000120	1	3	7568	459	1709	93800
6	6358500000150	3	4	10002	501	2014	98800
7	6358500000100	1	3	7560	459	1709	90600
8	6358500000070	1	3	10781	449	1771	97200
9	6358500000140	4	2	9033	421	1479	85600
10	6594300000220	1	3	7861	444	1939	97800
11	6594300000150	1	3	13040	444	1939	90000
12	6594300000300	1	3	7700	444	1940	97800
13	6594300000250	3	3	9800	444	1939	90000
14	6594300000010	1	3	8400	459	1706	89800
15	6594300000100	1	3	11085	444	1939	90000
16	6594300000110	3	3	11022	444	1939	96600
17	6594300000080	1	3	19300	479	1681	79800
18	6268800040010	1	3	9191	441	1475	84000
19	6268800010070	1	3	8500	430	1515	82000
20	6268800010120	3	3	8800	441	1697	97200
21	6268800030090	1	3	7700	451	1732	82000
22	6268800030060	3	3	8580	524	1613	90000
23	6473900110150	0	3	11000	419	1777	86000
24	6473900600020	3	3	7125	422	1512	77200
25	6473900300060	3	3	7500	421	1403	74600
26	6473900700120	1	3	8040	454	1703	87000
27	6473900300160	1	3	7763	469	1503	72000
28	6473900500140	3	3	7125	458	1577	91000
29	6473900500080	3	3	7600	430	1394	78000
30	6473900050060	2	2	7410	455	1372	88000
31	6473900010570	3	3	8036	477	1472	97400
32	6473900010020	1	2	7500	460	1321	76000
33	6473900010250	1	3	7995	466	2065	97000
34	6473900010290	3	3	7500	471	1535	87800
35	6473900020060	3	3	8000	471	153!	79000
36	6473900110100	1	3	11000	427	1640	79800

Figure B.4 Means, Standard Deviations, and Simple Correlation Coefficients of Variables—First Analysis

```
MEANS

VARIABLE NO.   1 - PORCH =        1.8055
VARIABLE NO.   2 - BDRMS =        2.9444
VARIABLE NO.   3 - LT SZ =    8,978.5555
VARIABLE NO.   4 - GAR A =       455.5000
VARIABLE NO.   5 - LIV A =     1,670.4722
VARIABLE NO.   6 - PRICE =     86988.9000


STANDARD  DEVIATIONS

VARIABLE NO.   1 - PORCH =        1.0642
VARIABLE NO.   2 - BDRMS =        0.3333
VARIABLE NO.   3 - LT SZ =    2,277.2125
VARIABLE NO.   4 - GAR A =       25.0855
VARIABLE NO.   5 - LIV A =      199.4894
VARIABLE NO.   6 - PRICE =     6828.0200


SIMPLE  CORRELATION  COEFFICIENTS

    1        2        3        4        5     DEP VAR
 PORCH    BDRMS    LT SZ    GAR A    LIV A    PRICE

1.0000  -0.0313  -0.1746  -0.0069  -0.2225   0.0224
         0.9999   0.1511   0.2596   0.5082   0.2909
                  1.0000  -0.0168   0.3232   0.0686
                           0.9999   0.0720   0.3210
                                    1.0000   0.6598
                                             0.9999
```

Figure B.5   Summary of Comparable Sales—First Analysis

```
STEP NUMBER 1   ENTER VARIABLE 5

STANDARD ERROR OF ESTIMATE:   5205.38
ADJ COEFF DETERM:           .418814
DEGREES OF FREEDOM:          34
F RATIO:                     26.2216
CONSTANT TERM:               49260.5

VARIABLE        COEFFICIENT    S.D. OF COEFF.    T VALUE
  5 LIV A        22.5855        4.41062          5.1207

STEP NUMBER 2   ENTER VARIABLE 4

STANDARD ERROR OF ESTIMATE:   4919.33
ADJ COEFF DETERM:           .480935
DEGREES OF FREEDOM:          33
F RATIO:                     17.2144
CONSTANT TERM:               16311.5

VARIABLE        COEFFICIENT    S.D. OF COEFF.    T VALUE
  4 CAR A        74.8245        33.2339          2.25145
  5 LIV A        21.9069        4.17913          5.24197

STEP NUMBER 3   ENTER VARIABLE 1

STANDARD ERROR OF ESTIMATE:   4843.79
ADJ COEFF DETERM:           .496755
DEGREES OF FREEDOM:          32
F RATIO:                     12.5162
CONSTANT TERM:               12236

VARIABLE        COEFFICIENT    S.D. OF COEFF.    T VALUE
  1 PORCH        1126.44        789.177          1.42737
  4 CAR A        74.3876        32.7249          2.27312
  5 LIV A        23.2482        4.22089          5.5079

STEP NUMBER 4   ENTER VARIABLE 2

STANDARD ERROR OF ESTIMATE:   4808.05
ADJ COEFF DETERM:           .504154
DEGREES OF FREEDOM:          31
F RATIO:                     9.89659
CONSTANT TERM:               12661.4

VARIABLE        COEFFICIENT    S.D. OF COEFF.    T VALUE
  1 PORCH        1220.57        787.172          1.55058
  2 NBRMS       -3580.89        2945.92         -1.21554
  4 CAR A        85.0186        33.6402          2.52729
  5 LIV A        26.3048        4.88641          5.38325
```

Figure B.5   Continued

```
STEP NUMBER 5   ENTER VARIABLE 3

STANDARD ERROR OF ESTIMATE:   4803.71
ADJ COEFF DETERM:             .505047
DEGREES OF FREEDOM:           30
F RATIO:                      8.14275
CONSTANT TERM:                14710.9

VARIABLE         COEFFICIENT     S.D. OF COEFF.     T VALUE
  1 PORCH         1130.22          791.362          1.4282
  2 BDRMS        -3563.51         2943.32          -1.21071
  3 L1 S7         -.389959          .379485         -1.0276
  4 GAR A          83.5747         33.6393          2.48444
  5 LIV A          27.6346          5.05062          5.47153
```

Figure B.6   Comparison of Actual and Estimated Sale Prices of Comparables Showing Residuals and Percentages of Error— First Analysis

```
                    RESIDUAL ANALYSIS


OBSERVATION   PREDICTED Y     ACTUAL Y    RESIDUAL  % ERROR   # STD DEV
-----------   -----------     --------    --------  -------   ---------
         1       87144.10     91000.00     3855.87     4.24       0.56
         2       82705.70     85800.00     3094.30     3.61       0.45
         3       93187.00     93800.00      612.98     0.65       0.09
         4       89310.80     97200.00     7889.22     8.12       1.16
         5       87787.70     93800.00     6012.30     6.41       0.88
         6       97474.20     98800.00     1325.84     1.34       0.19
         7       87790.80     90600.00     2809.18     3.10       0.41
         8       87412.40     97200.00     9787.64    10.07       1.43
         9       84638.80     85600.00      961.21     1.12       0.14
        10       92775.80     87800.00    -4975.78    -5.67      -0.73
        11       90756.20     90000.00     -756.19    -0.84      -0.11
        12       92866.20     87800.00    -5066.20    -5.77      -0.74
        13       94280.10     90000.00    -4280.09    -4.76      -0.63
        14       87380.40     89800.00     2419.65     2.69       0.35
        15       91518.60     90000.00    -1518.55    -1.69      -0.22
        16       93803.60     96600.00     2796.44     2.89       0.41
        17       84110.40     79800.00    -4310.43    -5.40      -0.63
        18       79184.00     84000.00     4816.04     5.73       0.71
        19       79639.50     82000.00     2360.52     2.88       0.35
        20       87731.80     87200.00     -531.75    -0.61      -0.08
        21       87703.20     82000.00    -5703.23    -6.96      -0.84
        22       92432.90     90000.00    -2432.95    -2.70      -0.36
        23       83855.30     86000.00     2144.70     2.49       0.31
        24       81684.60     77200.00    -4484.62    -5.81      -0.66
        25       78442.60     74600.00    -3842.64    -5.15      -0.56
        26       87020.00     87000.00      -19.96    -0.02      -0.00
        27       82854.70     72000.00   -10854.70   -15.08      -1.59
        28       86489.60     91000.00     4510.45     4.96       0.66
        29       78907.10     78000.00     -907.10    -1.16      -0.13
        30       82895.90     88000.00     5104.11     5.80       0.75
        31       84820.60     87400.00     2579.41     2.95       0.38
        32       80739.10     76000.00    -4739.09    -6.24      -0.69
        33       98044.10     97000.00    -1044.13    -1.08      -0.15
        34       86269.10     87800.00     1530.87     1.74       0.22
        35       86074.20     79000.00    -7074.16    -8.95      -1.04
        36       81868.20     79800.00    -2068.18    -2.59      -0.30
```

Figure B.7   Residuals Percentage of Error—First Analysis

```
                         RESIDUALS  AS  A  PERCENT  OF  ACTUAL
6358500000230 *                      4.23                                    *   1
6358500000290 *                     3.60                                     *   2
6358500000110 *        0.65                                                  *   3
6358500000270 *                                      8.11                    *   4
6358500000120 *                           6.40                               *   5
6358500000150 *          1.34                                                *   6
6358500000100 *                    3.10                                      *   7
6358500000070 *                                           10.06             *   8
6358500000140 *          1.12                                                *   9
6594300000220 *                           -5.66                             *   10
6594300000150 *       -0.84                                                  *   11
6594300003300 *                           -5.77                             *   12
6594300000250 *                         -4.75                               *   13
6594300000010 *                 2.69                                        *   14
6594300000100 *        -1.68                                                *   15
6594300000110 *                 2.89                                        *   16
6594300000080 *                           -5.40                             *   17
6268800040010 *                        5.73                                 *   18
6268800010070 *                 2.87                                        *   19
6268800010120 *       -0.60                                                 *   20
6268800030090 *                               -6.95                         *   21
6268800030060 *            -2.70                                            *   22
6473900110150 *                 2.49                                        *   23
6473900600020 *                           -5.80                             *   24
6473900300060 *                           -5.15                             *   25
6473900700120 *     -0.02                                                   *   26
6473900300160 *                                           -15.07           *   27
6473900500140 *                          4.95                               *   28
6473900500080 *        -1.16                                                *   29
6473900050060 *                        5.80                                 *   30
6473900010570 *               2.95                                          *   31
6473900010020 *                           -6.23                             *   32
6473900010250 *        -1.07                                                *   33
6473900010290 *          1.74                                                *   34
6473900200060 *                              -8.95                          *   35
6473900110100 *            -2.59                                            *   36
```

Figure B.8   Selected Sales—Second Analysis

STEPWISE MULTIPLE REGRESSION
ANALYSIS

OBSERVATIONS

OBS NUM ***	PROPERTY I.D. # **************	INDEPENDENT VARIABLE					DEP VAR.
		1 PORCH *****	2 BDRMS *****	3 LT SZ *****	4 GAR A *****	5 LIV A *****	PRICE *****
2	6358500000290	1	3	8100	484	1457	85800
3	6358500000110	1	3	7575	520	1720	93800
6	6358500000150	3	4	10002	501	2014	98800
7	6358500000100	1	3	7560	459	1709	90600
9	6358500000140	4	2	9033	421	1479	85600
11	6594300000150	1	3	13040	444	1939	90000
14	6594300000010	1	3	8400	459	1706	89800
15	6594300000100	1	3	11085	444	1939	90000
16	6594300000110	3	3	11022	444	1939	96600
19	6268800010070	1	3	8500	430	1515	82000
20	6268800010120	3	3	8800	441	1697	87200
22	6268800030060	3	3	8580	524	1613	90000
23	6473900110150	0	3	11000	419	1777	86000
26	6473900700120	1	3	8040	454	1703	87000
29	6473900500080	3	3	7600	430	1394	78000
31	6473900010570	3	3	8036	477	1472	87400
33	6473900010250	1	3	7995	466	2065	97000
34	6473900010290	3	3	7500	471	1535	87800
36	6473900110100	1	3	11000	427	1640	79800

Figure B.9　Means, Standard Deviations, and Simple Correlation Coefficients of Variables—Second Analysis

```
MEANS

VARIABLE NO.  1 - PORCH =       1.8421
VARIABLE NO.  2 - BDRMS =       3.0000
VARIABLE NO.  3 - LT SZ =   9,098.3157
VARIABLE NO.  4 - GAR A =     458.6842
VARIABLE NO.  5 - LIV A =   1,700.6842
VARIABLE NO.  6 - PRICE =    88589.5000


STANDARD  DEVIATIONS

VARIABLE NO.  1 - PORCH =       1.1672
VARIABLE NO.  2 - BDRMS =       0.3333
VARIABLE NO.  3 - LT SZ =   1,605.3780
VARIABLE NO.  4 - GAR A =      31.2908
VARIABLE NO.  5 - LIV A =     202.1781
VARIABLE NO.  6 - PRICE =    5479.8900


SIMPLE  CORRELATION  COEFFICIENTS

     1       2       3       4       5    DEP VAR
   PORCH   BDRMS   LT SZ   GAR A   LIV A   PRICE

 1.0000 -0.1427 -0.1895  0.1232 -0.2878  0.0431
         0.9999  0.1005  0.4261  0.4410  0.4014
                 0.9999 -0.3764  0.5334  0.1066
                         0.9999  0.0870  0.5390
                                 1.0000  0.7721
                                         1.0000
```

Figure B.10   Summary of Comparable Sales—Second Analysis

```
STEP NUMBER 1   ENTER VARIABLE 5

STANDARD ERROR OF ESTIMATE:   3583.14
ADJ COEFF DETERM:          .572451
DEGREES OF FREEDOM:        17
F RATIO:                   25.1005
CONSTANT TERM:             52997

VARIABLE        COEFFICIENT    S.D. OF COEFF.    T VALUE
  5 LIV A         20.9283        4.17728         5.01004

STEP NUMBER 2   ENTER VARIABLE 4

STANDARD ERROR OF ESTIMATE:   2462.36
ADJ COEFF DETERM:          .798089
DEGREES OF FREEDOM:        16
F RATIO:                   36.5742
CONSTANT TERM:             16714.5

VARIABLE        COEFFICIENT    S.D. OF COEFF.    T VALUE
  4 GAR A          83.2604       18.6186         4.47189
  5 LIV A          19.8066        2.88159        6.87348

STEP NUMBER 3   ENTER VARIABLE 1

STANDARD ERROR OF ESTIMATE:   2222.09
ADJ COEFF DETERM:          .835571
DEGREES OF FREEDOM:        15
F RATIO:                   31.4899
CONSTANT TERM:             14425.3

VARIABLE        COEFFICIENT    S.D. OF COEFF.    T VALUE
  1 PORCH        1022.45        474.292          2.15573
  4 GAR A          77.5591       17.0087         4.55996
  5 LIV A          21.5828        2.72783        7.91208

STEP NUMBER 4   ENTER VARIABLE 3

STANDARD ERROR OF ESTIMATE:   2100.97
ADJ COEFF DETERM:          .853006
DEGREES OF FREEDOM:        14
F RATIO:                   27.1136
CONSTANT TERM:             22393.8

VARIABLE        COEFFICIENT    S.D. OF COEFF.    T VALUE
  1 PORCH        1051.87        448.789          2.3438
  3 LOT SZ       -.703438        .421954        -1.6671
  4 GAR A          62.0166       18.5888         3.33624
  5 LIV A          24.8207        3.22866        7.68762
```

Figure B.10   Continued

```
STEP NUMBER 5   ENTER VARIABLE 2

STANDARD ERROR OF ESTIMATE:   2025.46
ADJ COEFF DETERM:             .863383
DEGREES OF FREEDOM:           13
F RATIO:                      23.751
CONSTANT TERM:                22030.7

VARIABLE        COEFFICIENT     S.D. OF COEFF.     T VALUE
 1 PORCH         990.254         434.779          2.2776
 2 BDRMS        -2559.79         1782.04         -1.43644
 3 LOT SZ        -.670822        .407421         -1.64651
 4 GAR A         73.7264         19.6877          3.7448
 5 LIV A         26.2837         3.275            8.02554
```

Figure B.11 Comparison of Actual and Estimated Sale Prices of Comparables Showing Residuals and Percentages of Error— Second Analysis

```
                  RESIDUAL ANALYSIS


OBSERVATION   PREDICTED Y      ACTUAL Y    RESIDUAL  % ERROR   # STD DEV
-------------  -------------    --------    --------  --------  ---------
           1     83886.90      85800.00     1913.15     2.23      0.35
           2     93805.80      93800.00       -5.80    -0.01     -0.00
           3     97925.00      98800.00      874.97     0.89      0.16
           4     89029.40      90600.00     1570.57     1.73      0.29
           5     84725.00      85600.00      874.99     1.02      0.16
           6     90292.70      90000.00     -292.68    -0.33     -0.05
           7     88387.10      89800.00     1412.91     1.57      0.26
           8     91604.10      90000.00    -1604.13    -1.78     -0.29
           9     93626.90      96600.00     2973.09     3.08      0.54
          10     81161.80      82000.00      838.25     1.02      0.15
          11     88535.60      87200.00    -1335.63    -1.53     -0.24
          12     92594.70      90000.00    -2594.67    -2.88     -0.47
          13     84569.80      86000.00     1430.23     1.66      0.26
          14     88181.10      87000.00    -1181.09    -1.36     -0.22
          15     80565.70      78000.00    -2565.67    -3.29     -0.47
          16     85788.50      87400.00     1611.54     1.84      0.29
          17     98610.70      97000.00    -1610.70    -1.66     -0.29
          18     87361.50      87800.00      438.46     0.50      0.08
          19     82549.00      79800.00    -2748.98    -3.44     -0.50
```

Figure B.12   Residuals Percentage of Error—Second Analysis

RESIDUALS AS A PERCENT OF ACTUAL

Figure B.13   Final Summary of Data Analyzed

```
          HOME  FEDERAL  SAVINGS  AND  LOAN

              MARKET  DATA  ANALYSIS


PROPERTY ADDRESS   9290  132 ST  NO

APPRAISER                           DATE -

PARAMETERS FOR COMPARABLES SEARCH:

PORCHES    GENERAL    BEDROOMS   GENERAL    LOT SIZE    GENERAL
GARAGE AREA GENERAL    LIVING AREA GENERAL


COMPARISON GRID:
                                    COMPARABLE PROPERTIES
                     PROPERTY   **************************************
      ITEM           APPRAISED      #1           #2          #3
***************      *********   **********   **********   **********
DATE SOLD            10 80        9 82         10 82        10 82
LOT SIZE             7,575        8,400        11,000       11,000
CONSTRUCTION DATE    1976         1976         1972         1972
PORCHES              NONE         NONE         UNKWN        NONE
BEDROOMS             THREE        THREE        THREE        THREE
BATHS                TWO          TWO          TWO          TWO
LIVING AREA          1,720        1,706        1,777        1,640
POOL                 NONE         NONE         NONE         NONE
PARKING              2 GR'GE      2 GR'GE      2 GR'GE      2 GR'GE
COOLING              CNTRL        CNTRL        CNTRL        CNTRL
FINANCING            CNVTL        CNVTL        UNKWN        UNKWN
EXTRAS               N            N            N            N
SALES PRICE          $  93900     $  83800     $  96000     $  79900

ADDRESSES            # 1   9002  127LANE NO
                     # 2  11455  131 AVE  N
                     # 3  11450  132 AVE  N
```

(Continued)

Figure B.13   Continued

```
        STEPWISE  MULTIPLE  REGRESSION
             VALUATION  ANALYSIS

SUMMARY DATA FOR ALL COMPARABLE SALES ANALYZED:
    TOTAL NUMBER OF SALES ANALYZED . . . . . . . . . . . . .    19
    MEAN SALES PRICE FOR ALL SALES . . . . . . . . . . . $  88590
    STANDARD DEVIATION IN PRICE FOR ALL SALES . . . . . .  $  5480

SUMMARY DATA FOR THE MULTIPLE REGRESSION ANALYSIS:
    ADJ COEFF DETERM . . . . . . . . . . . . . . . . . . .  0.8634
    STANDARD ERROR OF THE ESTIMATE . . . . . . . . .       2025.46
    NUMBER OF VARIABLES IN REGRESSION EQUATION . . . . . . . .    5
    DEGREES OF FREEDOM . . . . . . . . . . . . . . . . .         13
    F RATIO  . . . . . . . . . . . . . . . . . . . .       23.7492

APPLICATION OF REGRESSION RESULTS FOR PROPERTY VALUATION:

    VARIABLE   SIGNIFICANCE    MULTIPLIER    DATA FOR    EXTENSION
     NAME       (T VALUE)      CALCULATED    SUBJECT    FOR SUBJECT
    ********   ************    **********    ********   ***********
    PORCH         2.2775         990.254      1.0000     $    990
    BDRMS        -1.4363       - 2559.79      3.0000     $-   7679
    LT SZ        -1.6463        0.670822   7575.0000     $-   5081
    GAR A         3.7445         73.7264    520.0000     $   38338
    LIV A         8.0251         26.2837   1720.0000     $   45208

    CONSTANT TERM OF THE REGRESSION EQUATION  . . . . . $   22031
    INDICATED VALUE FOR THE PROPERTY APPRAISED . . . . . $   93807

CONFIDENCE INTERVALS FOR THE VALUE ESTIMATE:

    DEGREE OF     RANGE OF CONFIDENCE     REASONABLE VALUE INTERVAL
    CONFIDENCE    IN PERCENT  IN DOLLARS    MINIMUM   TO   MAXIMUM
    **********    **********  **********   ************************
     68.26%       +/- 0.0228  +/- $  2025   $  91782       $  95832
     95.44%       +/- 0.0457  +/- $  4050   $  89757       $  97857
```

Example of Nonlinear Regression Analysis

The following table is part of an analysis that compares a county's retail sales per capita with the per capita sales of the state and the entire country.

Retail Sales per Capita—Metropolitan County

Year	Sales
1979	$4,470
1978	4,784
1977	4,301
1976	3,912
1975	3,395
1974	3,059
1973	2,635
1972	2,254

Source: Calculated from population and retail sales data in various issues of *Sales and Marketing Management, Survey of Buying Power*, 1973 to 1980.

The objective of the analysis was to predict the county's retail sales per capita for 1980 before the data were published. A basic calculation indicates a simple linear average growth rate of 14% per year. Projecting this average would indicate retail sales of $5,098 in 1980. However, this type of figure, like the Consumer Price Index, relates to the preceding value, not to the beginning value; therefore, the relationship is nonlinear.

Several types of curves can be fitted to this analysis using a hand-held calculator. First, the estimate can be improved somewhat by using linear regression to separate the slope and intercept figures. Moreover, this is not an extremely long-term trend. Simple linear regression produces these results: $a = -23,812.4$, $b = 363.095$, $r^2 = 0.942$, $S_{yx} = 219.07$, and predicted Y (retail sales per capita for 1980) = $5,235.

The exponential curve, expressed as

$$Y = ae^{bx}$$

reflects a positive or negative compounding over time. This equation is transformed into a linear format by substituting the natural logarithms of the Ys, the dependent variable, and entering the Xs in their original form. The equation becomes

$$ln\ Y = bX + ln\ a$$

Fitting the data to this type of curve yields the following results: $a = 1.13776$, $b = 0.106353$, $r^2 = 0.939$, $S_{yx} = 0.07143$, and predicted $Y = $5,638.

Another curve that may be considered when exploring nonlinear regressions on data is the logarithmic curve. The equation for this curve is

$$Y = a + b(\ln X)$$

In this equation the Xs, or independent variables, are not transformed. The natural logarithms of the Xs, the independent variables for 1972 to 1979, are used. With this nonlinear approach, the results are: $a = -115{,}052.34$; $b = 27{,}442.8$; $r^2 = 0.9538$ unadjusted, 0.9472 adjusted, and predicted $Y = \$5{,}203$.

Next the power, or geometric, curve can be used. This curve is expressed as

$$Y = ax^b$$

which may be transformed to

$$\ln Y = \ln a + b(\ln x)$$

To apply this equation the natural logarithms of both the independent and dependent variables are entered, and these data points are then regressed as if they were linear. The results of this curve are

$$Y = 2.63162E\text{-}12 \times X^{8.05383}$$

The b figure could easily be lost in a small calculator because 11 zeroes precede the first digit. The adjusted $r^2 = 0.968$, standard error $= 0.06823$, and predicted $Y = \$5{,}590$.

This nonlinear relationship may be explored in a slightly more complex form with a polynomial regression. In addition to the original Xs, this type of regression employs the specified powers of the Xs. This results in the following equation.

$$Y = a + b_1 X + b_2 X^2 + b_3 X^3 + \ldots + b_n X^n$$

The highest power used in the regression is called the *order*, or *degree*, of the equation. Using a second-order equation, the results are: constant $= 137089.9847499$, first-degree coefficient $= 3902.4547389$, second-degree coefficient $= 28.2440798$, coefficient of determination $= 0.929$, standard error $= 288.118$, and predicted $Y = \$5{,}656$.

Adding the cube of the Xs to the equation for a third-order polynomial regression produces these results: constant $= -37241.803694$, first-degree coefficient $= -376.947096$, second-degree coefficient $= 6.434948$, third-degree coefficient $= -0.056301$, $R^2 = 0.984$, standard error $= 160.889$, and predicted $Y = \$5{,}271$.

With fourth-order polynomial regression, the coefficient of determination declines to 0.979 and the standard error increases to 203.955. Although it is difficult to conceptualize exactly what the standard error measures in a fourth-order polynomial, it does indicate that the regression equation can be complicated past the point of diminishing returns.

One variation on polynomial regressions should be noted. Using the Cramer's Rule algorithm, a parabolic regression program seems to produce better results over the long term than the standard second-degree polynomial. In the present example, the results would be: constant $= -163746.7262$, first-degree coefficient $= 4073.3810$, second-degree coefficient $= -24.5714$, coefficient of determination $= 0.968$; standard error $= 163.227$, and predicted $Y = \$4,867$. It is interesting to note that the actual 1980 per capita retail sales figure was $\$4,843$; not all regression-based predictions will be this close. However, by testing the various techniques available, the validity of the work product can always be enhanced.

Appendix C
Financial
Tables

$\mathbf{T}$he formulas and financial tables presented in this appendix have been adapted from the Appraisal Institute's Capitalization Theory and Techniques course, Parts A and B, and from published financial tables.[1] Although the tables were developed for real estate appraisers, they should also prove useful to students of finance, lenders, investment consultants, and other financial analysts. Sample tables from the nine sets of financial factor tables are prefaced by the formulas, brief explanations, and practical examples. The tables illustrate continuous compounding and discounting factors; annuities changing in a constant amount; annuities changing in a constant ratio; sinking fund factors for annual payments with daily interest; the part paid off for monthly, direct-reduction loans; and straight-line J factors for income adjustment in mortgage-equity analysis.

---

1. James J. Mason, MAI, ed. and comp., *American Institute of Real Estate Appraisers Financial Tables*, rev. ed. (Chicago: American Institute of Real Estate Appraisers, with tables computed by Financial Publishing Company, 1982).

BASIC FORMULAS

Where:

I = income
R = capitalization rate
V = value
M = mortgage ratio
DCR = debt coverage ratio
F = capitalization factor (multiplier)
GIM = gross income multiplier
$EGIM$ = effective gross income multiplier
NIR = net income ratio

Subscript:
O = overall property
M = mortgage
E = equity
L = land
B = building

Basic Income/Cap Rate/Value Formulas

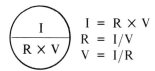

$I = R \times V$
$R = I/V$
$V = I/R$

Basic Value/Income/Factor Formulas

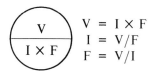

$V = I \times F$
$I = V/F$
$F = V/I$

Adaptations for Mortgage/Equity Components

Band of investment (using ratios)

$$R_O = M \times R_M + [(1 - M) \times R_E]$$
$$R_E = (R_O - M \times R_M)/(1 - M)$$

Equity residual

$$V_O = [(I_O - V_M \times R_M)/R_E] + V_M$$
$$R_E = (I_O - V_M \times R_M)/V_E$$

Mortgage residual

$$V_O = [(I_O - V_E \times R_E)/R_M] + V_E$$

Debt coverage ratio

$$R_O = DCR \times M \times R_M$$
$$DCR = R/(M \times R_M)$$
$$M = R/(DCR \times R_M)$$

Cap Rate/Factor Relationships

$$R = 1/F$$
$$R_O = NIR/GIM$$
$$R_O = NIR/EGIM$$

Note. NIR may relate to scheduled gross or effective gross income; care should be taken to ensure consistency.

Adaptations for Land/Building Components

Land residual

$$V_O = [(I_O - V_B \times R_B)/R_L] + V_B$$
$$R_L = (I_O - V_B \times R_B)/V_L$$
$$R_B = (I_O - V_L \times R_L)/V_B$$

Building residual

$$V_O = [(I_O - V_L \times R_L)/R_B] + V_L$$

Where:

PV = present value
CF = cash flow
Y = yield rate
R = capitalization rate
Δ = change
a = annualizer
$1/S_{\overline{n}|}$ = sinking fund factor
$1/n$ = 1/projection period
CR = compound rate of change
V = value

Subscript:

n = projection periods
O = overall property
I = income

Discounted Cash Flows/Present Value (DCF/PV)

$$PV = \frac{CF_1}{1 + Y} + \frac{CF_2}{(1 + Y)^2} + \frac{CF_3}{(1 + Y)^3} + \ldots + \frac{CF_n}{(1 + Y)^n}$$

Basic Cap Rate/Yield Rate/Value Change Formulas

$$R = Y - \Delta a$$
$$Y = R + \Delta a$$
$$\Delta a = Y - R$$
$$\Delta = (Y - R)/a$$

Adaptations for Common Income/Value Patterns

Pattern	Premise	Cap Rate (R)	Yield Rate (Y)	Value Change (Δ)
Perpetuity	$\Delta = O$	$R = Y$	$Y = R$	
Level annuity*	$a = 1/S_{\overline{n}|}$	$R = Y - \Delta 1/S_{\overline{n}|}$	$Y = R + \Delta 1/S_{\overline{n}|}$	$\Delta = (Y - R)/1/S_{\overline{n}|}$
Straight-line change	$a = 1/n$	$R = Y - \Delta 1/n$	$Y = R + \Delta 1/n$	$\Delta = (Y - R)/1/n$
Exponential change	$\Delta_O a = CR$	$R_O = Y_O - CR$	$Y_O = R_O + CR$	$\Delta_O = (1 + CR)^n - 1$

*Inwood premise: $1/s_{\overline{n}|}$ at Y rate; Hoskold premise: $1/S_{\overline{n}|}$ at safe rate

Straight-Line Change* in Income	Straight-Line Change* in Value	Compound Rate of Change
$\$\Delta_I = V \times \Delta 1/n \times Y$	$\$\Delta 1/n = \$\Delta_I/Y$	$CR = \sqrt[n]{FV/PV} - 1$
$\Delta_I = (Y \times \Delta 1/n)/(Y - \Delta 1/n)$	$\Delta 1/n = (Y \times \Delta_I)/(Y + \Delta_I)$	$CR = Y_o - R_o$

*In these formulas Δ_I is the ratio of one year's change in income to the first year's income.

Table Relationships

The following formulas may be used to convert the annual constant (R_M) for a monthly payment loan to the corresponding monthly functions.

Function for Monthly Frequency	Formula
Amount of $1	$S^n = R_M/(R_M - I)$
Amount of $1 per month	$S_{\overline{n}} = 12/(R_M - I)$
Sinking fund factor	$1/S_{\overline{n}} = (R_M - I)/12$
Present value of $1	$1/S_{\overline{n}} = (R_M - I)/R_M$
Present value of $1 per month	$a_{\overline{n}} = 12/R_M$
Partial payment	$1/a_{\overline{n}} = R_M/12$

In these formulas, I = nominal interest rate.

Present Value of Increasing/Decreasing Annuities

Straight-line changes

To obtain the present value of an annuity that has a starting income of *d* at the end of the first period and *increases h dollars* per period for *n* periods:

$$PV = (d + hn)a_{\overline{n}} - \frac{h(n - a_{\overline{n}})}{i}$$

To obtain the present value of an annuity that has a starting income of *d* at the end of the first period and *decreases h dollars* per period for *n* periods, simply make *h* negative in the formula.

Exponential-curve (constant-ratio) changes

To obtain the present value of an annuity that starts at $1 at the end of the first period and *increases each period* thereafter at the rate *x* for *n* periods:

$$PV = \frac{1 - (1 + x)^n/(1 + i)^n}{i - x}$$

Where i is the periodic discount rate and x is the ratio between the increase in income for any period and the income for the previous period.

To obtain the present value of an annuity that starts at \$1 at the end of the first period and *decreases each period* thereafter at rate x, simply make x negative in the formula.

Where:

r =	basic capitalization rate		
Y =	yield rate		
M =	mortgage ratio		
C =	mortgage coefficient	Subscript:	
P =	ratio paid off—mortgage	E =	equity
$1/S_{\overline{n}\rceil}$ =	sinking fund factor	M =	mortgage
R =	capitalization rate	P =	projection
$S_{\overline{n}\rceil}$ =	future value of \$1 per period	O =	overall property
Δ =	change	I =	income
J =	J factor (changing income)	1 =	1st mortgage
n =	projection period	2 =	2nd mortgage
NOI =	net operating income		
B =	mortgage balance		
I =	nominal interest rate		

Mortgage/Equity Formulas

Basic capitalization rate (r)

$$r = Y_E - MC$$
$$r = Y_E - (M_1C_1 + M_2C_2)$$

$$C = Y_E + P\,1/S_{\overline{n}\rceil} - R_M$$
$$P = (R_M - I)/(R_{MP} - I)$$
$$P = 1/S_{\overline{n}\rceil} \times S_{\overline{n}\rceil}\,P$$

Capitalization rates (R)

Level income

$$R = Y_E - MC - \Delta 1/S_{\overline{n}\rceil}$$

$$R = r - \Delta 1/S_{\overline{n}\rceil}$$

J-factor changing income

$$R_O = \frac{Y_E - MC - \Delta_O 1/S_{\overline{n}\rceil}}{1 + \Delta_I J}$$

$$R_O = \frac{r - \Delta_O\,1/S_{\overline{n}\rceil}}{1 + \Delta_I J}$$

Required change in value (Δ)

Level income   J-factor changing income

$$\Delta = \frac{r - R}{1/S_{\overline{n}|}}$$ $$\Delta_O = \frac{r - R_O(1 + \Delta_I J)}{1/S_{\overline{n}|}}$$

$$\Delta = \frac{Y_E - MC - R}{1/S_{\overline{n}|}}$$ $$*\Delta_O = \frac{r - R_O}{R_O J + 1/S_{\overline{n}|}}$$

Note. For multiple mortgage situations, insert M and C for each mortgage.

*This formula assumes value and income change at the same ratio.

Equity yield (Y_E)

Level income   J-factor changing income

$$Y_E = R_E + \Delta_E \, 1/S_{\overline{n}|}$$ $$Y_E = R_E + \Delta_E \, 1/S_{\overline{n}|} + \left[\frac{R_O \Delta_I}{1 - M} \right] J$$

Change in equity

$$\Delta_E = (\Delta_O + MP)/(1 - M) \text{ or}$$
$$\Delta_E = [V_O(1 + \Delta_O) - B - V_E]/V_E$$

Assumed mortgage situation

Level income   J-factor changing income

$$V_O = \frac{NOI + BC}{Y_E - \Delta_O 1/S_{\overline{n}|}}$$ $$V_O = \frac{NOI(1 + \Delta_I J) + BC}{Y_E - \Delta_O \, 1/S_{\overline{n}|}}$$

Mortgage/Equity Without Algebra Format

Loan ratio × annual constant	=	_____
Equity ratio × equity yield rate	= +	_____
Loan ratio × paid off loan ratio × SFF	= −	_____
Basic rate (r)	=	_____
+Dep *or* −App × SFF	= +/−	_____
Cap rate (R)	=	_____

Note. SFF is sinking fund factor at equity yield rate for projection period. Dep/App is the change in value from depreciation or appreciation during the projection period.

Where:

$$PV = \text{present value}$$
$$NPV = \text{net present value}$$
$$CF = \text{cash flow}$$
$$i = \text{discount rate in NPV formula}$$
$$n = \text{projection period}$$
$$IRR = \text{internal rate of return}$$
$$PI = \text{profitability index}$$
$$MIRR = \text{modified internal rate of return}$$
$$FVCFj = \text{future value of a series of cash flows}$$
$$i = \text{reinvestment rate in MIRR formula}$$

Subscript:
$$0 = \text{at time zero}$$
$$1 = \text{end of 1st period}$$
$$2 = \text{end of 2nd period}$$
$$3 = \text{end of 3rd period}$$
$$n = \text{end period of series}$$

Net Present Value (NPV)

$$NPV = CF_0 + \frac{CF_1}{1 + i} + \frac{CF_2}{(1 + i)^2} + \frac{CF_3}{(1 + i)^3} + \ldots + \frac{CF_n}{(1 + i)^n}$$

Internal Rate of Return (IRR)

$$\text{Where } NPV = 0; \ IRR = i$$

Profitability Index (PI)

$$PI = PV/CF_0$$

Modified Internal Rate of Return (MIRR)

$$MIRR = \sqrt[n]{\frac{FVCF_j}{CF_0}} - 1$$

$$MIRR = \sqrt[n]{\frac{CF_1(1 + i)^{n-1} + CF_2(1 + i)^{n-2} + CF_3(1 + i)^{n-3} + \ldots + CF_n}{CF_0}} - 1$$

Note. In these formulas individual CFs may be positive or negative for *PV* and *NPV* solutions; however, CF_0 is treated as a positive value for *PI* and *MIRR* solutions.

COMPOUND INTEREST (Future Value of $1)

This factor reflects the amount to which an investment or deposit will grow in a given number of time periods including the accumulation of interest at the effective rate per period. It is also known as the *amount of one.*

$$S^n = (1 + i)^n$$

Where: S^n = future value factor
          i = effective rate of interest
          n = number of compounding periods
and S^n = $(e)^{in}$ for continuous compounding
Where: S^n = future value factor
          i = nominal rate of interest
          n = number of years
          e = 2.718282

This factor is used to solve problems dealing with compound growth.

Example 1

What is the future value of $10,000 assuming interest at 6% compounded annually for 10 years?

$$\$10,000 \times 1.790848 = \$17,908.48$$

Example 2

What is the future value of $10,000 assuming interest at 6% compounded annually for 10 years and 7 months?

$$\$10,000 \times 1.790848 \times 1.035000 = \$18,535.28$$

This calculation assumes simple interest for any time that is less than one conversion period.

Example 3

A property is sold for $135,000, but five years previously it was sold for $100,000. What is the trend in its sale price expressed as a monthly compound rate of growth?

$$\$135,000 \div \$100,000 = 1.350000 \text{ (future value factor)}$$

Scan the table of future value factors, monthly frequency, for 1.350000 at five years. The closest match is found at a 6% nominal rate, so the monthly rate of growth is approximately 0.5%.

Example 4

How long would it take prices to double if a 6% rate of inflation is assumed?

$$2.00 \div 1.00 = 2.000000 \text{ (future value factor)}$$

Scan the table of future value factors at 6% nominal interest for 2.000000. Assuming annual frequency, the target is between the factors for 11 and 12 years. Visual interpolation indicates an answer of slightly less than 12 years. Mathematical straight-line interpolation produces an answer of 11.9 years.

$$(2.000000 - 1.898299)/(2.012196 - 1.898299) + 11 = 11.9 \text{ years}$$

   When money is invested or deposited at the beginning of a period in an account that bears interest at a fixed rate, it grows according to the interest rate and the number of compounding (conversion) periods that it remains in the account. To illustrate how and why this growth occurs, consider an investment of $1.00, a nominal interest rate of 10% with annual compounding, and an investment holding period of five years.

Original investment	$1.00
Interest, first year at 10%	.10
Accumulation, end of 1 year	$1.10
Interest, second year at 10%	.11
Accumulation, end of 2 years	$1.21
Interest, third year at 10%	.121
Accumulation, end of 3 years	$1.331
Interest, fourth year at 10%	.1331
Accumulation, end of 4 years	$1.4641
Interest, fifth year at 10%	.14641
Accumulation, end of 5 years	$1.61051

   One dollar grows to $1.61051 in five years with interest at 10%, so the future value of $1 factor at 10% annually for five years is 1.610510; $1,000 would grow 1,000 times this amount to $1,610.51, over the same five years at the same 10% annual rate. When interest is not collected or withdrawn as it is earned, it is added to the capital amount and additional interest accumulates in subsequent periods. This process is called *compounding*.

The results of compounding can be calculated with the formula $(1 + i)^n$, where n is the number of compounding periods and i is the interest rate per period.

n
1   $1.10 \times 1 = 1.10^1$ $= 1.10$
2   $1.10 \times 1.10 = 1.10^2$ $= 1.21$
3   $1.10 \times 1.10 \times 1.10 = 1.10^3$ $= 1.331$
4   $1.10 \times 1.10 \times 1.10 \times 1.10 = 1.10^4$ $= 1.461$
5   $1.10 \times 1.10 \times 1.10 \times 1.10 \times 1.10 = 1.10^5$ $= 1.61051$

Thus, the factors in this table, the amount of one or the future value of $1, reflect the growth of $1.00 accumulating at interest for the number of compounding periods shown at the left and right sides of each page of tables. For example, the 10% annual column reveals a factor of 2.593742 for 10 periods. This means that $1.00 deposited at 10% interest compounded annually for 10 years will grow to $1.00 $\times$ 2.593742, or just over $2.59. In other words, $1.10^{10} = 2.593742$. The factors for seven and eight years indicate that $1.00 (or any investment earning 10% per year) will double in value in approximately 7.5 years. Similarly, an investment of $10,000 made 10 years ago, earning no periodic income during the 10-year holding period, must be liquidated in the current market at $10,000 $\times$ 2.593742, or $25,937.42, to realize a 10% return on the original investment.

This factor reflects the growth of the original deposit measured from the *beginning deposit period*. Thus, at the end of the first period at a rate of 10% the original $1.00 has grown to $1.10 and the factor is 1.100000, as shown above.

6%   COMPOUND INTEREST (Future Value of $1)

Base:	2.718 282	1.005 000	1.015 000	1.030 000	1.060 000	
			Frequency of Conversion			
Months	Continuous	Monthly	Quarterly	Semiannual	Annual	Months
0	1.000 000	1.000 000	1.000 000	1.000 000	1.000 000	0
1	1.005 013	1.005 000	1.005 000	1.005 000	1.005 000	1
2	1.010 050	1.010 025	1.010 000	1.010 000	1.010 000	2
3	1.015 113	1.015 075	1.015 000	1.015 000	1.015 000	3
4	1.020 201	1.020 151	1.020 075	1.020 000	1.020 000	4
5	1.025 315	1.025 251	1.025 150	1.025 000	1.025 000	5
6	1.030 455	1.030 378	1.030 225	1.030 000	1.030 000	6
7	1.035 620	1.035 529	1.035 376	1.035 150	1.035 000	7
8	1.040 811	1.040 707	1.040 527	1.040 300	1.040 000	8
9	1.046 028	1.045 911	1.045 678	1.045 450	1.045 000	9
10	1.051 271	1.051 140	1.050 907	1.050 600	1.050 000	10
11	1.056 541	1.056 396	1.056 135	1.055 750	1.055 000	11
Years						Years
1	1.061 837	1.061 678	1.061 364	1.060 900	1.060 000	1
2	1.127 497	1.127 160	1.126 493	1.125 509	1.123 600	2
3	1.197 217	1.196 681	1.195 618	1.194 052	1.191 016	3
4	1.271 249	1.270 489	1.268 986	1.266 770	1.262 477	4
5	1.349 859	1.348 850	1.346 855	1.343 916	1.338 226	5
6	1.433 329	1.432 044	1.429 503	1.425 761	1.418 519	6
7	1.521 962	1.520 370	1.517 222	1.512 590	1.503 630	7
8	1.616 074	1.614 143	1.610 324	1.604 706	1.593 848	8
9	1.716 007	1.713 699	1.709 140	1.702 433	1.689 479	9
10	1.822 119	1.819 397	1.814 018	1.806 111	1.790 848	10
11	1.934 792	1.931 613	1.925 333	1.916 103	1.898 299	11
12	2.054 433	2.050 751	2.043 478	2.032 794	2.012 196	12
13	2.181 472	2.177 237	2.168 873	2.156 591	2.132 928	13
14	2.316 367	2.311 524	2.301 963	2.287 928	2.260 904	14
15	2.459 603	2.454 094	2.443 220	2.427 262	2.396 558	15
16	2.611 696	2.605 457	2.593 144	2.575 083	2.540 352	16
17	2.773 195	2.766 156	2.752 269	2.731 905	2.692 773	17
18	2.944 680	2.936 766	2.921 158	2.898 278	2.854 339	18
19	3.126 768	3.117 899	3.100 411	3.074 783	3.025 600	19
20	3.320 117	3.310 204	3.290 663	3.262 038	3.207 135	20
21	3.525 421	3.514 371	3.492 590	3.460 696	3.399 564	21
22	3.743 421	3.731 129	3.706 907	3.671 452	3.603 537	22
23	3.974 902	3.961 257	3.934 376	3.895 044	3.819 750	23
24	4.220 696	4.205 579	4.175 804	4.132 252	4.048 935	24
25	4.481 689	4.464 970	4.432 046	4.383 906	4.291 871	25
26	4.758 821	4.740 359	4.704 012	4.650 886	4.549 383	26
27	5.053 090	5.032 734	4.992 667	4.934 125	4.822 346	27
28	5.365 556	5.343 142	5.299 034	5.234 613	5.111 687	28
29	5.697 343	5.672 696	5.624 202	5.553 401	5.418 388	29
30	6.049 647	6.022 575	5.969 323	5.891 603	5.743 491	30
31	6.423 737	6.394 034	6.335 622	6.250 402	6.088 101	31
32	6.820 958	6.788 405	6.724 398	6.631 051	6.453 387	32
33	7.242 743	7.207 098	7.137 031	7.034 882	6.840 590	33
34	7.690 609	7.651 617	7.574 984	7.463 307	7.251 025	34
35	8.166 170	8.123 551	8.039 812	7.917 822	7.686 087	35
36	8.671 138	8.624 594	8.533 164	8.400 017	8.147 252	36
37	9.207 331	9.156 540	9.056 789	8.911 578	8.636 087	37
38	9.776 680	9.721 296	9.612 546	9.454 293	9.154 252	38
39	10.381 237	10.320 884	10.202 406	10.030 060	9.703 507	39
40	11.023 176	10.957 454	10.828 462	10.640 891	10.285 718	40

10% COMPOUND INTEREST (Future Value of $1)

Base:	2.718 282	1.008 333	1.025 000	1.050 000	1.100 000	
			Frequency of Conversion			
Months	Continuous	Monthly	Quarterly	Semiannual	Annual	Months
0	1.000 000	1.000 000	1.000 000	1.000 000	1.000 000	0
1	1.008 368	1.008 333	1.008 333	1.008 333	1.008 333	1
2	1.016 806	1.016 736	1.016 667	1.016 667	1.016 667	2
3	1.025 315	1.025 209	1.025 000	1.025 000	1.025 000	3
4	1.033 895	1.033 752	1.033 542	1.033 333	1.033 333	4
5	1.042 547	1.042 367	1.042 083	1.041 667	1.041 667	5
6	1.051 271	1.051 053	1.050 625	1.050 000	1.050 000	6
7	1.060 068	1.059 812	1.059 380	1.058 750	1.058 333	7
8	1.068 939	1.068 644	1.068 135	1.067 500	1.066 667	8
9	1.077 884	1.077 549	1.076 891	1.076 250	1.075 000	9
10	1.086 904	1.086 529	1.085 865	1.085 000	1.083 333	10
11	1.095 999	1.095 583	1.094 839	1.093 750	1.091 667	11
Years						Years
1	1.105 171	1.104 713	1.103 813	1.102 500	1.100 000	1
2	1.221 403	1.220 391	1.218 403	1.215 506	1.210 000	2
3	1.349 859	1.348 182	1.344 889	1.340 096	1.331 000	3
4	1.491 825	1.489 354	1.484 506	1.477 455	1.464 100	4
5	1.648 721	1.645 309	1.638 616	1.628 895	1.610 510	5
6	1.822 119	1.817 594	1.808 726	1.795 856	1.771 561	6
7	2.013 753	2.007 920	1.996 495	1.979 932	1.948 717	7
8	2.225 541	2.218 176	2.203 757	2.182 875	2.143 589	8
9	2.459 603	2.450 448	2.432 535	2.406 619	2.357 948	9
10	2.718 282	2.707 041	2.685 064	2.653 298	2.593 742	10
11	3.004 166	2.990 504	2.963 808	2.925 261	2.853 117	11
12	3.320 117	3.303 649	3.271 490	3.225 100	3.138 428	12
13	3.669 297	3.649 584	3.611 112	3.555 673	3.452 271	13
14	4.055 200	4.031 743	3.985 992	3.920 129	3.797 498	14
15	4.481 689	4.453 920	4.399 790	4.321 942	4.177 248	15
16	4.953 032	4.920 303	4.856 545	4.764 941	4.594 973	16
17	5.473 947	5.435 523	5.360 717	5.253 348	5.054 470	17
18	6.049 647	6.004 693	5.917 228	5.791 816	5.559 917	18
19	6.685 894	6.633 463	6.531 513	6.385 477	6.115 909	19
20	7.389 056	7.328 074	7.209 568	7.039 989	6.727 500	20
21	8.166 170	8.095 419	7.958 014	7.761 588	7.400 250	21
22	9.025 013	8.943 115	8.784 158	8.557 150	8.140 275	22
23	9.974 182	9.879 576	9.696 067	9.434 258	8.954 302	23
24	11.023 176	10.914 097	10.702 644	10.401 270	9.849 733	24
25	12.182 494	12.056 945	11.813 716	11.467 400	10.834 706	25
26	13.463 738	13.319 465	13.040 132	12.642 808	11.918 177	26
27	14.879 732	14.714 187	14.393 866	13.938 696	13.109 994	27
28	16.444 647	16.254 954	15.888 135	15.367 412	14.420 994	28
29	18.174 145	17.957 060	17.537 528	16.942 572	15.863 093	29
30	20.085 537	19.837 399	19.358 150	18.679 186	17.449 402	30
31	22.197 951	21.914 634	21.367 775	20.593 802	19.194 342	31
32	24.532 530	24.209 383	23.586 026	22.704 667	21.113 777	32
33	27.112 639	26.744 422	26.034 559	25.031 896	23.225 154	33
34	29.964 100	29.544 912	28.737 282	27.597 665	25.547 670	34
35	33.115 452	32.638 650	31.720 583	30.426 426	28.102 437	35
36	36.598 234	36.056 344	35.013 588	33.545 134	30.912 681	36
37	40.447 304	39.831 914	38.648 450	36.983 510	34.003 949	37
38	44.701 184	44.002 836	42.660 657	40.774 320	37.404 343	38
39	49.402 449	48.610 508	47.089 383	44.953 688	41.144 778	39
40	54.598 150	53.700 663	51.977 868	49.561 441	45.259 256	40

REVERSION FACTORS (Present Value of $1)

This factor is the present value of $1 to be collected at a given future time discounted at the effective interest rate for the number of periods between now and the date of collection. It is the reciprocal of the corresponding compound interest factor.

$$1/S^n = \frac{1}{(1 + i)^n}$$

Where: $1/S^n$ = present value factor
   i = effective rate of interest
   n = number of compounding periods

and $1/S^n = \dfrac{1}{(e)^{in}}$ for continuous compounding

Where: $1/S^n$ = present value factor
   i = nominal rate of interest
   n = number of years
   e = 2.718282

This table is used to solve problems that involve compound discounting.

Example 1

What is the present value of $10,000 to be received in 10 years, assuming an interest rate of 6% and annual compounding?

$$\$10,000 \times .558395 = \$5,583.95$$

Example 2

What is the present value of $10,000 to be received in 10 years and 7 months, assuming an interest rate of 6% and annual compounding?

$$\$10,000 \times .558395 \times .966184 = \$5,395.12$$

This calculation assumes simple interest for any time that is less than one conversion period.

Example 3

Assuming a 6% rate and annual compounding, what is the present value of the following cash flows: $1,000 in one year, $2,000 in two years, and $3,000 in three years?

Cash Flows		Present Value Factor		Present Value
$1,000	×	.943396	=	$ 943.40
2,000	×	.889996	=	1,779.99
3,000	×	.839619	=	2,518.86
Present value				$5,242.25

Example 4

A property is sold for $100,000, but five years previously it was sold for $135,000. What is the depreciation in its sale price expressed as a monthly compound rate?

$$\$100,000/\$135,000 = .740741 \text{ (present value factor)}$$

Scan the tables of present value factors, monthly frequency, for .740741 at five years. The closest match is found at 6% nominal rate, so the monthly rate is approximately 0.5%.

Example 5

How long will it take $1.00 to be worth $0.50 assuming a 6% rate of inflation?

$$.50/1.00 = .500000 \text{ (present value factor)}$$

Scan the tables of present value factors at 6% nominal interest for .500000. Assuming annual frequency, the target is between the factors for 11 and 12 years. Visual interpolation indicates an answer of slightly less than 12 years. Mathematical straight-line interpolation produces an answer of 11.9 years.

$$(.526788 - .500000)/(.526788 - .496969) + 11 = 11.9 \text{ years}$$

As demonstrated in the discussion of future value, $1.00 compounded annually at 10% will grow to $1.610151 in five years. Accordingly, the amount that will grow to $1.00 in five years is $1.00 divided by 1.61051, or $0.62092. In the 10% table, the present value of $1 factor for five years is .620921. In other words, $1.00 to be collected five years from today has a present value of $0.620921 when discounted at 10% per year. And $10,000 to be collected five years from today, discounted at the same 10% annual rate, has a present value of $10,000 × .620921, or $6,209.21. The $10,000 sum to be received in five years is a *reversion*.

6%   REVERSION FACTORS (Present Value of $1)

Base:

	2.718 282	1.005 000	1.015 000	1.030 000	1.060 000	
			Frequency of Conversion			
Months	Continuous	Monthly	Quarterly	Semiannual	Annual	Months
0	1.000 000	1.000 000	1.000 000	1.000 000	1.000 000	0
1	.995 012	.995 025	.995 025	.995 025	.995 025	1
2	.990 050	.990 075	.990 099	.990 099	.990 099	2
3	.985 112	.985 149	.985 222	.985 222	.985 222	3
4	.980 199	.980 248	.980 320	.980 392	.980 392	4
5	.975 310	.975 371	.975 467	.975 610	.975 610	5
6	.970 446	.970 518	.970 662	.970 874	.970 874	6
7	.965 605	.965 690	.965 833	.966 044	.966 184	7
8	.960 789	.960 885	.961 051	.961 261	.961 538	8
9	.955 997	.956 105	.956 317	.956 526	.956 938	9
10	.951 229	.951 348	.951 559	.951 837	.952 381	10
11	.946 485	.946 615	.946 849	.947 194	.947 867	11

Years						Years
1	.941 765	.941 905	.942 184	.942 596	.943 396	1
2	.886 920	.887 186	.887 711	.888 487	.889 996	2
3	.835 270	.835 645	.836 387	.837 484	.839 619	3
4	.786 628	.787 098	.788 031	.789 409	.792 094	4
5	.740 818	.741 372	.742 470	.744 094	.747 258	5
6	.697 676	.698 302	.699 544	.701 380	.704 961	6
7	.657 047	.657 735	.659 099	.661 118	.665 057	7
8	.618 783	.619 524	.620 993	.623 167	.627 412	8
9	.582 748	.583 533	.585 090	.587 395	.591 898	9
10	.548 812	.549 633	.551 262	.553 676	.558 395	10
11	.516 851	.517 702	.519 391	.521 893	.526 788	11
12	.486 752	.487 626	.489 362	.491 934	.496 969	12
13	.458 406	.459 298	.461 069	.463 695	.468 339	13
14	.431 711	.432 615	.434 412	.437 077	.442 301	14
15	.406 570	.407 482	.409 296	.411 987	.417 265	15
16	.382 893	.383 810	.385 632	.388 337	.393 646	16
17	.360 595	.361 513	.363 337	.366 045	.371 364	17
18	.339 596	.340 511	.342 330	.345 032	.350 344	18
19	.319 819	.320 729	.322 538	.325 226	.330 513	19
20	.301 194	.302 096	.303 890	.306 557	.311 805	20
21	.283 654	.284 546	.286 321	.288 959	.294 155	21
22	.267 135	.268 015	.269 767	.272 372	.277 505	22
23	.251 579	.252 445	.254 170	.256 737	.261 797	23
24	.236 928	.237 779	.239 475	.241 999	.246 979	24
25	.223 130	.223 966	.225 629	.228 107	.232 999	25
26	.210 136	.210 954	.212 585	.215 013	.219 810	26
27	.197 899	.198 699	.200 294	.202 670	.207 368	27
28	.186 374	.187 156	.188 714	.191 036	.195 630	28
29	.175 520	.176 283	.177 803	.180 070	.184 557	29
30	.165 299	.166 042	.167 523	.169 733	.174 110	30
31	.155 673	.156 396	.157 838	.159 990	.164 255	31
32	.146 607	.147 310	.148 712	.150 806	.154 957	32
33	.138 069	.138 752	.140 114	.142 149	.146 186	33
34	.130 029	.130 691	.132 013	.133 989	.137 912	34
35	.122 456	.123 099	.124 381	.126 297	.130 105	35
36	.115 325	.115 947	.117 190	.119 047	.122 741	36
37	.108 609	.109 212	.110 414	.112 214	.115 793	37
38	.102 284	.102 867	.104 031	.105 772	.109 239	38
39	.096 328	.096 891	.098 016	.099 700	.103 056	39
40	.090 718	.091 262	.092 349	.093 977	.097 222	40

10%   REVERSION FACTORS (Present Value of $1)

Base:	2.718 282	1.008 333	1.025 000	1.050 000	1.100 000	
			Frequency of Conversion			
Months	Continuous	Monthly	Quarterly	Semiannual	Annual	Months
0	1.000 000	1.000 000	1.000 000	1.000 000	1.000 000	0
1	.991 701	.991 736	.991 736	.991 736	.991 736	1
2	.983 471	.983 539	.983 607	.983 607	.983 607	2
3	.975 310	.975 411	.975 610	.975 610	.975 610	3
4	.967 216	.967 350	.967 547	.967 742	.967 742	4
5	.959 189	.959 355	.959 616	.960 000	.960 000	5
6	.951 229	.951 427	.951 814	.952 381	.952 381	6
7	.943 335	.943 563	.943 948	.944 510	.944 882	7
8	.935 507	.935 765	.936 211	.936 768	.937 500	8
9	.927 743	.928 032	.928 599	.929 152	.930 233	9
10	.920 044	.920 362	.920 925	.921 659	.923 077	10
11	.912 409	.912 756	.913 376	.914 286	.916 031	11

Years						Years
1	.904 837	.905 212	.905 951	.907 029	.909 091	1
2	.818 731	.819 410	.820 747	.822 702	.826 446	2
3	.740 818	.741 740	.743 556	.746 215	.751 315	3
4	.670 320	.671 432	.673 625	.676 839	.683 013	4
5	.606 531	.607 789	.610 271	.613 913	.620 921	5
6	.548 812	.550 178	.552 875	.556 837	.564 474	6
7	.496 585	.498 028	.500 878	.505 068	.513 158	7
8	.449 329	.450 821	.453 771	.458 112	.466 507	8
9	.406 570	.408 089	.411 094	.415 521	.424 098	9
10	.367 879	.369 407	.372 431	.376 889	.385 543	10
11	.332 871	.334 392	.337 404	.341 850	.350 494	11
12	.301 194	.302 696	.305 671	.310 068	.318 631	12
13	.272 532	.274 004	.276 923	.281 241	.289 664	13
14	.246 597	.248 032	.250 879	.255 094	.263 331	14
15	.223 130	.224 521	.227 284	.231 377	.239 392	15
16	.201 897	.203 240	.205 908	.209 866	.217 629	16
17	.182 684	.183 975	.186 542	.190 355	.197 845	17
18	.165 299	.166 536	.168 998	.172 657	.179 859	18
19	.149 569	.150 751	.153 104	.156 605	.163 508	19
20	.135 335	.136 462	.138 705	.142 046	.148 644	20
21	.122 456	.123 527	.125 659	.128 840	.135 131	21
22	.110 803	.111 818	.113 841	.116 861	.122 846	22
23	.100 259	.101 219	.103 135	.105 997	.111 678	23
24	.090 718	.091 625	.093 435	.096 142	.101 526	24
25	.082 085	.082 940	.084 647	.087 204	.092 296	25
26	.074 274	.075 078	.076 686	.079 096	.083 905	26
27	.067 206	.067 962	.069 474	.071 743	.076 278	27
28	.060 810	.061 520	.062 940	.065 073	.069 343	28
29	.055 023	.055 688	.057 021	.059 023	.063 039	29
30	.049 787	.050 410	.051 658	.053 536	.057 309	30
31	.045 049	.045 632	.046 799	.048 558	.052 099	31
32	.040 762	.041 306	.042 398	.044 044	.047 362	32
33	.036 883	.037 391	.038 410	.039 949	.043 057	33
34	.033 373	.033 847	.034 798	.036 235	.039 143	34
35	.030 197	.030 639	.031 525	.032 866	.035 584	35
36	.027 324	.027 734	.028 560	.029 811	.032 349	36
37	.024 724	.025 105	.025 874	.027 039	.029 408	37
38	.022 371	.022 726	.023 441	.024 525	.026 735	38
39	.020 242	.020 572	.021 236	.022 245	.024 304	39
40	.018 316	.018 622	.019 239	.020 177	.022 095	40

ORDINARY LEVEL ANNUITY (Present Value of $1 per Period)

This factor represents the present value of a series of future installments or payments of $1 per period for a given number of periods discounted at an effective interest rate. It is commonly referred to as the *Inwood coefficient*.

$$a_{\overline{n}|} = \frac{1 - 1/S^n}{i}$$

Where: $a_{\overline{n}|}$ = level annuity factor
   $1/S^n$ = present value factor
   i = rate of interest yield

This table is used in solving problems that deal with the compound discounting of cash flows that are level or effectively level.

Example 1

What is the present value of an ordinary annuity of $1,000 per month for 10 years, assuming an interest rate of 6%?

$$\$1,000 \times 90.073453 = \$90,073.45$$

Assuming payments are made in advance, the PV of this annuity would be

$$\$1,000 \times 90.073453 \times 1.005000 = \$90,523.82$$

or

$$\$1,000 \times 90.073453/.995025 = \$90,523.81$$

Example 2

What is the present value of an ordinary annuity of $1,000 per month for 10 years and 7 months, assuming an interest rate of 6%?

$1,000 × 90.073453	= $90,073.45
$1,000 × 6.862074 × .549633*	= 3,771.62
	$93,845.07

*Reversion factor for 120 months

Assuming payments in advance, the PV of this annuity would be

$$\$93,845.07 \times 1.005000 = \$94,314.30$$

or

$$\$93,845.07/.995025 = \$94,314.28$$

Example 3

Assuming a 6% annual discount rate, what is the present value of an ordinary annuity consisting of the following cash flows: $1,000 per year for five years, then $2,000 per year for five years, and then $3,000 per year for five years?

$$
\begin{aligned}
\$1,000 \times 4.212364 &= \$ \ 4,212.36 \\
2,000 \times (7.360087 - 4.212364) &= \ 6,295.45 \\
3,000 \times (9.712249 - 7.360087) &= \ \underline{7,056.49} \\
&\quad \ \$17,564.30
\end{aligned}
$$

Assuming payments are made in advance, the PV of this annuity would be

$$\$17,564.30 \times 1.060000 = \$18,618.16$$

or

$$\$17,564.30/.943396 = \$18,618.16$$

Example 4

If a 10-year ordinary level annuity of $1,000 per month has a present value of $90,000, what is the indicated interest or yield rate?

$$\$90,000/\$1,000 = 90.000000 \text{ (present value factor)}$$

Scan the ordinary level annuity tables at 10 years, monthly frequency, for 90.000000. The closest match is a 6% nominal rate.

Finding the present value of a future income stream is a discounting procedure in which future payments are treated as a series of reversions. The present value of a series of future receipts may be quickly ascertained using the precomputed present value of $1 per period factors for the selected discount rate provided the receipts are all equal in amount, equally spaced over time, and receivable at the end of each period.

If, for example, 10% per year is a fair rate of interest or discount, it would be justifiable to pay $0.909091 (i.e., the annual present value of $1 at 10%) for the right to receive $1.00 one year from today. Assuming that the cost of this right is $0.909091, the $1.00 received at the end of the year could be divided between principal and interest as follows.

Return of principal	$0.90909
Interest on principal for one year @ 10%	.09091
Total received	$1.00000

If approximately $.091 is the present value of the right to receive $1.00 of income one year from today at 10% interest, the present value of the right to receive $1.00 two years from today is less. According to the present value formula, the present value of $1.00 to be received two years from today is $0.826446. The present value of $1.00 payable at the end of two years can be confirmed with these calculations.

Return on principal	$0.82645*
Interest for first year at 10% on $0.82645	.08264
	$0.90909
Interest for second year at 10% on $0.90909	.09091
Total principal repayment + interest received	$1.00000

*Present value factor, 0.826446 × $1.00 = $0.82645 (rounded).

Similarly, the present value of the right to receive $1.00 at the end of three years is $0.751315, at the end of four years it is $0.683013, and at the end of the fifth year it is $0.620921. The present value of these rights to receive income at one-year intervals for five years is accumulated as the present value of $1.00 per year. This is known as the *compound interest valuation premise*, also referred to as the *ordinary annuity factor*. Therefore, the sum of the five individual rights to receive $1.00 each year, payable at the end of the year, for five years is $3.790787 (i.e., the 10% annual present value of $1 per period factor for five years).

Sum of Individual Present Values of $1.00

Payable at the End of the Period

Present value of $1.00 due in 1 year	$0.909091*
Present value of $1.00 due in 2 years	.826446*
Present value of $1.00 due in 3 years	.751315*
Present value of $1.00 due in 4 years	.683013*
Present value of $1.00 due in 5 years	.620921*
Total present value of $1.00 per year for 5 years	$3.790786**

*10% present value of $1 factor.

**10% present value of $1 per period factor is 3.790787; the difference is due to rounding.

The present value of $1 per period table for five annual discounting periods ($n = 5$) gives a factor that represents the total of the present values of a series of periodic amounts of $1.00, payable at the end of each period. The calculation presented above is unnecessary because multiplying $1.00 by the factor for the present value of $1 per year for five years produces the same present value ($1.00 × 3.790787 = $3.790787).

For appraisal purposes, the present value of $1 per period factor may be multiplied by a periodic income with the characteristics of an ordinary annuity to derive the present value of the right to receive that income stream. The future payments of income provide for recapture of, and interest on, this present value. Present value factors are multipliers and perform the same function as capitalization rates.

The 10% ordinary annuity factor for five years, 3.790787, represents the present value of each $1.00 of annual end-of-year collection based on a nominal annual discount rate of 10%. Tables and formulas for semiannual, quarterly, and monthly payments are also available. The ordinary annuity factor for semiannual payments in the 10% nominal annual rate table is 7.721735. If payment continues for five years, each $1.00 of semiannual payment represents $10.00 received, but reflects only $7.72 of the discounted present value of monthly payments for five years. In the table for a 10% nominal rate, the monthly factor is 47.065369, indicating that the present value of an ordinary annnuity income stream of 60 monthly payments of $1.00 each discounted at a nominal rate of 10% is 47.065369 × $1.00, or about $47.065.

Based on a 10% nominal rate, semiannual payments would involve an effective rate of 5%. In the 5% annuity table, the factor for 10 periods is 7.721735; this is the same factor shown in the 10% semiannual table for a five-year period. Thus, when tables are not available at the effective rate, annuity factors for more frequent payment periods can be derived using nominal annual rate tables. Preprogrammed financial calculators can be used to facilitate these calculations.

In computing the present value of an annuity income stream, it may be desirable to assume that periodic payments are made at the beginning rather than the end of each payment period. The present value of an annuity payable in advance is equal to the present value of an ordinary annuity in arrears multiplied by the base (i.e., 1 plus the effective interest rate for the discounting period: $1 + i$). Thus, the present value of semiannual payments in advance over a five-year period discounted at a nominal rate of 10% becomes $1.00 × 7.721735 × 1.05 = $8.107822, or $8.11, compared to $7.72 as computed for payments received at the end of each payment period.

6%   ORDINARY LEVEL ANNUITY (Present Value of $1 per Period)

Base:	1.005 000	1.015 000	1.030 000	1.060 000	
		Frequency of Payments			
Months	Monthly	Quarterly	Semiannual	Annual	Months
1	.995 025	—	—	—	1
2	1.985 099	—	—	—	2
3	2.970 248	.985 222	—	—	3
4	3.950 496	—	—	—	4
5	4.925 866	—	—	—	5
6	5.896 384	1.955 883	.970 874	—	6
7	6.862 074	—	—	—	7
8	7.822 959	—	—	—	8
9	8.779 064	2.912 200	—	—	9
10	9.730 412	—	—	—	10
11	10.677 027	—	—	—	11
Years					Years
1	11.618 932	3.854 385	1.913 470	.943 396	1
2	22.562 866	7.485 925	3.717 098	1.833 393	2
3	32.871 016	10.907 505	5.417 191	2.673 012	3
4	42.580 318	14.131 264	7.019 692	3.465 106	4
5	51.725 561	17.168 639	8.530 203	4.212 364	5
6	60.339 514	20.030 405	9.954 004	4.917 324	6
7	68.453 042	22.726 717	11.296 073	5.582 381	7
8	76.095 218	25.267 139	12.561 102	6.209 794	8
9	83.293 424	27.660 684	13.753 513	6.801 692	9
10	90.073 453	29.915 845	14.877 475	7.360 087	10
11	96.459 599	32.040 622	15.936 917	7.886 875	11
12	102.474 743	34.042 554	16.935 542	8.383 844	12
13	108.140 440	35.928 742	17.876 842	8.852 683	13
14	113.476 990	37.705 879	18.764 108	9.294 984	14
15	118.503 515	39.380 269	19.600 441	9.712 249	15
16	123.238 025	40.957 853	20.388 766	10.105 895	16
17	127.697 486	42.444 228	21.131 837	10.477 260	17
18	131.897 876	43.844 667	21.832 252	10.827 603	18
19	135.854 246	45.164 138	22.492 462	11.158 116	19
20	139.580 772	46.407 323	23.114 772	11.469 921	20
21	143.090 806	47.578 633	23.701 359	11.764 077	21
22	146.396 927	48.682 222	24.254 274	12.041 582	22
23	149.510 979	49.722 007	24.775 449	12.303 379	23
24	152.444 121	50.701 675	25.266 707	12.550 358	24
25	155.206 864	51.624 704	25.729 764	12.783 356	25
26	157.809 106	52.494 366	26.166 240	13.003 166	26
27	160.260 172	53.313 749	26.577 660	13.210 534	27
28	162.568 844	54.085 758	26.965 464	13.406 164	28
29	164.743 394	54.813 133	27.331 005	13.590 721	29
30	166.791 614	55.498 454	27.675 564	13.764 831	30
31	168.720 844	56.144 153	28.000 343	13.929 086	31
32	170.537 996	56.752 520	28.306 478	14.084 043	32
33	172.249 581	57.325 714	28.595 040	14.230 230	33
34	173.861 732	57.865 769	28.867 038	14.368 141	34
35	175.380 226	58.374 599	29.123 421	14.498 246	35
36	176.810 504	58.854 011	29.365 088	14.620 987	36
37	178.157 690	59.305 706	29.592 881	14.736 780	37
38	179.426 611	59.731 286	29.807 598	14.846 019	38
39	180.621 815	60.132 260	30.009 990	14.949 075	39
40	181.747 584	60.510 052	30.200 763	15.046 297	40

10%   ORDINARY LEVEL ANNUITY (Present Value of $1 per Period)

Base:	1.008 333	1.025 000	1.050 000	1.100 000	
		Frequency of Payments			
Months	Monthly	Quarterly	Semiannual	Annual	Months
1	.991 736	—	—	—	1
2	1.975 275	—	—	—	2
3	2.950 686	.975 610	—	—	3
4	3.918 036	—	—	—	4
5	4.877 391	—	—	—	5
6	5.828 817	1.927 424	.952 381	—	6
7	6.772 381	—	—	—	7
8	7.708 146	—	—	—	8
9	8.636 178	2.856 024	—	—	9
10	9.556 540	—	—	—	10
11	10.469 296	—	—	—	11
Years					Years
1	11.374 508	3.761 974	1.859 410	.909 091	1
2	21.670 855	7.170 137	3.545 951	1.735 537	2
3	30.991 236	10.257 765	5.075 692	2.486 852	3
4	39.428 160	13.055 003	6.463 213	3.169 865	4
5	47.065 369	15.589 162	7.721 735	3.790 787	5
6	53.978 665	17.884 986	8.863 252	4.355 261	6
7	60.236 667	19.964 889	9.898 641	4.868 419	7
8	65.901 488	21.849 178	10.837 770	5.334 926	8
9	71.029 355	23.556 251	11.689 587	5.759 024	9
10	75.671 163	25.102 775	12.462 210	6.144 567	10
11	79.872 986	26.503 849	13.163 003	6.495 061	11
12	83.676 528	27.773 154	13.798 642	6.813 692	12
13	87.119 542	28.923 081	14.375 185	7.103 356	13
14	90.236 201	29.964 858	14.898 127	7.366 687	14
15	93.057 439	30.908 656	15.372 451	7.606 080	15
16	95.611 259	31.763 691	15.802 677	7.823 709	16
17	97.923 008	32.538 311	16.192 904	8.021 553	17
18	100.015 633	33.240 078	16.546 852	8.201 412	18
19	101.909 902	33.875 844	16.867 893	8.364 920	19
20	103.624 619	34.451 817	17.159 086	8.513 564	20
21	105.176 801	34.973 620	17.423 208	8.648 694	21
22	106.581 856	35.446 348	17.662 773	8.771 540	22
23	107.853 730	35.874 616	17.880 066	8.883 218	23
24	109.005 045	36.262 606	18.077 158	8.984 744	24
25	110.047 230	36.614 105	18.255 925	9.077 040	25
26	110.990 629	36.932 546	18.418 073	9.160 945	26
27	111.844 605	37.221 039	18.565 146	9.237 223	27
28	112.617 635	37.482 398	18.698 545	9.306 567	28
29	113.317 392	37.719 177	18.819 542	9.369 606	29
30	113.950 820	37.933 687	18.929 290	9.426 914	30
31	114.524 207	38.128 022	19.028 834	9.479 013	31
32	115.043 244	38.304 081	19.119 124	9.526 376	32
33	115.513 083	38.463 581	19.201 019	9.569 432	33
34	115.938 387	38.608 080	19.275 301	9.608 575	34
35	116.323 377	38.738 989	19.342 677	9.644 159	35
36	116.671 876	38.857 586	19.403 788	9.676 508	36
37	116.987 340	38.965 030	19.459 218	9.705 917	37
38	117.272 903	39.062 368	19.509 495	9.732 651	38
39	117.531 398	39.150 552	19.555 098	9.756 956	39
40	117.765 391	39.230 442	19.596 460	9.779 051	40

ORDINARY ANNUITIES CHANGING IN CONSTANT AMOUNT
(Present Value of Annual Payments Starting at $1 and Changing in Constant Amounts)

$$PVF = (1 + hn)a_{\overline{n}|} - \frac{h(n - a_{\overline{n}|})}{i}$$

Where: PVF = present value factor
h* = annual increase or decrease after 1st year
n = number of years
$a_{\overline{n}|}$ = PVF for ordinary level annuity
i = rate of interest yield

*h is positive for an increase and negative for a decrease

This table is used to solve problems dealing with the compound discounting of cash flows that are best represented by a straight-line pattern of change.

Example 1

Assuming a 15% interest or yield rate, what is the present value of an ordinary annuity consisting of 10 annual cash flows that start at $10,000 and increase $1,000 per year?

$$\$10,000 \times 6.7167 = \$67,167$$

Assuming payments are made in advance, the PV of this annuity would be

$$\$67,167 \times 1.150000 = \$77,242$$

or

$$\$67,167/.869565 = \$77,242$$

Example 2

Assuming a 15% interest or yield rate, what is the present value of an ordinary annuity consisting of 10 annual cash flows that start at $10,000 and increase $300 per year?

$$\$10,000 \times (5.3584 + 5.6979)/2 = \$55,282$$

or

$$\$10,000 \times (5.018769 + 16.979477 \times .03) = \$55,281.53$$

Example 3

There are five years remaining on a lease that provides a level income of $1,000 per year. During this period inflation will cause purchasing power to decline an average of 10% per year (on a straight-line basis). What is the value of the income expressed in constant dollars and discounted at 6%?

$$\$1,000 \times (.90 \times 4.212364 - 7.934549 \times .10) = \$2,997.67$$

Proof:

Year	Income	×	Inflation Factor	×	PVF @ 6%	=	Value
1	$1,000	×	.90	×	.943396	=	$ 849.06
2	1,000	×	.80	×	.889996	=	712.00
3	1,000	×	.70	×	.839619	=	587.73
4	1,000	×	.60	×	.792094	=	475.26
5	1,000	×	.50	×	.747258	=	373.63
							$2,997.68

This table is similar to the ordinary level annuity table, but the annual receipts are converted into constant dollar amounts. For instance, assume that the amount to be received one year from today is $10,000, additional future receipts are expected to increase $1,000 per year for the next nine years, and 15% per year is a fair rate of interest. According to the 15% annual present value of $1 factor, it would be justifiable to pay $67,167 for the right to receive $10,000 one year from today and nine additional payments growing at $1,000 per year for nine additional years. The table indicates that the factor to be applied to the initial receipt is 6.7167.

Proof:

Year	Income	×	Present Value Factor	=	Present Value
1	$10,000	×	.869565	=	$ 8,695.65
1	11,000	×	.756144	=	8,317.58
2	12,000	×	.657516	=	7,890.19
4	13,000	×	.571753	=	7,432.79
5	14,000	×	.497177	=	6,960.48
6	15,000	×	.432328	=	6,484.92
7	16,000	×	.375937	=	6,014.99
8	17,000	×	.326902	=	5,557.33
9	18,000	×	.284262	=	5,116.72
10	19,000	×	.247185	=	4,696.52
Present value					$67,167.17

$$\frac{\text{Present value}}{\text{Initial receipt}} = \text{Factor}$$

$$\frac{\$67,167.17}{\$10,000.00} = 6.7167$$

10%   ORDINARY ANNUITIES CHANGING IN CONSTANT AMOUNT
(Present Value of Annual Payments Starting at $1 and Changing in Constant Amounts)

Base: 1.100 000

		Annual INCREASE of:					
Years	Slope	.00	.02	.04	.05	.10	Years
1	.000 000	.909 091	.9091	.9091	.9091	.9091	1
2	.826 446	1.735 537	1.7521	1.7686	1.7769	1.8182	2
3	2.329 076	2.486 852	2.5334	2.5800	2.6033	2.7198	3
4	4.378 116	3.169 865	3.2574	3.3450	3.3888	3.6077	4
5	6.861 802	3.790 787	3.9280	4.0653	4.1339	4.4770	5
6	9.684 171	4.355 261	4.5489	4.7426	4.8395	5.3237	6
7	12.763 120	4.868 419	5.1237	5.3789	5.5066	6.1447	7
8	16.028 672	5.334 926	5.6555	5.9761	6.1364	6.9378	8
9	19.421 453	5.759 024	6.1475	6.5359	6.7301	7.7012	9
10	22.891 342	6.144 567	6.6024	7.0602	7.2891	8.4337	10
11	26.396 281	6.495 061	7.0230	7.5509	7.8149	9.1347	11
12	29.901 220	6.813 692	7.4117	8.0097	8.3088	9.8038	12
13	33.377 193	7.103 356	7.7709	8.4384	8.7722	10.4411	13
14	36.800 499	7.366 687	8.1027	8.8387	9.2067	11.0467	14
15	40.151 988	7.606 080	8.4091	9.2122	9.6137	11.6213	15
16	43.416 425	7.823 709	8.6920	9.5604	9.9945	12.1654	16
17	46.581 939	8.021 553	8.9532	9.8848	10.3507	12.6797	17
18	49.639 539	8.201 412	9.1942	10.1870	10.6834	13.1654	18
19	52.582 683	8.364 920	9.4166	10.4682	10.9941	13.6232	19
20	55.406 912	8.513 564	9.6217	10.7298	11.2839	14.0543	20

		Annual DECREASE of:					
Years	Slope	.00	.02	.04	.05	.10	Years
1	.000 000	.909 091	.9091	.9091	.9091	.9091	1
2	− .826 446	1.735 537	1.7190	1.7025	1.6942	1.6529	2
3	− 2.329 076	2.486 852	2.4403	2.3937	2.3704	2.2539	3
4	− 4.378 116	3.169 865	3.0823	2.9947	2.9510	2.7321	4
5	− 6.861 802	3.790 787	3.6536	3.5163	3.4477	3.1046	5
6	− 9.684 171	4.355 261	4.1616	3.9679	3.8711	3.3868	6
7	−12.763 120	4.868 419	4.6132	4.3579	4.2303	3.5921	7
8	−16.028 672	5.334 926	5.0144	4.6938	4.5335	3.7321	8
9	−19.421 453	5.759 024	5.3706	4.9822	4.7880	3.8169	9
10	−22.891 342	6.144 567	5.6867	5.2289	5.0000	3.8554	10
11	−26.396 281	6.495 061	5.9671	5.4392	5.1752	—	11
12	−29.901 220	6.813 692	6.2157	5.6176	5.3186	—	12
13	−33.377 193	7.103 356	6.4358	5.7683	5.4345	—	13
14	−36.800 499	7.366 687	6.6307	5.8947	5.5267	—	14
15	−40.151 988	7.606 080	6.8030	6.0000	5.5985	—	15
16	−43.416 425	7.823 709	6.9554	6.0871	5.6529	—	16
17	−46.581 939	8.021 553	7.0899	6.1583	5.6925	—	17
18	−49.639 539	8.201 412	7.2086	6.2158	5.7194	—	18
19	−52.582 683	8.364 920	7.3133	6.2616	5.7358	—	19
20	−55.406 912	8.513 564	7.4054	6.2973	5.7432	—	20

15% ORDINARY ANNUITIES CHANGING IN CONSTANT AMOUNT
(Present Value of Annual Payments Starting at $1 and Changing in Constant Amounts)

Base: 1.150 000

		Annual INCREASE of:					
Years	Slope	.00	.02	.04	.05	.10	Years
1	.000 000	.869 565	.8696	.8696	.8696	.8696	1
2	.756 144	1.625 709	1.6408	1.6560	1.6635	1.7013	2
3	2.071 176	2.283 225	2.3246	2.3661	2.3868	2.4903	3
4	3.786 436	2.854 978	2.9307	3.0064	3.0443	3.2336	4
5	5.775 143	3.352 155	3.4677	3.5832	3.6409	3.9297	5
6	7.936 781	3.784 483	3.9432	4.1020	4.1813	4.5782	6
7	10.192 403	4.160 420	4.3643	4.5681	4.6700	5.1797	7
8	12.480 715	4.487 322	4.7369	4.9866	5.1114	5.7354	8
9	14.754 815	4.771 584	5.0667	5.3618	5.5093	6.2471	9
10	16.979 477	5.018 769	5.3584	5.6979	5.8677	6.7167	10
11	19.128 909	5.233 712	5.6163	5.9989	6.1902	7.1466	11
12	21.184 888	5.420 619	5.8443	6.2680	6.4799	7.5391	12
13	23.135 223	5.583 147	6.0459	6.5086	6.7399	7.8967	13
14	24.972 496	5.724 476	6.2239	6.7234	6.9731	8.2217	14
15	26.693 019	5.847 370	6.3812	6.9151	7.1820	8.5167	15
16	28.295 990	5.954 235	6.5202	7.0861	7.3690	8.7838	16
17	29.782 805	6.047 161	6.6428	7.2385	7.5363	9.0254	17
18	31.156 492	6.127 966	6.7511	7.3742	7.6858	9.2436	18
19	32.421 267	6.198 231	6.8467	7.4951	7.8193	9.4404	19
20	33.582 173	6.259 331	6.9310	7.6026	7.9384	9.6175	20

		Annual DECREASE of:					
Years	Slope	.00	.02	.04	.05	.10	Years
1	.000 000	.869 565	.8696	.8696	.8696	.8696	1
2	− .756 144	1.625 709	1.6106	1.5955	1.5879	1.5501	2
3	− 2.071 176	2.283 225	2.2418	2.2004	2.1797	2.0761	3
4	− 3.786 436	2.854 978	2.7792	2.7035	2.6657	2.4763	5
5	− 5.775 143	3.352 155	3.2367	3.1211	3.0634	2.7746	5
6	− 7.936 781	3.784 483	3.6257	3.4670	3.3876	2.9908	6
7	−10.192 403	4.160 420	3.9566	3.7527	3.6508	3.1412	7
8	−12.480 715	4.487 322	4.2377	3.9881	3.8633	3.2392	8
9	−14.754 815	4.771 584	4.4765	4.1814	4.0338	3.2961	9
10	−16.979 477	5.018 769	4.6792	4.3396	4.1698	3.3208	10
11	−19.128 909	5.233 712	4.8511	4.4686	4.2773	—	11
12	−21.184 888	5.420 619	4.9969	4.5732	4.3614	—	12
13	−23.135 223	5.583 147	5.1204	4.6577	4.4264	—	13
14	−24.972 496	5.724 476	5.2250	4.7256	4.4759	—	14
15	−26.693 019	5.847 370	5.3135	4.7796	4.5127	—	15
16	−28.295 990	5.954 235	5.3883	4.8224	4.5394	—	16
17	−29.782 805	6.047 161	5.4515	4.8558	4.5580	—	17
18	−31.156 492	6.127 966	5.5048	4.8817	4.5701	—	18
19	−32.421 267	6.198 231	5.5498	4.9014	4.5772	—	19
20	−33.582 173	6.259 331	5.5877	4.9160	4.5802	—	20

ORDINARY ANNUITIES CHANGING IN CONSTANT RATIO
(Present Value of Annual Payments Starting at $1 and
Changing in Constant Ratio)

$$PVF = \frac{1 - (1 + x)^n/(1 + i)^n}{i - x}$$

Where: PVF = present value factor

x* = constant ratio change in income

n = number of years

i = rate of interest or yield

*x is positive for an increase and negative for a decrease

This table is used to solve problems dealing with the compound discounting of cash flows that are best represented by an exponential-curve pattern of change.

Example 1

Assuming a 15% interest or yield rate, what is the present value of an ordinary annuity consisting of 10 annual cash flows that start at $10,000 and increase 10% per year compounded?

$$\$10,000 \times 7.1773 = \$71,773$$

Assuming payments are made in advance, the PV of the annuity would be

$$\$71,773 \times 1.150000 = \$82,539$$

or

$$\$71,773/.869565 = \$82,539$$

Example 2

Assuming a 15% interest or yield rate, what is the present value of an ordinary annuity consisting of 10 annual cash flows that start at $10,000 and decrease 3% per year compounded?

$$\$10,000 \times 4.5429 = \$45,429$$

Example 3

There are five years remaining on a lease that provides a level income of $1,000 per year. During this period inflation will cause purchasing power to decline 10% per year on a compound basis. What is the value of the income expressed in constant dollars and discounted at 6%?

$$\$1{,}000 \times .90 \times 3.4922 = \$3{,}142.98$$

Proof:

Year	Income	×	Inflation Factor	×	PVF @ 6%	=	Value
1	$1,000	×	.900000	×	.943396	=	$ 849.06
2	1,000	×	.810000	×	.889996	=	720.90
3	1,000	×	.729000	×	.839619	=	612.08
4	1,000	×	.656100	×	.792094	=	519.69
5	1,000	×	.590490	×	.747258	=	441.25
							$3,142.98

6% ORDINARY ANNUITIES CHANGING IN CONSTANT RATIO

(Present Value of Annual Payments Starting at $1 and Changing in Constant Ratio)

Base: 1.060 000

Annual Percentage INCREASE of:

Years	7%	8%	9%	10%	11%	12%	Years
1	.9434	.9434	.9434	.9434	.9434	.9434	1
2	1.8957	1.9046	1.9135	1.9224	1.9313	1.9402	2
3	2.8570	2.8839	2.9110	2.9383	2.9658	2.9934	3
4	3.8273	3.8817	3.9368	3.9926	4.0491	4.1062	4
5	4.8068	4.8984	4.9916	5.0867	5.1835	5.2821	5
6	5.7956	5.9342	6.0763	6.2220	6.3714	6.5245	6
7	6.7936	6.9896	7.1917	7.4002	7.6153	7.8372	7
8	7.8011	8.0648	8.3386	8.6229	8.9179	9.2242	8
9	8.8181	9.1604	9.5180	8.8916	10.2820	10.6897	9
10	9.8447	10.2766	10.7308	11.2083	11.7104	12.2382	10
11	10.8810	11.4139	11.9779	12.5747	13.2061	13.8743	11
12	11.9270	12.5727	13.2603	13.9926	14.7725	15.6030	12
13	12.9829	13.7533	14.5790	15.4640	16.4127	17.4296	13
14	14.0488	14.9562	15.9350	16.9909	18.1302	19.3596	14
15	15.1247	16.1818	17.3294	18.5755	19.9288	21.3988	15
16	16.2108	17.4305	18.7632	20.2199	21.8123	23.5534	16
17	17.3072	18.7028	20.2376	21.9263	23.7846	25.8301	17
18	18.4138	19.9990	21.7538	23.6971	25.8499	28.2355	18
19	19.5309	21.3198	23.3129	25.5347	28.0126	30.7772	19
20	20.6586	22.6654	24.9161	27.4417	30.2773	33.4627	20

Annual Percentage DECREASE of:

Years	7%	8%	9%	10%	11%	12%	Years
1	.9434	.9434	.9434	.9434	.9434	.9434	1
2	1.7711	1.7622	1.7533	1.7444	1.7355	1.7266	2
3	2.4973	2.4728	2.4486	2.4245	2.4006	2.3768	3
4	3.1344	3.0896	3.0455	3.0019	2.9590	2.9166	4
5	3.6934	3.6250	3.5579	3.4922	3.4278	3.3647	5
6	4.1838	4.0896	3.9978	3.9085	3.8215	3.7367	6
7	4.6141	4.4929	4.3755	4.2619	4.1520	4.0456	7
8	4.9916	4.8429	4.6997	4.5620	4.4295	4.3020	8
9	5.3228	5.1466	4.9781	4.8168	4.6625	4.5149	9
10	5.6134	5.4103	5.2170	5.0331	4.8581	4.6916	10
11	5.8684	5.6391	5.4222	5.2168	5.0224	4.8383	11
12	6.0921	5.8377	5.5983	5.3728	5.1603	4.9601	12
13	6.2883	6.0101	5.7495	5.5052	5.2761	5.0612	13
14	6.4605	6.1597	5.8792	5.6176	5.3733	5.1452	14
15	6.6116	6.2896	5.9907	5.7131	5.4550	5.2148	15
16	6.7441	6.4023	6.0863	5.7941	5.5235	5.2727	16
17	6.8604	6.5001	6.1685	5.8629	5.5811	5.3207	17
18	6.9624	6.5850	6.2390	5.9213	5.6294	5.3606	18
19	7.0520	6.6587	6.2995	5.9710	5.6700	5.3937	19
20	7.1305	6.7226	6.3514	6.0131	5.7040	5.4212	20

10%   ORDINARY ANNUITIES CHANGING IN CONSTANT RATIO

(Present Value of Annual Payments Starting at $1 and Changing in Constant Ratio)

Base: 1.100 000

Annual Percentage INCREASE of:

Years	1%	2%	3%	4%	5%	6%	Years
1	.9091	.9091	.9091	.9091	.9091	.9091	1
2	1.7438	1.7521	1.7603	1.7686	1.7769	1.7851	2
3	2.5102	2.5337	2.5574	2.5812	2.6052	2.6293	3
4	3.2139	3.2586	3.3037	3.3495	3.3959	3.4428	4
5	3.8601	3.9307	4.0026	4.0759	4.1506	4.2267	5
6	4.4533	4.5539	4.6570	4.7627	4.8710	4.9821	6
7	4.9981	5.1318	5.2697	5.4120	5.5587	5.7100	7
8	5.4982	5.6677	5.8435	6.0259	6.2151	6.4115	8
9	5.9575	6.1646	6.3807	6.6063	6.8417	7.0874	9
10	6.3791	6.6253	6.8837	7.1550	7.4398	7.7388	10
11	6.7663	7.0526	7.3548	7.6738	8.0107	8.3664	11
12	7.1218	7.4487	7.7958	8.1644	8.5557	8.9713	12
13	7.4482	7.8161	8.2088	8.6281	9.0759	9.5542	13
14	7.7479	8.1568	8.5955	9.0666	9.5724	10.1158	14
15	8.0230	8.4726	8.9576	9.4811	10.0464	10.6571	15
16	8.2757	8.7655	9.2967	9.8731	10.4989	11.1786	16
17	8.5077	9.0371	9.6142	10.2436	10.9307	11.6812	17
18	8.7207	9.2890	9.9115	10.5940	11.3430	12.1656	18
19	8.9163	9.5225	10.1898	10.9252	11.7365	12.6323	19
20	9.0959	9.7390	10.4505	11.2384	12.1121	13.0820	20

Annual Percentage DECREASE of:

Years	1%	2%	3%	4%	5%	6%	Years
1	.9091	.9091	.9091	.9091	.9091	.9091	1
2	1.7273	1.7190	1.7107	1.7025	1.6942	1.6860	2
3	2.4636	2.4406	2.4177	2.3949	2.3723	2.3498	3
4	3.1264	3.0834	3.0410	2.9992	2.9579	2.9171	4
5	3.7228	3.6561	3.5907	3.5266	3.4636	3.4019	5
6	4.2596	4.1664	4.0755	3.9868	3.9004	3.8162	6
7	4.7428	4.6210	4.5029	4.3885	4.2776	4.1702	7
8	5.1776	5.0259	4.8798	4.7390	4.6034	4.4727	8
9	5.5689	5.3867	5.2122	5.0450	4.8848	4.7312	9
10	5.9211	5.7082	5.5053	5.3120	5.1277	4.9521	10
11	6.2381	5.9946	5.7638	5.5450	5.3376	5.1409	11
12	6.5234	6.2497	5.9917	5.7484	5.5188	5.3022	12
13	6.7801	6.4770	6.1927	5.9259	5.6754	5.4401	13
14	7.0112	6.6795	6.3699	6.0807	5.8105	5.5579	14
15	7.2192	6.8599	6.5262	6.2159	5.9273	5.6586	15
16	7.4063	7.0207	6.6640	6.3339	6.0281	5.7446	16
17	7.5748	7.1639	6.7855	6.4369	6.1152	5.8181	17
18	7.7264	7.2914	6.8927	6.5267	6.1904	5.8809	18
19	7.8629	7.4051	6.9872	6.6051	6.2553	5.9346	19
20	7.9857	7.5064	7.0705	6.6736	6.3114	5.9805	20

15%   ORDINARY ANNUITIES CHANGING IN CONSTANT RATIO
(Present Value of Annual Payments Starting at $1 and Changing in Constant Ratio)

Base: 1.150 000

			Annual Percentage INCREASE of:				
Years	7%	8%	9%	10%	11%	12%	Years
1	.8696	.8696	.8696	.8696	.8696	.8696	1
2	1.6786	1.6862	1.6938	1.7013	1.7089	1.7164	2
3	2.4314	2.4531	2.4750	2.4969	2.5190	2.5412	3
4	3.1319	3.1734	3.2154	3.2579	3.3010	3.3445	4
5	3.7835	3.8498	3.9172	3.9858	4.0557	4.1268	5
6	4.3899	4.4850	4.5824	4.6821	4.7842	4.8887	6
7	4.9541	5.0816	5.2129	5.3481	5.4874	5.6308	7
8	5.4790	5.6418	5.8105	5.9851	6.1661	6.3534	8
9	5.9674	6.1680	6.3769	6.5945	6.8212	7.0573	9
10	6.4219	6.6621	6.9137	7.1773	7.4535	7.7427	10
11	6.8447	7.1261	7.4226	7.7348	8.0638	8.4103	11
12	7.2381	7.5619	7.9049	8.2681	8.6529	9.0605	12
13	7.6042	7.9712	8.3620	8.7782	9.2215	9.6937	13
14	7.9447	8.3556	8.7953	9.2661	9.7703	10.3104	14
15	8.2616	8.7165	9.2060	9.7328	10.3000	10.9110	15
16	8.5565	9.0555	9.5952	10.1792	10.8113	11.4959	16
17	8.8308	9.3739	9.9642	10.6062	11.3048	12.0656	17
18	9.0861	9.6729	10.3139	11.0146	11.7812	12.6204	18
19	9.3235	9.9537	10.6453	11.4053	12.2410	13.1607	19
20	9.5445	10.2173	10.9595	11.7790	12.6848	13.6870	20

			Annual Percentage DECREASE of:				
Years	7%	8%	9%	10%	11%	12%	Years
1	.8696	.8696	.8696	.8696	.8696	.8696	1
2	1.5728	1.5652	1.5577	1.5501	1.5425	1.5350	2
3	2.1415	2.1217	2.1021	2.0827	2.0634	2.0442	3
4	2.6014	2.5670	2.5330	2.4995	2.4664	2.4338	4
5	2.9733	2.9231	2.8739	2.8257	2.7784	2.7319	5
6	3.2740	3.2081	3.1437	3.0810	3.0198	2.9601	6
7	3.5173	3.4360	3.3572	3.2808	3.2066	3.1347	7
8	3.7140	3.6184	3.5261	3.4371	3.3512	3.2683	8
9	3.8730	3.7643	3.6598	3.5595	3.4631	3.3705	9
10	4.0017	3.8810	3.7656	3.6552	3.5497	3.4487	10
11	4.1057	3.9744	3.8493	3.7302	3.6167	3.5086	11
12	4.1898	4.0490	3.9155	3.7888	3.6686	3.5544	12
13	4.2579	4.1088	3.9679	3.8348	3.7087	3.5895	13
14	4.3129	4.1566	4.0094	3.8707	3.7398	3.6163	14
15	4.3574	4.1949	4.0422	3.8988	3.7639	3.6368	15
16	4.3934	4.2254	4.0682	3.9208	3.7825	3.6525	16
17	4.4224	4.2499	4.0888	3.9380	3.7969	3.6645	17
18	4.4460	4.2695	4.1050	3.9515	3.8080	3.6737	18
19	4.4650	4.2852	4.1179	3.9620	3.8166	3.6808	19
20	4.4804	4.2977	4.1281	3.9703	3.8233	3.6862	20

SINKING FUND FACTORS (Periodic Payment to Grow to $1)

This factor represents the level periodic investment or deposit required to accumulate to $1 in a given number of periods including interest at the effective rate. It is commonly known as the *amortization rate* and is the reciprocal of the corresponding sinking fund accumulation factor.

$$1/S_{\overline{n|}} = \frac{i}{S^n - 1}$$

Where: $1/S_{\overline{n|}}$ = sinking fund factor
i = effective rate of interest
n = number of compounding periods
S^n = future value factor

This table is used to solve problems that involve calculating required sinking fund deposits or providing for the change in capital value in investment situations where the income or payments are level.

Example 1

Assuming a 6% interest rate, what monthly, end-of-period deposit would be required to yield $10,000 in 10 years?

$$\$10,000 \times .006102 = \$61.02$$

Assuming deposits are made at the beginning of the period, what amount would be required?

$$\$10,000 \times .006102/1.005 = \$60.72$$

Example 2

Assuming a 6% interest rate, what monthly, end-of-period deposit would be required to yield $10,000 in 10 years and 7 months?

$$\$10,000/(1/.006102 + 1.819397*/.140729) = \$56.56$$

*future value factor for 120 months

Assuming deposits are made at the beginning of the period, what amount would be required?

$$\$56.56/1.005 = \$56.28$$

Example 3

What is the annual constant for a direct reduction loan at 12% interest with monthly payments for 25 years?

$$.12 + 12 \times .000532 = .126384$$

In actual practice, loan payments are rounded up to the nearest penny. Published tables of annual constants reflect this practice. In a typical table of annual constants, factors are calculated for each $1,000 of loan, so the sinking fund factor is rounded up to the fifth decimal place. On this basis, the constant for a 12%, 25-year loan would be

$$.12 + 12 \times .000540 = .126480$$

Example 4

Assuming a 12% interest or yield rate, what monthly payment would provide for interest and 40% amortization of a $100,000 loan in 10 years?

$$\$100,000 \times (.12/12 + .4 \times .004347) = \$1,173.88$$

Example 5

A property has an anticipated net operating income of $10,000 per year for the next five years. The trend in prices indicates a 15% increase in value over this period of time. What is the calculated value of the property assuming a 12% yield rate?

$$\$10,000/(.12 - .15 \times .157410) = \$103,747$$

When deposits are made at the end of each compounding period, sinking fund factors reflect the fractional portion of $1.00 that must be deposited periodically at a specified interest rate to accumulate to $1.00 by the end of the series of deposits.

If $10,000 is to be accumulated over a 10-year period and annual deposits are compounded at 10% interest, the factor shown on the 10-year line of the annual column in the 10% sinking fund table indicates that each annual deposit must amount to $10,000 × .062745, or $627.45.

6%   SINKING FUND FACTORS
(Periodic Payment to Grow to $1)

Base:	1.005 000	1.015 000	1.030 000	1.060 000	1.061 831	
			Frequency of Payments and of Conversions			
Months	Monthly	Quarterly	Semiannual	Annual	Annual Payment Daily Conversion	Months
1	1.000 000	—	—	—	—	1
2	.498 753	—	—	—	—	2
3	.331 672	1.000 000	—	—	—	3
4	.248 133	—	—	—	—	4
5	.198 010	—	—	—	—	5
6	.164 595	.496 278	1.000 000	—	—	6
7	.140 729	—	—	—	—	7
8	.122 829	—	—	—	—	8
9	.108 907	.328 383	—	—	—	9
10	.097 771	—	—	—	—	10
11	.088 659	—	—	—	—	11

Years						Years
1	.081 066	.244 445	.492 611	1.000 000	1.000 000	1
2	.039 321	.118 584	.239 027	.485 437	.485 006	2
3	.025 422	.076 680	.154 598	.314 110	.313 547	3
4	.018 485	.055 765	.112 456	.228 591	.227 971	4
5	.014 333	.043 246	.087 231	.177 396	.176 749	5
6	.011 573	.034 924	.070 462	.143 363	.142 703	6
7	.009 609	.029 001	.058 526	.119 135	.188 471	7
8	.008 141	.024 577	.049 611	.101 036	.100 374	8
9	.007 006	.021 152	.042 709	.087 022	.086 365	9
10	.006 102	.018 427	.037 216	.075 868	.075 218	10
11	.005 367	.016 210	.032 747	.066 793	.066 152	11
12	.004 759	.014 375	.029 047	.059 277	.058 646	12
13	.004 247	.012 833	.025 938	.052 960	.052 340	13
14	.003 812	.011 521	.023 293	.047 585	.046 977	14
15	.003 439	.010 393	.021 019	.042 963	.042 367	15
16	.003 114	.009 415	.019 047	.038 952	.038 369	16
17	.002 831	.008 560	.017 322	.035 445	.034 875	17
18	.002 582	.007 808	.015 804	.032 357	.031 799	18
19	.002 361	.007 141	.014 459	.029 621	.029 077	19
20	.002 164	.006 548	.013 262	.027 185	.026 654	20
21	.001 989	.006 018	.012 192	.025 005	.024 487	21
22	.001 831	.005 541	.011 230	.023 046	.022 541	22
23	.001 688	.005 112	.010 363	.021 278	.020 787	23
24	.001 560	.004 723	.009 578	.019 679	.019 201	24
25	.001 443	.004 371	.008 865	.018 227	.017 762	25
26	.001 337	.004 050	.008 217	.016 904	.016 452	26
27	.001 240	.003 757	.007 626	.015 697	.015 258	27
28	.001 151	.003 489	.007 084	.014 593	.014 166	28
29	.001 070	.003 244	.006 588	.013 580	.013 165	29
30	.000 996	.003 019	.006 133	.012 649	.012 247	30
31	.000 927	.002 811	.005 714	.011 792	.011 402	31
32	.000 864	.002 620	.005 328	.011 002	.010 624	32
33	.000 806	.002 444	.004 971	.010 273	.009 906	33
34	.000 752	.002 281	.004 642	.009 598	.009 243	34
35	.000 702	.002 131	.004 337	.008 974	.008 630	35
36	.000 656	.001 991	.004 054	.008 395	.008 062	36
37	.000 613	.001 862	.003 792	.007 857	.007 535	37
38	.000 573	.001 742	.003 548	.007 358	.007 046	38
39	.000 536	.001 630	.003 322	.006 894	.006 592	39
40	.000 502	.001 526	.003 112	.006 462	.006 170	40

10%   SINKING FUND FACTORS
(Periodic Payment to Grow to $1)

Base:	1.008 333	1.025 000	1.050 000	1.100 000	1.105 156	
		Frequency of Payments and of Conversions				
Months	Monthly	Quarterly	Semiannual	Annual	Annual Payment Daily Conversion	Months
1	1.000 000	—	—	—	—	1
2	.497 925	—	—	—	—	2
3	.330 571	1.000 000	—	—	—	3
4	.246 897	—	—	—	—	4
5	.196 694	—	—	—	—	5
6	.163 228	.493 827	1.000 000	—	—	6
7	.139 325	—	—	—	—	7
8	.121 400	—	—	—	—	8
9	.107 459	.325 137	—	—	—	9
10	.096 307	—	—	—	—	10
11	.087 184	—	—	—	—	11

Years						Years
1	.079 583	.240 818	.487 805	1.000 000	1.000 000	1
2	.037 812	.114 467	.232 012	.476 190	.475 024	2
3	.023 934	.072 487	.147 017	.302 115	.300 614	3
4	.017 029	.051 599	.104 722	.215 471	.213 843	4
5	.012 914	.039 147	.079 505	.163 797	.162 125	5
6	.010 193	.030 913	.062 825	.129 607	.127 932	6
7	.008 268	.025 088	.051 024	.105 405	.103 749	7
8	.006 841	.020 768	.042 270	.087 444	.085 821	8
9	.005 745	.017 452	.035 546	.073 641	.072 059	9
10	.004 882	.014 836	.030 243	.062 745	.061 212	10
11	.004 187	.012 730	.025 971	.053 963	.052 481	11
12	.003 617	.011 006	.022 471	.046 763	.045 334	12
13	.003 145	.009 574	.019 564	.040 779	.039 404	13
14	.002 749	.008 372	.017 123	.035 746	.034 427	14
15	.002 413	.007 353	.015 051	.031 474	.030 211	15
16	.002 126	.006 482	.013 280	.027 817	.026 609	16
17	.001 879	.005 733	.011 755	.024 664	.023 511	17
18	.001 665	.005 084	.010 434	.021 930	.020 831	18
19	.001 479	.004 520	.009 284	.019 547	.018 500	19
20	.001 317	.004 026	.008 278	.017 460	.016 464	20
21	.001 174	.003 593	.007 395	.015 624	.014 679	21
22	.001 049	.003 212	.006 616	.014 005	.013 108	22
23	.000 938	.002 875	.005 928	.012 572	.011 722	23
24	.000 841	.002 577	.005 318	.011 300	.010 495	24
25	.000 754	.002 312	.004 777	.010 168	.009 407	25
26	.000 676	.002 076	.004 294	.009 159	.008 440	26
27	.000 608	.001 867	.003 864	.008 258	.007 579	27
28	.000 546	.001 679	.003 480	.007 451	.006 811	28
29	.000 491	.001 512	.003 136	.006 728	.006 126	29
30	.000 442	.001 362	.002 828	.006 079	.005 512	30
31	.000 398	.001 227	.002 552	.005 496	.004 963	31
32	.000 359	.001 107	.002 304	.004 972	.004 471	32
33	.000 324	.000 999	.002 081	.004 499	.004 029	33
34	.000 292	.000 901	.001 880	.004 074	.003 632	34
35	.000 263	.000 814	.001 699	.003 690	.003 276	35
36	.000 238	.000 735	.001 536	.003 343	.002 955	36
37	.000 215	.000 664	.001 390	.003 030	.002 667	37
38	.000 194	.000 600	.001 257	.002 747	.002 408	38
39	.000 175	.000 542	.001 138	.002 491	.002 174	39
40	.000 158	.000 490	.001 030	.002 259	.001 963	40

12%   SINKING FUND FACTORS
(Periodic Payment to Grow to $1)

Base:	1.010 000	1.030 000	1.060 000	1.120 000	1.127 474	
			Frequency of Payments and of Conversions			
Months	Monthly	Quarterly	Semiannual	Annual	Annual Payment Daily Conversion	Months
1	1.000 000	—	—	—	—	1
2	.497 512	—	—	—	—	2
3	.330 022	1.000 000	—	—	—	3
4	.246 281	—	—	—	—	4
5	.196 040	—	—	—	—	5
6	.162 548	.492 611	1.000 000	—	—	6
7	.138 628	—	—	—	—	7
8	.120 690	—	—	—	—	8
9	.106 740	.323 530	—	—	—	9
10	.095 582	—	—	—	—	10
11	.086 454	—	—	—	—	11
Years						Years
1	.078 849	.239 027	.485 437	1.000 000	1.000 000	1
2	.037 073	.112 456	.228 591	.471 698	.470 041	2
3	.023 214	.070 462	.143 363	.296 349	.294 233	3
4	.016 334	.049 611	.101 036	.209 234	.206 957	4
5	.012 244	.037 216	.075 868	.157 410	.155 090	5
6	.009 550	.029 047	.059 277	.123 226	.120 922	6
7	.007 653	.023 293	.047 585	.099 118	.096 862	7
8	.006 253	.019 047	.038 952	.081 303	.079 114	8
9	.005 184	.015 804	.032 357	.067 679	.065 568	9
10	.004 347	.013 262	.027 185	.056 984	.054 959	10
11	.003 678	.011 230	.023 046	.048 415	.046 479	11
12	.003 134	.009 578	.019 679	.041 437	.039 592	12
13	.002 687	.008 217	.016 904	.035 677	.033 925	13
14	.002 314	.007 084	.014 593	.030 871	.029 210	14
15	.002 002	.006 133	.012 649	.026 824	.025 253	15
16	.001 737	.005 328	.011 002	.023 390	.021 907	16
17	.001 512	.004 642	.009 598	.020 457	.019 060	17
18	.001 320	.004 054	.008 395	.017 937	.016 624	18
19	.001 154	.003 548	.007 358	.015 763	.014 530	19
20	.001 011	.003 112	.006 462	.013 879	.012 724	20
21	.000 887	.002 733	.005 683	.012 240	.011 159	21
22	.000 779	.002 404	.005 006	.010 811	.009 800	22
23	.000 686	.002 117	.004 415	.009 560	.008 617	23
24	.000 604	.001 866	.003 898	.008 463	.007 585	24
25	.000 532	.001 647	.003 444	.007 500	.006 683	25
26	.000 470	.001 454	.003 046	.006 652	.005 892	26
27	.000 414	.001 285	.002 696	.005 904	.005 199	27
28	.000 366	.001 136	.002 388	.005 244	.004 590	28
29	.000 324	.001 005	.002 116	.004 660	.004 054	29
30	.000 286	.000 890	.001 876	.004 144	.003 583	30
31	.000 253	.000 788	.001 664	.003 686	.003 168	31
32	.000 224	.000 698	.001 476	.003 280	.002 802	32
33	.000 198	.000 619	.001 310	.002 920	.002 479	33
34	.000 176	.000 548	.001 163	.002 601	.002 194	34
35	.000 155	.000 486	.001 033	.002 317	.001 942	35
36	.000 138	.000 431	.000 918	.002 064	.001 719	36
37	.000 122	.000 383	.000 815	.001 840	.001 523	37
38	.000 108	.000 339	.000 725	.001 640	.001 349	38
39	.000 096	.000 301	.000 644	.001 462	.001 195	39
40	.000 085	.000 267	.000 573	.001 304	.001 059	40

SINKING FUND ACCUMULATION FACTORS (Future Value of Periodic Payments of $1)

This factor represents the total accumulation of principal and interest on a series of deposits or installments of $1 per period for a given number of periods with interest at the effective rate per period. It is also known as the *amount of one per period*. It is the reciprocal of the corresponding sinking fund factor.

$$S_{\overline{n}|} = \frac{S^n - 1}{i}$$

Where: $S_{\overline{n}|}$ = sinking fund accumulation factor
   i = effective rate of interest
   S^n = future value factor

This table is used to solve problems that involve the growth of sinking funds or the calculation of capital recovery in investment situations where the income or payments are level.

Example 1

Assuming a 6% nominal interest rate, how much money would be accumulated if deposits of $100 were made at the end of each month for a period of 10 years?

$$\$100 \times 163.879347 = \$16,387.93$$

Assuming the deposits were at the beginning of each month, how much money would be accumulated?

$$\$16,387.93 \times 1.005 = \$16,469.87$$

Example 2

Assuming a 6% nominal interest rate, how much money would be accumulated if deposits of $100 were made at the end of each month for a period of 10 years and 7 months?

$$\$100 \times (163.879347 + 7.105879 \times 1.819397^*) = \$17,680.78$$

*Future value factor for 120 months

or

$$\$100 \times (7.105879 + 163.879347 \times 1.035529^*) = \$17,680.77$$

*Future value factor for 7 months

Example 3

Assuming a 6% nominal interest rate and daily compounding, how much money would be accumulated in a Keogh Retirement Plan if deposits of $1,200 were made at the end of each year for 10 years?

$$\$1,200 \times 13.294699 = \$15,953.64$$

Assuming the deposits were made at the beginning of each year, how much money would be accumulated?

$$\$15,953.64 \times 1.061831 = \$16,940.07$$

Example 4

Given a $100,000 loan with monthly payments of $908.71 including nominal interest at 10%, how much will be paid off in 10 years?

$$[\$908.71 - (\$100,000 \times .10/12)] \times 204.844979 = \$15,440.53$$

Sinking fund accumulation factors are similar to the future value of $1 (amount of one) factors except that deposits are periodic (in a series) and are assumed to be made at the *end* of the first compounding period and at the *end* of each period thereafter. Thus, the initial deposit, which is made at the end of the first period, has earned no interest and the factor for this period is 1.000000.

If compounding at 10% per year for 10 years is assumed, a factor of 15.937425 reveals that a series of 10 deposits of $1.00 each made at the end of each year for 10 years will accumulate to $1.00 × 15.937425, or almost $15.94.

6%   SINKING FUND ACCUMULATION FACTORS
(Future Value of Periodic Payments of $1)

Base:	1.005 000	1.015 000	1.030 000	1.060 000	1.061 831	
			Frequency of Payments and of Conversions			
Months	Monthly	Quarterly	Semiannual	Annual	Annual Payment Daily Conversion	Months
1	1.000 000	—	—	—	—	1
2	2.005 000	—	—	—	—	2
3	3.015 025	1.000 000	—	—	—	3
4	4.030 100	—	—	—	—	4
5	5.050 251	—	—	—	—	5
6	6.075 502	2.015 000	1.000 000	—	—	6
7	7.105 879	—	—	—	—	7
8	8.141 409	—	—	—	—	8
9	9.182 116	3.045 225	—	—	—	9
10	10.228 026	—	—	—	—	10
11	11.279 167	—	—	—	—	11

Years						Years
1	12.335 562	4.090 903	2.030 000	1.000 000	1.000 000	1
2	25.431 955	8.432 839	4.183 627	2.060 000	2.061 831	2
3	39.336 105	13.041 211	6.468 410	3.183 600	3.189 137	3
4	54.097 832	17.932 370	8.892 336	4.374 616	4.386 516	4
5	69.770 031	23.123 667	11.463 879	5.637 093	5.657 740	5
6	86.408 856	28.633 521	14.192 030	6.975 319	7.007 565	6
7	104.073 927	34.481 479	17.086 324	8.393 838	8.440 851	7
8	122.828 542	40.688 288	20.156 881	9.897 468	9.962 760	8
9	142.739 900	47.275 969	23.414 435	11.491 316	11.578 769	9
10	163.879 347	54.267 894	26.870 374	13.180 795	13.294 699	10
11	186.322 629	61.688 868	30.536 780	14.971 643	15.116 727	11
12	210.150 163	69.565 219	34.426 470	16.869 941	17.051 413	12
13	235.447 328	77.924 892	38.553 042	18.882 138	19.105 723	13
14	262.304 766	86.797 543	42.930 923	21.015 066	21.287 053	14
15	290.818 712	96.214 652	47.575 416	23.275 970	23.603 258	15
16	321.091 337	106.209 628	52.502 759	25.672 528	26.062 677	16
17	353.231 110	116.817 931	57.730 177	28.212 880	28.674 164	17
18	387.353 194	128.077 197	63.275 944	30.905 653	31.447 123	18
19	423.579 854	140.027 372	69.159 449	33.759 992	34.391 538	19
20	462.040 895	152.710 852	75.401 260	36.785 591	37.518 009	20
21	502.874 129	166.172 636	82.023 196	39.992 727	40.837 794	21
22	546.225 867	180.460 482	89.048 409	43.392 290	44.362 846	22
23	592.251 446	195.625 082	96.501 457	46.995 828	48.105 855	23
24	641.115 782	211.720 235	104.408 396	50.815 577	52.080 300	24
25	692.993 962	228.803 043	112.796 867	54.864 512	56.300 489	25
26	748.071 876	246.934 114	121.696 197	59.156 383	60.781 618	26
27	806.546 875	266.177 771	131.137 495	63.705 766	65.539 821	27
28	868.628 484	286.602 288	141.153 768	68.528 112	70.592 229	28
29	934.539 150	308.280 125	151.780 033	73.639 798	75.957 034	29
30	1004.515 042	331.288 191	163.053 437	79.058 186	81.653 552	30
31	1078.806 895	355.708 115	175.013 391	84.801 677	87.702 292	31
32	1157.680 906	381.626 531	187.701 707	90.889 778	94.125 033	32
33	1241.419 693	409.135 393	201.162 741	97.343 165	100.944 900	33
34	1330.323 306	438.332 297	215.443 551	104.183 755	108.186 449	34
35	1424.710 299	469.320 826	230.594 064	111.434 780	115.875 751	35
36	1524.918 875	502.210 922	246.667 242	119.120 867	124.040 492	36
37	1631.308 097	537.119 271	263.719 277	127.268 119	132.710 069	37
38	1744.259 173	574.169 720	281.809 781	135.904 206	141.915 697	38
39	1864.176 824	613.493 716	301.001 997	145.058 458	151.690 520	39
40	1991.490 734	655.230 772	321.363 019	154.761 966	162.069 733	40

10%   SINKING FUND ACCUMULATION FACTORS
(Future Value of Periodic Payments of $1)

Base:	1.008 333	1.025 000	1.050 000	1.100 000	1.105 156	
			Frequency of Payments and of Conversions			
Months	Monthly	Quarterly	Semiannual	Annual	Annual Payment Daily Conversion	Months
1	1.000 000	—	—	—	—	1
2	2.008 333	—	—	—	—	2
3	3.025 069	1.000 000	—	—	—	3
4	4.050 278	—	—	—	—	4
5	5.084 031	—	—	—	—	5
6	6.126 398	2.025 000	1.000 000	—	—	6
7	7.177 451	—	—	—	—	7
8	8.237 263	—	—	—	—	8
9	9.305 907	3.075 625	—	—	—	9
10	10.383 456	—	—	—	—	10
11	11.469 985	—	—	—	—	11

Years						Years
1	12.565 568	4.152 516	2.050 000	1.000 000	1.000 000	1
2	26.446 915	8.736 116	4.310 125	2.100 000	2.105 156	2
3	41.781 821	13.795 553	6.801 913	3.310 000	3.326 524	3
4	58.722 492	19.380 225	9.549 109	4.641 000	4.676 327	4
5	77.437 072	25.544 658	12.577 893	6.105 100	6.168 069	5
6	98.111 314	32.349 038	15.917 127	7.715 610	7.816 676	6
7	120.950 418	39.859 801	19.598 632	9.487 171	9.638 643	7
8	146.181 076	48.150 278	23.657 492	11.435 888	11.652 200	8
9	174.053 713	57.301 413	28.132 385	13.579 477	13.877 493	9
10	204.844 979	67.402 554	33.065 954	15.937 425	16.336 789	10
11	238.860 493	78.552 323	38.505 214	18.531 167	19.054 693	11
12	276.437 876	90.859 582	44.501 999	21.384 284	22.058 401	12
13	317.950 102	104.444 494	51.113 454	24.522 712	25.377 964	13
14	363.809 201	119.439 694	58.402 583	27.974 983	29.046 599	14
15	414.470 346	135.991 590	66.438 848	31.772 482	33.101 010	15
16	470.436 376	154.261 786	75.298 829	35.949 730	37.581 766	16
17	532.262 780	174.428 663	85.066 959	40.544 703	42.533 698	17
18	600.563 216	196.689 122	95.836 323	45.599 173	48.006 353	18
19	676.015 601	221.260 504	107.709 546	51.159 090	54.054 489	19
20	759.368 836	248.382 713	120.799 774	57.274 999	60.738 620	20
21	851.450 244	278.320 556	135.231 751	64.002 499	68.125 624	21
22	953.173 779	311.366 333	151.143 006	71.402 749	76.289 413	22
23	1065.549 097	347.842 687	168.685 164	79.543 024	85.311 670	23
24	1189.691 580	388.105 758	188.025 393	88.497 327	95.282 667	24
25	1326.833 403	432.548 654	209.347 996	98.347 059	106.302 170	25
26	1478.335 767	481.605 296	232.856 165	109.181 765	118.480 436	26
27	1645.702 407	535.754 649	258.773 922	121.099 942	131.939 313	27
28	1830.594 523	595.525 404	287.348 249	134.209 936	146.813 467	28
29	2034.847 258	661.501 133	318.851 445	148.630 930	163.251 721	29
30	2260.487 925	734.325 993	353.583 718	164.494 023	181.418 550	30
31	2509.756 117	814.711 013	391.876 049	181.943 425	201.495 721	31
32	2785.125 947	903.441 034	434.093 344	201.137 767	223.684 118	32
33	3089.330 596	1001.382 375	480.637 912	222.251 544	248.205 750	33
34	3425.389 447	1109.491 289	531.953 298	245.476 699	275.305 967	34
35	3796.638 052	1228.823 303	588.528 511	271.024 368	305.255 923	35
36	4206.761 236	1360.543 518	650.902 683	299.126 805	338.355 284	36
37	4659.829 677	1505.937 989	719.670 208	330.039 486	374.935 228	37
38	5160.340 305	1666.426 280	795.486 404	364.043 434	415.361 756	38
39	5713.260 935	1843.575 325	879.073 761	401.447 778	460.039 359	39
40	6324.079 581	2039.114 724	971.228 821	442.592 556	509.415 060	40

DIRECT REDUCTION LOAN FACTORS (Monthly Payment and Annual Constant per $1 of Loan)

Payment: $\qquad 1/a_{\overline{n}} = \dfrac{i}{1 - 1/S^n}$

Annual constant: $\qquad R_M = 12/a_{\overline{n}}$

Where: $\qquad\qquad 1/a_{\overline{n}}$ = direct reduction loan factor
$\qquad\qquad\qquad 1/S^n$ = present value factor
$\qquad\qquad\qquad\quad i$ = effective rate of interest
$\qquad\qquad\qquad R_M$ = annual constant

Part paid off: $\qquad P = \dfrac{R_M - 12i}{R_{Mp} - 12i}$

Where: $\qquad\qquad R_M$ = actual annual constant
$\qquad\qquad\quad R_{Mp}$ = annual constant for projection period
$\qquad\qquad\qquad\ i$ = effective rate of interest

This table is used to solve problems dealing with monthly payment, direct reduction loans. Payments and constants for quarterly, semiannual, and annual payment loans can be obtained by calculating the reciprocals of the present value of $1 per period factors.

Example 1

What is the level monthly payment and annual debt service for a direct reduction loan of $100,000, assuming nominal interest at 10% and full amortization over 25 years?

$$\$100,000 \times .0090870 = \$\quad 908.70*$$
$$\$100,000 \times .1090441 = \$10,904.41*$$

*In actual practice, the payment would be rounded up to $908.71 and the debt service would be $908.71 × 12 = $10,904.52.

Example 2

How much of the loan in Example 1 would be paid off in 10 years?

$$\$100,000 \times .1544 = \$15,440$$

or

$$\$100,000 \times [(\$10,904.52/\$100,000 - .10)/(.1585809 - .10)] = \$15,440.52$$

Example 3

What discounted price would achieve a 14% yield for this loan?

Assuming full term:

$$\$10,904.41/.1444513 = \$75,488.49$$

Assuming a 10-year call:

$$
\begin{array}{lr}
\$10,904.52/.1863197 & = \$58,525.86 \\
(\$100,000 - \$15,440.53) \times .248603^* & = \underline{21,021.74} \\
& \$79,547.60
\end{array}
$$

*Present value for 120 months

Example 4

What is the level monthly payment and annual debt service for a direct reduction loan of $100,000, assuming nominal interest at 10% and full amortization over 25 years and 7 months?

$$\$100,000/(1/.0090870 + .082940^*/.1476586) = \$904.09$$

$$\$904.09 \times 12 = \$10,849.08$$

*Present value factor for 300 months

Example 5

How much of the loan in Example 4 would be paid off in 10 years?

$$\$100,000 \times [(\$10,849.08/\$100,000 - .10)/(.1585809 - .10)] = \$14,494.14$$

These factors, which are known as *mortgage constants for loan amortization*, reflect the amount of ordinary annuity payment that $1.00 will purchase. They indicate the periodic payment that will extinguish the debt and pay interest on the declining balance of the debt over the life of the payments. The mortgage constant may be expressed in terms of the periodic payments. A mortgage constant related to a monthly payment is the ratio of the monthly payment amount to the original amount of the loan. Whether payments are monthly, semiannual, or annual, the mortgage constant is usually expressed in terms of the total payments in one year as a percentage of the original loan amount. This is called the *annual constant* and is represented by the symbol R_M. As the loan is paid off and the outstanding balance is reduced, a new annual mortgage constant can be calculated as the ratio of total annual payments to the unpaid balance of the loan at that time.

A loan of $10,000 to be amortized in 10 annual end-of-year payments at a mortgage interest rate of 10% would require level annual payments of $10,000 × .162745, the 10% direct reduction annual factor for 10 years. If monthly payments were made at 10% over 10 years, the amount of each payment would be $132.15 (i.e., $10,000 × .013215). The annual mortgage constant in this case would be .158580, or 12 × .013215.

Direct reduction factors consist of the interest rate plus the sinking fund factor at the specific point in time. They are reciprocals of the corresponding ordinary level-annuity factors.

10%   DIRECT REDUCTION LOAN FACTORS
(Monthly Payment and Annual Constant per $1 of Loan)

Base: 1.008 333

| Months | Payment | Annual Constant | Part Paid Off Projection | | | | Months |
			1 Year	5 Years	10 Years	15 Years	
1	1.008 3333	—	—	—	—	—	1
2	.506 2586	—	—	—	—	—	2
3	.338 9043	—	—	—	—	—	3
4	.255 2299	—	—	—	—	—	4
5	.205 0277	—	—	—	—	—	5
6	.171 5614	—	—	—	—	—	6
7	.147 6586	—	—	—	—	—	7
8	.129 7329	—	—	—	—	—	8
9	.115 7920	—	—	—	—	—	9
10	.104 6404	—	—	—	—	—	10
11	.095 5174	—	—	—	—	—	11

Years							Years
1	.087 9159	1.054 9906	1.0000	—	—	—	1
2	.046 1449	.553 7391	.4751	—	—	—	2
3	.032 2672	.387 2062	.3007	—	—	—	3
4	.025 3626	.304 3510	.2140	—	—	—	4
5	.021 2470	.254 9645	.1623	1.0000	—	—	5
6	.018 5258	.222 3101	.1281	.7893	—	—	6
7	.016 6012	.199 2142	.1039	.6402	—	—	7
8	.015 1742	.182 0900	.0860	.5297	—	—	8
9	.014 0787	.168 9442	.0722	.4449	—	—	9
10	.013 2151	.158 5809	.0613	.3780	1.0000	—	10
11	.012 5199	.150 2385	.0526	.3242	.8576	—	11
12	.011 9508	.143 4094	.0455	.2801	.7410	—	12
13	.011 4785	.137 7418	.0395	.2436	.6443	—	13
14	.011 0820	.132 9843	.0345	.2129	.5631	—	14
15	.010 7461	.128 9526	.0303	.1868	.4942	1.0000	15
16	.010 4590	.125 5082	.0267	.1646	.4354	.8810	16
17	.010 2121	.122 5453	.0236	.1455	.3849	.7787	17
18	.009 9984	.119 9812	.0209	.1289	.3411	.6901	18
19	.009 8126	.117 7511	.0186	.1145	.3030	.6131	19
20	.009 6502	.115 8026	.0165	.1020	.2698	.5458	20
21	.009 5078	.114 0936	.0148	.0909	.2406	.4868	21
22	.009 3825	.112 5895	.0132	.0812	.2149	.4348	22
23	.009 2718	.111 2618	.0118	.0727	.1922	.3890	23
24	.009 1739	.110 0866	.0106	.0651	.1722	.3484	24
25	.009 0870	.109 0441	.0095	.0584	.1544	.3124	25
26	.009 0098	.108 1172	.0085	.0524	.1386	.2804	26
27	.008 9410	.107 2917	.0076	.0471	.1245	.2519	27
28	.008 8796	.106 5552	.0069	.0423	.1119	.2264	28
29	.008 8248	.105 8972	.0062	.0381	.1007	.2037	29
30	.008 7757	.105 3086	.0056	.0343	.0906	.1834	30
31	.008 7318	.104 7813	.0050	.0309	.0816	.1651	31
32	.008 6924	.104 3086	.0045	.0278	.0735	.1488	32
33	.008 6570	.103 8843	.0041	.0251	.0663	.1342	33
34	.008 6253	.103 5033	.0037	.0226	.0598	.1210	34
35	.008 5967	.103 1607	.0033	.0204	.0540	.1092	35
36	.008 5710	.102 8526	.0030	.0184	.0487	.0985	36
37	.008 5479	.102 5752	.0027	.0166	.0440	.0889	37
38	.008 5271	.102 3254	.0024	.0150	.0397	.0803	38
39	.008 5084	.102 1004	.0022	.0136	.0359	.0725	39
40	.008 4915	.101 8975	.0020	.0122	.0324	.0655	40

14%   DIRECT REDUCTION LOAN FACTORS
(Monthly Payment and Annual Constant per $1 of Loan)

Base: 1.011 667

| Months | Payment | Annual Constant | Part Paid Off Projection | | | | Months |
			1 Year	5 Years	10 Years	15 Years	
1	1.011 6667	—	—	—	—	—	1
2	.508 7669	—	—	—	—	—	2
3	.341 1412	—	—	—	—	—	3
4	.257 3340	—	—	—	—	—	4
5	.207 0541	—	—	—	—	—	5
6	.173 5380	—	—	—	—	—	6
7	.149 6011	—	—	—	—	—	7
8	.131 6513	—	—	—	—	—	8
9	.117 6928	—	—	—	—	—	9
10	.106 5283	—	—	—	—	—	10
11	.097 3957	—	—	—	—	—	11

Years							Years
1	.089 7871	1.077 4454	1.0000	—	—	—	1
2	.048 0129	.576 1546	.4653	—	—	—	2
3	.034 1776	.410 1316	.2882	—	—	—	3
4	.027 3265	.327 9177	.2005	—	—	—	4
5	.023 2683	.279 2190	.1485	1.0000	—	—	5
6	.020 6057	.247 2689	.1144	.7705	—	—	6
7	.018 7400	.224 8801	.0905	.6097	—	—	7
8	.017 3715	.208 4580	.0730	.4917	—	—	8
9	.016 3337	.196 0044	.0597	.4023	—	—	9
10	.015 5266	.186 3197	.0494	.3327	1.0000	—	10
11	.014 8867	.178 6399	.0412	.2775	.8342	—	11
12	.014 3713	.172 4553	.0346	.2331	.7007	—	12
13	.013 9510	.167 4124	.0292	.1969	.5918	—	13
14	.013 6049	.163 2588	.0248	.1671	.5021	—	14
15	.013 3174	.159 8090	.0211	.1423	.4277	1.0000	15
16	.013 0770	.156 9239	.0181	.1216	.3654	.8544	16
17	.012 8748	.154 4971	.0155	.1041	.3130	.7318	17
18	.012 7038	.152 4460	.0133	.0894	.2687	.6283	18
19	.012 5588	.150 7051	.0114	.0769	.2311	.5404	19
20	.012 4352	.149 2225	.0098	.0662	.1991	.4656	20
21	.012 3297	.147 9561	.0085	.0571	.1718	.4016	21
22	.012 2393	.146 8715	.0073	.0494	.1483	.3469	22
23	.012 1617	.145 9408	.0063	.0427	.1283	.2999	23
24	.012 0950	.145 1405	.0055	.0369	.1110	.2595	24
25	.012 0376	.144 4513	.0047	.0320	.0961	.2247	25
26	.011 9881	.143 8570	.0041	.0277	.0833	.1947	26
27	.011 9453	.143 3439	.0036	.0240	.0722	.1688	27
28	.011 9084	.142 9004	.0031	.0208	.0626	.1464	28
29	.011 8764	.142 5167	.0027	.0181	.0543	.1270	29
30	.011 8487	.142 1846	.0023	.0157	.0472	.1103	30
31	.011 8247	.141 8969	.0020	.0136	.0410	.0958	31
32	.011 8040	.141 6475	.0018	.0118	.0356	.0832	32
33	.011 7859	.141 4313	.0015	.0103	.0309	.0723	33
34	.011 7703	.141 2436	.0013	.0089	.0268	.0628	34
35	.011 7567	.141 0808	.0012	.0078	.0233	.0546	35
36	.011 7450	.140 9394	.0010	.0067	.0203	.0474	36
37	.011 7347	.140 8166	.0009	.0059	.0176	.0412	37
38	.011 7258	.140 7100	.0008	.0051	.0153	.0358	38
39	.011 7181	.140 6173	.0007	.0044	.0133	.0312	39
40	.011 7114	.140 5368	.0006	.0039	.0116	.0271	40

J FACTORS (Adjustment Factors for Changes in Income)

Ellwood: $\quad J = 1/S_{\overline{n}}\ [n/(1 - 1/S^n) - (1/Y_E)]$

Straight-line: $\quad J = (1/n - 1/S_{\overline{n}})/Y_E$

Where: $\quad J = $ factor

$\quad 1/S_{\overline{n}} = $ SFF at equity yield rate for projection period

$\quad n = $ projection period

$\quad 1/S^n = $ reversion factor at Y_E for projection period

$\quad Y_E = $ equity yield rate

This table is used to solve mortgage/equity problems that involve changing income. The factors can be substituted in any of the J-factor changing income formulas that solve for overall rates, change in property values, or equity yield rates.

The Ellwood-premise J factors reflect curvilinear income that changes from time zero in relation to a sinking fund accumulation curve; the straight-line premise J factors describe income changing in equal annual amounts after the first year.

In the following examples, the change in both income and value is +25% in five years and the mortgage terms are 70% ratio at 12% nominal interest with a 25-year term. The desired equity yield rate is 18%.

$$C = Y_E + P\ 1/S_{\overline{n}} - R_M$$
$$C = .18 + .0435 \times .139778 - .1263869$$
$$C = .0596934, \textit{ or } .0597$$

Example 1

Assuming the income of a property at time zero is $10,000, what is its calculated value using the Ellwood premise?

$$R_o = (Y_E - MC - \Delta_o\ 1/S_{\overline{n}})/(1 + \Delta_I J)$$
$$R_o = (.18 - .70 \times .0597 - .25 \times .139778)/(1 + .25 \times .4651)$$
$$R_o = .092509$$
$$V_o = I_o/R_o$$
$$V_o = \$10,000/.092509$$
$$V_o = \$108,098$$

Proof:

$$\text{Debt service} = \$108.098 \times .70 = \$75,668$$
$$\$75,668 \times .1263869 = \$9,563$$
$$\text{Reversion} = \$108,098 \times 1.25 - \$75,668 \times (1 - .0435) = \$62,746$$
$$\text{Equity} = \$108,098 \times .30 = \$32,429$$

Time	Income	−	Debt Service	=	Cash to Equity	×	PVF @ 18%	=	Value
1	$10,349	−	$9,563	=	$ 786	×	.847458	=	$ 666
2	10,762	−	9,563	=	1,199	×	.718184	=	861
3	11,248	−	9,563	=	1,685	×	.608631	=	1,026
4	11,823	−	9,563	=	2,260	×	.515789	=	1,166
5	12,500	−	9,563	=	2,937	×	.437109	=	1,284
Reversion					62,746	×	.437109	=	27,427
Total equity									$32,430

Example 2

Assuming the income of the property at the end of Year One is $10,000, what is its calculated value using the straight-line premise:

$$R_o = (Y_E - MC - \Delta_o\, 1/S_{\overline{n}})/(1 + \Delta_I J)$$
$$R_o = (.18 - .70 \times .0597 - .25 \times .139778)/(1 + .25 \times .3346)$$
$$R_o = .095294$$
$$V_o = I_o/R_o$$
$$V_o = \$10,000/.095294$$
$$V_o = \$104,938$$

Proof:

$$\text{Debt service} = \$104,938 \times .70 = \$73,457$$
$$\$ 73,457 \times .1263869 = \$9,284$$
$$\text{Reversion} = \$104,938 \times 1.25 - \$73,457 \times (1 - .0435) = \$60,911$$
$$\text{Equity} = \$104,938 \times .30 = \$31,481$$

Time	Income	−	Debt Service	=	Cash to Equity	×	PVF @ 18%	=	Value
1	$10,000	−	$9,284	=	$ 716	×	.847458	=	$ 607
2	10,500	−	9,284	=	1,216	×	.718184	=	873
3	11,000	−	9,284	=	1,716	×	.608631	=	1,044
4	11,500	−	9,284	=	2,216	×	.515789	=	1,143
5	12,000	−	9,284	=	2,716	×	.437109	=	1,187
Reversion					60,911	×	.437109	=	26,625
Total equity									$31,479

If the income were expected to change by +25% in five years and the yield rate were 16%, the J factor would be .4790 under the Ellwood (sinking fund) premise and .3412 on a straight-line basis. The appropriate factor would be inserted into the mortgage-equity formula.

J FACTORS
(Adjustment Factors for Changes in Income)

	16.0%		16.5%		17.0%		17.5%		
Years	Ellwood	Straight Line	Ellwood	Straight Line	Ellwood	Straight Line	Ellwood	Straight Line	Years
1	1.0000	.0000	1.0000	.0000	1.0000	.0000	1.0000	.0000	1
2	.7116	.2315	.7104	.2309	.7093	.2304	.7082	.2299	2
3	.5986	.3005	.5966	.2995	.5946	.2986	.5926	.2977	3
4	.5298	.3289	.5270	.3276	.5242	.3263	.5215	.3250	4
5	.4790	.3412	.4755	.3395	.4720	.3379	.4685	.3362	5
6	.4374	.3455	.4333	.3435	.4291	.3415	.4250	.3395	6
7	.4015	.3453	.3968	.3430	.3921	.3406	.3874	.3384	7
8	.3695	.3423	.3642	.3397	.3590	.3371	.3538	.3345	8
9	.3403	.3377	.3345	.3348	.3289	.3319	.3233	.3290	9
10	.3134	.3319	.3072	.3287	.3012	.3255	.2952	.3224	10
11	.2884	.3253	.2820	.3219	.2756	.3185	.2694	.3152	11
12	.2652	.3182	.2585	.3146	.2519	.3110	.2454	.3074	12
13	.2435	.3109	.2366	.3070	.2299	.3032	.2233	.2995	13
14	.2233	.3033	.2163	.2993	.2095	.2953	.2028	.2914	14
15	.2045	.2957	.1974	.2915	.1905	.2873	.1838	.2832	15
16	.1870	.2880	.1799	.2837	.1730	.2794	.1663	.2752	16
17	.1707	.2804	.1636	.2759	.1568	.2715	.1502	.2672	17
18	.1555	.2729	.1486	.2683	.1419	.2638	.1354	.2594	18
19	.1415	.2656	.1347	.2609	.1281	.2563	.1219	.2518	19
20	.1286	.2583	.1219	.2535	.1155	.2489	.1095	.2443	20
21	.1166	.2513	.1101	.2464	.1040	.2417	.0981	.2371	21
22	.1056	.2444	.0994	.2395	.0934	.2347	.0879	.2301	22
23	.0955	.2377	.0895	.2328	.0838	.2280	.0785	.2233	23
24	.0862	.2312	.0805	.2263	.0751	.2215	.0700	.2168	24
25	.0778	.2249	.0723	.2200	.0672	.2152	.0624	.2105	25
26	.0700	.2188	.0648	.2139	.0600	.2091	.0555	.2044	26
27	.0630	.2130	.0581	.2080	.0535	.2032	.0493	.1986	27
28	.0565	.2073	.0519	.2024	.0477	.1976	.0437	.1930	28
29	.0507	.2018	.0464	.1969	.0424	.1922	.0387	.1876	29
30	.0455	.1965	.0414	.1917	.0377	.1870	.0343	.1825	30
31	.0407	.1915	.0369	.1866	.0334	.1820	.0303	.1775	31
32	.0364	.1866	.0328	.1818	.0296	.1772	.0267	.1728	32
33	.0325	.1819	.0292	.1771	.0262	.1726	.0236	.1683	33
34	.0290	.1773	.0259	.1727	.0232	.1682	.0208	.1639	34
35	.0258	.1730	.0230	.1684	.0205	.1639	.0183	.1597	35
36	.0230	.1688	.0204	.1642	.0181	.1599	.0161	.1557	36
37	.0205	.1648	.0181	.1603	.0160	.1560	.0141	.1519	37
38	.0182	.1609	.0160	.1565	.0141	.1522	.0124	.1482	38
39	.0162	.1572	.0142	.1528	.0124	.1486	.0109	.1447	39
40	.0143	.1536	.0125	.1493	.0109	.1452	.0095	.1413	40

J FACTORS

(Adjustment Factors for Changes in Income)

Years	18.0% Ellwood	18.0% Straight Line	19.0% Ellwood	19.0% Straight Line	20.0% Ellwood	20.0% Straight Line	21.0% Ellwood	21.0% Straight Line	Years
1	1.0000	.0000	1.0000	.0000	1.0000	.0000	1.0000	.0000	1
2	.7070	.2294	.7047	.2283	.7025	.2273	.7002	.2262	2
3	.5906	.2967	.5866	.2949	.5827	.2930	.5787	.2912	3
4	.5187	.3237	.5132	.3211	.5078	.3186	.5024	.3160	4
5	.4651	.3346	.4582	.3313	.4514	.3281	.4448	.3249	5
6	.4210	.3375	.4129	.3336	.4050	.3298	.3971	.3260	6
7	.3828	.3361	.3736	.3316	.3647	.3272	.3558	.3228	7
8	.3487	.3320	.3386	.3269	.3288	.3220	.3191	.3171	8
9	.3177	.3262	.3069	.3206	.2963	.3152	.2861	.3098	9
10	.2894	.3194	.2779	.3133	.2668	.3074	.2561	.3016	10
11	.2632	.3118	.2513	.3054	.2398	.2990	.2288	.2928	11
12	.2391	.3039	.2269	.2970	.2152	.2903	.2039	.2838	12
13	.2168	.2958	.2044	.2885	.1926	.2815	.1814	.2747	13
14	.1963	.2875	.1838	.2800	.1720	.2727	.1609	.2656	14
15	.1773	.2792	.1649	.2714	.1533	.2639	.1423	.2567	15
16	.1599	.2711	.1477	.2630	.1363	.2553	.1256	.2479	16
17	.1439	.2630	.1319	.2548	.1209	.2469	.1106	.2394	17
18	.1292	.2551	.1176	.2467	.1070	.2388	.0972	.2311	18
19	.1159	.2474	.1047	.2389	.0944	.2308	.0851	.2232	19
20	.1037	.2399	.0929	.2313	.0832	.2232	.0744	.2155	20
21	.0926	.2326	.0824	.2240	.0732	.2159	.0650	.2082	21
22	.0826	.2256	.0729	.2170	.0642	.2088	.0566	.2011	22
23	.0735	.2188	.0643	.2102	.0563	.2021	.0491	.1944	23
24	.0653	.2123	.0567	.2037	.0492	.1956	.0426	.1880	24
25	.0579	.2060	.0499	.1974	.0429	.1894	.0369	.1819	25
26	.0513	.2000	.0438	.1915	.0374	.1835	.0319	.1761	26
27	.0454	.1942	.0385	.1857	.0326	.1779	.0275	.1705	27
28	.0401	.1886	.0337	.1802	.0283	.1725	.0237	.1652	28
29	.0354	.1833	.0295	.1750	.0245	.1673	.0204	.1602	29
30	.0312	.1782	.0258	.1700	.0213	.1624	.0175	.1554	30
31	.0274	.1733	.0225	.1652	.0184	.1578	.0150	.1509	31
32	.0241	.1686	.0196	.1606	.0159	.1533	.0129	.1466	32
33	.0212	.1641	.0171	.1563	.0137	.1491	.0110	.1424	33
34	.0186	.1598	.0148	.1521	.0118	.1450	.0094	.1385	34
35	.0163	.1557	.0129	.1481	.0102	.1412	.0081	.1348	35
36	.0142	.1517	.0112	.1443	.0088	.1375	.0069	.1312	36
37	.0125	.1480	.0097	.1406	.0075	.1340	.0059	.1278	37
38	.0109	.1443	.0084	.1372	.0065	.1306	.0050	.1246	38
39	.0095	.1409	.0073	.1338	.0056	.1274	.0043	.1215	39
40	.0083	.1376	.0063	.1306	.0048	.1243	.0036	.1186	40

INTERRELATIONSHIPS AMONG THE TABLES

Note that mathematical relationships exist among the formulas for the various tables. These relationships can be useful in understanding the tables and solving appraisal problems. For example, appraisers should know that the factors in the ordinary level annuity and direct reduction loan tables are reciprocals; the factors in the ordinary level annuity table can be used as multipliers instead of using the direct-reduction loan factors as divisors.

Reciprocals

Reciprocals are numbers divided into 1. Thus, the reciprocal of 10 is $1/10$ and the reciprocal of .5 is $1/.5$. The factors in some of the tables are reciprocals of those in other tables. This is indicated by their formulas.

Future value of $1 and reversion factors

$$S^n \quad \text{and} \quad \frac{1}{S^n}$$

The reversion factor at 12% for 10 years with annual compounding is .321973, which is the reciprocal of the future value of $1 factor.

$$.321973 = \frac{1}{3.105848}$$

Sinking fund accumulations and sinking fund factors

$$S_{\overline{n}|} \quad \text{and} \quad \frac{1}{S_{\overline{n}|}}$$

The sinking factor at 12% for 10 years with annual compounding is .056984, which is the reciprocal of the sinking fund accumulation factor.

$$.056984 = \frac{1}{17.548735}$$

Ordinary level annuity and direct reduction loan factors

$$a_{\overline{n}|} \quad \text{and} \quad \frac{1}{a_{\overline{n}|}}$$

The direct-reduction loan factor at 12% for 10 years with annual compounding is .176984, which is the reciprocal of the ordinary level annuity factor.

$$.176984 = \frac{1}{5.650223}$$

Summations

Ordinary level annuity factors

An ordinary level annuity factor represents the sum of the reversion factors for all periods up to and including the period being considered. For example, the ordinary level annuity factor for five years at 12% with annual compounding is 3.604776, which is the sum of all the reversion factors for Years One through Five.

$$
\begin{array}{r}
.892857 \\
.797194 \\
.711780 \\
.635518 \\
\underline{.567427} \\
3.604776
\end{array}
$$

Direct reduction loan factors

A direct reduction loan factor represents the sum of the interest, yield, or discount rate stated at the top of the table and the sinking fund factor. For example, the direct reduction loan factor at 12% for 10 years with monthly compounding is .1721651, which is the sum of .12 plus the monthly sinking fund factor of .0043471 times 12 (.12 + .0521651 = .1721651).

Conversely, the sinking fund factor can be obtained by subtracting the interest rate from the direct reduction loan factor. The sinking fund factor at 12% for 10 years with monthly compounding is .1721651 − .12 = .0521651. In addition, the interest rate can be obtained by subtracting the sinking fund factor from the direct reduction loan factor. Given a mortgage constant of .1721651 with monthly compounding for 10 years, the interest rate is .1721651 − .0521651 = .12000, or 12.0%.

Appendix D
Selected Readings and Information Sources

Books

Akerson, Charles B. *The Appraiser's Workbook*. Chicago: American Institute of Real Estate Appraisers, 1985.

_____ . *Capitalization Theory and Techniques: Study Guide*. Rev. ed. Chicago: American Institute of Real Estate Appraisers, 1984.

Albritton, Harold D. *Controversies in Real Property Valuation: A Commentary*. Chicago: American Institute of Real Estate Appraisers, 1982.

American Association of State Highway Officials. *Acquisitions for Right of Way*, Washington, D.C., 1962.

American Institute of Real Estate Appraisers. *The Appraisal of Rural Property*. Chicago, 1983.

_____ . *Appraisal Thought: A 50-Year Beginning*. Chicago, 1982.

_____ . *The Dictionary of Real Estate Appraisal*. Chicago, 1984.

_____ . *Guidelines for Appraisal Office Policies & Procedures*. Chicago, 1981.

_____ . *Readings in the Appraisal of Special Purpose Properties*. Chicago, 1981.

_____ . *Readings in Highest and Best Use*. Chicago, 1981.

_____ . *Readings in the Income Approach to Real Property Valuation, Volume I*. Chicago, 1977.

_____ . *Readings in Market Value*. Chicago, 1981.

_____ . *Readings in Real Estate Investment Analysis*. Chicago, 1977.

_____ . *Readings in Real Property Valuation Principles, Volume I*. Chicago, 1977.

American Institute of Real Estate Appraisers. *Readings in Real Property Valuation Principles, Volume II*. Chicago, 1985.

_____ . *Readings in the Income Capitalization Approach to Real Property Valuation, Volume II*. Chicago, 1985.

Andrews, Richard B. *Urban Land Economics and Public Policy*. New York: Free Press, 1971.

Andrews, Richard N. L. *Land in America*. Lexington, Mass.: D. C. Heath, 1979.

Babcock, Frederick M. *The Valuation of Real Estate*. New York: McGraw-Hill, 1932.

Barlowe, Raleigh. *Land Resource Economics*. 4th ed. Englewood Cliffs, N.J.: Prentice-Hall, 1986.

Bierman, Harold Jr., and Seymour Smidt. *The Capital Budgeting Decision*. 6th ed. New York: Macmillan, 1984.

Bish, Robert L., and Hugh O. Nourse. *Urban Economics and Policy Analysis*. New York: McGraw-Hill, 1975.

Bloom, George F., Arthur M. Weimer, and Jeffrey Fisher. *Real Estate*. 8th ed. New York: Wiley, 1982.

Bloom, George F., and Henry S. Harrison. *Appraising the Single Family Residence*. Chicago: American Institute of Real Estate Appraisers, 1978.

Bonright, James C. *The Valuation of Property*. Vol. 1. New York: McGraw-Hill, 1937.

Burton, James H. *Evolution of the Income Approach*. Chicago: American Institute of Real Estate Appraisers, 1982.

Canestaro, James C. *Real Estate Financial Feasibility Analysis Handbook and Workbook*. Chicago: American Institute of Real Estate Appraisers, 1982.

Carn, Neil, Joseph Rabianski, Maury Seldin, and Ron Racster. *Real Estate Market Analysis: Applications and Techniques*. Englewood Cliffs, N.J.: Prentice-Hall, forthcoming.

Clark, Louis E., Jr., and F. M. Treadway, Jr. *Impact of Electric Power Transmission Line Easements on Real Estate Value*. Chicago: American Institute of Real Estate Appraisers, 1972.

Conroy, Kathleen. *Valuing the Timeshare Property*. Chicago: American Institute of Real Estate Appraisers, 1981.

Davies, Pearl Janet. *Real Estate in American History*. Washington, D.C.: Public Affairs Press, 1958.

Desmond, Glenn M., and Richard E. Kelley. *Business Valuation Handbook*. Llano, Calif: Valuation Press, 1980.

Dilmore, Gene. *Quantitative Techniques in Real Estate Counseling*. Lexington, Mass.: D. C. Heath, 1981.

Dombal, Robert W. *Residential Condominiums: A Guide to Analysis and Appraisal*. Chicago: American Institute of Real Estate Appraisers, 1976.

Eaton, James D. *Real Estate Valuation in Litigation.* Chicago: American Institute of Real Estate Appraisers, 1982.

Foreman, Robert L. *Communicating the Appraisal: A Guide to Report Writing.* Chicago: American Institute of Real Estate Appraisers, 1982.

Friedman, Edith J., ed. *Encyclopedia of Real Estate Appraising.* 3rd ed. Englewood Cliffs, N.J.: Prentice-Hall, 1978.

Gibbons, James E. *Appraising in a Changing Economy: Collected Writings of James E. Gibbons.* Chicago: American Institute of Real Estate Appraisers, 1982.

Gimmy, Arthur E. *Tennis Clubs and Racquet Sport Projects: A Guide to Appraisal, Market Analysis, Development and Financing.* Chicago: American Institute of Real Estate Appraisers, 1978.

Graaskamp, James A. *A Guide to Feasibility Analysis.* Chicago: Society of Real Estate Appraisers, 1970.

Greer, Gaylon E. *The Real-Estate Investment Decision.* Lexington, Mass.: D. C. Heath, 1979.

Haggett, Peter. *Locational Analysis in Human Geography.* New York: St. Martin's, 1965.

Harrison, Henry S. *Houses—The Illustrated Guide to Construction, Design and Systems.* Rev. ed. Chicago: REALTORS® National Marketing Institute, 1976.

Heilbroner, Robert L. *The Worldly Philosophers.* Rev. ed. New York: Simon and Schuster, 1964.

Heuer, Karla L. *Golf Courses: A Guide to Analysis and Valuation.* Chicago: American Institute of Real Estate Appraisers, 1980.

Hoover, Edgar M. *The Location of Economic Activity.* New York: McGraw-Hill, 1963.

Institute on Planning, Zoning, and Eminent Domain. *Proceedings.* Albany, N.Y.: Matthew Bender.

International Association of Assessing Officers. *Assessing and the Appraisal Process.* 5th ed. Chicago, 1974.

——————— . *Property Assessment Valuation.* Chicago, 1977.

Jevons, W. Stanley. *The Theory of Political Economy.* 5th ed. New York: Augustus M. Kelley, 1965.

Kahn, Sanders A., and Frederick E. Case. *Real Estate Appraisal and Investment.* 2nd ed. New York: Ronald Press, 1977.

Keune, Russell V., ed. *The Historic Preservation Yearbook.* Bethesda, Md.: Adler and Adler, 1964.

Kinnard, William N., Jr. *Income Property Valuation: Principles and Techniques of Appraising Income-Producing Real Estate.* Lexington, Mass.: D. C. Heath, 1971.

Kinnard, William N., Jr., and Byrl N. Boyce. *Appraising Real Property.* Lexington, Mass: D. C. Heath, 1984.

Kinnard, William N., Jr., Stephen D. Messner, and Byrl N. Boyce. *Industrial Real Estate.* 4th ed. Washington, D.C.: Society of Industrial REALTORS®, 1979.

Kratovil, Robert, and Raymond J. Werner. *Real Estate Law.* 8th ed. Englewood Cliffs, N.J.: Prentice-Hall, 1983.

Mason, James J., ed. and comp. *American Institute of Real Estate Appraisers Financial Tables.* Chicago: American Institute of Real Estate Appraisers, 1981.

National Cooperative Highway Research Program. *Reports.* Washington, D.C.: National Academy of Sciences Highway Research Board, 1966-1979.

North, Lincoln W. *The Concept of Highest and Best Use.* Winnipeg, Manitoba: Appraisal Institute of Canada, 1981.

Noyes, C. Reinold. *The Institution of Property.* London: Longmans, Green and Company, 1936.

Olin, Harold B., John L. Schmidt, and Walter H. Lewis. *Construction—Principles, Materials & Methods.* 4th ed. Chicago: Institute of Financial Education and Interstate Printers and Publishers, 1980.

Perin, Constance. *Everything in Its Place: Social Order and Land Use in America.* Princeton, N.J.: Princeton University Press, 1977.

Ratcliff, Richard U. *Modern Real Estate Valuation: Theory and Application.* Madison, Wis.: Democrat Press, 1965.

_____ . *Urban Land Economics.* New York: Greenwood, 1972.

Reynolds, Judith. *Historic Properties: Preservation and the Valuation Process.* Chicago: American Institute of Real Estate Appraisers, 1982.

Ring, Alfred A. *Valuation of Real Estate.* 2nd ed. Englewood Cliffs, N.J.: Prentice-Hall, 1970.

Rohan, Patrick J., and Melvin A. Reskin. *Condemnation Procedures and Techniques; Forms.* Albany, N.Y.: Matthew Bender, 1968 (looseleaf service).

Roll, Eric. *A History of Economic Thought.* 3rd. ed. Englewood Cliffs, N.J.: Prentice-Hall, 1964.

Rushmore, Stephen. *Hotels, Motels, and Restaurants: Valuations and Market Studies.* Chicago: American Institute of Real Estate Appraisers, 1983.

Sackman, Julius L., and Patrick J. Rohan. *Nichols' Law of Eminent Domain.* 3rd rev. ed. Albany, N.Y.: Matthew Bender, 1973 (looseleaf service).

Schmutz, George L. *The Appraisal Process.* North Hollywood, Calif.: the author, 1941.

_____ . *Condemnation Appraisal Handbook,* rev. and enlarged by Edwin M. Rams. Englewood Cliffs, N.J.: Prentice-Hall, 1963.

Schwanke, Dean. *Smart Buildings and Technology-Enhanced Real Estate, Volume I.* Washington, D.C.: Urban Land Institute, 1976.

Shenkel, William M. *Modern Real Estate Appraisal.* New York: McGraw-Hill, 1978.

Smith, Halbert C. *Real Estate Appraisal.* Columbus, Ohio: Grid Publishing, 1976.

Smith, Halbert C., Carl J. Tschappat, and Ronald L. Racster, *Real Estate and Urban Development.* 3rd ed. Homewood, Ill.: Richard D. Irwin, 1981.

Sutte, Donald T., Jr. *The Appraisal of Roadside Advertising Signs.* Chicago: American Institute of Real Estate Appraisers, 1972.

Vane, Howard R., and John L. Thompson. *Monetarism—Theory, Evidency and Policy.* New York: Halsted, 1979.

Vernor, James D., ed. *Readings in Market Research for Real Estate.* Chicago: American Institute of Real Estate Appraisers, 1985.

Wendt, Paul F. *Real Estate Appraisal Review and Outlook.* Athens: University of Georgia Press, 1974.

White, John Robert. *Real Estate Valuing, Counseling, Forecasting: Selected Writings of John Robert White.* Chicago: American Institute of Real Estate Appraisers, 1984.

Witherspoon, Robert E., Jon P. Abbett, and Robert M. Gladstone. *Mixed-Use Developments: New Ways of Land Use.* Washington, D.C.: Urban Land Institute, 1976.

Wolf, Peter. *Land in America: Its Value, Use, and Control.* New York: Pantheon, 1981.

Building Cost Manuals

Boeckh Building Valuation Manual. Milwaukee: American Appraisal Co., 1967. 3 vols.
>   Vol. 1—*Residential and Agricultural*; Vol. 2—*Commercial*; Vol. 3— *Industrial and Institutional.* Uses 1967 cost database and includes wide variety of building models. Built up from unit-in-place costs converted to cost per square foot of floor or ground area. *Boeckh Building Cost Modifier* is published bimonthly for updating with current modifiers.

Building Construction Cost Data. Duxbury, Mass.: Robert Snow Means Co., annual.
>   Lists average unit prices on many building construction items for use in engineering estimates. Components arranged according to uniform system adopted by the American Institute of Architects, Associated General Contractors, and Construction Specifications Institute.

Dodge Building Cost Calculator & Valuation Guide. New York: McGraw-Hill Information Systems Co. (looseleaf service, quarterly supplements).
>   Lists building costs for common types and sizes of buildings. Local cost modifiers and historical local cost index tables included. Formerly *Dow Building Cost Calculator.*

Marshall Valuation Service. Los Angeles: Marshall and Swift Publication Co. (looseleaf service, monthly supplements).

>   Cost data for determining replacement costs of buildings and other improvements in the United States and Canada. Includes current cost multipliers and local modifiers.

Residential Cost Handbook. Los Angeles: Marshall and Swift Publication Co. (looseleaf service, quarterly supplements).

>   Presents square-foot method and segregated-cost method. Local modifiers and cost-trend modifiers included.

Sources of Operating Costs and Ratios

Only a few published sources are cited below. Attention is directed to the first item listed.

Robert Morris Associates. *Sources of Composite Financial Data—A Bibliography.* 3rd ed. Philadelphia, 1971.

>   An annotated list of 98 nongovernment sources, arranged in manufacturing, wholesaling, retail, and service categories. Subject index to specific businesses. Publishers' names and addresses included for each citation.

Building Owners and Managers Association International. *Downtown and Suburban Office Building Experience Exchange Report.* Washington, D.C.

>   Published annually since 1920. Includes analysis of expenses and income quoted in cents per square foot as well as national, regional, and selected city averages.

Dun & Bradstreet, Inc. *Key Business Ratios in 125 Lines.* New York.

>   Published annually. Contains balance sheet and profit-and-loss ratios.

Pannell Kerr Forster. *Clubs in Town & Country.* Houston.

>   Published annually since 1953. Lists income-expense data and operating ratios for city and country clubs. Geographical data broken down into four U.S. regions.

_____ . *Trends in the Hotel Industry.* Houston.

>   Published annually since 1937. Lists income-expense data and operating ratios for transient and resort hotels and motels. Geographical data broken down into five U.S. regions.

Institute of Real Estate Management. *Income/Expense Analysis: Apartments, Condominiums & Cooperatives.* Chicago.

>   Published annually since 1954. Data arranged by building type, then by national, regional, metropolitan, and selected city groupings. Operating costs listed per room, per square foot, etc. Formerly *Apartment Building Experience Exchange.*

Institute of Real Estate Management. *Income/Expense Analysis: Suburban Office Buildings*. Chicago.

> Published annually since 1976. Data analyzed on the basis of gross area and gross and net rentable office areas. Includes dollar-per-square-foot calculations; national, regional, and metropolitan comparisons; and detailed analyses for selected cities.

Laventhol & Horwath. *U.S. Lodging Industry*. Philadelphia.

> Published annually since 1932. Includes income, expense, and profit data as well as historical trend tables.

Laventhol & Horowitz and National Restaurant Association. *Table-Service Restaurant Operations*. Philadelphia.

> Published annually since 1976. Lists income-expense data and operating ratios. Supercedes Laventhol & Horwath's *Restaurant Operations* report.

National Retail Merchants Association, Controllers' Congress. *Department Store and Specialty Store Merchandising and Operating Results*. New York.

> Published annually since 1925. Merchandise classification base used since 1969 edition (1968 data). Includes geographical analysis by Federal Reserve districts. Known as the "MOR" report.

_____ . *Financial and Operating Results of Department and Specialty Stores*. New York.

> Published annually since 1963. Data arranged by sales volume category. Known as the "FOR" report.

National Institute of Real Estate Brokers. *Percentage Leases*. 13th ed. Chicago: 1973.

> Based on reports of 3,100 leases for 97 retail and service categories in seven U.S. regions. Data broken down by type of operation, area, center, and building. Regional and store averages given for average minimum rent, rent per square foot, average gross leasable areas, and sales per square foot.

Urban Land Institute. *Dollars and Cents of Shopping Centers*. Washington, D.C., 1978.

> First issued in 1961 and revised every three years. Includes income and expense data for neighborhood, community, and regional centers as well as statistics for specific tenant types.

Periodicals

American Right of Way Proceedings. American Right of Way Association, Los Angeles.

> Annual. Papers presented at national seminars.

Appraisal Institute Magazine. Appraisal Institute of Canada, Winnipeg, Manitoba.

> Quarterly. General and technical articles on appraisal and expropriation in Canada. Includes information on institute programs, news, etc.

The Appraisal Journal. American Institute of Real Estate Appraisers, Chicago.
> Quarterly. Oldest periodical in the appraisal field, published since 1932. Includes technical articles on all phases of real property appraisal and regular feature on legal decisions. Bibliographies for 1932-1969 and 1970-1980 available.

The Appraiser. American Institute of Real Estate Appraisers, Chicago.
> Published monthly, except July and August, News bulletin covering current events and trends in appraisal practice.

Buildings. Stamats Communications, Inc., Cedar Rapids, Iowa.
> Monthly. Journal of building construction and management.

Editor and Publisher Market Guide. Editor and Publisher, New York.
> Annual. Standardized market data for more than 1,500 areas in the United States and Canada, including population estimates for trading areas. List of principal industries, transportation, climate, chain store outlets, etc.

Journal of the American Real Estate and Urban Economics Association. Bloomington, Ind.
> Quarterly. Focuses on research and scholarly studies of current and emerging real estate issues.

Journal of the American Society of Farm Managers and Rural Appraisers. Denver.
> Semiannual. Includes appraisal articles.

Journal of Property Management. Institute of Real Estate Management, Chicago.
> Bimonthly. Covers a broad range of property investment and management issues.

Just Compensation. Sherman Oaks, Calif.
> Monthly. Reports on condemnation cases.

Land Economics. University of Wisconsin, Madison.
> Quarterly. Journal devoted to the study of economics and social institutes. Includes reports on university research and trends in land utilization. Frequently publishes articles on developments in other countries.

The following periodicals on debenture and equity investment are published by Moody's Investors Service, Inc., New York.

Moody's Bank and Finance News Reports.
> Twice weekly.

Moody's Bond Record.
> Monthly.

Moody's Bond Survey.
> Weekly.

Moody's Commercial Paper Record.
> Monthly.

Moody's Dividend Record.
> Twice weekly.

Moody's Handbook of Common Stocks.
Quarterly.

Moody's Handbook of Over-the-Counter Stocks.
Quarterly.

Moody's Industrials.
Twice weekly.

Moody's Investors Fact Sheets.
Irregular.

Moody's Municipals and Governments.
Twice weekly.

Moody's Over-the-Counter Industrials.
Weekly.

Moody's Public Utilities.
Twice weekly.

Moody's Transportation.
Twice weekly.

Property Tax Journal. International Association of Assessing Officers, Chicago.
Quarterly. Includes articles on property taxation and assessment administration.

The Quarterly Byte. American Institute of Real Estate Appraisers, Chicago.
Quarterly. Addresses use of computers in appraising.

The Real Estate Appraiser and Analyst. Society of Real Estate Appraisers, Chicago.
Quarterly. Technical articles, society news, and regular feature on legal cases. Consolidated bibliographies for 1935-1960 and 1961-1970 available. Previously published as *The Review, The Residential Appraiser*, and *The Real Estate Appraiser.*

Real Estate Issues. American Society of Real Estate Counselors, Chicago.
Semiannual.

Real Estate Law Journal. Warren, Gorham and Lamont, Inc., Boston.
Quarterly. Publishes articles on legal issues and reviews current litigation of concern to real estate professionals.

Right of Way. American Right of Way Association, Los Angeles, Calif.
Bimonthly. Articles on all phases of right-of-way activity—e.g., condemnation, negotiation, pipelines, electric power transmission lines, and highways. Includes association news.

Small Business Reporter. Bank of America, San Francisco.
Irregular. Each issue devoted to a specific type of small business—e.g, coin-operated laundries, greeting card shops, and restaurants.

The following periodicals on debenture and equity investment are published by Standard and Poor's Corporation, New York.

Standard and Poor's Bond Guide.
> Monthly.

Standard and Poor's Bond Record.
> Twice weekly.

Standard and Poor's Commercial Paper Ratings Guide.
> Monthly.

Standard and Poor's Daily Stock Price Record: American Exchange.
> Quarterly.

Standard and Poor's Daily Stock Price Record: N.Y. Stock Exchange.
> Quarterly.

Standard and Poor's Daily Stock Price Record: Over-the-Counter Exchange.
> Quarterly.

Standard and Poor's Dividend Record.
> Daily and quarterly.

Standard and Poor's Earnings Forecaster.
> Weekly.

Standard and Poor's Outlook.
> Weekly.

Standard and Poor's Registered Bond Interest Record.
> Weekly.

Standard and Poor's Stock Guide.
> Monthly.

Standard and Poor's Stock Summary.
> Monthly.

Survey of Buying Power. Sales Management, New York.
> Annual. Includes population totals and characteristics and income and consumption data presented in national, regional, metropolitan area, county, and city categories. Separate section for Canadian information. Population estimates between decennial censuses.

Survey of Current Business. U.S. Bureau of Economic Analysis, U.S. Department of Commerce, Washington, D.C.
> Monthly. Includes statistical and price data. Biennial supplement, *Business Statistics.*

Valuation. American Society of Appraisers, Washington, D.C.
> Three issues per year. Articles on real property valuation and the appraisal of personal and intangible property. Includes society news. Previously published as *Technical Valuation.*

Index